VOICES

JAMES MATTHEWS

VOICES

A Life of Frank O'Connor

New York ATHENEUM 1983

Library of Congress Cataloging in Publication Data

Matthews, James H., ———
    Voices : a life of Frank O'Connor.

    Includes bibliographical references and index.
    1. O'Connor, Frank, 1903–1966. 2. Authors,
Irish—20th century—Biography. I. Title.
PR6029.D58Z76 1983   823'.912   81–69161
ISBN 0–689–11272–6

For Justin, Heather, and John

Preface

FRANK O'CONNOR was the pseudonym of Michael O'Donovan, who was born early in this century in Cork, the largest city in the southwest of Ireland, and who died nearly sixty-three years later in Dublin, that nation's capital. During a broadcast for the BBC about provincial writers, O'Connor once said that he couldn't write outside Ireland because nowhere else in the world was his presence as a writer resented as much as it was at home. "An Irish writer without contention is a freak of nature," he proclaimed. "All the literature that matters to me was written by people who had to dodge the censor." When he made that statement in 1938 he had not yet been officially censored in Ireland, but he had already made himself something of a scourge in his homeland, an abrasive and self-appointed voice of the cultural conscience. Throughout his career, Frank O'Connor was a writer with contention.

Michael O'Donovan grew up in a slum, a frail boy jeered by the children of the neighborhood and tyrannized by a drunken father on whom he threw himself to protect his beloved mother. Later, as Frank O'Connor, he wrote countless stories about boy heroes fighting in some way to protect mothers, orphans, illegitimate children, and other helpless persons. Growing up in poverty forced him to fight the facts of his surroundings with the only tools he possessed—his mind and his voice. He talked and wrote in a ceaseless struggle against the forces of stupidity, repression, and stagnation that he believed were keeping his homeland smothered in darkness. He even fought *for* her, a rebel for Irish freedom and a holdout for Republican ideals during the Civil War—a boy warrior caught up in the romance of the fight, losing his spiritual virginity in the mountains of West Cork and his innocence behind the barbed wire of an internment camp in Meath. He started writing about this painful time in his own and his nation's history until he grew weary of guns and ambushes. Then he kept on writing about the curious habit of fighting among the Irish, about loneliness, the need for human contact, and the desolation caused by the failure to communicate. On and on, through a lifetime that paralleled and reflected the life of Ireland in this century, he fought one lost cause after another, improvised an education and a career, and, with more audacity than good sense, dug in his heels and stood for what he considered right and true.

Speaking at the graveside of W. B. Yeats in 1965, O'Connor observed that "in the summing up of any man's achievement there are two things to be taken into account—the man's character and the character of the circumstances he had to deal with." And just how does one discern the character of another person? How does one know that the portrait is a true, or even a reasonable, likeness of the "real" person? To write a life of Michael/Frank, as he was affectionately called by Mrs. Yeats, means listening to the voices of the people and the places he knew and wrote about; beyond that, it means listening to *his* many voices—his stories, poems, plays, novels, and travel books, as well as his journalism and literary criticism.

It was said of O'Connor that his voice was so low that barnacles clung to it and that in conversation with him "organ-tuners boomingly despaired of their diapasons." Anyone who speaks of him sooner or later mentions that voice. Vivian Mercier, for instance, claimed that "in resonance, range of pitch and breadth of control, it [was] one of the best untrained voices" (and it *was,* like everything else about him, untrained) he had ever heard. Toward the end of his life, in a television broadcast called "Interior Voices," he suggested that though poor eyesight caused him to miss visual details, his memory was "extremely tenacious of voice." He began writing stories without a clue as to how to go about it and only later discovered that what he was doing was simply "listening to voices in my head." He called his study of the short story *The Lonely Voice* and said that where Yeats, Synge, and the other Olympian figures of the Irish Literary Renaissance had their "presences" to offer eternity, he would have only his voices—his stories. In the last thing he ever wrote about Yeats, his greatest literary hero, O'Connor concluded that Yeats's "poems and plays spring from a continuous soliloquy, an unceasing interior monologue, interrupted only by voices from outside. It is not always easy to detect whose the voices are, or what, precisely, they are saying, because they represent the unwritten part of Yeats's biography."

Harold Nicolson once said that "Biography is the preoccupation and solace not of certainty, but of doubt." Writing a life of Frank O'Connor is like circling a stranger's house, circling and peering into that house from the outside, circling to know something of what or who is inside, never able to enter but content with momentary glimpses from many angles. Richard Ellmann, biographer of Yeats and Joyce, has wisely cautioned that even when authorized a biographer is intrusive. O'Connor once said that it would take more than one lifetime to discover the reason for all the ruins in Ireland; one wonders how many lifetimes it would take to tell all the stories of all the people who figure in O'Connor's story. Yeats argued that "nothing exists but a stream of souls, that all knowledge is biography."

The only reason to write about Michael O'Donovan is because of what he wrote under the name of Frank O'Connor. He believed with Yeats that what one writes is an allegory of one's life; one writes what one is, or in the words of Samuel Butler in *The Way of All Flesh,* "Every man's work, whether it be literature or music or pictures or architecture or anything else, is always a portrait of himself." Frank O'Connor, it can be said, lived a good story.

James Matthews
Stanwood, Washington
March 1982

Contents

Illustrations

VOICES

I

Inescapably Cork

Cork's poor are its kings.

SEÁN O'FAOLÁIN, *An Irish Journey*

MICHAEL O'DONOVAN was born and brought up in Cork City, Ireland; Frank O'Connor fled that city pleading to be let go. For the man and for the writer Cork was the place where all his ladders started. At every stage of his life Cork stares you in the face, for he was "unmistakably a Munster man, inescapably from Cork." No more or less than Joyce from Dublin or Yeats from Sligo, Michael O'Donovan/Frank O'Connor was an Irish writer from Cork. And no more than all the rest—Shaw, O'Casey, Beckett—he was close to home and far away, always loving it, always hating it.

I

Cork is attractive, even alluring. To many it is the most Continental city in Ireland; to some the most seductive town in Europe. Frank O'Connor knew it as a lovely place, even considering that, as his mentor Daniel Corkery observed, it was "flung higgledy-piggledy together into a narrow, double-streamed, many-bridged river valley, jostled and jostling, so compacted that the mass throws up a froth and flurry that confuses the stray visitor, unless indeed he is set on getting at the true size and worth of things."[1] O'Connor's Cork possessed a mobile charm more to be heard than seen—the river and the rain, the spires and the bells, the market cries and the dock whistles, the trams with their high-pitched scream and slow crawl—all that noise for so little progress. He once said of Cork that he could admire, as if he were a stranger, "the up and down of it on the hills as though it had been built on a Cork accent."

Cork was, and still is, a walking town. Like Belfast and Dublin, it was in O'Connor's youth populous enough to be diverse, almost cosmopolitan; lacking the spacious designs of those larger cities, it could be spanned, even circled, in a comfortable stroll. Seán O'Faoláin, a native of Cork who shared with O'Connor the habit of serious walking, once wrote that something kept "young Corkmen walking round and round their city for hours at night, planning and arguing, hoping and praising, reviling and loving."[2] The Mardyke, one of their favorite walks, is "a mile of trees and lamps at intervals lost in the leaves spanning the gravel. It starts with the weather-slated houses and ends on the green verge of the city."

An island city in an island country, Cork has been called the Venice of Ireland. At times the tides and winds push the water back into the streets of the flat, exposing the age of the place. In the Gaelic *Corraigh* means "Marsh," and indeed the city is compacted on these islands in the marsh, floating as it were at the mercy of the elements: soft and wet in the summer, hard and wet in the winter. Edmund Spenser addressed the graceful and threatening river that supports and divides the city as "the spreading Lee, that like an island fayre,/ Encloseth Cork with his divided flood." Cork has always been just that—a flooded and divided city.

Cork was divided, too, in a more elusive way, as all of Ireland has been divided, between the displaced and the displacers: Gaelic natives and alien imperialists each in turn, the Vikings, the Normans, and finally the English. Particularly at the outset of this century these two streams met in Cork like oil and water. At that time the power of Cork rested with the English while the vitality flowed from the native poor: the one within the walls, ruling from the commercial flat of the city and living on the fashionable heights; the other just outside those "walls," barely surviving in the picturesque dilapidation of miserable cabins and tenements improvised from decaying mansions discarded by the rich as they moved up. Tivoli, Montenotte, Sunday's Well, Grand Parade, South Mall, the Western Road, and Lee Fields looked as nice as a fine portrait and felt as solid as hard cash. Blackpool, Barrackton, the Cattle Markets, Fair Hill, Shandon Street, and the other fringe areas of the city all smelled heavy like life and sounded harsh like teeming reality. The two streams together formed the essential character of this "shoneen"* town where, as O'Connor wrote, "the old crafty alien race/ And craftier peasant fight it out."[3]

Whatever else can be said of O'Connor's Cork—the parks and walks and hills, the churches and shops and theatres, the docks and bridges and factories—it is a city that has managed in this century to produce some great people, some from the oil and some from the water. O'Connor was one of the native born, but he spent his life trying to mix the unmixable elements of his home, trying to harness the energy of their contention. The contradictory streams of Cork surfaced in nearly everything he wrote or did. His life of continual struggle and contention in large measure came from the inner turmoil of divided Cork. The Cork of O'Connor is not the topography of place but the biography of people, not the sights but the sounds.

I I

Surrounded on three sides by hills, cut by the river, and pushed against the sea, Cork is pocketed and close. Dublin and Belfast may have been as provincial as Cork at the turn of the century, but their size allowed some anonymity. In Cork squalor and untidiness were exaggerated by closeness. Cork was small enough to be familiar, yet to young men like O'Connor and O'Faoláin it was so small as to be constricting. It was a place to get out of, quick, and they did— soon enough to preserve their sanity and integrity, but late enough to remain saturated with the place and its people. Both men listened to Daniel Corkery carefully enough to measure Cork by its true size and to find the true worth of things in its close texture. To them it was still a city of claustrophobic provincialism, where life was "deadly dull, strangled by inhibitions." O'Connor, it

---

* Or *shauneen* (John with diminutive suffix). An Irish term of derision for a would-be John Bull, a native pretender to alien English fashion.

has been said, looked "not into clean and coloured domestic content, but out over a threshold of unquiet at badly-lighted streets where sodden figures move uncertainly in the rain."[4] O'Faoláin went so far as to say that on a summer afternoon, when the fishermen are drying their nets and the angelus rings "in various tones and at various speeds all over the city," then "Cork becomes without pretension the Lilliput it is."[5]

To their credit, however, both men paid tribute to the cultural richness of their hometown, acknowledging the city's rare offerings of theatre, music, and learning. O'Connor knew it to be the "most musical city in the United Kingdom"—visiting singers said so. It was also the most attentive to great literature—"visiting Shakespearean actors confirmed it."[6] As O'Faoláin acknowledged: "As far as the popular theatre went, Cork was well-served. . . . Cork still has its theatre, and that is a valuable thing." Needless to say, O'Faoláin and O'Connor were well served by this strange mix of Irish and continental culture. O'Faoláin learned his lessons at the stage door of the Opera House, just around the corner from his home. O'Connor learned his in the rough streets of the Barrack Stream and in the attics of his mother's employers and the library near City Hall. Both were doubly fortunate to have come under the tutelage of Daniel Corkery, the master teacher and Irish nationalist who gave so many Cork boys something to live for as well as to die for.

That the spirit of rebellion should arise strongest in Cork and its environs is hardly surprising. After the uprisings of 1798 it had been a closely watched town with a full barrack of English troops; but it remained a natural hub of restlessness. Following the Famine and the Land Troubles of the nineteenth century, thousands of people flocked to Cork looking for work or passage to America. Those who stayed, like the families of O'Connor and O'Faoláin, settled in the dingy outskirts and worked the docks, the breweries, or the other industries controlled by the English. But their hearts remained in West Cork or Kerry or some other rural home. Cork gave rise to the most vigorous resistance against this system because there the disparity between the Anglo-Irish ascendancy and the native Irish was most exaggerated and irritated.

In Cork poor boys like O'Connor and O'Faoláin could dare to rebel, dare to ask for more than a divided city and a divided country could give them. One journalist called the place a "city of tattered grace, probably the most seductive and loquacious in Western Europe." Cork was indeed a city of words, battling words and lyrical words; though it was unique, it also reflected the qualities that in the stereotypes of English melodrama passed for Irish—fighting, drinking, cursing, and charming. In the slums of Cork, boys like O'Connor and O'Faoláin could sharpen their claws on the language of people living at "blood-heat": the coal urchins dressed in brilliant garb and locked in screeching battle while their mothers in colorful shawls shouted fish prices and their fathers swaggered on the docks or in the pubs.[7] These were the folks who mobbed Dan Lowry's music hall around the turn of the century, filling the second-floor gallery from which they judged performances with brutal gibes and well-timed witticisms. "Slagging," it was called, and the navvies and coal-heavers, the charwomen and "shawlies," were masters of the art. In that shifting ambiguity of words—the only medium of expression, other than violence, the poor can afford—O'Connor and O'Faoláin found the peculiar energy of their poems and novels and stories.

I I I

O'Connor's story begins with Mick O'Donovan and Minnie O'Connor, an ex-soldier and an orphaned charwoman, both of whom grew up in the native stream of Cork. About his father's background, little is actually known beyond the scant remarks of O'Connor himself. Michael O'Donovan was born in Donnybrook on April 1, 1869, and grew up in the area of Cork known as the Barrack Stream, a colorful and rough neighborhood in the shadow of the English barracks above the city to the north. His father, Thomas Donovan, was a common laborer, usually out of work. His mother, Julia Connalee, a peasant woman from Aghada, took in washing from the officers in the barracks. The O'Donovan family was trapped in a sort of idle poverty, surviving on the intermittent beneficence of the army, the factories of Blackpool, or the docks. It was a close family, tied together by the customs of the neighborhood. O'Connor contended that his father moved his young family back to this area because there he was highly respected, and there he was at least certain of a decent funeral. Mick was among Cork's "strutting poor," with exaggerated dress and exaggerated loyalties. His family was nostalgic about home and family tradition, melancholy about their daily existence, and anxious about the future. Mick, a strong, handsome young man, apparently felt this sense of worry more keenly than his brothers. Unskilled and uneducated, he finally turned to the only source of glamour he knew, the British army. At the age of nineteen he enlisted with the Munster Fusiliers. For a time he was stationed at Fort Charles in Kinsale and later he fought in South Africa.

While serving with the fusiliers, Mick O'Donovan became quite friendly with a young man named Tim O'Connor, brother of a thirty-year-old woman named Mary Theresa from the Blarney Street area known as Irishtown. Their mother, a country girl from Donoughmore, worked as a charwoman and, finding widowhood and poverty too hard to handle, went mad and eventually died in the Cork asylum. Their father was a laborer in Arnott's Brewery until his accidental death. The children, four in all, ended up in orphanages in various parts of the city. It was from her home in the Good Shepherd Convent in Blarney Street that Minnie, as she was always called, went at the age of fourteen to take domestic positions in the homes of well-to-do families. "There was little of the agony of the orphan child that Mother did not know," wrote O'Connor in *An Only Child* in poignant sympathy for her homelessness: first the orphanage, then her mother's burial "among strangers," and finally the succession of temporary jobs from which she always seemed to be displaced with capricious cruelty.[8] There was a Protestant family on Gardiner's Hill, then a Catholic lodging house on Richmond Street—both disastrous situations for a lonely and vulnerable girl. Only in the house of Ned Barry, a man of about forty, and his unmarried sister, Alice, did she ever find anything resembling permanence, staying there nearly eight years. At that point in her life it was the only home she had ever really had; and though she had received proposals of marriage, Ned was the only man she had ever really loved. When Alice married, the nuns forced Minnie to leave, because a "man who married his housekeeper was too obvious a subject for ridicule." Homeless once again, she became "almost insane with worry and fear and loneliness," even to the point of entertaining thoughts of suicide. In her restlessness and loneliness Minnie took a number of jobs after that, including one in England that lasted only six months and another brief job in Limerick. Finally, in 1901, "she took a job with the family of a naval paymaster in Queenstown." By this time she had met her brother's friend Mick O'Donovan.[9]

Though the relationship was anything but happy, Minnie insisted throughout her life that Mick had raised her from the gutter where the world had thrown her. Presumably she meant the physical and emotional circumstances of the orphanage and the uncertainty of domestic service. Constantly shifted from family to family, nearly raped by a newspaper reporter in one house, and generally buffeted about in orphaned poverty, Minnie nevertheless seemed to have maintained her natural dignity and gaiety. At age thirty-six, partly out of desperation, she finally married her brother's friend. That was on October 8, 1901, at the Church of St. Finbarr's South in Douglas Street.

With no money, "they went to live with his parents, who then had a house in Maryville Cottages in Barrackton that they could not afford to keep on their own." Minnie was "disgusted and horrified by the dirt and drunkenness," but when she complained, Mick supposedly replied, "It's done now and it can't be undone."[10] That cruel statement "rankled in her mind for forty years." Sometime after Christmas, 1902, Mick left for the South African campaign, and Minnie, who was nothing if not independent and resourceful, moved back into digs over a shop in Douglas Street, as far across Cork from the O'Donovans and the Barrack Stream as she could get. It was there on September 17, 1903, with her landlady, Mary O'Connell, acting as midwife, that she gave birth to her only child, Michael Francis O'Donovan.[11]

2

Mother's Boy

. . . in his imagination he lived through a long train of adventures. . . . But when he had sung his song and withdrawn into a snug corner of the room he began to taste the joy of loneliness.

JAMES JOYCE, *A Portrait of the Artist as a Young Man*

I

SHORTLY after Michael was born, his mother chanced to encounter Ned Barry on a Sunday morning at Mass, six years after their abrupt separation. While Minnie was busy trying to hush her crying son, her beloved boss came out of the church, stopped and patted the baby's head, and continued on his way. She was so shocked by his pale appearance that she said nothing. She ran after him, but upon reaching his house, she was scornfully sent away by the new housekeeper. A few months later he was dead, and Minnie sat with the sister until after dark in the house where the three of them had been so happy. The emotional end of the improvised home occurred at the very time she was beginning to create, in the face of an unhappy marriage, a new and lasting home for herself and her child.

Michael O'Donovan was an only child and, by his own admission, "the classic example of the Mother's Boy." He took his pseudonym from her maiden name; the first title he considered for his autobiography was "Mother's Boy." He was born while his father was away at war, and he grew up almost entirely under his mother's care. Because there were his father's absences, military and otherwise, and because he was a frail, even sickly, child, his mother lavished upon him all the parental attention she had longed for as an orphan.

Big Mick returned to Cork from the South African campaign within a year of his son's birth and promptly moved his family to Blarney Lane. Minnie opened a small shop, a disastrous enterprise due as much to her own altruism as to her husband's hand in the till and elbow on the bar. "This was the one period of her life that she always refused to speak about, and it was clearly a horror to her." But at least she was on familiar grounds, close to such comforting reminders of a happier time as the convent, where she went regularly to show her baby to the nuns, the house of Ned Barry, and the small shop owned by a man who had once wanted to marry her. Young Michael's memories, then, began here in what is still called Irishtown, a slum area that "begins at the foot of Shandon Street, near the river-bank, in sordidness, and ascends the hill to something like squalor." The O'Donovans lived near the top in what may be "properly described as a cabin, for it contained nothing but a tiny kitchen and a tiny bedroom with a loft above it." This was one of the ruts of Cork's Native Stream, located on the edge of the "open country" and at the back door of the "classy quarter of Sunday's Well."

O'Connor's memories of life in Blarney Lane exaggerate the differences between his parents. His mother appears the long-suffering, loving, understanding, gentle saint every Irish boy seems to have for a mother. His father emerges as the bellicose, hard-drinking, angry tyrant every Irish boy claims for a father. Perhaps such images are merely part of the sociology of poverty, of family life in a repressed society. Or perhaps they are part of the psychology of a child's memory, which locates all that is loving in one place, all that is harsh in another. If Michael inherited a brooding, violent melancholy from his father, then most certainly it was his mother who gave him that simple, unworldly innocence that characterized both his writing and his actions. These "were the two powers that were struggling for possession of my soul," he confessed in *An Only Child*. O'Connor was sensitive enough to recognize that struggle, deluded enough to oversimplify it, and talented enough to embody it in living stories, some tragic and some hilariously funny. Those compelling stories resonating from the Blarney Lane years, "My Oedipus Complex," "Man of the House," "The Drunkard," and so many others, all hinge on the natural subjectivity of a child's view of things.

The image of his father was one of public display, of a man who gloried in the trappings of the military and the opinions of his neighbors. Whatever else in the world he was or was not, he was first a soldier; he grew up with that image and he lived his entire life with it, marching in parades wielding a fierce drumstick, drinking with old comrades, and telling old war stories. One favorite story was that during a review held by Queen Victoria, she asked a general about the "distinguished-looking man in the second rank" and was told, "That, Your Majesty, is Michael O'Donovan, one of the best-looking men in your whole army."

O'Connor's own description of his father in *An Only Child* bears out that tall tale: a fine-looking six-footer of muscular build and soldierly erectness; a long Scandinavian head with unusually broad features; a careful dresser with old-fashioned tastes—blue serge suit, starched shirtfront, and bowler hat. Again and again a character resembling his father appeared in O'Connor's stories, a man of the pubs and the docks, given to lengthy harangues about the old days in the fusiliers, a huge man, "quiet enough when he was sober, but when he was drunk . . ."[1]

After returning from the South African campaign, Michael's father was mustered out of the British army with a small pension; he worked, when work was available, as a navvy, or unskilled laborer. Where the father was robust and gregarious, the son was frail and timid. Each morning Big Mick washed himself under bracing cold water behind the house and taunted his son, who huddled close to his mother near the tiny stove for warmth. His image of himself as a vigorous, self-sufficient man among men was devastated by the sight of this sensitive boy whose chronic fever and congestion kept him indoors with his mommy and his kittens. However, years later O'Connor admitted that he seemed to inherit much of his father's disposition, "which was brooding, melancholy, and violent."

Thus Big Mick became the source of his son's most vivid folklore because they were at once so different and yet so alike. For instance, he loved music and played the drum in a local band. As Michael was the only child, he was forced to accompany his bellicose father on Sunday band outings. Most of the bandsmen were, like Michael's father, "ex-bandsmen of the British Army." The choice of bands depended on politics, for there were but two bands: the Blackpool Brass and Reed Band for which Big Mick originally played owing to his fierce devotion to the flamboyant William O'Brien; and the Molly Maguires, a better band musically but its members were supporters of John Redmond. Apparently Michael's father preferred music to politics because for the sake of music "he even endured the indignity of playing for Johnny Redmond." His son may not have inherited the brute physical power necessary to wield a great drum, but he most certainly inherited the old soldier's propensity for public display and his love of music.

Michael was sent with his father on those Sunday outings because his mother believed he could restrain her husband from drinking too much. More than once, however, Big Mick left his son outside a pub with a bribe of a few pennies while he and his comrades talked and drank. At the time it was no joke to Michael, though later he could laughingly write about wandering home across a dark city after having been left outside a Crosshaven pub or about sneaking his father's porter and then being escorted home roaring drunk bellowing "The Boys of Wexford" to the mortal embarrassment of his sober father. Michael had squired his father on similar drinking jousts only to "bring him home, blind drunk, down Blarney Lane." If Mick was a drummer in the classic manner, he was also a tippler in a classic way. And though he always returned to his image of himself as a "home-loving body," his son distrusted him with a mixture of hatred and fear.

One night, for example, Big Mick stumbled home in search of more money to continue his debauch. First he begged and whined for the price of a round, then he grew violent. Smashing Minnie's few kitchen ornaments to bits, he threatened to put an end to the whole thing with the razor he waved about menacingly. Then he threw the two of them out in the cold wearing nothing but their nightclothes. There they sat huddling and shivering on Blarney Lane until neighbors, who were familiar with this ritual of savagery, took them in. After that horror, whenever his father brandished the razor at his mother, Michael went into hysterics and rushed his father with his fists. That drove his mother to hysterics, for she knew that she was as helpless as her weak son to stop a slashing. Later, in adolescence, Michael not only had recurring nightmares about these scenes but developed "pseudo-epileptic fits that were merely an externalization" of these nightmares.[2]

This endless insecurity exaggerated the effects of poverty and kept Michael and his mother emotionally on edge. Mick's drinking created a vacuum of affection that his wife and son filled with each other. The turmoil in the house ceased only when Mick went out drinking. Michael developed such a hatred of his father that he took to avoiding the word *father,* carefully and contemptuously using *he* or *him* instead. But his mother corrected his insolence and insisted on filial piety. As a boy, he was unable to comprehend her loyalty; but later he surmised that had she left her husband, she would have been forced to take a domestic job and put her son in an orphanage—"the one thing in the world that the orphan child could not do."

Her fear was the orphan's fear of displacement, of being thrown out on the street. Their only dependable income was her meagre earnings as a char-woman (about ten shillings a month), and even this Mick often demanded for his "entrance fee," the price of the first round of drinks. The longer the binge, the more destitute the family would become: "The shopkeepers refused Mother even a loaf of bread, and the landlord threatened us with eviction, and Father could no longer raise the price of a single pint." Only then would he give it up. "Sour and savage and silent, he began to look for another job. He rarely went back to the job he had left, and in those days I believed it was be-cause he had lost it."[3] Rather, Mick in his pride was unable to face the humilia-tion of admitting to his fellow workers what he had done.

While Mick was working—and apparently he was a fine worker—he saved with a vengeance, providing for that "rainy day," which always meant many wet days. Trousers would be patched, shoes cobbled, and hair trimmed in the backyard—all in the interest of frugality. Sweets, books, or Christmas gifts were only proof to Mick of his wife's "fundamental improvidence." When sober, he was an extravagant skinflint and a self-righteous teetotaller, abso-lutely convinced that he was the best father and husband in the area. Then something would set him off—a funeral or a chance meeting of an old com-rade-at-arms.

That was the end of Father in his role as home-loving body. Next evening he would slink upstairs to the locked trunk where he kept his savings, and then go out again. The rainy day had at last arrived. He would return in a state of noisy amiability that turned to sullenness when it failed to rouse a response.

On such occasions Michael could not bear his father's maudlin attentions and often would either shriek insults or run away sobbing hysterically. Mick would snarl at Minnie that the whelp was "better fed than taught." Offended and feeling guilty he would then brace up for an even longer carouse.

The savings were usually exhausted in a week, and then Minnie would trek to the pawnshop—first with his blue suit, then with the clocks, his watch, and his military medals, and finally with his "ring paper," the authorization by which he drew his army pension (about one guinea each month). To Michael, when she left the house and turned down the hill with some item wrapped be-neath her shawl to keep the humiliation from the neighbors, "it meant an im-mediate descent in the social scale from the 'hatties' to the 'shawlies'—the poorest of the poor." When they had reached bottom again, the debauch ended and they once more climbed out of the hole. Loans were secured, the ring paper was restored, and the suits and clocks were retrieved. The family could once again attend Mass together at the Dominican Church on Sand Quay; life returned to "normal" and money would begin to pile up for the next rainy day. Mick would return to his teetotal domestic routine: rising early to wash under the tap at the back of the house, taking tea to Minnie in bed, and sitting pla-cidly in the evenings reading the *Cork Echo* aloud. Michael usually sat alone in a corner absorbed in his own boys' weekly. Minnie may have accepted the brief spell of harmony, but her son was suspicious, knowing that sooner or later it would be shattered again.

In the spring of 1910 Michael's father moved the family, this time once and for all, back to his old neighborhood, the Barrack Stream. A house had become available in Harrington Square,

> an uneven unlighted piece of ground between the Old Youghal Road and the Ballyhooley Road that seemed to have been abandoned by God and was certainly abandoned by the Cork Corporation. One side was higher than the other, and a channel had been hollowed out before the houses on the lower side to give ingress, while at the end of this one lonesome pillar commemorated some early dream of railing the place off. In England such sites are politely known as "non-adopted," a word that well-suits their orphaned air.

Mick O'Donovan was returning to the locality of his parents because he was homesick anywhere else. He was almost entirely a creature of habit: a man given to one town, one neighborhood, one house, and one woman. What the move meant to a sickly boy and his mother was an uprooting known only too well to an orphan. Torn from the place of her orphan past, Minnie spent the first night in the filthy, run-down kitchen of the new house weeping. Michael simply carried his kittens and sat in the corner listening to the bickering. If Blarney Lane had brought to his mind certain contrasts between his parents, then Harrington Square blew those contrasts out of all proportion. Being an only child, Michael felt his own powerlessness in the face of these cruel contrasts with what he called "hysterical clarity." The hereditary powers struggling within him—the O'Donovan gloom and the O'Connor gaiety—were focused most clearly in the differences between the women: his mother on the one hand and the women of his father's family on the other.

Minnie O'Connor was "dainty in everything she did," fastidious, tidy, and proper. Though over forty at the time, Minnie possessed that naive view of the world expected of women half her age. *Mozartean* was the term her son later used to characterize her temperament. "She knew that when people were happy they laughed, and she laughed with them," he wrote; "she never teased and could never understand teasing, which was the amusement of people like Father, who do not believe in the world of appearances." In addition, she was an excellent, resourceful cook and an attentive housekeeper. Unlike her husband, who was openly friendly and a backslapper, Minnie was one to keep to herself and not share in the tea-and-tart circuit of the square. And though she loved classical music (especially Schubert and Mozart) and Victorian novels, she seldom paraded her interests; she was not considered at all pretentious, or a "maker-outer," by the ladies of the neighborhood, even though she had little in common with them besides poverty. A small woman with long dark hair, Minnie took great pride in her appearance. In fact, her son, looking back years later, admitted that her list of failings comprised vanity, along with a kind of obstinacy.

Her mother-in-law, by contrast, was as untidy as Minnie was neat. To her oversensitive grandson she seemed dirty, loud, and common—the essence of the O'Donovan family. She drank too much, in his estimation, and was given to the same "alcoholic emotionalism" as her son. To top it all off, she came to live with them after her husband died; Michael was then nine years old. Despite this loathing of his grandmother, a loathing more of the "drunkenness, dirt, and violence" of the situation than of the woman herself, O'Connor managed to write two of his most humorous stories about her. In "First Confession" a young boy tells the priest of his compelling wish to murder his granny because she takes porter and snuff, goes around in bare feet, gives pennies to his sister, and gets his father to beat him. In "The Long Road to Ummera" an Irish-speaking old woman, with all the boisterous charm of Michael's grandmother, insists on being buried in the home of her people in the mountains of West Cork. O'Connor admitted that the voices of the story are those of his townee father and peasant granny, voices he never forgot. And it cannot be forgotten, either, that it was this coarse peasant woman who first taught him Irish and introduced him to the native Ireland outside Cork City. Though the motif of the orphan runs throughout his fiction, O'Connor used his mother's image sparingly in his early writing and his father's image freely—suggesting perhaps that for him intense bitterness was easier to assimilate than intense affection.

I I

Cork, indeed all of Ireland at the end of the first decade of the twentieth century, was stirring with nascent political passion. The faction fighting between the bands in which Michael's father played represented the pervasive discontent of native Irishmen over the policies of the British government. Oppressive employment practices gave rise to an abortive labor movement led in Dublin by Jim Larkin.[1] Michael's father was a fierce supporter of Larkin, buying the *Irish Worker* and even staying out on strike once or twice. But poverty has a way of smothering the protest it ignites. Though the Barrack Stream to which Big Mick moved his family was considered a cut above the Blarney Lane area, it was still an impoverished neighborhood full of desperation and malice. It would be his home until his death thirty years later, but the home of his son only until Michael was old enough to join the rebels, old enough to find a job, old enough to leave.

All in all, the move to the Barrack Stream proved to be an important juncture in Michael O'Donovan's young life; Harrington Square was to become the shaping place of his fiction. In a letter to an American editor O'Connor once confessed that his "square" was not really a square at all, "as it's only two rows of small houses in a deserted lot; the remaining two sides are provided by houses on the farther side of two roadways." Each house had the same ground plan with a "tiny hallway, a small front room and a kitchen back of them." Everything took place in the dimly lit kitchen, which had "two doors opposite one another, one leading into the hallway, the other into the backyard."[5] A single window was situated beside the back door.

Just about anyone familiar with O'Connor's "juvenile" stories could envision the place; it was his home, his point of reference in Cork's native stream. Slightly more well off financially than Blarney Lane, this area was nevertheless considerably rougher, "like all places attached to military barracks." Rougher meant "women who went with soldiers, and girls who went with officers, and sinister houses where people drank after hours." It also meant the charm of regular bugle calls and parades with marching soldiers and pipe bands. Life around the barracks was a moving, changing, noisy stream. In "The Duke's Children" O'Connor's narrator, feeling betrayed by his family situation, remarks "[It wasn't only the] poverty that repelled me, though that was bad enough, or the tiny terrace house we lived in, with its twelve-foot square of garden in front, its crumbling stumps of gate-posts and low wall that had lost its railing." It was rather the "utter commonness." What Michael missed in these rough, transient surroundings was the "breath of fineness," the spark of charm, and the texture of civility.

Frankly, Michael O'Donovan was a misfit, a snob by conviction as he implied in "The Genius." He was called a "blooming sissy" by the boys of the square, which he didn't like, though he preferred it to fighting. His way of meeting the incessant challenges of the neighborhood toughies "was to climb on the nearest wall and argue like hell in a shrill voice about Our Blessed Lord and good manners." Even his father taunted him about being so sickly and frail that he would not wash under the cold tap like a real man. Thus looked down upon, he chose to assume an aloof posture.

> The boys from our neighborhood usually gathered outside Miss Murphy's shop at the foot of the Square, while the respectable boys of the Ballyhooley Road—the children of policemen, minor officials, and small shopkeepers—gathered outside Miss Long's by the Quarry. I lived in a sort of social vacuum between the two, for though custom summoned me to Miss Murphy's with boys of my own class who sometimes went without boots and had no ambition to be educated, my instinct summoned me to Miss Long's and the boys who wore boots and got educated whether they liked it or not.

Caught between two groups, Michael always seemed to be "lonely and unwelcome." To both he was a freak: to the poorer boys because he used affected language and to the others because he was only a pretender.

Belonging nowhere else, he attached himself more closely to his mother, meeting her at the houses of her wealthy employers, where he was sometimes permitted to explore their ample libraries and attics, or indulging in voyages of fantasy while gazing from windows overlooking the harbor. In reality he might not have been a boy of the neighborhood or a respectable, educated boy, but in his imagination he was any boy he wished. In "The Genius," for example, the boy narrator thinks himself an explorer traveling the roads and lanes around the barracks and copying his "adventures in a book called The Voyages of Johnson Martin, with Many Maps and Illustrations, Irishtown University Press, 3s. 6d. nett."[6] About that time he received a prize of five shillings from a Catholic boys' paper for a poem of his they published. There is even an apocryphal story, perpetuated by dust-jacket blurbs, that by the age of twelve Michael had put together a collected edition of his own writings. The point is that through fantasy he escaped from his common situation and became a writer after all.

Another avenue of escape for the dreamer of Harrington Square was his pink-washed attic room with its skylight window. There he spent many rich, lonely hours reading, sketching, or running his own private theatre. His theatre was a boot box with a proscenium arch cut in one end; his actors were cut from illustrations in books, mounted on pasteboard, and stuck to pieces of

wood. He particularly liked grand opera because in addition to elaborate set-
tings it gave him the opportunity of being principal tenor, orchestra, and chorus as well. On good days he would climb out on the roof to the high back wall
and sit alone for hours commanding a great view of his neighbors' yards. Here
he was not only equal to his surroundings but transported above them; from
squalid disorder he had improvised his own refined order.

And if not in his attic retreat composing some imaginary edition of songs
or staging some theatrical production, if not on the back wall mapping out
some imaginary battle, Michael would climb to the edge of the quarry above
the Ballyhooley Road to survey the entire area below: the spires of the churches,
the masts and funnels of the ships at the quays, the blue hills beyond. From
there he "felt like some sort of wild bird," abstracted and distant from the life
moving below him—"the horse and cart coming up the road, the little girl with
her skipping rope on the pavement, or the old man staggering by on his
stick,"—all unaware of the "eagle eye" observing them from his secure nest.[7]

Reading was another of the heights he scaled, "and a more perilous one,"
for as he said, "it was a way of looking beyond your own back yard into the
neighbors'." The neighborhood outcast escaped from his surroundings and
found in the printed word what Eileen O'Faoláin called "a variety show in his
own mind."[8] The premier acts of that show were the storybooks and boys'
weeklies he read with such fervent devotion from the time he could read at the
age of five until he left school for good and began to educate himself. He found
himself drawn to the children in these pages, who were always being "kid-
napped by tramps and gipsies." He liked to think that something of the sort
could happen to him; he became Billy Bunter, the fat boy, or Tom Merry, the
all-around hero. Murder and intrigue and schoolboy adventures abounded in
the stories in *Boy's Own Paper, Gem, Magnet,* and *Marvel,* magazines popu-
lated by English boys whose lives evidenced values and expectations far above
young Michael's.[9] The style of these boys' magazines was as dramatic and exaggerated as what his father read to him from the newspaper. Usually the
characters were boys of estate, of mannered schooling. They possessed marvelous codes of behavior, which Michael found lacking in the Barrack Stream
where survival was the yardstick of action. Above all, these boys were "getting
a really good education" and he felt "that some of it was bound to brush off"
on him. So Michael read and dreamed and speculated about what it would be
like if his father owned a factory and they lived in Sunday's Well and he wore a
blazer to school. But resplendent as his fantasy world was, Michael eventually
had to face the reality of his life. It was "misery to return from the heights" and
face the difference between the two worlds, the one in his head and the one at
his feet.

Needless to say, many of his later stories of childhood, so rich in autobiographical detail, are the refinement of his lifelong struggle with fantasy and reality. In so many of these stories his boy heroes find themselves trapped in a
dilemma caused by their taking their fantasies and reading too seriously. The
contrast between life lived in the pages of the boys' weeklies and life in the
poor areas of Cork caused more than one trauma for young Michael. In *An
Only Child* he tells how all of his reading at Christmas time inflated the magic
of the season. The words and pictures radiated holly and candles and snow and
gleaming windows, representing "the contrast between light and dark, life and

death; the cold and darkness that reigned when Life came into the world." But the promised magic and feasting never seemed to materialize at 8 Harrington Square. His father and mother quarreled about money, and the postman never arrived with the Christmas Eve delivery. Still, he was happy when his mother took him across the bridge to shop at the toy shop on North Main Street. "There in the rainy dusk, jostled by prams and drunken women in shawls, and thrust on one side by barefooted children from the lanes, I stood in wonder, thinking which treasure Santa Claus would bring me from the ends of the earth." Small candles and stale cakes on Christmas Eve; on Christmas morning, nothing but the toy he had picked out the day before. "Nothing had happened as it happened in the Christmas numbers"—no snow, no holly, no gleaming windows, no special visitors, no precious gifts. Only Christmas Mass "and the choir thundering out *Natum videte regem angelorum* as though they believed it, when any fool could see that things were just going on the same old way."[10] The season of imagination slipped away and the world of reality broke harshly upon him.

I I I

Disillusionment might be reasonably expected to swamp a poor boy at Christmas, a time of naturally lofty hope. More remarkable was the disillusionment Michael felt at school. The boys' weeklies had inflated his educational expectations to the point where there was no vital connection between his idea of education and what he actually got. "So I adored education from afar, and strove to be worthy of it, as later I adored beautiful girls and strove to be worthy of them, and with similar results."

As far as we know, he managed well enough at first in the school on Strawberry Hill near the house in Blarney Lane, but then he was only just beginning to read, to enter his mental variety show. Though Michael was sick often and unable to attend school regularly, he did learn to read and write with ease. By the time he enrolled at St. Patrick's National School in St. Luke's Cross, just down the hill from Harrington Square, he knew all about "proper education." The headmaster of this boys' school was a man whose stupidity apparently matched his brutality. To him small boys were criminals conspiring with consummate cunning to undermine his educational purposes. Consequently for Michael, going to school each morning was more to be dreaded than going to the dentist.

Then, when Michael was about nine years old, a new assistant came to St. Patrick's and made an immediate impression. What the young dreamer saw in Daniel Corkery was a limping man with a round face radiating enthusiasm; what he heard was a harsh, staccato voice sounding a note of subversion. From the first day, Corkery kept his boys in to do Irish. It was the first time Michael heard the language. *Muscail do mbisneail, a Banba,* Corkery scrawled on the board, commanding them to write it out many times. "Waken your courage, Ireland." The next day Michael asked about the two pictures Corkery had hung in the classroom in place of the usual charts. Corkery smiled and told the inquisitive boy that he had painted the pictures. So Michael decided that he would be a painter too; at home he discovered that the cost of paints and brushes was prohibitive.[11] Printed in script below Corkery's picture of a blind fiddler was a poem in Irish. Michael copied the poem and took it to his grandmother, whose first language was Irish; she did not fancy the poem, but she taught him a few verses of her own. The next day he returned to Corkery armed with his first Irish sentence, something about asking a girl for a kiss. At Christmas Corkery gave book prizes; Michael's was W. Lorcan O'Byrne's *Kings and Vikings*.

Corkery was a passionate nationalist; he was also a painter, a writer, and a lover of music. He was a gentle, approachable person and a dynamic teacher. With marvelous control he managed to move deftly about the classroom, despite a lame leg, and to speak with clarity and impact, despite a speech impediment. He captured Michael's heart and imagination. "I am a natural collaborationist," O'Connor wrote; "like Dolan's ass I go a bit of the road with everybody, and I enjoyed having a hero among the hereditary enemy—schoolmasters."

Good students often make good teachers better, and Michael captured Corkery as well, hounding him for books in Irish, stumbling through sentences learned from his granny, and after school, walking behind him up Gardiner's Hill. He began to imitate Corkery's mannerisms: the way he tipped his hat, the careful way he enunciated each word, and even the way he limped, resolutely trailing his crippled foot. In *An Only Child* O'Connor confessed that he imitated those he loved, and Corkery was his "first and greatest love."

At about the age of nine Michael began to complain of severe headaches. For over a year they plagued him. His father suspected him of scheming to avoid the unpleasant life of the schoolyard. His mother was baffled and worried. Finally a doctor sent him to have his eyes examined, and after that he had to wear black glasses and stay home from school for months. Already branded a sissy by the tough boys of the Barrack Stream, he now had to carry the label of "specky four-eyes." To make matters worse, the only eyeglasses the family could afford, huge lenses in black wire frames, called attention to themselves. Had it not been for his healthy crop of black hair and his long face, he might have appeared to be all glasses.

Michael did not return to St. Patrick's after the months of absence; he was sent instead to the Monastery of Our Lady's Mount, a school run by the Christian Brothers. North Mon, as it was called, was ostensibly a school for poor boys.[12] Recalling the switch, O'Connor suspected that his mother had wanted him to succeed as the son of a friend had succeeded, complete with picture in the *Examiner* and a university scholarship. The problem was that North Mon was located so far from Harrington Square that on rainy days he reached school wet and chilled. The only consolation he could salvage from the long walk was adventure—a parade near the barracks, a ship entering the slips, or just a sprightly spring day. So even if he arrived at school dry, he arrived late, not a practice guaranteed to please the monks.

At first the school seemed comfortable enough. Michael had escaped from the dullness of the National School, and for a time the brothers treated him with the same attentiveness he had received from Corkery. He felt special. His compositions were often displayed along the partition as examples of good writing. It was not long, however, before his joy soured. The monks decided that he had a "defective ear," and refused him permission to join singing classes. Moreover, the monks realized that he was a dreamer, the worst possible disease for a scholar. He simply didn't fit; he asked embarrassing questions and he read too much. They were convinced, with good reason, that Michael would never be a "passer of examinations," a quality on which the reputation of North Mon had long rested. They therefore recommended him to Trades School where he could learn something useful, and so with righteous dispatch got him out of their hair to protect the prestige of the school.

Michael meanwhile went on about the business of learning on his own. He had always improvised in order to survive, not only in the restricting routine of school but also in the dull habits of home. Like all melancholy men, his father made the house his cave—dark, dull, and unimaginative. "As nothing would persuade Father but that he was a home-loving body, nothing would persuade me but that I belonged to a class to which boots and education came natural." While his father tinkered with clocks and brackets and pipe bowls, Michael read his boys' weeklies or the sixpenny Shakespeare he had found. His mother, who worked hard all day as a charwoman, tried to liven the house with gay curtains and fresh paint. Still, the emotional ambiance was insecure, sad, and close—except when he escaped into his books and dreams or was alone with his mother. Naturally, when Mick senior decided to go off to war again, Michael felt a huge burden lifted.

A new war for an old soldier means the chance to be young again, to swagger and dare and feel the excitement of combat. So, when the Great War broke out in 1914, Mick O'Donovan accepted the call from His Majesty's forces without hesitation. Those tall tales of South Africa were wearing thin among his comrades in the pubs of the Barrack Stream, and besides, even the hardships of military life look inviting to a man caught in a "bad marriage." Mick's departure left Minnie and Michael alone again to share the boy's passage into adolescence. "Mother and I had never been happier."

Mick was away for nearly two years, during which time his son burrowed deeper into his own private world; he had given up school but not education. He read the English schoolboys' weeklies avidly and followed faithfully the campaigns of the British army on war maps pinned to his attic wall. For a while he read everything he could find on Irish history, and even wrote an essay in which he chronicled all the atrocities the English had committed upon the Irish that he could gather.[13] Every day he went to early Mass with his mother to pray for the safe return of his father. Occasionally he walked in the country to watch Corkery paint, but usually he just went to the Free Library near City Hall. Having exhausted the supply of books in the children's department, he ventured into the adult section with his mother's card; and there he found more books on Ireland, as well as art books and novels. His favorite writer for a time was Canon Sheehan, but later he moved on to Hugo and Dumas. He learned Goethe's "Symbolen" by heart because Sheehan "shared with the authors of the boys' weeklies a weakness for foreign languages, and printed lengthy extracts from Goethe in the original."[14] Thus inspired, he went on to learn German and Russian from the Hodder and Stoughton Self-Educator texts so popular at the time. He memorized whole passages because he could not afford to buy books, and learned by pretending because he had no teachers. When his father returned early in 1916, they were even greater strangers.

3

The Incorruptibles

Perhaps, after all, you are right, and I am only a Don Quixote, and the reading of all sorts of wonderful books has turned my head.

HEINRICH HEINE, *writing on Cervantes*

ON Easter Monday, 1916, small groups of ill-equipped and unorganized Irish patriots, hoping to stir their countrymen to arm against the English rule, stormed the General Post Office and a few other strategic points in Dublin. Though instantly crushed by the military force of the British Empire, this uprising became a symbolic gesture precipitating an eight-year chain of events leading to the establishment of an Irish Free State.[1] At the time of the Rising Michael O'Donovan was only twelve years old. When it was all over—the Black and Tan War, Partition, and the Civil War—he was twenty. "A revolution had begun in Ireland, but it was nothing to the revolution that had begun in me," he said later.[2] For the nation and for the "smart boy of Harrington Square," it was a time of growing up and of brutal encounters with reality; it was a time of adolescence.

I

Cork, in 1916, was still a divided city. The insurgency and political unrest that had fermented for centuries was reaching the brim, but for such a loquacious city it was a surprisingly quiet unrest, a rebellion building fearfully because of vigorous police activity.[3] Life went on pretty much as usual, except for little parties of men drilling at sunset or illicit news sheets being circulated. The underground swell seeped above ground. Not only were natives learning Irish, they were proposing to drop English altogether. Names were changed from Murphy to O'Murchadha, from Whelan to O'Faoláin. "One can still almost date that generation by its Liams, Seans, and Peadars." Books in Irish, not all of them good by any means, were published in great numbers; and little magazines, many offering little more than enthusiastic rhetoric, appeared with increased frequency.

The Easter Rising may have been the most significant public event of 1916, but to Michael it was only background noise. To him the discovery in a shop window of the book *A Munster Twilight*, by Daniel Corkery, proved a greater shock and a more significant immediate influence.[4] He gloated over his discovery, borrowed the book from the library, and read it through "without understanding a word." Then he saved a shilling to buy his own copy. There and then he put aside the boys' weeklies and plunged with equal exuberance into Corkery's world of Irish literary nationalism.

Daniel Corkery, already a surrogate father to Michael, lived at the time in a small house on Gardiner's Hill with his mother and sister. There, surrounded by books and paintings, he presided over a small group of eager disciples— young ones like Michael and Seán O'Faoláin and older ones like Denis Breen, who had worked in Corkery's theater in Queen's Street. Corkery may have been what O'Connor later termed a "provincial intellect," but to his protégés he was all the intellect they knew. He gave them music, art, theatre, Irish verse, and Russian fiction; but what mattered most was the spirit of his teaching—the enthusiasm, idealism, and intensity of it.

Michael's mother had always sung to him, and in spite of the Christian Brothers' ruling that he had a defective ear, he had always enjoyed music. An evening of singing light melodies or listening to the gramophone was one of the trappings of middle-class life that he envied. Occasionally Corkery took him to a recital or to the opera. On Corkery's gramophone they listened to Bach, Beethoven, and Mozart: "I practically learned the Seventh Symphony and the Mozart Concerto by heart, and for years judged everything by them."[5] Because he considered himself culturally disadvantaged, Michael strained to master what was considered the best, to meet the measure of refinement set by his mother and the English school stories.

The thing Michael did best was to read. Not that his tastes were what anyone would call refined; he just loved to read. Corkery began to lend him well-chosen volumes from his own bookcase. The first was Browning, of whom Michael had never heard. He had memorized thousands of lines in German and Irish, but the only English poet he had heard of was Shakespeare whom he had decided he should dislike on principle. From Shelley and Browning, Corkery moved him carefully to Chekhov and Turgenev, then to Whitman and Tolstoy. It was like bringing along a young racing colt slowly with short sprints and then gradually moving to the longer runs. After Michael published a translation into Irish of a sonnet by Du Bellay in the *Sunday Independent,* Corkery invited him to join the literary group that met at his house.

Above all else, Corkery gave to Michael his first understanding of Ireland. Though he had received some inkling of rural Ireland and a smattering of the Irish tongue from his peasant grandmother, Michael's sense of nationality was only beginning to blossom. After all, his models in those boys' weeklies were primarily English, and nationalism in a poor neighborhood is generally more shadow than substance. He had groped for his personal identity in the noisy streets and in his attic den. Now Corkery forced him to grope for his cultural identity in the library and in the Gaelic League Hall, the place that came to serve as his teenage hangout. The shock of the Easter Rising and the discovery of *A Munster Twilight* brought Corkery back into his life, and for a while Michael had a mentor again and, while his father was away at least, a sort of father. One day, as he says, he woke to find the romance of his childhood depart with a wave of the hand, but he always remembered it for what it had been— "a child's vision of a world complete and glorified." New people and different ideas claimed his attention, but he never really lost that innocence. Invisible Presences or Interior Voices—whatever he chose to call them—were to remain perennial acts in the variety show running inside his head.

I I

At the age of fourteen Michael was an ex-scholar chafing against the bit of unemployment. His reading was restless and unsystematic—novels, histories, and "high-class magazines" such as the *Times Literary Supplement* or the *New Statesman*. In addition he carefully read the advertisements in the *Examiner* for jobs that demanded a smart boy. He even went to the Technical School and the School of Commerce at night to pick up whatever he could in the way of arithmetic, typing, and bookkeeping, but all he ever got out of these practical courses were two quotations. From a bookkeeping text he pulled this saying: "In business there is no such thing as an out-and-out free gift." And in typing exercises one phrase caught his ear: "The splendour falls on castle walls." What struck him years later was that these two simple assertions, so indelibly riveted somewhere between his ears, "represented the two irreconcilables that I was being asked to reconcile in myself."[6]

Michael's first job was in a wholesale drapery business. Actually his priest got him the position, but the piety and regimentation of the place were too much for him. He was sacked for being a dreamer. His next job, as a messenger for a chemist, came to pretty much the same end. Again he went back to his attic to work on his Greek or Irish or whatever splendor had caught his attention. There was an "even briefer spell at a job printer's." While his new boss was showing him the ropes, he asked if Michael could spell. To which the smart boy replied smartly: "Oh, that's my forte!" Such language would have been suitable in a dream world but not in a dirty print shop. That very evening the man who had recommended Michael for the job told his father about the incident. Realizing that he had made a fool of himself, Michael was too mortified to return the next day. "It was part of the abnormal sensitiveness induced by daydreaming."

Finally he worked as a "junior tracer" with the Great Southern and Western Railway at Glanmire Station, just down the hill from his house. His job was to trace missing goods by checking dockets and storage sheds between the station and the Goods Office on the quay. It did not take him long to realize that he was out of place here too. The bookish ways of the library held little weight in this fast-paced and practical world of goods and consignments. The language was not even the same. Besides, his eyesight was a severe handicap, making him appear even more awkward and mawkish than he actually was. A gangling daydreamer might easily trip over boxes or misplace invoices—even without bad eyes. Moreover, everything at work seemed as common as things at home. There were no blinding illuminations, though he often dawdled near the passenger trains departing for Dublin, dreaming of the day he would escape. Among his fellow workers his naive inattention was seen as dullness. He came in for more than his share of ragging, usually about matters of sex. "There was, for instance, the matter of '1 Bale Foreskins' which appeared on a docket and was invoiced to Kingsbridge by some bored young invoice clerk." Michael did his duty and traced the shipment with his usual earnestness, "enquiring of the Dublin boys if perhaps a bale of foreskins might not still be lying round somewhere." Only after considerable difficulty did he finally recognize the practical joke. Though humiliated and enraged by the insult, he never retaliated. He endured the daily horrors only to draw his meagre weekly pay. Always out of place, lonely, and trapped within himself, he made this dreary reality disappear at seven o'clock when he walked up the hill toward home.

One talent, however, found some practical application at the railway—his Irish. In mockery of his love of the language and of the pin he wore on his coat, the other workers called him the Native. Oddly enough, in Ireland at the time "the mere fact that you spoke Irish could make you be regarded as a freak." As if Michael—frail, clumsy, bespectacled, and dreamy—were not enough of a misfit already. His boss, Joe Power, perpetuated the label but exploited Michael's translating ability from time to time, particularly when some Englishman, more Irish than the Irish, refused to converse in anything but Irish, which of course no one but Michael could speak. To O'Connor, recapturing these incidents, almost as hallucinations, it all seemed an indication of a sort of double life.

> One life I led in English—a life of drudgery and humiliation; the other in Irish or whatever scraps of foreign languages I had managed to pick up without benefit of grammar, and which any sensible man would describe as daydreaming, though daydreaming is a coarse and unrealistic word that might be applied by sensible men to the beliefs of the early Christians. That was the real significance of my passion for languages: they belonged entirely to the world of my imagination.

It was a double life he would always lead.

Unable to reconcile the real and the imaginary, Michael was sacked again. Joe Power, a decent and clever man, happened to read one of Michael's first groping literary efforts. His advice, like Harold Macmillan's years later, was "for God's sake, stick to writing." And on the Saturday night he lost his job, Michael read his first paper at the Gaelic League Hall—in Irish, on Goethe. That event summed up his adolescence: a poor dreamer improvising an education and slipping into high-class literary life through the servants' entrance.

However, he was again without work. The Free Library once more became his headquarters; there he read whatever book came into his hand and watched the advertisements for jobs suitable to his education. Sometimes he just wandered the streets, looking for something or someone but not knowing what or whom. Michael at fifteen more than coincidentally resembled the "hero" of "The Procession of Life," a story contained in *Guests of the Nation,* O'Connor's first volume of short stories. In it a boy, locked out of the house by his obstinate father, wanders along the quays seeking some measure of human contact. Quays and libraries, whores and drunken fathers, lost jobs and lost opportunities, all figured in the procession of life as it marched past Mickey Donovan at sixteen.

I I I

It was a procession of literature in which Michael chose to march, led for a time by Corkery. Another of Corkery's followers was Seán O'Faoláin, whom Michael met one wet, sleepy night in 1918 at a Gaelic League meeting. The place was a hayloft on Queen's Street across from Corkery's theatre, An Dun. The room had been labeled An Grianan, meaning "a queenly solarium" in Irish. However, a stable occupied the ground floor, and the noises and smells of the horses filtered gently up. O'Faoláin remembers that he was "eighteen then, Michael was fifteen, slightly hooped, all specs, eyes and brow, and eyes myopic, the teeth ingratiating, the brow magnificent and prophetic of the genius he would display fifteen years later. He wore knicker-bockers, long, woollen, hand-knitted stockings and . . . black boots." Being poor, the two literary enthusiasts would simply "walk around in the rain, sheltering in doors, talking literature."[7]

Michael looked up to O'Faoláin for being everything he wanted to be— "handsome, brilliant, and, above all, industrious." Corkery pitted the two against each other, often driving an already self-conscious Michael mad with jealousy. But he supported their efforts—Michael's in translation and Seán's in reviewing. His theatre, his plays, his novels—and, above all, his presence— broke the boredom of Cork for them. He gave them Russian literature and Gaelic literature. He made the two boys literary men, two of Ireland's greatest.

The term *Incorruptibles* was coined by Geraldine Neeson, the wife of Sean Neeson, who was later head of broadcasting in Cork, not long after meeting Michael and Seán at Corkery's play *The Yellow Bittern* in 1920.[8] To her they were arrogant but earnest; "world beaters" she called them. Seán was on his way to college, and Michael was simply on his way, hurling himself at life in the same way he hurled himself at the wind or rain when he walked. Michael and Seán were great walkers and talkers; Michael especially walked hard and talked constantly—fixing the world's problems and writing the world's books all over again as he went. Being incorruptible and impatient to get somewhere, anywhere, he hurled himself at Ireland.

The backdrop for the literary procession of O'Connor and O'Faoláin was Cork under siege. After the 1916 Rising this garrison town became nervous and conspiratorial. Trust vanished and the factionalism became even more noticeable. Insurrection was in the air. Most people of the middle class were trapped by cross allegiances; they nodded assent to the ideals of nationalism but gave in to the practical demands of the pocket. Seán O'Faoláin's father was a retired member of the Royal Irish Constabulary, and Michael's father was a pensioned private in the Munster Fusiliers; both men held fairly clear British sympathies. Their sons, however, took the rebel path and joined the Irish Volunteers shortly after the fighting began in 1919.

Though he had already been on the fringes of rebel activity, Michael saw little action. Watching the older O'Faoláin riding a commandeered lorry with a rifle made him even more anxious and impatient to take part. So when in the spring of 1920 Corkery handed him the opportunity to go to Dublin for a special course in Irish, he jumped at the offer. It was a Gaelic League school "formed to train teachers of Irish, who would later cycle about the country from village to village, teaching in schools and parish halls."[9] Actually, he spent more time around the bookstalls on the quays than he did in the study of Irish. Although at the end of the summer he was granted a certificate qualifying him to teach Irish, he was probably not qualified at all. He returned to Cork, and for a time he "cycled eight or ten miles out of the city in the evenings to teach in country schools by lamplight." Always unlucky in his jobs,

Michael lost this one too, though not for dreaming. This time it was the strict curfew, which prohibited long bicycle rides at night.

This curfew had been imposed on Cork after the murder of the Lord Mayor, Thomas MacCurtin, and the hunger strike of his successor, Terence MacSwiney, whose plays Michael knew well. When MacSwiney's body was returned from Brixton Prison in November 1920, the city became edgy. The Black and Tans paraded ostentatiously, victimized and tortured suspects at will, and kept continual pressure on the rebels. Then, on the night of December 11, some of the British forces swept into the center of the city well after curfew and, in reprisal for a particularly effective ambush the day before, began looting and burning building after building. Though there was only one fatality, the effect was traumatic to the entire city. O'Connor remembered seeing from the back door a red glare mount over the valley of the city. "For hours Father, Mother, and I took turns at standing on a chair in the attic, listening to the shooting and watching the whole heart of the city burn." The next day he toured the rubble and mourned the loss of "the handsome red-brick library" that had been so much a part of his life for nearly ten years.

Two months after this devastation Michael met a young man named Jack (or Sean) Hendrick, a "pale, thin-lipped young clerk in an insurance office," who had been sent by Daniel Corkery. Michael was three years Hendrick's junior but about ten years his senior in "his knowledge of literature and the qualities of mind which he brought to it."[10] He was then, as Hendrick described him, a "tall, bony, awkward-looking lad. He wore steel-rimmed spectacles, had a wonderful sweep of brow and spoke in a rich deep voice." Hendrick's purpose in seeking out this protégé of Corkery was to engage his help in starting a literary and debating society.

For a boy like Michael, Hendrick was just what he needed: someone with all the middle-class virtues and contacts a poor boy lacked and with the personal traits a dreamer wouldn't bother to cultivate—"methodical, cool, and thoughtful." Sean was brilliant but totally lacking in ambition. Michael was just breaking out of the confines of his ghetto neighborhood; he was beginning to look beyond his immediate family. His years of "lonely daydreaming" had left him emotionally and socially backward. The sensitive mommy's boy was terrified of strangers, irritable or uneasy in new situations, jealous of what security he knew, and exacting of those acquaintances he had made, so exacting and intense that he often drove them away. He could be dazzling and entertaining or churlish and morose. Insecure to a fault, he generally exaggerated his own self-importance and dominated conversation. Sean Hendrick was oblivious of this surface smoke and accepted Michael's frustrating excesses. He listened when Michael talked too much about things he did not understand. He broke through Michael's excessive shyness by introducing him to his own friends around Gardiner's Hill.

Home had become intolerable for Michael. His father had returned at the end of the war with his pension and his new stories. His constant nagging about what Michael was or, rather, was not doing with his life drove Michael, like the boy in "The Procession of Life," out into the streets. Home was probably unbearable just because it was home, which for an adolescent is often a shabby thing, especially when compared with friends' houses. But for Michael normal adolescent dissatisfaction was magnified both by the circumstances of his life, which were almost as bad as he believed them to be, and by the character of his melancholy, dreaming makeup. His shy, gaunt, shortsighted awkwardness, and the emotional residue of the years of family strife, made him ashamed of himself, of his parents, and of the little place in Harrington Square. When any of his new friends from up the hill called, he hustled them out of the house and dragged them somewhere else—"for fear Father would start telling funny stories about his army days or Mother reveal that she was only a charwoman."

Sean Hendrick was magnificent leavening for Michael's capricious risings and fallings; he was reality to Michael's romance and romance to Michael's reality. He was an agent of freedom. For one thing, Sean conspired with Michael in that natural adolescent game of love, which for a mommy's boy is a painful form of emancipation. Sean's sister's friends the O'Leary girls, Kitty, Ita, and Maire, became part of Michael's circle of acquaintances, an improbable occurrence without Sean's intervention. Kitty, who eventually married Sean, remembers Michael as tall, gaunt, and bony but attractive to the girls. He had good teeth, thick, even sensuous lips, and dark hair through which he constantly ran his hand. He loved to spend the evening at her house on Ashburton singing German songs while she accompanied him on the piano.

O'Connor once said that he loved girls and education from afar—with much the same results. It was bad enough that he was shy, self-conscious, and lonely; but his fantasy-producing faculty exaggerated every female relationship to the extent that he would fall hopelessly in love only to be crushed desperately by any imagined slight. Like the adolescent heroes of "A Romantic," "Judas," and *The Saint and Mary Kate,* Michael attached a value to girls as sexual beings and objects of adulation all beyond suitable proportion. He also exaggerated his own desires and carried extreme guilt about what he perceived to be his lustful nature. He was so naive that he hadn't a clue what the language of sex meant, let alone how to accomplish in reality what he spent so much time reading and dreaming about.

I V

Michael's role in the Irish struggle for freedom was much the same mixture of romance and reality. The time of the Troubles was to him something of a relief, because it acted as a sort of safety valve for his own angry emotions: "Indeed, it would be truer to say that the Irish nation and myself were both engaged in an elaborate process of improvisation. I was improvising an education I could not afford, and the country was improvising a revolution it could not afford." In this endeavor, too, Sean Hendrick conspired with Michael, the two of them caught up in the rhythms of the times. Hendrick was unable to induce Michael to join a debating society, but Michael managed to enlist Sean in the Volunteers in May 1921, shortly before the Truce. Nearly two years before, Michael had joined, in the face of his father's threats and with the encouragement of Corkery and his mother. Which is to say that Michael's anti-British sentiments were probably more personal than ideological.

Young rank and filers like O'Donovan, O'Faoláin, and Hendrick were given "safe" jobs, such as carrying dispatches, digging up information (useful or not), scouting, or trenching roads. If nothing else, playing at war was better than boredom. The curfew had stripped Cork of what fun it had ever allowed—in Cork, O'Faoláin once quipped, sin is not committed, it is achieved. The young rebels slouched around in trench coats with hats cocked over one eye, or paraded in a field near the Rathcooney road. O'Faoláin added a little style by wearing yellow gloves. Sometimes when an ambush or barrack attack was imminent, they watched the roads or dropped trees across them to stall reinforcements. "Otherwise," O'Faoláin observed in *Vive Moi!,* "we hung around, drilled, waited, felt nervy, groused, and were supremely proud and happy whenever even the most modest task made us feel we were really doing something positive in the struggle for independence."[11] They were young then and it was a love affair of sorts, for they were completely caught up in the romance of rifles and uniforms and press releases. When the armistice came and there was no longer anything for them to do, they woke and found their innocence gone, found themselves hardened, almost grown up, and even a little contemptuous of people who indulged in false sentiment. They had burned out their fantasies and found only the case-hardened reality of modern Ireland.

The Truce came "a little before noon on Monday, July 11, 1921." Michael was not yet eighteen, but he strode like a man into Cork with the armored cars and tanks to take the barracks. For the Incorruptibles it meant a summer in the open, drinking and dancing and parading. But the euphoria ended with the long days of summer, and in the chill of winter the Anglo-Irish Treaty granted them everything but a republican government and control of Ulster—everything but a united Ireland—more than they expected, less than they could accept.

The Treaty brought an end to hostilities with Britain but precipitated a bitter Civil War. Between December 6, 1922, when the Treaty was signed, and the middle of June, the nation waited while two imaginary governments jockeyed for position. The nationalist movement was split between Free Staters, who followed Michael Collins and Arthur Griffith to accept the Treaty, and Republicans, led primarily by Eamon de Valera, who refused to compromise on two major points: the oath of allegiance to the Crown and the concession of the six counties of Ulster to Britain. Looking back with the judgment of years, O'Connor marked this event as "merely an extension into the fourth dimension of the improvisation" that had begun after the crushing of the insurrection of 1916.[12]

Michael took the Republican side partly because he was still incorruptible and partly because it was Corkery's side. He had joined, at Corkery's invitation, an informal group of intellectuals who called themselves the Twenty Club, meeting each Sunday to hear papers on Tolstoy, French theatre, or some other highly irrelevant topic. They later issued a virulently Republican periodical called *An Lóng* (Irish for "the ship") for three numbers (May to July 1922) until it was suppressed by the Free State government.[13] The stamp of Corkery and his talented protégés is obvious. The tone of all three numbers is uncompromising but optimistic. Michael's contribution to the first issue was two poems: "Invictus," which laments the betrayal of dead rebels by compromise, and "Mozart," a sonnet in the style of Corkery, which celebrates freedom and the forces of vibrant life. The poems by Michael, the reviews by O'Faoláin—in fact, everything about the short-lived enterprise—were adolescent, passionate, and self-conscious, just as they all were at the time.

In February 1922 Michael and Hendrick were sent as delegates to the Ard Fheis in Dublin; they were to replace two officers of the Irish Republican Army. The issue was the Treaty, and their instructions were to reject it. But no vote was taken; the general feeling in Ireland was to avoid a split. By the summer, however, Treaty and anti-Treaty factions had become irreparably divided. On June 28 violence resumed when Michael Collins, the man who had engineered the fight against British forces, used brute force to oust a Republican squad from the Four Courts. Harsh military injunctions, including execution for being caught with a weapon, followed that initial mistake. Eleven months of bitterness, reprisal, and atrocity filled the national vacuum. Boys like Michael and Hendrick returned to action, first as censors of the *Cork Examiner* and then as writers for *An Poblacht,* which meant that they were really publicity runners for Erskine Childers.[14]

An ex-British army officer serving the Irish cause, Childers seemed an imposing figure to the impressionable boys, though he was a small man who dressed unobtrusively. Conscientious to a fault, he carried out the trivial details of the Republican cause with cold efficiency. Despite a stiff price placed on his head by the provisional government, Childers was careless about being tailed. In at least two instances Michael and Sean, the most unlikely of saviors, rescued him from alarming situations. To be caught with a gun meant summary execution, and Childers was one man the Republican forces could not afford to lose.

Late in July 1922 Michael accompanied Childers to Republican headquarters in Fermoy. It was an honor for him, but he was more delighted with the countryside than the martial display at the barrack square. The uniforms and bandoliers and Lewis guns struck him as a bit ostentatious, particularly when displayed at meals where the atmosphere was strained and artificial enough. That night, he noticed that Childers was reading Dumas and Fenimore Cooper, which struck him as rather unheroic. Michael was reading Dostoevsky or Whitman, while casting himself in the part of young Tolstoy, war correspondent at Sebastopol.[15] Somehow he couldn't quite fit his romantic image of war with the pedestrian realities of Childers's habits.

The next day Childers sent him with some dispatches to Kilmallock, where a front-line headquarters had been set up in Ashill Towers, a pseudo-Gothic castle more suited to Michael's romantic tastes. Unlike the barracks at Buttevant and Fermoy, with their parade grounds and officers' mess, this operation was an improbable improvisation of guerrilla proportions, down to its armored cars and the shells hand made for a captured Big Gun. From Kilmallock he was sent north to Croom in County Limerick, armed with a carbine; his mission was to fetch reinforcements. But his attention was more on the visit to the ancient place of the O'Donovans than on his mission, which he accomplished without a hitch. After that Childers sent him to Buttevant with dispatches for the divisional commander, Liam Deasy. When Deasy seemed to give the dispatches a casual eye, Michael felt deflated. He had risked his life only to be patted on the head and sent to bed, like the young girl in "Soirée Chez Une Belle Jeune Fille" whose first assignment as a courier met the same indifferent greeting. The dispatches, however, received due attention—Deasy was made of the same steel as Childers; and Michael was sent back to Kilmallock with more dispatches.

Somewhere between Charleville and his destination Michael and his driver were stopped unexpectedly by a column of Free State soldiers behind Republican lines. It was a Sunday when all the troops were either at Mass or heading for home. The half-uniformed men who emerged from some hedges were probably as surprised at finding a courier on the road as Michael was at seeing guns pointed at him. Instead of eating the dispatches, which his reading would have dictated, he simply tore them up and tossed the pieces to the summer wind. He cursed his captors viciously, more out of frustration than hatred: On his first day of real action he had allowed himself to be taken prisoner, and his dream of Tolstoy at Sebastopol had blown up in his face.[16]

After having been held for a few hours in a commandeered farmhouse, Michael and some other prisoners from an action the day before were rescued by front-line Republican troops who had returned from Mass. However, the rescue was not without considerable gunfire, chaos, and even death. Just before dark a rifle grenade exploded upstairs, killing the leader of the Free State column. Surrender was immediate. The entire charade had taken the better part of a perfectly fine Sunday. The hilarity and hysteria of it all only convinced Michael that he was not cut out for soldiering. He'd read about the exhilaration of "baptism under fire," but this skirmish he found rather dull.[17] All he wanted was to see the prisoners to Buttevant without incident or reprisal and to make for Cork by the first car so he could get the story into print. He did not know it at the time, but, if nothing else, this war was giving him more material than he could ever use—stories of men switching sides, of dead boys' caps, of Big Guns and armored cars striking fear more by noise than by accuracy. Unlike Childers, Michael and the rest were amateurs, and amateurs have a way of overlooking details.

One detail that someone, perhaps even Childers, had overlooked was the possibility of an invasion of Cork from the sea.[18] In early August that was exactly what happened. Michael and Sean had only just finished their news releases about the enemy's defeat when they noticed Republican soldiers fleeing the city. Headquarters was in a frenzy, and it was every man for himself. Michael and Sean headed for Corkery's cottage in Inniscarra. Corkery fed them, pushed them off toward Macroom, and followed later after deciding that his boys were probably incapable of taking care of themselves. The army was disbanded the next day in favor of a return to the guerrilla tactics used against the Black and Tans. For some reason, Michael and Sean were assigned to continue publicity activity. With a printing press commandeered from a local job printer, they set up their operations in a schoolhouse at Ballymakeera and later in a farmhouse in Reananarree. It was a primitive setup in one of the wildest parts of Ireland, a strictly Irish-speaking area in the rugged mountains west of Macroom. It was Michael's first time in a totally Irish-speaking environment. Corkery, who had introduced him to Irish, had departed for Gougane Barra, and Hendrick, who knew no Irish at all, fretted over the machines. Michael was in his glory. He sat for hours in one particular farmhouse listening to the magical sounds of the language spoken as it ought to be spoken. He also fell in love with the farmer's eldest daughter, of whom he wrote in *An Only Child*: " [Her] gentle, blond, lethargic beauty was as breath-taking as her Irish, and she spoke that as I had never heard it spoken before, with style. Unfortunately, I had no notion of how to make love to her, because she appeared to me through a veil of characters from books I had read. Most of the time she was Maryanka from *The*

Cossacks." One has only to read "September Dawn," a story in *Guests of the Nation,* to realize that eventually he turned the whole experience back into literature.

On August 22 news came that Michael Collins, the commander in chief of the Free State troops, had been shot and killed in an ambush at Beal na mBlath, only ten miles away from Ballymakeera. Everyone rejoiced except Childers who remained silent and wrote an article praising his old friend.[19] It is somewhat ironic that of all the people in this war, it was Collins and Childers, two very unheroic heroes, to whom Michael was drawn. Both were men of details, of letters and dispatches. Michael's role in the war was that of journalist, whose details were words rather than bullets. And words, after all, were the imaginative core of this particular revolution. It was a journalist, Arthur Griffith, who inspired the nationalism of Sinn Fein in his paper the *United Irishman.* The experiences at Ballymakeera also put Michael in direct contact with the other half of Irish nationalism, that which was inspired by Hyde and Pearse: the Gaelic Revival. Michael's devotion to learning Irish was also part of the campaign of words, perhaps the only important way anything is fought in Ireland. Significantly, he kept to both pursuits his entire life—journalism and Irish.

Early in September Corkery appeared again and ordered him to return home. There had been rumors of drink and the farmer's daughter, both untrue because Michael was still seeing things through a veil of literature. Corkery was adamant and Michael was not sure whether to be flattered or infuriated. Off they went to Cork in a commandeered lorry, the ride made torturous by blown-out bridges and fallen trees. Though he was in Cork once again, Michael still acted like a rebel on the run, always looking for enemy troops and seldom sleeping at home. The retreat from Cork in August had brought increasing chaos to the Republican ranks.

The death of Collins, instead of being a victory, only served to lubricate the slide to disarray. Childers was being blamed for ambushes he had no part in; the war of words was part of the enemy's strategy as well. By October he had become the object of such vigorous pursuit that even Republican troops avoided him for fear of being captured and shot with him. After an incredible journey across Ireland Childers and his cousin David Robinson were captured in County Wicklow.[20] By the time of Childers's execution in November, things had fallen completely apart for the Republican cause, and for the young Michael O'Donovan, now living from hand to mouth, from one hiding place to another. When he heard of the execution, he wrote the date over Whitman's elegy to Lincoln in the copy of *Leaves of Grass* he had carried constantly for over a year. "Like everything else I did at the time, it reeked of literature, and yet when I recite the lines to myself today, all the emotion comes back and I know it was not all literature."[21]

4

Freedom

We had fed the heart on fantasies,
The heart's grown brutal from the fare;
More substance in our enmities
Than in our love . . .
W. B. YEATS, *"Meditations in Time of Civil War"*

I

MICHAEL'S role in the Troubles ended abruptly. On a cold, clear morning in February 1923, he was captured unceremoniously by Free State soldiers. Had he been carrying a gun he would have been executed. At the courthouse he was promptly sentenced, then marched in late afternoon to the Women's Gaol in Sunday's Well. His fugitive existence of the past four months had so disoriented him that imprisonment seemed almost a relief. It took responsibility from his hands: At least he knew when he would eat and where he would sleep. The next morning before dawn he was awakened by a flashing torch and the faceless growl of a guard, who marched him down a corridor for a lesson: In a cell a young boy lay writhing on the floor, so ravished by the bayonets and rifle butts of overzealous soldiers that he seemed a swollen "lump of dough"; the boy was shot a few days later. In an autobiographical piece, "A Boy in Prison," written nearly ten years later, O'Connor recalled his feelings at the time: "I saw him as an embodiment of us all, young, poor, bewildered, struggling against we knew not what; his mother perhaps making a miserable living as a laundress in some slum."[1] His belief in the magical improvisation, already stretched by the atrocities of guerrilla fighting, nearly snapped. The boy's empty face haunted him for years. Since he could not be too sure he himself would not be next, fear as much as pity stirred him to nausea. The romance of self-determination had come to this brutality; the highest hopes of Michael and a generation of Incorruptibles were dashed in atavistic reprisal.

Conditions in the prison were intolerable even to young rebels used to sleeping in barns and ditches. The place crawled with rats and other vermin. Three of the boys slept on the floor and one on the radiator under the window; that left no room to walk about in. On top of the physical discomfort, Michael found the company equally unbearable; in fact, he was a snob, and he considered his cell mates to be uneducated and unimaginative. Behind the prison was a convent; the nuns who lived there administered the penitentiary for fallen women. Every morning Michael noticed a nun at an open window waving to them—only one.

And in the solitary figure of that nun who had not yet detached herself
from the world of passions that we represented, there was for me some-

thing terrible lonely and heartbroken, and for years the thought of her made me lonely too until at last I put her into a story called Nightpiece with Figures.[2]

While the others cursed and complained, during the day he read books smuggled to him by Corkery, who had also sent tobacco and cigarette papers, not so much for the pleasure of smoking as for the discipline of rolling one's own cigarettes. Indeed, Corkery understood Michael perfectly at the time. Their letters were written in a kind of literary code. The variety show in Michael's mind made prison bearable, almost interesting. The first person he got to know in prison, he wrote to Corkery, resembled Baburin in Turgenev's "Punin and Baburin." Another prisoner, "a ragged, toothless, underfed-looking man with blue eyes and a cropped skull," tried to keep his fellow inmates amused, but to Michael he was "a Pantaloon with a tragic heart." Corkery even came to visit him disguised as Martin Cloyne, the hero of his own novel *The Threshold of Quiet.*[3]

Early one morning in April Michael and hundreds of other prisoners "were taken in lorries through the barely-wakened city" to Glanmire Station. With ten or twelve others he was jammed into a tiny carriage for a train ride to one of the permanent internment camps; he hoped it would be Newbridge, where his friend Sean Hendrick had been taken. At Limerick Junction it became obvious they were on the way to Dublin. Indeed, they arrived at Kingsbridge Station, then sat on a sidetrack for hours, only to be shunted across town to the Amiens Street Station. Soon the curious prisoners could discern the familiar smell of the sea off to their right. An hour or so out of Dublin the train stopped at a small station in flat farm country. Distant searchlights scanned the area "picking out white-washed cottages and trees in their first leaf and flattening them against the night like pieces of theatre scenery." The weary and hungry bunch marched toward a group of nondescript buildings inside a high barbed-wire fence. It all struck Michael as a shifting fantasy, the way the lights beamed on one building after another. The only fixtures in this kaleidoscopic scene were "the barbed-wire entanglements and the main gate which were lit with great arc lamps and the little wooden hut outside which we halted, and in which we must be received."[4]

They stood for hours in the bitter cold. Shortly before dawn they staggered through the main gate to receive from the quartermaster a hut assignment. Michael had been unable to eat the rations on the train, so while carrying his eating and sleeping gear across the compound he fainted from exhaustion and hunger. Apparently, he had begun to show symptoms of the stomach trouble that was to plague him for years. With the help of the military police and a few prisoners, he was placed in bed, the first real bed he had felt for months. There he awoke the next morning to sunlight and fresh air. "I felt I was dreaming." Actually, he was locked inside the Gormanstown Internment Camp, an abandoned American aerodrome from World War I.[5]

Despite all the modern facilities of an American military installation, including good plumbing and well-lit barracks, Gormanstown was still a prison. Michael was in a long hut at the west end of the camp. Twenty-five to thirty beds were lined up on either side of a high partition running down the center of the hut.

Still, Michael was better off than he had ever been. After the Women's Gaol in Cork this was a place of "privacy and culture." The camp held nearly a thousand internees, and it was easy "to maintain the illusion that one was in a town; there were classes, lectures, plays, concerts, debates, books." The food was dull but regular, and for a while Michael's stomach problem disappeared. The summer of 1923 was unusually pleasant. Michael slept well and woke early for a cold shower and a brisk walk—two miles around the compound. As usual he took advantage of enforced solitude to listen to his Interior Voices; gradually the horrors of the Civil War faded from his mind, "the sleepless nights, the aimless skirmishes, and the futile, sickening executions." He offset the curse of boredom with the routine of study—he taught Irish and German and took lessons in French—and, as a teacher, was excused from fatigues.[6]

The most startling discovery he made while preparing his classes in Irish was that the language had a grammar. "For me, languages had always been a form of magic, like girls, and I would as soon have thought of taking liberties with one as with the other." He recited all the poetry he knew, and found that poets used certain word forms not from personal taste but on the basis of definite grammatical rules. As with every other "discovery" in his life, Michael took this one further than necessary. Grammar suddenly became an obsession with him; he began to hunt for subjunctives, accusatives, and misplaced modifiers. Grammer, he later concluded, was "the bread-winner of language as usage is the housekeeper, and the poor man's efforts at keeping order are for ever being thwarted by his wife's intrigues and her perpetual warnings to the children not to tell Father. But language, like life, is impossible without a father and he is forever returning to his thankless job of restoring authority." That oblique generalization represents something very close to the center of Michael O'Donovan's personality. The process is pure intuition with a flash-point finality, and the domestic imagery captures his fundamental world view, a pattern of paralyzing opposition in his life and his writing, variously expressed as the tension between judgment and instinct, head and heart, reason and imagination.

This sudden discovery of the rational structure of language was probably symptomatic of his "emergence from a protracted adolescence." At the same time as he was learning to measure his own ideas, he was forced to look outward. Objectivity accompanied realism in his growth as a person and his development as a writer. Surrounded by a greater array of human beings than he had ever known in Cork, Michael began to listen to voices other than those in his own head. "We had our share of fat-heads in the camp," he wrote, "and maybe a crook or two, but on the average, the prisoners were far finer types than we would have met in a normal lifetime in Ireland—better educated, more unselfish, thoughtful, and interesting." The person he was closest to was Tom Walsh, an Irish-speaker from Clare, who not only agreed with Michael's political heresies but also remembered reading a poem of Michael's.

Among the other interesting men he came to appreciate were Fred Cogley, who taught Spanish, and Frank Gallagher, a Shelley enthusiast who had been a close friend of Erskine Childers.[7] He also learned a few things from Sean T. O'Kelley, who later became president of Ireland, and Sean MacEntee, later minister of finance in de Valera's government. O'Kelly loaned Michael a French edition of Anatole France, and MacEntee gave him outright a copy of

Heine, which Michael had coveted since Corkery had recommended the German poet for anyone in prison. Then there was the quartermaster, a small man from North Cork, who "had a capacity for swearing and bad language that beat anything" Michael had ever heard, even in the Barrack Stream. What Michael noted was not what the quartermaster swore about but the sheer artistry with which he did it. Michael never went to college—a fact that rankled him throughout his life—but Gormanstown was as rich as any college could ever have been, both in scholarship and hard knocks.

Gormanstown was not without its unpleasant moments, some of which made Michael's emergence from adolescence exceedingly painful. One night, while listening to a group of Cork boys singing ballads about brave Irish heroes dying for the glory of Ireland, Michael flashed back to that "lump of dough" on the floor of the cell in the Women's Gaol. The nightmare of betrayal soured these songs for him and he said so. The worship of martyrdom struck him as sentimental ignorance, for he believed that the boy in all his misguided idealism hadn't wanted to die. Michael was adamant and the entire hut blew up in shouting. He went so far as to insist that even Patrick Pearse had not really wanted to die. The fury of the place was immeasurable. Michael stormed off to bed in a "blind rage" about the senseless attitude that glorious death justified living. "I didn't want to die," he insisted. "I wanted to live, to read, to hear music, and to bring my mother to all the places that neither of us had ever seen, and I felt these things were more important than any martyrdom."

Not long after that episode another incident ignited his self-righteous rage and isolated him further from the other prisoners. A "shadow" organization had been developed; it "duplicated completely the enemy organization" so that the Republican prisoners had little contact with Free State gaolers. They received mail from their own postmaster, were inspected by their own officers, and so forth. It seemed "all very dignified and practical" to Michael until one prisoner, whom O'Connor identified as Murphy, objected to some petty regulation of the shadow hierarchy. His refusal undermined the entire fiction of this arrangement and brought into question the validity of majority rule. Murphy was tried by his fellow prisoners, convicted, and sentenced to solitary confinement. At night Michael and Walsh crept to Murphy's prison-within-a-prison and talked to him. When Murphy went on a hunger strike, it was in defiance of his fellow Republicans, "people who were in prison for refusing to recognize majority rule and who had even been excommunicated for it."[8] At a prisoners' meeting it was proposed to release Murphy but to boycott him. The only dissenting voice was Michael's; it was his first "unpopular stand without allies," but it was not to be his last.

Toward the end of the year, as autumn flattened into gray winter, anxiety in the camp heightened. The cease-fire ordered by de Valera had little effect because of his refusal to recognize the new government. The prisoners were little more than pawns in a political standoff. Quietly and with no discernible pattern, prisoners were being released. When a room became available in the Limerick hut, Michael and another studious fellow named Joe Kennedy claimed it. The arrangement worked well for a time because most of these prisoners were friendly and independent. His new roommate, however, was "chock-full of mystical nationalism," which Michael found even more exasperating than mystical religion. Living in the presence of an invisible God was one thing; living in the presence of an invisible Ireland was more than he could tolerate. While Kennedy carried on like a prophet, Michael played the cynic. They ceased talking and began pinning poems over their beds to label their conflicting faiths—Kennedy's in "Death's Iron Discipline" and Michael's in "The Tree of Life." To MacSwiney's dictum that victory goes to those who endure pain and death, Michael responded with Goethe's declaration that a "man must be either a hammer or an anvil."

Two days after Kennedy returned to a hut more congenial to his fierce nationalism, another incident took place, which forced Michael to wash his hands of both sides. On the one hand, "Free State authorities gave parole as the Catholic Church gave the sacraments—in return for a signed declaration that one would behave oneself for the future." On the other, the Republican prisoners opposed anything of the sort and considered any parolee a traitor. It happened that the mother of a boy from Kerry was ill; she was a widow with a large family who would be orphaned if she died. A wire came begging the boy to return before she died. He refused to sign, a decision that hit Michael's most vulnerable spot: Not only did he love his mother, but he knew about orphans. His vigorous campaign to get the rule bent so the boy could go home without losing face met brutal reminders of "the principle of the thing." The woman died. When the boy learned about her death, his mind snapped from the guilt. "It was a pity," Michael mused, "that God hadn't made mothers with the durability of principles." Michael knew nothing then about mental illness, but sitting the next day by the boy's bed in the hospital trying to penetrate that vacant stare, he learned to hate those "abstractions that reduce life to a tedious morality." He had already heard from another Kerry prisoner the tale that he later cast as "Guests of the Nation," but his inducement to write that story of the thoughtless adherence to abstract duty was probably the sound of the newly orphaned boy sighing out his guilt.

The last straw was the hunger strike, which was called for all Republican prisoners throughout the country.[9] The purpose was to gain release by embarrassing the government. To Michael the spectre of mass martyrdom was a Shelleyan fantasy gone sinister. He and two others, Walsh and Buckley, voted against the strike, and immediately after the vote was taken, Michael went to the camp hospital with bronchitis. When he returned a few days later, he found the Cork hut in a sullen gloom, and the men there hissed him vehemently. The Limerick bunch were holding up much better and treated him as a friend. The next day a few of the Cork boys gave in but were told by the contemptuous kitchen staff that they had to give twenty-four hours' notice. Michael, Walsh, and Buckley gave them their own food. One of the boys asked Michael if he remembered the time they rescued him at Kilmallock—as if to say that they were now even.

That evening Michael visited his friend Moriarty. The remarkable thing was that his best friends respected his decision even though they stood with the majority. It was his custom to share his copy of the *Irish Statesman* with Moriarty, but that night he withheld the current number because it contained a furious article by George Russell (AE), the editor, denouncing the hunger strike.[10] Moriarty guessed why Michael had not brought the paper, and demanded to see it. When two soldiers burst into his room and replaced his mug of salt water with soup, Moriarty jumped up in rage and threw the soup out the window, just missing Michael who had been sitting on the sill. This was too much for Michael; he ran to his hut, got the paper, and tossed it through the window at Moriarty. The next morning Moriarty and a few other Limerick boys were in line for food. Not a word was spoken.

A week later the strike was called off. The entire camp became hysterical as hungry men groveled at the barbed wire for soup slopped from huge buckets. One Free Stater noted to Michael with cynical glee, "Well, professor, the pigs feed." He was right; animal treatment had reduced good men to animals. To Michael it was the end of "something noble, priceless, and irreplaceable." It was as if a friend had died. Even his own victory seemed empty, and he felt no satisfaction or vindication, only the humiliation of his friends as if it were his own. In many ways it was. Michael heard a voice somewhere that night: "The country! Oh, God, the bloody country!" For one reason or another Michael was to voice that same frustrating cry many times in the next four decades.

11

If he entered prison with a sigh of relief, then Michael endured it like any other prisoner: with an eye to release. A poem he wrote in November in response to the hunger strike, entitled "For the End," whispers the hush of incarceration and the hope of freedom.[11] The poem is a sigh of resignation for the passing of Romantic Ireland. Shortly after his release he wrote a poem called "Life," which awkwardly voices his belief in the living heart, the dancing skirt, and the kiss around the corner.[12] Michael O'Donovan was not a philosopher in the systematic or abstract sense. But he was thoughtful, and the folk wisdom of these poems emanated from the mental hardening he had received at Gormanstown. Climbing down from the lofty heights of literature, he found what was to be the subject of his finest writing: the pulse of common people. Romance had begun to give way to Realism.

Not long before Christmas Michael was sitting with Walsh in another hut when someone burst in and excitedly said, "O'Donovan, you're wanted." Michael did not even move; he was afraid to find out if it was a call to life or death. Such messages were common camp jokes, cruel glints of fear or hope. The Civil War had been officially ended with de Valera's announcement of a cease-fire in November; it was only a matter of time until they would be released, but hope was kept neatly in check, for a general amnesty had not yet been offered.* In less than a year—through the language classes, the prisoner boycotts, the hunger strike, and all the rest—the volatile idealist had learned a little self-control. He returned to his room, stunned and apprehensive. Walsh helped him pack up his little library—"my sixpenny anthologies of German and Spanish poetry, my anthology of Gaelic poetry, my beloved Heine, *Hermann und Dorothea,* and a school history of the Crusades in French"—all that had kept him in touch with the cultured world to which he aspired. He left his clothes behind because the books had done more to keep him alive, but he took his memories.

After the formalities of release Michael walked through the gates with a small group of former prisoners. There were no searchlights; it was broad day-

* General Amnesty was declared in March 1924, releasing all internees.

light. He wanted to run and run and never stop, into the fields and over the hills. Instead he walked automatically down the narrow road flanked by high hedges toward the railway station. "For the first time I felt the presence of that shadow line that divides the free man from the prisoner." On the train from Drogheda to Dublin he sat dazed, his attention fixed on a baby in the arms of a young woman in his carriage, fixed on one of the beautiful things he had missed for nearly a year. Beause there was no train to Cork that afternoon he spent the night in a hotel in Parnell Square. The next morning he left for Cork.

Homecoming turned out to be stiff and awkward. His father, who still harbored resentment of Michael's politics, welcomed him and then took the opportunity to launch another drinking bout. His mother laughed at first, for the end of the ordeal. The entire time he was at Gormanstown she had found extra work in order to send him weekly parcels of cake, cigarettes, cocoa. No sacrifice was too great, though Michael often felt guilty about it. Once he had written to her saying that when he got out he would never again be a burden to her. The reply, lyrical and ambiguous, was indicative of her view of life: "If there were no wild boys there would be no great men." After the laughter of the first few days, however, Michael's mother cried a great deal, for the beginning of the end. She had depended on his dependence on her for twenty years. Now he was back but so dramatically changed by his prison experience that she felt no satisfaction. Seeing him after a year's absence, she realized his manhood more drastically than if he had simply matured gradually before her eyes. He was a man now, ready to follow his dreams, and she knew it.

For nearly a month Michael did very little. He was still recuperating from the bronchitis, and the turmoil of the events surrounding his release had caused his stomach to flare up again. Over tea in the kitchen he talked endlessly with his mother about his plans (or his lack of plans) for the future. On the rare clear days he walked the streets of Cork smelling and seeing and listening. Mainly he listened to the drizzle on the roof as he sat in his pink-washed attic by the orange crate that he had long ago improvised as a bookcase. A bird alone again, he idled through his old books from which he had been separated for so long that he had forgotten their existence. It was like renewing old friendships.

His old friends around town, except for Sean Hendrick and the O'Leary girls, kept their distance. Because he now refused to attend Mass, he was branded an atheist. Though this wasn't exactly true, he certainly had no use for the church. Like many rebels, he felt betrayed by the excommunication of rebels. Once he quoted Yeats as saying that an Irish writer isn't worth his salt until he has lost his faith. Michael had indeed lost his faith, at least his faith in the empty pietism and death-in-life Catholic-Nationalist establishment. Actually, he had lost faith in all the big abstractions. He had also lost his taste for politics. At a political meeting the week after his release Corkery had rescued him from a group of enraged young people, most of whom had never touched a gun; word of the hunger strike had preceded him, and he was considered a traitor. The injustice of the label hurt Michael; after all, he loved Ireland dearly and was spending hours teaching Irish and translating Irish verse. But he had lost his faith in the politics of violence, in the national hysteria that led to brutalized boys and starving martyrs, and he had the nerve to say so. This, however, was Cork, the home of MacSwiney, who had popularized hunger strikes.

Michael was at home but he was out of place. He had crossed that shadow line of manhood a person crosses from bondage to freedom, from dependence to independence; and it made him wonder if he would ever again be completely at ease with the people he loved, with "their introverted religion and introverted patriotism." The passage is natural to growing up; for Michael O'Donovan it was exaggerated by the national rite of passage. The nation had filled its vacuum with violence. At the end of it all, there was a vacuum still, a vacuum of leadership and imagination, a vacuum filled by pietism and nationalism. The road to national integrity was as rocky as Michael's road out of Cork. Michael's vacuum in Cork was a spiritual one which he filled with literature—poems and grammar and Continental novels. But then, he had always filled his vacuum of loneliness with his reading. His interior life had always been rich.

The significant difference was that after Gormanstown he added to his Interior Voices those of other people with stories to tell. He had indeed crossed from high-minded poetry to realistic fiction, from the romance of the sagas to the grammar of Irish. Recalling this time of passage at the end of *An Only Child*, O'Connor actually sounds very much like a mystic believer: it was, he concludes, the thought of these people's voices "that turned me finally from poetry to storytelling, to the celebration of those who for me represented all I should ever know of God."

After his return to Cork Michael sorted through his war memories, roamed the streets, studied Irish, and wrote poetry. The poems he wrote that year were melancholy and Cork-conscious. In such poems as "Theocritus on Sunday" and "Before the Mirror" he seems to be searching for something vague and lyrical.[13] He exaggerates subjective visual images, especially shadows and darkness. For all their pretense and subjectivity, however, the poems signal a writer of talent and thoughtfulness. To his credit O'Connor left most of these poems in manuscript and never tried to publish or rewrite them.

From the first, O'Connor was most at ease with dramatic verse, particularly the dramatic monologue. In a poem like "Duet" (1924) his understandable obsession with love finds a twisted, dynamic expression in the confrontation of a lovesick young man and a headstrong farm girl. The ambiguity O'Connor felt about the fighting is reflected in the voice of the young soldier in "On Guard" (1925).[14] He feels trapped by the folly of it all and as dawn approaches he is told by the poet to keep his post because "his youth will not come again." Folly and loneliness ring true in the empty night of illusion. Even at this time in his life it was the lonely voice that brought Frank O'Connor to attention.

Nowhere is O'Connor's integrity of poetic voice more evident than in the Irish poems and translations he started shortly after his release from Gormanstown. As he once said, the best of Irish verse rests on some dramatic situation or motif, such as a revenant figure telling his tale. His first substantial poem like this was "Suibhne Geilt Aspires," a translation of which he later published in the *Irish Statesman*.[15]

> I am Sweeney they call the Mad,
> I am as tall as any tree,
> I am a tree without its roots
> And yet the mountains nourish me.

The voice is authentic mainly because it is not at all the poet's voice; subjectivity is entirely subsumed in objectivity. The influence of Corkery and the Munster poets is obvious in another poem written about the same time, a sparse, almost primitive poem, called "The Winter of Earth":[16]

> Cold is winter time, the wind
> drives the stag from height to height,
> belling for the mountain's cold
> untameable, he strays tonight.
>
> . . . .
>
> In the icy winter's dawn
> I that now am young no more
> once with mighty hand the spear
> swung in the bare light so hoar.

That is genuine O'Connor—simple yet heroic; it is primary and not derivative poetry. Michael had started to look and listen instead of borrowing images from his extensive private reading.

By the spring of 1924 Michael had become thoroughly disenchanted and restless. Like most "ex-gaolbirds," he was denied access to whatever jobs the Free State government made available. Besides, he was without the proper educational pedigree. Most of his friends were doing something with themselves: Seán O'Faoláin had completed his degree at University College, and Sean Hendrick was working for an insurance firm. Both also had been more successful at romance than Michael. Sean Hendrick and Kitty O'Leary were nearly engaged, while Séan O'Faoláin and Eileen Gould would soon marry. Michael was close to desperation, a failure and alone. Whether he ever contemplated suicide, like the young woman in his poem "Alone," or whether he ever awoke in a strange hotel room with a whore, like the young rover in "A Romantic," it is impossible to say for sure. But in his discouraged state he might have resorted to anything.

Cork had closed in on him again. Like Browning, he found himself too intense and bitter, too melancholy and self-conscious.[17] His judgment said that to be a lyric poet was the highest vocation; his instinct compelled him to listen to the tales of the little people he had met in rural cottages, in prison, and in the wet streets of Cork. Groping but resolved to find himself as a writer and his roots as an Irishman, he screamed at Cork for freedom.

5

From Cork to the World's Side

. . . in Cork you do not commit sin; you achieve it. You do not, likewise, enjoy life in Cork; you experience it. . . . To succeed here you have to have the skin of a rhinoceros, the dissimulation of a crocodile, the agility of a hare, the speed of a hawk. Otherwise the word for every young Corkman is—"Get out— and get out quick*!"*

SEÁN O'FAOLÁIN, *An Irish Journey*

BECAUSE Cork had been the focal point of Republican activity, the turmoil of the Revolution and Civil War seemed to linger there longer than it did elsewhere in the country. It was a city still edgy from years of bloodletting. Every war of national liberation is marked by slow and tentative recovery, though it is often most torturous in places where the animosity has been most concentrated. Thus Cork in the spring of 1924 seemed to be cloaked in a residue of violence and emotional dislocation. The Troubles had been largely symbolic, so naturally sentimentality and symbolism persisted. The problem was to reconcile romance and reality, which for Michael meant finding a job.

I

As so often before, it was Corkery who saved the day. One weekend in May while Michael and Hendrick were visiting Corkery's house in the country, he told Michael of a job opening. His old theatre friend Lennox Robinson was now secretary of the Carnegie Trust in Ireland. In this capacity he was organizing rural libraries and needed young men and women to train as librarians. As Corkery unfolded the scheme Michael decided that this was "the very job" for him and that he was the very person Robinson was looking for. "It was not so much that I wanted to be a librarian, or even knew what being a librarian meant; it was just that never in my life had I had enough books to read and this was my opportunity."[1] So the next week he met Robinson in the restaurant of the Glanmire Station—the same wretched place from which he had embarked for Gormanstown. But Robinson's offer sounded even more wretched. He would have to spend a year or two as an apprentice librarian somewhere in the north with a salary of thirty shillings a week. At the end of that time, if he didn't starve first, he would qualify for a salary of two hundred and fifty pounds a year, more than he had ever dreamed of earning. With his mother's urging (she would add what she could to his salary, somehow) he took the job. She knew what Michael was only beginning to discover: Even at the age of twenty it was the only real job he was qualified for. She packed his bag and he set out for Sligo.

Sligo demanded considerable adjustment, but after Gormanstown Michael seemed able to take anything, including the deprivation caused by his meagre salary. His lodgings, situated just below the Sligo Cathedral, took nearly his entire weekly earnings. His only expensive vice was cigarettes; he still drank with reticence because of his father's excesses. He posted his laundry to his mother once a week, an act of frugality on his part that also gave her a sense of still having a son.

The head librarian, Robert Wilson, was convinced that Michael was too clumsy, disorganized, and absentminded to make a good librarian; but he shared Michael's interest in Yeats and Russian novels. Wilson also shared Michael's love of music and, because Michael had no gramophone of his own, invited him from time to time for dinner, conversation, and music. Michael was totally out of his element on those occasions. Already sensitive about his lack of social poise, he was overwhelmed by the excessive propriety of Wilson's English wife. One afternoon, anticipating one of those evenings, he purged his unpleasant mood by writing to Hendrick. An hour at the Wilsons', he confided, "means that I must make an unmannerly and noisy cup of tea behave itself while I dispose of it as gracefully as possible, modulate my Rabelaisian laughter to the dulcet mirth of my host, refrain from expressing the obscene sentiments which I feel when certain subjects are broached."[2] Michael at the age of twenty had never dined out. His naturally exaggerated shyness made him seem more gauche than he actually was.

Ill at ease in society, Michael was at home only when he was reading or writing. To Hendrick he wrote that books alone reconciled him to the "barbarous mediocrity of the small town life" he saw around him. His reading was more extensive than thorough: Yeats, Joyce, Chekhov, and Turgenev, as well as such up-to-date writers as Knut Hamsun and Romain Rolland. One of the advantages of being a librarian—even in a provincial outpost—is that one's reading need not be provincial, especially if one can rummage through the book packages before anyone else. However, being a librarian in a small town meant maintaining a proper public posture. Not long after Michael arrived in Sligo, Lennox Robinson was forced to resign his position because of the turmoil resulting from a story he published about "a simple country girl who believed she had been visited in the same way as Christ's mother."[3] Michael had already begun writing stories, so the incident was a grim warning to him.

Two months after his arrival in Sligo he took his first trip outside Ireland, to London for a week-long library conference sponsored by the Carnegie Trust. He survived the stormy November passage from Belfast to Liverpool but had more difficulty with the undue attentions of Mr. Wilson, who hovered about explaining music and architecture in Liverpool Cathedral. In London he was able to escape to the bookshops; there he "moved in a lover's trance through the wet twilight," clutching whatever treasure he had skipped lunch to afford. His horizons were broadening, but he still felt the lust of most provincials "for the strange book or print or packet of cigarettes or bottle of wine that may bring back into the gloom of some provincial town a flash of glory from the world outside."

At Christmas Michael returned to Cork, a custom he would faithfully observe for the next ten years or so. In Sligo he had been homesick for his mother's dim kitchen, his father's cluttered backyard, and his own attic room.

With Hendrick and O'Faoláin he took all the old walks and talked out the same old solutions to the world's problems. On the Sunday evening after Christmas he went with them to Corkery's house on Ashburton, but it was not the same. Corkery, holding forth on architecture, happened to speak disparagingly of the Liverpool Cathedral. When Michael objected, Corkery pounced on his protégé:

"What do you know about it?" he asked. "The photographs are there. The detail is *very* bad."

To which Michael replied in a mixture of deference and assertiveness:

"Oh, nothing, but I was there at Matins a few weeks ago, and I thought it very impressive."[4]

The stunned silence was telling. Having made a fool of his old master, Michael had caused an irreparable break. He had cut one of the cords, though not the last.

Michael returned to Sligo for only a brief time. In February he was transferred to Wicklow where a new library was opening. Again lodgings took most of his salary; but this time, instead of putting up with Protestants playing "God Save the King" or an ex-British soldier's drink and guns, Michael had to cope with a nervous old widow and her brow-beaten son. Had his life been "normal," however, devoid of such characters as his deaf-mute uncle, Minnie Connolly, or the Widow Soames, perhaps he would not have resorted to fiction at all. They were, after all, part of that rich carnival of common life outside himself, which he was beginning to discover and to write about.

He listened to the story of Stephen, the widow's son, a miserable story of working to support his mother and courting the same sweet servant girl for fifteen years. He listened through the walls the night Stephen returned from a Redemptorist mission and informed his mother of his decision to marry. The immensity of her disaster drew Michael's empathy, on the basis of his own close relationship with his mother, as keenly as the boy's lonely frustration drew his sympathy. "But I saw it from the outside," he later concluded, "my material, as you might call it." The range of his experience was stretching in Wicklow as surely as it had in London.

His new boss, Geoffrey Phibbs, was as insolent and aloof as Wilson had been solicitous and gentle. At first he treated Michael and the other assistant with curt disdain. But Michael in his innocence gave Phibbs dutiful respect and soon they were the best of friends. He would not have thought of sharing his literary efforts with Wilson, but he let Phibbs read everything he wrote. Phibbs might have behaved in a high-handed fashion, but he loved poetry as no one Michael had ever known. It did not even matter to him that Phibbs disregarded anything in Irish. To Michael he was a source of wonder. "I was fascinated by the sheer mental agility that went with his physical agility, which was considerable." Phibbs was interested especially in things modern; Michael tended to be old-fashioned. In reading, Phibbs preferred the difficult, Michael the simple. Phibbs loved bright modern pictures, Matisse for instance, whereas Michael liked Rembrandt. Phibbs listened to Stravinsky on the gramophone, whereas Michael gloried in the slow movement of a Beethoven quartet. And Phibbs flashed off three or four poems in a day, whereas Michael tortured himself just to produce one a week. But they were poets nevertheless, or at least they considered themselves poets and enjoyed acting as if they were.

Phibbs was responsible for Michael's entry into the Dublin literary circles.

He had fabricated a pompous "manifesto" against Yeats and the Literary Renaissance. Because AE had dismissed the tirade as adolescent, Phibbs decided to visit the old man. Early in March they took a train to Dublin and went directly to his offices in Merrion Square. Phibbs despised AE, so Michael was prepared to feel the same. But the benevolent, burly old man leaned back, puffed his vile-smelling pipe, stroked his great beard, and dispelled Michael's antagonism. As the two impetuous pretenders were leaving, AE put his arm around Michael's shoulder and told him to send something along for publication.[5]

Michael sent his verse translation of "Suibhne Geilt Aspires," and when AE published it in the next issue of the *Irish Statesman,* it carried, for the first time, the pseudonym Frank O'Connor.[6] He had probably been toying with the idea of using a pen name ever since Lennox Robinson's forced resignation. Now, for reasons of discretion and caution—traits not generally associated with Frank O'Connor—and probably also contempt for his father's family, he adopted his own middle name and his mother's maiden name.

The prominence AE and the *Irish Statesman* gave to the name of Frank O'Connor thrust Michael into literary view. That year he published two more translations, a number of audacious letters to the editor, and one book review. The occasional guinea or two he reaped from these efforts made it possible to spend a night in a hotel or to visit Seán O'Faoláin in Dublin, where they went to the galleries, the bookshops and, of course, the Abbey Theatre. He even mastered his timidity enough to visit AE's Rathgar house. By the fall of 1925 he had become a regular Sunday evening guest at AE's, along with such other regulars as Osborn Bergin, the Celtic philologist, and C. O. Curran, a noted Dublin barrister. AE considered him one of his "discoveries," and "as all Russell's discoveries had to be pronounced on by Yeats," Michael was soon invited to one of Yeats's Monday evening gatherings. Michael, the shy, socially inept provincial, must have been terrified to find himself trying to make conversation with the likes of Yeats and his aristocratic literary comrade Lady Gregory.

In all fairness, Michael deserved the attention he was getting. His verse translations were as good as any poems in the *Irish Statesman* that year. His letters to the editor, written with Phibbs, were obstreperous attacks on the older generation of poets, whose worn-out language he claimed was like "rashers gone cold."[7] He praised native Irish poets for their simplicity and poetic imagination and called for a renewal of that sort of poetry. Yeats, who came in for the most pointed criticism, nevertheless saw through the adolescent veneer; Michael may have had obstinate literary opinions, but at least he felt strongly about poetry (something Yeats had not seen since Joyce) and those opinions were even stated well. AE's replies were patient but forthright; poets, he suggested, could use whatever words they liked so long as they made poetry. It was also obvious that besides being a first-rate poet (AE considered Michael's translations superior to Mangan's), Michael possessed an incredible understanding of traditional Irish poetry. It was not long before he took regular reviews from "Frank O'Connor" on books in Irish.

Against all odds, Michael O'Donovan was finding acceptance as Frank O'Connor. Phibbs had engineered an increase in Michael's salary to two pounds ten a week, allowing for regular trips to Dublin and a new wardrobe— green shirts, tweeds, and black bow ties. It was the poet's pose, a tribute to

Phibbs's unorthodoxy, and Michael played the part with enthusiasm. Returning to Wicklow from Dublin, he usually carried a stack of books from AE's ample bookcase and reports of new literary acquaintances—George Moore, Sarah Purser, Seamus O'Sullivan, Francis Stuart. Michael was giddy in the rarefied atmosphere into which Russell's attention had thrust him. The poor boy from Cork was suddenly somebody, and quite naturally he enjoyed it.

I I

It never occured to Michael O'Donovan that he would not return to Cork. Like his father, he was, at that age, a one-town man. AE warned him that he would be miserable back in Cork, but nothing could cure him of the notion that Cork needed him and that he needed Cork. In December 1925 he accepted the position of the new librarian of Cork County.

His salary of two hundred and fifty pounds a year was more than he or anyone he had known as a boy had ever earned. At five pounds a week it was outrageous compared with his mother's ten-shillings-a-week earnings as a charwoman; his father's pension was one pound four a month. With this salary Michael achieved a certain status. His father was pleased that the job carried a respectable pension. To his mother the title and his picture in the *Cork Examiner* were reward enough. A library post was definitely "rising in the world," even if it was the only job he was in the remotest way suited for. It didn't even matter to his mother that he was now writing under a different name. At least he was home.

That was precisely the problem. For the next three years, in spite of earning enough to afford a better house for his parents and himself, Michael lived at 8 Harrington Square. Because his father refused to move, the old house was simply improved a bit. His mother bought a gas stove and installed new lights in the kitchen and front room so Michael could read and write without bothering his weak eyes. Michael bought himself a Morris chair like Corkery's and a used typewriter, some prints to liven the place, and a gramophone. His father tolerated a few changes, so long as they didn't interfere with his habits. Bookcases were admitted but not an indoor toilet. By returning, Michael had upset the vast complacency of his father's world, a world that had suffocated his mother. Indeed, it was the close texture of this home that finally took its toll on the young writer as well.

In Cork, as perhaps in provincial places everywhere, the forces of parochial conservatism were aligned against the local boy making good, or at least against him making it too good. Cork was home; it was where his friends still lived; yet within a month he could not stand the place. It was one thing to be exiled from it, relying on memories of the hills and quays and mists, relying on letters and hasty holiday visits. It was quite another thing to be exiled within it, encountering daily and petty problems and the close texture of his Cork world. His response, looking back on the situation, was that he was "beginning to get a picture of Ireland, the real Ireland, lonely and dotty. This was no longer the romantic Ireland of the little cottages and the hunted men, but an Ireland where everyone was searching frantically for a pension or a job."[8]

The independence Michael felt by virtue of his ample salary was nothing compared with the lift he got from having a few things published. The question he had to answer during his three years in Cork was what kind of a writer he would be. This meant not only a struggle with his personal tastes and temperament but an even more profound grappling with his place in the national literature. His early writings, particularly his essays, were clearly based on lofty, elitist ideals. Gormanstown, however, brought him back to earth, closer to people and to the uneasy and common realities of Irish life. The dilemmas facing him in 1926 were whether to write in Irish or English and whether to write poetry or fiction. His search for his roots was simultaneous with his search for a suitable voice. His articles and reviews reveal a deliberate and studious effort to plumb his Irish heritage. He considered it the task of any serious Irish writer to find his roots in the buried past—before the Flight of the Earls, before Cromwell, before the English stripped Ireland of its unique cultural heritage. In this regard he was following Corkery's cultural nationalism without espousing Corkery's strident political ideas. Michael had translated and studied Irish, even taught it. Some of his own early writing was done in Irish ("Solus" in *An Lóng,* the Turgenev essay, and a few extant poems). But English was still his primary language; it was, in fact, the primary language of all but a few residents of Ireland.[9]

One of the most engaging columns in the *Irish Statesman* was called "Literature and Life." It reflected AE's belief that the one could hardly exist without the other.[10] Such people as Oliver St. John Gogarty, Lennox Robinson, P. S. O'Hegarty, and Sean O'Casey contributed essay-reviews to this column and gave the magazine a remarkable range of literary investigation as well as a coherent depth of scholarly and critical insight. O'Connor's reviews for the "Literature and Life" column show him continuing to struggle for the essence of the national literature. Time and again, for instance, he uses the phrase "at our best" to express his conviction that Irish culture in the past was capable of rising above the ordinary. His article on Egan O'Rahilly (January 30, 1926) was actually a review of Seamus O hAodha's recent study of O'Rahilly. O'Connor commends O hAodha in a manner that shows he knows enough to appreciate just how good the essay is and how good O'Rahilly was. What he finds so rare in O'Rahilly is the artist concerned with his art rather than the shape of his own personality. That distinction appears again and again in O'Connor's criticism, a distinction between the poet of instinct and the poet of judgment, the objective writer who becomes all things and the subjective writer who makes all things become himself. What he has betrayed is that he is not a critic of all, but a writer foraging about for inspiration, for some bedrock place upon which he could fabricate his own art. Ending his praise of O hAodha's little book, he injects a note of petulant frustration about contemporary Irish culture, a note heard again and again from O'Connor, the champion of lost causes, calling for Irish universities to play a greater role in the cultural life of the nation by producing books for Irish readers.

Sprinkled liberally through these review articles were Michael's own translations from the Irish. During his three years in the Cork library he worked hard on these translations for a book on Irish culture.[11] Eventually, most of them found their way into *The Wild Bird's Nest* (1932) and *The Fountain of Magic* (1939)—after considerable revision. Still, the bulk of his creative efforts between 1926 and 1928 was original poetry in English. His translations seemed so effortless and lucid because in them he had so little of himself invested; they were the voices of others, revelations of personalities not his own. His own poems showed him struggling with his own voice. O'Faoláin and the rest of the Cork crowd saw him as their poet.[12] Even Michael had begun to assume that role, but it was an uneasy one because the voice was not authentic. In poems such as "Two Impressions" he has moved from the bitterness he felt after Gormanstown to boredom in the face of the vanity of writing and all other human wishes. The young prisoner who quoted Goethe in response to Shelley and MacSwiney has been replaced by a voice, suspended between romance and reality, indulging in the forlorn abyss of youthful doubt. In sum, it is the poetry of a young man enthralled by his ability to handle language, though unsure exactly what to do with that ability. Indeed, the inclination of his verse to the storied moment and the dramatic rendering of character suggests the instincts of a storyteller. Yet the inclination of his finest stories toward the "tone of a man's voice speaking" suggests the equally strong instinct of a lyric poet.

Michael was also struggling at the time to find his own authenticity in relation to Ireland. Other than his translations, the two poems most clearly about this quest for an ancestral past are "On Moyrus" and "In Quest of Dead O'Donovans," both published in the *Irish Statesman* in 1927.[13] During the Civil War Michael had been intrigued on his visit to Croom to find there the ruined fortress of the O'Donovans who were expelled from Croom in the twelfth century. Thus "On Moyrus" opens with this blunt assertion: "On Moyrus stands a pyramidal tomb which commemorates the O'Donovan family." Like many of the Irish poems he was translating, "On Moyrus" is a dream-vision poem. The opening stanzas give a narrative account of an isolated man "on the last ledge of rock" where the waves of the "outer sea" beat "cold monotonous." There he stands next to the pyramid and listens not to the waves or seabirds but to an interior voice:

> "O, if these dead dream, their one thought
> Is their own utter loneliness,
> With no succession, by their God
> Abandoned on an alien shore!"

In reply the "long grey wave" breaks his deeper silence with voices of "ghostly inarticulate grief." In the face of the sea's darkening surge the lonely man muses about the frustration of dreams shared with the dead. The colloquy continues; as the waves wash his feet he sighs that it is "but one man's grief." The waves conclude by asserting cryptically, "We are the desert where you dwell,/ And what you dream us!" To the still waves and a silent heart the man asks if there is "bitterer death" than these darkened dreams. There is no answer from the voiceless wave; the poem hastens to a narrative conclusion:

> Beside their tomb his choice was made,
> And many a time unmade before
> The loneliness of these, his kin,
> Took up its dwelling in his mind.
>
> He stood on the last ledge of rock,
> He did not turn, as though he feared
> The desolation, or knew not
> Which side lay Ireland, which the sea.

In the end the poet-speaker is trapped between the past and the present, suspended between one world dead and the other powerless to be born. The voice is lonely and absolutely authentic, primarily because O'Connor has succeeded in objectifying his intensely personal struggle with Ireland.[14]

I I I

Michael's personal growth during these three trying years in Cork was not unlike his development as a writer. His intellectual struggle to find his place within the Irish literary tradition occurred simultaneously with his efforts to find his place in society. Though living at home, he was no longer bound by his father's house or his mother's love, for his circle of friends had gradually enlarged. Evenings when he was not writing he often spent with Sean Hendrick at the home of the O'Leary girls, singing songs or listening to the gramophone in the parlor. He still suffered mercilessly in the presence of young women, often making a fool of himself. But more than one woman found his company compelling, whether on long walks listening to him talk or on evenings at the theatre.

Michael's confidence was bolstered mainly by his status in Cork as the head librarian. Of course, everyone knew that "Mick-Mihal" (as he was affectionately known in his hometown) was the Frank O'Connor whose poems and stories were beginning to appear in Dublin magazines, making him fashionably notorious. Still, it was the library that brought him his greatest satisfaction. Minutes of the General Library Committee, as well as those of the various subcommittees of which he was the prime working member, testify to the serious and diligent manner with which he tackled his job.[15] He may have antagonized some members of the County Council by his choice of banks, his choice of books, and his choice of clothing (tweeds and green shirts were not considered appropriate business attire), but he won them over with his consistent performance.

Michael was faced with the task of opening a library from scratch. The old Carnegie Library behind City Hall had been burned in the Black and Tan War. The new county-libraries scheme was initially funded by the Carnegie Trust. An abstract of accounts shows that in 1926 Michael was responsible for a budget of almost three thousand pounds, nearly half of which went for book purchases. He had already been through the committee wars in Wicklow, but Cork proved, at least at the outset, a tougher nut. In Cork the barriers to opening a library were infinitely more subtle—and rather more personal—since he was a local boy. His makeshift office in the courthouse was inadequate even for a poor boy who had made whole universes in his attic; he did all of his correspondence at home.

When he first presented plans for better offices, he was publicly belittled by a jealous local teacher, Tubby Donoghue, whom they called the Beet because of his nose. Donoghue implied that an uneducated boy from the Barrack Stream could not possibly know anything about the complexities of renovation, rents, and interior decorating. Michael was especially sensitive, and therefore vulnerable, to the derision that came with poverty. But, though stung by Donoghue's attack, Michael kept his composure, fought the issue indirectly through the committee, and, by force of reason and probably a good deal of charm, won the battle. His new offices were located in rooms over a shop at 25 Patrick Street.

Michael had some experience with libraries, but he had none with finance. In *My Father's Son* he tells a story about the furor raised over his choice of a bank for the huge Carnegie Trust check. Apparently, he misjudged the intensity of vested interests on the council; no matter which bank he chose, someone was bound to take offense. The Munster and Leinster Bank was a newly established Catholic-owned enterprise; the Provincial Bank was a venerable Protestant institution. On the night when the bank issue was to be discussed, a number of the committee members were locked from the committee room and "only those who knew the architecture of the building were in their seats on time." Almost all of the members who had gotten in were planning to vote for Michael's innocent decision to lodge the money in the Provincial Bank nearby instead of in the Munster and Leinster.[16]

Actually, the bank dispute was a real issue, and Michael's mistake showed his lack of worldly sense. Even after 1922 anti-Catholic bias continued to influence the leaders of commerce in hiring and lending decisions, and advertisements for jobs still often read "RCs need not apply." Michael's decision to lodge three thousand pounds at the nearest, rather than at the politically appropriate, bank was no small matter at the time. But Michael was not thinking of Catholic unity or Protestant discrimination when he lodged the check; he simply wanted to get the thing out of his pocket. The workings of the mercantile mentality, the petty intrigues of those his mother always called the maker-outers, were beyond his innocent comprehension. Still, he managed to survive and to build a useable library for Cork and an effective book distribution system for the entire county.

Michael's annual reports were thorough and deliberate, serious and factual, without any trace of literary show. For instance, his first report on May 22, 1926, explained the work done by himself and his one assistant supplying twenty local centers, and called for additional help to expand the operation to over a hundred centers. Though he cared little for the technical details of library organization, preferring to chat with the patrons about books, he managed to develop a satisfactory facility. He fought for salary increases for his assistants and insisted that a van be purchased for delivering books to communities outside Cork City.[17] In fact, during the last two years of his stay in Cork he spent as much time in the villages of West Cork as he did in his office in Patrick Street. Traveling about this wild country made him realize that he "was a townie and would never be anything else." He felt that these country people were closer to their environment than he was to his. From time to time he stopped longer than necessary to listen to some story or other, but generally the country depressed him. Little by little he was beginning to feel trapped by Cork.

Probably the main reason for his depression was the illness that seemed to plague him constantly in Cork. His lungs never really recovered from the severe bronchitis (more likely pneumonia) he had suffered in prison. His naturally frail constitution and thin, sunken chest made him susceptible enough to illnesses of the lungs in the damp, cold marsh of Cork. Added to this, he smoked excessively. And when it wasn't his lungs, he was plagued by a chronic stomach problem: "Nervous gastritis," his mother called it, and she attempted to keep it under control by cooking bland foods. Early in July 1926 he became seriously ill, exhausted perhaps from worry and overwork, but nevertheless ill enough to require two weeks in hospital and six weeks of convalescence.

Actually, Michael simply drove himself too hard, writing nearly every night after work. He often remarked to Corkery and Hendrick that he envied O'Faoláin's ability to work so consistently at his writing. Obviously, he underestimated his own difficult schedule as well as the consistency of his own writing habits; he also forgot to take into account that O'Faoláin was a full-time student. Besides, Michael's method of doing anything was to become totally absorbed and to work at a frantic pace until the project was completed or scrapped, and then to collapse. He once wrote to Phibbs: "I'm working like a brute beast, and I think I deserve a holiday. . . . It's only in my stories I'm getting what I want though I slave more at poetry than at anything else."[18] In August 1926, while still recuperating from his mysterious ailment, he accepted O'Faoláin's invitation for one last fling before Seán left for Harvard. They went straight to Oxford, and the impression of their brief visit stayed in O'Connor's mind for years—"the joy of seeing a whole town that was still a work of art in itself and the sick feeling that we had nothing like it at home."[19] Depressed by the cultural deprivation of Cork, they continued on to the Continent, ending up in Damme, a hamlet toward the sea from Bruges, where they spent nearly a week totally lost in the foreignness of it all. Not an hour after arriving, Michael, in one of his customary flashes of spontaneity, revealed what O'Faoláin called "his own secret image of the Full Life. He bought an enormous-brimmed black poet's hat . . . put it on, sat in an outdoor cafe, sank into a blissful coma of narcissism, immobile as a waxwork the livelong day."[20] Travel added greatly to Michael's sense of himself. His salary was sufficient to cover his yearly holiday, which he usually took in Glengarriff, and as head librarian he was obliged to travel to Dublin and London on business. In 1927 he made two trips on library business, both times to Dublin, where he met Phibbs and went to the theatre.

Theatre had long been a recognized part of the cultural atmosphere of Cork City, too. During the nineteenth century English touring companies on their way to Australia, America, or South Africa sailed from Queenstown (Cobh) and often gave a final performance in the old Cork Opera House, which continued well into Michael's youth to be the center of popular theatrical activity in Cork. In 1909 Daniel Corkery founded the Cork Dramatic Society in a small room above the Gaelic League Hall in Queen's Street. When the Gaelic Leaguers moved across the street, the entire place became a theatre. It was called An Dun. Michael Farrell wrote in *The Bell* years later: " 'It was all Daniel Corkery,' say those who were there. 'He produced us, taught us, would have nothing but perfection, he *was* The Dun.' "[21] Most of the works produced at An Dun were new plays written by such local dramatists as Con O'Leary, Lennox Robinson, T. C. Murray, Terence MacSwiney (later mayor and martyr), and, of course, Daniel Corkery. Their impact was felt as far as the Abbey Theatre in Dublin, but political opposition and lack of funds combined to close An Dun in 1913.

During the next fifteen years rival groups such as the Leeside Players, the Munster Players, the Father Matthew Players, and the Cork Shakespearean Society produced an assortment of plays—popular and "arty," local and Continental—in an assortment of places: the Opera House, the A.O.H. Hall, and Gregg Hall. In August 1927 Micheál MacLiammóir and Hilton Edwards brought their touring company to Cork. After the performance a social gathering was held at the home of Sean Neeson, head of broadcasting in Cork, and his wife, Geraldine. Among the guests was Michael O'Donovan, who spent most of the evening rapt in conversation with MacLiammóir, whose obsession at the time was drama in Irish. He encouraged Michael—who knew nothing about theatre but, obviously, a great deal about the Irish language—to revive drama in Cork. MacLiammóir's other obsessions, French and Russian theatre, also matched Michael's own enthusiasms.[22]

With that inspiration Michael, Sean Neeson, and J. J. Horgan (a director of the Opera House) put together the Cork Drama League. Subsidized by such citizens as Mr. Dermot Forde-Nagle, the League sought only one hundred members, each subscribing at an annual rate of one guinea. Subscriptions were few. Nonetheless, rehearsals began before the year ended. As Sean Hendrick recalls:

> That Michael knew nothing about producing plays and I knew nothing about stage-managing them did not trouble us at all. We both agreed that our drama group could not be run by a committee. The producer was to be given a free hand in the choice of both plays and cast and members were bound to accept the parts allotted them. There were to be no stars and an all-round uniformity of performance was to be aimed at. Stage fussiness was to be banned. No movements or gestures were to be allowed except those dramatically significant.[23]

The Incorruptibles simply read all they could about theatre—stage design, lighting, acting—and improvised a theatre as they had a war.

Michael convinced Lennox Robinson to allow them to do his play *The Round Table,* which had been so successful at London's Court Theatre in 1925 with Sybil Thorndyke in the leading role. Robinson not only consented to waive royalties but rewrote the play for a Cork audience. The "curtain raiser" was to be Chekhov's *The Bear,* directed by Joseph Gilmore (Sean Neeson's stage name), with Geraldine Neeson and Frank O'Connor playing the major roles. Rehearsals were held in a studio of the radio station run by Neeson. Ironically, the station was located in a wing of the Women's Goal in Sunday's Well where Michael had been held prisoner during the Civil War. According to Hendrick, no producer ever

> threw himself into the job with such an intensity of nervous energy as our producer. At every rehearsal there was never the slightest doubt as to who was in control. "Enthusiasm's the best thing. . . . Only we can't command it; fire and life are all, dead matter's nothing." Michael's enthusiasm swept fire and life into a fair share of dead matter. Producing a play, composing a poem, attacking the subtleties of grammar—all called forth the same daemonic energy.[24]

According to Michael, the theatre was simply the best available "escape from the unreality of my work."

The reality of casting for *The Round Table* gave Michael great anguish, particularly the role of Daisy Drennan, a determined girl managing a family while dreaming of far-off places. One evening Geraldine Neeson brought a friend to the studios to show her what was happening and to arrange a bit part for her in the play. Nancy McCarthy, a shy young chemist, watched and listened from a distance, and the girl playing the part of Daisy struck her, too, as incapable of "yearning for the mysterious East." When Michael called a recess, Geraldine introduced Nancy to him. He looked her over and then asked her to read the part of Daisy. "I-I-I'll t-try," she stumbled in embarrassment. Michael threw up his hands and stalked over to Sean Hendrick and whispered, "My God, the damn woman stutters." He glared at Geraldine, a dignified woman not normally given to practical jokes, and shrugged as if to say "She can't be any worse than what we have now." With his head in his hands Michael prepared for the debacle he was sure she would make of the part. Instead, Nancy took the stage and read "as though all her life she had been doing nothing else."[25] Michael not only gave her the part but walked her home that night. From then on she was his leading lady.

The debut of the Cork Drama League on February 20, 1928, in Gregg Hall was given high praise by Cork and Dublin newspaper reviewers. Nancy received acclaim for her performance as Daisy Drennan, and Michael was singled out both for his producing and for his acting. He played Smirnov, "the Bear," opposite Geraldine who played Popova. The program included this statement of purpose, most likely written by Michael:

> The Cork Drama League has been founded in the hope of providing for Cork a local theatre which will adequately express the best of Southern thought and emotion. English drama—no matter how significant it may be in its own setting, or how important it may seem in countries where it has been absorbed by the national theatre—can have no beneficial effect upon a country which is subjected to cultural influences only from one source.
>
> The Cork Drama League proposes first of all to perform Irish plays, and more especially plays by local authors; it proposes secondly to give the best of the American and Continental theatre, of Chekhov, of Martine Sierra, of Eugene O'Neill and those other dramatists whose work, as a result of the dominating influence of the English theatre, is quite unknown in Cork.[26]

That was more than a subtle reference to Father O'Flynn's Cork Shakespearean Society; it was an outright challenge. Unfortunately, the primary purpose ("Southern thought and emotion," plays by local authors, even "Irish plays") was apparently lost in the shuffle of getting started. What "local" plays were produced in the six year life of the League—Corkery's *The Yellow Bittern,* Teresa Deevy's *Temporal Powers,* Robinson's *The Round Table*—hardly owe their existence to the League. The secondary purpose, however, was fulfilled all too well, as Farrell observes, with plays "in abundance by Ibsen and Quintero, by Sierra, de Musset, Molière, by Chekhov and the other Russians."

For his second production Michael chose Chekhov's *The Cherry Orchard;* Nancy and Geraldine were assigned the leading female roles. The play had been scheduled for April 1928; but one night while walking Nancy home after rehearsal Michael complained of severe abdominal pains. The next day he was taken to the Bon Secours Hospital for an emergency appendectomy. Because he refused confession, customarily made by all patients before an operation, surgery was delayed so that Nancy could convince him to see a priest. That evening one of the nuns asked Nancy about her relationship with him, about his parents, and about his religious beliefs. She informed Nancy that he was refusing, quite obstreperously, to take confession, and asked Nancy's intervention. "It doesn't surprise me, Sister," Nancy replied. "When he was in the internment camp he didn't sign a promise to lay down arms against the existing government. He and the rest were refused sacraments. So he decided if he could do without sacraments in prison, he could do without them altogether." Though devout herself, Nancy was not about to try to change Michael. When she told him of the incident the next day, he was furious that she had been catechized in this way. He vowed never again to enter a Catholic hospital; he kept the vow.

The Cherry Orchard was performed after only a month's delay. Following the highly successful opening night, Michael presented a neatly penned poem, entitled "The Play," to Nancy McCarthy.[27] Michael's poem celebrates Nancy's loveliness but laments the continual frustration of his affections. It ends with a "cry of languor":

> "Oh, that our lives were gathered up into that fold
> Where artifice resumes her yoke on flesh and blood,
> And flesh and blood alike are kindled"   artifice
> That even within this darkness of our body keeps
> Communion with the brightness of a world we dream.
>   May 9, 1928
>   Ich liebe dich,
>   M

As poetry "The Play" left a lot to be desired, but as an expression of his desires it was more than adequate. Sentimental perhaps, but genuine above all else; he had "fallen in love in a completely hopeless way with [his] leading lady."

Throughout the summer of 1928 Michael continued to court Nancy with determination. For a time she lived in Sunday's Well and they would walk up the Mardyke; later she took lodgings near Victoria Quay, and they would walk down the Marina. Nancy usually listened while Michael talked about the people of the square, about his theories of drama, or about Mozart or Browning, all the time opening up to her worlds she had never known before. She saw herself as just a simple chemist, but to Michael she was the epitome of Woman.[28]

The fact is that Nancy was also opening up a world of emotions inside Michael that was as strange to him as the world of Mozart, Degas, and Joyce was to her. He was impatient to fathom the change and to press his ardent cause. One special evening in July, for example, he took her home to meet his mother, the first time he had ever taken a girl home. Minnie was extremely wary of Nancy. She served them cocoa and biscuits in the kitchen and then withdrew awkwardly. On later visits, Nancy recalls, Michael would usually talk about books but never above love. He was enthusiastic about Joyce at the time and gave her copies of *Dubliners* and *A Portrait of the Artist as a Young Man*. Patiently he explained to her what these books were all about. Fondly he read

Browning and Whitman and even some of his own poems—the translations but not the love poems, at least not at home. It was all shattering to her, and though she reveled in the strange newness of his attention, she was apprehensive about his affection.

During their walks Michael talked incessantly, "carrying on," she called it, about pregnant girls and "living" with someone or about going off together somewhere—anything daring and unlike Cork. Nancy, who worked in a pharmacy owned by a well-known Protestant, would reply sharply, telling him about the letters she saw regularly from girls seeking aborting agents. While she reminded him of the consequences of the behavior he was advocating, he lectured her about pious middle-class values. In the face of his arrogance she simply stood her ground. She had been raised in a big family where everyone saw to it that no one's bubble went unburst for too long, and it seemed to her that Michael's bubble was badly in need of bursting. But his arrogant self-assertion, she soon discovered, was born of a deep insecurity. He would criticize her severely about such minor habits as keeping her mouth open during an entire evening with the poet Padraic Colum. He even accused her of stammering just to infuriate him. When Michael loved someone, he wanted that person to be perfect, and in spite of all his blustering talk about "advanced" sexual activity, he was shy and moral, not just reticent but downright chaste.

In September of that year Michael made a trip to Dublin. His stomach problem had been worsening, so he had decided to go to the Richmond Hospital for a week of X rays and observation. Although he said he found Dublin a dreary place, he was beginning to feel confined by Cork, and this prompted him to apply for the post of librarian at a Dublin suburb. When the tests were concluded, he went on to England for another week to study libraries in Lincoln and Nottingham, and on his way back to Cork he stopped in Dublin "for a medical exam in connection with the job."[29] As absorbing as the Cork Drama League and his relationship with Nancy were, the close texture of life in his hometown was prodding him to make provisions for leaving Cork.

Upon his return to Cork in the fall, the League began rehearsals for a production of Ibsen's *A Doll's House*. Michael continued to walk Nancy home every night even though she was then living in Victoria Avenue. And every night he walked alone back across town in restless dismay. Cork was closing in on him, as if it were determined that the local boy not make good. His frenzied activity in the theatre may have enlarged his circle of friends and brought him his first lover, but it also forced his hand publicly, somewhat in the manner of the Lennox Robinson resignation.

In fact, it all started the winter before with Lennox Robinson, who was visiting Cork with the Abbey company on tour. After a production of his *Crabbed Youth and Age* Robinson gave a press interview in which he singled out the Cork Drama League for special commendation. Father O'Flynn, director of the Cork Shakespearean Society, which O'Connor said "performed Shakespeare with the dirty words left out," launched a frontal attack on Robinson and the upstart Drama League in a series of caustic and pietistic letters to the editor of the *Cork Examiner*.[30] Michael replied that theatre had a venerable tradition in Cork, and that as for filthy language, O'Casey could be played without the blue pencil sooner than *Measure for Measure*. With that Father O'Flynn turned his sights toward Michael, tagging him a friend who dallied in the filth of O'Casey and Ibsen. "Mick the moke," he branded Michael, with disparaging comments on the integrity of his Irishness.[31] In response to O'Flynn's letters, always signed "The Producer," Sean Hendrick wrote a few appropriately nasty replies under the name Spectator. But Corkery never uttered a word in Michael's defense, though in one letter O'Flynn referred to Donal O'Corcora only to be corrected by Michael in his next letter. All this "row and racket" troubled Michael at the time and came back to haunt him when rehearsals began for the Ibsen play nearly a year later.

First a young actress refused to say a line containing the word *mistress*. A young actor supported her refusal because it would be publicly embarrassing to his uncle, a bishop. "I was beginning to realize," O'Connor later quipped, "that Cork standards of literature and my own could not exist for long side by side." Then on the night of dress rehearsal (Sunday, November 25, 1928) the leading man decided he couldn't perform. Apparently Father O'Flynn had been applying pressure through ecclesiastical channels. As a result, Sean Hendrick postponed the show for one night and Michael began feverishly to digest the part himself. On Tuesday the play went off without a hitch in the A.O.H. Hall on Morrison's Island; Robinson's *Crabbed Youth and Age* was the curtain raiser. One reviewer praised Nancy's performance as Nora, adding that had the "audience not been made aware of the fact, few indeed would have thought that Mr. O'Connor had to prepare the part in the space of a day. His acting in the final scene was particularly fine."[32] It was a critical success, but the enthusiasm of the reviewers was not shared by the good people of Cork. The Cork Drama League was by now deeply in debt, and Frank O'Connor was ready to leave Cork.

6

The Bookman

FRANK O'Connor was only twenty-five when he finally moved to Dublin once
and for all. He had stretched Cork to the limit; it would take only a decade for
him to do the same with Dublin, but for the present, for better or worse, Dublin became his new home. It was to be the place of his most productive years as
a writer. He assumed the post of librarian of the Pembroke District Library at
the end of 1928 and resigned that post in 1938.

I

When Michael left Cork on December 1, 1928, he took the train to Waterford
rather than the more direct route to Dublin in order to spend some time with
Geoffrey Phibbs and his new wife, a painter named Norah McGuinness. Phibbs
met him at the station but seemed distracted. The atmosphere at Leitrim
House, their bungalow above Wicklow town, was equally tense. Norah tired
early of the usual discussion of books, music, and sex. As soon as she went off
to bed, Phibbs began talking about complications that had arisen in the marriage. For some reason he had always confided his love affairs to his less sophisticated friend. Michael was intrigued by Phibbs's iconoclastic views on
love and sex, but found it strange that someone with such "advanced" attitudes should confide in a naive country boy. Thus this confession made him
wonder just how advanced Phibbs's attitudes really were. He only then started
to see in Phibbs, what years later, after he had experienced a few tangled love
affairs of his own, he came to realize about himself: He, like everyone else, was
trapped sooner or later by his own nature. And what he concluded about
Phibbs was probably just as valid about himself: "He was inescapably trapped
because in him the gap between instinct and judgment was wider than it is in
most of us, and he simply could not jump it."

Phibbs served to expand Michael's view of life and literature, though his
carefree bohemian attitude represented as much what Michael feared as what
he admired. The most superficial emblem of that irresponsibility was Phibbs's
notoriously bad spelling and grammar. Michael admired the way Phibbs
turned out his poems on the spot, furiously and without heed to details. Michael always corrected the spelling while Phibbs gloated. In contrast, Michael
labored for hours over his writing before daring even to approach the type-

writer. This carefulness was equally apparent in his approach to romance. Though he came to assume a pose of impulsive abandon in his personal affairs, he never lost what Phibbs derisively called a "sintactical exactness of mind."

One reason Michael had accepted the job in Dublin was the chance to spend more time with Phibbs and Norah. He did spend three weekends with them, but on his return from Christmas holidays in Cork he learned that they were moving to London. Their departure in January made his life in Dublin "terribly and monotonously quiet." He soon found his first residence unsuitable, because, as he wrote to Nancy McCarthy, it was "neither too bright nor comfortable and far too Catholic." As a study, however, it proved interesting to him, primarily because of his fellow lodger, a pious and organized fellow whom he immediately cast as the hero of a novel he had begun to write. In his isolation he read a great deal more than he had in Cork, and, according to his letters, he even started a play. Then he decided to move to simpler digs in Ranelagh, a bit farther from the library. As homesick as he was for Cork and as friendless as he felt, the task of opening a library was even more disconcerting to him. In the first place, the building itself, a compact mock-Georgian barn huddled behind the Royal Dublin Society in Anglesea Road, was better suited for the fire brigade than books and readers. The books donated by civic-minded people in Ballsbridge proved to be largely worthless. Above all, he had to find an assistant who knew something about the technical details of a library.

The morning Dermot Foley climbed the stairs toward Michael's office for an interview, Michael was storming about, cursing some "eejit" or another. They met on the stairs, and the interview began there, Michael leering down and Dermot gazing up.[1] Michael's superior air and the echo of his formidable voice almost overpowered the quiet, self-effacing young librarian. However, Michael needed a person with the experience he lacked, and this officious Dubliner had a more competent air than anyone he had interviewed thus far: Most of them had not known Schubert from Shakespeare or Marie Antoinette from Maria Edgeworth. Dermot had been sent on the recommendation of the local Labour party, so Michael knew that he would get at least one favorable vote from the Library Committee. With no apparent malice, Michael sent Dermot to see the committee chairman, a wealthy businessman. Dermot knew the man by reputation and shrieked, "But don't you realize that he's a Freemason?" "Never mind what he is," Michael insisted, "I want him to support you when the committee meets."[2] Dermot went off, angry at having been subjected to such a "display of arrogance and crude manners." He was nonetheless intrigued, and he beguiled the Freemason with his scrupulous poise and, by a slim vote, became Michael's assistant on March 1, 1929.

At first Dermot loathed his new boss; his abrupt manner and constant shouting were upsetting. "There were only two of us at first," he remembered, "and into the empty rooms he would sweep like a gale, leaving in his wake a malediction on invoices, the typewriter, the slovenly charwoman."[3] It was a relief when his unruly boss with the "mop of unruly hair" stormed off into town to scald some poor bookseller. Dermot had been told that this "raw recruit from Cork" was something of a literary fellow, but at first Dermot thought he was nothing more than an overbearing bully.

In time, however, Dermot discovered that "the raging eyes and roaring voice concealed a shy and even inexperienced man with unexpected streaks of gentleness." Even the lack of manners he came to see as due less to the Cork slums than to Michael's preoccupation with the variety show inside his head. Dermot persisted in his efforts to introduce those technicalities of organization he knew were necessary for a good library. Gradually his methods met less resistance, and the tension between them began to ease.

I I

At twenty-five Michael O'Donovan was very much as he had always been: the smart boy of the square fighting invisible dragons, the shy and sensitive mother's boy, the curious and voracious reader, and the formidable friend. Though not tall, he seemed to be, owing as much to his thin frame as to his huge head, thrown back in laughter or tilted forward at a curious angle while his fingers ran automatically through his black hair. Everything about him was notable in a nervous sort of way: the black moustache, the black wire eyeglasses, the cigarette glued to his fingers, and the outlandish attire. Above all, there was his voice, which "seemed to come up from the bowels of the earth" to hypnotize or overpower. His nervousness was exaggerated by his eagerness to succeed in Dublin.

That was how he arrived in Dublin in December of 1928—naive, explosive, inquisitive, ambitious, and, more than anything else, lonely. He may have come to hate Cork, but at least he could depend on it to be what it seemed—provincial, parochial, pietistic. Dublin was not all that different, though bigger and more cosmopolitan; yet to a young man out to make his mark in the world it was the center of all opportunity. It was a writer's town and Michael was out to become a writer.

Dublin proved to be as good a place for walking as was Cork, and to Michael a writer's town was a town for walking and talking. The wide curving streets of the south side of Dublin from College Green and Leeson Street to Ballsbridge and Lansdowne Road were perfect for long strolls and helped ease the difficulties Michael was having adjusting to a new city. He walked the tree-lined streets of this dignified and quiet Protestant suburb lost in his own mind. The Grand Canal and the road along Sandymount Strand especially caught his fancy; neither place was the Mardyke nor the Marina, but both were suitable for thoughtful walks.

Between Ranelagh where he eventually settled and Pembroke (Ballsbridge) where he worked, he came to know every street, every lamp post, every bench. Like Cork, Dublin was cut to liveable proportions around villages, small pockets of various identifiable populations. Where Cork had Montenotte, Sunday's Well, Blackpool, and the Marsh, Dublin had its own pockets of diverse life, many of which were also associated with writers: Yeats's Sandymount, O'Casey's North Circular Road, and AE's Rathgar. Michael adopted Ballsbridge near Grand Canal, not far from the area that nurtured the young Beckett. He walked and read and dreamed and made it home; that is, he tried to make it seem like Cork. Even in later years he never lived in Dublin but that he lived in or near this area.

Like the heroine of his first novel, Michael found Dublin disappointing at first, because "it wasn't sufficiently like Cork." His letters to Sean Hendrick and Nancy McCarthy during those initial months were full of hopes, regrets, and lists of people to whom he wanted to be remembered. He called his letters "songs of home-sickness."[4] For the same reason—that it wasn't Cork—he found Dublin exciting. His extended fits of melancholy could be offset by a visit to the bookstalls on the quays, to a concert, or to a play. The new city, "in all its myriad aspects," was a challenge to his restless spirit. Only the accent of the people left him lonely: so harsh, monotonous, and nonchalant, not at all like the "sinuous, excitable, whirling timbre of the southern voices."[5] Michael was in Dublin but not of it. He told Nancy, "I hate Dublin with a hatred that ever grows more intense; in the impudent autobiographical note I sent round with my stories I have incorporated the clause 'Lives in Dublin, but not by conviction.' "[6]

If he arrived in Dublin nervous and brimming with expectation, then the town he arrived in was ready for him; Dublin at the time was itself nervous and brimming. Any capital city is dominated by politics, and in the capital of a new nation politics not only dominates, it obscures. While rural Ireland was still blanketed in post-Famine fatigue, Dublin was already infected with post-Treaty frenzy. Ex-gunmen from the country migrated there in search of newly created civil service jobs. Partition dominated conversation; domestic issues, such as housing, education, social welfare, and economic recovery, were drowned out by the endless debates on such issues as the Irish language.

Irish independence meant little more than freedom from British domination; though a few revolutionaries envisioned entirely new social institutions, little was done to change the economic and legal structure left by the British. William T. Cosgrave, head of government after the death of Michael Collins, had no real blueprint for a new Ireland.[7] The Pro-Treaty party, or, as it was then called, Cumann na nGaedheal, moved with extreme caution for fear of giving Eamon de Valera's new Fianna Fáil party grounds for attack. The economy worsened with the Great Depression. As unadventuresome as it was, the new government managed a few modest achievements, such as the Shannon River project and civilian control of the military; but fear of violence and the atmosphere of reprisal motivated most policy decisions. The Public Safety Act of 1928 outlawed the IRA, and the Censorship of Publications Act of 1929 proved as harsh and repressive as any British statute. The homegrown and "ingrown" leadership was tentative, partly from inclination and partly from inexperience.[8] Michael and the other young artists of his generation, many of whom had been rebels and prisoners, could not have helped feeling the emotional vibrations of division, suspicion, and instability that engulfed the city.

Dublin in 1928–29 was about as chaotic culturally as it was politically. The shifting political alignments were part of a whole process of shifting priorities that naturally affected the intellectual climate of the nation. The renewed interest in the Gaelic language was as ideologically diverse as Partition. The issue was whether Irish writers, as Corkery insisted, must write only in Irish or whether, as AE argued, they should expand the English language with their native idiom. Irish writers were also battling the forces of a puritanical church and a chauvinistic government that threatened to curtail severely all intellectual and artistic expression. A new nation was rising out of the ashes of dissension and war; a new literary spirit was emerging out of an equally corrosive atmosphere of competition.

Where unrest and uncertainty lurk, opportunity often appears as well. As the Abbey Theatre stagnated, a new theatre, the Gate, opened under the creative and youthful leadership of Micheál MacLiammóir and Hilton Edwards.[9] The fading of the Abbey meant the ebb of the heralded Literary Revival and the flow of a new literary movement, a phenomenon AE defined as "five or six writers who live in the same town and hate each other cordially." So instead of having only the church and state to contend with, this second wave of writers—O'Flaherty, Colum, Clarke, O'Connor, O'Faoláin, Stuart—had each other to fight. AE hoped that these talented young men would make the same spiritual impact on their generation as Yeats, AE himself, and others had made on their own generation.

Dublin was still a city of exaggeration and talk; debate, they say, is as natural to Dubliners as is drink. Always full of writers, wits, and conversationalists, it had become, as one wag phrased it, a "city of spoiled Prousts." Since the eighteenth century it had been a place of personality, a city of gossip and cliques and characters, of great figures and little ones clamoring to be great. During the time of recovery, after the Civil War, everyone took himself so seriously that the strident rhetoric of the political figures was matched by the self-righteous clamor of artists and thinkers. Michael O'Donovan came to Dublin as Frank O'Connor, to conquer it, to save Irish literature; he succeeded to the extent that he became, within a few years, notorious in Dublin as the slightly abrasive conscience of Irish literature.

To Michael, who continued to see everything through a veil of literature, Dublin was Swift and Swift was Dublin. In a sense Swift was the first of the men who were "hurt into greatness" by Ireland's rejection of their work, men as various as Yeats and Joyce, Parnell and Wilde. Dublin still resembled the Georgian town of Swift, Burke, and Goldsmith. Its elegance was subtle and unstudied; its lure was a brilliant oral surface of wit and irony. The voice heard by Michael when he first came to Dublin was the harshly vindictive political rhetoric of a depressed and confused town talking to itself. Listening to it, he became more fiercely nonpolitical and moved to the edge of things. Like Swift, he was an exile in Dublin, an outsider snarling and bellowing at its "dreary hopelessness."

By contributing regularly to the *Irish Statesman* and associating regularly with AE and his circle, the new Pembroke librarian was close to the nerve center of post-Treaty Ireland. AE was not afraid to use the magazine for comment and intelligent debate on such issues as housing, agriculture, old-age pensions, and the Irish language. His aim was to "advance the Irish character" by calling attention to Ireland's basic values. And the small sums given to young writers like O'Connor for their work helped advance a few reputations.

The most lively controversy at the time O'Connor came to Dublin was censorship; it would remain a bone of contention with him for the rest of his life. During the fall of 1928 Cosgrave introduced a censorship bill that polarized the Roman Catholic hierarchy and the intellectual community. The proposed legislation provided for "the prohibition of the sale and distribution of unwholesome literature . . . and the establishment of a censorship of books and periodicals." In essence, it was an extension of long-standing British statutes. To many, the powers of the proposed Censorship Board were not strict enough, while to others, including AE, Yeats, and Shaw, any form of censorship represented a threat to freedom of expression. Nevertheless, the bill was passed into law by the Dáil, Ireland's parliament, in July 1929.[10] Enforcement of the law resulted in the banning of works by every important writer of that generation: O'Faoláin, O'Casey, O'Flaherty, Gogarty, and, of course, O'Connor.

Libel was another, more subtle, form of censorship. When O'Connor arrived in Dublin, the *Irish Statesman* was in the middle of a fierce legal struggle, which eventually led to its demise. The trouble had begun with an *Irish Statesman* review critical of an edition of Irish songs, to which the editor of the book responded with virulence. AE backed the reviewer; at stake were the standards of scholarship and the image of Irish intellectual life. Yeats and the rest of Ireland's literary community stood behind AE's battle for integrity, but suit for libel was instigated in October 1928. The proceedings were long and highly publicized; they were also extremely expensive. Though no verdict was rendered, the *Irish Statesman* was forced to absorb all legal fees; this financial burden in turn forced the paper to cease publication in 1930.[11]

I I I

If Michael O'Donovan had lost a few of his illusions in the Troubles, and a few more in the libraries of Sligo, Wicklow, and Cork, then administrating the Pembroke Library in Dublin merely polished his realism. His first job as librarian was to enlighten the local library committee officials about the purpose of a public library. The biggest obstacle he met here was the force of Catholic piety, which had recently been strengthened by the Censorship of Publications Act. Although he had learned some diplomacy from the priest in Wicklow and the bank clerk in Cork, he nevertheless still found stupidity and puritanical narrowness hard to tolerate. When he moved to Dublin, he adopted an ethic of expediency in dealing with the committee officials and, by contrivance and subterfuge, worked to establish a library that would serve the public well.

As librarian in Cork he had decided that if people could not or would not come to the books, then he would take the books to them. As he traveled about West Cork discovering what people wanted to read, he also tried to change their reading habits by introducing them to the literature of Russia and France, anything other than the pallid stuff sanctioned by the church. The conflicting aims of serving the needs of common readers while trying to raise their consciousness constantly disturbed Michael the librarian; it also disturbed Frank O'Connor the writer. It was a contradiction between his judgment, which was elitist, and his instinct, which was close to common, everyday reality.

In fact, Frank O'Connor's career as a librarian was a kind of postgraduate education. His formal schooling had ended at age twelve, but he had continued his education in the Free Library near the Cork City Hall. Having educated himself in a library, he always contended that libraries were for poor kids, old men, and other autodidacts dreaming their own inner culture. Where schools represented the principle of authoritative learning, libraries stood for self-education. He resisted the standard English notion that a good library meant a certain number of books covering a certain number of topics for a certain number of mythical researchers. He was interested in real readers, not in hypothetical scholars. He believed in books, for, to his mind, freedom was equated with the ability to read, and to read exactly what one wished to read; to control books and ideas was to stifle free thought. Provincialism and ignorance were, to Michael, worse oppressors than the Vikings or the English. He spent his entire life fighting the sort of attitude that left Ireland without publishing houses, without an effective system of libraries, "without even such a rudimentary thing in the whole country as a chair of Irish Literature." He believed that better libraries meant a better country, a free country that was not merely a province of England.

The condition of libraries in Ireland after the Civil War was shockingly inadequate, particularly outside the cities. The Carnegie Trust had endeavored to salt the small towns of the British Isles with funds sufficient to start and continue lending libraries. Besides dilapidated buildings and deteriorated collections where libraries had once existed, the main problem was public indifference and official suspicion. Generally, titles had to be approved by some committee of self-important citizens from a list of Three Thousand Books constituting the basic stock of acceptable books. The fallacy of this basic-stock idea did not dawn on Michael until he got to Pembroke. "I assure you," he told a group of librarians, "that a man's loss of faith was nothing to the realisation that our beautiful basic stock really wasn't worth a damn, and that the only best books in the world are the books that people want." If that meant boys' weeklies, sentimental historical romances, and detective "shockers," then that's what he bought. He always insisted that "the best librarian is the one who hands out the most books to the most people."[12]

He added to that pronouncement another important qualification: the capacity to get on with committees. "I would say to young librarians who feel frustrated that you can get a committee to do anything you want within reason provided you approach them properly." Though Michael had raged at stupid committee members and narrow-minded priests, and though he had antagonized polite patrons by refusing to dress or act politely, he met with not a single call for his resignation, either for incompetence or for literary impropriety, during his three years in Cork and ten years in Dublin. By trial and error he learned to cooperate enough to bring his libraries to some degree of respectability. Mainly he learned to work with his associates, which was no mean feat for an opinionated only child and a self-educated dreamer. His apprenticeship in the Carnegie Trust libraries had been in large measure an apprenticeship in life. He was forced to deal with more kinds of people than he would ever have met in a university or in his own room reading and writing—much as he had been made to do in prison.

Naturally, he developed firm friendships with some of the people with whom he worked. He valued friendship highly, for his friends were collaborators in his enthusiasms—books, music, and Ireland. Geoffrey Phibbs was his first great library friend, Dermot Foley his second. Dermot was as different from Michael as Michael was from Phibbs. He was Dublin middle-class: practical, stable, and properly educated. He was as horrified by Michael's country manner as he was intrigued by his wild talent. Michael seemed to him oblivious of every social grace. He was repelled, for instance, by the ring of stains on the wall of the lavatory where Michael sat every morning reading, smoking, and spitting, habits acceptable perhaps in a slum neighborhood, but hardly in

Dublin's fashionable south side. Michael was also oblivious of his own personal appearance, often showing up at the library in rumpled clothes; and his hair never seemed to be combed. In spite of their differences, the two young librarians soon became good friends.

The week before Easter* Michael announced to Dermot that he was leaving the next evening on the mailboat for London and Paris, and that the only thing he needed before he sailed was a pair of tennis shoes. By this time Dermot had come to realize that his boss was inept at anything practical, from driving a car to buying clothes, so he simply loaned him his own shoes and watched the spectacle at the pier: "All he possessed was an attaché case, a raincoat and a walking-stick; and with the artist's black hat daringly cocked, he headed for Europe." According to O'Connor's account in his autobiography, he arrived in London "one cold and grey Good Friday" intent on rescuing Geoffrey Phibbs, who had left Norah and was living with Robert Graves and Laura Riding, the American poet. Michael's gallant efforts were frustrated entirely: Laura Riding made a fuss about his smoking, and Phibbs made jokes of everything he said. "We drank absinthe and ate salad," O'Connor recalled; after that he was escorted politely out.[13] For all practical purposes, it was the end of their friendship.

In what he called a "suicidal mood of loneliness," he left that night for Paris, intent on meeting James Joyce. Primed to talk about Joyce's work and the glories of the literary vocation, Michael met only questions from the great novelist about how such and such would be said in Cork and whether or not a certain store still stood on a certain street in Dublin. It was on this occasion that Michael asked Joyce about the picture in his hallway. Joyce said that it was Cork, to which Michael replied that he knew very well what the city looked like, but it was the frame he was curious about. Joyce smugly repeated that it was cork, leaving Michael only slightly better off than when he came.[14]

For the remainder of the spring and throughout the summer, Michael and Dermot toiled to impose some degree of order upon their library. The night before the Pembroke District Library opened officially, they were working frantically on the final details. Michael was particularly nervous that night, complaining about his gastritis, chain-smoking as usual, and stalking from one station of the library to the next. Dermot was upstairs in the children's section. Having heard no explosions for some time, he crept down the stairs to see if Michael had fallen asleep. Instead he found Michael creeping up the stairs. "Jesus, Dermot! It's nearly three." They both sat down for a reflective smoke. Michael broke the silence: "I'd never have opened this without you. Mind, you wouldn't have opened it without me either." It was the first time Michael had given Dermot recognition as a colleague and as a friend.

The following day, September 27, 1929, the library opened. Only one person from the other libraries in the area chose to attend, and he praised their ambitious project. Unable to contain his pleasure over the collection of Continental literature he had gathered, Michael pulled a French novel from the shelf and handed it to the man, a shy, thorough librarian. "What do you think of this?" he challenged. The man looked at the binding, spotted an error in the

* Easter in 1929 fell on March 31.

classification number, and pointed to it. Michael exploded in laughter, unable to fault the one professional librarian thoughtful enough to honor his opening, even though he failed to comment on the collection. Michael was certain of his knowledge of books, and selecting books gave him great pleasure, though, as Dermot observed, he would often "give tongue when cataloguing books, lashing into the bonehead whose masterpiece lay before him and pontificating on the subject, no matter what that was."[15] At the time he was obsessed by French and Russian literature; to this day the stamp of his taste is evident in the Pembroke Library.

His office was a tiny cubicle, about ten by ten feet, with a large mahogany desk, two straight-backed oak chairs, a fireplace on one wall, and two Medici prints on another. To the right of the desk was a window overlooking the parade ground of the Royal Dublin Society. Except when Yeats, AE, or Lennox Robinson came for a visit, or when he was reading, Michael was out of the office, roaming among the patrons trying to catch a glimpse of what they had chosen to read so he could recommend something better. When he tried to work at the lending desk, he turned Dermot's careful system inside out in no time. To Dermot, "he was the most impractical man I ever knew."

Every day, for example, Michael walked to work from his lodgings in Ranelagh reading a book. Dermot often anxiously watched him cross the bridge with his head down, heedless of the traffic. At the front gate he mechanically took the key from his coat pocket and opened the postbox, and the book was abandoned as he pounced on the mail. This momentary fascination usually took one or two circuits of the ground floor, a few explosions, and perhaps even a dramatic rendering of particularly memorable passages—memorable, that is, by their stylistic perversity. When he finally climbed the stairs to his office, the library staff could breathe easily again and return to their chores. Michael was a strict and demanding boss; to some, he was a tyrant who considered the library his own palatial grounds and the staff his own retinue. This royal manner toward his staff and the oracular mien in all matters literary were instinctive measures of defense against an "extraordinary vulnerability and innocence," traits that Dermot had come to realize lay at the very core of Michael's character and that were the reason for his profound sense of personal loneliness.[16]

Michael left his stamp on Pembroke not only by his book selections but by his attention to the Children's Library. Recalling the hours he had spent in the Free Library in Cork as a boy, he insisted on giving the boys and girls of the community, both the rich and the poor, a place of their own. He turned the spacious well-lighted area upstairs into a cheerful room for children. He arranged a schedule for fortnightly talks and other special events, held in the late afternoon hours.[17] Padraic Colum often told fairy tales; usually Dermot or Michael gave readings or played music. Here Michael was at his entertaining best, raving about Mozart or Schubert, miming the exploits of some Irish hero, or gesturing wildly as he read in Gaelic. He even formed a choir but reduced the whole scheme to a muddle the first afternoon by ignoring the staff notation of the sheet they were using in favor of the "tonic sol-fa" method, and plowing along with a rhythm none of the children could follow.[18] Finally he flung the book at Dermot, who had some choral training and some patience for the squirming ways of children. Order was restored, and Michael was invited to be the assistant conductor.

It was that spirit of unbridled adventure that formed the basis of Michael's relationship with Dermot. They complemented each other like two plough horses, one frisky and full of wild energy, the other trained and steady. He lifted Dermot "out of common-place adolescence to contemplate an entirely new world." Dermot, on the other hand, brought Michael back to earth, and Michael felt comfortable enough with him to reveal his "extraordinary vulnerability and innocence" beneath all the "calculated arrogance and pomp." Dermot was Michael's sounding board, the one person with whom he needed no mask, from whom he did not need to conceal his insecurity; and Dermot gave Michael acceptance in return. Music was the cement of their friendship. No matter how distraught Michael was made by the library or by his writing, he blossomed to life whenever Dermot came to his flat with a new recording. They always ended one of their evenings with a Beethoven quartet or a Russian folk dance.

After music their other point of collaboration was walking. On most days Dermot worked until six or seven, long after Michael had gone home to write. But occasionally they walked home together; at such times Michael would talk about some book he had just read or would quote poetry, perhaps Yeats or Verlaine. Both fearful and enthralled, Dermot would simply "listen in silence to the ceaseless flow of it." One memorable occasion "took the form of a sixteen-mile walk from Rathfarnham and over the mountains into Enniskerry, where we were just able to crawl in a bus and reach the Theatre Royal for a concert by John Sullivan, Joyce's Irish tenor from the Paris Opera. We went quite wild with joy that night."[19]

I V

Before Dublin Frank O'Connor had seen himself primarily as a poet, though he once confided to Phibbs that stories came more easily and gave him greater satisfaction. Another friend, Sean Hendrick, noticed that after Gormanstown Michael had begun to turn from romantic poetry to realistic fiction. The shift was due as much to a natural fascination with character, drama, and situation as to some drastic moral disillusionment, however. The young writer simply turned from a verse of the personal voice to a prose sounding the voices of those who, he said, represented all he ever knew of God. Shortly after his release from prison, in the "first flush of remembrance," Michael began writing about his war experiences, mostly effusive poems but brief prose sketches as well. In prison he had listened carefully to fellow prisoners talk endlessly of their war experiences, and he took bits and pieces of their anecdotes and turned them into sketches. While serving as county librarian in Cork, he tinkered with these sketches in the first of his writing journals.[20]

His first published stories, most of which were written in the shadow of Daniel Corkery's *A Munster Twilight,* were exuberant but lacking in control. Moreover, the subject of war had not yet been fully assimilated within O'Connor's mind. Like the nation, perhaps, he was still smarting from the effects of violence, rhetoric, and partial victory. "War," a story written in 1926 and published by AE in the *Irish Statesman,* renders his own capture by Free State troops on the road to Kilmallock.[21] Though relatively unsuccessful—as with most of his early stories, O'Connor chose never to reprint or rewrite it—"War" nevertheless anticipated some of the writing that eventually came together in his first volume of stories. It also revealed his compassion for suffering people and his natural ability to capture people in some telling moment; already the marks of the typical O'Connor story had begun to emerge: simple and collo- quial diction, brisk dialogue, and a layering of tragic and comic emotions.

Prompted by AE and Sean Hendrick, O'Connor once again turned his hand to these war sketches in 1929, forging the reminiscent vignettes into short stories. The stories had been knocking about in his mind, gathering force and direction as he walked the wet streets of Cork; but only after he moved to Dublin was he able to work them out fully in his own peripatetic and improvi- sational way. Michael finished writing "Guests of the Nation" late in March 1930. He later felt that writing it had been something of a breakthrough. After all, he hadn't the slightest idea how to write stories. He certainly knew nothing about the sort of facts with which most other storytellers seemed to salt their prose. Quite by accident he discovered himself laughing and crying as he wrote "Guests of the Nation." He knew he had written a good story, but for the life of him he could not tell why. The demise of AE's *Irish Statesman,* he wrote to Nancy on April 3, 1930, had forced him to seek outlets for his stories in America: " [This] may be a blessing for me, really, though I shall have to bottle up my rage against the Gaels." At the same time he observed, "John Hendrick would smile at my all-too-careful preparations, my violence of self-criticism, but never mind, I shall write so that every word will have a meaning."[22] What- ever it was, rage against Corkery's national consciousness or against his own fumbling prose, something was bottled up in Michael, making him quarrel- some at the library and moody at his flat. His stomach alternated between bad and worse. Exiled in Dublin, writing out the demons of his war experiences, and missing his mother and Nancy, he considered himself the loneliest crea- ture on God's earth.

Thus, when he received a telegram from the *Atlantic Monthly* accepting "Guests of the Nation," his exuberance was volcanic. He grabbed his amazed landlady, twirled her rejoicingly around the kitchen, kissed her smartly, and rushed off to tell the news to Dermot. That morning the library was a noisy shambles until the two decided to take their celebration to Glendalough, the secluded mountain valley just south of Dublin known for its ecclesiastic ruins. Off they went for a great weekend of careless abandon underwritten by the $150 the American magazine was to pay O'Connor for the story. What they forgot was that the money wouldn't come until later. Dermot, chuckling at their stupidity, was forced to take the bus back into Dublin to borrow enough to cover their lavish celebration, while Michael drank and waited in the Royal Hotel—Yeats often went there for short holidays—until Dermot returned.

Unfortunately the enthusiasm with which that story was received by the editors of the *Atlantic Monthly* failed to emerge in Britain, where Michael was trying to find a publisher for an entire volume of war stories. Various literary friends encouraged him to send his set of stories to Edward Garnett, the noted English critic who had already "discovered" Liam O'Flaherty and who would soon do the same for Seán O'Faoláin. Garnett's judgment apparently ranked somewhere near gospel in the minds of British publishers, so it seemed fatal to Michael's career when Garnett returned the stories with the acrid comment that Frank O'Connor had no power of observation.[23] Furthermore, he recommended that the young writer read O'Flaherty. Michael was more dismayed than crushed—certainly Garnett could be no more critical of his writing than he was himself.

At this point AE stepped in and wrote to his own publisher, Macmillan, with the following recommendation:

> ... May I supplicate attention for his mss. He is a young man of very great talent, an admirable poet and something of a scholar. His translations from Gaelic are the best I know. His stories are I believe about the civil war in Ireland and he had exceptional opportunities for gathering intimate knowledge of this dark period in our history. But his interest in writing these stories is not political but human. That is his interest is in the characters not in the political situation. I recommended James Stephens to your attention a good many years ago. I have come across no young Irish writer since in whose future I have more confidence.[24]

That was in August. In September, still waiting to hear from Macmillan, Michael wrote to Nancy that he was not really worried about the book. "I am exalted when I am writing a good story," he told her; "when it is written I have little or no interest in it, except to revise; and then only when the old glory flashes over it again for an instant." Even recognition must not have excited him very much, because he sent off only a few of these war stories to magazines. What he needed, he suggested to Nancy, was an "adoring wife," one who would be more interested in his work than he was. "She would say all the venomous things about editors that I do not say when I get back a manuscript. She would loathe every writer who was preferred above me; while I only lean back and wonder at human impudence."[25] Perhaps the insouciance was a trifle forced, but apparently he was less bothered by the Garnett snub than were AE and Nancy.

When the contract finally came from Macmillan in October, Michael was too harried by a proposed scheme to reorganize the public libraries in Dublin, too worried about his health, and too lovesick to take much notice. Macmillan offered Frank O'Connor only a nominal advance but made generous provision for the publication of his novel and a second volume of stories. With the anticipated publication of *Guests of the Nation* Frank O'Connor was on his way. Michael O'Donovan, however, was still adrift. His "infertile in-between periods" of loneliness and boredom were exaggerated by Nancy McCarthy's staunch refusal to marry him and by his chronic stomach problem. For weeks on end that fall he lived on little but baby food. Then he developed painful boils on his neck, which his physician, Dr. Richard Hayes, believed were the outward evidence of some sort of gangrenous abscess. Finally, the Greater Dublin Act, which annexed Pembroke township along with Rathmines into Dublin, brought the Pembroke District Library under the authority of the Dublin Corporation.

Believing that officials had rigged the new qualifications to exclude him, Michael stormed the main library offices. Rebuffed soundly, he returned and actually cried on Dermot's shoulder. He assumed that their library was being stripped out from under them, "the only literary library in Ireland." Though this did not happen, they did lose the independence they had enjoyed under the District Council. Soon his afternoon programs were taken over by the Gaelic League, and his assistants were replaced by people from the Central Library staff. Then a group of vigilante protectors of the public conscience raided the library in search of books on Russia. O'Connor was opposed to communism, but he was equally opposed to this sort of arbitrary censorship. A library, he believed, should contain "a totality of experience in which the voice should come to the individual." Dermot, as disgusted as Michael was by the incursion of all this bureaucracy, decided to accept the position of librarian for County Clare in Ennis. He would leave Dublin late in 1931, and Michael, again faced with the loneliness of a long-distance friendship, would return to his books and to his writing. "Henceforth my maxim must be," he proclaimed to Nancy: "I've got a job and I'm going to sit on it."

7

The First Confessions:
Women, War, and Words

Chameleons feed on light and air:
Poets' food is love and fame.

SHELLEY, *"An Exhortation"*

"THE loneliest creature on God's earth is a young writer trying to find himself." In this observation about the tortures of his first two books, *Guests of the Nation* (1931) and *The Saint and Mary Kate* (1932), Frank O'Connor was probably referring to his fumbling search for a suitable literary style. What he might have added was that there is no one more lonely than a passionate and naive young man from a provincial town fumbling for a suitable social style in a big city. A self-taught amateur in all things, he simply improvised love as he had his education. It was the loneliest time of his life, a time spent vacillating between manic intensity and severe melancholy.

1

The flurry of activity from 1929 to 1930 in which O'Connor wrote the stories published in *Guests of the Nation* was characteristic of the way he approached every volume of stories he ever produced. He would write a story or two under some spontaneous spell and then begin to sense a larger picture, a set of stories, cohesively related by some thread or other. In a blaze of enthusiasm he would write more stories in the same voice. Then, frustrated by their crudity, he would doggedly rewrite the very stories that had generated the whole notion in the first place.

The stories that eventually came together in *Guests of the Nation* were conceived in Michael's mind as a unified volume, somewhat in the manner of Corkery's *A Munster Twilight* and Joyce's *Dubliners,* even more in the manner of George Moore's *The Untilled Field,* the book that O'Connor believed contributed a new simplicity of form and style to the prose fiction of the Irish literary movement.[1] Moore's stories, like those of Turgenev and Chekhov in whose shadow they were written, seemed to O'Connor to bridge the gap between poetry and realism. He had always assumed that he could make the world more palatable. That he tried is testimony to his romanticism; that he knew in the end that it was a futility was the mark of his realism. Realism, at least as it was practiced by O'Connor, is like the stubbornness of the amateur or the candor of the child—audacious, tactless, and bothersome.

Against the odds, Michael learned Irish and became a writer; against the odds, a ragtag bunch of amateurs fought the mighty British to a draw. Seán O'Faoláin, Peadar O'Donnell, and many other rising young writers of Michael's generation took part in that violent affair, believing in the possibility of a far-reaching social and cultural revolution in Ireland, rather than simply a change in the ruling class. It all turned sour in their mouths when they realized the lack of spiritual vitality within the new establishment. The past, with its sentimental nationalism, had become intractable, and the future, managed largely by mediocrity and commercial practicality, offered little hope for meaningful change. So they turned instead to a revolution at once more personal and tentative, to their poems and plays and stories and novels. Everything Frank O'Connor wrote carried the weight of the pugnacious idealism and contentious realism that flow through *Guests of the Nation*.

Of the fifteen stories in the volume, all but the last four deal with the Troubles, from the Easter Rising to the Civil War. Some of the stories take place in or near Cork City with its wet streets, quays, steep hills, pubs, churches, lanes, and shops. Most of the actual fighting stories are set in the countryside outside Cork, in the rugged mountains around Macroom, or the gentle hills around Mallow. But place is never the primary dimension in an O'Connor story; setting for him is atmosphere, emerging as a complement to the voice of the story. Thus most of the stories are wrapped in darkness, casting the disarray and desolation in silhouetted relief. Even time is vague, for the historical moment transcends natural time.

Offhandedly Michael called *Guests of the Nation* his "war book" in a letter to Nancy with an equally casual reference to Isaac Babel's *The Red Cavalry,* which had just been translated.[2] Babel's war stories contained a violence mingled with elegance and lyricism. "My First Goose" and "The Death of Dolgushov," two stories about the effect of outright brutality on sensitive individuals, undoubtedly touched a nerve in Michael, whose war memories still plagued him—not what had happened so much as how he had reacted. Reading Babel's stories, O'Connor saw a way to span poetry and realism by redirecting intense moral concerns through stringent aesthetic form. Inevitably what he took from Babel was not the subject but the manner of the stories: control, brevity, objectivity, and lyrical apprehension of human problems.

Intense as his response to Babel was, O'Connor actually relied more heavily on another Russian for the conception of his own war stories. Turgenev's *Sportsman's Sketches* remained O'Connor's model for a volume of stories— each story discrete and whole, yet related by some thematic ambiance to the other stories in the volume.[3] What unity *Guests of the Nation* possessed was both tonal and thematic, however, for inevitably O'Connor's mind gravitated from idea to situation, from theme to character. For a storyteller, life is a highly fragile and personal affair unified not by grand abstractions but by the inconvenient, elusive, and diverse patterns etched by common humanity across the surface of events. Invariably O'Connor's imagination forced itself through the picturesque, the historical, or the abstract to some situational flash point, some point of vivid impact.

The violence and idealism of the events of 1916 to 1923 created in Ireland a mood of national hysteria. At least that was the tone of voice O'Connor heard when trying to capture those events in prose six years later. In fact, *Guests of the Nation* vacillates between the extremes of hysteria and melancholy, thoughtless act and numbed thoughtfulness. Benedict Kiely detected in these stories a "genuine bliss-was-it-that-dawn-to-be-alive romanticism," an adolescent enjoyment of the guns, the ambushes, the flying columns.[4] Indeed, this hysterical romanticism swirls across the surface of all but the last four stories.

"Jumbo's Wife," "Alec," and "Machine Gun Corps in Action" are examples of romanticized violence of the sort O'Connor found in Isaac Babel. In these stories war exposes the folly and weakness of character, as well as the normal responses of people under pressure. The failure of the stories is not that O'Connor idealized violence but that he failed to control its comic energy. Situation dominates character, and the voice is blurred.

However, "Laughter" delivers a more clearly realized comic story from an equally absurd misadventure. Boys playing soldier find all the ingredients of a daring ambush: revolvers, Mills bombs, trench coats, and dark alleys. The story is the fictional account of the poem "Ambush"; written by O'Connor in 1924, the poem is about the time he, Seán O'Faoláin, Sean Hendrick, and Vincent O'Leary tried to sabotage a Free State convoy.[5] In "Laughter" the hysteria is controlled; thematic tragedy gives way to the comic twist of character. An old woman emerges from "the gloom of an archway" and comes toward the fleeing boys. Stanton and Nolan (Hendrick and O'Faoláin) continue, but Cunningham and Stephen (O'Leary and O'Donovan) stop to speak. "They were above the city now, and it lay far beneath them in the hollow, a little bowl of smudgy, yellow light." The old woman asks if it was shooting she heard "below be the cross." With "wild, happy eyes" Cunningham replies that it wasn't shooting at all but a deaf woman in a shop below spending a winter night "blowing paper bags!" A laugh shakes the old woman's frail body, and she hails the "young devil" disappearing with his comrade "under the gloom of the trees." The laughter of this survivor persists in the face of hysteria and gloom, the two extremes between which young Michael O'Donovan ran his course.

As surely as violence and hysteria, along with their safety valve of comic hilarity, dominate the surface of *Guests of the Nation,* a more serious and thoughtful voice operates below that surface, a voice full of compassion and bitterness. The humor of "Laughter" and "Machine Gun Corps in Action" is the comedy of disorder, of natural nervous tension in the face of violent death. After all, war is not a normal situation, at least not for amateur warriors. O'Connor distrusted the cold, organizational mind of the professional soldier, for whom fear and disorder have been disciplined away. If romantic hysteria, nervous laughter, and chaotic fear represent the natural responses of plain people to the stress of war, then disillusionment, accompanied by loneliness and melancholy, emerges just as naturally from the violence and stress. After *hysteria* the other word used throughout the volume more than might normally be expected is *melancholy.*

Although *Guests of the Nation* carries no dedication, it is most certainly for Sean Hendrick, to whom "September Dawn" had been dedicated when first published in a magazine, and by whose side Michael O'Donovan spent most of his battle time in 1921 and 1922 running dispatches for Erskine Childers and turning out publicity sheets on a commandeered printing press. For both of them the romance of war was second only to their love affair with language and literature, so Michael began writing his war stories to capture something of the romance and the agony of the whole affair. "September Dawn," the story O'Connor wrote for Sean Hendrick, seems to recreate the feelings the two young rebels were left with at the end of the fighting.

For those in a disheveled flying column love is only a fleeting chance. After disbanding their column, because they "want to live for Ireland, not die for it," the two young rebels of "September Dawn," Hickey and Keown, beat a haphazard retreat from Mallow to the safety of the mountains of West Cork. Their frantic journey is devoid of glory or romance; they snatch bits of food on the run, not daring to stop. The retreat is made more treacherous by the finest autumn in years, its oblique "shafts of sunlight" creating telltale shadows. At nightfall they reach the cottage of Hickey's aunt. A young woman is there helping the old lady, and to the frightened, lonely patriots on the run her simple beauty fills the emptiness.

This glimmer of romance suspends the two rebels between the fear of death and the desire for life. Hickey, sleepless and thoughtful, realizes that his life has been aimless and the cause for which he is risking his life will mean little in the long run. His desire for love returns "with all the dark power of nocturnal melancholy surging up beneath it; the feeling of his own loneliness, his own unimportance, his own folly." The swirling wind wakes his comrade, who imagines that his pursuers have come. Only Hickey's fist silences his sniveling; violence intrudes even into the natural serenity. At dawn he watches the gray fog lift, exposing the withered leaves and broken branches. In the kitchen below he finds the girl returning with a bucket of turf. Without speaking, he kisses her: "for him in that melancholy kiss an ache of longing was kindled." Grotesques and silhouettes caught in the death-dealing hysteria of war find a hope as barren as the autumn dawn, a life-affirming melancholy, which pervades the entire volume.

As the emotional center of *Guests of the Nation*, "September Dawn" seems to combine the numbed thoughtfulness of some of the stories with the thoughtless frenzy of others.[6] The romance of war with its tragic violence and comic disarray has been diverted to an affirmation of love and friendship. The hysterical fear of death has become the melancholy acceptance of life. In a similar way, "September Dawn" represents a standard of O'Connor's technique, an indication of that delicate merging of romanticism and realism that would give his finest fiction a special edge. The lyricism of O'Connor's adolescent poems has been modulated into a kind of poetic realism; the passage of the two rebels in the story reflects the process of change in the entire volume, from fearful and fumbling adolescence to resigned and sober manhood.

The last four stories of *Guests of the Nation* operate in a temporal vacuum, suggesting perhaps that the personal growth happens with or without the pressure of war or catastrophe. The man in "After Fourteen Years" could be visiting Bantry at almost any historical moment, for history pales in the face of personal considerations. He could just as well be returning there after an absence of forty years, because life for him has settled into polite encrustation; it is settled and there is nothing to hope for. The same can be said for the protagonist of "The Death of Henry Conran," whose death was reported prematurely; perhaps the report was not premature, after all, for he seems more dead than alive. Death weighs heavily in "The Sisters" as well: two sisters live alone; one cares for the other, the "mad" sister, and then dies suddenly, leaving the mad one on her own. Whereas the war stories concern the particular change from adolescence to maturity, these three stories deal with the general reality of passing from one condition in life to another, but they share with the entire volume a sense of return, a backward look at once melancholy and hopeful.

The final story of the volume returns to the crisis of adolescence. "The Procession of Life" ties together much of the volume, both in tone and theme. The narrator is a man looking back on an incident that seems to him particularly expressive of the confusion and anxiety of growing up. What traps the young hero of the story is his provincial Cork environment in general and his brutal father in particular. Larry's beloved mother has been dead almost a year; his obstinate father, on the night in question, has locked him out of the house. (Michael at the same age found himself locked out almost every time he went to the Gaelic League Hall with Corkery.) Alternately elated and miserable, he wanders along the quays, which are "lonely and full of shadows," until he finds a watchman's sentry box. The river makes "a clucking, lonely sound against the quay wall." Larry is adrift and lonely, seeking some measure of human contact, but the grizzled old watchman chases him away when a lady of the night appears. He sneaks back, and the scene becomes a portrait of loneliness: three of the loneliest creatures imaginable huddled at one of those places of futility that are to be found at any public-works site in Ireland. To Larry the woman seems a "magical creature"; her perfume, "overpowering and sweet." At the same time the watchman falls under her spell. The old and the young, the bitter and the naive, share a radical lonesomeness. The woman's touch sends "shivers of pleasure through him" while the watchman's competitive reproof makes him cower. A constable arrives and resolves the standoff by sending the woman away and telling her to meet him later. At the end of the story Larry disobeys the policeman's order to stay with the old man and returns home jaunty and confident and ready to defy his surly father.

Seeking to capture in his own volume of stories something of the unity of Turgenev and Moore and Joyce, O'Connor gave special force to the stories that open and close *Guests of the Nation*. "The Procession of Life" stands apart from the rest of the volume in its treatment yet complements the overall theme of passage from romance to realism. The voice is lyrical but not strictly autobiographical. Loneliness is embodied rather than indulged, for the voice generates a life of its own in a detached reminiscence characteristic of nearly every story in the volume. The title story, which opens the volume, also stands apart. In "Guests of the Nation" O'Connor backs far enough away from the violence to expose its futility, but not so far as to miss its tragic implications.[7] Thrown together by the vagaries of war, Irish rebels and their English hostages come to personal terms over cards and negotiate a momentary truce through conversation and argument. At that point politics negate personal feelings; abstract retribution literally blows apart real friendship. After "assassinating" the two helpless hostages, the hero-narrator finds himself emotionally desolate: "It is so strange what you feel at such moments, and not to be written afterwards," he muses. "I was somehow very small and very lonely. And anything that ever happened to me after I never felt the same about again."[8]

O'Connor has not indicted the rebels or their cause; neither has he vindicated violence. Rather he has isolated its horrible effects at the moment of impact. For him, human dignity and rationality inevitably yield to the sudden impulse, to the unpredictable and passing moment. Although there is nothing quite like it in the rest of O'Connor's writing, "Guests of the Nation" contains those qualities that are unmistakably O'Connor: simplicity, tight narrative design, and lively drama carrying sparse revelations in language that is direct and alive. Most of all, it embodies the "lyric cry in the face of destiny."

Like most of his stories, "Guests of the Nation" came from someone else, though O'Connor stamped it with his own particular sympathies. It was in the Gormanstown Internment Camp that he heard the essential germ of the story about the killing of two English soldiers in reprisal for the killing of some Irish rebels.[9] Apparently there had been circulating in Kerry for some time a rumored tale about two English defectors who had been working on farms for some time before a zealous rebel leader, perhaps even O'Donovan Rossa, took them as spies and ordered their execution.[10] A variation on the anecdote had it that the two were to be murdered in the milking shed of an isolated Kerry farm. When the simple farmer objected to disallowing the men benefit of clergy, his strong-willed wife thrust him aside, took the gun, and shot the two Englishmen herself.

No matter where O'Connor got his story and no matter how obliquely he grafted it onto different characters and situations, "Guests of the Nation" emerged in the telling as a tightly designed and provocative story. It has become a classic story, honored by many imitations, including Brendan Behan's *The Hostage.* In "Guests of the Nation," as in few of his other early stories, O'Connor rises above mere contrivance and literary fumbling to voice the sort of primary affirmation that he himself insisted was vital to great literature.

I I

It is said that Turgenev once told Tolstoy that he could not write unless he was in love. Frank O'Connor would probably not have said it that directly, but it is obvious that his greatest productivity came when he was romantically involved with a woman. By the same token, his barren interludes as a writer occurred when he felt himself to be in a vacuum of love or when he was caught in tangled relationships that blurred the mystique of love for him. His strong and stormy friendships with men were collaborations in shared enthusiasms; his relationships with women were romantic pursuits of magic on the one hand and stability on the other. He saw love, as he did the rest of life, through a veil of literature and idealized women from afar.[11]

Actually, in the company of women Michael was so sensitive that he never seemed to know whether he was standing on his head or his feet. Once he surprised Dermot Foley by agreeing to attend a meeting of a notoriously "precious" literary group, then surprised him "still more by turning into a pub and swallowing a double whiskey, since he seldom drank at that time."[12] What Dermot did not know was that Michael always took a drink or two whenever visiting strangers, to brace himself for the ordeal. But it did not help much, for he had only to enter a strange situation to make a complete fool of himself. After one particularly embarrassing evening at the home of Francis Hackett, the novelist and historian, and his Danish wife, the writer Signe Toksvig, Michael had to be defended at great length by his old friend Joseph O'Neill, who concluded that "O'Connor never does himself justice except when he sits down to write."[13]

In society Michael was ill at ease, awkward, and naive. From shyness he talked too much and regretted most of it afterwards. One never knew whether he would be contentious, giddy, churlish, or totally silent; but alone, reading or writing, he was totally at ease and marvelously controlled. It was the same double life he had been leading since childhood, one in the real world of "drudgery and limitation," of jobs and manners, and one in his imaginary world of chivalric daydreams and foreign languages, music, and poetry.

One of the weaknesses of a "mother's boy" is the lifelong need for a female presence. Michael was helpless around the house, unable to perform even such simple chores as making breakfast, choosing a suitable lamp, or hanging a picture on the wall. He confessed to being "hagridden" without a woman to look after him. His inability to cook the proper foods exacerbated his chronic stomach problem, as did his "rut of occasional meals and general abstraction." "Whether or not there is a woman looking after me," he once wrote to Nancy, "can usually be observed by noting whether or not there is a large stain of cigarette ash on the front of my pants."[14] And although Michael hated to be alone, he needed solitude for writing. He was desperate for the magic and inspiration of a loving relationship, yet equally insistent on time and space for dreaming. Throughout his life he sought the constant, enduring, and silent presence of the sort his mother gave him.

Shortly after Michael took an upstairs room at Molly Alexander's house in Ranelagh, his mother came to Dublin for the first of a string of lengthy visits. They needed each other, the spoiled poor boy and the aging orphan-mother. From the very first Minnie got on well with her son's new landlady, who attended to him and loved him from afar. Minnie spent her time tidying his digs and writing letters back to her husband in Cork. She worried about his drinking, so she also wrote to her friends, particularly Minnie Connolly, in the square; nothing could cure her of the belief that Big Mick needed her mothering attention as much as her son. During the day she shopped with Molly in the village or went by herself into town. In the evening she and Michael and Molly enjoyed extended tea and conversation. Within a few days Minnie was as homesick as Michael. They talked mainly of Cork; rather, she regaled him with anecdotes about the place. After tea they generally walked; Michael listened as Minnie made Ranelagh and Ballsbridge and Donnybrook hospitable: which is to say that she, too, tried to make them seem like Cork. At night she always retired early as much for Michael as for herself. Though nearly seventy, she was still energetic; she was also perceptive enough to know that her son the writer would be needing to write.

Before moving to Dublin, Michael's romantic involvement with young women had been remarkably tame. In Cork, besides his decorous courtship with Nancy McCarthy, he had been "pals" with the O'Leary girls and had entertained fantasies about another Cork beauty, Natalie Murphy. In Dublin his female pals included Mary Manning, Anne Crowley, and Irene Haugh.[15] For some reason he felt constrained to inform Nancy of each new woman in his life, always the same gallant, bouncy, sassy sort of girl. Not long after arriving in Dublin he fell hopelessly in love with Meriel Moore, an actress at the Gate. He even went so far as to land a part in a silly comedy in which she played the female lead, just to be near her. Later it was a Gaiety actress, named Ruth Draper, who owned a motorcar and took him on gay rides to Wicklow. There was also Ethel Montgomery, a married woman twice his age whom he met at AE's. "That's the sort of woman I'd like to marry—if ever," he told Dermot one Sunday evening after she had interrupted the burly old saint's monologue with an outburst of laughter.[16] The more irrepressible a woman's gaiety and the more spontaneous her wit, the more she reminded him of his mother.

Molly Alexander, his young landlady, had been placed in a vulnerable position by her husband's frequent absences from home. She decided to take in a lodger as much for the security of a man in the house as for the additional income. Because he was wrapped up in his long-distance romance with Nancy and because Molly was a married woman with children, nothing romantic ever developed between them, but they managed to share one of the closest friendships Michael was ever to enjoy with a woman his own age. She woke him every morning, served him breakfast in the tiny kitchen at the back of the house, and tidied his room during the day. Often they would sit and talk after tea; just as often Michael would eat and retire to his room to write.[17] It was in her house that he wrote the stories of *Guests of the Nation.*

Molly Alexander was a simple, unpretentious person toward whom, Dermot asserts, Michael was "warmth itself." With her there was none of his cast-iron arrogance. To her he was a simple man, easy to talk to. Any man who loved his mother as much as Michael did couldn't be all bad, she thought. She admired his diligence in writing every evening after working a full day in the library. Occasionally she would read whatever pages were in his typewriter. Once she questioned him about what he was writing, and asked him if he would ever read something of it to her. Sheepishly at first, running his fingers through his hair, and then with great pomp, he read to her from "The Sisters," which pleased her because he had taken it from an incident she had related to him one evening.

The nearly two years at Chelmsford Road in Ranelagh were good years for Michael. It was in Molly's sitting room downstairs that he and Dermot spent hours listening to music on his prized gramophone. Usually it was Mozart or Beethoven, but occasionally Dermot could convince him to tolerate Schubert or Bach. One evening, in a particularly mischievous mood, Michael produced a new acquisition: Mozart, he claimed. Dermot squirmed impatiently until Michael rose to turn the disk. "Who the bloody hell is that really?" Dermot roared. "It can't be Mozart." Michael, with a gleam in his eye, simply replaced the needle and sat down again to listen to the other side. When it was over, Dermot, who deferred to Michael in almost everything except library technicalities, broke the silence: "Well, if that's Mozart, then I'm Brahms." "How did you know?" Michael replied. "Know what?" "That was actually Brahms," Michael confessed gleefully. "Blackguard," Dermot shouted over Michael's booming laughter. "I'll never trust you again." "Sir," said Michael, "and I shall never question your taste in music again." Their laughter woke one of Molly's children.

In October 1930, shortly after Macmillan's final acceptance of *Guests of the Nation,* Michael moved from Molly's house in Chelmsford Road to Anglesea Road. The book had sapped his spirit completely, and he had grown restless and irritable. Molly, like so many of the women in his life, had been drawn to him as much by his practical helplessness as by his creativity and had loved him and mothered him. Uneasy now at her attention to him, he desired his own place with his own furnishings. Moreover, the few friends who had made Dublin liveable for him were disappearing—Dermot to Ennis, Norah and Geoffrey Phibbs to London; and Nancy was as obdurate as ever. The provisions of the Greater Dublin Act had turned his position at the library into a mere job, and his stomach was in outright rebellion. Finally, he was having difficulty getting a fix on his novel. Soon after he was settled in his new lodgings, his mother came for a long visit and, finding him ill and melancholy, set about making things right. By the time she left in December he had recovered enough from the gastritis and from the string of exasperations to take up work on his novel again.

I I I

In April 1931 Michael mentioned by way of an aside in a letter to Nancy that his novel, *The Saint and Mary Kate,* was about half finished. Though he had no way to know it, his relationship with her was also about half finished. He had already endured three years of frustratingly proper courtship, most of it carried on through the post. Yet to come were three more years of self-imposed torture. The difficulties stemmed from the conflict between her chastity and piety and his audacity and impiety. But she represented security to Michael, and she was, above all, from Cork. By his own admission to her, this was not really a love affair,

> and because of that I think all the more of that queer little lane off Winter's Hill, and that night or rather that morning after The Round Table; the little window all lit up and the people who said the rosary inside; I think of it as if it were something out of a book that I had read long ago and of which I could remember nothing else, not even its author nor its name.[18]

As he was in love with writing, so Michael was at this time in love with love, trapped by the mystique of romantic moods and romantic words.

Actually, Michael was so absorbed in the loneliness and worry of his writing that this need for love was simply disconcerting to him. What he sought from Nancy was clarity. For instance, in one winter letter he opens with this paragraph:

> What a mean creature you are! And how weak I am! For just as I had made up my mind never to write to you again I began reconstructing the Castleblayney story (which may yet prove a masterpiece) and fell again so hopelessly in love with the typescript Nance that the very real cold-blooded inconsiderate Nance was dissolved in a romantic shower of gold.[19]

At times, however, he could cut through his self-absorption and be compassion itself, particularly at moments of crisis for Nancy (only crises that had nothing to do with himself). When her friend Gracie O'Shea died in July 1929, he wrote two very supportive and tender letters. Toward the end of the first, after observing how suffering acts as a merciful opiate on itself, he concludes:

> It is very rough on you now, but you will be all right. You have what I have not got and what I grudge you whole heartedly, tremendous resilience. . . . It will all pass—quicker than you know. But while you can grieve, do. It is one of the few things worth while and perhaps the purest

thing in our lives. I wish I could be more helpful, but you know me for
what I am, a dour doleful heathen who contemplates the universe with a
scowl and sees in everything a snare.[20]

Actually, the strength he saw in her was not resiliency but rather a realistic assessment of her abilities and a resigned acceptance of life's limited hopes. At
the time she was simply more mature than he.

Michael believed that what he needed was a strong woman: "not a knock-
kneed hypercritical hypersensitive pathological case like myself." In a gesture
of self-dramatization he ended another letter by exclaiming: "Russell is right
about me; I am a romantic and the realism is only a kink. Realism be damned!
It's only a sort of spiritual cold storage."[21] Nancy was realist enough to know
that marriage with Michael would not work; she had simply adjusted to it. Michael may have known it, too, but persisted in trying to buck the tide. Loving a
woman, distant and unattainable, was the chivalric way, the "literary" way.

Since he saw life through a "veil of literature," even his lovers became
part of the texture of his literary life. His letters to Nancy resembled those of
Chekhov to Olga Knipper, which in fact he once instructed her to read.[22] Michael was testing the limits of his artistic vision against her congenial intelligence. His tone was usually confessional. He shared with her the travail of
writing, his moods of anguish and self-doubt, and occasionally even his tentative delight in his abilities. But he complained again and again of her superficial gossip when what he said he needed was a good story, even though she
had always (though perhaps unwittingly) supplied him with material. He also
needed objective details about Cork for his novel, and Nancy enthusiastically
assisted him during the spring of 1931 by taking countless photographs
around Cork. When Michael saw the photographs, he wrote to her, "I shall
never, never begin a novel again without going over my ground with a camera.
The detail one gets wrong is not so important as the detail one misses."[23] In
this way Nancy was as much a collaborator in his early writing efforts as a
sounding board for his highly volatile opinions and for his stifling depressions.
She believed in him, probably more than he did himself, and encouraged him
constantly. She resisted his pressure to live with him on moral grounds, but
she cared enough about him to know that she would hinder him from writing
the masterpieces she knew he had in him.

The novel, begun in October 1930 and half finished in April 1931, was
nearing completion in June. Michael had detached himself almost completely
from his little library in Pembroke since the Greater Dublin Act, even going so
far as to write in his office during the day. AE spent hours with him poring over
his novel, struggling with him "for mastery of the theme." All O'Connor could
say was that it was his religious novel. AE considered it a philosophical mouthpiece. On June 14 Michael wrote to Nancy:

I don't like to speak too much of the novel at this closing stage (scowls at
typewriter and attempts to readjust the ribbon) but it may be a masterpiece. Anyway in spots it is long miles ahead of what I have done before
and it is simply burning its way about in my mind. I wish whether you go
to Switzerland or England you would call here and read and discuss it
before it is sent off. It must be finished for the end of July.

Then, flushed with confidence, he retorts to her latest bubble-bursting criticism of his arrogance:

(Irritably) Why of course, girl, I am a genius. Realize that when I left Cork two and a half years ago I was writing in prose nothing but balderdash, that when I was here for six months I wrote After Fourteen Years and have progressed from that through September Dawn, through Guests to Conran and the Patriarch, and am now engaged in leaving these behind me at the rate of two hundred and twenty miles an hour. And all this in spite of physical ailments and a shyness of human beings such as no writer before me ever had.

By the end of June 1931 the old self-doubt had returned. "The book is a glugger," he wrote on a dismal Saturday morning. On the Thursday before he had thought consolingly that if it was not a masterpiece, it was at least a "readable bit of humorous writing." Then on Friday night even that hope had fled, thrusting him from an improvisational fury to disconsolate melancholy.

The truth is that I know nothing whatever of novel writing or didn't while I was writing it. A novel—I define for your benefit—is the smallest number of characters in the least number of situations necessary to precipitate a given crisis. But what use are definitions when my book is the greatest number of characters in the greatest number of situations leading up to a non-existent crisis? It's deplorable. A man with half my talent would have done it ten times better. I have Mozart's fatal gift of melody only my melodies are characters; characters for which a real novelist would have given his soul spring up at every page and I enjoy myself, and then—no more.[24]

Dermot Foley, who had not yet departed for Ennis, laughingly chided Michael, saying that this was merely the opinion of the weekend. And, in fact, on the Monday when he finally posted the letter to Nancy, Michael could scribble at the bottom of the last page his fervent thanks to Saint Anthony for having rediscovered the subject of the book.

But his emotions continued to roller-coaster. Three days later he wrote again to Nancy:

How great and rich the times are now. Wednesday a visit from Norah McGuinness, Thursday a gathering peace about my book, Friday a letter from A.E. (consoling me) and tonight a letter from you (consoling me). . . . Not that I have reached anything like my old exultation, but reading certain bits I was profoundly moved by a sort of physical tenderness which I know is in myself though it is in nothing I have written up to this; and I understand why it is that for months I have felt a curious passion for birds and dogs and children, because ultimately we become what we write even if the change is not perceptible to others.

The rest of the letter is playful. He chides her for misreading Lawrence, whose stories he finds the only English stories worth reading. Then he requests a snapshot of her in bathing attire. "You never know what it will inspire," he quips. Finally, in a scribbled postscript, he lets her know that he has settled on a title for his novel: It was to be called *The Saint and Mary Kate*.

Meanwhile he had received proofs of *Guests of the Nation* and sent them to Nancy, cautioning her not to show them to anyone. He found it amusing that Macmillan editors had recommended reconsideration of "all Anglo-Saxon words beginning with 'b'," suggesting "jade" instead. He also expressed slight dissatisfaction with the publisher's exaggerated enthusiasm about the title story. When the volume finally appeared in September 1931, reviewers paid little attention to his own personal favorites. They also compared him to Turgenev, which seemed to Michael somewhat out of proportion, if not downright blasphemous.[25] All the lavish praise for his promise as a writer prompted him to scribble "We Shall See!" on the copy of the Macmillan announcement he sent to Nancy. At the end of the letter in which the announcement and a few clippings were enclosed, Michael admits that it is a "disgruntled egotistical letter": but still, "one publishes a first book but once, and whether one lives or dies the bloom will soon be off the rose."[26]

More than anything else, what disturbed O'Connor was not hearing from Corkery, to whom he had sent a special signed copy. "Catch me do it again," he wrote to Nancy. This was his first big step into the world of writing, and he received no acknowledgment of it from the man who had given him his start; not much, actually, from anyone in his hometown. "Oh, Cork! Cork!" he wrote to Nancy.

Then, Michael's annual July holiday in Glengarriff with his mother degenerated into a feud with his father. By September he had again been caught in what he called a "Byronic depression." Overwork and poor eating habits caused his stomach problem to flare up again. The Anglesea lodgings where he had written *The Saint and Mary Kate* now felt confining and inhospitable, the library even less congenial. So in the fall, feeling displaced and restless, he decided to move once again. In December he and an acquaintance named Paddy Corr took a flat in a huge house called Trenton,* just across from the Royal Dublin Society.

By the beginning of 1932 O'Connor had become quite at sea about his novel. Actually, he was at sea about nearly everything—suffering the agonies of gastritis and painful boils, drinking too much, and entertaining a "chorus girl." He wrote to Nancy that with all the pent-up hatred in his heart he hated everything about the book. "Why didn't I stick to short stories which I know I can do on my head instead of mucking about with a form of which I know nothing and for which I care less?" *Guests of the Nation* went into a second edition, which meant a bit of money for O'Connor, who had received no advance from Macmillan for the forthcoming novel. He confessed to Nancy not only a monetary motive in writing *The Saint and Mary Kate*—to make enough to be able to retire to Spain to write another—but a more personal one: to best Corkery's only novel, *The Threshold of Quiet*. "At least the Saint is an artistic failure!"[27] he exclaimed to her. His stories had been praised for all the wrong reasons, he thought, and he was sure that his novel would "annoy everybody except the artists so it [would] cancel out." This pattern would persist throughout his life: Writing for the common reader, he would always gather more acclaim from the intelligentsia. In advance reviews of *The Saint and Mary Kate* he was given glowing praise by the *Observer* but accused by the

---

* Houses in the British Isles occasionally have names as well as a street address. For instance, the first house in which O'Connor stayed in Dublin was called Castleville.

Derry Journal of writing on a dung heap. This pattern, too—praise from England and America and condemnation from Ireland—would continue throughout his career.

The Saint and Mary Kate was Frank O'Connor's religious love book, a testament to the magic of love and the exuberance of faith. The treatment was entirely from without, for the drama was all too within the passionate variety show in his own mind. When Nancy observed that the characters seemed to her like museum pieces, he agreed, though claiming the same could be said of a Dostoevsky novel or an Elizabethan play. "It's just a question of approach. Seen close enough anything appears monstrous while if one stands far enough away (Guests) the most monstrous thing appears natural." But what he observed later of Corkery's *The Threshold of Quiet* may be as true of his own novel: "a work of art in the Freudian sense of a spiritual conflict in the author's mind given external expression."[28]

If *The Saint and Mary Kate* is the work of a young man groping for a suitable theme, it is also the work of an Irishman writing to locate a cohesive Irish consciousness. On one hand, the novel is a private quest and an act of love, and as such it reveals something of the character of the man who wrote it. On the other hand, it is a public portrait and an act of defiance, and to understand it is to catch a glimpse of the nature of O'Connor's circumstances. For him, to do battle with the provincial narrowness of Cork was to encounter his own provincialism; to answer Corkery was to confront his spiritual father.

O'Connor once said that Ireland always looks out on the world through windows and doors. Mary Kate McCormick and Phil Dinan (the Saint) peer from the dark, confining monotony of a Cork tenement called the Dolls' House toward the light and freedom of the outside world.[29] Their tragedy of innocence, as O'Connor himself termed it, resembled the double doors so prevalent up and down the untidy, noisy lanes of this Irishtown—half open and half shut, the brutality of circumstance blocking the delicacy of hope. O'Connor neither romanticizes poverty or condemns wealth; the abstraction of social class dissolves before the richness of emotion and language within Cork's Native Stream. Far enough away to appear natural, close enough to be monstrous—that is the impact of the desperate, volatile poverty of the Dolls' House, an eighteenth-century house once occupied by the rich and, since the Famine, taken over by the poor.

The first half of the novel, set entirely in the Dolls' House, presents the opposite responses of Phil and Mary Kate to their blighted and restrictive surroundings. Each is dependent only upon himself: she because of her mother's way of life and he by his mother's death. His studious piety drives him further into himself, and her sentimental fantasies isolate her from those around her. In the second half of the novel Phil, against his better judgment, travels to Dublin to rescue Mary Kate who has gone to visit the man she supposes to be her father. Phil's fight with McCormick and the strange events on the road back to Cork force Phil and Mary Kate together. Returning home for her is anguish; she has sought her past and found it empty. Phil, however, is "tasting in innocence the joy of discovery," the discovery of a future. But the past intrudes on him as well when his mother appears to him in an apparition. "A loneliness filled the room that did not come from the night outside, but from the night within himself, as though there were reaches of his nature that he had never known of or walked in." In the end he retreats into the sanctity of his abstractions, and the novel closes on a note of unresolved separation.

While writing *Guests of the Nation,* O'Connor had sketched out a story in his journal about a character modeled after a fellow lodger whose compulsive attention to detail, whether counting the number of steps between Castleville and the nearest chapel or collecting overdue debts from friends, seemed almost saintly to an undisciplined, impetuous librarian.[30] Indeed, Phil's "fidgets" resemble the compulsive efficiency of Michael's fellow lodger as his bookish seriousness mirrors something of Michael's own efforts to make life rational. The problem is that the Saint reflects nothing of Michael's other side, the romantic poor boy of Harrington Square who had survived the squalor of his surroundings by the intensity of his dreams.

O'Connor's Hamlet, as he wrote to Nancy, is not the saintly boy but the spontaneous girl. Michael had often heard about the daughter of a prostitute who lived in his square, a girl who went off in search of her father and never returned. He found himself as captivated by his heroine as was AE, who speculated about what she would be like to live with. Mary Kate is the epitome of the O'Connor woman—unpredictable, bright-eyed, witty; a creature of instinct rather than intellect.[31] It is a boy's image of girls, full of worship and fear. Many of the girls in *Guests of the Nation* display that same carefree insolence: Norah in "Jo," Helen in "Soirée Chez Une Belle Jeune Fille," and the nun in "Nightpiece with Figures." They are all a bit like Ita O'Leary, Natalie Murphy, and Eileen Gould (O'Faoláin)—all unorthodox girls from lively, secure homes unlike Michael's own. At the time he wrote *The Saint and Mary Kate* he was in love, though no nearer marriage, with an image, more fanciful than real, of the quicksilver girl confronting the desolation around her with an amusing irrelevancy and a laughing eye.

As compelling and sensitive as it is in parts, *The Saint and Mary Kate* is not a successful novel. For one thing, O'Connor took an abstraction—the opposition between two conflicting ways of life, represented by Mary Kate and Phil—and let it dictate his plot. For a novelist such an approach may work no hardship, but for a storyteller like O'Connor it was too restricting. The theme was one that he would elucidate in more subtle ways in later stories, but here it is imposed on situation and character, thereby calling attention to itself instead of emerging naturally from the whole. Consider the poignant scene in which the two travelers share their feelings about love while huddling together inside a ruined cabin:

> "Everybody," said Eternal Boy as though he had not heard her, and quite unaware of that wan little smile Eternal Woman gave him in the darkness, "has some passion that eats him up, and his will power is the only weapon he have against it. I haven't a strong will power, and I never had, but bad as it is it's all that stands between me and a shocking life."[32]

Mary Kate, who has not only just kissed Phil but confessed to being in love with her supposed father, doubts that her saintly companion has any passion at all. Phil, "his overburdened conscience staggering like an old ass mounting a hill," admits that " 'tis lust." Mary Kate chuckles to bury her grief; a "poet though she did not write," she has been groping for her past. Phil, by contrast, has been trying to change the course of his future. But on the way back to Cork his past, in the form of his dead mother's ghost, brings him up short, while Mary Kate finds that she must face the future without the comfort of an imaginary father. The two sides of Michael's character, represented by Phil, the scholar, and Mary Kate, the adventuress, switch coats for a moment. Phil turns to his feelings, while Mary Kate begins to think in a very rational manner. The dislocation of these two youngsters in time and space thus emanates from the tragic gap between dreams and realities, between emotions and thoughts.

On the other hand, and perhaps it is to his credit, O'Connor's inclinations as a storyteller get in the way of his novel. He is too easily diverted from his deterministic "tragedy of innocence." O'Connor himself believed that a novel required a society, not just a vague backdrop; but here he appears so intrigued by the people he is describing that he barely elaborates upon the world in which they live, the world that supposedly crushes their dreams. Still, the setting of the novel is drawn with such swift sympathy that it strikes the reader as absolutely genuine, which Seán O'Faoláin believed was "the only real tribute" Cork's poor ever received. When O'Connor sketches a tenement feud, or the face of one of Cork's "characters," or the tone of an overheard conversation, he appears diverted by the potential story he sees in the sketch; the passing glances become frozen moments rather than parts of a carefully sustained progress.

All in all, parts dominate the whole in *The Saint and Mary Kate,* and the part that dominates most exquisitely is character. Shortly after the novel appeared, Michael confessed in a letter to Nancy, "The older I get the more I love people—all sorts of people, drunk and sober, vicious and virtuous, clever and stupid—particularly the stupid!"[33] He might have hated Cork in general, but he loved the individual people of Cork, particularly the odd ones. Because of his sympathy and lively interest, one can almost forgive Babe McCormick, Mary Kate's mother, her selfishness and vanity. Mary Kate's aunt, Dinah Matthews, a charwoman, is the gentle persevering sort of woman Michael's mother was; and Mr. Vaughan, Mary Kate's surrogate father, is more than vaguely reminiscent of Michael's father—captivating when sober and horrifying when drunk.

The two characters, besides the hero and heroine, who are given most memorable life, however, are Dona Nobis and Gregory Mahon, the saintly washerwoman and the eccentric carpenter. These two ancients provide the novel with a sort of religious polarity: between her orthodox theological piety and his occult madness. Dona Nobis, Babe's oldest crony, had been affectionately named by her tenement neighbors from a phrase in the hymn she sings continually. She is a pious old maid who knows more about saints and scriptures and less about practicalities and local gossip than anyone else in the tenement.[34] Dona Nobis resembles the closest friend of Michael's mother, Minnie Connolly, whose only hero was Saint Teresa, the source of O'Connor's inscription to the novel.

In contrast to Dona Nobis's "library of pious meditations" stand the "mysterious presences" seen by Gregory Mahon, the old carpenter to whom Phil has apprenticed himself. Since Saint Joseph had been a carpenter, Phil wished to be one, too, and though he eventually masters the mysteries of the trade, he can never comprehend the old man's strange belief in three malicious spirits—Felim, Selim, and Thedd. Still, it is Mahon who divines that Phil and Mary Kate have been blown together by the creative force of Thedd: "a white flame of passion must go up from the Marsh, and every sort of amorous allusion was used to incite Phil toward her—without immediate success." Phil's faith is tested daily by old Mahon, modeled, many Cork people believed, on Daniel Corkery who was originally a carpenter by trade. The continual on-slaught of Gregory's theology, a combination of rocking-chair philosophy and senile eroticism, creates a religious energy that counters the exaggerated piety of Dona Nobis. The old female saint and the old male romantic mirror the young saintly hero and the young romantic heroine.

Inevitably *The Saint and Mary Kate* stands not on its own merit as a novel but on what it reveals about the personal and artistic concerns of Frank O'Connor at the beginning of his career. He was a lyric poet who felt ill at ease behind the mannered mask of verse. He was a storyteller interested more in recreating flash points of human existence than in constructing a logical arti-fice. And he was a lonely young writer trying to find himself. *The Saint and Mary Kate,* to an even greater extent than his first stories, uncovers the issues, the characters, and the voices that characterize all of his writing: love and lone-liness and self-delusion; the little people, innocents, outcasts, dreamers, ec-centrics, and lovers; and the voices of sympathy, of belief, and of humor.

When O'Connor finished his novel, all that remained was the small mat-ter of a dedicaton. He had considered no one except Nancy McCarthy, but when he asked her, she flatly refused. Supposing her reticence had something to do with her job, he implored her to reconsider. What she could not tell him, or even admit to herself, was that she was close to a nervous breakdown. In her estimation the Saint went mad at the end of the novel and she wanted no part of any identification with madness. Locked in his own "fit of gathering doom," Michael had no way of understanding her reasoning. Her refusal stung him deeply, and he eventually dedicated the novel to his mother.

When *The Saint and Mary Kate* appeared in February 1932, Michael had already decided that the novel had actually happened to him: "Me as Mary Kate, someone else as the saint"—"someone else" obviously being Nancy.[35] He had begun by writing a book about the Saint but had let it become Mary Kate's book, realizing perhaps that AE was right about realism. He became his heroine simply by following his instinctive enthusiasms. Unfortunately, it was not long before he turned, for various reasons, back to the "cold storage locker" of his intellect.

8

Fathers, Saints, and Scholars

*Here and there, human nature may be great in times of trial,
but generally speaking it is its weakness and not its strength
that appears in a sick chamber; it is selfishness and impatience rather than generosity and fortitude, that one hears of.
There is so little real friendship in the world.*

JANE AUSTEN, *Persuasion*

FRANK O'Connor once mused that the real weakness of the mother's boy is not that he is inclined to become involved with women, having of course a satisfactory mother already, "but that he is liable to get into emotional relationships with older men."[1] Michael's disrespect for his father led him to be drawn to older literary men, like Corkery and AE, or men like Dr. Richard Hayes, whose interests were compatible with Michael's intense intellectual craving. Michael's adolescent devotion to Daniel Corkery was as much due to his intense need for a surrogate father as to his desire for learning; but when he left Cork, he was rejecting Corkery's narrow, pietistic nationalism. He left the fathers of his past and went to Dublin in search of new ones.

I

Michael's first and most emotional attachment in Dublin was to George Russell (AE). Michael was drawn to AE's house in Rathgar for the weekly ritual of literary conversation; always on Sunday evenings (the routine was the same) from about eight o'clock until about ten when Mrs. Russell would serve tea. AE may have been what O'Connor later described as a "creature of habit," whose life "ran in patterns," but to the young upstart from Cork he was a fountain of freshness. Michael never left AE's house or his editorial offices in Merrion Square "without an armful of books." When Michael was confined to the hospital because of his stomach ailment in 1926, AE sent parcels of books intended to raise Michael's soul above the troubles of the flesh. It was the sort of attention Michael had received only from his mother. AE's emotional abundance dissolved Michael's shyness and his guarded way with people. Out of a curious paternalism for young writers AE, as Michael recalled, "would find you a new doctor, a new wife, a new lodging, or a new job, and if you were ill would cheerfully come and nurse you."[2]

Distrusting Cork people in general and Cork doctors in particular, AE had insisted that Michael come to Dublin to be examined by his own doctor, Frank Purser. When AE heard of the Pembroke opening, he had besieged the District Council, claiming that Michael was the only legitimate literary librarian in all of Ireland. And though AE played no role in locating lodgings in Dublin for

Michael, he tried constantly to locate a wife for his protégé. AE looked on his literary discoveries as his sons. John Eglinton, AE's first biographer, noted that while Yeats remained aloof from most aspiring young writers, "nothing delighted Russell so much as the discovery of new talent, and when any youthful poet presented himself, the big man would rise up and embrace him like a father."[3] AE encouraged and published long before they became established such writers as James Stephens, Padraic Colum, Seamus O'Sullivan, Austin Clarke, and Frank O'Connor. Someone in Dublin tagged them AE's "canaries." It is enough now to say that AE was a generous friend to a generation of Irish writers.

AE, according to Dermot Foley, was Michael's "point of repose," the one man "to whose judgment he deferred as to none other, not even to Yeats."[4] For nearly ten years Michael looked to AE for personal and literary guidance. Their friendship was one of mutual admiration and respect, unlike the inflated hero worship that dominated Michael's relationship with Yeats.[5] O'Connor was probably incapable of comprehending Yeats's platonic mind, but he was more than sympathetic with the instincts of AE, who exuded warmth and generosity. Where Yeats was distant and formal, AE was familiar and casual. Michael visited AE's house on Sunday evenings and stayed late. On Monday evenings at the Yeatses' he always left with the other "guests." Yeats deigned to visit Michael in his office at Pembroke (and later at his flat in Ballsbridge), but never without a specific invitation. AE would show up unannounced even at Michael's modest lodgings in Ranelagh. Idols, like Yeats, had to be toppled, but a "comforting father" was a rare find.

Whether on a Sunday-evening visit to AE's house or on one of AE's unannounced but regular visits to Michael's lodgings ("My dear fellow, I hope I'm not interrupting you," he always said while entering and tossing his hat and coat on the sofa), the conversation was generally the same. AE sat nervous and intent, "a little flushed and flurried and distracted, running his hands through his hair and beard." He never seemed to relax. He always inquired about Michael's writing, which was usually "going badly." Michael wrote in "brief excited fits" most often followed by "months of idleness and depression, or— what was worse—of fruitless and exhausting labour on some subject" he was not yet capable of tackling, like his proposed book on Irish literature. AE would dig up some generalization meant to give the young writer courage to continue. "My dear fellow, you see you are passing through what the Indian philosophers call the dark fortnight," AE would muse, and then proceed with his set speech. Not even AE's assurance of a bright fortnight to follow comforted O'Connor. He was looking for a subject, not a proverb; AE just "sat back and sucked his old pipe." Then he would tell a story that Michael had heard many times before.[6] It wasn't a bad story, but Michael refused to deal with a theme ready-made; he preferred to find his own themes in the stories he borrowed, and besides, he knew nothing of that particular time and place. So AE would simply pull out another set speech, which began, "I wonder if you remember that phrase of Leonardo's where he advises young painters to seek the subject of battle pictures in the stains of old marble?"

The fact is, Michael could not see how any of this was much help in giving shape to his stories. Exasperated, he decided that on the whole, like most Irishmen, he was inclined to blame his inability to find a theme on "the drabness of Irish life," and to think that if he could only get out of the country, everything would begin to flow again. AE vehemently opposed this attitude and cautioned Michael to "sit down at home and let experience come to [him]." He claimed never to have sought for anything; it had all come. He called it the "doctrine of psychic attraction." To this he added "the doctrine of the diversity of inner and outer," which asserted that whatever "afflicted you, whether it was the stupidity of Irish priests or acute gastritis, it was dangerous to try to get rid of it, because it might be that it was this which made you a writer."[7]

If all else failed, AE turned to the Mahabharata, advising O'Connor to practice meditation. Michael was impressed enough to read in the Bhagavad Gita. In his self-consciousness he was appalled by his own "flighty, will-o'-the-wisp of a mind which leaped from one subject to another, from theatre to storytelling and from storytelling to verse, earnestness to satire, finishing nothing, wearying of everything, sentimental, materialistic." He decided that he had no spiritual faculty at all; AE concurred but added that he was merely like every other Irishman.

One evening O'Connor particularly exasperated AE, who felt that genuine encouragement should lift someone's spirits, but Michael remained discontented and morose. Finally AE leaned forward and said, "You know, you remind me of an old hen who has just laid an egg and is going round complaining. Did you ever hear a hen that has laid an egg? She says, 'Oh, God! God! God! God! There are going to be no more eggs!' That's what she says, you know."[8] With that, he finished his tea, peered over his spectacles at Michael, then glanced at his watch. It must have been exactly twenty minutes before eleven, the time he usually left, because he gasped, "I must be going," rose quickly, and "fumbled his way downstairs for the last tram." He came as he left: always at the same time and in the same manner. "He always stood right in the tracks, signalling frantically with both arms to the driver, and then, without a backward glance, bundled himself on and was half-way up the stairs before the tram restarted."

AE represented something very authentic to Michael. The habitual sameness of his conversation, the repetitive themes of his verse and painting, even the clichés that checkered his editorial prose, were merely his way of addressing his "universe of spiritual essences." At times in his presence the vagueness, benevolence, and platitudes vanished in a spontaneous flash of either malice or inspiration. O'Connor preferred to remember a man "quick, gay, spontaneous, with just that little touch of southern malice," a man who, when he threw back his head and laughed, shook in all his fat; at such times it seemed "there was a real incandescence about him." Most often that spark appeared to O'Connor when AE was recommending a new book. His enthusiasm for literature knew no bounds, and he taught Michael in the same excited spirit that Corkery had exuded years before, with the enthusiasm of the mystic—vague about the edges but brilliantly focused at the core. Corkery had introduced Michael to Heine, Browning, and the Russians; AE flooded him with French novels—Hugo, Dumas, and Balzac. In Sligo Michael had read Rolland, Hamsun, Rimbaud, and Yeats. In Wicklow he and Phibbs had read Shelley, Joyce, and Landor. When he came to Dublin, AE got him to read Dante, Plato, and Pascal. He insisted that he read George Moore, Somerville and Ross, and

Swift. He even surprised O'Connor by admitting that he, like Yeats, delighted in detective novels, or "shockers." If nothing else, AE encouraged rather than diminished the vacillation in O'Connor's reading between the lowbrow and the highbrow, the literature of the people and the literature of classical tradition.

AE always read "shockers" on holiday, which he took every year at the same house in Donegal; there he "painted exactly the same sort of pictures," wrote to the same friends, and composed the same sort of verse. Once he wrote to O'Connor from Donegal a letter that revealed, to O'Connor at least, a "real heart-throb of grief and bewilderment." He wrote in response to his latest reading of Dante:

> I would like to write an epic, but I am afraid it would require several vir-
> tuous and noble lives to prepare for it. If I had been noble and austere
> when I was young I might have been able to write the first sentences of
> an epic. After that titanic piece of imagination, Il Purgatorio, I feel lyrics
> are small things. You see, I have my own despondencies. I am not exempt
> from the dark fortnight. I think I am just emerging from it. In fact I al-
> ways am emerging and slipping back. The dark fortnight has got me by
> the hair of my head.[9]

It is likely that AE's disquietude was an expression of a profound and constant spiritual restlessness. He anchored himself in habit to keep his mysticism in check, not allowing it to totally disconnect him from the world and people around him.

Among other things, AE appeared to Michael disconnected from women, because he often spoke of them as "pleasant decorative things," nice to have around so long as they kept their mouths shut. He was, however, curious about Michael's love life. One night he was particularly intrigued by a bawdy story Michael had heard from a young woman. AE took it all in and then re-plied: "Nature intended me to be a lyric poet, so I *never* met a girl who told stories like that. She intended you to be a realistic novelist, so she just throws girls of that sort in your way."[10] On another occasion he inquired of Michael if he had flirtations with pretty girls. Michael admitted that he had, though he was a bit shy about just how few.

"And do the girls get you to write poems to them?" AE asked.

"They do," Michael replied uncomfortably.

"That's right," AE gurgled. "Write as many poems as they want but take care none of them marries you. That's the devil of it."[11]

AE might have been "unhappy in his marriage," but he was forever try-ing to find a wife for Michael. One of his choices was the Paris correspondent for the *Irish Statesman,* Simone Tery. Seeing a chance to help his young protégé and at the same time assure the woman's presence in Dublin, for his own satisfaction, he invited both of them to dinner. However, the two strong-willed writers saw through his scheme and "glowered at one another" the en-tire evening.

Not long after that unsuccessful evening AE left for an extended tour of the United States. He and Michael corresponded whenever one of them was away from Dublin; few of their letters have survived. One of Michael's was written as he sat by himself on New Year's Day, 1931, brooding over his future as a writer. He seems to have given up the pretense that life is charming and a comfortable job desirable. "Realism is just ice, and myself like a pat of butter or a fish in cold storage, looking with mild interest at all the other pats of butter and fishes about me, and thinking how real they look." Why, he wonders, had he not realized this before? Then he enlists AE's continuing assistance in the struggle to find a compatible woman: a "real hot flame to melt me out of it," because, he laments, "there aren't any women in Ireland." The censorship has abolished them, he adds sardonically. He begs AE to either find him a "good live flame" or visa his "spiritual passport to another country."[12] AE could accomplish neither.

In furthering O'Connor's literary career, however, AE was eminently more successful. He was instrumental in making O'Connor's name familiar to Irish readers by publishing his poems, articles, and stories in the *Irish Statesman*.[13] In more than one editorial AE observed that O'Connor was one of Ireland's finest poets and verse translators. He also admired O'Connor's critical writing, and often entrusted important reviews to the young librarian. On April 13, 1929, under the pseudonymn Y.O., AE wrote an extensive review of an exhibition of works by young Irish painters held at the Hibernian Academy. Toward the end of the review, as further evidence of his belief in O'Connor's abilities, he observed:

> There are some good portraits by Sean O'Sullivan, and I thought a portrait of "Frank O'Connor" an admirable likeness of the young poet. I hope this picture will not get lost, for I feel sure some time   more than a half a century from this, I hope—there will be a biographer for Frank O'Connor, a biographer who will be very glad to get a portrait of his subject as he is to-day.

On the back of his next letter to Sean Hendrick, Michael copied AE's words of praise, appending this pastiche of an Emily Dickinson poem:

> To make a biographer takes one mistress and one song
> One mistress and a song
> If that be long
> Two mistresses perhaps will do
> If rhymes are few.[14]

The portrait did not survive, but O'Connor lived up to AE's high hopes, both as a translator and as a writer of fiction.

AE played a significant role in Michael's development as a poet and translator of poetry. Not only did he publish O'Connor's first verse translations but he introduced the young provincial to Ireland's leading literary figures. AE counted several of Ireland's finest Celtic scholars among his closest friends. Undaunted by Michael's lack of educational pedigree, AE was enthusiastic about the talent and knowledge of his new discovery and introduced him to such people as T. F. O'Rahilly, Robin Flower, Edmund Curtis, Joseph O'Neill, and Richard Best. But AE's closest friend was Osborn Bergin, recognized as the greatest of all the Celtic scholars. Michael was introduced to him on one of his very first Sunday-evening visits to the house in Rathgar and, though he was one of the few "uninitiated" (German-trained philologists), Bergin did talk to him about Irish literature. He found Michael's translations interesting, though not necessarily accurate. Then, too, Michael was a friend of AE, which counted for something with Bergin. Of course, Michael always seemed to be on his best behavior around AE's scholar friends: He showed genuine admiration of their expert knowledge, and sensing his position as a "belletristic trifler," he deferred to their scholarly judgments with dutiful respect. He held no competitive grudges against them as he so often showed toward other writers.

Bergin, like AE, was a lonely man who took refuge in reading detective novels; and being a librarian, Michael was usually in a position to supply them with new whodunits. Listening to the two old men banter about AE's projected "shocker," called "The Murder of a Celtic Scholar," in which Bergin was cast as the chief suspect in the murder of some historian who had been "unscrupulous with his sources," gave Michael more than one evening's chortle. Their joking and gibing about each other's love lives also amused Michael, though he was never quite sure how to react to it. And finally he took delight in hearing about Bergin's hatred (AE seldom spoke of people he disliked, if in fact he disliked anyone) of such people as George Moore, Yeats, and Joseph O'Neill, all of whom had slighted him in some trivial way. To Michael his pettiness was merely an indication of his humanity. Michael once wrote that a "scholar's work is often as much a self-portrait as a writer's," and he found it significant that the poetry Bergin loved most was poetry in which the passion was subsumed in the form.[15]

One of Bergin's students, a man who eventually replaced him as the foremost Celtic scholar, was Daniel Binchy. He and Michael met in 1927 in AE's offices at Merrion Square. Binchy was finishing his studies under Bergin before leaving for Germany to continue his work, and Michael had not yet moved to Dublin. The two protégés immediately clashed, for they were "two very angry and very youthful know-alls." But because they shared a fondness for AE and Bergin they eventually became close and enduring friends. Michael may not have thought much of Binchy's politics or his reading of Heine, but Binchy was a Celtic scholar and that was good enough. Over the years he came to Binchy for assistance with his most difficult linguistic problems. Michael respected Binchy's knowledge; Binchy on his part greatly admired Michael's intuitive grasp of the structure of language. More than once, Michael grumbled that a poet would never say such and such in a certain way; more often than not, Binchy could give textual corroboration of Michael's instinct. Once, when Binchy was troubled by something in Mauriac, Michael grabbed the book impatiently and translated the French straightaway.[16] Binchy knew French better than Michael, but he could not listen as well as Michael or grasp the underlying meaning as readily. Binchy may not have understood Michael's blazing energy or the violent shifts of Michael's emotions, but he marveled at Michael's perseverance in the very difficult study of Old and Middle Irish and at his unshakable loyalty to Irish culture.

"The ideal thing is for the poet translator to have a scholar friend," O'Connor wrote years later. The reason, he concluded, from his observation of the extraordinary attraction between Russell, "that soft-hearted Lurgan poet," and Bergin, "that hard-hearted Cork scholar," was that "the poet could never say anything but 'Yes' and the scholar could never say anything but 'No.' "[17] O'Connor was fortunate not only in being a bit of both but also in having friends who were scholars and friends who were poets. His work as a translator of Irish verse, begun under the eye of Daniel Corkery, had been furthered by

AE and Yeats, on the one hand, and Bergin and Binchy on the other. O'Connor recognized his deficiencies and was willing to collaborate, for the goal of a translator, to him, was not personal aggrandizement but the recreation of something memorable of its own accord.

The Wild Bird's Nest, published in 1932 by Yeats's Cuala Press, brought together seventeen verse translations of Irish poetry dating from the seventh through the seventeenth centuries.[18] Many of these poems had first appeared in the *Irish Statesman,* and as early as 1926 O'Connor had conceived of a book about Irish poetry, comprising in large measure his own translations but containing critical evaluation of the Irish poetic tradition as well. At the time *The Wild Bird's Nest* was published he had already decided to print only the translations, feeling that he still did not know enough to say anything definitive about the tradition of Irish poetry. Besides, Yeats was interested more in poetry than in commentary for the Cuala series.

AE's introduction, "An Essay on the Character in Irish Literature," underscores what O'Connor himself had recognized for some time: the idea that ancient Irish poetry reveals a "primeval culture of imagination." The mythic heroes, Angus, Lug, and Lir, emanated from a clear and simple mind, AE argued, and whatever truth lay in them "was poetic or spiritual truth, a relation of myth and image to deep inner being." AE goes on to observe two poles in this literature: a visionary intuition and "a cold, hard, yet passionate realism." The one creates faerie adventure in many-colored lands, while the other is "made through intensity of brooding over life." O'Connor's translations belong mainly to the second kind, according to AE. He even suggests that the dominating mood of the latest Anglo-Irish literature—meaning O'Connor, O'Faoláin, O'Flaherty, Clarke, and the rest—has its roots in this ancient, brooding realism.

Possessing no philosophical system, this poetry "enables the poet to interpret his experience to himself" in a manner more dramatic than lyrical. The immediacy of its impact lies in the vividness of the voices, giving the sense of persons caught in the act of revealing themselves. In the poems of *The Wild Bird's Nest,* to which he would return again and again throughout his life, O'Connor achieves the effect of "being there" by maintaining a fidelity to the voice, by merging his own poetic voice with that of the ancient poet.[19] But it is not the personality of the poet or the translator we hear, only the voice, crying out the sorrows of great misfortune, political or emotional. For example, the lament of the Old Woman of Beare for her vanished youth and that of the observer of the charred remains of Kilcash reveal not some religious consolation but that brooding recognition of reality that AE described as "bleak, cynical, and ironical." About O'Connor's achievement AE wrote: "The alchemy of the brooding mind distils no precious knowledge."

I I

After AE and his scholarly circle, the two men with whom Michael felt most comfortable in those early Dublin years were a physician, Dr. Richard Hayes, and a young priest, Tim Traynor.

His friendship with Tim Traynor seems at first glance a bit surprising.

That Michael held little regard for the official church had been obvious since Gormanstown. Perhaps he had exaggerated his battles with priests during his library posts in Wicklow and Cork and had kept open the wounds of the skirmish with Father O'Flynn over the Cork Drama League. But the fact is that one of the men in Cork whom Michael held in highest regard was Michael MacSwiney, a quiet, scholarly priest who had been sent by a vindictive bishop to Kinsale after the Troubles. Since this post was tantamount to exile for one so active in the intellectual life of Cork, his friends, including Michael, Nancy, and Sean Hendrick, had often cycled down for a visit carrying books and sherry. Tim Traynor was also one of MacSwiney's friends, though at the time he and Michael had not yet met. Later, when Traynor was a curate in Dublin, the O'Faoláins brought Tim and Michael together.[20] It turned out that Traynor and Michael had a number of other mutual friends, including Nancy, Natalie Murphy, and Tim Buckley, the lame tailor of Gouganne Barra. No one had ever thought of bringing them together before, fearing fireworks from Michael, but when they finally met in Sandymount there was no explosion at all; in fact, the two became fast friends.

Traynor was a stocky, swaggering man with a pugilistic face, "beefy and red and scowling, with features that seemed to have withdrawn into it to guard it from blows; a broad, blunted nose and a square jaw."[21] He intrigued Michael because he was everything he seemed to be yet not what Michael expected him to be—part devil, part saint, given to conspiracy and malicious manipulation but also to generosity and empathy. In *My Father's Son* O'Connor explains that Traynor's "temperament and imagination constantly overflowed the necessary limits of his vocation as they would have overflowed the limits of almost any calling, short of that of a pirate." This emotional expansiveness caused him to alternate between excitement over some new passion (a book or a painting, some new gadget or new idea) and depression over the frustrations of his vocation, of a marriage or career that might have been had he not become a priest. But he had no more intention of taking Michael's petulant advice and leaving the priesthood than Michael had of taking his—"For God's sake, Michael, if writing causes you so much anguish then give it up."

Traynor owned a motorcar, a luxury Michael could not have afforded even if he had had the patience to drive. On Saturdays they often went to the Wicklow mountains or up the coast past Skerries or to a racetrack, either Leopardstown or the Curragh, where Michael placed bets for Traynor, who was not allowed to gamble. Occasionally they drove as far as Ennis to visit Dermot Foley or to West Cork to visit their old friend, the Tailor. Their conversation usually took the form of gossip, not so much because Michael had anyone to talk about but because Traynor, perhaps in betrayal of clerical confidence, had to unburden himself of the manifold surprises he encountered in his parish work. To Michael these conversations were merely grist for the mill, for they contained stories in the raw, particularly Traynor's anecdotes about the lives of married people. At that time marriage was as much of a might-have-been for him as it was for Traynor, though he held it in higher regard than did the priest, who he said "comforted himself with the usual seminary sour grapes" about the torments of marriage. The result was a kind of mutually beneficial collaboration in which Traynor was able to talk to someone about his problems and O'Connor was able to get a variety of material from a single source, material that resulted in such stories as "The Frying Pan," "The Holy Door," and "Uprooted."

Like O'Connor, Traynor had a "peculiarly intense relationship with his mother." Both women had been entirely devoted to raising their sons, insisting on a proper education, on proper music, and on proper dress. They were two fastidious women ambitious for their sons, disappointed that their boys fell prey to the normal foibles of adolescence, but inevitably gratified by the results of their sacrifices. And two more dutiful sons could hardly be imagined than Michael O'Donovan and Timothy Traynor, two men who seemed to most everyone else absolute iconoclasts. What O'Connor observed about his friend might have been true of himself as well: "All the imaginative improvisation was only the outward expression of a terrible inward loneliness, loneliness that was accentuated by his calling."[22] And, "cut off from ordinary intercourse," priests and writers shared the same loneliness. Michael and Tim were two "bloody fools," each of whom kept the other honest by refusing to buckle to his pontifications; two brooding, lonely men who preserved some measure of sanity by laughing at each other.

If O'Connor's friendship with a volatile young priest struck Dubliners as unlikely, then his friendship with a proper, middle-aged physician probably seemed unimaginable. In fact, the two friendships appear even more strange when one realizes that Hayes and Traynor thoroughly disapproved of each other, and that each of them spent more than one fruitless conversation with Michael trying to convince him of the worthlessness of the other. Hayes, whose brother was a very proper and dutiful priest, believed that Traynor was a disgrace to his vocation. Traynor, on the other hand, thought that Hayes was a pompous and self-seeking man. No matter what they thought of each other, however, they were both right for Frank O'Connor. The Tailor, who knew them both, wisely saw through them, labeling Hayes "the Old Child" and Traynor "the Saint," nicknames that captured the men behind the masks.

Michael had never been satisfied with his medical care. Not even Frank Purser, AE's friend and physician, seemed able to diagnose his various ailments with any degree of reliability. During the winter of 1930–31 he suffered from one painful boil after another. Tired of enduring Michael's constant foul mood, Dermot Foley recommended that he call on a highly respected doctor he knew. Michael recoiled in fear and snarled something about hating all doctors. After Michael had carried on about X rays, needles, scalpels, and outrageous fees, Dermot calmly suggested that he go home and let him get some work done. He knew Michael's mother was visiting and was sure she could do something with his roaring temper. She was having afternoon tea with Molly Alexander when Michael stormed in and offered nothing more than a disgruntled mumble about how he felt. She pleaded with him to see a doctor; he recoiled again but she stopped him short by insisting that he go for her sake. He relented and set off back down Anglesea Road, past the library and toward Guilford Road in Sandymount to find Dr. Richard Hayes.[23]

Richard Hayes was in charge of a crowded dispensary near his house; officially he didn't take private patients, but in fact he looked after nearly everyone in Ringsend on a well-if-it's-that-bad-but-only-this-once basis, generally without pay. Hayes lived in the family house, a modest Georgian redbrick cautiously set back from the road behind a high stone wall. The day Michael first came to call was the housekeeper's day off, so the doctor answered the door himself. Michael ceremoniously announced the reason for the call, and Hayes calmly upbraided his presumptuousness for calling at that hour of the day with no introduction and less grace. He went on to say that he didn't take private patients and knew nothing about boils. He informed Michael that if he wanted an X ray, a miracle drug, or even, God forbid, a lancing, he would have to go somewhere else. By this time Michael had changed his opinion of the man from impertinent and pompous to delightfully eccentric. Michael distrusted a respectable doctor or lawyer or priest, but a renegade was something else. His protests met further elegant reproach, which, it turned out, was Hayes's way of accepting a patient. Finally, he asked Michael's name and occupation. Rather than calling himself "Michael O'Donovan, Librarian," he pulled himself erect and in grand Yeatsian fashion announced, "Frank O'Connor, Poet." When Hayes asked him to enter, Michael was so disconcerted that he did so at once, following Hayes like a dutiful puppy to a small room off the hall. From that day on they were friends.

It seemed a ridiculous friendship to everyone in Dublin, including Seán O'Faoláin, who years later gave this fictional description of two men resembling Hayes and O'Connor walking arm in arm like father and son along O'Connell Street:

> The doctor straight and spare as a spear, radiating propriety from every spiky bone of his body, as short of step as a woman, and as carefully dressed from his wide-brimmed bowler hat to the rubber tip of his mottled, gold-headed malacca cane; the poet striding beside him, halting only to swirl his flabby tweeds; his splendid hydrocephalic head stretched behind his neck like a balloon; his myopic eyes glaring at the clouds over the roofs through the thick lenses of his glasses; a waterfall of black hair permanently frozen over his left eye; his big teeth laughing, his big voice booming, he looked for all the world like a peasant Yeats in a poor state of health.[24]

By all accounts, O'Faoláin's description was hardly invention at all.

Tim Traynor scoffed at them and gave the association less than a year. Traynor's obsession at the time was psychoanalysis, and he was quick to pontificate that the two eccentrics, the urbane doctor and the provincial writer, had invented each other. As with every problem he faced, Traynor reduced the friendship to sex, though he knew Michael better than to call his friendship with Hayes a homosexual relationship. What he meant was that they both needed encouragement to continue a bachelor life, for they both detested celibacy. Traynor was right but for the wrong reasons. O'Connor invented Hayes (and vice versa) but only insofar as he invented any friend or father or lover— to offset his terrible feeling of loneliness. Almost every evening they walked the broad streets of Ballsbridge or along Sandymount Strand. Michael drew furiously on one cigarette after another, his head cocked back in strutting celebration of some line of poetry, while Hayes smoked thoughtfully on his slender pipe and saluted gracefully every person he knew, bending "his long frame in two like a jack-knife, his walking stick thrust out from behind his back like a tail and his punchinello face distorted with amiability." For several years this was Michael's "dearest friend": "the man," he wrote, "who replaced Corkery in my affections, to whom I went in every difficulty and who gave me advice that was always disinterested and sometimes noble."[25]

Richard Hayes was not a very public person, preferring the quiet of his study to the hubbub of medical practice or the swirl of committee rooms. Medicine consumed less of his time and interest than did history, more precisely the history of Franco-Irish relations. One of the reasons he stayed in his modest position at the dispensary was the time and privacy it afforded his research on France.[26] He even declined an offer to be made governor-general, a titular representative of the British Crown in Ireland. The day the rumor of the nomination broke in the Irish press, Hayes and O'Connor walked and talked as usual along the strand. Michael argued that if Hayes did not accept, then some "bloody government eejit" would get himself appointed. Hayes remained adamant for some time. Then something struck him about the whole affair and he began to laugh, not his usual sedate chuckle but a hearty O'Connor roar. Michael was stunned. He saw nothing funny about it. The only thing he saw was a man so vain that he would not lower himself to mere civil responsibility. Reading Michael's mind, Hayes said, "And you're right, of course. I am mad with vanity." They toasted their mutual arrogance with fine French brandy that night.

Hayes remained reticent about his past, even with Michael, who was beginning to believe that most men he knew, except perhaps Dermot Foley, tended to be both "uninquisitive and unrevealing" about such things. Only by accident, for example, did he learn that Hayes had distinguished himself in the 1916 Rising. One evening Michael invited Hayes to his Ballsbridge flat along with James Montgomery, then the film censor. Montgomery's wife, Ethel, dabbled in palmistry. That evening she read everyone's palm. Though O'Connor never mentions what she saw in his own hand, he does allude, in *My Father's Son*, to what she saw in Hayes's: a "terrible crisis here. It's as though you'd died and then started to live again." He remembers that Hayes was somewhat disturbed and left earlier than usual, after which Montgomery excitedly revealed that Hayes had been "sentenced to death and then reprieved." Michael was skeptical, of course, but Montgomery assured him that his wife hadn't even a clue who Hayes was.

The incident might have passed without further comment except that Hayes raised the subject himself, a few days later, confessing that Ethel had indeed struck a very tender chord. In an effort to ease his friend's discomfort, Michael acknowledged that there was a great deal about the Troubles he wanted to forget too. Hayes patiently explained that coming close to execution was not really a crisis. "I was once in love, and then it was with a girl who had tuberculosis. I was a doctor, and I knew how long she had to live. I couldn't bear the thought that my children might be the same way, so I gave her up."[27] Normally, the impetuous writer, hungry for a story, would have probed for further information; but sensing that Hayes was already at emotional bedrock, Michael kept silent. The episode emerged in his autobiography, greatly enhanced by the years, as an emblem of the kind of troubled ambiguity buried in the human soul that he had sought to uncover in his stories.

I I I

Not long after he had begun to attend AE's Sunday evening gatherings, O'Connor received an invitation, passed to him by AE, from Yeats, who was then residing in Merrion Square. Monday evenings at the home of W. B. Yeats were all-male affairs and the topic was sex, except when Lady Gregory was visiting. Michael had the misfortune to find himself alone that first evening with Yeats and Lady Gregory, two of the most Olympian figures of the Irish Literary Renaissance. "To my complete confusion," he wrote in *My Father's Son*, "Lady Gregory wore a mantilla as though for an audience with the Pope." Uneasy in social occasions of any kind, Michael was terrified when they involved women. Having grown somewhat comfortable in the casual, enfolding atmosphere of AE's home, he was overwhelmed by the mannered formality of Yeats. He found himself "alone in a dim, candle-lit room when Yeats entered, tall, elegantly dressed, sternly looking with a sideway glance." Yeats's immaculate attire and deliberate gesture were as unlike AE's rumpled clothes and vague manner as Dublin was to West Cork. Everything about the house and the great poet struck Michael as graceful and expensive with just "a touch of dandyism in the lofty, ecclesiastical stare, the ritual motion of the hands, the unction of the voice, and an occasional elaborate mispronunciation."[28]

When Michael moved to Dublin three years later with more than a few affectations of his own, he came to realize that, like himself, "Yeats was a desperately shy man who had the effect of driving other shy people slightly dotty." The celebrated pomposity, insolence, and arrogance that Dublin wits imputed to Yeats escaped the young provincial. What he saw, looking from behind his own mask of arrogance and bravado was "a boy's tense eager face," which looked out at the world as though "trapped and despairing." Mrs. Yeats was quick to spot the similarity between her husband and this new recruit. "I knew you were shy," she told him once at a party, "because you did exactly as Willie does when he's shy, you ran your hand through your hair."[29] She called him Michael/Frank and pampered him just as she did her own Willie. The touch of dandyism, the bearing of a bird, the pose of vagueness, Michael came to recognize as protective measures against timidity much like his own. What struck O'Connor most forcefully was that Yeats "lived a deep interior life and all the outside things counted practically for nothing."[30]

Still, Michael's admiration never went much beyond hero worship. He was unable to become close to Yeats because of the tacit rivalry between Yeats and AE, who held all Michael's loyalty. He could look up to Yeats, even glory in the lofty presence; but AE gave what Yeats could not possibly give—warmth and understanding. Where Yeats was great in Michael's eyes, AE was good. Even Mrs. Yeats pointed out this difference to W. B. himself: He was a poet but he could not be what AE was—a saint. To Michael AE was "as warm and homely as a turf fire." Yeats, on the other hand, was fatherly too, but in a more imposing, Victorian way—detached and shadowy.[31] Nevertheless, it was Yeats and the swirling currents of his artistic energy that could inspire O'Connor into poetry. AE gave him courage to face life, but Yeats gave him a standard against which O'Connor could measure his talent.

Characteristically, Michael constructed a personal symbolism from the contrast between his two literary fathers, expressing it as a fable of light and shadow, of objectivity and subjectivity. Yeats reminded him of some unbelieving aristocrat: "fascist and authoritarian . . . nationalist, lover of tradition and hater of reason." On the other hand, he saw Russell as the northern democrat "with leanings toward communism; pacifist, internationalist, despiser of tradition and class, and, in spite of his mysticism, a thoroughgoing rationalist and humanitarian."[32] Though he remained loyal to AE, perhaps out of provincial instinct, Frank O'Connor worshiped Yeats from afar; AE nourished his heart, Yeats his head. He deferred to AE, whom he loved, while he fought with Yeats, whom he respected. But eventually it was the Yeats element that won out; in the crises of the 1930s O'Connor moved away from the shadows of AE to the cold air of realism.

Shortly after Michael arrived in Dublin, Yeats called at the Pembroke Library to enlist his support in a campaign against the newly passed Censorship Act. Michael, always ready to take up a worthy cause, joined a select group of writers and intellectuals, including G. B. Shaw, AE, Yeats, and Gogarty, to lodge official protests and write indignant letters. Michael was flattered that Yeats was even aware of him, considering that he had not yet published a book. AE was a bit skeptical about the idea, partly because it was Yeats's and partly because he preferred to continue his editorial arguments in the *Irish Statesman*. He was an idealist, not a showman. But Yeats was an organizer as well as a man of the theatre; by organizing he could get younger men to carry on a campaign he was too old to wage by himself.

One of the first targets of the Censorship Board was Shaw, whose *Black Girl in Search of God* met with disfavor among the Catholic hierarchy. The book was banned as being "in its general tendency indecent and obscene," though the charge hung only on a few woodcuts of a naked girl. Being a librarian as well as a writer, O'Connor objected to this abuse of power and presented to Yeats and Shaw a plan to defy the ban by selling copies of the book at the Abbey Theatre. Not even de Valera would "be idiotic enough to prosecute both Shaw and Yeats," O'Connor argued. Instead, Yeats chose to lead a deputation to the Ministry of Justice, but rather than simply offering the petition they had brought with them, Yeats delivered a speech on the sanctity of the nude. Needless to say, they not only lost that skirmish, but their efforts had little effect at all on the power of the Censorship Act.[33]

One tangible result of Yeats's campaign against the Censorship Act was his Irish Academy of Letters. As early as 1926 he had tried to start something like a literary society. In the summer of 1931 he again appeared at Michael's Pembroke office, this time to solicit his participation on a committee to launch Yeats's latest brainchild. Even in that initial meeting Michael questioned Yeats—on the inclusion of the dramatist and former Abbey director St. John Ervine. True to form, Yeats did not mention that Shaw was behind this choice; he only lifted his head and said, "Why worry about literary eminence? You and I will provide that."[34] This was just before *Guests of the Nation* had appeared. The planning committee met through the winter of 1931–32. Lists of possible members were submitted and argued over; rules of incorporation and bylaws also stimulated endless debate. Finally, letters of invitation were sent to nearly thirty Irish writers. Among those who refused membership (by letter or by silence) were James Joyce, Douglas Hyde, Sean O'Casey, and O'Connor's old mentor, Daniel Corkery.[35]

On September 14, 1932, at Jammet's, a fashionable Dublin restaurant, the Academy held its first formal meeting. Shaw was elected president (either because of or in spite of his absence on the occasion), with Yeats as vice-president and AE as secretary-treasurer. Discussion was so animated that someone jokingly called to the staid waiters for boxing gloves. Instead, Walter Starkie cooled the conversation with his violin. Yeats may have provided eminence to his Academy—and while he lived it was his—but despite his own immaculate manners the group never suffered from an abundance of decorum.

The second annual meeting of the Academy proved especially disturbing to O'Connor. The idea of a formal dinner at the Dolphin he found vexing enough, but he also carried with him the nagging feeling that AE was being treated unfairly. He shared AE's suspicion that the Academy was a plot by Yeats to give prizes to his protégés. Though Yeats was ill at the time, he came to the dinner, sat at the head table, and in fact announced the establishment of the Harmsworth Award and the Casement Award. To top it all off, Oliver Gogarty, the master of ceremonies for the evening, puckishly described O'Connor as "a country boy with hair in his nose and hair in his ears and a briefcase in his hand." Actually, Michael was as much dismayed by the sedate formality of the evening—owing to the presence of ladies, invited for the honoring of the Harmsworth family—as he was by Gogarty's unnecessary remarks. Animated literary conversation would have suited him better than formality and animated pettiness. He left early and alone.

The next formal dinner meeting of the Irish Academy of Letters was a gentlemanly affair, as Seán O'Faoláin describes it in *Vive Moi!*, with "no Yeats to give it glamour, no Gogarty to give it sparkle." O'Faoláin, acting as master of ceremonies, sat at the head table with Lord Dunsany, the first recipient of the Harmsworth Award. O'Connor delivered an intemperate speech on nationalism to the chagrin of Dunsany, who was being somewhat disagreeable because of references to his refusal to join the Academy, but to the delight of O'Faoláin, who toasted "to the Nation." With that they managed to get very drunk, or at least so Michael claimed in a letter to Nancy the next day.[36]

Before the fourth annual banquet meeting O'Connor and O'Faoláin called on Yeats to plead the election of Ernie O'Malley, a former commandant of the IRA, to membership in the Academy on the strength of his recently published book *On Another Man's Wound,* which they considered the finest book of any kind on the Troubles. Having heard in advance from F. R. Higgins about this mission, Yeats greeted them with a chuckle and asked, "What do you two young rascals mean by trying to fill my Academy with gunmen?" Yeats and AE, along with other older writers, had supported the Treaty, while the younger writers had been zealous supporters of de Valera and the anti-Treaty forces. Nevertheless, Yeats had made them founding members of his Academy, more on the basis of promise than for achievement, in the hope of stimulating a new literary revival in Ireland. He had already informed the two "rascals" that they would be his successors: O'Faoláin would save the Academy and O'Connor the Abbey, both of which needed saving, certainly, but not by these two, for they had different dreams. At the next banquet Yeats publicly bestowed benediction on O'Connor and O'Faoláin and further stunned his audience by announcing that "the future of Irish literature was with the realistic novel."[37]

In *My Father's Son* O'Connor exaggerated to some extent the intrigue and contentiousness that surrounded his relationship with Yeats. Indeed, he stood up to Yeats on many occasions when no one else dared. Yeats may have seemed to O'Connor at various times a "bully," a "born organizer," "tone deaf," and a "notorious fat-head," but their relationship went far beyond the intrigues of council minutes and Abbey feuds. Theirs was a literary friendship, for Michael's internal literary variety show required a larger-than-life hero. He and Yeats, he said, had long, wandering discussions about Hegelianism, pacifism, and communism, during which they frequently worked themselves into passionate arguments. O'Connor was fortunate to have come into Yeats's circle at the time of the poet's second youth, the time of his late enthusiasms.

However, Yeats's "phantasmagoria" was often beyond the comprehension of Michael's provincial realism. He seemed almost incapable of allowing himself to understand Yeats's vacillation between extreme incongruities. Michael loved abstractions, but only if they led to a story. He squirmed impatiently at any mention of things mystical and once even challenged Yeats to produce an experience that could not be explained on strictly rational grounds. Yeats paused a moment, then began a story about visiting a medium to find out if a young woman's charge that she was pregnant by him was true or not. The medium, in a deep trance, had produced some indecipherable writing which experts later ascertained was an archaic form of Hebrew. Satisfied that he had produced a rationally unexplainable experience, Yeats tossed his head back triumphantly. Enthralled by the incident, Michael, now hot on the trail of a story, begged for more.

> "Never mind what sort of Hebrew it was written in," I said. "Did it tell you whether you were the father of the child or not?"
> The practical Corkman! [Yeats] sat back wearily—rationalists are so hard to argue with.
> "Oh, no, no," he said vaguely. "It just said things like 'O great poet of our race!' "[38]

To Yeats that was important; for O'Connor the story had been lost.

Though O'Connor stood with the "rationalists, liberals, and humanitarians" and wrote like a novelist—"out of the logic of circumstance"—whenever he saw certain plays of Yeats's or Synge's his native Gaelic blood would respond, he always said, making him ashamed of the alien language in which he wrote. Yeats seemed to know that about him and spoke of the validity of folk beliefs only once. At a lunch gathering Michael mentioned something about a tale to which Yeats had said, "Why do you deliberately close your eyes to those things? You know quite well they were once the religion of the whole world!"[39] It was this sort of intuitive mysticism, filling Yeats's life and work with depth and luminous appeal, that left O'Connor "abashed and miserable." He called Yeats's folk sense a "great mass of shadow," comparing it to the Rembrandt print above his mantelpiece.

Another incident suggests that their perceptions may not have been so different as they seemed. One evening in 1934 O'Connor and some friends, including Seán O'Faoláin, were gathered at Yeats's house. As he occasionally did, Yeats read a new poem as a sort of test run. Afterwards he reportedly commented to Higgins: "O'Faoláin and O'Connor were here, and I read them the Meru poem, and O'Faoláin said he understood it and he didn't, and O'Connor said he didn't understand a word of it, and he understood it perfectly."[40] Yeats was probably as wrong as he was right; O'Faoláin had an amazing facility for holding incongruity in suspension, though he often overlooked a simple truth underlying the complex ideas; O'Connor, on the other hand, while perceiving the simple, often frustrated himself with surface complexities. Yeats's next poem, "Ribh in Ecstasy," began, "Although you said you understood no word."

On another occasion Yeats mentioned to Michael that he had used the translation of Grania's song to Diarmuid, which O'Connor had entitled "Lullaby of Adventurous Love," as the basis for his new poem "Lullaby." Later that evening O'Connor, asked to recite something aloud, produced a fourteenth-century English lyric and began to read: "I am of Ireland/And of the holy land/Of Ireland." As Richard Ellmann reports the occasion, "Yeats took fire at once from the words, snatched wildly for a piece of paper, and gasped 'Write, write'. The result was 'I am of Ireland', in which the woman's lines were at first very close to the original."[41] Both poems appeared in *Words for Music Perhaps*.

In fact, more than one poem in that volume owes something to Frank O'Connor. For instance, Yeats attempted to render a female voice in a series of dramatic monologues strikingly similar to the dramatic lyrics that abound in Irish poetry and that O'Connor had been translating for five years or more. Crazy Jane, though admittedly based on a real-life character named Cracked Mary who lived near Coole Park, resembles in more than a vague way O'Connor's Hag of Beare, who, cloistered in a convent, complains of her lost youth. Likewise, the poem "Three Things" is reminiscent of O'Connor's "Prayer for the Speedy End of Three Great Misfortunes."

On yet another occasion Michael was invited to dinner, and Yeats eagerly confessed, "O'Connor, I've stolen another poem from you." Michael, glancing sheepishly at Mrs. Yeats, said only, "Did you make a good job of it?" Yeats tilted his head back and replied, "I made a *beautiful* job of it." Yeats was referring to his poem "The Curse of Cromwell" in which he took this line nearly verbatim from O'Connor's version of O'Rahilly's "Last Lines": "His fathers served their fathers before Christ was crucified."[42] Everything was grist to Yeats's mill, every remark, every poem, every incident. He may have been what O'Connor called a "born plagiarist," but was no more or less so than O'Connor himself who spent a lifetime plundering stories from the casual anecdotes of friends.

What Yeats borrowed or stole from Michael/Frank was more than recompensed by his contribution to O'Connor's own writing. He gave as freely as he took, for he regarded literature as a cooperative activity, particularly among friends. At the same time collaboration with Yeats often meant that Yeats's ideas gained the upper hand; when he agreed to help another writer, he usually rewrote whatever the other person had written. Once Gogarty invited Michael to come along to Yeats's flat to see about some poems he had left for Yeats to read. "He's writing a few little lyrics for me," Gogarty commented with a wry laugh, "and I'd like to see how he's getting on." But, especially after offering to publish O'Connor's translations, Yeats labored generously with O'Connor over them.[43] When he saw lines that stumbled, fell, or otherwise weakened the sound of the poem, he would intone alternate versions over and over again, almost as if Michael were not there at all.

Such was the case the evening they argued long after dinner over the refrain from "The Grey Eye Weeping," one of the Egan O'Rahilly poems included in *The Wild Bird's Nest*. The problem line read: "Has made me travel to seek you, Valentine Brown." Yeats recited it "over and over again, at various pitches, beating time with his right hand." Though Yeats was indeed a masterful technician, he overestimated, according to his young collaborator, his ear for music. Michael, of course, had a similarly high opinion of his own musical gifts, so they often argued. In this case he not only thought that Yeats had inadvertently dropped a beat from the original, changing an Alexandrine to iambic pentameter, but considered Yeats's line redundant. "You can say 'Has made me travel to you' or 'Has made me seek you' but you can't say 'travel to seek you,' " Michael contended. "Why not 'Has made me a beggar before you, Valentine Brown'?" (Either reading fits the sense of the original, which was composed extempore by O'Rahilly after taking a poem to Sir Valentine Brown only to receive a flat refusal.) But Yeats snapped irritably, "No beggars! No beggars!"[44] The line stood as Yeats had intoned it.

"The Grey Eye Weeping" was one of seven verse translations by Frank O'Connor included in Yeats's edition of *The Oxford Book of Modern Verse* in 1936. In his introduction to that extremely personal selection Yeats asserted that O'Connor had made such poets as O'Rahilly "symbols of our pride," wandering as they did among the Irish peasantry after the flight of the earls, "singing their loneliness and their rage." He then tells of showing a book by Day Lewis to Lady Gregory shortly before her death. She responded, according to Yeats, "I prefer those poems translated by Frank O'Connor because they come out of original sin."[45] Whether or not it was because of that sense of "original sin," Yeats thought highly enough of O'Connor's translations to steal from them, rewrite them, and print them. In *On the Boiler,* for example, he made this suggestion to Irish poets: "Translate into modern Irish all that is most beautiful in old and middle Irish, what Frank O'Connor and Augusta Gregory, let us say, have translated into English." Not only was Yeats fascinated by the themes of decay and passing and lost love, and by the tone of ironic yet passionate regret in the original poems, he was also impressed, according to Richard Ellmann, by the way in which O'Connor seemed to have captured "their severe, unsentimental vigour." Knowing no Irish himself, Yeats fell on O'Connor's poems with hungry enthusiasm. He had used the idiom of these folk poets for years, but only in his old age, when he was attempting to strip his own verse to the bone, was he able to feel so close to the original.

The give-and-take of this collaboration with Yeats proved exhilarating and instructive for a young writer like Michael O'Donovan, and certainly the Cuala publications, *The Wild Bird's Nest* (1932) and *Lords and Commons* (1938), also proved helpful to the reputation of Frank O'Connor, for after the demise of the *Irish Statesman* in 1930 these small, attractive volumes helped keep his name alive among Irish readers. By the same token, the prominent place Yeats gave him in the Irish Academy of Letters as a council member and as an adjudicator of the Gaelic awards also served to keep him conspicuously among the Irish literary elite. And finally, his appointment, at Yeats's insistence, to the Board of Directors of the Abbey Theatre sealed his notoriety and made him fair game for Dublin's critical marksmen.

Of his three literary fathers, Corkery, AE, and Yeats, it was Yeats who made the most lasting personal impression on Michael/Frank. It was in the image of Yeats that Michael was fashioning himself in Cork when he assumed the "poet's mien"—black hat, tweed suit, green shirt, black tie. Later he came to read poetry aloud in the high bardic style of Yeats, with the same curiously delicate inflection and the same stately, oracular intonation. He assumed not only the outward manner of Yeats but also an ample portion of the great poet's cast of mind. Though they seemed to Richard Ellmann "the last romantic and the last realist,"[46] Yeats and O'Connor quarreled endlessly because they were too much alike. O'Connor spent his entire life fighting one Irish dragon after another, vacillating, as Yeats had, between idealized image and real fact; but unlike Yeats, who strove to bring life into a unified whole, O'Connor grasped life in bits and pieces. But he often managed to accomplish what he once said only Yeats could do: that is, "from two fallacies and one bit of nonsense" forge a theory that not only worked but "illumined other things besides."[47] Both were essentially self-educated men, whose theories, though perhaps assumptive, erratic, even silly, were always original. Genius was the standard against which O'Connor measured everything human; it was his word for the very best. It was the genius of Yeats that he was honoring when he said, "I thought he was the greatest man in the world!"

Throughout his life O'Connor wrote about Yeats as about no other writer, always with respect and always from a biographical point of view, as he believed what Yeats had once pronounced: What a man writes is an allegory of his life. His stories, too, soon fell under the shadow of Yeats's wisdom. Once when they were collaborating on a poem, Yeats scolded O'Connor: "You must always write poetry as if you were shouting to a man across the street who you were afraid couldn't hear you and trying to make him understand."[48] In his old age Yeats had found the knack of placing a commonplace word or phrase in the right spot—to restore "the tone of the human voice speaking," he told O'Connor. The advice of the poet became the very ground of O'Connor's prose.

9

Bones of Contention

There is internal war in man between reason and the passions.
PASCAL, *Pensées*

I must seek mankind in mankind and no longer in books ...
my distinction of heart and understanding will be useful to
me, even as a bard.
STENDHAL, *The Private Diaries*

I

By the time advance notices for *The Saint and Mary Kate* had begun appearing in March 1932, Michael had worked himself into a state of growing misery and depression about the book. While Irish reviewers kept up the barrage of harsh treatment, English reviewers remained unusually complimentary, and the two men whose opinion O'Connor held most highly, AE and Yeats, were both enthusiastic about the novel.[1] Though Yeats did not suffer, as AE did, from an infatuation with the heroine, he held the novel in high enough esteem to recommend it to his friends. Writing to Olivia Shakespear from his retreat in Glendalough, he mentioned that he had brought with him Virginia Woolf's *Orlando,* "which I shall probably find faint of pulse and dislike and *The Saint and Mary Kate* by Frank O'Connor, one of my Academicians to be. I recommend it to you—a beautiful strange book."[2]

Despite all the "clutter" about *The Saint and Mary Kate,* Michael's self-esteem remained low, and he was further distressed by physical illness. At the end of March his stomach was in outright revolt and he was suffering from painful boils just at the hairline of his neck. Nancy, whom he had been courting for four years, remained virginal and elusive. To top it all off, Seán O'Faoláin's book of stories *Midsummer Night Madness* had appeared, complete with a glowing introduction by Edward Garnett, the same person who had earlier dismissed Michael's stories.[3] Fortunately, Richard Hayes, his "angelic doctor," prescribed an extended sick leave in May, giving Michael time to devote to *The Wild Bird's Nest.* AE's wife had died in February, leaving him in a sort of vacuum as well. The occasion of the Eucharistic Conference in June was excuse enough for them both, with Bergin, to leave Dublin on holiday. They all met in June in Glengarriff, where Michael had let a cottage overlooking the bay. While Michael and Bergin swam, AE perched in the rocks "sketching and commenting to the Celtic gods on the thunder that rolled promisingly in the distance."[4] In the evenings they all went over Michael's translations and argued about AE's ideas on the Irish Character. It was a delightful holiday made better by Nancy's arrival at the end of June.

Those few days were to be the most intimate and unencumbered time they would ever enjoy together. Michael had recuperated considerably and was again at the top of his form, and Nancy, just returning from a fortnight in Galway, was relaxed and exuberant. Though the presence of two elderly men in a small cottage with Michael seemed sufficient chaperonage, Nancy stayed at the Eccles Hotel. The arrangement was proper enough to make her feel totally at ease. She was taken by AE's gentle warmth and by Bergin's grumbling wit; even Michael seemed a bit softer in their company. He read some of his new translations to her, including the title poem which he intended to use in dedication to her:

> I will climb a high, high tree
> And rob a wild bird's nest,
> And I'll bring back whatever
> I do find
> To the arms I love the best
> —he said
> To the woman I love the best.

But she demurred, as she had about his novel, and *The Wild Bird's Nest* was dedicated instead to AE. Michael was undaunted, however, and Nancy left for Cork with his persistent marriage proposals ringing in her ears. "A marriage contract for two highly-strung people" was his way of phrasing it in a letter in July.

Michael returned to Dublin in August without money enough for cigarettes but with material enough for a winter's writing. In fact, he had too much material, and it made him feel that he was scattering his energies. Even his reading in Glengarriff had been more voluminous than focused: *Crime and Punishment, War and Peace* (for the fourth time), *Tristram Shandy,* and Wolfe Tone's autobiography. His journals show that after AE returned to Dublin, Michael cycled in the countryside around Glengarriff, meeting people and collecting stories. In Bantry he visited Anne Crowley, whose magnificent contralto voice thrilled him, and continued to write regularly to her, encouraging her musical aspirations.[5] His conversations with people around Clonakilty renewed his interest in Michael Collins, and he began making preliminary notes for a book about this rebel leader whose life seemed to Michael as enigmatic as the circumstances surrounding his untimely death on a West Cork road. Besides a play version of *The Saint,* he was also working on another novel, the hero of which, he confessed to Nancy, was too much like himself, for Michael felt he was "still too youthful to laugh at [his] youthful self." He still considered himself a poet with "little notion of how to write a story and none at all of how to write a novel." He wrote to Nancy that *Guests of the Nation* and *The Saint and Mary Kate* had been "produced in hysterical fits of enthusiasm, followed by similar fits of despondency, good passages alternating with bad," and he could no longer read them. The translations of *The Wild Bird's Nest,* however, had been produced in pure devotion.

Frank O'Connor had turned out three books in one year, and they were three qualified successes in three very different modes. Though the prestigious London firm of A. D. Peters, the literary agents for AE, had agreed to represent him, O'Connor still considered himself a librarian fumbling with writing. Acclaim gave him only lukewarm satisfaction, while attack chilled him to the marrow. He may have scoffed at his detractors, but inside he fought to prove them wrong, for he was always more ready to believe criticism than praise. Fighting the burden of his provincial beginnings, Frank O'Connor was always his own harshest critic. His public notoriety brought pressure for "something bigger," but the fiercest expectations were still his own.

I I

In September 1932 Dermot Foley passed through Dublin on his way back from Wales, where he had spent a week with his girl friend. Dermot's obvious happiness magnified Michael's own loneliness and he soon fell into a deep melancholy. The Academy council meetings bored him, and his flat-mate, Paddy Corr, was talking of leaving. The only social contact he had enjoyed since returning from Glengarriff was with Seán O'Faoláin, whose routine approach to his writing both infuriated and impressed Michael. One night, however, he went to a bachelor party, tangled with a particularly trenchant Gaelic Leaguer, and the next day, full of regret for his intemperance of speech and drink, wrote to Nancy a letter of self-pity, lamenting the necessities of social intercourse and the poverty of the Irish mentality.[6] In his gathering gloom he again entertained the idea of leaving "the bloody country."

Since Dermot always seemed to be salve for his melancholy and a source of new stories, Michael decided to spend a weekend in Ennis at the end of October. Upon his return he wrote to Nancy: "Dermot is a delightful creature, full of energy and imagination. I'm glad to say love seems to have won the day against religiosity, and I think he'll marry the quaker lass, in church or out."[7] But Nancy's life was in too much of a turmoil for her to answer Michael's hints. Her mother, who had been ill for some time, was dying. Because of her reticence, Nancy would not have left Cork to visit him in Ennis or Dublin even without a family crisis. Nancy's mother died in November; shortly after he heard of her death, Michael also got word of a job opening: Cork's new city library needed a head librarian. Homesickness and nostalgia got the better of common sense, and he applied for the position. "As one changes," he wrote to Nancy, "one's environment too should change; it's all wrong that Frank O'Connor who wants to write a wild intellectual novel should be tied to the same desk as that affected by the boy who wrote the Saint."[8] But at the same time he knew that Cork would be purgatory. AE asked Michael to consider the notion of bringing out a book while living in Cork—he would spend all his time wondering where the next brick was coming from, AE insisted. At the end of the month, while attending a library conference in Cork, Michael sat for an interview before the same committee with which he had worked four years before, but an amalgamation of opposition forces led by a priest had its way and the job went to Denis Cronin, Michael's old assistant. Michael refused to go home for Christmas, the first one he'd missed in ten years.

He began 1933 as he had 1932, sick and alone. The material he had gathered during the previous summer remained untouched in his notebooks. One piece of writing to find light that winter was a strange story entitled "There Is a Lone House," published in the obscure *Golden Book* (January 1933).[9] In style it is quite unlike the stories O'Connor had written up until that time, and in theme it anticipates many of his later stories—the strange, intuitive ways people find to ease their loneliness. In this story a traveling man stops for a cup of tea at the home of an unmarried woman. The woman, who has been brutalized by her uncle, is detached and awkward, but the traveler's "childlike" way, his whistling, and his attempts at poetry appeal to her. She allows him to stay so that he can whitewash the outhouse, dig the potatoes, and mend the fence, but insists that he sleep in the shed. Guilt and fear separate them, but loneliness and despair draw them to each other, until one night she allows him to enter her bed.

That O'Connor chose never to reprint this story may be due more to personal reticence than to literary judgment, for though the events were fabricated from a story he had heard somewhere in West Cork, the people involved and the nature of their emotions were all too real. The relationship of the man and the woman resembles Michael's relationship with Molly Alexander, even though Michael and Molly had never been physically involved. He had, when he lived at her house, been the "man of the house," and Molly in return had provided him with motherly attention and admiration of his work. The woman of the story is a composite portrait of many of the women Michael had known, including Molly, while the traveling man is most clearly a portrait of Michael himself—shy and boyish with women and uncertain of his artistic talents. At the same time the story may also be a working-out of his ideal love story, a fantasy of the way he hoped his relationship with Nancy would end. What a man dreams, perhaps tells as much about him as what he actually does and says.

Sometime that spring the playwright Denis Johnston and a few prominent Dublin actors, perhaps stimulated by the recent shooting of *Man of Aran* by Robert Flaherty, decided to make a film adaptation of "Guests of the Nation." Though done on an amateur basis using silent film at a time when "talkies" had taken over the cinemas, it was an ambitious undertaking; in fact, it was the first film produced entirely in Ireland by Irish artists.[10] O'Connor had no official hand in the project, but he took an active interest in it, advising Denis Johnston and Mary Manning on the script and even visiting the shooting site in the Wicklow hills. Even the energetic optimism of this amateur film crew was not enough to offset another bout of gloom. His flat-mate had decided to move, leaving Michael with the financial burden of the huge house across from the library, so while his mother was visiting in April he moved to a tiny basement flat on Raglan Road which she and Molly Alexander helped to make hospitable. Then, while standing in the rain watching the shooting of the film, he caught a fierce cold, which, combined with his continued frustration at Nancy, kept him in a terrible temper. For the first time in his life he was even short with his mother, who stayed in Dublin less than two weeks.

Then, almost overnight, he snapped out of it. His writing journal shows evidence of two plays, a radio script, and a few reviews. Even his relationship with Nancy received a momentary infusion of energy. For years he had tried to talk her into taking a holiday with him in some anonymous place. Finally, she agreed to spend the first fortnight of July with him, and his angry frustration melted with her acquiescence. Early in June Michael wrote a very loving letter proposing an excursion to Donegal. After complaining about his stomach and his new novel, he commented that the photo she had sent was very "kissable." Lamenting her chronic chastity, he bluntly assured her, " [as] a cause of sin I prefer you in the flesh." Long walks and Russian verbs, he added, only served to delay his ardor, the accumulation of which might be too much for her "moral fibre." Then there appears a sketch (he often included tidy little pencil sketches in his letters) of a man and woman in bed, back to back and clearly avoiding each other, with the caption "The End" lettered above the pillows. "Nothing personal," he added. "I am thinking of using this for a tail piece in my new book."[11]

The plan for their vacation was to stay in Dunfanaghy and to visit Irish-speaking villages. Nancy told her father only that she was going to the Donegal Gaeltacht (an Irish-speaking region) with a friend; with nine other children to look after, he hadn't the time to think that the friend was not a woman. When Michael met her at Kingsbridge Station in Dublin, he found his plans neatly curtailed. First, she insisted that they stay in separate hotels in Donegal; not wishing to upset her sense of propriety, Michael agreed. Next, she expressed reluctance over visiting the O'Faoláins, who had just returned from teaching in England. At the time, Michael was full of admiration for his old friend, who had chucked a steady job to make a living by writing. They also had a baby on whom he doted like a proud uncle. Michael insisted until she admitted that she did not want to have anything to do with anyone who wrote censored stories. Hastening out of the station, he turned to her and bellowed, "How in the name of God can you say you don't like somebody you haven't even met? Where's your sense of fair play?" She conceded, and they went directly to the guest house in Dun Laoghaire where Seán and Eileen were staying until a house became available. Every ounce of her prejudice toward Seán evaporated during the course of the evening. Eileen and Nancy hit it off splendidly, and the baby, Julie, was the center of attention. Needless to say, Michael was more than pleased about the success of the first part of the plan—an omen, he thought.

His hopes were shattered the next day. The train ride to Sligo was harrowing enough, but then on the coach to Dunfanaghy they were subjected to the rude jabbering of a coarse stranger. Their tension from the entire trip multiplied instantly when they found that the hotels Michael had booked were miles apart; so the vacation was to be more of a walking marathon. For three mornings Michael walked from his hotel to Nancy's, cursing the whole way; each evening he walked all the way back. Their meals were especially tense, and plans for visiting Irish-speaking villages evaporated. Then Michael began resurrecting the travails of their courtship and correcting her faults. One evening he remarked that her stammer was put on for effect, and she ran from the table in tears. For three days they did not speak to each other. He would walk past her hotel bound for a pub, while she watched his parade from her room. Neither made any effort to negotiate a truce. On the fourth day he stopped before the hotel, looked around furtively, and entered. Nothing was ever said about those three days or about his unkind remark, and their holiday "courtship"—such as it was—picked up where it had been left off. When they departed they were as nervous and standoffish as they had been when they'd arrived.

They resumed corresponding immediately upon her return to Cork but fell back into the same pattern of his passionate fury met by her cordial caution. Michael was so agitated by the frustrations of their relationship that he began mentioning other women in his letters, hoping to induce Nancy to reciprocate his affections. One such woman was Anne Crowley. Though he never had what could be termed a love affair with Miss Crowley, he had become very fond of her. He once received letters from both women on the same day, each putting a collar on his romantic notions. To both he responded, "You women are a conspiracy."[12] He took ill again, forcing his mother, presumably the one woman in his life not part of a conspiracy against him, to extend her visit to care for him. Only the arrival of a young poet named Patrick Kavanagh ("You'd love him," he wrote to Nancy, "a huge handsome lad with a hawk nose and wild blue eyes") and the presence of Seán O'Faoláin made life bearable. For a time at least he was able to escape from the writing vacuum which had tormented him for two years, the "peculiar curse of Ireland," he explained to Nancy, "this moral apathy, indifference." Even though his romance with her was crumbling, his writing, thanks to O'Faoláin, was taking focus. But Frank O'Connor wanted both love and literature.

August in Dublin that year was more exasperating than ever. Open clashes between the old guard of the IRA and the young idealists of Eoin O'Duffy's Blue Shirts, a movement with a distinctly fascist character, once again brought anxiety about civil war.[13] AE had changed drastically in the months after that soothing holiday in Glengarriff; he now railed about the policies of the government that Eamon de Valera had formed after the election of 1932. With his *Irish Statesman* gone, AE had no rational outlet for his opinions about Ireland, and he began talking more seriously about leaving the country. Yeats's fascination with the obstreperous fascist crowd left him quite distraught. The Literary Revival, to his mind, was dead and gone.

Earlier that year AE had called on Michael with the ominous announcement that he had just received a premonition of his death. Not sharing AE's mystical apprehension of spiritual things, Michael heard only the voice of a man afraid not of death but "of the pain and humiliation that would precede it." As they walked home AE bubbled with speculation about speaking to Socrates and avoiding Tolstoy after he'd arrived in heaven. A few weeks later he visited Michael again but in lighter spirits. They talked of poetry. Walking toward Rathgar, Michael quoted from a poem he was writing:

> A patriot frenzy enduring too long
>   Can hang like a stone on the heart of a man,
> And I have made Ireland too much of my song;
>   I will now bid those foolish old dreams to begone.

AE halted there at the corner of Appian Way, threw up his arms in a frenzy, and cried: "That's exactly how I feel. I have to get out of the country before it drives me mad."[14]

By May 1933 he had made up his mind to leave Ireland. He put his house up for sale, took a flat in London, and left for his July holiday in Donegal. The house was sold in his absence. When he returned, he began divesting himself of all his possessions; he invited Michael to take whatever of his belongings he wanted, but Michael refused. Only the intercession of F. R. Higgins brought Michael to visit the quickly emptying house: Higgins argued that AE would be hurt if Michael did not come and that greedy parasites would soon strip the place clean. Reluctantly Michael went along with Higgins but nearly wept when he saw AE's tragic face. The burly old saint insisted that Michael take two exquisite little watercolors he had done in Glengarriff and a set of broadsheets by Jack Yeats, the brother of W. B. and a painter Michael admired very much. Before AE left on the first of August he went round to the Pembroke Library to try to see Michael one last time; he wrote to Bergin the next day, lamenting that the library was "closed and dark and blind."[15] Supposing Michael to be on holiday again—Michael was in fact at his darkened flat in Raglan Road; stifled by the heat, tortured by his stomach, he stared endlessly through cigarette haze at the dismal ceiling—AE turned as usual without looking back. His departure created a void in Michael's life.

In September Michael did leave Dublin on holiday. This time he went to Sligo, then to Mayo and to Ennis where he stayed with Dermot. He arrived in Cork on the weekend of his thirtieth birthday to celebrate with Nancy and his mother. He had as gifts for his two favorite women the two watercolors AE had given him. As it happened, his mother was distressed about Big Mick's latest drinking bout and Nancy was especially distracted by problems in her family. Michael returned to Dublin angry and bewildered. By now he had apparently come to realize that the courtship was hopeless.

Over a month passed with no word from Nancy. He could not understand the silence. What troubled him about Nancy was that he thought she "externalized" herself, refusing to follow the interior life he felt she possessed.[16] As with his remarks about her stammer, Michael was not so much being censorious as, he thought naively, encouraging—"because I'm sufficiently fond of you to want you to make something of your life." Holding tenaciously to the idea—perhaps instilled in him by his mother—that he could change things, Michael implored Nancy to understand that he just could not let her go. "Six years, during which all I succeeded in doing was to make a mess of my own life, six years of evasion on your part, first because I hadn't £500 a year, second because I wasn't a good Catholic and then something else."[17] There followed another month of silence on her part and another month of torrid writing on his. At the end of November Michael was ready to chuck the whole thing—"all the emotion in the world isn't worth a spark of human kindness." Nancy, he felt, was unable to make up her mind, but he was prepared to marry her instantly. He could not, however, continue this "hide-and-seek business." On December 28 he confessed: "So far as I can see I'm finished as a writer and my health is, if anything, worse, but you are the only woman I care enough about to try and make a success of it for."

Not really the moral coward he made her out to be, Nancy was only a highly strung small-town girl afraid of what she might do to the two of them. In February 1934 he asked for no more letters, ending with the words "I love you, hopelessly and crazily, and I'll never say it again, if I can help it."[18] From then on his letters ceased to open "Dear Nance"—they just started. On St. Patrick's Day he went to Cork but spoiled everyone's weekend with his moroseness. Apologizing to Nancy later, he wrote, "When these melancholy fits come on me they are absolutely uncontrollable and suicidal." Exactly one month later, on April 17, he received a letter from Nancy in which she announced her marriage. He responded with unusual savagery: "I shall never forgive you and twenty eternities won't be enough to wipe out the shame and rage and bitterness and hatred of now."[19] In his self-pity he refused to offer congratulations but admitted a certain relief that "the lies and shams and hypocrisies are gone." The private torture forced him to the "edge of madness." On the twenty-third he sent a telegram to her saying "Everything All Right Good Luck."

The fact is that everything was not all right. He had actually fallen apart; his next letter to Nancy (April 26) made almost no sense and the handwriting was practically illegible. The letter frightened her with its references to "ghostly hallucinations" and to the hospital. On the same day she received a letter from Seán O'Faoláin expressing his and Eileen's worry about Michael's behavior. Friday they had found him dumpy and silent, and Sunday he had blown in on them talking wildly of Cork and the desperate state of the "bloody country." To Nancy Seán wrote: "You are too nice a girl to ruin anybody's life. Remember Michael is given to terrible exaggeration and even ends by believing his own dramas." Seán expressed the wish that she had confided in them so they would have known what to guard against—"Anarchists? or a broken heart?" Two days later Eileen wrote to Nancy saying that she and Seán had brought Michael to stay with them and that he had seemed to cheer up. Then, enlisting the help of Richard Hayes, they persuaded him to take another sick leave, and within a week Michael left for Glengarriff.

On May 11 from Casey's Hotel in Glengarriff he wrote to Nancy a thoughtfully tender letter. He said he had pocketed his pride and swallowed the bitterness: "I don't want you to think that I don't blame myself bitterly too: I do, but remember that all these years I've been living in the dark, loving you passionately and trying to keep my love alive against coldness and indifference." His naivete and self-centered "interior life," he confessed, kept him from realizing how his criticism of her stammer or laughter at her singing might have affected her. He said he had thought it enough that all along he had considered her the finest woman in the world, and it was only now, realizing that things he had said had hurt her, that he cursed every word. The strain of a long-distance romance must have been unbearable for him. It wasn't the news of the marriage that bothered him as much as the gossip of his breakdown: "The worst thing about a collapse is facing the people who saw you collapse; it's worse when they know the cause. Where you are concerned all the pride I had went when I picked up the traces after three years." So ends Michael O'Donovan's first severe slide into what he later called the abyss of subjective horror.

I I I

For all the distress Michael had to endure, the break with Nancy and his subsequent breakdown were the best things that could have happened to him. For one thing, it brought him closer to his male friends, Richard Hayes, Tim Traynor, Dermot Foley, and Seán O'Faoláin, all of whom thought the world of Michael and supported him through the good times and the bad. For another, it forced him to come to terms with Cork; by clinging to the illusion of marrying Nancy he had also clung emotionally to his home. He returned briefly to Cork in June, but the visit only reopened the old love-hate relationship. Corkery would not see him at all, and Sean Hendrick was too busy with business and personal matters to spend much time talking about poetry. Nancy, of course, was out of the picture; but Michael's father was in unusually fine form, strutting and swaggering about the house reliving the old days of neighborhood bands and military glories. Michael returned to Dublin with Cork ringing in his ears and began a burst of writing activity that carried well into the fall. Thus the violent wrenching of his soul broke a three-year logjam in his creative life and precipitated four or five years of his most productive writing.

O'Connor was obviously writing out the Cork demons. The first thing he wrote that summer was a story in the manner of D. H. Lawrence. In "The Man Who Stopped" a talented man bearing a close resemblance to Sean Hendrick simply stops one day in a Cork street, forever.[20] O'Connor believed that his old friend was frittering away his life in an insurance office. While nothing impressed him more than a person making full use of his mental faculties, nothing displeased him more than waste of talent. "A Boy in Prison," written the same week, wrings out the residue of bitterness left by the Gormanstown experience.[21] In "The English Soldier" and "Lofty" he is probing life in the shadow of a military barracks and dealing with the character of his father. Finally, "Orpheus and His Lute" and "Repentance" (which he later titled "First Confession"), written at this time though not published until the following winter, both show him trying to put a laughable face on the emotional disarray and impoverished hopelessness of his childhood in Cork.

Though obviously autobiographical, all these stories mark the emergence of the detached narrative manner that was to become characteristic of O'Connor's stories. He had begun to back far enough away from himself to be able to laugh, proving once again his belief that things that look monstrous when seen too close appear quite normal when viewed from afar; but he was nevertheless finding the process of "externalization" difficult. In a letter to Dermot Foley he wrote: "I've sold a fair share of stories but I don't love what I write. Hard, cold and cautious, but I've been saturating myself with music and glamour and poetry and hope for the best."[22] According to AE's "doctrine of the diversity of the inner and outer," the reaction to experience rather than the experience itself is what makes a writer what he or she is. Frank O'Connor was writing about the "material" he knew best, about the things he'd experienced growing up in Cork, but instead of dealing with his own ambivalent feelings of bitterness and affection, he stayed entirely outside of himself, preferring the safety of other "voices" to the frightening desolation of his own.

In *Guests of the Nation* O'Connor had written the hysteria of revolution out of his system, but by 1934 he felt Ireland needed another transformation. "Oh, this bloody country," he moaned again and again to anyone who would listen. The banning of O'Faoláin's novel, *A Nest of Simple Folk,* in 1933 had made his blood boil. He and the younger members of the Irish Academy of Letters made their objection to this act known by sending endless letters to the editors of Dublin's newspapers. Although the shadow of censorship made literary life frustrating in Dublin in 1934, it was an exciting time to be a part of that life. On one hand, a new crop of writers had emerged to claim the ear of Irish readers. Men such as Denis Johnston, Paul Vincent Carroll, Peadar O'Donnell, Patrick Kavanagh, Austin Clarke, Francis Stuart, Liam O'Flaherty, Seán O'Faoláin, and Frank O'Connor were drawn together by the belief that they held the key to Ireland's future, that the eclipse of Yeats and AE and the rest of the Olympian generation did not have to mean intellectual darkness. They dreamed of a new literary theatre, for instance, that would generate the best plays—in English and in Gaelic—from Irish writers. On the other hand, the Fianna Fáil party, with Eamon de Valera acting as head of government, used the natural conservatism of Catholicism and Nationalism to sanction severe measures that limited the freedom of these headstrong young writers, whose writings were seen as threatening to the growth of a stable establishment.

The issue of artistic freedom kept Frank O'Connor perpetually uneasy in Ireland; at the same time he was still "fumbling for a style." Having found the romanticism of violence unproductive, he turned from the subject of a nation at war to smaller and less colorful situations. The title of his next volume of stories, *Bones of Contention*, published by Macmillan in 1936, suggests petty dissension, not revolution on a grand scale. The characters of the stories in this collection are not soldiers or lovers; they are peasants, drunk musicians, and tired old men. Their struggles are, for the most part, isolated, parochial, and spontaneous. These are the "laney folk" among whom Michael grew up and to whom he listened as intently as he did to his own interior voices. The title story is indicative of the prevailing mood of the stories that he came to envision as a unit. Written in 1932 from an anecdote he had heard from both Nancy and his mother, "Bones of Contention" concerns the monumental and eminently funny feud that erupts when a stubborn, hard-drinking old woman, resembling Michael's grandmother, insists on supervising the funeral of an old friend. The cliché title captures the irony of the whole episode: the intensity of the "battle" over a corpse does not raise it above the merely trivial, and all the fiery words and nasty contention only temporarily upset a normally quiet lane.

During the autumn of 1934 the incredible capacity of the Irish for verbal battling once again demonstrated itself to O'Connor. Late one night after a party at the home of John Garvin, another civil servant with literary connections, O'Connor found himself in a taxi with three other gentlemen, all talking about what was wrong with the "bloody country." After the first man was dropped off at his residence with hearty farewells, the remaining three passengers began to criticize his views on the matter. The next gentleman was let out at his house; as soon as the cab pulled away the remaining passengers took to criticizing his theories on the country. At the third stop O'Connor stepped from the taxi and walked cautiously toward his house, leaving Edward Sheehy, editor of *Ireland Today*, alone with the taxi driver. After a few blocks of silence Sheehy leaned forward in the seat and asked the driver who he thought was right about what was wrong with the country. The driver gave a wry smile and said they were all off the mark: what was wrong with the country was the endless talk about its problems. Sheehy told John Garvin the story the next day, and Garvin passed it on to O'Connor two days later over lunch. The story "What's Wrong with the Country?" was written almost as it happened.[23]

But talk was what Frank O'Connor thrived on. Most of the stories that came together in *Bones of Contention* were told to him by other people. His journals are filled with bits and snatches of conversation, choice figures of speech and fragments of stories picked up from friends and strangers. In conversation with friends Michael could be either affable or morose, whichever suited his mood, until a story started to unravel. Then he would become attentive: his ears would prick up and he would lean forward in his chair. Suddenly self-conscious, the friend would apologize and try to move the conversation to another topic. But if Michael had gotten the scent of a story, he would insist that the person continue while he impatiently probed for the essential details, the background, the names of the people involved. He might interject a quote from a story by Maupassant to encourage the teller to continue, or, chafing for more, wave the reluctant friend away from digression. It was the story he was after, and most likely he had already begun to write it in his head; sometimes even the title would pop out of some cliché or other the teller would use, and Michael would pounce on it with delight. And if the anecdote ended with a thud, he would press impatiently for some unexpected twist that might bring sense to the incident or that would suggest a theme for the story. So it was that the slightest memories of friends or temporary companions in trains or pubs became sparks of inspiration for his voracious story-collecting appetite.[24]

During the six-month period from May to November 1934, O'Connor had written at white-hot pace, making it the most concentrated creative burst in his career. Lovat Dickson alone bought five stories at five guineas each, and the *Yale Review* paid nearly eighteen pounds for "The English Soldier." In June *Life and Letters* bought "May Nights," a curious story about two tramps sitting by the road waiting for something to happen.[25] Buoyed by the additional funds and optimistic of continued success, Michael decided in January 1935 to move back to Trenton, the huge house he had once shared with Paddy Corr; but this time he rented the place by himself, hoping to do more entertaining. He had been maintaining a full social calendar since August—evenings at the O'Faoláins or with Richard Hayes; concerts with Anne Crowley, who had recently moved to Dublin; regular lunches with John Garvin, who loved to talk with Michael about Joyce; and weekend jaunts with Tim Traynor. He was not often found in the Pearl or any of the other "literary" pubs, though he occasionally had a drink with Patrick Kavanagh when they chanced to meet in Hanna's, a bookstore they both patronized in those years. But by March his writing had dried up and his stomach was once more in revolt, so that not even a larger flat was sufficient to brighten his spirits. For nearly a month he was a virtual recluse, perfunctorily meeting his duties at the library and then retiring to his bed, where he would lie sleepless for hours, smoking endlessly and staring at the high ceiling. After Michael had not appeared at a St. Patrick's Day party at the O'Faoláins' house in Killiney, Seán and Eileen called on him two or three times, but not even their efforts could shake him from his depression.

Then, around the first of April, Dermot came up from Ennis for a surprise visit, prompted by a letter from Seán and Eileen about Michael's dismal condition. Before making his way to Ballsbridge, Dermot called on Irene Haugh, an old friend of his and Michael's from the days of the *Irish Statesman*. She too warned him about Michael's depression. In the course of their conversation Dermot asked about her brother Kevin, who had come to Ennis once with Michael and Irene. It happened that Kevin Haugh, then serving in the Ministry of Justice as a deputy prosecutor, was working on the highly publicized trial of a woman accused of poisoning her husband. Dermot had heard rumblings about the case in Ennis, which was not far from the West Clare village where the murder had taken place, so he decided to sit in on the trial. When he arrived at Trenton, he found Michael exactly as he had been warned he would—shabbily dressed, lying on his bed smoking, a half-empty decanter of whiskey on the table beside him. Without so much as a nod of pity, Dermot bustled officiously about the room talking about the horrors of provincial life. Then, after putting a Russian folk song on the gramophone (he always played Russian music when Michael needed cheering up and Beethoven when he was already in good spirits), he told Michael that they were going to the Four Courts for a trial.

Michael thought at first that it was a silly idea, but he was glad to see Dermot and so went with him to watch the proceedings. During recess Michael and Dermot talked with Kevin Haugh, who predicted an acquittal. Michael asked if the accused woman was actually guilty of murdering her husband, and Kevin admitted that she was, but that her neighbors would perjure themselves before testifying against her. Dermot surmised aloud that the woman must have had many friends, but Mr. Haugh explained that, on the contrary, she was practically an outcast because it was rumored that she had a lover. When the trial resumed, Michael sat as near to the front of the courtroom as he could get, transfixed. When it was all over and the woman was indeed acquitted, Michael left the courtroom in a hurry, giving Dermot only enough time to wave at Kevin Haugh across the room. Outside, Michael was ecstatic. Down the quays he marched, Dermot in pursuit, trying to listen to the flurry of words. The melancholy had fallen away and the old magical gleam had reappeared. "A story was on him," Dermot realized.

The story was "In the Train," one of O'Connor's richest and best known. Somewhere between the Four Courts and O'Connell Street, where they caught the tram to Ballsbridge, Michael had begun to write it in his head. The rest of the weekend he was at his most charming, giving Dermot credit for pulling him out of the quagmire. He finished the story within the week and sent it off to A. D. Peters almost as it came off the typewriter. Lovat Dickson snapped up the story at once.[26]

The theme on which O'Connor had fastened that day at the Four Courts was justice. The way his relationship with Nancy had ended had made him believe there was no such thing as cosmic justice, while repressive activities in Ireland since the Treaty had given ample evidence that civil justice was illusory as well. Maintaining that "abstract considerations like justice, truth and personal integrity melt before the personal element," O'Connor turned his attention to the problem of how people cope with injustice in a chaotic and senseless world. His technical problem was to capture the drama of a murder trial without using the courtroom cliché. He circles the trial itself and diverts attention to the gallery of people surrounding the woman on the train, taking them all home, where justice is a personal matter. The policemen swap stories and the peasants converse about the weather until the conspicuous arrival of a "young woman in a brown shawl." The train rumbles westward carrying a group of people divided by their own personal problems, including drink and domestic discord, but united by their suspicion of the woman. O'Connor offers only a glance at the woman herself. As the train nears its destination the story quickens; even though she is suspended in her moment of tragic injustice, the acquitted woman's life hastens relentlessly on like a train.

Literature to Frank O'Connor was a moral art, not a parlor game for the intellectual elite. What was important in a story was not only the person telling it but the person listening to it. Because he always views characters from without, O'Connor only offers guesses. Neither the peasants nor the policemen evoke much sympathy; they are judged by their own contradictory ethic. Neither is the young woman exactly spotless. This ambiguity compels the reader to collaborate with the storyteller. When a drunken policeman snarls that there will be one happy man in Farranchreesht, he brings into the open the rumor that the woman killed her husband for a lover. Unfortunately her adamant denial does little to erase the implication. O'Connor maintained that one had to get beyond what people are saying to what they are thinking; in this story he digs behind what they are *not* saying to what they are thinking and why. He has played out his hunch and elaborated his idea of justice, but it is still hunch. The truth, as Yeats had taught him, cannot be known, only embodied. The story ends suspended, and knowledge is as tentative as the law is arbitrary.

"In the Train" was the story that turned the corner for O'Connor, that brought into focus the personal despair with which he had been struggling in the trying time since his breakup with Nancy. But rather than penetrating his own intense emotions, he once again sought detachment in voices outside himself. As a result, technique dominates emotion in most of the stories in *Bones of Contention.* For a storyteller like O'Connor narrative point of view dictated the handling of the material. In every story except "A Romantic," which is strongly autobiographical, the narrative voice is detached, calling attention to the persons in the story rather than to itself. Such phrases as "for as the old man said to me of him" or "as they all said" create in the story "Peasants," for example, the impression of a story overheard, almost as gossip, from the peasants themselves about the unpleasant memories left behind by a former priest. "Orpheus and His Lute," the comic account of the drinking habits of the Irishtown Brass and Reed Band, is told entirely from the outside, even though it is almost purely autobiographical.[27] Though his most obvious model of the *seanachie,** a native Irish teller of tales, was the lame tailor of Gougane Barra—who once objected that Michael's stories hadn't enough "marvels" in them—O'Connor was also following Yeats's dictum that poetry should be spoken as to a man across the street. Whatever the sources for his technique might have been, O'Connor's stories began to carry what Yeats had called the quality of a "man's voice speaking."[28]

When O'Connor followed his instincts, when he let a story tell itself, he created life. In his best stories he usually provides just enough setting to give a particular incident background. Dan Bride, the old man of "Majesty of the Law," appears totally at harmony with his rough-hewn, archaic environment. Helena, the felon of "In the Train," is cast in momentary relief by O'Connor's description of Farranchreesht. The occasion crystallizes both stories, completing for a hesitant moment the incomplete slice of life. To an even greater extent this is true of "Michael's Wife," the most evocative story in *Bones of Contention.* In 1935 O'Connor's mother and father came to Dublin. During this visit Big Mick toured all the military barracks in town and all the graves of the Irish patriots buried in Dublin. Michael consented to accompany him one afternoon to Glasnevin Cemetery. On the way back his father insisted that they stop at a bar near Cross Guns Bridge—for old times' sake, he said. Though un-

* Also spelled *seanchaidhe, seanchai,* or occasionally *shanachie* (an American variant), the Gaelic word for a local storyteller, whose *sagen* (long tales about local events) and *seanchas* (tidbits of local lore) have been raw material for social historians and poets alike.

easy over the thought of another of his father's drinking bouts, Michael agreed to go in with him. After ordering stout for his son and lemonade for himself, Mick embarked on a nostalgic conversation, speaking as if Michael were one of his Cork cronies. During that conversation he asked his son's advice about convincing Minnie to apply for the old-age pension. He said she was "close on seventy and would sacrifice a perfectly good pension of ten shillings a week from mere vanity." The events of that day—the cemetery visit, the ritual drink, and the conversation—constituted one of the few times Michael and Big Mick had had anything like father-son rapport.

Pondering the incident after his parents returned to Cork at the end of the week, Michael tried to recall when he had last felt close to his father. For over a year he had been toying with his childhood memories, recalling his father's drum, his military medals, and his drinking bouts. But now he remembered the few occasions upon which he and his father had shared something besides hatred. The one that kept surfacing was the time he and his father had been walking near Courtmacsherry on one of the hills overlooking the sea. A farmer joined them as they were watching an American liner making for Cobh. The liner reminded the farmer of his dead son, who had gone to America, married a girl from Donegal, and then ceased to write. The son's wife came for a visit, alone, stayed for a while to recover from a recent illness, and then left. Only later did they learn that their son had died before his wife ever left America. The moment captivated Michael—the liner, the bewildered old man telling his tale to strangers, and his father impatient to return home. The old man's story and his question "Why would she do a thing like that to us?" haunted O'Connor until he wrote "Michael's Wife."[29]

Unlike the stories that follow it in *Bones of Contention*, "Michael's Wife" contains nothing of provincial edginess, verbal squabbling, or social chaos. Irony is toned down, and the sense of occasion arises naturally from a highly evocative presentation of place. In its merging of locale and incident, "Michael's Wife" resembles the dramatic lyrics of the ancient Irish poetry O'Connor was translating. It is not lyrical, as some critics have argued, because of the rich descriptive language. It is lyrical because of the voice heard resonating within the surroundings. And it is dramatic because the voice, at once discrete and expansive, harmonizes the people and the occasion.

"Michael's Wife" bears O'Connor's "comment" on those instinctive ways in which people communicate the incommunicable and share their humanity. Abstractions cease to matter, but the story has indeed pulled the reader into the story, testifying most eloquently to O'Connor's theory of the lonely voice. Other stories may reveal what he thought about War, or Love, or Justice, but "Michael's Wife" reveals what he felt. It is as autobiographical as anything O'Connor wrote—not because it is about his personal experience but because it is a personal experience. That he later repudiated as sentimental his so-called lyrical stories shows how far he let the cold and cautious realist dominate the intense, improvising romantic.

O'Connor constructed *Bones of Contention* with the same careful attention he had given to *Guests of the Nation*. Though Maupassant influenced his approach to some of the individual stories, he turned to his adolescent idol Turgenev for the conception of the volume. The final story, "A Romantic," balances the first, "Michael's Wife"; and these two, so different in tone from the ten wry, detached stories in between, make a sort of emotional envelope. "A Romantic" builds on a string of quick, almost cinematic movements unveiling the shifting moods of a young dreamer in love. Originally entitled "Love," it is about a boy in love not only with three different girls but with the idea of love. Noel, the dreamy messenger boy of the story, resembles the young Mick-Mihal of Harrington Square in more than a casual way. Aged seventeen when the story begins, he has "jet-black hair and a dark-skinned face with features of a curious intensity." The first girl he falls in love with is Anne Ferriter, a girl above his social station who sends him into "melancholy rapture." She is a portrait of O'Connor's ideal woman: a quicksilver girl with "imperious eyes" and spontaneous tongue. But Noel dares not kiss her, "afraid he might scare the vision"—it is this "vision" that makes life bearable to Noel, trapped in a menial job and a miserable home with a father who is given to drink. The next girl, Joan Glynn, the sister of a friend, is a "creature of instinct and fantasy." He kisses her without illusion, but goes back to Anne again and again. Then Helen Dwyer, a staunch Gaelic Leaguer, begins to dominate his dreams with "her melancholy, sensuous mouth," "her brilliant dark eyes," and her delicate face. With her he savors "the melancholy joy of resignation" leading to the first embrace.[30] The story continues, scene by scene, conversation by conversation, as Noel turns from one girl to another, always presenting himself in a different pose. At age twenty—now well-dressed, sporting a moustache, and carrying himself in a "masterful, incisive manner"—his pursuit of love continues. The reason he is attractive to women may be found in a sentence which, by all accounts, describes Michael O'Donovan as well: "At the same time, under his aggressiveness, his masterful, argumentative manner, there was still something helpless and appealing that begged for understanding and affection."

In the next few quickening cinematic frames O'Connor pushes his protagonist to the breaking point, forcing him eventually to face "a real world he hated." Noel proposes to Anne, then to Helen, but both girls refuse him, so he despairs of even bothering to ask the third girl and wanders around town. O'Connor's description of Cork is vibrant; the lanes, the quays, the ships, the spires, the hills, all seem but melancholy hallucinations to a young man distracted to the point of considering suicide. By the final frame the fantasies have played themselves out. Noel awakens in a strange bed with a strange woman. All the hallucinations of the night before "exist in an ideal world far, far above him; a world that contained the magical lost beauty of Anne. First love and last, there was no one like her." A real world clatters noisily outside and a real woman, her breasts exposed, sleeps next to him. He has fed on fantasy and has awakened to find it brutally empty.

That O'Connor even attempted to write such a story after his calamitous courtship with Nancy suggests how far he had come in finding a measure of peace for himself. Whether or not he ever woke with a strange woman is impossible to know; but the "wild fancies," the "extraordinary melancholy," and the "sense of appalling desolation," he most surely knew—again and again. And that he intended to give special weight to the only personal story of the volume by placing it at the end is verified by the poetic epilogue that follows it. He opens *Guests of the Nation* with a love poem to Nancy celebrating the joy of returning to Ireland; he ends *Bones of Contention* with a valediction of sorts. "Epilogue" leaves the volume somewhere between hope and despair:

> By the creaking gate
> Now my guests are sped,
> I ask pardon for
> Every word I said—
> Some to please a friend,
> Some to praise the State—
> A tree in the wind.
> Now, maybe too late,
> To the stars I cry,
> Trembling from head to toe,
> "From magic we come,
> To magic we go."

I V

By the middle of the thirties O'Connor had come to accept both his limitations as a verse maker and his inclinations toward prose fiction. By that time, however, he had written a respectable pile of poems, to say nothing of his translations, so when his agent apprised him of the possibility of doing a "slim volume" for a poetry series published by Nelson, O'Connor decided to print the best that he had, and call an end to his career as a poet. Except for some occasional verse, he published no more original poetry after the appearance of *Three Old Brothers* in 1936.

Arranged chronologically from "Three Old Brothers" and "Sweeney" (originally "Suibhne Geilt Aspires"), written in 1925, to "Self-Portrait," written in 1935, the twenty-five poems included in *Three Old Brothers* represent about one-third of O'Connor's verse output during those ten years. The first fourteen poems were all written before 1930, the last publication year of the *Irish Statesman,* in which eight of these poems first appeared. Most of these poems are dramatic monologues of the sort found so frequently in the ancient verse O'Connor was translating. But his penchant for dramatic lyrics and dramatic monologues also grew out of his adolescent passion for the poetry of Robert Browning. Like Browning he sought to externalize emotion, to objectify personal concerns too intense to meet head-on, too profound to avoid altogether. What O'Connor later said of Browning and Shakespeare was more than likely pointed at himself as well: Absolute objectivity is a form of gigantic egotism.

The poems written after 1930, however, have a more personal flavor. Even the three translations he chose to group together under the heading "Echoes" deal with a personal crisis—faith and the loss of faith. In fact, the mood of loss and disillusionment so dominates these later poems that it seems likely they were written during or shortly after Michael's emotional crisis over Nancy. "A Statue of Life" is three lyrics about the most important things in O'Connor's life: the little people of Cork's Native Stream, his mother, and the Imagination. The final lyric begins:

> What are the forms of life but illusion?
> Every passion, every institution,
> Imagination built them all,
> And having built, must bring them to their fall.

The answer in the second octave is the disappointment of an image maker with the inability of words to last:

> The patterns change because they are fiction
> Which we create out of some contradiction
> Within the channels of our blood,
> Dream words misspelt, misunderstood.

Finally, the speaker asserts, with characteristic O'Connor distrust of abstraction that when myth has been replaced by theory men are left with perdition.

> So I would put a statue up
> That the imagination's cup
> May fill again and Joan and Jack
> See a golden age come back.

The voice in this poem speaks of a sensibility beyond that of the forlorn romantic poet of "The Grand Vizier's Daughters," a voice content with more modest returns on its artistic investment. "Prologue and Epilogue" continues to explore the lonely desolation of a soul without love or imaginative spark. Through the deserted anteroom of the poet's heart pass silent ghosts in review.

"Self-Portrait" by contrast is all pose and swagger. It is the voice of a poet watching other people watch him be a poet with sardonic delight.

> Last Sunday morning,
> Sitting on the tram,
> I found myself beside a priest,
> A fat and gloomy man;
> I looked over his shoulder
> And I read *namquam*.
> Now I happened to be reading
> *Les Amours de Madame,*
> And even though he scowled at me
> I didn't give a damn.
> And that just shows you
> The sort I am.

That's as much a self-portrait of Michael/Frank as the proverbial dog's bark. It does show, however, how much he enjoyed being the abrasive conscience to a race of pietists intent on banning his work.[31]

V

As early as 1931 O'Connor had shown interest in writing a book about Michael Collins. As the fever of the Troubles subsided he became more and more intrigued by the myths surrounding Collins, and when Father Traynor mentioned something about knowing one of Collins's mistresses, Frank O'Connor took fire. The official attitude of respectful silence on the subject of Collins struck him as ludicrous. On one hand, the Irish people wanted a plaster saint, and on the other, the Irish political establishment preferred that Collins be forgotten altogether. In December 1931 Michael had written to Nancy, who had been friendly for years with a niece of Collins's, about his proposed book.

Michael asked Nancy to ask the young woman what she remembered of her uncle, his traits and interests. O'Connor wanted to present Collins, he said, as a human being, not as some sort of "dynamo." Then in January 1932, after talking until well after midnight with Robert Barton, one member of the Treaty delegation who had voted with Collins, Michael wrote to tell Nancy that, like himself, Collins suffered from the agonies of gastritis. About the same time, he met the son of Erskine Childers and discovered that what he'd suspected since the Civil War days was true: Childers and Collins, contrary to popular opinion, had indeed been good friends, and the gun Childers was shot for having was a present from Collins.

Meanwhile Traynor continued to track down details of Collins's sex life. In March 1932 he arranged for Michael to meet Mrs. Llewelyn Davies, who had known Collins intimately and had been madly in love with him. Describing that interview to Nancy, Michael wrote: "She talked of him as 'the most beautiful creature she had ever seen' and described him with the sun in his hair and told me (as she acutely remarked when I was going) 'nothing, absolutely nothing.' " The woman completely repelled O'Connor: "if M.C. slept with that woman he must have had a stomach for women. I'd rather go to bed with one of her own Medici prints." Then he asked Nancy to do him the favor, as he put it, "of not being a Mrs. Ll. Davies and storing me up."[32] What he could not understand was what attracted such a man as Collins to this kind of woman, as well as to "savage gunmen." Even at this stage of his investigation, while he still conceived of the book as a novel, O'Connor was hard pressed to encompass all the contradictions surrounding Michael Collins.

The crisis with Nancy forced the Collins project to the back of O'Connor's mind. It was difficult enough for him to understand his own tangled relationships with women without trying to sort out the affairs of a national hero. He also had another diversion at the time. In the fall of 1933 Richard Hayes had invited him to join him in Mayo to recreate the disastrous journey of a French brigade led by General Humbert in 1798. Michael agreed, though he could only afford a week away from the library. Over the ensuing year he spent considerable time helping Hayes prepare the book, his third about the historical connections between the Irish and the French. When the book, entitled *The Last Invasion of Ireland*, was finished, Hayes wanted to include O'Connor's name on the title page, but the publisher, M. H. Gill, refused. By this time *The Wild Bird's Nest* and *The Saint and Mary Kate* had been attacked by the Catholic Truth Society, and Michael's outspoken opposition to the censorship laws had given him the reputation of being an iconoclast. Hayes was embarrassed by the affront, but Michael insisted that any mention of his name, including the use of a few translations by him, be deleted. Hayes did acknowledge his debt to Frank O'Connor in his preface to the book, which appeared in 1937.[33] In turn, O'Connor dedicated *Bones of Contention* to Richard Hayes.

In the course of his work with Hayes, Michael was impressed by the readiness with which people of all kinds offered information and documents to Hayes. He was also struck by the integrity of Hayes's patriotism and the depth of his understanding of the political history of Ireland. It was Hayes, thinking perhaps that Michael needed something to divert him from self-pity, who encouraged him to resume work on the Collins book. Except for some secret files obtained by Father Traynor, O'Connor had access to few reliable documents.

And his reputation cut him off from access to many people. But Hayes seemed to have everyone's ear. Not only was he respected for his role in the 1916 Rising and the Black and Tan War, but he was a staunch Fianna Fáil man and a personal friend of de Valera. There was nothing, it seemed, the old patriots wouldn't do for Hayes, so when he interceded on Michael's behalf, they generally agreed to talk with him, whether they intended to say anything or not. Since Michael knew nothing about interviewing, Hayes often went with him to the interviews to ease the situation or to ask questions that had not occurred to Michael. At times he even invited people to his own house to meet Michael.

Hayes was warily sympathetic to Michael's feelings about the degree to which Irish nationalists had been prepared to be cruel. By this time Michael had become disgusted with both sides of the Treaty questions for keeping the wounds open. Though Hayes did not share Michael's severe disillusionment, he understood it, and even corroborated Michael's tales of the sordid acts of violence at Gormanstown. Hayes had encountered more brutality than had Michael, but his temperament was different. Having known people on both sides, he cautioned Michael to consider the intensity of feeling and the humanity of even the most violent gunmen. One evening at John Garvin's, while discussing the execution of Patrick Pearse, Hayes was unusually relaxed and talkative. Michael pushed the theory that Pearse might have wondered at the end if it was worth dying for—the cause he had championed, the people he had led, the violence he had fostered. Hayes, who knew what it was like to face execution, agreed with the plausibility of this speculation. He was taken by Michael's acute feeling for the subtle contradictions possible within people but was repelled by Michael's snap judgments. He knew that Michael would write the book because it was burning within him. He also knew that his young friend had a few bones to pick, and he thought he could exercise some influence in the direction of tact and objectivity.

There was a streak of paternalism in Hayes, not only regarding Michael but toward the men who had figured in the fight for Irish independence. For example, Seán O'Faoláin and Frank MacDermott were working at the time on the manuscripts of Wolfe Tone's autobiography, the book Michael Collins was said to have read constantly in prison. They discovered references to a mistress, which Tone's son had omitted in the published book. The thought of defacing the reputation of Wolfe Tone sent Hayes into what Michael called one of his "sudden, old-maidish fits of self-righteousness." He wanted Michael to persuade O'Faoláin not to publish the offending passages, but Michael enjoyed the thought of Tone's impropriety as much as Hayes abhorred it.

Hayes patiently went through all the published material on Collins with O'Connor, correcting inaccuracies of fact and formulating appropriate questions for the interviews. He arranged for Michael to meet Piaras Beaslai, Collins's first biographer, early in 1935.[34] Hayes had served with Beaslai as a representative in the first Dáil Éireann in 1919. He also knew Dorothy Macardle, who was at the time preparing her book, *The Irish Republic,* and invited her to his house one evening to help Michael. O'Connor's notebooks indicate that nearly forty interviews took place during the spring and early summer of 1935.[35] The list of people whom Hayes persuaded to talk to O'Connor reads like a veritable honor roll of the rebellion and a checklist of Irish politics thereafter—excepting Eamon de Valera, who would say nothing about his old neme-

sis; W. T. Cosgrave, the former head of government; Sean MacEntee, whom
Michael knew from Gormanstown and who was a cabinet minister under de
Valera; Richard Mulcahy, a general of the army; and Ernest Blythe, a prominent Free State figure who later reviewed O'Connor's book for the *Sunday Independent*. General Mulcahy was particularly eager to explain the enmity between Cathal Brugha, the minister for defense, and Collins. A few weeks after
his interview, Mulcahy caught O'Connor's eye in a Dublin bookshop and
beckoned him over. As Michael approached, Mulcahy held out a copy of Frank
Pakenham's newly published *Peace by Ordeal* (1935). Half sighing and half
chuckling, he said, "Nobody in future generations will ever realize what idiots
we were."[36]

W. T. Cosgrave reluctantly spoke with Michael one afternoon but supplied very little information. Ernest Blythe offered copious gossip about Kevin
O'Higgins, the justice minister who was murdered in 1927, about Arthur Griffith, leader of Sinn Fein, and even about de Valera.[37] To his mind Collins was
incapable of getting along with any of the other rebel leaders, not just the hot-
headed Brugha. Blythe also talked freely about Collins's love affairs, observing
that he was drawn to "sophisticated women." In fact, the entire interview with
Blythe, judging from O'Connor's notes, must have been lengthy and chatty.
O'Connor was looking for personal anecdotes that revealed Collins the human
being, and not so much for hard information. He was more interested in seizing on the "essential details" of character, and out of the legend was emerging
for O'Connor a character.

What was perhaps the most dramatic interview took place on a Tuesday
evening at the end of May. Hayes had invited Michael to his house in Sandymount to meet a man who was not as famous as Blythe, Cosgrave, or Mulcahy
but who, Hayes knew, was actually closer to Collins. Joe O'Reilly had been
with Collins in London, in the Easter Rising, and in British prisons at Stafford
and Frongoch. When Collins returned in 1918, he tapped O'Reilly to be his
aide-de-camp. For the duration of the fighting O'Reilly served Collins as "courier, clerk, messenger boy, nurse, slave." If O'Connor wanted to know Collins
the living man, then O'Reilly, Hayes insisted, would be the best bet. The evening was pleasant enough, but all of Michael's questions seemed to meet with
the same cordial reticence. O'Reilly was willing to chat about unimportant details, to produce facts about where Collins slept and how many letters he answered, but offered nothing that illumined Collins's emotions or his motives.
Even Hayes pursued a line of questions, "but he too got nowhere." At about
ten o'clock Michael was ready to give up, when an extraordinary thing happened. He had asked O'Reilly how Collins acted when he had to have someone
shot, and at first the response consisted of more of the same cordial misdirec-
tion. Then, as O'Connor describes the scene in *My Father's Son*, O'Reilly

> jumped up, thrust his hands in his trouser pockets, and began to stamp
> about the room digging his heels in with a savagery that almost shook the
> house. Finally he threw himself onto a sofa, picked up a newspaper,
> which he pretended to read, tossed it aside after a few moments, and said
> in a coarse country voice, "Jesus Christ Almighty, how often have I to tell
> ye. . . ?" It was no longer Joe O'Reilly who was in the room. It was Mi-
> chael Collins, and for close on two hours I had an experience that must

be every biographer's dream of watching someone I had never known as though he were still alive. Every gesture, every intonation was imprinted on O'Reilly's brain as if on tape.[38]

Without the aid of a tape recorder or a notebook, however, O'Connor had to re-create the entire scene in the early hours of the morning, scribbling out the voices of a young man and the returned ghost of his commandant.

Even more remarkable was that O'Reilly returned the next evening. The episode had made as profound an impression on him as it had on Hayes and O'Connor. He had been unable to sleep, he said; the voices kept banging around in his head. He returned, he said, because he had to talk about it. "He did so for the rest of the evening," O'Connor says, "and once again Collins was there." O'Connor spent another full evening listening to the voices and an-other early morning recording the scene in his notebook. He filled over eight pages with his compact scrawl, and much of these eight pages was later in-cluded word for word in the published book, which O'Connor titled *The Big Fellow*. From O'Reilly more than anyone else O'Connor got a picture of the in-tensity and power of Collins in moments of stress, of his diabolical temper and his stormy swearing. Where more important people in the IRA saw only the cool and efficient side of Collins, O'Reilly saw the angry outbursts, and as the aide-de-camp, he was often the main target of them. When the book was finally published, Traynor, who had not been present at the interviews with O'Reilly, singled him out as one whose testimony was unreliable; but O'Connor and Hayes believed the "handsome, brightly spoken, golf-playing man" and his ghosts.

After the book was published in 1937 O'Reilly was rumored to be going about Dublin enraged with O'Connor and threatening to shoot him. Walking down Grafton Street two years later, Michael ran into O'Reilly, who mumbled: "I've been trying to see you. Come in here for a cup of tea." Not knowing what to expect, Michael obliged. O'Reilly was embarrassed and evasive until Mi-chael insisted that he say what was on his mind. He told Michael that he wanted a half-dozen copies of *The Big Fellow* to give to friends. The book had gone out of print and there were no copies available in Dublin. Whether or not O'Reilly had really wanted to shoot O'Connor is hard to say; it is curious, how-ever, that no matter what complaints many old gunmen made in Dublin about O'Connor's book, most of them shook his hand in private. After all, in most cases he had told not only Collins's story but their own stories as well.

Throughout O'Connor's research on the book his friend Father Traynor took an active interest, often accompanying him on various interviews. He ar-ranged for Michael to meet with Liam Tobin and Frank Thornton, members of a highly secret squad answerable only to Collins. Tobin talked freely enough, but when the book appeared, he denied everything he had said. The interview with Thornton took place at Father Traynor's residence. His memory was most vivid, particularly about the events of Bloody Sunday and the executions Col-lins supervised himself. Even more remarkable was that he brought with him to that interview files of the secret squad that documented Collins's move-ments and decisions. Because Collins was such a stickler for accuracy, they must have been very thorough files indeed. After the book was finished, Traynor expressed dissatisfaction with O'Connor's use of this material, contending that he had listened to "the most unreliable people, who were interested in building up their own reputation."[39]

When one deals with a man's life, particularly a man with a reputation as variegated as Michael Collins's, truth seems an almost unmanageable mixture of objective fact and subjective response. O'Connor was pluralist enough to accept that it was more than likely that each of the men interviewed was telling the truth about Collins: not the whole truth, but part of the truth. What was emerging from the gossipy anecdotes, ghostly recreations, and self-serving reminiscences was a composite image. Various men told only what they knew, exaggerating those incidents in which they had the greatest part. O'Connor listened as Fintan Murphy described Collins as a "lonesome fucker." He tried to understand Diarmuid O'Hegarty's opinion about Collins's vanity. He tried to reconcile stories of Collins's drinking bouts and visits to prostitutes with avowals of his temperance and chastity. To some, Collins was ruthless and cold-blooded; but to Diarmuid Lynch and Liam Devlin, who saw him weep the night Brugha was killed, he was a maudlin sentimentalist.

Again and again O'Connor was struck, he said, by the "extraordinary consistency" of all the different stories, but this "consistency" was probably a superficial one imposed by the biographer on his subject. Although he often quoted line by line from his notes, the living image of Michael Collins, the man and the character, was more than a little his own, a composite of selected impressions from the Cork days with Childers and MacSwiney, from Gormanstown, and from these eyewitness accounts. O'Connor had once said that where the scholar deals with facts and says no, the poet deals with images and says yes. He admitted in his foreword that he would rather all the documentation disappear than the living image. He may have left a trail of misshapen facts behind him, but he created something alive.

In an assessment of the book he produced, the question turns not on facts but on motives. Why did Frank O'Connor write *The Big Fellow*? Certainly not for the same reason that O'Faoláin wrote biographies of two of Collins's antagonists, Eamon de Valera and Countess Markievicz; nor was his approach like that of O'Faoláin. O'Faoláin was a professional man of letters, capable of the most exacting scholarship and objectivity, but O'Connor was a fumbling, improvising amateur. Perhaps his passion for Collins was like Yeats's fascination with the legendary Cuchulain. Yeats's dictum—that what a man writes is an allegory of his life—can be applied here: No more and no less than his stories, his translations, his novels, or his criticism, O'Connor's biography of Michael Collins was a personal statement. *The Big Fellow* was a labor of love; writing it, he told Foley, left him on a seesaw between exultation and despair. "It swells and swells, contracts and contracts at every enthusiastic or chilling word. AND everyone agreeing it will raise a storm!"[40]

"I have written not for Collins' contemporaries, but for a generation which does not know him except as a name. His friends are properly jealous of his reputation, but sometimes in safeguarding reputations we lose something a thousand times more valuable, the sense of a common humanity." O'Connor wrote the book to preserve a great and misunderstood career; to both Free Staters and Republicans the name of Michael Collins had been obscured by a mixture of fact and myth tinged with animosity for what he represented to the new government. Disillusioned by the homegrown tyranny of the Catholic-

Nationalist establishment, O'Connor felt that the "cold touch of normality" replaced the heat of genius. Apathy and mercantile pettiness had replaced the "day of lofty ideals." For most people, O'Connor felt, when genius "is absent we sigh for it, when it is present we grow weary of its violence and impetuousness." O'Connor had been part of the events of which he wrote, even serving time for his refusal to recognize the Treaty engineered by Collins, and in outlining the life of Collins, he becomes part of his story. Not stopping to ponder whether men make history or history men, O'Connor identifies Collins with those six intense years in which the Irish people forged a new identity.

V. S. Pritchett once told O'Connor that one could describe the character of any Irishman as that of either Swift or Goldsmith—"We are all either the hammer or the anvil, and Swift was unmistakeably the hammer." Quite clearly O'Connor conceived of Collins as the hammer and de Valera as the anvil; nor is there any doubt about where his sympathies lie. For O'Connor the "imaginative improvisation," begun by the martyrs of 1916 and carried on by big men like Collins, had to be kept alive by succeeding generations to assure an Ireland free in the highest sense.

O'Connor's treatment of Collins's death in 1922, etched so deliberately in sympathy, is at once transcendent and humane. To O'Connor the loneliness of Collins became apotheosis when he was killed by a Republican bullet near his home in County Cork. "The countryside he had seen in dreams, the people he had loved, the tradition which had been his inspiration—they had risen in the fallen light and struck him dead." The death of Collins and Griffith destroyed Sinn Fein and with it the hopes of O'Connor's generation.

> It destroyed the prospect which, we are only just beginning to realise, Collins' life opened up: fifteen years—perhaps more, perhaps less—of hard work, experiment, enthusiasm; all that tumult and pride which comes of the leadership of a man of genius who embodies the best in a nation.[41]

For O'Connor the tragedy of Michael Collins was that life in Ireland had returned to normal, to the deadening ruts of conventional thinking and pious timidity, almost as if genius had not ventured through at all.

IO

The Abbey: A Fantasy in Five Acts

Players and painted stage took all my love,
And not those things that they were emblems of.
W. B. YEATS, *"The Circus Animals' Desertion"*

I

ALL around him O'Connor saw signs of a deteriorating sense of destiny in Irish life. He was writing a biography of Michael Collins as much to answer the mediocrity and encrustation of post-Treaty Ireland as to proclaim the possibility of heroic belief and action. Yet he was repelled by the gathering attraction of fascism, including Yeats's flirtation with the Blue Shirts movement. Michael could not countenance this obviously self-defeating ignorance. Besides, Michael had not much political conviction; his ideals for Ireland were of a more spiritual nature. The real reason for his feeling of spiritual emptiness, however, was the absence of AE. He had known for about a year that the old man was dying of cancer, but it was not the imminence of AE's death that chilled him as much as the likelihood of his own social exile. AE had been his point of repose amid the swirl of Dublin events, that steadfast center without which things would most surely fall apart.

On July 17, 1935, AE died in Bournemouth; his body was returned to Dublin for burial. The funeral on Saturday the twentieth was attended by all the most distinguished people of the Free State. The only significant departure from the normal Church of Ireland committal service was the reading of the passage from Ecclesiastes that begins "Let us now praise famous men, and our fathers that begat us." Before the final prayers Frank O'Connor spoke a "few words of farewell" on behalf of the Academy of Letters, offering the gratitude of two generations of Irish writers for the generous encouragement of this great man. With barely contained tears he was also praising a father. Then, cocking a slightly jaundiced eye at de Valera, who stood directly opposite, O'Connor declaimed:

> Circumstances have ordained that in Ireland the modes of life would be few and inadequate; that the genius and sensibility of our race have been directed into two main channels—religious and political. . . . Now the greatest service AE rendered to Ireland was to help in the creation of new modes of life, to stand apart as a symbol of a more complete and comprehensive existence.[1]

AE faced death, O'Connor continued, with the "invisible gaiety" (a phrase he did not use again except in reference to his beloved mother) that looked for new worlds to see. Had he devoted himself to one art alone, O'Connor contended, AE might have been among the world's greats, but then he would not have been AE—and "Ireland, and we, would be poorer for that." He concluded by leaving this great man, his spiritual father, "in the faith that all that we loved in him has been joined to the lightning and its glory forever."

Afterwards Yeats loudly praised the speech as noble and then asked in a whisper if Michael had copies for the press. At the time he might not fully have realized Michael's loss, but within a month or two Yeats could capitalize on the vacuum left by AE in O'Connor's life to bring him into the life of the Abbey Theatre. According to Peter Kavanagh, "Yeats would probably have appointed O'Connor in the first instance, but O'Connor was a 'discovery' of AE."[2]

Among the dreams Frank O'Connor had carried with him when he fled Cork in 1928 was to be part of that bigger-than-life enterprise known as the Abbey Theatre. Undaunted by the disastrous history of his improvised Cork Drama League, which he blamed on provincial narrowness, Michael persisted in his conviction that the theatre needed him—or that at least he needed the theatre. He was certain from the examples of Corkery and Yeats that to be an Irish writer he must exploit the public voice of the stage. The very man who had encouraged O'Connor's fledgling theatre in Cork, Micheál MacLiammóir, had taken the dare and opened a new theatre in Dublin. The Gate, as it was called, promised to be a lively and cosmopolitan alternative to the Abbey. Still, O'Connor had eyes only for heroes, so theatre in Dublin to him meant the theatre of Synge, Lady Gregory, and Yeats.

Actually, he had arrived a bit too late; the Literary Renaissance was coming to an end. Earlier that year (1928) Yeats had rejected *The Silver Tassie,* a new play by the Abbey's most popular playwright, Sean O'Casey. Unsatisfied with Yeats's criticisms of the play—he found it unduly experimental—O'Casey forced the issue in the pages of the *Observer,* thus infuriating Yeats and alienating himself even further. O'Casey's departure for London also furthered the decline of the Abbey Theatre. In spite of a government subsidy the theatre fell further into debt, limiting the kind of plays it could produce to crowd pleasers and slapdash comedies. Only the brilliance of the players kept the box office open. As the Abbey declined, the Gate prospered, forcing the Abbey to compete by producing "European classics." By the end of the decade the audience had assumed control—an audience that, according to Peter Kavanagh, demanded and received flattery, "soft sentiment and superficialities."[3] A theatre begun by the idealism of Yeats and Lady Gregory and revived by the realism of O'Casey was wilting as the dreamers died and the bitter voices departed.

Lady Gregory's death in 1932 left Yeats alone and demoralized; by default he left control of the management of the theatre to Lennox Robinson, who, according to Hugh Hunt, "was rapidly falling a victim to alcoholism." When the Cosgrave government fell in the same year, the Abbey lost Ernest Blythe, a former minister of finance, whose efforts had helped to secure the annual subsidy. The process of replacing Blythe on the Board of Directors brought Yeats into direct confrontation with Eamon de Valera. Yeats refused to accept the nomination of William Magennis as the government representative and sought Frank O'Connor's help in convincing Dr. Richard Hayes to accept the seat instead. Though unfamiliar with the world of the theatre, Hayes finally agreed because he, too, disliked Professor Magennis.[4] Eamon de Valera's Fianna Fáil government pursued a policy of strict nationalism intended to make the country self-sufficient, which meant reducing all unproductive expenditures, including the Abbey subsidy. For some time the Abbey budget had been buttressed by a lucrative American tour. Sensitive to the criticism of Irish-American groups, which held that the Abbey players gave the wrong impression of Irish life, de Valera insisted that *The Plough and the Stars* and *The Playboy of the Western World* be withdrawn from the upcoming tour. Yeats refused to bow to the request, and the government inserted a note in the tour program stating that it accepted no responsibility for the selection of plays.

As Yeats approached the age of seventy he became more and more uneasy about the future of his theatre. His own uncertain health demanded escape from the debilitating Dublin winters, but he had to assure support for his policies in his absence. Recognizing his own lack of energy and will, he sought to bring new life to the Board of Directors, which in 1934 consisted of himself, Robinson, Hayes, and Starkie, whom Yeats had kept on in defiance of de Valera. A good deal of controversy arose as soon as he announced his reorganization plans. In February O'Connor and O'Faoláin wrote letters to the *Irish Times* protesting the revival of old plays, the discourteous treatment given to new dramatists, the scheme for producing Continental plays, and the proposed Board.[5] Believing in the validity of a theatre along the lines of Yeats's and Lady Gregory's, they called for the appointment of an honest to goodness "man of the theatre" with his own vision. Art, they insisted, is made by individuals, not groups or schools. They believed in the potential of individual Irish writers to write good plays, given the chance.

In April, despite the protests, Yeats reorganized the Abbey Board. By doubling the size of the Board of Directors, which determined everything from budget to new plays, he effectively stripped Robinson of his control without bruising his ego. The man had become a deadweight on the theatre, but Yeats was not one to throw his friends to the dogs. He brought in F. R. Higgins, an affable poet who had by now replaced Robinson as Yeats's best friend; Brinsley MacNamara, the author of some of the more successful plays in the Abbey stock; and Ernest Blythe. That summer Yeats got his "man of the theatre" when he engaged Hugh Hunt, a young producer from England who had come to Dublin with a recommendation from the poet John Masefield.[6] The appointment made no sense to O'Connor at the time because it seemed to split the theatre between two producers, Hunt and Robinson. At this point O'Connor was still outside looking in, so he had to content himself with writing nasty letters to the papers and listening to Hayes's blow-by-blow accounts of greenroom maneuverings.

The Abbey's new season opened in August 1935 with a production of the play Yeats had rejected seven years before, O'Casey's *The Silver Tassie*. A better play could not have been deliberately chosen to stir public opinion and bring the Abbey back into the limelight. Joseph Holloway, observer of all things theatrical in Dublin, noted in his diary that the critics slated the play and that the clergy resented its blasphemous parts.[7] O'Casey even sent a rebuttal to the *Irish Press* (published August 20). However, when Brinsley MacNamara joined the attack, criticizing the very Board of which he was a member (albeit the only Catholic member, as he was quick to note in a rambling and pietistic diatribe in the *Irish Independent*), Yeats moved swiftly to keep the tempest from upsetting the cup. On September 3 the Board of Directors replied in the *Irish Press* to MacNamara's allegations.[8] The next day MacNamara tendered a forced letter of resignation in which he accused Yeats of personal attack. Yeats immediately asked Frank O'Connor to fill the vacant seat.

Thus, Michael entered the boardroom for the first time a few days after his formal election on October 11. He was full of nervous apprehension; for MacNamara had been a friend, and though Michael disagreed with the substance of his attack on O'Casey, he admired his stand. Still, here he was, the portraits of Synge and Lady Gregory looming large and the arrival of Yeats imminent. As usual Michael smoked ferociously and ran his fingers through his hair. When Yeats finally entered the room, Michael stood up, almost in salute. Then, noticing the others resolutely lodged in their accustomed chairs, he sheepishly sat down. Yeats noticed the whole thing too, particularly the look of chagrin on Robinson's face.

Yeats now had the gadfly he wanted. He knew from disputes with Michael on the Academy Council that he could be depended upon to keep things stirred up and to fight for the best interests of Irish artistic expression. Moreover, he could count on Michael to fight in the open, perhaps in a too trusting manner, thereby leaving himself open to hurt, but always out front. He once cautioned Michael about his naive belief that people were for the most part not really out to do him harm, in response to which Michael asked if he should treat his fellow Board members as a "gang of masked conspirators."[9] Yeats chose to let him find out for himself.

From the very first, O'Connor was out of step with the rest of the Abbey Board of Directors. He came to the task with more than his usual dose of enthusiasm and idealism, but his childlike innocence was matched by a childish impatience. Assuming that what he considered the right thing to do was an opinion shared by anyone in his right mind, he recoiled in spontaneous indignation when that person did not act accordingly. Thus that quality of innocence that so many found compelling in Michael carried with it an equally unattractive petulance when things didn't go his way. On the other hand, the other members of the Board resorted to more traditional methods of getting their way. Hayes, who knew little about theatre, restricted his attention to financial affairs, except when some political or religious indiscretion in a play under consideration set him off on what O'Connor called "old-maidish tizzies." Higgins joked and glad-handed everyone but carried stories to every corner of Dublin about greenroom deliberations. Blythe, who O'Connor said looked "like a Buddha in grey plaster," usually just doodled Gaelic phrases on his pad and voted whichever way the wind blew. He was solid to the point of permanence, and he outlasted them all. Finally, Robinson "merely sat back in his chair, sucked his pipe and replied in monosyllables."[10] This thoughtful silence, full of mature caution and control, had a dampening effect. It was part of an elaborate greenroom game, which everyone but O'Connor could play to perfection. If he had the genius, then they all had the sagacity. His spoiled-boy tantrums were simply more obvious than their adult manipulations.

At the next few meetings O'Connor's role in the greenroom game became painfully obvious even to him. When a new play came before the group, Robinson reduced it to rubble with ingratiating smoothness. Michael soon saw why no new Irish plays had been appearing: Threatened by new talent, Lennox had been sweeping them all under the table. Immediately Michael struck back and spoke indignantly about the destructive stagnation caused by this belittling of young writers. There was more than a slight personal edge to this attack because a play of his had been quite unceremoniously rejected a year or so before. But he couldn't help feeling some remorse, for Lennox was a good man who was caught in his own despondent inertia. Drinking made his personal dissatisfaction all the more pitiable. The awe and gratitude O'Connor once felt for Robinson, who had given him the job in the Carnegie library system, slid through pity to animosity. When his heroes were toppled, Michael confused their loss with his own and felt betrayed.

Actually, F. R. Higgins, a fellow poet, was more dangerous than Robinson, more devious than Yeats. Being an intriguer he saw intrigue everywhere; being amiable, he kept away from direct confrontation. O'Connor took things at face value and had "no shyness about fighting for any reasonable cause," so Higgins used him as the fall guy for unsavory Board decisions. Joseph Holloway, for instance, laid blame at O'Connor's feet for almost every questionable or controversial action of the Abbey Board from 1935 on.[11] Only Higgins's jocular gossip could have given such ideas to Holloway, a priggish, narrow-minded man, perhaps, but one sincerely devoted to theatre, and an honest mirror of Dublin opinion. Like everyone else, he was prepared to believe the worst about O'Connor. Higgins once brought uncontrollable laughter to the entire Board, O'Connor included, by telling in boisterous detail how he had gotten rid of some bothersome writer simply by saying that Frank O'Connor had turned down the play. "I use O'Connor all the time as an excuse," he roared. "You have no idea of the character that man has in Dublin."[12]

I I

The one person at the Abbey with whom Michael did not quarrel was Hugh Hunt, who was, by his own admission, "totally ignorant of Irish politics; and even more so of the traditions of the Abbey."[13] Only twenty-four and handicapped with an obvious Oxford accent, Hunt was immediately drawn to O'Connor, the only person at all close to him in age. Everything about Michael—his imposing features, booming voice, disorderly appearance, and impetuous manner—was in contrast to Hunt, who struck Michael in turn as a model of self-control. On Sundays they often took long walks in the Dublin hills, talking endlessly about the Abbey. Michael goaded Hunt about his British manner, and Hunt made fun of Michael's singing voice. As different as they were, they became allies; they disagreed about nearly everything in the theatre, but they respected each other. Out of mutual self-interest they supported each other and survived—at least for a few years—the Abbey intrigues.

Yeats intended Hunt and O'Connor to pump new life into the Abbey— Hunt by producing competence on the stage, O'Connor by generating new writing. Hunt did his job, and gave the actors, who had become slovenly under Robinson's tired direction, a new standard to aim at.[14] Long rehearsals were unheard of, and building character was overlooked, as the actors were simply allowed to dredge up old roles. Hunt gave meticulous attention to everything—the text, the lighting, even the wardrobe. At the same time, O'Connor championed such proven young dramatists as Teresa Deevy, Paul Vincent

Carroll, Denis Johnston, and George Shiels. Where Hunt, a theatre man to the bone, emphasized visual effects and deliberate action, O'Connor, a literary man all the way, simply wanted veracity and passion.

By the time the new list of plays for 1936 came up for consideration, Hunt and O'Connor had begun to make their methods felt. The production of Teresa Deevy's *Katie Roche* in March was well received. Hunt got creative performances from such Abbey regulars as Eileen Crowe, F. J. McCormick, and Arthur Shields. In April George Shiels's *The Passing Day* packed the theatre and gripped the attention of the audience. Hunt might have tended to squeeze the poetry from some of the old plays in favor of dramatic effect, but he would not permit any loss of dignity or off-the-cuff vulgarity. O'Connor, who agreed with Yeats's insistence on poetic declamation (the "Senecan" style, he labeled it), argued with Hunt from time to time but generally stayed out of the way.

For some time O'Connor had been eyeing the financially troubled hardware store next door. When he presented his scheme to buy the store in order to add one hundred seats to the house, he cautioned secrecy by the Board members so the proprietors would not inflate the price. At the next meeting Higgins reported sadly that Robinson "had sent the stage carpenter round to the hardware store to inquire the price." That was the last straw. Michael stormed from the room to Hunt's office and thundered, "Will you accept a contract as manager for the next two years?" Hunt was too stunned to refuse. O'Connor returned to the greenroom and rammed through a resolution appointing Hunt.[15] Angered by Robinson's blunder, the Board voted with O'Connor for once.

By this point Michael's emotional loyalties had been completely shredded. In anger he had not only stripped Robinson of his influence but also deprived him of his main source of income. The man who had given Michael his first job had now been sacked by him, a reversal almost too dramatic even for a theatre. The guilt was more than Michael could handle. After a few sleepless nights he took Robinson to lunch to see what could be done. As usual he took the direct approach, feeling that there was really no polite way to confront "an older and more distinguished man" about a problem such as alcoholism. Robinson agreed to see a specialist if Michael would only find some job for him in the theatre. O'Connor had no choice but to put the man in charge of the Abbey School of Acting, a new scheme of the Board's to bring new acting talent into the theatre. His first choice had been Shelah Richards, a prominent Dublin actress. Within a month Robinson had let drink make a shambles of what had been one of the brightest hopes for the future of the Abbey Theatre.[16]

The ascent of Hugh Hunt made Robinson redundant in other ways as well. Over the years his casual indifference to financial matters—"Every theatre in the world carries an overdraft," he often claimed—had brought the Abbey close to bankruptcy. Uneasy over continual threats from bank managers, the rest of the Board voted during the summer of 1936 to redistribute the company shares, effectively stripping Robinson of his controlling interest. Meanwhile Hayes and Blythe pushed for tighter fiscal management. Blythe saw no reason for keeping a full orchestra, and Hayes argued that carrying two producers was luxury enough, but having two secretaries—"Eric Gorman for correspondence and Robinson's brother, Tom, for accounts"—was ridiculous.[17] By August Tom was sacked and the orchestra reduced.

The absence of Barry Fitzgerald and four other senior Abbey actors, engaged elsewhere in a film of *The Plough and the Stars,* gave Hunt the opportunity to use new players in revivals of Synge's *The Playboy of the Western World* and Yeats's *Deirdre.* He proved that an Englishman could stage these great Irish plays without the familiar faces or the old acting style. Even die-hard traditionalists like Holloway were satisfied. Though he filled the theatre, Hunt found his productions the center of "acrimonious debates in the Board room."[18] In the absence of Yeats, who had delayed his return from Majorca, Higgins took it upon himself to upbraid Cyril Cusack, the young actor who played Christy Mahon in *The Playboy,* for stripping the role of its "porthery." When Yeats finally returned in late July, he launched a savage attack on Hunt. O'Connor defended Hunt and his new approach. He also objected to Yeats's criticizing a play he had not even seen. Yeats turned on him, accusing him of not supporting efforts to find a more suitable producer of the Irish plays than Hunt, to which O'Connor calmly said that he refused to reply to greenroom gossip, knowing quite well that Higgins had been behind the entire misunderstanding.

Needless to say, Hunt's production of Yeats's own play a few weeks later faced the same silly acrimony. Actually, the trouble started months before when O'Connor sought permission for a production of his favorite play of Yeats's, *The Player Queen.* But Yeats would not go along with Hunt's desire to have an English actress, Jean Forbes-Robertson, play the leading role, insisting instead on a young Irish actress of whom nothing favorable had been heard. O'Connor refused to use her, so Yeats refused to give them any play but *Deirdre.* Hunt decided to go ahead with the production of this simple tragedy of young love, though the entire arrangement was calamitous. In the first place, Miss Forbes-Robertson, a highly polished actress of the English stage, was too "sophisticated" for the role—to O'Connor it was "like asking the perfect Zerlina to play Isolde." But even more unsuitable was the casting of Micheál MacLiammóir as Naisi, Deirdre's beloved, which may be comparable to asking a perfect Wotan to play Siegfried.[19]

Though not entirely well, Yeats appeared opening night (August 10). O'Connor had given his seats to friends and came only to "check the takings." The house was full and by the applause, he surmised from the foyer, highly impressed. Yeats, refusing even calls for the author, left the theatre muttering "Terrible! Terrible!" Curious, Michael came the next night and found the production worse than terrible. All the rhetorical power of the play, what he called its "Senecan starch," had been sacrificed to Shakespearean atmosphere. However, the audience loved it, and the receipts were the biggest in Abbey history.

Nevertheless, on Wednesday Yeats came to the theatre furious again at Hunt and bent on closing down the play. Learning of this, MacLiammóir refused to continue a second week. O'Connor was trapped between his belief that Yeats was right about this particular production and his belief that in the long run Hunt would revitalize the theatre. Yeats had his way, and Hunt was "debarred from all further productions of Synge, Lady Gregory and Yeats."[20] Disgusted by the constant fuss, Hunt resigned his position as manager but agreed to stay on as producer of new plays only. For the remainder of the year he put together solid productions of plays by Cormac O'Daly, George Shiels, Teresa Deevy, Maeve O'Callaghan, and Paul Vincent Carroll. After Christmas he produced *Blind Man's Bluff* by Ernst Toller and Denis Johnston. The popularity of this murder story prompted Johnston to suggest that Michael recast his story "In the Train" as a play. Reluctant to undertake the project alone, Michael got Hugh Hunt to agree to a collaborative venture.

At the end of May 1937 *In the Train* was staged at the Abbey. In less than three months O'Connor and Hunt had hammered out the play, amidst all their other activities. O'Connor wrote a scenario based on his story and then Hunt transformed it into a useable script. Hunt found little wrong with O'Connor's plot, characters, or dialogue; but when he tried to implement his own theatrical ideas, he met great resistance. His idea of using the accused woman's neighbors as a chorus, "in the manner of a German impressionist play," for instance, struck his collaborator as nonsense.[21] O'Connor could no more stop thinking like a writer than Hunt could stop thinking of theatrical gimmicks, but on the chorus Hunt won out. Then early in rehearsals Hunt asked Michael to give the cast some impression of how he felt the characters in the story should speak. Michael obliged and surprised everyone with his performance. However, when they tried to duplicate his delivery, he stormed from the back of the theatre yelling "No! No! No! That's not it at all." For the next few minutes he kept interrupting. Finally, he walked to the front and said to the lead actress, "There's a girl in Cork who could act ye off the stage." From then on Michael was barred from rehearsals.[22]

Despite the difficulties of collaboration, *In the Train* was astonishingly successful. As always, opening night at the Abbey was a gala affair. The audience, which included the entire Board of Directors except Lennox Robinson, was generous in its response, particularly to Ann Clery and F. J. McCormick, whose performances as the acquitted woman and the drunken traveler were exceptional. O'Connor was most taken by Denis O'Dea's portrayal of the policeman. About the only objection voiced by theatregoers, including the ubiquitous Holloway, was that the chorus was a bit artificial.[23] While Hunt moved about the theatre that night with professional composure, O'Connor was as skittish as an expectant father, accepting best wishes of the first-nighters with sheepish pride. At the end of the play he answered calls for the author with an awkward bow and a few words of thanks to Hugh Hunt.

This expression of gratitude was as genuine as was his nervousness. Michael may have been sarcastic, unbending in his views, even cruel at times to other members of the Board, but beneath the scoffing was something genuine, born of a childlike vision of life. Hunt accepted Michael's thanks as he had his excesses, and thrived on his warmth and enthusiasm. And Michael never neglected to give Hunt the credit for whatever success their collaborative efforts might have achieved on the Abbey stage and in the Abbey greenroom. Twenty years later he still believed that the opening-night performance of *In the Train* proved that Hunt was the very man they needed to bring life to the Abbey tradition. "I knew that night," he wrote in *My Father's Son*, "that Hunt could give us the thing I had dreamed of for years, a theatre that could express the poetic realism that I admired in Liam O'Flaherty, Seán O'Faoláin and Peadar O'Donnell."[24]

Yeats, however, took the opportunity to admonish his protégé. In the greenroom on that opening night Yeats simply said: "O'Connor, you have made a *terrible* mistake. You should have explained in the first scene that the woman was the murderess. You must never, NEVER, keep a secret from your audience." Though stung by a rebuke where he had expected praise, Michael soon came to realize just how right Yeats had been. Try as he might, he was never able to think or write for the stage.

Shortly before the opening of *In the Train* the Directors learned that for the first time in years the Abbey Theatre could boast a credit balance—not much of one, but enough for great rejoicing. After the meeting at which the joyous news was presented, Yeats asked O'Connor to walk with him as far as the bus stop. When they reached their destination, Yeats dramatically pronounced that he had been watching Michael for some time, and that even though he opposed many of his decisions publicly, he had known they were necessary. "Thirty years ago I should have done them myself, but now I am an old man and have too many emotional associations," he said. He thanked Michael and turned to look for the bus. Michael had no idea how to fill the silence. As the bus mercifully approached, Yeats turned toward him and, almost as an afterthought, asked him to consider becoming managing director.[25]

Michael wasn't sure which stunned him more, the speech or its addendum. He knew Hunt deserved the credit for the temporary recovery of the theatre. He also knew that the job of managing director was more than he could handle. Most of the winter he had been in poor health; but then, AE had always told him that any Irish writer worth his salt, except perhaps Padraic Colum, had a pain in the belly. The real trouble was that the theatre business, coming as it did after library hours, left little time for writing. Since finishing his book on Collins, he had done little but tinker with some plays; he had worked on no stories, which in itself might have contributed to his frayed nerves. Managing the Abbey would mean that much less time for writing. It was a thankless job anyway, and it paid nothing, but he wasn't sure if he could refuse Yeats.

III

Meanwhile Michael's mother, who was staying with him at the time, had taken a terrible fall. On her birthday Michael had brought home a bottle of champagne to celebrate the occasion. After a festive dinner he went out for his customary walk while she busied herself with the dishes, singing gaily and generally enjoying the effects of her first champagne. Hearing the gate from Northumberland Road swing open, she rushed to greet him and fell headlong down a small flight of stairs. Seeing her at his feet, hearing her moan, Michael went into such hysteria that the couple who owned the house, the McGarrys, had to make her comfortable and summoned Richard Hayes. After examining her, Hayes took Michael aside and warned him of the worst: Even if she survived obvious fractures to the pelvis and shoulder, she would probably never walk again. Nevertheless, he rang a specialist, who confirmed Hayes's opinion and directed that she be taken immediately to a nursing home on Eccles Street. Michael accompanied her in the ambulance, waited until she was settled in, and then walked home across town after midnight, blaming himself and wondering how to break the news to his father in Cork.[26]

What Hayes had told him while they waited for the specialist—that Minnie had endured chronic appendicitis her entire adult life—intruded again and again in his mind as he walked. He grimaced to think of her stoicism over the years, in the face of physical pain and a "bad marriage" as well. The next day he found her resigned to death, though lively enough to report some stories she had heard from the nurses. But at the end of the week he knew she would survive when she asked him to comb her hair so she would not look so frightful. In ten days she was able to go home to Michael's flat, where the McGarrys had prepared the ground-floor sitting room for her. For over a month Michael attended to her. Around Dublin Frank O'Connor may have been thought an arrogant bully and an uncompromising gadfly, but around home Michael O'Donovan was an affectionate and dutiful son, a little boy who thought nothing too good for his mother. Thus his mind was more than occupied when Yeats sprung the notion of managing the Abbey on him.

For some time Michael had planned to take his holidays in Switzerland in order to consult a famous doctor there about his bothersome stomach. He decided to take his mother along, so early in July they embarked on their adventure, first to London, then to Paris, and finally to Lucerne. Unfortunately, he learned nothing helpful from the famous doctor. His mother, however, supplied him with countless stories from the interesting people she met. Though it was an "intolerable chore" for Michael, who had not only to see to her needs but also to alter some of his own plans (like tramping over the Alps into Italy, as Irish pilgrims had done centuries before, because he was a "born pilgrim"), the whole trip was, as he described it, "the fulfillment of a prophesy, the accidental keeping of promises made to her as a small boy, when she came in exhausted by a hard day's work and I airily described to her . . . the wonderful journeys we should make when I was older and had come into my own." Perhaps because he had traveled so extensively as a boy in the dreamworld of his own mind, he insisted on traveling so much as a man, trying always to rediscover that pilgrim dreamworld.

Eventually Michael had to come back to the realities of Dublin—bureaucratic restrictions imposed on him by the Library Service, harsh criticism of his biography of Collins, and disunity at the Abbey. All these needling frustrations only magnified a deeper discontent that showed itself in his need for intimate female companionship. Shortly after Michael returned from Switzerland, a new face appeared in Dublin: Evelyn Bowen, a Welsh actress married to Robert Speaight, the famous British actor and drama critic. While her husband was on tour in America with the original cast of T. S. Eliot's *Murder in the Cathedral,* Evelyn had come to Ireland to observe the workings of a national theatre company; she wanted to organize something similar in Wales. At first she was just another actress, another flirtation, to Michael. Though enchanted by him—she told some of her friends that the one person she had come to Dublin to meet was the man who had written "Michael's Wife"—she was still married, after all, and he was one of Dublin's most notorious personalities. What's more, she had a young child and any number of attractive suitors to deal with. Nevertheless, starved for the magical comfort of a lover, Michael paid suit to Evelyn Bowen throughout the fall.

Facing O'Connor when he returned from Switzerland was the task of putting together a winter season with a company of actors disgruntled that they had not been included in the upcoming American tour. Mr. de Valera gave a farewell luncheon for the touring Abbey Players. Only three years before, de Valera had tried to dictate the plays to be performed on tour, favoring plays that would present the most flattering picture of Ireland. Yeats had called his hand on that occasion. This time de Valera was thinking past Yeats, maneuvering to control the most visible expression of Irish culture and to assure, as Peter Kavanagh suggested, that it would "express the Ireland of his own imagination."[27]

At the luncheon O'Connor made a speech on behalf of the Board of Directors, which held a rather sharp edge. The chronicle of the Abbey, he contended, was a chronicle of the country, from the natural sentimentality of a subjective nation, through a healing phase of realistic self-laughter, to a phase only beginning to open up, a phase in which Ireland would have to take itself seriously. To him that meant tragedy and with it satire. Then, with an eye again cocked daringly at de Valera, and probably at Blythe and Robinson as well, he asserted that the theatre wanted young writers to express "the emotions and development going on all around us, to interpret the Ireland of today with its problems and tendencies." O'Connor was simply reiterating what he and O'Faoláin had been harping about for years.

On September 30, 1937, the main Abbey troupe, led by F. R. Higgins, embarked for New York, leaving O'Connor and Hunt to carry on with the second company. Internal problems apparently plagued the tour from the start, causing Higgins to stay in New York. In Dublin O'Connor set about finding new plays. George Shiels revised his play *Cartney and Kevney* for staging early in November, while Paul Vincent Carroll came up with a one-acter, *The Coggerers,* which played with a revival of *The Playboy of the Western World* later in that month.[28] O'Connor, who always read the newspaper with an eye for "material," saw a story that fall about a murder case. Recalling a conversation he had had with Shiels about *In the Train,* he hastily stuffed the clipping into an envelope with a note to Shiels: "Here, you're a playwright. Do something with this." The result, a few years later, was *The Rugged Path,* which ran longer than any play in Abbey history.[29] Also that fall O'Connor convinced O'Faoláin to finish a play and talked another Corkman, T. C. Murray, into writing one despite rumors of a long-standing feud between them.

During the writing of *The Big Fellow* Michael had often talked with Richard Hayes about the assassination in 1882 of two important British officials by a secret society known popularly as the Invincibles.[30] Popular sentiment around Dublin had always held that Joe Brady and the other young radicals who took part in the murders were brave patriots betrayed by a vile informer. O'Connor believed that the event split the Fenian movement between political negotiation and criminal violence. However, he was most interested in the actual people, whom he considered simple, sincere men frustrated into misguided violence by the ineffectiveness of political posturing. Assassination was their only answer to the British policy of systematic brutality, to the arrest of Parnell, and to the massacre of some children in a mob rejoicing at Parnell's release. To him the drama emanated less from the event and its cause than from its effects on the people involved.

Following the production of *In the Train* Michael had suggested to Hunt the idea of a play about the Phoenix Park murders. Hunt confessed to having no knowledge of Irish history but was willing to give it a try; for nearly a month the two of them dug up everything they could find on the Invincibles. Then

O'Connor wrote a scenario. Yeats had always told him that, when writing a play, what he first needed to do was to get the fable right. If he could not put it on the back of a postcard, then he did not have a play. But in trying to portray a group of people who had allowed exaggerated emotion to run wild, O'Connor let his own enthusiasm run wild: His scenario was twenty pages too long. Hunt cut it to seven scenes and sent Michael back to write the dialogue. On balance, this collaborative process went very well, O'Connor creating the story and characters, Hunt providing dramatic coherence and localizing effect.[31]

Once again Hunt asked Michael to stay away from rehearsals, not an easy thing considering his concern that Hunt would overplay the terrorism as he had in the writing stage. He also knew that this was a Dublin play needing the O'Casey touch. Though far from the Dublin voice, Michael's dialogue was nonetheless closer than the cockney harshness favored by Hunt. When finally asked to attend a rehearsal, Michael said nothing. He was befuddled, for instance, by Cyril Cusack in the role of Tim Kelly. Then it struck him that Cusack was underplaying the part and creating a sense of loneliness not apparent in the lines. As it turned out, Cusack's improvisations kept the play from sliding monotonously into melodrama.

In the middle of the dress rehearsal Hunt and O'Connor were summoned to the foyer, where they found two very old women wearing black shawls over their tattered clothing. One of them stepped forward, identified herself as Joe Brady's sister, and held out a parcel. "Ye'll be wantin' these for Joe," she said. "What are they," asked Hunt. "His things, and the crucifix, sir." "Whose things," Michael asked impatiently. "Joe's things. His suit, the wan he had on him when they took him, sir, and the ivory crucifix that her ladyship gave him." "You mean the actor playing Joe's part will want the suit," said Hunt politely. "Thank you indeed, but Mr. O'Gorman will not need them." "Oh, no sir. Joe'll be needing them, won't he?" said the other woman, quite as if she had no idea what a play was. Hunt returned to the stage muttering, while Michael watched the women disappear into the rainy night. Years later both he and Hunt would regret not having accepted the relics offered in an act of incredible innocence.[32]

The next evening was unusually charged with tension. Radio Eireann had its broadcasters out for the usual opening-night interviews with the usual opening-night celebrities. Joseph Holloway, the perennial first-nighter, observed "an air of eagerness and excitement in the animated scene. The orchestra played Irish airs."[33] Actually, the excitement emanated from a rumored protest demonstration by dissident left-wing groups. Michael, accompanied by his old friend Dermot Foley and his new companion Evelyn Bowen, entered the theatre in a state of agitated self-consciousness. Chatting with Hunt, Hayes, and O'Faoláin in the foyer, he expressed concern about the gathering crowd—although they were obviously Dubliners, their faces were not regularly seen at the Abbey and it seemed likely to him that they were former rebels. The possibility of violence grew with the appearance of "Yeats' old girl friend Maud Gonne," who still had considerable influence in certain rebel circles. However, at curtain time she took her place in the stalls with Dorothy Macardle and Jack Yeats. The play began without incident.[34]

Some in the audience were stunned, as the curtain went up, to see Hunt's ingenious stage design, a split-level arrangement that served as different public houses in the opening scenes and separate cells in the closing scenes. But the blustering rebel banter with which the play opened set everyone at ease, for the time being. Here, they thought, was the old Abbey gang clowning to the hilt. The older Fenians and the young Invincibles, safely segregated in their own public houses, attacked each other verbally. These self-styled patriots were dressed in the most exaggerated stage-Irish manner and carried on in the coarsest way. Holloway in his diary condemned the author for resorting to gutter language. O'Connor, who was raised among the swearing and swaggering poor, knew that street people would express their indignation over official British acts of brutality in anything but lace-curtain conversation. Through this slightly ironic atmosphere, which Roger McHugh called "blathering ineptidude," cuts the brash act of Joe Brady and Tim Kelly—the murder of Lord Frederick and Thomas Burke in Phoenix Park.[35]

Immediately, the boisterous chatter subsides. The murderers take refuge in a pub near the park where they cast uneasy shadows of pride and guilt and fear. The audience apparently was uneasy too, judging by Holloway's account:

> The audience laughed heartily at much of the play. Such as the scene where the Invincibles come into the pub for a drink after their deed of blood had been accomplished. They cut such a droll figure all muffled and slouching that the audience could not refrain from laughing, and who could blame them, for anything more unlike men trying to avoid attention could not be imagined.[36]

Actually, Holloway perceived the switch from farce to tragedy; he simply judged it melodrama rather than irony. At this point Hunt pulled another theatrical trick out of his bag, one that neither O'Connor nor the critics really liked. To announce the murders he sent paperboys through the audience hawking newspapers with the bold headline "Phoenix Park Murders—Extra! Read all about it." The dissension brewing in the first scene boils over after the murder. The Fenians offer a reward and some of the Invincibles resign in protest, but none escapes capture.

After the intermission the action of the play takes place in Kilmainham jail. Here O'Connor's hand is more visible. History had given Brady and Kelly ample attention, though public opinion had exaggerated their heroism. But the figure who intrigued O'Connor from the first was James Carey, the informer. In his research O'Connor found him a man not at all weak or opportunistic, rather one who stumbled into a conspiracy he wanted no part of because of its gross mismanagement. O'Connor's rendering of Carey is made all the more subtle by its juxtaposition to the overly efficient Inspector Mallon. What occurs is a struggle of wills that Mallon wins by playing on Carey's vanity; he makes Carey think he is being betrayed by Curley, the man who in the opening scene defeated Carey for the chairmanship of the Invincibles. More out of pride than fear, Carey informs. It is Carey's fall, not the execution of Brady and Kelly, that proves the Invincibles not invincible. In scene 4 one of the warders talking to Brady about Carey says: "Oh, he's a terrible man. First he wanted to be ringleader of the Invincibles and now nothing will do but to be ringleader of the Informers. . . . First in everything! First in everything! Oh, pride is a terrible sin, Mr. Brady, a terrible, terrible sin!"[37]

Awaiting execution, Brady is visited by the sister of one of the murdered men, a nun, who entreats him to repent the one act giving his life any meaning at all. His defiance of the church is more than slightly reminiscent of young Michael O'Donovan's when he returned to Cork from Gormanstown. Likewise, Brady's curse on the Irish people for wanting murder and then being repelled when they get it sounds the playboy motif with which O'Connor was becoming so fascinated. "No, 'twas the names they were afraid of: 'murder,' 'knives,' 'assassins,' " Brady shouts. "Like the crawling reptile Carey, Ireland ran away from the name they put on her and went whining to her prayers. But one day, mark my words, she'll do the same thing to Parnell, and then he'll know what we went through in the long nights at Kilmainham." By that point the audience had become primed for the culmination—the tragic apotheosis of the Invincibles in the grand Irish manner.

According to newspaper accounts, Tim Kelly, the choirboy drawn into the web of intrigue out of devotion to the older Joe Brady, sang to Brady in the next cell the night before their hanging. As Cyril Cusack sang the hymn, "Hail, Queen of Heaven," a chorus situated backstage came in softly and hesitantly, like prisoners saluting those soon to be hanged. If Hunt had not managed to draw the audience into the play with his paperboys, he accidentally managed it here, for the audience joined in—hesitantly and softly at first, then with boldness and triumph. Michael nearly came out of his seat at the sound. He grabbed the hands of Dermot and Evelyn in his own personal triumph. The audience was ecstatic. Joseph Holloway wrote that he left the theatre as the curtain descended, cheers ringing from the audience—"evidently more impressed than I was by the crude picture they had just seen limned of a very painful episode in our country's history."[38] Obviously, Holloway was not around when O'Connor answered repeated calls for the author. Again he thanked them on behalf of himself and Hugh Hunt. To his mind this acceptance of a play about such a "dangerous subject" signaled a new maturity of outlook in Ireland.

After the performance a lavish party was given by Robert Collis, a prominent pediatrician and sometime playwright. The magic of the evening had not yet worn off, so for a while Michael held forth in grand style, singing and telling stories. By the time Evelyn had excused herself and gone home, Michael had begun to worry about the morning press notices. Well before dawn he left the party to pace the streets with Dermot and Willie O'Gorman, who had performed so admirably as Joe Brady. Though Michael scoffed and claimed not to give a damn about the critics, he was obviously anxious. Peter Kavanagh in the *Irish Press* gave the play cautious praise, while Andrew Malone, drama critic for the *Irish Times,* was not so generous. Michael read the morning notices at the newsstand. So upset was he with Malone's remarks that he threw down the paper and walked all the way back to his flat, then took to his bed and stared at the ceiling for two days.

The notices stung his pride and upset him momentarily, but Lennox Robinson's actions utterly infuriated him. During a debate at the Gate about the political implications of the play, Robinson had condemned O'Connor and Hunt for dramatizing an event "that was bound to cause pain to the relatives of the men who had been hanged by the British fifty years before."[39] At no time when considering the play had Robinson raised any such objection, and in fact had offered O'Connor a few helpful suggestions to improve the dialogue. Mi-

chael heard about Robinson's stab in the back from Hayes, who was so outraged that he asked for a special meeting to consider Robinson's immediate
dismissal. After all, Brinsley MacNamara had been unceremoniously forced to
resign for a similar breach of public decorum.

Once again Yeats moved to defuse an explosion. He invited O'Connor to
tea and explained his position. "Personal reasons," he said, meaning loyalty to
a dear, if somewhat bothersome, friend. At the next meeting of the Board Yeats
entered the greenroom with the slow dignity of a king. As usual, only Michael
stood in salute, an odd gesture in this instance, considering the occasion. After
Hayes had stated his case for Robinson's dismissal, Yeats spoke: "Every member of this Board realizes that Lennix Robinson is no longer responsible for his
actions."[40] While Robinson sat anchored in despondent inertia, Yeats dictated
the terms—a published apology. O'Connor worshiped Yeats more than he
hated Robinson; he voted with the majority to kill Hayes's resolution. But
when Hayes read Robinson's statement, he was furious. It was little more than
self-justification. He insisted that Michael confront Yeats. A "handsome apology" came by return post, written, as it turned out, not by Robinson but by
Yeats. As Hunt would later observe, "Further trouble followed."[41]

I V

This unfortunate turn of events left O'Connor in a strong position at the
Abbey, temporarily. No one could have predicted that Robinson would be able
to turn even this ignominy to advantage. However, with all he had to think
about, O'Connor found it hard to protect his flanks against conspiracy. He had
a theatre to manage, a library to supervise, and an ailing mother to care for.
But his greatest distraction was Evelyn Bowen, with whom he was now being
linked by scandal-hungry Dubliners. Seán O'Faoláin's play *She Had to Do
Something* was scheduled for production the day after Christmas. From the
outset O'Faoláin had insisted that the title role be played by Evelyn.[42]
O'Faoláin wanted a foreign actress to play the part of a foreign woman who,
feeling the claustrophobia of a provincial Irish town, decides she must do
something to bring a little life to the place. To his mind Evelyn filled the
bill.

Naturally, the Abbey actors held a rather proprietary attitude toward
"their" theatre. Jobs were scarce enough as it was without another leading
role going to another exile from the London stage. How, they argued, could a
truly Irish theatre flourish under such conditions? When the cast was announced, a delegation came to Hunt demanding that one of the regular leading
ladies play the part instead of Evelyn Bowen. Hunt refused. They threatened to
strike. Ironically, O'Connor found himself in the unaccustomed role of peace-
maker. It would have been difficult enough to soothe the ruffled feathers of a
second company stuck at home with no chance of landing fat Hollywood contracts without the additional suspicion of personal bias. It was general knowledge that Michael and Evelyn were a bit more than casual friends. Shortly
after becoming a director, Michael had sought advice from his only real friend
among the Abbey actors, Arthur Shields, brother of the famous F. J. McCormick. Shields had told him: "Treat us as though we were children. Nice chil-

dren, of course; children that you're fond of, but not as grown-ups." O'Connor either ignored or forgot that extraordinary piece of advice and as a result never had the confidence of the actors.

Actually, his bad blood with the players was to some extent of his own making. Though given to histrionic declamation, O'Connor was utterly incapable of presenting a false face. He shouted if displeased, usually in strong language; he waxed enthusiastic if happy, often in absurdly glowing terms. He never learned to act with actors, to play the fatherly critic and whip-wielder. He either insulted them by showing them up or patronized them by showering them with excessive praise. As so often in his life, he was an amateur among professionals, which meant not only that he was distrusted but that he distrusted himself. The professional theatre person or linguist or literary critic distrusted even O'Connor's most penetrating intuitions merely because he was not pedigreed. And he himself, underestimating those intuitions or overestimating the proven ways of established professionalism, vacillated between deference and rebellion. As it happened, he managed to quell the threatened strike by forcing auditions before the entire Board of Directors. However, as rumors of his affair with Evelyn quickened, many in the Abbey observed this act of diplomacy with rather bemused skepticism.

She Had to Do Something opened as planned. When the curtain fell, the audience gave Evelyn and the rest of the cast polite, almost enthusiastic applause.[43] When the author was called, the house erupted in contradictory jeers and bravos. O'Faoláin took the opportunity to insult the audience, comparing its puritan response to his play to the puritan response of provincials in the play to a visiting ballet company. He reminded them of what AE had maintained years before: The Abbey had to remain heretical or close its doors. To O'Faoláin the integrity of the writer was at stake. What he could not say was that the integrity of the actors, forced to placate a stage-Irish audience, was also at stake. He could not say what Joyce had said years before: The Irish theatre had fallen into the hands of the rabblement.

Less than a month after O'Faoláin's play closed Michael called on Evelyn unexpectedly one evening and unceremoniously proposed marriage. "But I don't love you," she protested. "Oh yes you do. You just don't know what love is," he asserted gallantly. "How can you say that, you don't know anything about me." "I know enough," he replied. "You think love is an emotional, physical reaction between two people. But it's not, it's spiritual." "I know that too," she insisted. "You do not and I'm going to save you from a string of promiscuous affairs." Michael kissed her earnestly and left feeling confident and heroic. After his jaunty departure, Evelyn reflected on the whole stunning performance. She recalled once telling him about a confrontation with one of the actresses in her husband's company. The woman claimed to be in love with Speaight, and in response to Evelyn's laughing dismissal she sarcastically informed her that not only had she slept with him but that all of the other girls in the chorus of *Murder in the Cathedral* had slept with him too. Michael had listened carefully to Evelyn's account, interested not so much in the infidelity as in why she was telling him. Wondering if she had exaggerated the story to justify her own behavior in Dublin, he had challenged her to find out the truth. She thereupon wrote to Speaight in America and inquired about the allegation. The response came in a telegram from Chicago: "Opening night great success, play well received, own performance acclaimed. Notices excellent. Sorry True. Bobbie."[44]

By the end of the year it was common knowledge that Evelyn Bowen and Frank O'Connor were more or less living together. On New Year's Day, 1938, Hugh Hunt was returning to Dublin from Christmas holidays in England and met Robert Speaight on the Holyhead boat. Knowing what Speaight would find, Hunt was extremely uneasy. What he didn't know was that Speaight was only traveling to Dublin to see his young son and to entreat Evelyn to cooperate in his efforts to secure an annulment so that he could marry another woman. The sordidness of the entire episode set the tone for the tangled domestic affairs of Michael and Evelyn.[45]

As controversy over O'Faoláin's play swirled, pressure mounted on O'Connor. Of course, his relationship with Evelyn caused him no end of grief. As much as he tried to dismiss the rising gossip, he could not escape the fact that it undermined his position at the Abbey and exaggerated his notoriety. Scoff as he would at public opinion, Michael cared a great deal about how people felt about him, particularly as his reputation now affected Yeats's theatre. Furthermore, he had been ill continually since returning from Switzerland. His physician, Richard Hayes, could find no physical cause for Michael's chronic stomach pain, the boils on his neck, or his loss of weight. He was extremely concerned about Michael's erratic diet, his inordinately high blood pressure (medication for which Michael refused to take), and his chainsmoking. No amount of warning from Hayes, no amount of pleading to slow down, could deter Michael, however, from his intense and obsessive commitments.

O'Connor was more than normally uneasy about his next play, *Moses' Rock,* scheduled for production in February 1938. The success of *The Invincibles* had tempted him to continue the same historical theme in a trilogy of Fenian plays. However, *Moses' Rock* was not proving quite so easy, possibly because it was a more creative effort than *The Invincibles,* closer in substance and tone to his short stories. The historical circumstances surrounding the last days of Parnell were to serve in the second play as a backdrop for a drama closer to O'Connor's instincts: the drama of little people struggling with personal relationships. It is a love story involving a young woman and three suitors, each of whom stands out by virtue of his political allegiance. The problem facing O'Connor was that he was taking on the two main forces in Irish life: nationalism and Catholicism. Parnell is said by one suitor, a journalist, to have the solid support of the Irish people. The family doctor adds cynically that such support reminds him of Moses' rock, and cautions the young journalist to remember the power of the church.

Three years later, in a preface for a planned publication of the play, O'Connor wrote that *Moses' Rock* was part of his attempt to bring more plays into the Abbey "containing a criticism of Irish life," because it seemed at the time that "Irish literature was waking up to the realities of life about it."[46] Reflecting on the play itself, he claimed that "this little fantasy" came into his mind during his work on the life of Collins. Mixing with men like O'Reilly, McLeahy, Mulcahy, and the rest, listening to their memories of the Fenian movement, he realized that their Ireland "was a simpler, more heroic affair. It was an Ireland full of ideals, an Ireland at war with the gombeen man." Many who saw his play in 1938 felt the glow of that past time and were entertained by it, but the critics again were split. O'Connor was rubbing nerve endings many believed better left unrubbed. And though no one said it aloud, not a few in Dublin whispered that the whole subject of extramarital affairs and divorce hit rather close to O'Connor's own doorstep.

Seeing O'Connor in one of the back rooms of the Abbey on the opening night of *Moses' Rock,* T. C. Murray wished him luck. O'Connor made this curious reply: "It would want to be. I need it." At the time Murray thought this strange and said so a few minutes later to Joseph Holloway.[47] He would not have thought it quite so strange had he known Michael's physical condition at the time. For indeed he was so ill, so overwrought from the pressure of the past four or five months that, shortly after the curtain fell, he collapsed. Evelyn was terrified, but Hayes was on the spot immediately. A week later Michael seemed no better and his weight had dropped below 140 pounds. Hayes was seriously concerned because his tests had ruled out ulcers. Suspecting cancer, he ordered an extended sickleave from the library and from the theatre.

During his convalescence Michael received a note from his publisher Harold Macmillan expressing concern about another missed deadline. He advised Michael to decide whether he wanted to be a good public servant or a good writer, because it was impossible to be both. In February he and Evelyn talked about Macmillan's advice. Was it possible, they wondered, to live together on his income as a writer? They had talked about marriage, but the annulment proceedings undertaken by Speaight were expected to drag on for nearly a year. Evelyn insisted on caring for Michael, but living together unmarried was impossible in Dublin. So, with the help of O'Faoláin, the couple found a house to rent in County Wicklow, far enough from Dublin to assure peace and detachment, yet near enough to the train to keep him within striking distance. By March Hayes had become convinced that Michael had terminal cancer; he gave Michael five years to live, a prognosis at once generous and incorrect. On April 1, 1938, Michael retired from the Library Service with an annual pension of seventy-five pounds.[48] He was only thirty-four years old.

V

Shortly before the first Abbey company was due to return from America, Lennox Robinson hatched the idea of holding a festival, as he said, "to represent the work of the Irish National Theatre during thirty years."[49] From the start O'Connor opposed the idea; rather than promote fresh plays, such a festival could only indulge the past. Though he did not say it in so many words, he also knew that it would insinuate Robinson back into the limelight. With Higgins back in town to support Robinson the idea became a certainty.

Once again O'Connor was in a situation—humiliating at best, self-destructive at worst—inflicted on him for operating outside the rules of the tribe. Nearly ten years in the capital had not erased Michael's provincial manner; he brought scorn on himself by an open contempt for the pettiness of Dublin literary and theatrical life. Nor had a decade of literary prominence erased a gnawing sense of inferiority about his lack of formal education; he continued to move with deference to his betters, with uneasy respect for his equals, and with unmasked contempt toward dolts. For too long he had played by the rules of his boys' weeklies, by romanticized codes of honor and decency. But Hayes, Robinson, Higgins, and Blythe, to say nothing of de Valera and the bishops, played by a different set of rules. If O'Connor had been an outsider in Dublin, he was even more isolated away from it. Speaight's annulment proceedings had been stalled by Evelyn's refusal to lie about their marriage, so he was now suing for divorce in English courts on grounds of her adultery with Michael O'Donovan. "Responsible for a woman and her son, waiting for the end of ecclesiastical and divorce court proceedings," O'Connor felt himself over a barrel.[50]

On June 3, 1938, O'Connor sent a brief letter of resignation to Yeats. Hayes had tried to dissuade him, which Michael appreciated, but he was extremely sensitive about living openly with Evelyn. He certainly didn't want to resign, but a puritanical sense of obligation, inherited he claimed from his mother and from Daniel Corkery, compelled him. Yeats responded with a gentle letter that referred mainly to the recent Cuala edition of *Lords and Commons.* A postscript added, almost as a casual afterthought: "I say nothing about your resignation because I have much to say on the subject in the Board meeting on Friday. Your book is beautiful and moving."[51] By the end of the month Michael reconsidered, throwing himself into the frantic planning of the first Abbey Festival.

So far as the program was concerned, O'Connor lost on all counts. His animated advocacy of Colum's *Thomas Muskerry* killed any chances of staging that little masterpiece. Instead, Robinson insisted on Shaw's *The Shewing up of Blanco Posnet.* O'Connor also pushed for Yeats's two new plays, *The Herne's Egg* and *Purgatory,* and for his own favorite, *The Player Queen.*[52] Yeats still wouldn't release *The Player Queen,* however, because of the old slight. That meant settling for *Kathleen ni Houlihan* and *Purgatory.* Thus, as Hugh Hunt describes that first Abbey Festival, on "twelve successive nights [August 8–20, 1938] seventeen plays, many of them the one-act classics of the Abbey's repertoire, were presented to an audience, a large percentage of which was gathered from America, Britain, and the Continent. By day there were lectures on the Abbey and its dramatists, exhibitions of pictures and manuscripts connected with the theatre, and visits to places of cultural interest."[53]

During deliberations by the Board in Yeats's absence, Hayes lodged strong objections about *The Herne's Egg.* He even threatened to resign, so adamant was he about the obscenity of the play. Unable to see his argument, Michael asked him after the meeting exactly what was obscene about the play. Hayes explained that Higgins had told him that Yeats himself had told him that "the seven men who rape the princess should represent the seven sacraments." The idea struck Michael as outrageously stupid and theologically naive, but no amount of arguing would change Hayes's mind. Exasperated to the limit, Michael brought the issue up at the next meeting, offering to produce the play at his own expense. Yeats turned on him in anger and asked why he hadn't insisted on producing the play over Hayes's objections. "You had the majority behind you."[54] O'Connor backed down, unable to recall the exact details of the previous meeting. Later he asked Hayes about the vote. Only Blythe had supported O'Connor, on the dubious grounds that the play was so obscure anyway that no one would understand it enough to object to it. Higgins, who had confused Hayes in the first place, apparently had carried back to Yeats the story that O'Connor had been the one to change his position, assuming that even Yeats was prepared to believe the worst about the headstrong provincial from Cork. Shortly before Yeats left for the south of France that fall, Hayes, a man as upright as he was pious, set Yeats straight about the entire matter. Though Yeats never apologized directly to O'Connor, he did make his feelings perfectly clear to Higgins.

Unable to do much about the list of plays, O'Connor asked to deliver one of the morning lectures, specifically the one on J. M. Synge. Actually, he was not exactly bursting with things to say about Synge, but ever since the publication in 1931 of Corkery's *Synge and Anglo-Irish Literature* he had wanted to respond. O'Connor considered Corkery's conception of Irish literature too exclusive; Irish literature was more than Land, Nationalism, and Church. Because Corkery demanded that writers represent these three elements, he dismissed Yeats, Shaw, and nearly everyone else he could not find at a "hurling match in Thurles."[55] Since he was fond of Synge's work, Corkery had written his book to justify Synge's presence on the Irish side, even to the point of excusing his Protestantism. Thus O'Connor was not only lecturing on Synge—to salvage his work for the other side, whatever that was—but championing all the Olympians of the Literary Renaissance, especially Yeats. In a personal sense, he was rejecting a father, as it were, while preparing to bury another. Less than a year later Yeats would die and the last of his literary fathers would be gone.

As always in his literary opinions, O'Connor hit close to home in this lecture, risking more self-exposure here than in his stories.[56] If his plays failed to express the "allegory of his life," his criticism managed to say more about him than about his chosen subject. When he began by asserting that the staying power of Yeats, Lady Gregory, and Synge stemmed from their audacity, their almost heroic decision to stay in Ireland and fight it out, he was justifying—if not to the small audience assembled for the lecture in the Gresham Hotel on August 9, 1938, then at least to himself—his own stubborn resistance to Irish Nationalism and Irish Catholicism. When he said that nationalism was as inescapable as one's sex or hometown, he was speaking as an artist who had learned that art came from individuals, not from representatives of schools, movements, or cultures. Corkery, Moore, and Sheehan refused to fight, in O'Connor's opinion. Shaw, Joyce, and eventually O'Casey fled the fight. Among the audacious and the tenacious of the so-called Literary Revival were Synge, Lady Gregory, and Yeats. O'Connor would not have been arguing the point if he had not counted himself, too, among the audacious and the tenacious of the post-Revival generation.

Having given his answer to why Synge, Lady Gregory, and Yeats were Irish writers, O'Connor had to answer why they stayed to fight and what they fought against. They stayed, he asserted, because of a philosophy that "everything must be created anew." What they fought was a middle-class optimism of which nationalism represented only one aspect. Aesthetically, the middle class depended on progress, on the appreciation of the value of things in time. The view of life held by the Olympians was "ascetic," by which O'Connor meant a chosen impoverishment which stripped all thought and language and form to their basic, concrete source.

O'Connor attached his notion of "museum theatre" to Yeats's theory of

depreciating purity of form. Yeats's theory holds that the ascetic anchors himself in some bedrock and "re-invents the wheel," as it were, daily. Thus,
O'Connor maintained, Lady Gregory could speak of the art of original sin,
Synge of the simple collaboration of audience and artist, Yeats of unities and
extremities. The intervention of a middle class which O'Connor equated with
Corkery's priests and patriots, adds needless ornamentation, superfluity, and
abstraction. On a fundamental dichotomy, articulated in this lecture, rests the
opposition that dominates all the rest of O'Connor's critical writing: pure versus impure, instinct versus judgment, objective versus subjective, thesis
(Yeats) versus antithesis (Joyce). Indeed, the idea allows him very neatly to
explain why Synge does not fit into Corkery's categories. But more than that it
allows him to explain why he does not fit Corkery's categories himself. Corkery's criticism of Synge was not wrong, it was beside the point because he
failed to see what Synge, Lady Gregory, and Yeats were doing. O'Connor believed that Corkery once wrote from the ascetic impulse himself, that he once
stripped Irish life and language bare, and that he once triggered a revolution in
the soul of two Cork boys, fathered them into a literary life, and then orphaned
them by selling out to the tyranny of middle-class abstractions just to obtain a
university chair. He was, O'Connor lamented at the very end of the lecture,
"the greatest artist of his generation," but he had left them. O'Connor never
forgave Big Mick for throwing his wife and son out on the streets; he never
forgave Daniel Corkery either.

Turning to Synge's plays, O'Connor spoke about them briefly in terms of
this purified aesthetic. He makes no mention of the theory of collaboration that
would buttress his later criticism. But like anyone trying to juggle dichotomies,
he becomes entangled in the dilemma. In fact, he remained suspended his entire life between this Great Man Aesthetic (the Ascetic hero) and his own Little Man Ethic (the values he inherited from the slums of Cork), trying at once
to keep to the High Road of Style and the Low Road of Subject. Ironically, it
was the Irish-Catholic middle class that he captured so faithfully and sympa-
thetically in his fiction, not the peasantry or the gentry. "Between-ness" always seemed to hound his literary path. In that tension is the base of his
unique contribution and the ceiling to his greatness. It explains why he did not
soar any higher, why he never wrote a big novel or a truly compelling play.

The very next evening the Abbey crowd heard Yeats's own last words in
the play *Purgatory*. The Old Man, addressing his son immediately prior to that
climactic moment in which a light in the window reveals a young girl, says in
confessional finality:

> I ran away, worked here and there
> Till I became a pedlar on the roads,
> No good trade, but good enough
> Because I am my father's son,
> Because of what I did or may do.

The idea of *Purgatory* is that crime inherited by blood can never be purged, no
matter how carefully the inheritor tries to wipe out all its traces. At the fall of
the curtain Yeats rose to address the Abbey audience—for the last time, it
turned out. He said, "I have put nothing in this play because it seemed picturesque: I have put there my own convictions about this world and the next."

Cyril Cusack, sitting next to O'Connor in the stalls that night, considered the applause reverential not to the play but to the man, the "poetic father-figure" of a theatre.[57] But O'Connor had ears only for the heroism and the loneliness. To him the Old Man in the play was the old man in the stalls who had written the play, voicing the loneliness of the artist, the outcast, the beggar, and the blind man. The next day, after Higgins's lecture, O'Connor vigorously defended the play to an American priest who had questioned its orthodoxy.[58] He called it a "testament of beauty and poetry." Once again O'Connor might have been unveiling the allegory of his own life more than Yeats's; *Purgatory* perhaps reminded him of the inequality of his own parents, aristocratic mother and tramp father, who begat a genius.

Following the Abbey Festival Michael's moods fluctuated between manic exuberance and severe melancholy. His own health had improved under Evelyn's care, but he was concerned about Yeats's declining health. The intrigues at the Abbey were disconcerting to him, but the lecture on Synge had purged some of his rage, for he had put Corkery in his place and felt that he had staved off, for a time, the Catholic-Nationalist assault on Anglo-Irish literature. He even felt some renewed optimism about his novel, which was due in the hands of his publisher by the end of 1938. But no sooner would he gather momentum in his work than his concentration would be shattered by the annulment business or by a letter from O'Faoláin about intrigues at the Abbey. As much as he needed solitude to recover his health and to write, he still missed his friends and the activity surrounding the theatre. Soon he and O'Faoláin, distraught over the conservative turn the Abbey's policies were taking, began a barrage of correspondence to the editor of the *Irish Times*, arguing that the original conception of the Abbey was being betrayed.[59]

For all practical purposes the first Abbey Theatre Festival marked the end of more than Frank O'Connor's brief tenure. It was the end of something far greater, and indeed many of the participants that fortnight knew it. Within a few years most of the fine Abbey players would leave for more lucrative and challenging positions. Cyril Cusack claimed that the exodus of actors was due to the conflict between Yeats's notion of a theatre purified and ceremonial and an actor's natural desire for a "theatre theatrical."[60] O'Connor's position was that without the infusion of new plays the theatre would die. To that end, he opposed any rudeness to writers. For instance, earlier that summer the Board, in the absence of Yeats and O'Connor, had rejected Paul Vincent Carroll's *The White Steed*. Hunt had written to O'Connor asking his intervention. Michael had not yet read the play but was furious at the thought of a first-rate writer being treated so thoughtlessly. He asked Yeats to reconsider the decision.

Early in September Yeats called a special meeting of the Board of Directors to review the *White Steed* decision.[61] By coincidence O'Connor was in Dublin en route to London where he was to make two wireless broadcasts for the BBC. What he thought would be merely a skirmish in the greenroom turned out to be a major confrontation. Yeats read his own report; though critical of the play, he graciously offered to sponsor a production elsewhere. O'Connor's report said exactly the same thing, though later Higgins carried the tale to Carroll that it was O'Connor alone who had axed the play. Yeats apologized to Michael for thinking that he had called for a reconsideration of the play on grounds of his friendship with Carroll. He asked Michael to respond personally to Carroll. In a letter neither gracious nor malicious O'Connor simply apologized for the discourteous treatment and explained that the decision had been upheld for artistic rather than moral reasons. Later Carroll used this very letter to attack O'Connor and his plays. Like everyone else in Dublin, he remained ignorant of the lengths O'Connor often went to in order to help people; all he recalled was the candor of his criticism.

The upshot of all this intrigue was the resignation of Hugh Hunt in October. For three years Michael had backed Hunt at every turn, protecting him as he had been protected by Yeats. But after the Festival and *The White Steed* debacle, Hunt had lost all optimism for the future of the Abbey. Since producing *Shadow and Substance,* Hunt and Carroll had become fairly close friends, so when Carroll asked him to go to New York to direct *The White Steed* Hunt accepted, leaving O'Connor to finish on his own the final play of the Fenian trilogy, *Time's Pocket,* and to withstand the maneuvering certain to follow the expected death of Yeats.

Shortly before Hunt's departure in November, the Board of Directors held a dinner to honor him for his service to the theatre. Only a few days before the dinner O'Connor received his invitation, addressed to "Mr. Frank O'Connor and Friend." He exploded with vindictive fury at what he considered a slap in the face, and refused to attend. O'Faoláin, surprised not to see Michael at the dinner, wrote the next day asking the reason. He received the full force of Michael's wrath. He answered in effect that Michael had overreacted, as usual. After all, he himself had received an invitation addressed in exactly the same manner.[62] He did admit, however, that he did not have Michael's reasons for feeling paranoiac. Later in the month a dinner was given for Tanya Moiseiwitsch, the talented designer who had been brought to the Abbey by Hunt and whose resignation followed immediately on the heels of Hunt's. On this occasion O'Connor received no letter of invitation at all. Again, O'Faoláin was curious about Michael's absence, but this time he said nothing. Rather, he began poking around. It turned out that Blythe had insisted that O'Connor not be invited to the dinner.

By now it had become obvious that O'Connor was being pushed from the Abbey Theatre. To fill the vacuum left by Hunt's departure, he proposed Denis Johnston, but Yeats merely replied that a man like that would want to have things his own way. When Yeats returned the post of managing director to Higgins, O'Connor's stock fell irretrievably. His only responsibility was editing a commemorative issue of the Abbey's newly resurrected publication the *Arrow.*[63] With the departure of Yeats to his winter retreat in the south of France, O'Connor was forced to carry the battle alone. With Yeats gone, O'Connor believed that "mediocrity was in control, and against mediocrity there is no challenge or appeal."[64] The give-and-take of talented people may be noisy and at times bitter, but from it emerges creative synthesis; mediocrity merely endures. O'Connor knew, too, that talk of an increased government subsidy to enlarge the theatre meant the possibility of censorship, against which he and Yeats and AE had fought so vigorously ten years earlier.

Meanwhile O'Connor was losing sight of his writing again. Late in October he put aside his novel in order to finish a play. One couldn't work in the theatre even as long as he had, he said in a letter to O'Faoláin, unless he either fell in love with it or ignored it: "I am in love with it, that's all." And as long as he held forth about new writers he was obliged to produce new plays himself. Nearly a year before he had written a story entitled "The Fenians," which he intended to use as the basis for the final play of his Fenian trilogy.[65] Hunt had offered to write the script, but then one thing after another came up during the year, all leading to Hunt's resignation. As sick as Michael had been, he still couldn't be cured of the idea that the Abbey needed him—or that he needed the Abbey—intrigue or not. *Time's Pocket*, when it was finished, echoed with the same bitter and tired voice heard in the novel he was writing, called "The Provincials," but eventually titled *Dutch Interior*. In both works he was striking out at the forces in Ireland aligned against the legitimate claims of young people upon the future. And in 1938 the future offered very little in the way of hope to Michael O'Donovan.

He ended the year with a bad play and a missed deadline on his novel. Promise now lay in the past, unfulfilled, and the future seemed to hold only regret. The costly and tedious annulment proceedings had stalled and Evelyn was pregnant. So, the week after Christmas they traveled to London together to answer Speaight's formal divorce action.[66] From London they visited her family in Wales and then went to Chester to await the final decree of divorce, scheduled for the end of January. There Michael received a letter from Yeats forwarded by O'Faoláin expressing concern about the Abbey. Michael immediately sat down and wrote a thoughtful response, defending Frank Dermody, Hunt's successor as artistic director, against the "malicious inventions" of newspaper critics and expressing his own concern about the negotiations for a State Theatre. This letter was never sent. On his way to post it, Michael caught a glimpse of a headline in the *Daily Telegraph* announcing the death of Yeats.[67] That night Michael walked the old Roman walls of Chester, mourning his hero and raging over the pettiness that remained. In that mood of fear and bitterness he and Evelyn were married in the Chester Registry Office on February 11, 1939. They returned at once to Ireland.

Frank O'Connor was soon removed from the Board of Directors of the Abbey Theatre. The *Arrow*, the Abbey publication of which he had been appointed editor by Yeats, was placed under the final control of Blythe, Robinson, Higgins, and Hayes. By requiring him to submit to them everything he wrote, they effectively stripped him of his last vestige of influence. On May 12, 1939, O'Connor posted an angry letter of resignation to the National Theatre Society. This time Yeats was not there to cool his fiery heir. The resignation was accepted with all the official words of regret.[68]

In all fairness to his fellow directors, O'Connor's demise was more his own doing than theirs. They did not so much conspire against him as let him hang himself on his own intensity. They fought only in the sense that inertia naturally opposes any active force. O'Connor's strength, that passionate attention of will to anything he believed in, was his downfall. Hayes was not really treacherous, just easily influenced by prevailing moods. In fact, O'Connor admitted he was a truly pious man, in the very best sense, and also a rare combination of gentleman and scholar. Higgins might have been devious, but not in a deliberately malicious way; he just talked too much and thought too little. Blythe was simply limited, in interest and intellect, the reason, no doubt, for his longevity on the Board. And Robinson just sat back and watched the bloodletting. O'Connor had the literary talent they lacked, but he lacked the worldly wisdom they possessed in abundance. He was probably right, in principle; but they survived inevitably not because they were devious but because they were closer to the prevailing mood of Ireland in 1939, closer to Corkery's thirty thousand spectators of a hurling match.

O'Connor fought for nearly four years; had he stayed longer, he would have been continually frustrated by compromise. His eventual ouster from the Abbey Board and the progressive deterioration of his reputation were only natural given his temperament and his virulent stand on current issues. All this happened to O'Connor because of who and what he was and because of where Ireland was (or perhaps where it wasn't) at the time. It is as hard to imagine Hayes or Blythe or de Valera acting against public expediency as it is to imagine Frank O'Connor compromising, placating, and submitting to authority. His failure to succeed in the Abbey says as much and perhaps more about his character, and indeed more about the character of his circumstances, than the eventual success of his writing in England and America.

*   *   *

The last time O'Connor saw Yeats was late in 1938, a few days before Yeats left for the south of France. Michael had gone round to his house to ask his permission to dedicate *The Fountain of Magic* to him, a gesture of gratitude and profound respect. Yeats blushed and said gruffly, "Delighted." As though that were not sufficient, the aloof tyrant of the Irish Literary Renaissance added quietly, "Honored."[69] Although he was the most acclaimed poet of his time, that was probably how he felt, perhaps shifting from one foot to the other or running his fingers through his hair like a small boy. Honored perhaps as a father might be honored by the unexpected and tardy courtesy of a heretofore recalcitrant son. Unfortunately, he did not live to see a copy of the book.

For O'Connor *The Fountain of Magic* was the culmination of a decade of effort to capture in Irish verse that world "in which imagination and thought are pure." It was a labor of love and the fruit of literary kinships with Yeats and AE, now ended. Ended too was a phase in the life of Michael/Frank. The passing in turn of AE, of the glory of the Abbey, and of Yeats marked the passing of an innocence, a magic that, as AE said, "distils no precious knowledge" but "lives and dies within the mood that creates it."

II

Retreat to Woodenbridge

There is not in the wide world a valley so sweet
As that vale in whose bosom the bright waters meet.
THOMAS MOORE, *"The Meeting of the Waters"*

I

WHEN O'Connor left Dublin for Woodenbridge, a tiny village in the mountains of County Wicklow, in March 1938, he put his scattered bachelor life behind him and took on the responsibilities of marriage. Equally important, he left the security of regular employment and entered the instability of full-time writing. Michael was in a frame of mind when he left Dublin that could only be described as despairing. He believed what his friend and physician, Dr. Richard Hayes, had told him: that he had only five years to live. But for the first time in his life he had a woman other than his mother to care for him, a passionate, vibrant woman who could give him the physical and emotional love he so desperately needed. He also needed peace, some respite from the tension of the Abbey wars, and Woodenbridge seemed a perfect retreat. Located in the Wicklow Mountains in the Vale of Avoca celebrated by the poet Thomas Moore, it was literary, quiet, and isolated. It seemed the perfect place for a convalescent writer, but it was not altogether satisfactory for Michael, who was caught in restless despair, unable to write and incapable of not writing.

Hayes was never able accurately to diagnose Michael's persistent gastric pains. X rays revealed nothing significant, and rest seemed the only remedy. In his adolescence Michael had suffered from pseudo-epileptic fits, generally caused by tension between his parents. He "outgrew" those frenzied attacks but not the extreme physical sensitivity to stress and tension. His fierce drive and sense of purpose created an inner ecology of intensity. He worked at a white-hot pace, whether writing or directing a play or opening a library. Finally, in exhaustion this intensity gave way to a severe "melancholy," as he termed it, triggered perhaps by nothing more than an argument or a friend's slight. He would take to his bed for days, smoking endlessly, eating next to nothing, and staring idly at the ceiling. Friends found him irritable and inconsolable. Whenever he suffered a particularly violent attack of this "nervous gastritis," an angry scarlet stigma would appear on the bridge of his nose. It went away when the attack had run its course, which is to say when Michael found something of enough interest to kindle his enthusiasm again.

As soon as they moved into Lynduff, Evelyn put Michael on a strict diet. For the first week she allowed him only milk. In the second she added eggs (soft-boiled) and cereal. By the third week he was able to eat boiled vegetables and chicken. Gradually she added more substantial food until he was able to cope with an ordinary diet. Michael had abused his body by his abysmal habits, so simply by eating wholesome food regularly, he began to gain weight. Over the years, when a gastric attack recurred, Evelyn returned him to this strict regimen, which usually pulled him out of it. Because he lost weight when he was writing seriously, he became convinced that added weight would at least give him some physical reserve against the inevitable attack.

Lynduff was a farmhouse set against the hill below the demesne wall of a huge estate overlooking the fairway of the golf links and the Avoca River. Michael fancied himself to be something of a squire, but he detested the pedestrian details of day-to-day country life. At first, Evelyn's Welsh upbringing bobbed to the surface after her years in the city. She threw herself into those mundane chores necessary to maintain a country household and nurse an irritable, idling writer-husband. She planted a huge vegetable garden and bought a few hens. Since it was possible to hire "help" cheaply, she was able to have a nursemaid for her infant son, Paddy Speaight. When, within a month or two, Michael's mother came for an extended visit, her presence gave them respectability in the small village; no one ever suspected that for some time they were not, in fact, married.

Like his father, Michael was temperamentally unable to sit still for very long. However he may have enjoyed a relaxing holiday at a country retreat, he was uncomfortable when not moving in familiar circles. By the beginning of the summer he had become restless. As idyllic as Lynduff seemed, it hadn't enough stimulation to keep his writing sharp. Michael was accustomed to a life crammed with crisis; he worked best when his mind was raging and taut. In *My Father's Son* he wrote that he had to escape to survive, but having survived, he chafed to return:

> A writer is as conditioned to his methods of work as any old horse, and I found that the long day's leisure away from the activities that interested me was simply something I was not trained to take advantage of, so that when I did sit down to work at my usual hour after supper the day's idleness had already drained and dispirited me so that I wrote without aim or conviction.[1]

Little wonder, then, that he complained in his letters to Dermot Foley and to Seán O'Faoláin about his "bloody novel" and about his inability to write.

In April, however, Michael finished the first story he had written in months. "Mac's Masterpiece," which appeared in the May issue of *London Mercury,* is neither wholly autobiographical nor wholly invention: Like most O'Connor stories, it is a bit of each.[2] Yet for some reason it stands out as a personal statement, a story with which he tried to write his way out of a rut. In the first place, it is a Corkery story. Nothing could send Michael into a creative rage faster than the thought of that old man whom he once viewed as a master, but whom, as O'Faoláin believed, "the compression of provincial life had made sour and arid and opinionated." Corkery still lived with his sisters in Cork, but he remained close to the nerve center of his star pupils, even though they now disagreed with nearly everything he stood for. In his study of Synge and in occasional pieces for Catholic magazines, Corkery was holding forth about nationalism, religion, and the land, attacking young writers (in English) for not using the Irish language, and calling for an end to their immoral writing.

In the second place, "Mac's Masterpiece" is the story of a man who takes to his bed in a fit of gigantic melancholy only to be bothered out of it by his protégés. Once out of bed, he begins a novel about the Irish soul. O'Connor, of course, more than once took to his bed, and Mac's conclusion that the Irish soul is torn between idealism and materialism is probably O'Connor's secret as well as Corkery's. Corkery's only novel, *The Threshold of Quiet,* was the one book Michael was trying to write around, believing that it dealt with the "resignation and loneliness of the provincial intellectual."[3] The novel that he was trying to write at the time, though eventually entitled *Dutch Interior,* was still called "The Provincials."

Finally, the characters of the story seemed to come directly from O'Connor's memories of the Corkery circle. Mac, or Dan MacCarthy, is a fifty-four-year-old teacher at the "monk's school"; he is eccentric, intellectual, and ineffectual. Boyd, his foil, resembles the young Michael O'Donovan, particularly after Gormanstown: a chemist, he is slightly built, sickly, but keen of mind and argument. The conflict between Boyd, an idealist gone sour who considers himself a realist, and Mac, a tormented, melancholy romantic, gives the story a sense of strain. O'Connor believed that Stevie Galvin in *The Threshold of Quiet* represented the antiself of Martin Cloyne, the novel's hero. Boyd and Mac may be said to bear the same relationship, while the tension between them is mitigated throughout by Mac's two other protégés, Corbett, a newspaperman resembling Sean Hendrick, and Devane, an organist resembling Seán O'Faoláin. They soften the feud between Boyd and Mac but are unable to understand the complexity of it. The two men, the mentor and the protégé, are full of love and hatred for each other, opposites who both repel and attract each other. The climax is forced not by will but by circumstance, by the pressure of Cork society, which is on edge because of rumors that Mac is writing them into his book. It is the curse of the tribe, he declares: "They hate to see anyone separating himself from the tribe."

With his beloved wife, Elsie, Mac steps out of his fastidious self-control to rage about roasting them all. His original idea had been "to show the struggle in a man's soul between idealism and materialism," to watch the dreaming quality of the Irish "dragged down by the mean little everyday nature of the Celt." Now he sees another theme emerging: "I am the Celt. I feel it in my blood. The Celts are only emerging into civilization. I and people like me are the forerunners. We feel the whole conflict of the nation in ourselves." Mac's ideas soar, but the idea of his novel falls heavily upon him, and he begins to feel as if everyone in Cork were out to get him. The loneliness is overwhelming; even the old gang finds him too contentious. After a final argument with Boyd in a pub, he walks home along the river. For a time he had persisted in his grand obsession and had written his uncompromising book, but as the voices of the tribe closed in on him he came to see himself as a fool. "In the early morning he went downstairs, made a bonfire of his novel, and sobbed himself to sleep."

"Mac's Masterpiece" contains all the bitterness and frustration O'Connor felt with post-Treaty Ireland run by a Catholic-Nationalist establishment of priests and former gunmen, all his soured idealism over the capitulation of a truly national theatre to the mercantile pietists. Perhaps he had found with Mac that he was the Celtic soul, and that he could not really detach himself at all. Or perhaps the strain of outward circumstances—his relationship to Cork, the Abbey Theatre wars, the persistence of the Catholic Truth Society, de Valera—was just too much for his frozen will and weak stomach to withstand any longer. By the end of the first summer in Woodenbridge it had finally dawned on him that he could not exist on two levels—"the level of the imagination in what concerns yourself and the level of reason in what concerns others—for sooner or later the two will change places." But he was not yet ready or able to reconcile the "idealism" with the "materialism." He turned paranoiac, feeling, as did Mac at the end of the story, "the sense of a hundred malicious faces peering over his shoulder."

I I

After the Abbey Board met in September to review the *White Steed* decision, Michael went on to London for two special BBC broadcasts. Under any conditions he would have been nervous about making these broadcasts, but after the confrontation in Dublin his stomach was tied in knots. Since his first wireless talk, a conversation with L. A. G. Strong on provincial writers, Evelyn had been coaching him to deliver his voice in a more natural way.[4] She was convinced that if he remained relaxed and confident, he would do brilliantly. It was her idea to invite Dermot Foley to go to London with Michael; with Dermot there in the studio Michael would have someone to joke with before the broadcast and someone to look at while he was actually in front of the microphone. On September 15 O'Connor read one of his stories, "The Lodgers." Dermot was ecstatic about Michael's performance, but Londoners seemed preoccupied with reports of Chamberlain's visit to Munich. "Everything here is war," Michael wrote to Evelyn.[5] The next night he was scheduled to read "A Fistful of Verses." Just before eleven o'clock a young man "with alarm in his face," in Dermot's words, "burst into the room jabbering something about a hitch and an important announcement." Michael was devastated as the man, who turned out to be a BBC announcer, gave the news that Chamberlain was returning from Munich quite unexpectedly. Then, almost as if nothing had occurred, he beckoned Michael into the studio, and as Dermot sat glued to his chair he heard "a stunned nation being told that Frank O'Connor would now read some medieval Irish verses."[6]

Michael and Dermot returned to Dublin the next day instead of staying on in London for the round of concerts and theatre they had planned. Back at home the uncertainty caused by the threat of war aggravated Michael's knotted emotions. He was inconsolable about the broadcast, which even Evelyn had thought superb. Predictably, he suffered a relapse of gastritis, but Evelyn's diet pulled him out in a week. His novel sat like a lump of resistant clay on his desk. Looking out across the river and toward the hills behind the village, Michael would often sink into melancholy.

However, for the most part that first year in Woodenbridge radiated domestic tranquility. Evelyn played the devoted wife to perfection and made the old farmhouse as comfortable a place as Michael had ever known. The daily patterns established during those months of full-time writing continued for the remainder of O'Connor's writing career. After an early breakfast he would write for about three hours. By this time the mail would have arrived; Evelyn would bring it to him with coffee, which they would enjoy together while he read the mail aloud. He would then return to his work, usually revising the previous day's writing. Dinner, the main meal of the day, was generally served around one o'clock, after which he and Evelyn (or his mother when she was visiting) took a long walk. Walking was Michael's only regular physical exercise, more nearly resembling a conviction than a pastime. On these walks, which often reached five or six miles, Michael usually carried on a monologue about the novel as an art form, the Abbey, or the state of affairs in Ireland, cursing like a boy kicking at a tin can. Occasionally, they stopped for a drink at the Cow Shed, the local pub just behind the Woodenbridge Hotel.

Returning to the house—across the bridge, over the golf links, and along the road at the base of the hill—they relaxed until evening. Evelyn prepared a light meal while Michael, in the manner of a country squire, sat back with a book and a smoke. The nurse watched Paddy, careful not to let him interrupt the master, whose temper was unpredictable. He paid attention to the boy during this time before the evening meal only when it suited him and only when Paddy, already fed, was in gay spirits. After eating, Michael resumed his work, writing until about nine o'clock. Over biscuits and milk (tea when his stomach was quiet) he and Evelyn talked about the day's writing. From time to time he would read aloud to her from one of two books in French, the memoirs of Saint-Simon or the story of a French priest in Tibet. Evelyn knew no French, so he simply translated the text into English as he read to her. During these quiet times together Michael was at his enchanting best; Lynduff was idyllic and their marriage blissful.

The only break in this daily regimen of work, walks, and readings was an occasional visit from Dermot. At such times, anything could happen. Once Dermot offered to mend a punctured tire on Evelyn's bicycle. Michael, who had tinkered ineffectually at the job for two weeks, flew into a rage about Dermot's middle-class competence and then stormed down the road. Dermot repaired the bicycle, and they all laughed about it later. On another visit Evelyn confided to Dermot that it was very difficult to cook for Michael. He refused to eat coarse foods like turnips and cabbage, insisting on tender green vegetables, potatoes, and plain cooked meats. That winter Evelyn, pressed to find sufficient delicacies, recollected something about nettles from an old French cookbook of her mother's. Enlisting Dermot's collusion in the conspiracy, they climbed the wooded hill behind the house to gather nettles, which grew in abundance just below the demesne wall of the Ballyarthur estate. While Dermot chuckled in delight, Evelyn nervously boiled and pureed the nettles. "Where did you find spinach this time of year?" Michael queried at dinner. "Up near the wall," Evelyn replied casually. "Well, don't let them catch you," he retorted, and helped himself to more nettles. Evelyn sighed in relief while Dermot choked in sheer delight.

Because he was technically still a Director at the Abbey Theatre, O'Connor had been invited to judge the dramatic competition at the Sligo Feis during Easter week, 1939.[7] He confessed to O'Faoláin that he had been a bit nostalgic about seeing the old town again and eager to "point out to Evelyn the gate where [he'd] kissed the hospital nurse and the house where [he'd] saved the poor fallen woman from having her brains blown out by a mad whore of an ex-

army officer." As it happened, however, Evelyn was having a difficult pregnancy so Michael, leaving her in the care of his mother, went to Sligo alone.
Instead of enjoying warm memories of a town he'd once known, he found the
cold, parochial dullness of a "northern" town neatly divided between Catholic
and Protestant. He stayed in the Grand Hotel, while another team of judges
(besides drama, competitions were also held in dance, instrumental music,
and voice) were lodged at the Imperial Hotel around the corner. In one of his
daily letters to Evelyn he laughingly sketched the situation:

> Here in this little town are two independent Feises, two sets of adjudica-
> tors and the competitions are arranged so that one set of adjudicators can
> make an appearance at both. The adjudicators at one stay at a Protestant
> Anglo-Irish hotel; we at a Catholic-Nationalist hotel and do not meet. It's
> a perfect French comedy.[8]

Ireland was still divided and it bewildered O'Connor more and more.

Michael was "bored stiff" by the town and by the amateur theatricals,
particulary those in Gaelic. He should have known not to expect much; after
all, he had judged children's plays in Dunmanway and Wexford. "The local
dramatic society was of professional standard. A local publican played a comic
part with a timing that was almost French," O'Connor wrote later about the
festival. But the next afternoon a team from Bundoran, a town on the Donegal
Bay, was so bad that he took the stage and denounced them in front of the entire audience. When he left the Town Hall an hour or so later, the whole Donegal troupe was waiting for him. " 'Tis easy for you to talk," said a young man
on the verge of tears. "Let me tell you that play was studied in a cold schoolhouse by the light of a candle."[9]

While in Sligo, Michael was entertained by the Mulcahy family. The four
Mulcahy daughters were celebrated beauties, one of whom, in a fit of temper,
had put out her sister's eye with a fork. Maeve was the lively one, full of vitality
and, best of all for Michael, full of fascinating stories. From the very first he
was captivated by her. Máira, the girl with the glass eye, struck him as the
most melancholy and thoughtful of the lot. She was the reader of the family.
But Michael was intrigued by them all and wrote some of his most poignant
stories about them, the most obvious being "The Grand Vizier's Daughters."
Their father, an ex-Republican, was most hospitable to Michael but insisted on
arguing about Collins. Michael wrote enthusiastically to Evelyn about the
Mulcahy family, and for the next few years he kept in touch with all of them.

Michael returned home by way of Dublin, in order to attend one last
meeting of the Abbey Board. It was at this time that he realized once and for all
that Higgins had won, that there was no longer a place for him in the Abbey.
Out of artistic principle he had resisted the decision to bring the *Arrow* under
the control of the entire Board. Yet the most disturbing thing about the entire
business was that Hayes had even agreed with the decision. Though Hayes
still thought of himself as Michael's dearest friend, Michael was not so sure of
that. It had been months since he had last visited Woodenbridge, and on that
occasion he had taken Evelyn aside and warned her not to marry Michael. "If
he lives," Hayes cautioned, "he will leave you at the first opportunity."[10] Actually, Michael had already been brutally candid with Evelyn: that his work, he
explained to her, was the most important thing in his life; he would see her and

the children in the poor house before he would let them interfere with his writing. Now Hayes was interfering and Michael was not at all pleased. He left the theatre blinded by rage and humiliation and a sense of personal loss. At O'Faoláin's house in Killiney later that day, trying to unwind, O'Connor chanced to read Austin Clarke's review of *The Fountain of Magic*.[11] Clarke insisted that O'Connor showed no "sense of rhythm" and that he had completely exaggerated the magical element in Irish verse. Under any circumstances Michael would have recoiled in violent indignation at such criticism, but coming directly on top of the rude treachery of his "friends" at the Abbey, Clarke's review ignited an emotional time bomb.

Michael returned to Woodenbridge in a foul temper. Even before he boarded the train the ugly stigma had blossomed forth again. A few days later, while Michael was chafing under Evelyn's corrective diet for the gastritis, Dermot Foley arrived for an ill-timed visit and drove Michael to further despair with his "smalltown stories" and enthusiastic chatter. Michael quipped in his next letter to O'Faoláin, "in default of taking me life I wrote the only decent thing I've written since I came here."[12] The story was "Bridal Night," one of the few stories he never revised; it wrote itself exactly as he had heard it from Hayes who had heard it in Mayo during a research excursion for his book on the French Invasion of 1798.

The story, however, did little to lessen O'Connor's deepening personal gloom. In a way it wasn't really his story at all; he had acted merely as a conduit for a situation, giving little of himself. Michael at this time needed to objectify his own subjective agonies rather than simply to mirror something entirely outside himself. He later repudiated "Bridal Night" and such stories as "Michael's Wife" because they were too emotional. Actually, the problem was that the emotion operated apart from his own loneliness and doubt. The novel he was writing represented a total investment of himself, and for this reason he fought it every step of the way. Just as his own poetry failed where his translations succeeded—in objectifying the lonely voice—so "Bridal Night" failed (or so he later thought) to capture something genuine.

Michael's mother stayed at Woodenbridge most of the spring of 1939, and in her doting presence he was a model of charm and decorum. Her attentions relieved some of the pressure on Evelyn who by now had been taxed to the limit by his raging moods and the demands of his special diet. Though pleased with her son's general health, Minnie still voiced her opposition to the diet dictated by Evelyn, particularly the large quantities of milk, for in her experience milk had often been the source of sickness. Now, with a war imminent, tuberculin-tested milk had become scarce, especially in a place like Woodenbridge, so Evelyn decided to buy a cow in order to have plenty of milk for the new baby. Hearing of a pub sale in Avoca, she ventured forth one morning to attend the auction—very bold and very pregnant. Her bid went unchallenged by a crowd of bemused farmers, who could not understand how a pregnant woman on foot would be able to drive an obstinate shorthorn down the road. About halfway back to Woodenbridge she met Michael and his mother strolling along in conversation. Rather than rejoicing in her acquisition or offering to help herd the beast home, they seemed embarrassed by the spectacle and refused even to walk with her.

They named the cow Mary Kate. A local man did the milking in return for half the milk. Even at that they had more than they could consume—cream, butter, even milk for the chickens. For the rest of the summer it was milk and eggs in every conceivable fashion—custards, puddings, soufflés, creamed vegetables, cream over tarts, butter on nearly everything else. Michael even kept a jug of milk on his desk. When Dermot visited in August, he was astounded when he and Michael went down to the river for a swim.

"My God, Michael," he blurted. "You've added flesh."

"It's this country life," Michael said, rather pleased with himself.

"I'd say it's the married life myself," Dermot replied.

A week after she bought the cow, Evelyn took the opportunity of Minnie's presence to go to Dublin to be treated for a back problem caused by the pregnancy. Michael managed well enough, judging from his letters to Evelyn, except on the nurse's day off or on days when it rained too hard for a long walk or a "cycle spin." He was apparently industrious enough to have a planter box for flowers built outside the kitchen window. Evelyn returned in about a week, relaxed and reassured about the coming birth. A month later she was back in Dublin at the Leinster Nursing Home, and on July 18 she gave birth to a baby boy, whom they named Myles. By August they were all back together in Woodenbridge.

Michael had assured Evelyn in the hospital that their finances were more than adequate to hold them through the coming war. He was drawing a fifteen-pound monthly advance from Macmillan and nearly as much from Knopf, in addition to an annual pension of seventy-five pounds and various royalties. The Sligo Feis had paid ten guineas, and Radio Eireann had asked him to do a series of readings over the winter. The American magazine market was returning substantial royalties as well, particularly *Harper's Bazaar*.[13] That year, they had earned well over the three hundred pounds he had figured they needed to survive, and 1940 looked promising.

His novel, however, held little promise. What momentum he had gained over the summer halted when Evelyn returned with the baby. It wasn't so much the baby as the visits of such friends as Dermot, Norah, Maeve, and even Father Traynor. Then Michael's mother decided to return to Cork in order to give Big Mick the opportunity to visit his new grandson. Michael was on edge as it was; all the commotion around the place conspired against his getting any writing done at all. The thought of his father coming only added to his anxiety. When he met the train, he found his father staggering from the carriage absolutely drunk. He managed to get the old man home and to bed, but not before young Paddy saw him. The look on the child's face stung Michael's memory— he had faced the same disaster at the same age. That night he lay awake, "shivering as if in a fever" and replaying in the variety show of his mind the nightmare of his childhood. In *My Father's Son* the story continues:

> I must have fallen asleep, for in the early hours of the morning I found he had got out, and knew what had happened. He was rambling mad through the countryside, looking for a public-house and hammering at the door for a drink. Later I went to search for him and when I found him said, "This can't go on. I have trouble enough in this place already." "I know, I know," he muttered stupidly. "I shouldn't have come. I'll go back by the next train. I'll be better at home." "I'm afraid you will," I said

and later that day saw him off from the little station. My heart was torn with pity and remorse because I knew that was no way to behave to a dog, let alone to someone you loved, and yet I could not control the childish terror and hatred that he had instilled into me so long ago when he threw us out in our night clothes on the street, or attacked Mother with an open razor.[14]

Michael never saw his father again. Obviously the old man was not welcome in Woodenbridge, and Michael felt little inclination to go to Cork himself. Circumstances provided a convenient excuse: When Germany invaded Poland, England declared war and the Irish Free State declared neutrality. Travel became difficult within Ireland when coal supplies were drastically reduced, limiting the amount of electricity for trains.

Torn between feelings of guilt for what he had done and loathing for what his father had done, Michael buried himself in his writing again. As he had said in a letter to Evelyn when she was in the hospital having the baby: "One should NEVER NOT FOR ANYTHING break a spell of writing; it's impossible to find the original spyhole in the immense wall of reality." With nearly five hundred pounds already advanced to him from Knopf and Macmillan for a novel, O'Connor had to produce something soon. His period of grace was running out: for months Knopf had been after O'Connor's agent to let them see the novel, and Macmillan sent a reminder with every month's installment of the advance.[15] To keep them quiet, O'Connor sent six chapters to his agent at the end of August and promised the rest of it by the end of the year, but he still was far from satisfied with what he had written. Only a few months before, he had written to O'Faoláin:

> You needn't be either terrified or envious of the novel—it's no good! Potentially, I still think, very good: a lovely design but I can't fill it. It's too ambitious—there are vast empty spaces where the implications elude me entirely, where they flap about like canvas unpegged in a high wind. That's why I say "simplify" and reread the Workhouse Ward in despair. I too can make a story of two people chattering and create them with past and future out of one crude situation, riding them like a jockey, but a race that is all falls and running after a runaway horse—that's not a work of art but a bloody endurance test.[16]

For more than a year he and O'Faoláin had kept a steady stream of letters flowing across the desk of the editor of the *Irish Times* about such things as censorship. But what little social conscience Michael had was now being drained by the novel. "We serve no purpose," he told O'Faoláin, "unless it be to create ourselves."

At the end of November he finally sent off the last of his novel, more as a gesture of futility than triumph. "I AM FED UP WITH MY BLOODY NOVEL," he wrote at the end of a letter to Dermot.[17] He wasn't writing any stories, and his novel lacked unity. He felt like a writer one day and a "glogger" the next. He was only "buying time," as O'Faoláin often said, doing hack work just to get by. Although he was revising his last play, *The Statue's Daughter,* at the time, he told Dermot there was no use trying to write for the theatre anymore.

I I I

In *The Saint and Mary Kate* O'Connor confronted the narrowness of his provincial home through the romantic quest of two poor kids for freedom and faith. Full of hope and blazing dreams, they gaze out on the larger world of possibility through the windows and doors of a blighted tenement. The young people of his second novel, *Dutch Interior,* continually escape from respectable, middle-class homes and secure, routine jobs into darkened Cork streets where they peer back through windows and doors, hoping to find warmth and life. But the doors are closed and the windows heavily curtained. The parts dominate the whole in *The Saint and Mary Kate:* A face, or a conversation, or a momentary encounter carries away the reader's attention, diluting the effect of the novel as a whole. In *Dutch Interior* O'Connor at least turned that corner, though perhaps with a vengeance. The impressionistic form, which really appears formless, is calculated to present a tapestry meaningful only on a large scale. Being too close to the issue (once again a vaguely deterministic notion of people trapped by their environment), O'Connor sought detachment by way of technique. The narrative, such as it is, develops from the static, suffocating atmosphere of a city, rather than from the motion of people's lives. The emptiness of the characters in *Dutch Interior* is the emptiness of the world of things that surround them—streets, clocks, churches, shops, and walls. The characters are not much more than symptoms of a diseased provincial town and are acted on almost solely from without. One is, in fact, meant to be less interested in the characters than in what has trapped them. What Peter Devane, one of the protagonists, sees of the passengers on a newly arrived steamer at the quay almost exactly equals what O'Connor allows us to see of his characters—vague silhouettes.[18]

The faces are those of O'Connor's old friends in Cork—Sean Hendrick, Dan Harrington, Seán O'Faoláin and Eileen Gould, the O'Leary girls, Natalie Murphy. They are all cast as silhouettes, suspended in "time's pocket" because in ten years' time their lives will make no difference to anyone in the world. In the half-light of hopelessness the river and the bridges and the trees all seem as unreal as the masked faces of the people on the trams, "masked like dancers in the quest of novelty, purpose or desire." Framed by windows and doors, *Dutch Interior* is a portrait of the gradual compression of provincial existence.

Time passes and the children grow to be young adults with no future, only time, repeating itself in a relentless, static flow like the omnipresent river. The wild geese flee or die, leaving tame geese like Peter "among the dead people, those for whom life held nothing!" For Stevie Dalton, the same young man who appears in "Mac's Masterpiece," the only escape is in the books he finds in his brother's library. Peter Devane, another of Mac's protégés, finds refuge in the shadowy womb of the library. Even in the church where Stevie finds himself there is "nothing to be seen but the red sanctuary lamp and its festoon of chains at the heart of darkness."

The second half of *Dutch Interior* opens in the daylight of spring rather than in the winter twilight. But the "air of hopelessness and gloom" persists. Gus Devane returns from America only to find himself intruding on the tidy, placid life of his brother, Peter. In the chapter entitled "Grania's Lullaby"

O'Connor brings most of the main characters together. After a round of the usual banter about Ireland, theology, and whiskey, Peter is induced to play a composition of his, something from an opera on Diarmuid and Grania he had started sixteen years before. During his performance things begin to fall into place. The methodical magic of the song frames the whole picture again. Stevie and Eileen Madden are trapped in a hopeless love affair. Peter, with the uncertainty of a prodigal's brother, later pauses to gaze at the house where he had spent his life and wonders what he has missed. "Over all the electric lamps in the long dingy Victorian street that stretched before him, a circle of mist was drawn like a bag." For Peter and the rest, time has steadily slowed; they have settled into middle-age complacency. There are no more rebels, only survivors. The book ends with ghosts, those imprecise abstractions of the past, and an empty room, extending like a "dutch interior" into nothing.

The evening Gus Devane returns home, his brother, Peter, and Stevie Dalton, the two primary characters of the novel, walk the misty streets of Cork and try to talk. Stevie had accompanied Gus to the monk's school that afternoon to see their old teacher, Mac, who had capitulated to the compression of this provincial city in "Mac's Masterpiece." Peter Devane points to a history book on a dusty shelf of an "old curiosity shop" and broodingly follows a twisted train of thought. " 'The conflict of personality and character. There's a subject for you, mister!' " This conversation, overheard at the very outset of the second part of the novel, sounds that Yeatsian notion O'Connor was struggling to embody. Stevie, bewildered, asks what he means: " 'Character is personality gone to seed,' Devane said intensely, thrusting his long fanatic head forward at Stevie inside the shield of the umbrella 'When 'tis all shaped and limited by circumstances, and there isn't a kick left in it.' "[19] They stop in front of a "whitewashed, evil-smelling latrine with a gaslamp askew over its entrance"; Peter's countenance seems "to stand out against a misty background of quay and terrace hillside and towers. 'That's what I am, mister,' he snarled with a croak of mirth, 'a character!' " O'Connor has molded the idea to fit Devane's melancholy state, but the Yeatsian vacillation between the eternities of soul and race, character and circumstance, cast a shadow on his conception of this novel. This is the dichotomy that had paralyzed him and that he found too large to bring into focus in this novel.

Though the characters of *Dutch Interior* change considerably in the sixteen years between the first and second parts of the book, no clear line of cause and effect emerges. They find they change only because Cork itself does not change. O'Connor moves from character to character, bullying his narrative and forcing his characters all back together in the social and domestic morass of their hometown. At first it's Peter Devane, the poor boy, whose life at school resembles Michael's at North Mon. Peter is a dreamer, a scaler of heights, rejected by his classmates, and set apart from the laney boys by his ideals. Then Stevie Dalton assumes the Mickey O'Donovan look, reading Heine, Browning, and Russian history. Eventually Peter becomes a musician whose opera about Diarmuid and Grania remains an incomplete masterpeice. He wears a melancholy face and complains constantly of a bellyache. Stevie, the respectable and dutiful clerk, acts out Peter's love song in his affair with Eileen. The voices of O'Connor's past, the tales of the lives of his friends, rise from the wet of the Marsh and the rubble of the Barrack Stream.

At the time, Thomas Hardy was O'Connor's favorite poet, but it was

Hardy the novelist, the master of local color, he was listening to while writing this novel. He had come to believe that nineteenth-century realism was akin to the paintings of the Dutch masters, who concentrated on the domestic and civil life of the middle class. For him, Hardy's novels stood out as supreme examples of the sort of provincial realism he was trying to achieve in his own writing. Here, for example, is a sentence from Hardy quoted years later by O'Connor in his study of the novel, *The Mirror in the Roadway*:

> The lamplights now glimmered through the engirdling trees, conveying a sense of great snugness and comfort inside, and rendering at the same time the unlighted country without strangely solitary and vacant in aspect, considering its nearness to life.[20]

And here is a sentence from *Dutch Interior*:

> The front of the painted houses was already beginning to dim, and their colours to blend lightly into one another, into the green of the trees and blue of the sky, as though a brush laden with water had been drawn lightly across all, concealing the figures at the open windows, while, high above, the face of the markethouse clock became visible.

O'Connor's Cork not only bears a strange resemblance to Hardy's Casterbridge but evokes the feeling one might get from a Breughel painting. His way of hearing or seeing from outside frames things in haunting relief.

While the literary idiom of O'Connor's exposition creates a static surface, the colloquial idiom of his characters creates dramatic tension. The dialogue abounds with such Corkisms as "whisht," "oh, law," "gligeen," "cockalorum," "connyshuring," and "screeds," all uttered as if by a shawlie on Coal Quay or a navvy on the docks. Like Hardy, however, O'Connor keeps his distance, preferring to hover as a sort of "disembodied presence"—what he often called a revenant figure. Even though his alienation from the skin-deep piety and respectability of Cork dictates the surface of the novel, O'Connor remains detached, too, from the inner lives of his characters, in the manner of an eavesdropper. Without a discernible voice to unify the rich imagery or a center of consciousness to focus the vigor of the dialogue, the novel fails to generate the emotional power O'Connor sought.

Whatever bitterness O'Connor felt about provincial life, its crushing effect on creativity, is undercut by a detached cynicism that lays a good deal of blame on the apathy and insecurity of people everywhere. To him a provincial is one who must escape from his home or be swallowed, but once gone, he finds that home is the only place he really understands. And home, of course, is not just one's hometown; it is the house of one's parents, that place of first memories. Below the social life of O'Connor's Cork, then, lay the more universal chaos of domestic life. Family life in *Dutch Interior* is stifling and contentious. The Devane brothers live in poverty, supported by their mother, a charwoman in the homes of the rich. Their father is a drunken man, barely visible to the two boys. For the Dalton boys the mother is the invisible presence, throwing barbs at her dyspeptic husband from her kitchen cave. Old Dalton is a frustrated civil servant, entirely trapped in respectable meaninglessness, frustrated and taking it out on his kids. "Better fed than taught" is an oft-repeated grumble, reminiscent of the usual complaint of Michael's own father.

The girls in the novel, especially Eileen Madden, marry for security rather than for love. The men marry for convenience. In the stagnation of provincial life all the marriages are "bad marriages," but the "secrets in houses" can't be forgotten. Oddly enough, O'Connor dedicated *Dutch Interior* to Evelyn.

Besides Hardy, the other writer O'Connor had in mind while writing this novel was Chekhov, whose own second novel was *Tales from the Lives of My Friends*, a sequence of vignettes about nine characters vaguely connected by friendship and a mutual environment.[21] Chekhov left that novel unfinished, because the scheme was too vague to carry a plot. Like Chekhov, the man to whom Yeats once compared him, O'Connor appears, in *Dutch Interior*, unable to sustain a narrative about the blighted lives of two men without indulging in quick glances toward the other lives they cross. The finest portions of the book are almost diversionary, the subjects perhaps of separate short stories. As a result, the larger unity of the novel is compromised, though it was in the cumulative effect of the whole that O'Connor invested himself and his ideas. As flawed as it is, *Dutch Interior*, because it was written at the break-point of O'Connor's career, remains a portrait of his artistic conscience.[22] It shows him to be a moralist, a lyric poet ill at ease behind the mannered mask of symbolism, and a storyteller interested more in the flash points of human existence than in the sweeping artifices of the intellect. Yeats often told him to hammer his thoughts into unity; he never really did.

Dutch Interior is good enough to make one wonder why it isn't better. Like the writer's own mind, it is too full, too undisciplined to strike clear. A reviewer called *Time's Pocket*, O'Connor's theatrical rendering of the same provincial theme, a "novelist's play." *Dutch Interior* might well be a "poet's novel," for it contains some of O'Connor's most lyrical prose.[23] The ghostly presences that move through his early love poems are also framed in the half-lit anterooms of this novel. The imagery of such early stories as "September Dawn" and "Nightpiece with Figures" is still present—shadows, silhouettes, twilight, melancholy, doors and half-doors, light and half-light, sullen voices, silence, and brooding. "From magic we come/ To magic we go," but in between lies emptiness and dim light and loneliness.

The year 1940 marks a dividing line for a generation of writers O'Connor called the "strayed revellers of the Irish literary revival, which by 1940 was all over and done with."[24] Trapped between conflicting allegiances and impulses, they appeared to be middle-aged, middle-class, middle-everything. For Frank O'Connor, especially, isolated in Woodenbridge, 1940 marked the beginning of a decade of disgrace and doubt. In the 1920s he had been treated as a promising young writer, understandably excessive and uneven. But in the 1930s he became an established writer and public figure with all the attendant pressures and expectations. With the completion of *Dutch Interior* it was almost as if he were starting all over again. He may simply have gone to Woodenbridge to write until he died; but he lived and wrote his way through his own personal abyss.

12

A Separate War

I want to be angry! I don't want to listen!
ALCESTE, in MOLIÈRE's *Le Misanthrope*

TOWARD the end of 1939, as O'Connor was finishing a novel and Europe was beginning a war, three things happened to change the pace and direction of his writing. In November Radio Eireann asked him to read some of his stories over the radio. His broadcasts for the BBC in 1938 had won such acclaim that Irish radio officials were anxious to keep his talent at home. Then, shortly after the birth of Myles, Evelyn and Michael began cycling together and found themselves intrigued by the incredible number of architectural monuments scattered around the countryside, so they decided to collaborate on a book about Romanesque architecture in Ireland. Finally, at Christmas Denis Johnston returned from London to meet with O'Connor and O'Faoláin about a scheme to revive Yeats's idea of a national theatre dominated by writers. The immediate result was a brief revival of the Dublin Drama League.[1] More significantly, their conversations led ultimately to the birth of *The Bell,* the most influential literary publication in Ireland in the 1940s.

Broadcasting, old churches, and journalism replaced the theatre as O'Connor's public forum. It goes without saying that he kept writing stories—that was his private challenge, his "lonely, personal art"—but he still believed that writing was 75 percent pure journalism. "Chekhov," he asserted, "is about 90%." People who might not have been buying books or sitting in libraries were probably reading newspapers, buying magazines, listening to the wireless, and occasionally attending the theatre or cinema. So O'Connor made radio broadcasts, cycled about Ireland in an effort to stir up public interest in ecclesiastical ruins, and wrote for every imaginable publication in Ireland, England, and even America, from street dailies to literary quarterlies. Not just his stories but all of his writing sounded the "voice of a man speaking." It also sounded the voice of one man fighting—his own separate war.

I

Marriage at first brought some measure of tranquility to O'Connor's life. Until then his life had been marked by struggle and upheaval, by blazing attachments and brutal severances, by abrupt moves from flat to flat and idea to idea. Evelyn's dutiful attention freed him from almost every domestic concern. Yet the marriage, begun in the chaotic entanglement of annulment and divorce proceedings, never seemed entirely harmonious. Michael and Evelyn were too much alike—impetuous and emotional, given to self-dramatization, and absolutely firm in their own opinions. Though they enjoyed listening to music and singing in the evenings, they argued about how to interpret the score. Having no notion of standard musical scoring, he improvised a sort of tonic sol-fa notation. He fancied himself a singer, and nothing could convince him otherwise, even his mother's chiding him about singing too loudly and with a queer rhythm. About the theatre they agreed for the most part, though Evelyn's taste ran more to comedy than did Michael's. Books were his realm and in this she deferred readily to him.

It was Evelyn, however, who sparked his interest in twelfth-century architecture. While touring with an acting company in England in the early thirties, she had discovered that nearly every town held something of interest—an old church or abbey, a Roman ruin, or a castle. Instead of wasting her days waiting for the nightly performance, she took to exploring architectural relics. When she and Michael went to England to be married, she suggested that they wait out the probationary period after the divorce in Chester because of its old Roman wall and fine abbey. In the months that followed she occasionally talked about other English churches and castles she had visited, because it was one subject upon which he could not claim to be an expert. Finally, he decided that they could make the same sort of explorations in Ireland on bicycle.

The only difficulty was that Evelyn had never ridden a bicycle. Undaunted, they left the baby with a nurse in September, took the train to Dublin, and bought a single-speed Raleigh for Evelyn. With Michael cursing loudly, she practiced nervously and slowly, zigzagging and tumbling along the banks of the Grand Canal. The next day, they set off for Naas, some twenty miles inland. When they finally arrived, Evelyn was so stiff from the unaccustomed exertions that she had to be lifted from her new bicycle. By the next day she had recovered, and they set off on a three-day marathon to visit Dermot Foley in Ennis. Michael had never been more than casually interested in architecture, even on his travels in France and Italy. Evelyn's exuberant stories had aroused his natural curiosity, but his imagination had not yet caught fire. Then, cycling into Roscrea that second evening, they found themselves "passing this plain little Romanesque front."[2] Michael jumped from his bicycle to have a better look. "Bloody marvelous," he declared.

After supper Evelyn went directly to bed, exhausted from the day's trek, and Michael returned to the little church to ponder why it had meant more to him than any building he had ever seen. Nearly two years later, while delighting in a row of eighteenth-century houses in another out-of-the-way Irish town, he decided that what had drawn his attention was the "art with which a builder erects a house so that to the memory it spells 'home.' " In other words, what had been communicated by that little church in Roscrea was that sense of domestic harmony that he often called a "desirable vision of life." And the book that started out as a survey of Romanesque architecture in Ireland became a book about the people he met and the places he visited while cycling through the Irish countryside. He would eventually call it *Irish Miles.**

At Roscrea they changed their plans in order to examine more churches of the same sort, heading toward Cashel by way of Thurles and Holy Cross. Michael was smitten by the imposing ecclesiastical fortress on the Rock of

---

* An Irish mile is an old measurement equal to 1.273 statute miles.

Cashel and vowed to return there as soon as possible. In Limerick they were met by Dermot Foley, who had commandeered his library's van on the pretense of delivering books in East Clare. Michael told him of his discovery in Roscrea and the Romanesque glories of Cashel. Since coming to County Clare, Dermot had taken to exploring old churches himself in order to offset the drabness of small-town living, so he decided to take a roundabout way back to Ennis to show them the tiny and unusually well preserved churches at Killaloe and Tuamgraney. Michael was moved by the exquisite stonework of both churches and pleaded for more. The next day Dermot suggested that they might like to meet a gentlemen in Limerick named Stan Stewart, a chemist who knew practically everything there was to know about old churches in the area. The introduction was as successful as it was brief; Michael and Stan became instant friends.

Shortly after this excursion the war broke out. Irish neutrality brought severe restrictions on fuel, food, and such supplies as sewing needles, tire rubber, and paper. As transportation became more fitful, visitors ceased coming to Woodenbridge. Food was plentiful for a time, because of Evelyn's little farm, but soon sugar, tea, and flour became scarce. American and British outlets for Michael's stories dried up, shrinking the family income and forcing O'Connor to write for his life. Like any serious artist, he was never satisfied; like any unpedigreed provincial, he drove himself to achieve excellence. The harder he worked, the less success he seemed to have; and the more he worked at his writing and broadcasting, the more he raged in discontent or retreated into his "black moods."

O'Connor could be ruthlessly demanding about his work and surly about personal problems, but at his best he was a most charming and engaging person. "At his best" was a phrase he often used about books and people, a phrase that paints an apt picture of how he met life and how he had to be met. As the pressures mounted he often snapped impatiently at Paddy and Myles, but he would just as often gather them to him with quiet affection to sing or to read to them. Though demanding of Evelyn, roaring about noise around the house or a late meal, he was generally a tender and devoted husband. In public he could grumble about "this bloody country" one moment and defend it vigorously against all comers the next. But there was nothing guarded or deliberate about him. To his close friends he was a spirited companion, whose obvious genius and infectious enthusiasm made him a source of constant surprise and wonder. His energy was boundless, and to accompany him on his cycling or walking expeditions meant keeping up with his voracious pace as well as with his flamboyant conversation.

Even when under great pressure, Michael found time to help people in need; the rage melted and the writing was put aside. Early in 1940, for example, an old friend fleeing France just ahead of the invasion came to Woodenbridge with her illegitimate child because there seemed no one else in Ireland willing to take her in. At some time during her stay she asked Michael and Evelyn how they had coped with the gossip and the hostility they had encountered before they were able to marry. As Evelyn explained what had happened and how they had tried to be honest without flaunting their marital arrangement, Michael listened thoughtfully. Finally, he interrupted, pointed sternly at the young woman, and said "Wear your failure like a feather in your cap." "I don't understand why you think I'm a failure," she replied. "Don't ever for a moment fool yourself that they don't know all about the child and don't ever forget that they think it shameful even though you don't. Retain your dignity and your pride. By wearing the feather you can laugh at yourself even if they can't." She never forgot the advice, nor the man who offered it. In time her son returned again and again to the O'Donovan home and became, for all practical purposes, a member of the family. His story—the illegitimate child searching for a father—became the theme that O'Connor wrote in so many variations over the next twenty years.

Michael's kindness extended as well to his literary acquaintances, but the man he was kindest to in those trying years was Patrick Kavanagh, another impoverished provincial who had come to Dublin to follow the literary life.[3] They had both lived in the Ballsbridge area, meeting at such places as Parson's Bookshop. Neither had ever been part of the fashionable crowd. O'Connor kept largely to himself, a "bun man," as Kavanagh called him, who was more likely to be found in restaurants or tea shops than in the pubs. Kavanagh was a "pint man" who circled such establishments as the Palace and the Pearl.

From the first, O'Connor was one of Kavanagh's greatest admirers. Shortly after AE died, Michael took it on himself to ask Macmillan to consider Kavanagh's poems. O'Connor believed that Kavanagh's writing not only cut through the insular complacency and pretentious posing of the time but gave poignant witness to the immense strength of rural Ireland. Kavanagh in turn admired O'Connor. "I liked his short stories very much," Kavanagh wrote in *The Green Fool*, "because they had artistic and intellectual honesty—and there was a great deal of humbug writing being turned out everywhere."[4] They were both simple men dedicated to common folks and distrustful of intellectuals and fanatics who warped reality to fit their abstractions. They were among those "strayed revellers" of the Literary Renaissance. In the 1940s they found themselves, as Kavanagh wrote, "between two stools." Censorship, closing markets, and libel suits brought an intellectual darkness and forced many of their fellow writers to follow Joyce into exile. O'Connor, O'Faoláin, and Kavanagh chose the more difficult exile within Ireland.

I I

Throughout the winter and spring of 1940 Michael and Evelyn were unable to do much cycling other than short jaunts to Wexford and Glendalough. Bad weather, a sick baby, and publishing deadlines conspired to keep them busy at home. Dermot regularly sent packages containing works on architecture, thus enabling Evelyn, despite all the distractions, to do some research on Irish churches and to compile thorough notes on all the sites they intended to visit that summer. They planned their next cycling expeditions carefully. Michael bought guidebooks, maps, knapsacks, and rain gear. They decided to carry with them everything that might cost money—bread, butter, cheese, tomatoes, fruit, even milk. The most clever tactic they devised was to carry a teapot and tea. If they saw an interesting cottage, or if they needed to rest, one of them would go to the cottage door and ask, "Would you be kind enough to give me some hot water?" knowing, of course, that every Irish cottage had a kettle on the hob.[5] In most cases they would be asked in and given not only tea but homemade bread and conversation.

Michael was scheduled to give a broadcast talk in Dublin at the end of May. The week before the broadcast he and Evelyn boarded the train with their bicycles at Kingsbridge Station, bound for Limerick. From Limerick each day they cycled out in all directions, returning to the city before dark. They visited the church in Mungret, the friary at Askeaton, and Manister Abbey near Shanagolden. On the advice of Stan Stewart they also took a loop trip through Patrickswell and Adare to Rathkeale, circling back into Limerick by way of Croom. There they turned off the main road in search of a Cistercian abbey they had been told was thereabouts. Soon a car approached, and as they edged to the side of the road Michael tumbled from his bike. He started to curse the driver, but Evelyn cautioned that it was a Garda car.* A little while later the same automobile came up behind them again, slowed down, and went by. Eventually, they got to Monasteranenagh and walked about the place admiring what was left of the cloisters and refectory. Poking around the ruins of the belfry, they came face to face with the men they had seen in the car. It suddenly struck them that they were being followed, because police weren't normally to be found inspecting ruined churches.

In the hotel that evening over drinks with Stan Stewart they talked about what had happened. The owner of the hotel, knowing Stan and figuring that if they were his friends they must be respectable folks, told them that the moment they had left that morning two gardaí had been in to search their bags. Apparently, they were suspected of being German spies. Parachute incidents during May south of Dublin and in Clare had made the police especially concerned about espionage activity.[6] And why would a man and a woman be out cycling around the countryside in foul weather looking at deserted ruins?

Not long after Michael and Evelyn returned to Woodenbridge, a Garda sergeant from the area began turning up in the village rather more often than usual. On two or three occasions he even called on the O'Donovans; he was a collector, he claimed, of Wicklow and Wexford folk songs. Not suspecting anything, Michael was as helpful as he could be, considering that he knew little about local folklore. Sometime later a friend, Charles Davidson, told them he had been asked by the gardaí to report anything suspicious about the O'Donovans. Noticing some flags in a field not far from the golf course near Lynduff, he remembered the sergeant's warning and jumped to the conclusion that the O'Donovans were indeed German spies, and that the flags were markings for a parachute drop. But, he reasoned, if the planes could not spot the flags, no parachutists would land in Woodenbridge and the O'Donovans would not be arrested, so Davidson tore up all the flags. A few days later he overheard a country engineer cursing the eejit who had stolen all the survey flags for a special drainage project.

While all this intrigue was swirling behind his back O'Connor was at work on more writing projects than he had ever managed to keep alive at one time: six or seven different stories (including "Orphans," "The Long Road to Ummera," and "Day at the Seaside"), portions of his translation of Brian Merriman's poem *The Midnight Court*, a radio play entitled "Malachy," and prelimi-

---

* The national police force of Eire is known as the Garda Siochana. The plural form, indicating more than one police officer, is *gardaí*, literally "guardians of the peace."

nary sketches for the Romanesque architecture book. At the request of
Roibéard OFaracháin of Radio Eireann he was also writing a series of broadcasts, eventually called "The Dublin Hill Discourses," drawn from his cycling
experiences.[7] Everywhere he went, stories were there for the taking. O'Connor might have been reading Stendhal and Trollope at the time, but he was listening to people talk in obscure pubs and across stone fences as he cycled in
search of ruins.

Broadcasting forced O'Connor to improvise a fictional style that was at
once entertaining enough for the "common reader"and substantial enough for
his own literary standards. After reading his first story over the air in London,
he had listened to the recording with "the same despair which the born raconteur probably feels when he sees his favourite anecdote in print"; he had
discovered himself to be "helpless, hopeless, drivelling and incompetent" behind the microphone.[8] He sought for models of good wireless readers but
found none. It was Christopher Salmon of the BBC who helped him to see that
while a reader can peruse leisurely back and forth over the printed page taking
in great gulps of material, the listener is forced to follow "at a fixed and unal-
terable rate."[9] Michael decided to emulate the old Irish *seanachie* sitting in
some out-of-the-way cottage enchanting his visitors in the web of his own personality.

In sum, he decided to become the entertainer he so naturally was. All he
had learned from Maupassant and Joyce had to be thrown out the window; no
more of the intricate orchestration and subtle harmonies of the printed page,
and no more of the detached voice, diffused in the "elaboration of cross-refer-
ences." The listener demanded entertainment, simple drama, not subtle allusion, and for this the radio storyteller had to "use all his power of personality
and dramatization to subdue an audience." (Had he discovered this "secret" a
few years earlier, he might have made a better showing in the theatre.) With
Evelyn's help he began practicing his readings, learning to catch the cadence
of each phrase, to delight in the gusto of each emotion. If he had been a musician, he said of the experience, he would have accompanied himself on the
piano. Since he wasn't, he fell back on the actor's tools to exploit the personality and tone of his voice. It was as Yeats had told him about poetry: He should
write as if he were shouting to a person across the street.

With all this attention to the resources of the spoken word banging
around in his head, Michael could not help being extremely sensitive to the
actual sound of the voices he heard in Sligo, where he again served as an adjudicator of dramatic recitations during Easter week, 1940. For years he had
been listening to his "voices," as he called them, recording with amazing accuracy the way people talked or said certain phrases. His ability to mimic people
and his inclination toward theatrics were natural instincts. In Sligo this time,
instead of railing at the contestants, he found himself coaching them. He
wrote enthusiastically to Evelyn about a brilliant performance of *The Rising of
the Moon* given in Irish by a railway porter, who happened to be from Cork, and
his troupe of lads from Donegal. The politics of two independent festivals with
two sets of judges housed at two different hotels still bewildered him, but the
combination of the voices and the Mulcahy family brought him back to Dublin
in high spirits. His special documentary talk on AE that week was inspired.

A few weeks later he returned to Dublin to participate in a special hundredth anniversary tribute to Michael Davitt, founder of the Land League. Accompanying him back to Woodenbridge was Maeve Mulcahy, with whom he had been infatuated since his first Sligo visit. Maeve was the typical O'Connor girl—vivacious, witty, and impetuous. Above all, she was a treasure house of stories, and the one she told Michael on this visit became "The Grand Vizier's Daughters." Evelyn tolerated the visit only because she knew that the attraction the young woman held for him was not unlike the attraction of a new idea or an old church—a focus for his blazing enthusiasm. She understood him well enough to know that he was not a "womanizer," his reputation notwithstanding. Love to him was like friendship, an intellectual and emotional collaboration, and since he was not a sensualist, his affairs were short-lived.

Writing to Dermot Foley the first week in June, Michael lavishly praised Maeve, adding that he was depressed: "health, war, love affairs and work." Then, a few weeks later, after returning from a long jaunt to Kerry, he mused in another letter to Dermot (who by this time was wondering when he would see his old friend again):

> The wife business is bad, very bad because none of us knows the day or the hour. It's so easy to say "What the hell did he see in her?" but the awful moment when one says "What the devil did I see in her?" one rarely thinks of. You see, one grows and grows, and no human being can tell if the other partner is going to grow too, or if it does when it may not stop suddenly and one begins to tear at the halter, seeing all the succulent green pastures ahead.[10]

All things considered, it was little wonder that Evelyn was eager, in spite of the fact that she was pregnant again, to accompany Michael on the ambitious cycling excursions he was planning for the summer. She needed to be alone with him, away from children, female visitors, and mother-in-law.

Toward the middle of June Michael and Evelyn embarked on their western tour. The miles were long but relatively flat. Michael was most interested in going to Mount Melleray, a monastery he had visited with Nancy McCarthy years before. A story, dredged from his writing journal, was working in the back of his mind, and he wanted to check the details. (The story eventually became "Song Without Words.")[11] From Cappoquin they followed the Blackwater River to Lismore ("Cormac MacCarthy had given it two chapels," O'Connor wrote in *Irish Miles,* as if to justify the visit) and on to Fermoy, where Evelyn protested about his avoidance, once again, of Cork. But he was adamant about not going, and they continued straight on to Killarney by way of Mallow. Besieged by all the hotel porters of the town, who sought their business, the tired couple escaped to a guest house on the Tralee Road conveniently near the Aghadoe Church, "the main interest of which," O'Connor confidently claims in *Irish Miles,* "is that its peculiar capitals enable you to trace the mason who did it from Holy Island in Lough Derg, through Clonkeen in Co. Limerick."[12] That sort of brash assumption probably made thoroughly trained specialists in Romanesque architecture quiver, but it gave an otherwise obvious travel book an entertaining petulance.

From Tralee they cycled seven or eight miles out to Ardfert to see the "remains of an admirable cathedral church and abbey in the Early English style, and a Romanesque chapel"; the chapel, which he noted "must have been a beauty," had been savaged beyond restoration. Because of a fierce westerly wind that knocked them from their bicycles every time they got up, they decided the next day to take the bus as far as Dingle, a distance of about twenty-five miles. At Dingle they set out again, every mile contested by the same wet wind. As they crested the hill on the road into Murreagh, the wind sliced the clouds enough to illuminate the scene in the valley ahead—the fences and checkered fields, the whitewashed cottages and sentinel hay stooks, the rocks, waves, and foam of the coastline. It was to this valley, which O'Connor called a "Munster Thebaiad," that early Christian monks came to follow their lonely faith in beehive huts scattered like wild birds' nests on the inhospitable slopes.[13] Michael and Evelyn made straight for the Gallarus Oratory, the finest example of beehive architecture, and then on to the ruins of a twelfth-century church at Kilmalkedar.

No sooner were they sheltered from the wind by the chancel wall than a child poked his head through a hole in the wall and stuttered something about a guide. When they produced sixpence he disappeared, only to return with a young man who told them more than they wanted to know about the place. Suddenly the guide ceased his zealous and mellifluous discourse: A "tall, gaunt, Spanish-looking man" had come in and was glowering at them all. The two boys ran off, leaving the petrified couple to fend for themselves. Trying to preserve their dignity, they too walked past the newcomer; Michael paused by the doorway and, hoping to give the appearance of having some reason for the trespass, pointed out to Evelyn something about corbels for a wooden roof. Instantly the man corrected him. It wasn't wood, he said: "t'was shlates."

It turned out that this imposing fellow was the caretaker, indignant over years spent picking up slates knocked from the graves by marauding bands of vandals. In his little cottage, over a kettle of tea, he showed them the carved stonework, including a sundial, he had salvaged from the area around the church. Cycling back to Tralee with a boisterous sunset helping the wind push them along, the two amateur archeologists still chattered excitedly about the old man and his church. "We shot downhill past Madman's Glen and along the shore of Tralee Bay as the moon rose, shouting joyously to one another."[14] Behind them lay not merely miles but whole ages. O'Connor never returned to this part of Kerry, but he also never had an unkind word to say about it.

All the miles and all the ruins had by this time exacted a great toll on Evelyn. Michael must have had more than enough of scenic wonder and wet roads because he consented without resistance to her suggestion that they board the train to Limerick, where they were to meet Stan Stewart for the Tipperary portion of their adventure. He insisted, however, on stopping at Listowel, "a reader's and a writer's town." Whenever his travels had brought him west of the Shannon, he had made a point of visiting Dan Flavin, a remarkable local bookseller who had single-handedly introduced the young people of the area to French literature, to Joyce, and even to the stories of Frank O'Connor. Flavin had run a milling operation that had been burnt out by the Black and Tans during the Troubles, after which he put all the money he received as compensation into a bookstore.[15] O'Connor once said that if Flavin liked a book, he did not want to part with it, and if it was one he did not like, he did not want to sell it; in this way his store became a sort of lending library. The main reason Michael wanted to stop in Listowel this trip was to meet the young teacher Flavin had convinced to take over the bookstore on his retirement the year before. Bryan MacMahon turned out to be a very engaging person, full of stories about the Blasket Islands and the folk culture of North Kerry.[16] He was also a promising writer, whose career would soon be given a boost by O'Connor.

Stan Stewart's house on Shelbourne Road in Limerick proved to be a much-needed place of recovery. Stan took great delight in fussing over the expectant mother, who was content to stay in while her excitable husband roamed the town. Two days in Limerick, a city Michael considered the "pleasantest in Ireland," were refreshing enough to put them all on the road in search of Romanesque architecture once again. Stan's idea of cycling, however, ran more to pub stops and gentlemanly conversation than to feverish, athletic peddling. And since Stan could not leave the chemist shop for too long, they took the train to Caher where they set off for Michael's obsession, Cashel, taking a meandering route along the river Suir. In *Irish Miles* O'Connor gives his cycling companions names, oddly enough drawn from Molière. Stan Stewart, for instance, is called Géronte, the garrulous, credulous old fellow in *The Doctor In Spite of Himself,* whose trifling absurdities are held up to gentle ridicule. Evelyn is called Célimène, the worldly coquette of *The Misanthrope* loved by Alceste, a noble spirit disgusted by a corrupt society.[17] Though he never refers to himself as Alceste, O'Connor's tone suggests unremitting identification. "Between the western wind and the small rain, the towns that are bad for a cup of tea and the ruins of churches and castles that no one cares for, the usual danger with Célimène and myself is misanthropy," he wrote in *Irish Miles*. Misanthrope or not, this Irish Alceste plundered the country for material to feed the consuming variety show in his own mind.

Meanwhile *Dutch Interior* had finally appeared, and though it did not exactly fall still-born from the presses, its publication hardly inspired a great deal of notice.[18] Even O'Connor was unable to generate much excitement about the event, and for once he didn't rage about indifferent reviews. Nor was he very surprised when on July 10 the Irish Censorship Board banned the book for obscenity and indecency.[19] He had voiced violent objection to the banning of O'Faoláin's *Bird Alone* in 1936; in the pages of the *Irish Times* he had already made something of a nuisance of himself over the repressive treatment of Irish writers. About this latest indignity, O'Connor had very little to say, at least publicly. Instead, a day or two after hearing about the banning, he and Evelyn went off on another long-distance cycling expedition.

I I I

In September 1940 Michael received a letter from Christopher Salmon of the BBC asking him to appear with T. S. Eliot on the Home Service series "The Writer in the Witness Box."[20] He agreed, but Eliot was forced to cancel; so O'Connor appeared instead with L. A. G. Strong in a discussion about the writer as entertainer. He returned to Dublin pleased with himself, richer by twenty guineas, but stunned by the devastation caused by the heavy German bombings. Within a week Salmon wrote offering him £150 for a series about drama to be broadcast in January. Michael was intrigued by the topic, but the stipend—roughly half of his projected yearly income—tipped the scale; his affirmative reply was wrapped around a pound of butter, an item made scarce by war rationing in Britain. Dealing with actors, playwrights, and critics forced Michael back into the arena into which he had put so much of his energy in the 1930s and from which he had received more pain than satisfaction. Scars from the Abbey wars had hardly healed, and his newest play, *The Statue's Daughter,* was proving difficult to stage in a town nervous about any sort of controversy.

Lennox Robinson's *Roly Poly,* an adaptation of a Maupassant story about a French prostitute's refusal to submit to the wishes of a Prussian officer, had just been forced to close at the Gate because of protests to the Irish government from the German legation.[21] Shortly thereafter, on November 21, 1940, Micheál MacLiammóir wrote to O'Connor explaining why it would not be advisable for him to produce *The Statue's Daughter* at that time. The atmosphere in Dublin was so sensitive that it would be inviting trouble to put on a play by an already controversial writer that dealt with such an obviously controversial topic as the illegitimate daughter of a national hero. If the portrayal of a prostitute had outraged government officials, then it was not difficult to imagine the response to a play about an equally unmentionable topic. For MacLiammóir the problem was not so much neutrality (the German legation protested nearly everything anyway) as what he termed the "sex-cum-religion obsession" of the Catholic-Nationalist leaders whom he called the Hoodlums. He had not anticipated such a response to Robinson's play by the "national Hoover-the-carpet movement," but he was certain now that O'Connor's play would cause more than a "minor stink."[22] Though admitting to O'Connor that raising a stink would have pleased him, he wouldn't risk anything that would close the theatre or hasten a general censorship of theatre in Ireland.

The previous winter O'Connor, O'Faoláin, and Denis Johnston had hatched the idea of forming a group of writers to control their own plays; now the original idea had evolved, in the hands of Seán O'Faoláin, into something a bit more ambitious. O'Faoláin was feeling the effects of Ireland's neutrality on publication markets as severely as was O'Connor, but which one of them actually stumbled on the idea of a new magazine is hard to say. O'Connor's combustible mind, which worked, as O'Faoláin himself once observed, like a man with a machine gun in a shooting gallery, could produce such ideas every minute. O'Faoláin, on the other hand, possessed a steadier mind, suited more to sifting and implementing ideas than to generating them, and in the end it was Seán O'Faoláin who made *The Bell* a reality. He was the one who engineered the details of printing, layout, advertising, and advance publicity—all those matters about which Michael couldn't have cared less.

During the summer of 1940 the new venture had been taking shape. Every time he came to Dublin, Michael met with Seán to cement the first two issues. For years they had both been publishing in every imaginable sort of publication, so they had more than a vague idea of the design and content they wanted. AE's *Irish Statesman,* the format of which had been a general survey of the social, political, cultural, and intellectual life of Ireland, served as their abiding model. O'Faoláin, who was to handle most of the editorial details, decided for practical reasons on a monthly publication resembling *Horizon* and *Commonweal.*[23] He set up editorial offices in Parkgate Street, installed the nov-

elist and social critic Peadar O'Donnell as magazine editor, and circulated
among his friends in the Irish Academy of Letters notice of the coming publication. In time almost every prominent Irish writer sent something to *The Bell*,
to say nothing of the score of young writers, including Brendan Behan, Bryan
MacMahon, and James Plunkett, who were first published there. Though
O'Faoláin was able to pay only modest commissions, at least it was something
at a time when for Irish writers there was next to nothing.

While pulling together the details of publication that summer, O'Connor
and O'Faoláin also hammered out a statement of policy which had been shaped
in their battles for artistic freedom with Yeats and AE in the Irish Academy.
Yeats had tapped O'Connor to save the Abbey and O'Faoláin to save the Academy; neither was entirely successful, but at least they had attempted to uphold
the spirit of Yeats. The title, O'Faoláin said in his editorial announcement in
the first issue, was chosen because it was a "spare and hard and simple word."
Turgenev might have been on their minds, too, since *The Bell* had been the
title of a periodical associated with the Russian writer in the mid-nineteenth
century. Whatever the source might have been, the name had "a minimum of
associations." Their hope was to create new life, new symbols, new associations. "Our only job was to encourage life to speak. When she speaks, then
THE BELL will itself become a symbol, and its 'policy' will be self-evident."[24]

Instead of calling for readers, O'Faoláin asked for writers, because the
magazine could be creative only insofar as Ireland was creative. For years
O'Connor and O'Faoláin had tried to raise Ireland's artistic consciousness, but
the magazine was their most magnificent gesture, a gesture of their radical
faith in Ireland, which had to be aired openly or else capitulate to the forces of
philistinism, puritanism, and chauvinism. The magazine succeeded not because it changed the moral or cultural outlook of the Irish peple, but because it
was able to nose out "bits of individual veracity, hidden in the dust-heaps of
convention, imitation, timidity, traditionalism, wishful thinking." The editors
asked subscribers to hold them accountable to "the real thing, the thing that is
alive and kicking, as against the thing that is merely pretending to be alive."
O'Connor and O'Faoláin might have left their old mentor behind in the marsh
of Cork, but they had not yet forsaken Corkery's admonition always to write
with something to say, to put truth before mere craftsmanship. The first issue
of *The Bell* appeared early in October 1940.

For months Dermot Foley had been after Michael to visit Ennis again and
to tour that rocky region of Northwest Clare called the Burren, a magnificent
"badlands" which Cromwell avoided because he found there no tree from
which to hang a man. Small-town life was closing in on Dermot, and he needed
the intellectual stimulation Michael always provided. He might also have felt
the need to shore up an ebbing friendship; Michael's allegiance was flowing toward Stan Stewart, an unfettered bachelor (Stan was separated from his wife)
who offered what the married librarian could not—unmitigated hero-worship.
Michael was anxious to take advantage of the splendid autumn weather, but
Evelyn was eight months pregnant. Her doctor gave guarded approval and a
few instuctions about what to do should labor commence. The thought of her
ham-fisted husband delivering a baby beside an isolated Clare road stretched
Evelyn's courage considerably; gambling against such an occurrence she de-

cided to risk it. Dermot met them in Limerick, where they had spent a night with Stan, and drove them in the library van to the home of another friend in Corofin.

Going into Clare, O'Connor wrote later in *Irish Miles,* "was like going into a land of skeletons, a cemetery of civilisations. On every road there were ruined cottages, by every ford and gap was a ruined tower, in every village the ruins of a Georgian Big House and a church of any century from the tenth to the nineteenth."[25] In one such village a group of women watched with intense curiosity as Michael, Evelyn, and Dermot resolutely pushed their bicycles uphill. Dermot later learned from a local policeman that reports of a buried child were flying about the area—why else would a pregnant woman and two middle-aged men be venturing into that desolate place? The morbid rumors were illfounded, however, for Evelyn cycled back from the rock plateau as pregnant as when she went in. On November 27 in the Leinster Nursing Home she gave birth to a daughter, whose unusual name was taken from a medieval Irish romance, which Michael had recently translated, about a Munster poetess named Liadain (meaning "gray lady").

About the same time, Christopher Salmon wrote proposing that Michael give what was called a "Postscript" to the BBC evening news on the Sunday following Christmas. O'Connor accepted on the condition that the broadcast originate from Dublin. With that the trouble began, because Irish officials were extremely sensitive at the time about anything that might endanger neutrality; any hint of sympathy for either England or Germany brought outcries from the legation of the other. Under sanctions of an Emergency Powers Act all public media were clamped by severe censorship.[26] Mr. Patrick Little, minister for posts and telegraphs, and Dr. T. J. Kiernan, director of broadcasting at Radio Eireann, decided that a broadcast for the BBC by Frank O'Connor would compromise neutrality, even though his script contained nothing in the way of propaganda. His reputation for causing trouble would have been sufficient reason, but there was also the matter of Garda surveillance of O'Connor for suspected espionage activity.

Eventually the diplomatic efforts of Christopher Salmon proved successful and on December 27, St. Stephen's Day, O'Connor gave a thirteenminute broadcast on the BBC Home Service entitled "Across St. George's Channel."[27] In deft, vivid strokes he recreated his last visit to London, a city under siege. His voice glistened with emotion: "I came prepared to be frightened. I hadn't come prepared to be bewildered, and that, I am afraid, is what I was." The blackouts, the sirens, the names of boys killed in action, the debris—"It was too stunning; I could not grasp it now." There was no cultivated detachment or contrived artistry in the talk, only the sound of a man feeling deeply. His memory of England was like a child's impression of a house once visited, "a distillation of hundreds of little incidents," a perfume compounded of kindness, courtesy, decency, order. What he noticed about the English was "a sort of simplicity; a singleness of mind and purity of intention; a touch of knight-errantry one loves, even though one pokes fun at it." Then he added: "a mind that looks outwards on life rather than in upon itself, that does not exploit or dramatize itself, that does not raise its voice."

At the very end of that talk O'Connor confessed, "I like old festivals, old customs, old friends, and I am glad to think that while I am speaking to you, some of the wren boys with their blackened faces are still knocking at cottage doors throughout Ireland. They are part of the permanent things of life."* These are the sentiments of the eternal provincial, one whose values are simple and rock-hard; the voice of one who at this "neighbourly season" would knock at the door and sing the Wren Boys' Song, a song of hope and cheer. It was one of Frank O'Connor's finest hours.

In a hotel lounge full of card-playing Britons Christopher Salmon listened that evening to his friend speaking from across the Irish Sea. To Michael he wrote, "I thought it a noble occasion and your voice was vigorous and strong." Unfortunately, O'Connor's admiration for the courage of the British people was seen by Irish officials as a tacit condemnation of Irish neutrality. Mr. de Valera was said to be especially outraged to discover that the broadcast had actually originated from Dublin studios. Though he may have secretly shared O'Connor's admiration of the British persistence in the face of German barbarism, de Valera was trapped between old rebel animosities and new international alliances. Too many IRA gunmen still felt that England's adversity was Ireland's opportunity; a united Ireland was still an unrealized dream for these rebels who had spent a lifetime fighting for it. But one leading politician, James Dillon, a deputy leader in Fine Gael, contacted O'Connor after the broadcast with congratulations. It was the first word of praise O'Connor had received from the officials of his native land in some time. If the banning of *Dutch Interior* earlier that year had not alienated O'Connor already, then the foot-dragging and prior censorship of his Christmas broadcast most certainly pushed him toward Britain—away from a place he couldn't stand to live in yet couldn't stand to be apart from.

Though O'Connor had met resistance to his request to leave Ireland, the Irish government issued him a temporary travel permit at the beginning of 1941. When Evelyn and her baby daughter were comfortably settled in Woodenbridge with a full-time nurse, Michael felt free to travel to England. Salmon had arranged for O'Connor to anchor a series of conversations with prominent actors, playwrights, directors, and critics of the London stage which was to be called "Curtain Up!"[28] Although O'Connor wasn't as nervous as he had been for his first broadcast in 1936, he felt uneasy at the prospect of talking extemporaneously with such imposing persons as John Gielgud, Tyrone Guthrie, Stephen Spender, Edith Evans, and Desmond MacCarthy. "I am a nervy person, and I should be afraid of cracking up and being an embarrassment to my friends," he wrote to Evelyn, who couldn't understand his self-doubt. His provincialism gave him more than one moment of insecurity in the presence of celebrities. "Nerves don't matter in writing," he said to Salmon. "They are everything in broadcasting; those terrible fifteen minutes when you must be on top of your material and of your public, and ready to laugh at the microphone."

Salmon had convinced BBC officials to consider O'Connor for full-time employment. However, to obtain a staff position one had to pass a general-knowledge examination. Salmon assumed that with Michael's breadth of reading and amazing memory he would sail through this formality, but while tak-

---

* A Celtic folk custom in which a party of masked and costumed male singers goes from house to house on Boxing Day waving sprigs of holly on which bits of cloth representing the wren are hung. For their song the Wren Boys expect some sort of gift.

ing the exam, Michael went completely blank. He was unable to identify even such simple facts as the name of a port on the Persian Gulf or the name of England's first laureate. When he left the examination room, knowing that in all likelihood he had failed, he lit a cigarette and all the answers came to him in a flash. "So there you are," he thought, "unschooled and out of work." He did indeed fail the exam, but Salmon arranged for him to work for the BBC on a free-lance basis for the remainder of the war.

In the opening broadcast of the "Curtain Up!" series O'Connor had to introduce what the theatre was all about without criticizing the current West End plays. In the first broadcast (January 17) he talked with the actor Lewis Casson who said he had started acting as a child. O'Connor recalled making a toy theatre as a boy, agreeing with Casson that children live by make-believe. In a subsequent discussion with John Gielgud he induced the famous actor to do one or two speeches from *Macbeth* to show how blank verse could be used to create a sense of make-believe. In his broadcast with the critic Desmond Mac-Carthy he capitalized on this concept of theatrical make-believe by staging a little drama with himself as "the young novelist who wants to write a play and has a subject ready made to his hand" and MacCarthy "as the old man in the theatre who tears the young novelist's story to pieces and puts it together in terms of the theatre." The "Curtain Up!" series was received with enough acclaim that O'Connor was asked to return in April for a broadcast talk with Val Gielgud, director of radio drama for the BBC and brother of the famous actor.

Between broadcasts Michael stayed outside of London to escape the bombings.[29] On days when rehearsals and broadcasting required him to be in London, he stayed at the Berners Hotel near Oxford Street. The twelve weeks passed very slowly for him, and his letters to Evelyn complained of their separation, even noting the time left until his return. By the second week of February he had written from Chipping Campden: "I am in the last stages for lack of a woman. Every line I write I have to sit back and say 'Is this literature or suppressed sex?' " When he finally returned home, he believed he had become a wiser man.

The incident that prompted this belief occurred toward the end of January at the home of L. A. G. Strong. Also visiting that evening was an old friend of the Strongs', a Dutch psychiatrist named Metman who specialized in the interpretation of dreams.[30] Reluctantly he interpreted the few dreams Michael could remember, but suggested that Michael take a notebook and pencil to bed and write down each dream the moment he awoke. Michael wrote to Evelyn that Metman had diagnosed his stomach problem as being due to impaired breathing caused by chronically inflamed adenoids. "He also expounded my 'falling' nightmare as a tendency to abstraction—life trying to pull me down to the ground floor." Some years before, Michael had spent hours talking with Father Tim Traynor, who considered himself something of an expert on Freudian theory, about such things as dreams. But in London he found a real expert, an interesting interpretation, and a practical suggestion as well. He returned to Dublin bent on recording his dreams.

Michael also returned with the assurance of three broadcasts in April and regular free-lance work after that. Though he disliked traveling and was terrified of the bombings, Michael was anxious for another opportunity to meet the Dutch psychiatrist. In April he took with him a rapidly filling dream notebook.

Conversation at the Strongs' again turned quickly to dreams. One of Michael's had to do with Hitler, Mussolini, and Franco, a natural enough combination considering the war. The events of the dream itself, however, made no sense. Another dream had to do with things happening on the left—running and falling on the left-hand side of the road or being stabbed in the left arm. This time Metman, equipped with more dreams than he cared to hear, began asking Michael questions in the manner of a verbal Rorschach: What did he think of first when he heard such words as *mother, bed, dog, knife,* and so on? When asked what *left* meant to him, Michael responded automatically "The heart." Metman concluded that Michael's head was trying to kill, or in some way free itself from, his heart.

By the time he got back to Woodenbridge a few days later and settled into his writing once again, O'Connor had decided that what this all meant was that he had been allowing feeling to dominate his writing. "It's all in the technique," he told Evelyn. She wondered about stories like "Michael's Wife," her own favorite, and the one he wrote in such a blazing flurry after Dermot's visit, "Bridal Night." But once Michael's mind was made up, not even facts could always change it. "The hell with feeling, it's the technique that matters," he repeated with finality. That was all there was to it; he just wouldn't write that way any longer—at least not if he could help it. That gap between instinct and judgment, which Michael had first discerned in Geoffrey Phibbs, then in Father Traynor, and finally in his own father, apparently cut deeply through his own being as well.

I V

The demands of broadcasts did not seem to keep O'Connor from writing stories. "The Long Road to Ummera," originally a broadcast story, appeared in the first issue of *The Bell.* From the day he put his drunken father back on the train in Woodenbridge, Michael had been plagued by memories of his family. Perhaps he needed to justify that cruel but necessary decision, because when walking or cycling with Evelyn, he often lapsed into tales of what it had been like growing up in the desperation of poverty, seeing his mother work too hard and his father drink too much. Evelyn encouraged him to put into his stories some of what he told her. Those were stories that she felt cut to the bone; they were also the kind of stories that gave him some detachment from his memories. "The Long Road to Ummera" was written at Evelyn's suggestion after she had heard O'Connor mimic a conversation between his father and his grandmother.

For some reason Michael's mother was, at that time, willing to reminisce about their life in Cork. Michael asked her to talk about her own family. She had never said much about her upbringing, except to talk about the convent which had been her only home. When she agreed one evening to tell her life story, he went so far as to take notes as he listened to things he knew nothing about. For once he didn't interrupt. The next day he set to work writing her story, exactly as she had given it to them that evening. This first-person account of an orphan girl was published anonymously in the first two issues of *The Bell.*[31] Few guessed who had written "Orphans" because it was hardly an

O'Connor story at all; it was his mother's story and Michael made sure that O'Faoláin sent the fifteen pounds directly to her.

In addition to the stories, O'Connor contributed substantially to *The Bell* during those early issues, pieces including book reviews, essays, and translations, but his primary contribution was as poetry editor. In this capacity he wrote "The Belfrey," a section reserved for new poets. The manuscripts that poured into the Parkgate offices provided ample testimony to the immediate impact of *The Bell* on a nation full of writers. Even after Peadar O'Donnell had mercifully siphoned off the worst, O'Connor had more than he could handle. In the second issue (November 1940) O'Connor chose a poem by Bryan Mac-Mahon, the young writer from Listowel, because the music of it had been in his head for days. In December, bound by a pact with himself to print the thing he liked best, O'Connor chose "Maguire," a poem by a young Belfast poet, because it struck him as "very Irish in its arrogance and unreasonableness." In the next issue he chose a poem by John Hewitt to illustrate his belief that "the real problem of Irish literature is the problem not of language but of idiom; that unique use of words which instantly produces the sense of Ireland."

Among the poets whose work O'Connor rejected was his old friend Geoffrey Phibbs, now writing under the name of Geoffrey Taylor. After seeing the first number of *The Bell*, Phibbs sent some poems to Michael along with an invitation to visit him in Tallaght. Michael did not answer the letter. He received another early in November asking if he would at least answer the letter even if he did not like the poems. Michael wrote a brief note from London and returned Phibbs's poems a week later.[32] The trouble was that with the constant clamor over his broadcasts, the arrival of the baby, and the relentless flood of bad verse, Michael was in such foul spirits that he could neither visit Phibbs nor write a gracious letter.

Phibbs, however, graciously visited Evelyn in the Leinster Nursing Home shortly after Liadain was born. In a note sent to Michael at Woodenbridge, he wrote, "Your daughter is a credit to you." Then, in response to O'Connor's translations of the Liadain poems in *The Bell*, Phibbs offered this praise: "You can't help being a poet. A sluttish poet, but still a poet. I may have come back to erin in time to unslut you." He advised Michael to keep writing stories. Finally, he observed that Irish writers could not afford to be serious until they realized that it all did not matter: "You, poor devil, still think it does, and what a byronic playboy of the wicklow world you get into over it all. Unwind yourself. But gently, so as not to wake the baby, bless her heart."[33] It was good advice, similar to that which Seán O'Faoláin was to give Michael a few months later.

From the time O'Connor had first arrived in Dublin he had stayed close to the action, writing reviews and letters to editors that infuriated nearly everyone with their hard-nosed opinions on nearly everything, particularly the theatre. In April 1941 he passed through Dublin after a cycling trip in Kilkenny and Kildare with Evelyn and stayed to meet with Mrs. Yeats regarding some Cuala Press business.[34] They decided to take in the Abbey production of *The Money Doesn't Matter*, by Louis D'Alton, a playwright Michael knew and admired. They stayed for two acts, leaving in protest when it became obvious to them that Denis O'Dea was playing his part as a caricature of Lennox Robinson. Everyone Michael spoke to about the play had recognized the caricature and had felt the same embarrassment it caused him. Naive and idealistic as

usual, Michael could not understand why no one had spoken out during the
play's amazingly long run of eight weeks.

As soon as he returned to Woodenbridge Michael wrote an indignant letter to the *Irish Times* expressing his disgust.[35] At the bottom of his typescript
he scribbled a note to R. M. "Bertie" Smyllie, the editor, imploring him to print
the letter and explaining his protest: "Whatever Robinson's faults may have
been, he was a distinguished figure, and for the directors of the theatre to permit one of their members to be portrayed as a dipsomaniac and thief is the
foulest treachery, which shows what little respect they have for their responsibilities." Smyllie published the letter and, a few days later, D'Alton's reply.
Jonathan Swift might have relished the ensuing battle, which transformed an
actor's tasteless performance into a cause of epic proportions.

In May Michael sent to O'Faoláin a carefully written but fervid article
about the incident for the next issue of *The Bell*. O'Faoláin took it immediately
to a solicitor, then agreed to print it only if Michael would accept some changes
that would protect the magazine from libel. His patience with Michael was
wearing thin, but he still wanted him to continue writing the "Belfrey" column. He wrote to Michael and tried to explain that *The Bell* could not succeed
unless it maintained AE's standards of constructive intelligence. The "noble
indignation" of Yeats was right for Yeats, but not for street urchins like himself
and Michael. "The people are OUR people, our fathers and mothers. They will
take it from Yeats—from Parnell—but not from Mikey Donovan, nor even from
Frank O'Connor, unless Frank is prepared to follow Yeats, and never, never,
never go down to the gutter where familiarity breeds . . . familiarity."[36]

In the postscript to that letter O'Faoláin reveals more than a little of his
exasperation:

> You sit down there on your backside and do the highflutin artist, while
> up here, painstakingly, I am doing a spot of real construction. That may
> not at all be how you see it. OK. I am merely telling you how I see it, and
> that's that. To me your irascibility is sheer nihilism. To me you are a mag-
> nificent anarchist. You drop out of the Abbey, You drop out of the Acad-
> emy, You want to drop out of the Bell. You will probably drop out of
> Cuala. A grand time for abit of excitement and let somebody else do the
> patient work. Can you imagine how your wildly explosive emotionalism
> strikes me, then? It just gives me a very large pain. I am beginning to be-
> lieve, enfin, that you are just a bloody genius, and your notion that you
> are a man of action is a gigantic delusion, and you should be told go away
> and write masterpieces—as, I have not the least doubt, you will do, and
> are doing.

O'Connor's statement, published in June and headed "Stone Dolls," approached the issue of taste and standards on four fronts.[37] He began by asserting that D'Alton's play, though ample in merit, galvanized the characters into
"a terrible parody of life." The actor who played the offending part stooped to
caricature, thus calling attention to the model rather than to the artistic creation. The caricature of public figures on the stage may be a time-honored dramatic device, but in Ireland, O'Connor claimed, the "whole social order is
framed against it," because of the principle that "a man's private life is his
own." The next target was the Board of Directors of the Abbey Theatre, who,

he wrote, had failed in their responsibility to the public conscience. Instead of raising the sights of the people, the directors had allowed the standards of the Abbey to slip from the dignity of Yeats to a level that "would not be tolerated in a Dublin slum." Finally, O'Connor turned on the critics. He especially condemned Denis Johnston's judgment that the play was "an amusing piece of foolery which, without professing great profundity, proved an excellent vehicle for the Company and gave an opportunity for one or two rather scandalous but very funny characters."[38] Johnston's tone of urbane tolerance infuriated O'Connor, because to his mind it betrayed the notion that nothing in the theatre really mattered very much, at least to the real problems of real people, an attitude that O'Connor found morally repugnant.

The conclusion to "Stone Dolls," powerfully flamboyant yet almost laughable in its eccentricity, lifts the entire piece from polemic to *apologia*. O'Connor recalls visiting the ruins of an Irish abbey and observing two tombs: "a Norman tomb of the thirteenth century" and another "from the fifteenth century when the Irish were again masters in their own house." Of the first, showing two crusaders, he says he found it "hard to contemplate without emotion the noble, sensuous flowing line, the delight in an ideal of human dignity and beauty." The second shows the twelve apostles, which he found to be "squat, lifeless, shapeless doll-like figures," as though "some Censor of the soul" had wiped out any trace of organic life and had "replaced it by the angular, graceless lines of the stone doll." Censorship and caricature represented to him an absence of "internal tension" gained by "straining after a desirable vision of life."

Denis O'Dea brought libel action against O'Connor, O'Faoláin, and *The Bell*, but he received little more than a few pounds for his trouble. Louis D'Alton did not so much answer O'Connor as undertake to instruct him, in the July issue of *The Bell*, on the difference between comedy and tragedy, the fallacy of quoting Yeats, and the gap between what O'Connor preached and what he practiced in his own plays. Such hyperbole and *ad hominem* reasoning hardly served to clarify anything; like O'Connor, D'Alton showed himself wrong even where he was right. He did not do his own play an ounce of good by labeling *The Invincibles* the beginning of the Great Decadence.[39]

Denis Johnston's reply in his regular theatre column for the July issue was calmer but no less irate; by this time even the unflappable lawyer/playwright had become fed up.[40] Dismissing plays one doesn't like by invoking pretentiousness or bad taste was no different, he argued, from raising the bogies of the "anti-national" or the "indecent," the usual ploy of the Censorship Board. In effect, Johnston found O'Connor guilty of opposing censorship by government edict while favoring censorship by critical tirade. Above all, Johnston disliked being dismissed as urbane, merely for laughing "at vulgarity and at gossip and at imitations of the innocuous mannerisms of my friends." Actually, Johnston said, the main harm done by the play had been to induce O'Connor to raise a furor by committing an "unsolicited rescue."

O'Faoláin's response to O'Connor's campaign was as balanced as his private letter had been shrill. In public O'Connor and O'Faoláin always seemed to defend each other, while continuing, like brothers, to fight in private. In his June editorial O'Faoláin argued that the entire incident proved that Ireland was still groping for standards.[41] He admitted that he didn't like what had been done on the stage of the Abbey only a little more than he didn't like what O'Connor was doing. Only a month before, O'Faoláin had argued eloquently for Ireland to maintain its traditions, insisting that a man like O'Connor, who defended tradition against the mediocrity of new fads and tired imitations, would always find himself torn between the old and the new. In June O'Faoláin reaffirmed his support of O'Connor, in spite of the nuisance he had made of himself, and in doing so affirmed that *The Bell* would continue to "let life speak for itself." It would neither encourage nor stifle controversy, preferring "to encourage people to speak of the things they like, rather than the things they dislike—that a kind of natural selectivity may reveal some kind of natural desire for, as Frank O'Connor says, a 'desirable vision of life.' " All that was barren and destructive, including the "recent unpleasant incident at the Abbey," could not be changed in a moment; only with time could the standards and tastes of the nation be brought into line with what he termed "our dreams about a great, modern Ireland." As always, O'Faoláin seemed to be fighting for exactly the same things O'Connor was fighting for, but in a very different way.

The question remains: Why did O'Connor choose to fight about an issue that was probably none of his concern? While O'Faoláin and Johnston felt comfortable taking the long view, O'Connor did not. He was a fighter, unwilling to compromise, and always ready to champion a lost cause. He took everything seriously, especially his self-appointed task of rescuing the helpless and saving Ireland from itself. He was also a chest thumper, not a back stabber; a grievance was something he handled on the spot, face to face. He could no more overlook a caricature he considered "monstrous and repulsive" than he could forgive government censorship, even if what he advocated—muzzling O'Dea—was itself a form of censorship. He had little love and less respect for Lennox Robinson, but he believed in acting on one's principles. For a moral absolutist that meant unequivocal action. O'Faoláin and Johnston, who preferred to choose their battles, felt that publicizing the unfortunate incident would expose Robinson to more public shame. Besides, they warned, wild ranting would be dismissed and the real issue would be obscured. The fact is, O'Connor wanted to live everything at larger-than-life size; since he could not stomach the petty or the trivial, he often elevated the trivial to the heroic to justify his attention.

It must be remembered that at the time O'Connor was understandably angry about recent government interference with his livelihood. Moreover, the wounds from his bitter feud with the Abbey Directors were still festering, so naturally he equated the shameful standards of taste in the Abbey with the shameful treatment he had received. (The same group of men who had demanded control of everything O'Connor wrote for the *Arrow* had, in O'Connor's estimation, now stooped to allowing ridicule of one of their own.) On an even deeper personal level he felt betrayed by Richard Hayes, once his closest friend. Evelyn's disclosure that Hayes had warned her not to marry him still stuck in Michael's memory, particularly her assessment that Hayes was jealous of her. Nothing made Michael more uneasy than homosexuality, nothing infuriated him quite so instantly as the implication of unnatural affection in his own relationships. In that spirit, he had begun to let it be known around Dublin that he would have no more to do with Richard Hayes.

Sometime in April Michael had written a cruel letter to Hayes announcing the irrevocable termination of their friendship. Hayes had heard what his old friend had been saying about him, and had chosen to ignore it. He had watched O'Connor's latest outburst over the D'Alton play with only mild indignation. But Michael's letter hurt him deeply. On May 4 Hayes wrote back responding point by point to Michael's charges that he had conspired against him; he denied any knowledge of the infamous dinners from which Michael had been excluded and denied all adverse statements imputed to him by Michael.[42] "That expression 'hatred of you' is dreadful when I think that since what you call 'the break' between us I have never ceased to regard you with the same affection and hold you in the same high opinion that I always did." As witnesses to his integrity he offered his new wife and a mutual friend, Niall Montgomery. "Resolutions of mine to suggest that you were a habitual drunkard" Hayes dismissed as "too disgusting to notice." However, he vigorously defended his stands on the editorial policy of the theatre magazine and the resolution to change the articles of association when O'Connor refused to resign his membership in the National Theatre. Hayes's postscript disavowed any desire to resume the friendship or even to offer an apology for "supposed statements and actions." He wanted no reply to his letter; he received none.

13

On Sandymount Strand

Am I walking into eternity along Sandymount Strand?
JAMES JOYCE, *Ulysses*

A visiting American once asked O'Connor what he thought was the most re-markable thing in Dublin; O'Connor replied by taking the man for a walk on Sandymount Strand.[1] In the late summer of 1941 O'Connor found himself faced with the necessity of moving his family back to Dublin; his financial situation was steadily deteriorating and in Wicklow no opportunity existed for Evelyn to supplement their income. So, he merely walked along the strand and took the first house he found for rent. For the next few years 57 Strand Road would be the center for the widening gyre of his life. He cherished solitude as ruthlessly as any writer, but he needed the sort of interaction available in Dublin. He moved to ease the financial pressure and to get closer to the center of activity, but within two years he would be nearly destitute and for all practical purposes an outcast.

I

While Frank O'Connor was fighting his novel, cycling around Ireland in search of ruins, and generally storming about the "bloody country," everyone else was feeling the effects of a very lean year. That winter petrol supplies had run dry, while coal, fertilizers, and steel had been cut back sharply. By April tea and sugar had come to be severely rationed. These were the days of monu-mental turf piles in Phoenix Park, of turf poachers, and of black-market prices. Rationing of gas and electricity prompted the appearance of the "glimmer men," government inspectors searching for unlawful use of residual gas in the lines. A stiff fine was imposed on anyone found using a stove during "glim-mer," or restricted, hours. Still, the Irish as a whole ate better than the British because of their plentiful supply of meat, bacon, eggs, and butter.[2]

Life at 57 Strand Road went on much as it had done at Lynduff. In the spring Evelyn planted a small vegetable garden behind the house. She man-aged to get a job now and then, reviewing a play or acting at the Gate, but being closer to town, they spent more on books, drink, and other little luxuries. Michael had always smoked Player's cigarettes, though now and then he in-dulged in a pipe with good tobacco bought in Fox's across from Trinity College.[3] His daily routine remained much the same: writing in the morning, walking in the late afternoon, and reading in the evenings.

The house in Sandymount was a typical Dublin detached terrace house with a "return," or addition, in back. O'Connor's study on the top floor over-looked the strand; he always insisted on making the best room of the house his study. An imposing sign on the study door, visible from the bottom of the stairs, read "AUTHOR!" On the north wall of this room was a fireplace, and bookcases filled the rest of the room. Folding doors opened into his bedroom. The main floor of the house was a few steps above street level. From the front door a long hall ran to the back of the house, with stairs at the end. To the right of the entry was the sitting room, from which Dublin Bay and Howth Head could be seen. Behind the sitting room, toward the back of the house, was the room that was soon occupied by Donny, the children's name for Michael's mother. In the basement was a dining room and maid's quarters. The return, a structural feature commonly added to Dublin houses to increase the space, held the kitchen at ground level and a nursery above that. The house was comfortably furnished but modestly decorated. Michael's main contributions, other than those in his study, were his old Morris chair and a new gramophone in the sitting room and a Rembrandt print, *Man in the Golden Helmet,* in the dining room.

Home to Michael O'Donovan, however, always meant his mother. She remained the one fixed point of his life. Minnie had carefully kept all mention of Big Mick's deteriorating health from Michael, partly because she wanted to keep her son from anxiety and partly because she believed he did not understand the man. Having had the patience to live with him, she had the patience to let him die in his own way, not his son's. With the severe tea rationing, he had turned to his only remaining resource, and he died, on March 13, 1942, as he had lived, "blundering drunk about Cork in the last stages of pneumonia."[4] In her loyalty Minnie always blamed the drink and not the man. "He took me from the gutter where life had thrown me," she sighed.

At the funeral Michael mourned honestly, not so much in public display as in bitter confusion over the loss of someone both dear and dreaded. His cousin Christy O'Donovan told him of a "big black stain that appeared about his heart when he died."[5] Michael could never determine what that stain meant, but the image of it haunted his dreams for years. An incident at the funeral did little to clarify his ambiguous emotions or to soften his already notorious hatred of the church. The priest who buried his father seemed unduly impatient and irritable; Christy later told them that the man was afraid of being late to an important football match. Reporting the offensive incident in his next letter to Dermot, Michael curtly concluded, "you'll be glad to know he got in for half time."[6] After his father's death Michael always made sure that his mother had enough money to have Mass said for Big Mick, knowing "how lost and embarrassed that shy, home-keeping man would be with no Minnie O'Connor to come home to, no home, no Cork, no pension, astray in the infinite wastes of eternity."[7]

Two days after the funeral Michael's mother closed the door at Harrington Square and returned to Dublin with her son. She remained under his roof, wherever it happened to be, until her death ten years later. Because Minnie received a small pension, her presence in the house was not a financial strain on her son. Actually, despite her advancing age, she contributed to the family in many ways. Her presence alone dispelled Michael's fury, and her irrepressible good humor buffered the nervous tension that often sprang up between Michael and Evelyn. She doted on the children, particularly when Evelyn and Michael were away cycling or when Michael was in England.

Michael's mother, who knew how to improvise in the face of poverty, gave inestimable support to Evelyn's frugal household management during those lean war years. She helped by knitting sweaters from the shoulder down in order to be able to reknit cuffs and sleeves, which wore out quickly. Evelyn was an excellent seamstress herself and often made warm vests and leggings for the children from Michael's worn trousers. When wheat shipments were stopped, the only flour available was so improperly milled that it all had to be sieved through silk or rayon stockings before it could be used, a measure Michael's mother had learned from one of the rich ladies for whom she worked during World War I.[8] In spite of the constant strain and sacrifice of making do, things at Strand Road were about the same as conditions elsewhere in Ireland during the Emergency—difficult, challenging and, at times even a bit comical.

I I

O'Faoláin's blistering letter to Michael about the D'Alton affair had referred to Michael's tendency to drop out of undertakings such as the Abbey and *The Bell*. O'Faoláin was correct in his accusations, though perhaps for the wrong reasons. By nature Michael was a person of intense feelings, given to wild emotional outbursts of love and of hatred. What he knew to be absolutely wrong he rejected without reservation or rationalization. By the same token, he loved people and held certain beliefs with the same unquestioning intensity. There was nothing contrived about his friendships, his enthusiasms, or his loves.

The fact is that he contributed to the Abbey primarily as a man of action and not as a man of thought. He gave it everything he had, conserving nothing. After participating actively in the founding of the Irish Academy of Letters, O'Connor gradually lost interest after the death of AE. And for nearly a year he supported O'Faoláin's efforts at *The Bell* with fervent optimism, dropping out finally because the bulk of unreadable manuscripts was just too much. In each case it was not recalcitrance or malignance that soured him, but a congenital inability to play the necessary political games. O'Faoláin called it "irascibility" bordering on "sheer nihilism," though others used the word *uncompromising*. Although Michael never lied, he also never exercised tact, which he said was "putting on airs." His values and his manners were those of the Cork slum from which he came—straightforward and simple. O'Connor's brand of idealism, his almost naive honesty, might have made enemies of some, but it was what endeared him to many others.

For nearly two years Mrs. Yeats had wanted him to serve on the editorial board of the Cuala Press. Though he thought highly of her and felt some indebtedness to the press for publishing his translations, he had resisted because of the looming presence of F. R. Higgins. When Higgins died in January 1941, Mrs. Yeats turned again to Michael/Frank, as she always called him. He accepted primarily because she was the widow of W. B. Yeats.[9] As a member of the Cuala Board of Editors, he was most outspoken in his support of the publication of Patrick Kavanagh's "The Great Hunger," which he considered the finest poem of its time. As always, he promoted what he felt represented Ireland *at its best*.

Late in October 1941 the idea Denis Johnston had first proposed to O'Connor and O'Faoláin, an idea overshadowed by, though not forgotten with, the inception of *The Bell*, finally became a reality with the founding of the Dublin Drama League.[10] At the very first meeting of this organization of people from all the theatres in Dublin, Johnston and MacLiammóir put forward O'Connor's *The Statue's Daughter* to be the League's first offering. Mrs. Yeats, acting as Honorary Secretary of the DDL, informed Michael of the decision and asked if he would object to Michael Farrell, an undistinguished playwright and actor, as producer.[11] Farrell was no great admirer of O'Connor; his review of *In the Train* had been so condescending that O'Connor held no great fondness for him either. But Farrell was a known commodity in Dublin theatre circles, and like everyone else in town at the time, he needed the work. O'Connor accepted the choice, but from the first reading of the script Farrell resisted the play. He wrote at least three long letters to O'Connor outlining his criticism and suggesting extensive alterations. Oddly enough, O'Connor patiently obliged him. Farrell was never fully satisfied and even went so far as to tell the critic Gabriel Fallon to go easy on him because all the faults in the play were the author's. Rancor swirled from other corners of the DDL as well. Ria Mooney, the brilliant actress who had made a great success of the Abbey School of Acting, still held the D'Alton affair against O'Connor. She had been loud in her disapproval of *The Statue's Daughter* when it had been circulated in the Abbey offices, and continued her campaign by asking a number of Dublin actors not to audition for parts.[12] As a result, the play was rehearsed and staged under a heavy fog of contention.

Ironically, this kind of anticipatory furor is precisely what the play is all about. A committee, raising money to erect a statue in memory of a local hero of the Troubles, is thrown into confusion by a rumor about town that he had an illegitimate daughter. Costello, a local journalist who is at once curious and skeptical about the rumor, asks if the committee wants to hear about the real Brian O'Rourke or about a plaster saint. Those who had fought beside him, joked with him, and drunk with him are torn between the memory of the human being and their memorial to his gathering legend. O'Rourke's sisters claim that the rumor is a British plot to discredit a man who never womanized, smoked, drank, or swore. In the last act of the play Peter Paul, the one who started the rumor in the first place, calls it his "holy duty" to blow up the statue because it "stands for something we never put up with."[13] Joan, the alleged daughter of O'Rourke, fires back: "It stands for life and you stand for death. It stands for reality, and you stand for sham; for hypocrisy." If her words are melodramatic, they nevertheless make the point. She has been threatened by the same sort of people who "censor every decent book in the library." While the Gaelic League Committee worries about the possibility of a riot, Costello practices his speech.

O'Connor called his play a fantasy, intending it as a political twist on the Playboy motif—when whispered about, the peccadilloes of a hero only add to the lustre of the legend, but when they turn up in the flesh, they topple the idol. He did not have Terence MacSwiney, who died after his hunger strike in 1920, in mind any more or less than he had Michael Collins or Charles Stewart Parnell in mind. His concern was not the sexual immorality of Irish heroes but the hypocrisy of the hero makers who fear all that is human and cling to pietistic and nationalistic abstractions. If Joan is the emotional center of the play, then Costello, the tired, idealistic newspaperman, is O'Connor's thematic mouthpiece. He claims that Ireland "is no place for idealists," and warns Joan that in "ten years time, if you haven't grown hard and coarse and cynical like all the others you may become what I am now." Lonely is what he is— lonely, his friends say, from forty years of telling the truth no one wants to hear.

Costello may not represent O'Connor (in fact, he resembles Corkery), but his speech is one that O'Connor had been making in one form or another since Gormanstown, about the betrayal of revolutionary ideals by an "incredulous and cynical generation." To his mind, "it's just because of our skulking fear of life that we try to turn Brian O'Rourke into legend and hide his relationship to Joan's mother." Costello is for telling the truth, which in the end turns out to be no truth at all: Peter Paul had invented the whole thing. The statue is unveiled one night only to be damaged a few minutes later by a time bomb set by a Virtue and Decency mob. In the final scene Costello jokes that the land mine was as "efficient as everything else that comes from the university. The statue is still there." Walking Joan home at the end of it all, Costello muses that he is like the statue, blown up many times but still there. "We live in faith, and I've kept true to the faith I had as a boy; that life can be a thousand times nobler and finer than anything we imagine."

Though O'Connor called his play a fantasy, it was actually a message play, but the message was not what Irish audiences wanted to hear, especially during the Emergency. Besides, they had heard it before in his broadcasts and letters to the editors, and it bored them. Not so many years before, women protesting over O'Casey's *The Plough and the Stars* claimed that there was not a whore in the entire island. Now it was alleged that there were no bastards either, at least none who should be talked about. O'Connor's own marriage to a divorced woman, rumors of his various flirtations, and the recent banning of his "indecent" novel seemed to prejudice response to *The Statue's Daughter*. Debate centered so much on the impropriety of dealing openly with impropriety that the fundamental irony of the play was missed.[14]

In November, during the squabbling over the play, O'Connor was visited by Cyril Connolly, an old friend from London who was in Ireland putting together a special issue of his magazine *Horizon*.[15] Though he interviewed a number of important people in government, Connolly was mainly interested in seeing wartime Ireland through the eyes of its writers. He heard from everyone he talked to that the problem of Irish writers was that with no rich or patron class they must depend on American and British markets, now all but closed by neutrality, which left Irish writers at the mercy of internal rivalries, libel actions, and government censorship. In his editorial introducing the Irish issue of *Horizon* two months later, Connolly reasoned that neutrality was simply the political manifestation of Irish nationalism, that cultural phenomenon Irish writing tried to reflect and understand. His view of Dublin, "disengaged from the fabulous embrace of Joyce," who had died in January 1941, was a place of excitement and envy, charm and enmity. His claim was to cut through some of the prejudice that existed on both sides of the Irish Sea: British impatience with Eire, and Irish suspicion of Britain. To this end he asked O'Connor for a piece on the future of literature in Ireland after the war. O'Connor eagerly accepted and urged Connolly to publish Patrick Kavanagh's long poem on rural Ireland, then called "The Old Peasant" and later retitled "The Great Hunger." Connolly agreed, Kavanagh accepted his offer, and the poem was published along with O'Connor's essay.

Controversy over *The Statue's Daughter* had barely cooled when copies of the January 1942 issue of *Horizon* were promptly seized by authorities and the magazine was banned. Gardaí from the vice squad even raided the flat in Haddington Road where Patrick Kavanagh lived, at near-starvation level, with his brother Peter.[16] They asked the writer if he had written "that filthy poem," pointing accusingly at "The Old Peasant." Although the poem hints at masturbation, it probably was considered obscene for its general implication that something was dreadfully wrong in a country where a farmer could live an entire life stifled by his mother and hungry for sexual love. But without O'Connor's scathing article, which among other things mentioned contraception, it is unlikely that Kavanagh's poem by itself would have prompted the Irish government to ban that issue of the magazine.

Many people felt that O'Connor's essay "The Future of Irish Literature" was an airing of dirty linen in public, but the question he believed he was raising was how literature in Ireland could survive the war. By Irish literature he did not mean Shaw or Elizabeth Bowen; rather he was thinking of the sort of national literature that "permits a young man or woman growing up in Cork or Helsinki or Kalamazoo to look at life about him through the medium of a racial outlook and philosophy, without his instantly beginning to pine for London and Paris and Rome."[17] Such a literature, he argued, began with Yeats and Synge as part of a national awakening that sought to locate "the cause of its defeat in itself rather than in its external enemy."

The common enemy, he asserted, had always been "the imitation of English ways—the provincialist, the 'gombeen man'—a very expressive Irishism for the *petit bourgeois;* and the Tammany politician who had riddled every institution with corruption." In that framework literature served to forge a sense of national dignity, a goal that O'Connor claimed had been subverted since the Revolution. When it became more important to know Irish and to go to Mass than to be competent and caring, provincialism had won.

There is nothing abstract or academic about O'Connor's argument; the attack is frontal, which fact as much as anything he said brought down the wrath of the government. O'Connor could no more mask his opinions in subtle language than he could write a subtle play. Instead of freedom, the Irish had simply accepted homegrown tyranny, he believed. The same line is taken by a character in *The Statue's Daughter,* who asks the committee if they want a country run by thieves, scoundrels, and pious hoodlums. Economics and birth control, however, were less O'Connor's concern than were the decay of the Abbey Theatre and the capricious censorship of books and films.[18] In the next two sections of his essay he argued that because of this poisoned atmosphere Irish writing in his generation was dominated by its subject. When an Irish writer looked beyond "slums and cabins," he found "nothing but a vicious and ignorant middle-class" and an alien aristocracy. O'Connor found this pattern particularly in Kavanagh's *The Green Fool*—"the novel every Irish writer who isn't a rogue or an imbecile is doomed to write when the emptiness and horror of Irish life begins to dawn on him."

The period of awakening was over, O'Connor claimed, but the character of the next period was not yet clear. War altered everything, even "Mr. DeValera's dream of a nonentity state entirely divorced from the rest of the world." *
In the meantime, he asked, "what can the Irish writer like Patrick Kavanagh do? How is he to compose this fundamental quarrel with his material?" As much as he wanted to take O'Faoláin's advice and stay in Woodenbridge to write masterpieces, he was compelled to return to Dublin and fight for lost causes:

> I am bewildered by the complete lack of relationship between Irish literature and any form of life, within or without Ireland. Blandly, sentimentally, maundering to itself, Irish literature sails off on one tack, while off on another go hand in hand Mr. DeValera and the Church, the murder gangs and the Catholic secret societies. It may be argued that they are the business of publicists, not of artists, but there are no publicists, there is no public opinion, and if the artists do not fight, who will? And if we don't fight, and new circumstances don't settle Mr. DeValera's hash for us, what is to become of Ireland or Irish literature?[19]

I I I

For nearly two years Frank O'Connor's voice had been heard regularly on Radio Eireann; his talks and readings were extremely popular with Irish audiences. In January 1942 three of his finest stories were dramatized: "Majesty of the Law" on the first, "The Long Road to Ummera" on the eighth, and "In the Train" on the fifteenth. Congratulatory mail poured into the broadcasting station.[20] However, O'Connor's own welcome at Radio Eireann suddenly ceased. When the January issue of *Horizon* was banned toward the end of the month, vice-squad detectives did not raid the O'Donovan house in Strand Road, but pressure was soon felt there. When O'Connor called at the broadcasting center in the General Post Office Building, he could not seem to find anyone in. When he wrote, he received no reply. At the end of February he was entirely without work and had no idea why. He moped around the house, speaking to no one, or sat in his study smoking and staring at the strand. Throughout March he met one obstacle after another in his attempts to obtain a permit to travel to London for broadcasts. Only a few days before his father died, he was finally cleared to leave Ireland, and Michael went to London as soon as his mother was settled in the Sandymount house. During that next week Salmon arranged for O'Connor to broadcast two stories from Dublin in June and to return to London in July to take part in another panel discussion for the "Living Opinion" series.[21]

As soon as he returned to Dublin O'Connor expressed to O'Faoláin his anger over the passport difficulties and his suspicions about his treatment at Radio Eireann. O'Faoláin nosed around a bit and learned that secret instructions had been issued: O'Connor was not to be allowed to broadcast, nor was he to be informed of this decision. In May, to test this policy, he submitted "The Gambler," the first of a series of stories that he had previously agreed to broad-

---

* O'Connor's spelling of de Valera here is not so much a mistake as a reflection of a common inconsistency in Irish/English spelling (e.g. Brian Merriman/Bryan Merryman).

cast. He received no acknowledgment. A month later he went to the office of Roibéard O'Faracháin, the talks officer, to retrieve the manuscript. O'Faracháin claimed it was not in the building. A few days later the manuscript was returned with a note from someone else at Radio Eireann; the manuscript, the note said, could not be accepted. On July 3 BBC officials, having heard that O'Connor would not be able to get out of Ireland for the scheduled broadcast of his story "Song Without Words," requested the use of studio facilities at Radio Eireann. The request was refused.[22]

On July 6 O'Connor, unaware of the negotiations between the BBC and Radio Eireann, attempted to board the mail boat for Holyhead. At the gangway he was turned back. He showed his visa, issued on June 23 by request of the London Permit Office. He was then shown an order from the Dublin Permit Office stating that he was to be "picked up" if he attempted to embark. He went straight to the office of the United Kingdom representative to Ireland, demanding an explanation of this discourteous and humiliating incident. The person with the unenviable task of soothing the wounded giant was Shevawn Lynam, assistant to the press attaché, John Betjeman, who was out of the office at the time. Though they were later to become friends, even neighbors, on this occasion Michael treated her most rudely.

Instead of waiting for Betjeman to return, Michael stalked off to wire Salmon in London. Then he went home to write letters to Betjeman and the British Passport Control Office. A week later the BBC broadcast had to be canceled, whereupon Michael wrote a long letter to Harold Macmillan, the only person he knew whose opinion would command attention at the Home Office, explaining what had happened. But Macmillan's efforts, whatever they were, had no effect. The matter lay in Dublin and not with the British Home Office. Frank O'Connor was virtually being kept a prisoner in his own country.[23]

By August WAAMA, a Dublin association of writers, actors, and musicians, took up O'Connor's cause. Gabriel Fallon organized the campaign behind the scenes so as not to bring O'Connor any more notoriety by publicizing the incident. O'Faoláin, on the other hand, wanted a public airing. He told Michael that he and their other friends would fight "tooth and nail" for him. "But I doubt if we'd ever get you into the Dail! We fight for the absolute right of public criticism here of any and all institutions." On August 11 O'Connor wrote to Mr. Patrick Little, who as minister for posts and telegraphs had cabinet-level jurisdiction over all broadcasts; he told Little he had been informed that his proposal for a series of short stories on Radio Eireann had been rejected on the personal instructions of Mr. Little. O'Connor wished to know what the objections were, and requested an interview. He received no acknowledgment and no reply. In the meantime Fallon and O'Faoláin had made contact with other officials at Radio Eireann, but they, too, met with little success. As nearly as O'Faoláin could discern, it was partly a "moral issue," stemming from the annulment business. Fallon was certain the issue was political, having to do with O'Connor's broadcasts for the BBC and with the *Horizon* article, which, among other things, criticized government broadcasting policies. O'Faoláin responded in a letter to Michael: "If it's the *Horizon* article they are nuts. That is legitimate."

Even Michael's old friend Daniel Binchy, then serving with the Irish diplomatic service, became involved. When Mr. Little returned from his holidays,

Binchy talked with him on O'Connor's behalf. About the passport restriction Little simply stated that it was "a question of policy" and that the decision could not be altered. When it was pointed out that this amounted to depriving a man of his livelihood, he disavowed any such intention and offered to accept programs if submitted under a *nom de plume,* such as Proinnsias O'Conchubhair, Micheal O'Donnobhain, or the like. O'Connor flatly refused this compromise, and to keep his sanity, he went off cycling with Dermot and Stan.

By September Michael and Evelyn had practically become destitute. At the end of one letter O'Faoláin even offered Michael a loan or an advance on a series of articles for *The Bell.* Of course, O'Connor was not alone; these were lean times for most writers and actors. Patrick Kavanagh, one writer pushed to the brink of desperation by the war, had never known anything but lean times. Shortly after the *Horizon* incident he too called on John Betjeman, to offer himself as a spy in Lisbon. For years his only source of income came from occasional book reviews for the *Times* or *Independent,* a column of "homespun chat" for the *Irish Press* under the pseudonym Piers Plowman, and a regular column of film and theatre criticism for the *Standard,* a Catholic weekly. For some reason (perhaps it was the *Standard* column) Kavanagh also made regular visits to the residence of the Reverend John C. McQuaid, Archbishop of Dublin, on which occasions he often received a meal and a small sum of money. Apparently, on one such occasion Kavanagh happened to mention something about the plight of Frank O'Connor, a fact that surprised and intrigued the archbishop.

The following Monday evening a stranger appeared at the O'Donovan house in Strand Road. Michael was reading when he arrived, so Evelyn showed the gentleman to the study. A short time later Michael shouted for Evelyn to come up. Not knowing who the man was or the nature of his call, she assumed that Michael wanted tea, so she delayed until it was ready. When she came to the door of the study, Michael was extremely agitated. "Tell that to her," he commanded. The tea cooled as the gentleman, an emissary from the Legion of Mary, a prominent association of Catholic laymen, explained that their marriage and the thorny annulment proceedings were a source of great embarrassment to the church.

"Now listen to his proposal," Michael roared, stalking toward the window, his fingers racing wildly through his hair, cigarette ashes flying down his shoulders. Calmly, the man told her that work would be made available to Michael again if they separated. Evelyn was stunned. "But we have a family," she implored, on the verge of tears. "The marriage is not recognized by the Church" was the reply. "Why? Austin Clarke was married in a Registry Office and no one bothers him," Michael yelled. Evelyn continued for a few minutes about what was to become of the children, then stopped short and in her most composed stage manner asked for proof. Michael whirled in disbelief. The man said confidently, "What proof do you want?" "Three months work at Radio Eireann for me. Then we'll talk about separation."

Two days later she had the job, and for three months she had more work than she had bargained for. She acted in radio plays, made a series of broadcast talks on Irish churches, reviewed and wrote scripts—anything and everything the heads of departments at Radio Eireann wanted done.[24] Dermot wrote that she should be called "Slavey" Bowen. She often came home late after a play or broadcast only to collapse into bed. Michael, whose views of the family were rather Victorian—authoritarian father who provides the means, passive mother who manages the daily affairs, and dutiful children who are seen and not heard—found the whole arrangement a bit shattering to his pride. In effect, he had been blacklisted, prohibited from all employment in Ireland. Since the days of the Abbey wars he had become increasingly paranoid; it was becoming obvious that he had good reason. His novel had been censored after publication, his scripts had been censored before broadcasting, and now he was being censored before the fact altogether.

Censorship, however, was not limited to Frank O'Connor. In March 1941, for example, Kate O'Brien's novel *The Land of Spices* was banned; and its author joined the roll call of Irish writers banned, officially or otherwise, under the 1929 Censorship of Publications Act.[25] Officially, *The Land of Spices,* a delicate and sensitive novel about convent life, was thought to be "in its general tendency indecent." Actually, what drew the violent response of the five censors was a single sentence alluding to homosexuality. Then, in October of that same year, a prohibition order was served on *Laws of Life,* a cautious medical book by a noted British gynecologist, Dr. Halliday Sutherland. The publisher was Sheed and Ward, a house of impeccable standing in Catholic circles; Dr. Sutherland was himself a Roman Catholic who went out of his way to explain Catholic teaching on procreation and contraception. The book was also banned for being "in its general tendency indecent."

There the matter lay except for skirmishes in the dailies and a continuing assault by O'Faoláin in *The Bell.* In spite of the systematic banning of books by reputable writers, Irish and otherwise, only minor opposition had been mounted during the 1930s, and after the demise of the *Irish Statesman* in 1930 no organ of protest against censorship existed in Ireland until O'Faoláin founded *The Bell* in 1940. There were angry letters from people like O'Connor following the banning of books like O'Faoláin's *Bird Alone* and Francis Hackett's *The Green Lion.* The Irish Academy of Letters, PEN, WAAMA, and the Irish Society for Intellectual Freedom tried valiantly and courteously to bring pressure to bear on the government to at least consider an appeals procedure. But nothing changed the administration of the censorship: "Innocuous at first, it became silly during the 1940s and vindictive during the 1950s," O'Connor later wrote.

Post-Treaty Ireland may be best described as ingrown: at least that is how John Ryan, a well-known Dublin writer, editor, and pub owner, describes it. In *Remembering How We Stood* he is especially caustic about de Valera's "Gaelic mandarins" who did everything they could to keep Ireland closed to "fresh winds of opinion and the germs of new ideas."[26] The primary instrument of "this self-appointed and self-perpetuating oligarchy," Ryan believes, was the censorship law, "which the founding fathers, in their sea-green incorruptibility, had managed to have enacted even in the teeth of the brave and eloquent opposition of Senator William Butler Yeats, lay like a heavy blight on the cultural landscape of the time." In effect, there existed between the Catholic-Nationalist establishment and the intellectual community a kind of strange sustaining opposition. Auden, after all, claimed that Ireland hurt Yeats into poetry. One wonders too, recalling John Montague's line a generation later about Puritan Ireland being a "myth of O'Connor and O'Faoláin," how much these writers could have grown as artists without the bruising tension that existed between them and their "material."

On September 28, 1942, Eric Cross's *The Tailor and Ansty* was banned. The prohibition was made public on October 2, and within a few days Frank O'Connor posted another heated letter of protest to the editor of the *Irish Times*.[27] The principle of censorship mattered less to him than the principle of human decency; banning a book was one thing, but insulting Tim Buckley and his wife, the innocent subjects of that book, was another. O'Faoláin entered the fray with an equally intemperate letter in which he threw caustic barbs at the "five addle-pates" on the Censorship Board, whose incompetency was "a humiliation to the people." Both O'Connor and O'Faoláin had known the old couple of Gougane Barra for years and saw in them the very stock of native Ireland. They also knew Eric Cross, the English chemist who had gone to the West Cork Gaeltacht (Gaelic-speaking region) in the late 1930s to record the adventures of one of the last of the Gaelic storytellers.

When Cross finished his book about Tim Buckley the Tailor and his wife, Ansty, he had O'Connor write the introduction, partly because that was what the Tailor wished. After the banning Cross wrote again expressing gratitude for O'Connor's gallant efforts.[28] Close to seventy-nine at the time, the Tailor had enjoyed the reviews of the books as he had enjoyed everything else in life—with gusto. "Life's a blue bag, knock a squeeze in it now and then," he would say with a twinkle. When the banning came, he had to endure all manner of unpleasantness—pietistic hooligans jammed his door and chased his cow, neighbors avoided the cottage, and three priests even forced the old man to burn his copy of the book. But he took it with stoic ease. "Take it slow and easy and it will take you slow and easy," he always said about life. Cross could not be so magnanimous; he wanted a fight.

Within a month the battle reached the Senate of Ireland. On November 18 Sir John Keane, a Protestant landlord, responded to the controversy by bringing a motion before Seanad Éireann calling for a reconstitution of the Censorship Board. He insisted that he was not questioning the principle of censorship, only its practice. Keane's case rested primarily on the injustice exhibited in the banning of *The Land of Spices*, *Laws of Life*, and *The Tailor and Ansty*. However, his entire speech went far beyond these books, even beyond the scope of his motion, to a consideration of the whole subject of censorship. He suggested that the Board was too removed from the stream of Irish life, too Victorian and academic, to make representative decisions. He called attention to an unofficial "literary Gestapo," including customs officials who by their own initiative restricted access to books. What he wanted, he said, was "clean, fresh air on the facts of life."[29]

What he got was an angry response from his Seanad colleagues, who upheld the Board's actions as necessary even if occasionally excessive. Others actually advocated strengthening the Board in order to censor any book portraying Ireland unfavorably or subverting Christian morality. One senator attacked Keane for his choice of allies, arguing that Irish standards were being dictated from England: "Every Irish writer who is acclaimed by completely unimportant English critics immediately establishes himself in this country as an outstanding pundit on all matters of literature, philosophy, politics and the ordering of society. That is our weakness. We have no critical standards." Kate

O'Brien had previously won the Hawthornden Prize in England: Eric Cross and Dr. Sutherland were English; O'Connor and O'Faoláin had both received more liberal acclaim in Britain than in Ireland.

Senator-Professor William Magennis, chairman of the Censorship Board, dominated the entire debate. O'Connor later called him "a windbag with a nasty streak of malice," who "in a torrent of irrelevancies interspersed with innuendos" simply deluged the opposition. Magennis called the Tailor a sex maniac and Ansty a moron. He accused Sir John Keane of taking his arguments from the letters of O'Connor and O'Faoláin in the *Times*. On *Laws of Life*, which he termed "the fornicator's *vademecum*," he launched an even more sarcastic attack: "Let me now come to the book, the banning of which involves this terrible thing that shocked the heart and conscience of Frank O'Connor and Sean O'Faoláin and their associates."[30] About the remainder of Magennis's two-day tirade little else need be said; its length and vehemence carried the day. Sir John Keane's motion was defeated, 34 to 2, on December 9, 1942.

But the issue was far from settled. Letters continued to appear in the Dublin dailies. A Council of Action, formed in November and comprising "recognized associations," brought to the minister of justice concrete suggestions for assuring that the administration of the Censorship Act would not "prevent liberty of thought or discussion" in Ireland. Staunch supporters of the act also continued the debate, feeling perhaps that the opponents of censorship had dominated the public spotlight. One clergyman published a fierce attack on the editor of the *Irish Times* and on the self-styled "literati" who started the "storm of protest" in the first place. Not content just to defend the Board's right to prohibit "indecent" publications, he called for the prohibition of all works subversive to the Christian way of life.

For O'Connor, however, the matter was closed. The "business of the artist," he had always maintained, "is with his art and not with the problems that will be decided far more finally and successfully by the illiterate *Mussolinis* of the world." When he received another letter from Eric Cross imploring him to keep attacking the censorship, he wrote to his old friend Sean Hendrick, asking him to communicate to Cross that if that simply meant going out with a toolbox and removing it, he would do so immediately.

> The Censorship will not be removed until either clerical pressure has been removed from the two political parties or a foreign power reminds us that we didn't get our freedom to establish another little Fascist tyranny and Dev comes rushing round to O'Faoláin and myself begging us to explain to the world that Ireland is really a democratic country where every man can say what he pleases. As to the possibility of either you will know what to say.
>
> I have now discovered why I always wanted a house on Sandymount strand. It's the nearest I can get to England.[31]

"Blast them all," he roared at O'Faoláin, "where's your Arts and the Free Man with the politicians and the priests? It's Gormanstown all over again." To Stan Stewart he wrote: "Blast Ireland, blast Catholicism, blast Protestantism. . . . And I spent ten years trying to save this country from itself when I should have been saving myself from the country."[32]

I V

Just before Christmas, as Evelyn's three-month "proof" period was drawing to an end, Larry Morrow, a director at Radio Eireann, noticed her sullen mood and asked what she and Michael would do next. She told him that Michael's literary earnings were still too meagre to support the family; not only was he prohibited from working in Ireland, but he was prohibited from leaving to work in England. Morrow thought of an old Belfast friend, Sam Fergusson, who worked at the ministry of Industry and Commerce. Off they went to Jammet's, where Fergusson dined regularly. Unfortunately, he couldn't help her, he said, because all of his hiring was done through the Civil Service Commission, which was tightly controlled by de Valera. But he knew someone who might be able to help.

The next morning (December 23) Evelyn went to Fergusson's office from which she was sent to an office in Nassau Street for an interview. On Monday, January 4, 1943, Evelyn began work as a secretary for British Ship-builders, Ltd. The next day she asked her new boss, a Mr. Toms, why she had been given the job, considering the political sanctions against her husband. He was, he explained, actually the UK liaison officer for labor in Dublin for the sole purpose of recruiting Irish labor for wartime industry. Furthermore, his activities had the tacit approval of Mr. de Valera himself. If the existence of such "fronts" was to become known publicly, de Valera would find it difficult to maintain Irish neutrality, with rising opposition in the Dáil following America's entry into the war.[33] So, he said, "Mr. de Valera is faced with stalemate. He can't touch you. He can't starve you into submission." Evelyn held that position until after the war; it paid three guineas per week, enough to pay the rent and buy food.

When, four years earlier, O'Connor decided to take Harold Macmillan's advice and turn to writing full-time, there was no looking back. He had to keep writing. Through the drought of 1942 he worked steadily and seriously on his stories and his book on churches, assured at least of his contract with Macmillan. Many of these stories and a few of the cycling articles served double, even triple, duty—as broadcast pieces, as magazine articles, and as works in collections. The most obvious example of this strategy was *A Picture Book*, a travel book about Ireland which O'Connor did in collaboration with Elizabeth Rivers.[34] The project had begun that summer in part because of Betty Rivers's friendships with Maeve Mulcahy and Norah McGuinness and in part because of O'Connor's editorial work on her book about the Aran Islands for Cuala Press. On two occasions, at Cashel and Clonfert, she met O'Connor on the spot to do sketches for her woodcuts. O'Connor's text served as accompaniment for her drawings. Some of it he had used before, in "The Dublin Hill Discourses"; the rest he extracted from his book on churches and cycling (eventually titled *Irish Miles*), which he sent to his agent in December under the tentative title "No Place Like Home."[35]

Home certainly wasn't what it once was. Evelyn's work load kept her away more than ever before, and Michael's dogged writing schedule, resembling at times a manic frenzy, kept him edgy and distant. Neither of them were up to much socializing. A few friends called regularly, however, including the actresses Meriel Williams and Patricia Hutchins, two of Evelyn's old friends, and Larry Elyan, an actor from Cork. The Romanesque interest brought them into contact with Michael Duignan and Françoise Henry, both scholars at University College, Dublin. Molly Alexander came by now and then to see Michael's mother. But most of his other friends from the 1930s were gone, having left Ireland or feuded with Michael. Denis Johnston was now in the Middle East as a war correspondent for the BBC. Hayes saw Michael once after his final letter, in Parson's Bookshop at Baggot Street Bridge; he approached warily and said something about at least shaking hands, but Michael simply turned his back. Father Traynor still lived in Sandymount but never visited the house, probably as much because of pressure from his superiors as because of his dislike of Evelyn. Maeve Mulcahy no longer visited because of Michael's accusation that she had taken his copy of *On the Boiler,* a dubious charge which particularly shocked Evelyn. All in all, life at 57 Strand Road gradually withered under the pressure of suspicion and discontent.

Toward the end of the year O'Connor wrote to O'Faoláin promising something on James Joyce for *The Bell.* He had yet to make his peace with the man he acknowledged as Ireland's greatest novelist. Not long after visiting Joyce in Paris in 1929, O'Connor wrote an extensive review of *Work in Progress* and of the essays by Beckett, Jolas, McGreevey, and others. In that article, published in the final issue of the *Irish Statesman,* his admiration for Joyce was undisguised. Joyce's greatness, in the opinion of the young librarian-cum-writer, was that he refused to be content with the greatness of *Ulysses* and fall back on imitations of himself. "Only the very great have that tirelessness, that restlessness," O'Connor concluded.

Now, writing for *The Bell* in February 1943, two years after the death of Joyce, O'Connor's admiration has hardened to a kind of writer-to-writer respect. He tries to explain the discomfort he feels knowing that *Ulysses* is the greatest book of his time but still preferring to read something by George Moore. He finds the first half of *Ulysses* incomparable: "It is, what Joyce intended it to be, the whole of life; the complete man in the complete world."[36] After that Joyce's strength became his weakness, that tendency to remain withdrawn from his work giving us parody and associative mimicry for style. *Finnegans Wake* represents to O'Connor "an extension of Joyce's problem and his solutions to it." Where *Ulysses* was concrete life, the last work is "universal history, universal language." Joyce's adventurous style "is touched with megalomania." Instead of characters, there are principles; "the men are earth and the women water; they change their shapes and reappear in all the great stories of history and mythology, and the language changes with them." Joyce's intellect, which O'Connor describes as "curious rather than profound, elaborate rather than subtle," has let the puns and jingles and parodies take control.

Here is O'Connor—aware by now that he will never write the great Irish novel and that the best he can hope to offer eternity is a few "voices"—trying to summarize the greatness of the most influential figure in twentieth-century literature in a 4,500-word "post-mortem." Admitting that Joyce was the greatest figure of his time, O'Connor wonders why he feels such a "strong sense of artistic failure" about Joyce's work. Artistic failure was something O'Connor lived with every day, that gnawing discontent born of the gap, known only to the artist himself, between conception and execution. His own failure was giving in to the diversionary surface of *Dutch Interior* over the potential depth of

"The Provincials"; Joyce's failure was succumbing to mediocrity in the middle of *Ulysses,* a mediocrity relative only to the incomparable brilliance of those sections that to O'Connor are "saturated in the poetry of everyday life." He feels that failure even more particularly in the revisions of *Finnegans Wake.* "It seems to me that every rewriting has added to the pedantry. . . . I feel it as a sort of disintegration of the material, as though the mind behind had softened from abstraction through pedantry into mere whimsy." Rewriting, O'Connor observes, is "always a clue to a writer's mind," and he was one writer who knew a great deal about rewriting.

Reading O'Connor on Yeats, one gets a feeling of completion, of a man with his hero worship in perspective. But reading O'Connor on Joyce, one gets the feeling of work in progress. He admired Yeats as he did women and education—that is, from afar—and tried to get close by imitating his manner and adapting Yeats's theories of theatre and poetry to his own fiction. He feared Joyce as he feared his own heart, and backed away, condemning the virtuosity and rationalism. In the end, however, he could never identify spiritually with either Yeats or Joyce. Yeats, after all, was an Anglo-Irish aristocrat living in Ireland but never entirely of it; Joyce, on the other hand, was Catholic middle-class, exiled from Ireland but forever of it. Yeats, the last Romantic, was capable of unifying by mystical simplicity the contrary and the irreconcilable; Joyce, the last Realist, vainly tried by force of will and reason to sift through the fragments of ordinary life for some sort of universal order. Between the two O'Connor always seemed suspended, unable to let his genius run free to one extreme or the other. "James Joyce: A Post-Mortem" stands with the rest of O'Connor's literary criticism as the overheard personal musings of a man almost entirely caught up in the world of literature and trying desperately to keep his feet on the ground.

In the meantime he was trying to keep bread on the table. Christmas that year (1942) had been enhanced by the presence of Stan Stewart and an unexpected visit from Sean Hendrick and his wife, Kitty, who filled the house with Cork gossip for Michael's mother. Another welcome gift that Christmas was a travel permit for Michael. He had been corresponding with Christopher Salmon about working for the BBC as soon as he could escape; and a few days after receiving notification from John Betjeman (rather than the Dublin Permit Office itself), O'Connor boarded the mail boat again. He was scheduled to take part in a special program on the Welsh to be broadcast from Central Wales on January 22, 1943.[37] On the boat he met an Irish priest returning to his parish in England, who told him a story of how he had nearly shot a soldier stealing onions from his garden.[38] O'Connor later turned the priest's little anecdote into "The Sentry," showing that he was as capable of admiration for a man of the cloth as he was of contempt. From Wales he went on to London for another broadcast and two recording sessions.

In March O'Connor received a letter from Hector Legge, editor of the *Sunday Independent,* proposing a series of weekly articles. "I have in mind articles that will point the finger at what is wrong in Ireland," Legge wrote, adding that O'Connor would have to adopt a "nom de plume—or de guerre!"[39] They arranged to meet in town on Friday, March 12, at Fuller's Cafe in Grafton Street. During the course of conversation Legge explained that the pseudonym was absolutely necessary because use of anything by Frank O'Connor was "unofficially" frowned upon. The same suggestion had infuriated O'Connor when put to him by Patrick Little, but he was fond of Hector and now closer to being completely broke. In his letter Legge had suggested something like "The Inquisitor," but left the choice to Michael, insisting only that it not be just an Irish version of Frank O'Connor or Michael O'Donovan. He was risking enough as it was, and if readers guessed the identity of the author, the impact would be lost to prejudice. For the next two years the stinging opinions of "Ben Mayo" intrigued, infuriated, and baffled Irish readers. Even Seán O'Faoláin once asked Legge, "Who is this Ben Mayo?"[40]

True to form, O'Connor's first installment, on March 28, 1943, entitled "Irish Ruins Shocked Visitors," hammered away at the dreadful condition of Ireland's national monuments. Ruined medieval abbeys in England were carefully kept and neatly marked, Ben Mayo asserted, but in Ireland, where abbeys had survived in remarkably complete condition, even architectural masterpieces were overgrown with weeds or used as handball courts. No attempt was made to mark the layout, so a visitor's time was wasted. All this struck Ben Mayo as "the very worst form of national propaganda." Not only did such scandalous indifference hurt tourism, it was a serious loss to an Irish worshiper who might find great inspiration in the "inherent sanctity and dignity of a building where his ancestors . . . have worshipped." Ben Mayo's suggestion: "Let us have a Society for the Preservation of Ancient Buildings!" Fifteen years later the Irish Georgian Society was founded by the Honorable Desmond Guinness to preserve and restore eighteenth-century buildings. Not until the late sixties was the same attention given to the equally magnificent medieval structures.

The Ben Mayo articles were marked by a probing sensitivity to current affairs in Ireland. That spring O'Connor looked at the crime wave and Dáil Éireann's response to it; a Finnish plan providing pensions for writers; and the banning of foreign dance music by Radio Eireann. He chided the government for hiding realities and wasting time on trivial matters like jazz and then called on the Irish people themselves to save Ireland from "unemployment, agricultural disorganization, an impractical system of education, and bad social conditions." In May Ben Mayo called attention again to the destruction of old houses of historic and architectural interest by land speculators and to another old hobbyhorse of his, the dismal condition of libraries outside the major cities. Again and again O'Connor's faith in the intelligence of "the little people" surfaced; people who could not or would not read, he claimed, were easy prey to tyrants and hooligans—though he could not say it in so many words, he meant the priests and the politicians.

In June he questioned de Valera's obsession with the Irish language. Ben Mayo asked whether Ireland could afford to let "people rot in slums, die of tuberculosis, emigrate" just to propagate the Irish language. To him the Gaelic Revival was meant "to preserve what was vital in its own tradition against the inroads of commercial internationalism. . . , to give our people a pride in themselves." Instead, he wrote, "we are now faced with a sour doctrinaire mysticism which rates human life at less than the prestige of appointing a Gaelic-speaking doctor." Compulsory Irish, to the jaundiced eye of Ben Mayo, not only failed to contribute in any practical way to the progress of the nation, it had even done what hundreds of years of foreign domination failed to do: It made people loathe the Irish language. Preserving the language was as dear to O'Connor as preserving the national monuments, but not in bad translations of Dickens or bad approximations of Irish on road signs and trams and certainly not at the expense of human welfare.

A few weeks later, extolling the pleasures of cycling in Ireland, Ben Mayo sounded more like a tourist board publicist than a social inquisitor.[41] But he returned quickly to form, asking irritating questions about educational reform, slum conditions, and social welfare. Commenting on the neglect of the book industry in Ireland, he recalled "the lesson which Swift preached over two hundred years ago—that our country's life blood is its manufacturers."[42] The Irish should be able to buy goods manufactured in Ireland, O'Connor believed, and that meant not only clothing, furniture, and bicycles but books as well, books written and printed at home.

What Ben Mayo had to say was not radically different from what Corkery and others had said twenty years before during the limited life of the *Irish Tribune,* or from what AE and others had said fifteen years before in the *Irish Statesman,* or from what O'Faoláin and others were saying at the time in *The Bell.* It wasn't always profound or even particularly well written, at least not by normal Frank O'Connor standards of prose. Yet the Ben Mayo series, improvised by a charitable editor to offset the indignity and financial squeeze of a tacit blacklisting of Frank O'Connor, illustrates, as well as his plays, his novels, his travel books, and even his stories, the character of the man and the nature of his circumstances. The voice of Ben Mayo was argumentative and provocative in the manner of the radio talk shows and eccentric newspaper columns so popular in Ireland today. Had O'Connor been an American serving up this sort of regular fare to the public he might have been a national figure, in the manner perhaps of an H. L. Mencken. But he was writing at a time in his country's history when nobody wanted to make a folk hero of a person who told the truth no one wanted to hear.

Frank O'Connor took Ireland seriously, perhaps too seriously, glorying in the best and fulminating at the worst. Ninety-six times over two and a half years, he wrote from the heart without exposing his face. The standards he advocated for cinema, tourist groups, labor unions, schools, and committee rooms were based on those simple slum values he clung to his entire life: respect for others, hard work, candor, self-defense, and common sense. His fantasy "Getting a Toy for Christmas" lifted a few hearts at a time when Irish children had only dreams to soften their Christmas pillows. His letter to Santa Claus the next week flipped the coin to harsh reality by asking Santa for an end to slums and mud cabins, for electric lights and proper schools, for good libraries and social halls, and for the greatest gift of all, a sense of purpose.

The extra money from the Ben Mayo series and from a successful revival of *The Invincibles* at the Gaiety (curiously enough, produced by Louis D'Alton) allowed Michael and Evelyn to afford a cycling holiday that summer (1943).[43] She talked him into visiting Cork, which, except for the day or two at the time of his father's funeral, he had avoided since their marriage. They took the train through Wicklow to Waterford, then cycled the coast to Youghal and on to Cork, where they met Stan Stewart. They all stayed for two days in the Victoria Hotel, longer than Michael would have cared to stay: More than an overnight visit brought melancholy memories of his unhappy childhood and frustrated adolescence. Unlike Thackeray, Evelyn heard no newsboys discussing Horace on the street and saw no shawlies arguing on the quays, but from the first she was smitten by Michael's town.

Walking down Summerhill from Harrington Square one afternoon with Evelyn, the sculptor Seamus Murphy and his wife Mairgread, Michael ran into Nancy McCarthy who, in an old raincoat and walking shoes, looked for all the world like one of Cork's "characters." She had the afternoon off and had planned to take a long walk in the country. Near the Coliseum, where she planned to catch the Blarney bus, Nancy spotted Michael's unmistakable walk—head up and hands held behind his back imperiously. She was mortified, not having seen him in nearly ten years and looking herself like something swept in on the tide. Evelyn looked trim and well groomed. When Michael introduced them she gave Nancy a cold, appraising look as if to say "So you're the Nancy I've heard so much about." They all walked together to Mac-Curtain Street exchanging banalities, until Nancy stopped and gave a weak excuse about an appointment. There was an amused look on Michael's face when she attempted to shake hands with Evelyn. He surveyed the scene—Nancy with her hand out feeling every bit an eejit, and Evelyn with her hands held smartly at her sides in stubborn resistance. So Nancy just smiled sweetly and said: "One of the misfortunes of m-m-meeting a McCarthy is that you're compelled to s-s-shake hands with them. We shake hands with each other when we meet." There was an ear-to-ear grin on Michael's face as Evelyn relented and shook hands.

The next day Michael, Evelyn, and Stan cycled to Kinsale, then along the coast toward Michael's favorite West Cork towns. To Michael, life there was exciting, "for it combines sordidity with a violence of emotion and a vigour of phrasing."[44] This was the country Michael associated with Somerville and Ross; it was also the locale of the Tailor. From the melancholy of Cork, Michael was taking Evelyn to the romance of Macroom, Ballingeary, and Gougane Barra. As they cycled from Inchigeela, Michael's heart, he wrote, "began to leap again as it leapt when [he] was a boy." Beside a whitewashed cottage, "gipsy brightness among the desolation," they saw "an old woman with a man's hat plastered down over her white locks." It was Ansty, the Tailor's wife, who directed them up the little mountain road to the brow of the hill where "with his withered leg stretched out, his round, yellow, baby face, his piercing little eyes, was the Tailor, teaching Irish to a couple of city childher."[45] They left him there and cycled on up to a hotel by the lake; on the island visible from the hotel were the remains of an old church and a holy well.

After supper they returned to the Tailor's. There were no neighbors now owing to the scandal over Cross's book, but he went on with his storytelling. "There never was a better storyteller or a more incurable philosopher." The story he told that night had to do with a faerie, Con na bPucai, and the priest with the cursed leg. When the visitors finally began to leave, they found themselves barricaded inside the cottage. "A stump of a tree had been wedged against the door outside: the persecution was still going strong." Ansty was furious, but the Tailor soothed her with the reminder, "At our age there is little the world can do to us." Going back over the hill O'Connor could feel, like an actual physical presence, "the sense of evil in the valley."[46] It was the last time Michael saw the Tailor, who died two years later.

They cycled on toward Limerick by way of Charleville where Michael relived that Sunday morning some twenty years before when he had motored from "Buttevant barracks with dispatches for Kilmallock." He was looking for the officer who captured him that day and for the farmhouse where he had been held prisoner for a time. He found neither. The nostalgia was wearing as thin as his patience in the dismal rain. Stan left them at Kilmallock and cycled back to Limerick; alone Michael and Evelyn caught the train back to Dublin.

V

On September 17, 1943, Michael O'Donovan turned forty, but except for the streaks of gray in his head of unruly black hair he was much the same as the young librarian of thirty, even the rebel of twenty. Michael/Frank was still a person of fierce sympathies and blunt hatreds, his faith often too buoyant, his disillusionment too heavy for those around him to understand. Peter Kavanagh, for instance, has described O'Connor at that time:

> a big man with a big head shaped like a horse. When he spoke he gave the impression of straining for something just over and behind your head. I met him a few times in the early forties and found him friendly but difficult to talk to. He had integrity despite his civil libertarianism. Patrick did not protest: he did not need to. O'Connor did, and I always felt embarrassed for him when he became thus involved. He seemed such an idiot though he was far from that. He was in fact a very superior person. He came to my defense on several occasions.[47]

At forty O'Connor still resented the sordidness of his surroundings and fought to expose injustice; championing lost causes and fighting shadows would be a lifelong ministry. In public he was still so sensitive he could embarrass himself by making regrettable gaffes. One never knew whether Michael would be charmingly magnificent, his great head thrown back in robust laughter or thrust forward in enthusiastic appreciation of something "grand," or whether he would be surly and contentious, glowering about some "rubbish" or other in the "bloody country." At home his family never knew when his spotaneous joy and warm affection would be buried by a moody silence or stormy outburst. Only when he sat down to write did he ever really do justice to himself.

The years had not blunted the story-making imagination of the only child playing at high opera in his attic room or the audacious young rebel playing at war in the hills of West Cork. Nor had time and acclaim eased his self-doubt; always the frail, bespectacled poor boy, he fought with the only tools he possessed, words, to prove himself. O'Connor wrote constantly, but since the bulk of his time was spent meeting deadlines for newspapers editors and broadcast directors, he seldom felt a sense of completion at the end of a day. Judging from his writing journals, he wrote everything in fitful longhand bursts, leaving his desk strewn with disorderly fragments. When O'Connor rewrote a story, he started from scratch; the same story often appears four or five times in the same journal, unrecognizable even by title or opening paragraph. He worked hard at his writing; it was the one thing that gave his life any meaning at all.

Contracts with Macmillan and Knopf had called for a novel in the fall of 1942, a book he had continued to dodge. As he confessed to Stan Stewart, it seemed "a colossus of a job, as my mind is small and intense, and to take it travelling through the thousand paragraphs of a novel is like embarking on a Siberian journey. I like short trips in fiction; Castlebar to Ennis is about my average; an excellent sprinter but why must I complete in a Marathon."[48] Since finishing *Dutch Interior,* O'Connor had written nearly twenty stories, some revised again and again, some only broadcast over the wireless, but most left in his writing journals, unpublished. He had "tinkered" on a volume of stories to satisfy his publishers, but it satisfied no one, particularly not himself.

That aborted volume, entitled "Mirror in Water," was to contain stories from those bachelor years when Maupassant was his great fascination. Such stories as "Flowering Trees," "The Storyteller," "Grandeur," and "The Climber" all carry a slight flavor of Maupassant—emotionally violent, enigmatic, stabbing.[49] They also have the Russian feeling apparent in his writing when it verges on autobiography, a feeling most evident in "A Rainy Day" and "Mac's Masterpiece." The people of Cork were his natural material, the people to whom he invariably listened when writing through his own crises. But he lived in Dublin now, and not on the north side of the river Liffey but on the fashionable south side where middle-class life circled him with a vengeance. He may have come to believe that many of the world's greatest storytellers were tramps, but he was desperately trying not to be one himself. He was an outcast perhaps because of his fiery temperament and his heritage of poverty, but he was still fighting to attain some sort of status in a country obsessed with respectability.

Four years of broadcasting had led O'Connor to the discovery that "the written word had robbed the story of its narrative impulse." The stories to be included in "Mirror in Water" were fashioned in the manner of Maupassant, Chekhov, and even Joyce, all of whose stories he felt "no longer rang with the tone of a man's voice speaking." The stories he chose for his next volume had been tested at the microphone, already stripped of literary sophistication and intricacy. O'Connor now felt that he knew to the syllable how his Irish subjects would sound. Furthermore, he now believed that the color and extravagance of his earlier stories had been conditioned by a youthful romanticism acted upon by a "supercharged nationalism." O'Connor's literary models were now no longer Hugo, Babel, and Maupassant; rather they were Jane Austen, Anthony Trollope, and A. E. Coppard, a yet little known English short-story writer. The Dutch psychiatrist's revelation of the fatal opposition between his head and his heart had convinced O'Connor that his writing needed tighter control.[50] Henceforth his aim was to scale down the issues in order to enlarge the people and magnify their voices—a strategy of containment, an art of restriction.

By September he had agreed to various changes in the contents of the new volume. "Soul of the Bishop" was dropped, and "The Star That Bids the Shepherd Fold" was substituted for "Last Post." His editor, Lovat Dickson, requested a brief foreword to explain the collection. O'Connor wrote:

A writer's development is as much a matter of interest to himself as is that of another writer and as much beyond his control. When I began to write stories it was with the mind of a young poet; spontaneity I valued most of all and I wrote in a fever, weeping, laughing, singing the dialogue to myself. That was how Guests of the Nation and The Saint and Mary Kate were written and any little virtue they have comes from it. And then the news of my "fool-driven land" dragged me away from writing and for years I only wrote two or three stories. Then the old passion came back and I cursed Ireland and began to write again. The new stories were quieter and I think intenser, and something of what I traded in gave them a little intellectual depth. And then the whirligig of politics came again for in a country ruled by fools and blackguards a writer must fight and think and waste his time in useless efforts to create an atmosphere in which he can exist and work, and when at last I settled down to literature as a career, I knew that the sort of thing I wanted to write now was so different from what I had begun with, so little and queer and I wrote it as if from a great distance and was terrified that I had lost my style. It came back to me two years later with two stories; the Miser and The House That Johnny Built and then again I sat for months looking at those stories and realizing that they were what I wanted to write and couldn't until at last it came to me in a flash that they were the sort of work of a man of forty and what I had been trying to do was the sort of lyrical tale I wrote at twenty-five; that though the tree of the Hesperides grew nothing but crab apples a man might still make a very palatable crab apple jelly.[51]

Dickson scrapped the foreword, perhaps the most telling statement O'Connor would ever make about his artistic growth, but used the last three words for the title of what turned out to be his finest volume.

"Bridal Night," the first story in *Crab Apple Jelly,* is powerfully impressionistic. What strikes the reader is not only the emotion but the aptness of it. In the course of conversation a faceless narrator casually asks a lonesome old woman about her family and uncovers a pathetic story. She has a son, but he has been in the asylum "these twelve years." Crying out her "sorrows like the wild birds," she tells of the lad's infatuation for his schoolteacher. "Denis was such a quiet boy, no way rough or accustomed to the girls at all—and how would he be in this lonesome place?" The crisis of her tale occurs after love had turned to madness. Haltered to his bed, waiting for asylum officials, the boy had called for the schoolmistress, who came to the distressed cottage and stayed with the boy until dawn. Thus comforted he let the officials take him without resisting. After bringing the story to such a catharsis, O'Connor turns outward in the final sentence: "Darkness had fallen over the Atlantic, blank grey to its farthest reaches." For O'Connor the story lies not in what the woman tells her visitor but in why she tells it at all. The mere telling of her story brings solace, a momentary release from the very words that haunt her.

O'Connor's so-called lyrical stories leave little doubt about the power of his prose to evoke highly poetic visual images. One of the most intriguing of these is "Uprooted," a story about two brothers that O'Connor had taken from his old friend Tim Traynor. Ned Keating, a teacher in Dublin, is bored by routine and respectable patterns. Tom, the more spontaneous and vigorous of the two, is a curate in Wicklow. Together they go back to visit their home in the west, where they are bustled about to meet forgotten relations. Neither has time to be nostalgic or time to regret. The committed priest thinks of what might have been and the uncommitted teacher of what might be, but they both fall back into the subjunctive pocket of time. As the two brothers leave home once again, they are uprooted with stark finality. In the "magical light" of dawn Ned's loss is the loss of the intolerably vivid world of childhood, a world supported only by the magic of words. His future is as "remote and intangible" as Tom's is futile and lonely. The lyrical moment is the uprooting itself, the suspending of human personality between the irremediable past and the intractable future.

Previously O'Connor had written little about priests, so the four stories in *Crab Apple Jelly* specifically about that misunderstood segment of Irish society stand out as something of a departure for him. Father Ring, the ubiquitous fund raiser and moral tyrant, appears in three stories about small towns. In "The Miser" he sets out to bilk a cranky shopkeeper who has suffered a stroke, but is bested when the old man dies penniless. In "The House That Johnny Built" and "The New Teacher" he is a sort of restrictive presence hovering about the town, wrangling over money and insisting on sexual decency. Benedict Kiely once wrote that the very sight of a collar was enough to make O'Connor's hair stand on end; indeed, O'Connor had the reputation of being a terrible anticleric. However, he had been close enough to such men as Father Traynor to feel something of the loneliness and frustration of a priest's life, to the point of eventually viewing the priest as a surrogate artist.[52] Father Devine, the young curate in "The Star That Bids the Shepherd Fold" (another portrait of Traynor), is as dignified and cosmopolitan as the French sea captain who jousts with the curate's tyrannical and boorish parish priest over a wayward lass of his flock. O'Connor's sympathy for the humanity of priests spills out, too, in that most gentle of his stories, "Song Without Words," the Mount Melleray tale about two monks in a monastery of silence who accidentally discover a mutual love of playing the horses (one of Father Traynor's most prominent vices).

The stories in *Crab Apple Jelly* represent the refinement of O'Connor's ability to exploit the "tone of a man's voice speaking." Nowhere is this attention to voices more evident than in "The Long Road to Ummera," a simple tale about an old woman's eccentric wish to be buried in the mountain home of her people, a request that, to her son, appears old-fashioned and impractical. Gabriel Fallon, who produced a radio version of the story, claimed it was so genuine that it helped his own mother die a little easier. By O'Connor's own admission, the main voices in the story were those of his own father and grandmother. It begins: "Always in the evening you saw her shuffle up the road." The narrator is personal and informal, speaking about his neighbors, not about strangers or "specimens." The old woman speaks entirely within the idiom of her adopted community. With little elaboration and less comment O'Connor ends the story: "They brought her the long road to Ummera, the way she had come from it forty years before." The voices in that story are lonely, though they resonate within the community; O'Connor's voice is lonely not in spite of his fidelity to Irish life but because of it.

Actually, *Crab Apple Jelly* is the least autobiographical volume O'Connor had yet put together. His new obsession with dreams pushed him further into himself, while his absolute dedication to technique protected him from exposing what he might have found there. What he blamed in Joyce he actually feared in himself. Technique was to become his way of achieving the artistic purity, the ironic detachment, that he so admired in the heroes of his maturity, Austen and Mozart. For example, "The Grand Vizier's Daughters" demonstrates the power of a storyteller to make his point without showing his hand. Not only was O'Connor telling a magnificent story about a father's way of gaining confessions of allegiance from his headstrong daughters, he was also experimenting with his medium, voices. The persistent problem of point of view is solved by the use of a narrator who overhears his uncle "on the skite again" regaling his daughters with a magical bedtime story designed to terrorize them rather than put them to sleep. "Song Without Words" shows O'Connor using for the first time the kind of opening that would become almost a trademark of the O'Connor story in the 1950s: "Even if there were only two men left in the world and both of them to be saints, they wouldn't be happy even then. One of them would be bound to try and improve the other. That is the nature of things." A cryptic generality is followed by a matter-of-fact telling of a marvelously compact and engaging little story, suggesting that O'Connor at forty had not only mastered his medium but begun to settle comfortably into it.

In a radio broadcast O'Connor once said: "An Irish writer without contention is a freak of nature. All the literature that matters to me was written by people who had to dodge the censor." The sexual repression of middle-class Irish life provided more than one Irish writer ready material for fiction. Many of them had attacked the clergy and exposed the sexual blight of a parochial society. O'Connor avoided both subjects until *Crab Apple Jelly,* refusing to wage a token war or to stoop to rhetoric. "The Mad Lomasneys" is one of his earliest and most successful stories about the strange way of love among the Irish.[53] The relationship between Ned Lowry and Rita Lomasney engages O'Connor's singular attention from their first, awkward encounter as adolescents to their strained and unfortunate parting. Rita is an independent girl, with a manner best described as rash and a voice that seems to laugh casually at life. Ned is rather unperturbably automatic, though also "clever . . . precise and tranquil." But O'Connor is not just playing the predictable against the unpredictable here. He is carefully accenting the subtle games played in middle-class Irish parlors and sidewalks, games of position, manners, and public image.

Rarely does O'Connor use overt symbolism or manipulate a story with devices. In this story, however, cigarettes serve to accentuate the self-consciously adult mannerisms of both Ned and Rita. Cigarettes emphasize Ned's calculated equilibrium and underscore Rita's impulsive and rebellious nature. After pouring tea for Ned and whiskey for herself, Rita condemns his sexual naivete while gesturing for a light. Later, when he admits that he would marry her, she abuses him for not having asked before she accepted a teaching job out of town. Once again a cigarette figures significantly; frustrated by her malicious flourish, Ned squelches "the butt of his cigarette on his plate" and offers to repeat his proposal of marriage every six months. The waiting game and the stalling game are played with brutality in a tidy, virtuous, if smoky, middle-class parlor in Cork.

The final section of the story contains no surprises, no sentimental revelations, no reversals, and no vindications. Rita marries someone else, and Ned begins to see "a gentle, humorous girl with a great mass of jet-black hair, a snub nose, and a long, pointed melancholy face." During one of Ned's friendly visits to the Lomasney home, a very pregnant Rita pokes fun at his Spanish-looking friend and asks, "Would Senorita What's-her-name ever let you stand godfather to my footballer, Ned?" Once again the cigarettes appear. Ned calmly forces the issue until Rita admits, "I made up my mind that I'd marry the first of you that called." Capricious and unreasonable, perhaps a trifle mad, but it is a way of solving a dilemma forced upon her as much from without as from within. She would never admit that she married the wrong man. "She looked mockingly at Ned, but her look belied her. He rose and flicked the ashes neatly into the fire." As he stands with his back to the fire Ned's façade collapses. He hurls the last remnant of the symbol of his carefully cultivated equilibrium into the fire, the love game having finally taken its toll on him.

When O'Connor sent off the manuscript of this volume of stories on July 15, 1943, he suggested the title "Small Towns."[54] While cycling about Ireland, he had become convinced that he was a townee and that in the rhythms of small-town life lay the stuff of his art. As much as he hated Catholic, middle-class Ireland with its exaggerated sense of self-importance and its hidebound attachment to custom and image, he had also begun to give it grudging sympathy. That tension between sympathy and judgment, in fact, is what gives *Crab Apple Jelly* both its variety and its power. It contains some of the savage criticism of Irish life apparent in *Dutch Interior,* without casting blame or seeking causes. If there is a unity in the volume, it is not a preconceived campaign but a natural coherence of manner and tone which O'Connor himself believed signaled an emerging artistic maturity. He felt he had moved beyond the archaic and merely insular features of Irish peasant life to the subtler rhythms of shopkeepers and clerks, teachers and chemists.

Of all the stories in *Crab Apple Jelly* "The Luceys" stands out as the paradigm of small-town Irish life. In it O'Connor continued to dig into the circumstantial pressures of small-town life that forced people to act in self-defeating ways. Years later, in a television talk called "Interior Voices," he confessed that this story—not "Guests of the Nation" or "First Confession" or even "My Oedipus Complex"—had for years been his favorite.

> I struggled with that story for the best part of twenty years, and I still seem to be struggling with it, because, whenever I re-read it, the voices in it are saying something new. It's the story of a man who sins against his family. Tom Lucey is the owner of a draper's shop and has one son called Peter: Ben, his younger brother, has a large family, the eldest of whom is a boy called Charlie. Charlie is Peter's friend, and when Peter gets into trouble over the embezzlement of his clients' funds, Charlie tries to make his father help, but Ben, a cautious man, refuses. "A man done out of his money is a mad dog," he says. So Peter changes his name, joins the English Air Force and is killed, and after that Tom refuses to speak to his brother. The difficulty of this story is that I knew the Irish small towns and was often horrified at the constricted lives people led in them, but I also noticed that in them I was always running into remarkable characters, men who in any other sphere would have been dominating figures. The difficulty of the story was to keep the issues small, but the men big.
>
> The voices of the three men are very clear in my mind, though I

heard none of them for more than a few hours in my life. Ben's is that of a man I was in gaol with, Charlie's that of a young man with whom I once had a couple of drinks in a country hotel, and Tom's that of an old tinker I used to know, who spoke with the old West Country accent of Raleigh's men.[55]

"The Luceys" is indeed a difficult story—for the reader as much as for the writer. If there is a fulcrum on which O'Connor's career teetered, it is this story, perhaps for the very reasons O'Connor offered in the television talk: its difficulty and its voices. Written at the very time he was trying to locate a mature style, "The Luceys" did not jump off the pen fully formed, as did "Bridal Night." And it certainly did not appeal instantly to listening audiences, as did "The Long Road to Ummera" or "Song Without Words."

The reason is that it was pure story, a distilled version of what he termed in that same television talk a "tragedy of character."

There are three sorts of tragedy, and with great respect to Aristotle, they are all equally important if treated by real writers. One is the tragedy of innocence—the tragedy of the orphan or the illegitimate child who can be destroyed by the inevitable complexity of life, by a death or an act of casual heartlessness. The second is the tragedy of authority, which one might illustrate from "Guests of the Nation." The third, and most difficult, is the tragedy of character, for here the villain, who in the former pair is external—either blind life or authority—is internal, part of the characters themselves. The characters in "The Luceys" seem to me to be trapped in their own characters as effectively as the orphan is trapped in the death of his parents, or the two Englishmen in "Guests of the Nation." Tom Lucey is trapped in his pride, Ben Lucey in his good-natured worldliness, and Charlie in the intensity of his family feeling. But to be the villain as well as the hero of your own life story, you have to be a very big man indeed, and my problem in writing the story was to find in an Irish Provincial town with all its limitations of outlook and circumstance, three men of true tragic capacity.[56]

The fact is that in "The Luceys," and in "The Mad Lomasneys" as well, O'Connor captured middle-class Irish life, with all its encrustation, crankiness, duplicity, and self-deception, as neither he nor anyone else had ever quite managed to do before. Simultaneously, he re-created a few of those voices that had long echoed inside his huge skull, voices that sounded his own provincial values and limitations. "Life is like that," those voices would say. At his best O'Connor listened from the back room instead of declaiming from center stage. Unfortunately, at forty he was as enamored of his own voice as he had been as a boy singing high opera to himself in his lonely attic loft. And the humanism that created the rich diversity of *Crab Apple Jelly* surfaced less and less as the clamor of his own subjective abyss became louder, more cacophonous.

14

English Miles

What our contempt doth often hurl from us,
We wish it ours again; the present pleasure,
By revolution lowering, does become
The opposite of itself.

SHAKESPEARE, *Antony and Cleopatra*

"AN Irishman's private life begins at Holyhead." With that bold sentence O'Connor started "English Miles," a book he never finished. He often joked that he lived in Sandymount in order to be within walking distance of the mail boat, but by 1944 his situation had ceased to be a joke. He had always counted himself among those who, with Yeats and Lady Gregory, dug in their heels and fought it out. But the Abbey battles, censorship, his virtual incarceration, and his blacklisting, had left him defeated and disillusioned. Nearly six years of comings and goings for BBC assignments in England had sparked something of a love affair with the place. But though he was drawn to England, he still held tenaciously to Ireland, as if locked in a comfortable but disquieting marriage, passionately loving and hating it at the same time. For the next few years, then, his private life and Holyhead would be irremediably linked.

I

In January 1944 O'Connor finally obtained permission to leave Ireland. Christopher Salmon at the BBC had interceded on his behalf with agencies all over England, having learned that Michael had been desperately seeking work.[1] Larry Morrow, who had left Radio Eireann, found a job for O'Connor at the Crown Film Unit's Pinewood Studios, but at the time he arrived in London, the job's status was in doubt. Shevawn Lynam, now working at the Ministry of Information, arranged a temporary assignment for him assessing the effect of the war on morale in local governments. Being an old librarian, Michael felt qualified to interview local officials; he chose a few towns with noteworthy cathedrals and set off. His first stop was Norwich, where he found few people willing to talk, even unofficially, about their jobs. Owing to the absence of the one person he had been instructed to interview, the town clerk, he was stuck there over the weekend with nothing to do but feel lonely. In an exasperated mood he wrote to Evelyn, "this sort of jaunt requires a holiday atmosphere; lots of grub, beer, and—you to exchange impressions with, and even a ruined chancel with you is more to me than a whole blooming complete Norman cathedral without you."[2]

One of the officials he interviewed in Lincoln, his next stop, was so engaging that Michael found time only for a glimpse of the cathedral. The only thing that could keep O'Connor from a cathedral was a story, and in this instance it was one about two local boys, brothers, who had joined the navy. One was killed; the other returned to Lincoln a nervous wreck. Mr. R., the municipal official telling the story, tried to cheer the boy up and halt his slide into drink. But when the boy went off to London for part of his leave, he still felt as if he had nothing left to live for. Then, just before his leave was up, he telephoned Mr. R. to ask him to serve as best man at his wedding. It turned out that he was marrying the girl his brother had been engaged to when the war had broken out. When he arrived home with the girl, Mr. R. offered him a drink, which he refused. "Off that now, Sir," he said. "We're saving up for a little home of our own after the war." Not since the old farmer in West Cork had told him the story of "Michael's Wife" had O'Connor been so moved. In "English Miles" he wrote: "I think of Mr. R. at least as frequently as I think of Lincoln Cathedral. Good men are like cathedrals; there's the devil of a lot to think about in them."[3]

Back in Windsor, where he had taken a flat to be near the Pinewood Studios, Michael discovered that he had been denied the Crown Film job. Two weeks later the impediment to his job clearance was discovered at the Ministry of Information: He had been confused with another O'Donovan who had failed to register for the National Service. With the mistaken-identity mystery solved, Michael received a script assignment, but it was little more than hack work. He had been in England for nearly a month before obtaining regular work, and his inability to provide adequately for his family troubled him deeply. In Dublin he would have had time to write, but he would have had no market; here in London he had contact with plenty of editors, but because of the distractions of temporary living conditions, air raids, and loneliness, he found it impossible to produce any stories.

"My Dublin is an affair of the affections," he said in a letter to Evelyn written one evening after a welcome all clear. "I realize more and more how little I depend on other sustenance; what a blooming introvert I am." As March slid into April he became more lonely. His letters to Evelyn were affectionate, even sentimental. In one he quoted from a recently published poem by John Betjeman, which reminded him of their cycling trips to ruined churches.[4] His letters also betrayed a gathering sexual frustration: a moonlit night made him long to "spoon" with her; he chafed under his "enforced celibacy." At Easter he wrote about shaking off his "introspections and morbidities and general fooling round": "The trouble is without a home and without a wife I am what I haven't been since I was eighteen or twenty and I behave in the same foolish, self-conscious way as an adolescent who doesn't belong anywhere." What these confessions betrayed, besides sexual longing, was a very real need for the routines of home, that pocket of domestic order where he was free to write.

Even a pleasant spring could not soothe his irritation; in letters he quarreled with his agent about a tax matter and with Mrs. Yeats about pending publications at Cuala Press.[5] He even went so far as to request Macmillan not to send advance copies of *Crab Apple Jelly* to any newspaper in Ireland but the *Times*, because, he said, "it gives enemies a chance to brew trouble."[6] The book was due in April, and for some reason he was unduly worried about its reception. At the end of his Easter letter Michael complained to Evelyn that he was lost without her; all of his Irish work seemed "absurd and lost in a hopeless past" and he himself, "a quaking mass of sensibility in a sort of avalanche of new impressions." "You are the only link between the past and whatever future I've got and I cling to the thought of you like a man in a high sea to a raft." Beneath the cast-iron shell of an aggressive world beater lurked a vulnerable and dependent boy. In a final confessional flourish to that letter Michael admitted to realizing how much *Crab Apple Jelly* was really Evelyn's book; "even more yours than the Late Poems are George's," he wrote.

Of all his English friends, O'Connor felt most comfortable with Dona and Christopher Salmon, both of whom worked at the BBC.[7] He looked forward to evenings or weekends with the Salmons for the poetry, the music, the gossip, and the cooking. Dona knew from her own correspondence with Evelyn that Michael was not feeding himself properly, so she invited him as often as her busy schedule would allow. Knowing how feckless he was about the mundane details of daily survival, she occasionally went out of her way to shop for him.

Michael's other companion at this time was Larry Morrow, and a more unlikely association could hardly be imagined. They had gotten to know each other at Radio Eireann; it was Morrow who supervised much of Evelyn's work in that vile "trial period" at the end of 1942 and who had taken the initiative to find her another job. A few months after that Morrow was sacked for allegedly profiting from free-lance work done under an assumed name. Though it later dawned on Michael that this bouncy, witty, gregarious fellow was unhappy about nearly everything, he found him a congenial companion. Cycling in the country, they tolerated each other's passion—Michael's for churches, Larry's for pubs—and still managed to cover many English miles.

From time to time Michael had mused aloud how nice it would be to find a place in the country away from the sirens where he could write. A week after Easter Morrow, feeling somewhat guilty over leaving Michael alone for the holidays, rang up with a beguiling proposition. He had just met a young woman, a teacher, who shared a small cottage in Hemel Hempstead with a former colleague now in the WAAF. Would Michael be interested in making a foursome of it on weekends? A week later Morrow took Michael to Hemel Hempstead. When they arrived, the young WAAF officer, named Joan, was dozing on the sofa. She rose and offered politely to throw together something to eat. Giddy and self-conscious as usual in the presence of a woman, Michael let himself get caught up in his own "impossible, romantic longings better suited to the age of eighteen," and volunteered to help even though he knew nothing about cooking. Joan, who had already met and been attracted—if frightened—by him, couldn't help being caught up in the warm torrent of his conversation. Because of the smallness of the cottage, the girls found Michael a room in the village. The next day they all went cycling together, with Michael and Joan sharing a tandem, but he was so nervous that he rocked them off into a ditch. The foursome was a success and the shared weekends continued; then, just before Pentecost, Larry did not go to the cottage, which made it possible for Michael to stay there. That weekend he and Joan became lovers.

From that beginning their relationship grew deeply intense, an attraction based as much on romantic ideas as on sex. She meant excitement and adventure at a time when he felt drab and listless. In conversation she sparkled, and they would talk for hours, usually about England. He had always said that the best way to know a place was to be in love with a woman from there. The benefits were mutual—at that time in her life Joan was seeking some sort of direction. She needed counsel as much as Michael needed mothering. She needed freedom from the strictures of her Methodist upbringing as much as he needed freedom from his Irish-Catholic past. Aware of her uneasiness— and, indeed, guilt—about his wife and family, Michael constantly assured her that he was not unhappy in his marriage and insisted that Evelyn understood.

However, Evelyn was having some difficulty understanding. Her letters ran more and more in the *de profundis* vein. He kept reassuring her that they were "indispensable to each other," that the separation was as hard for him as for her; and he continued to flood her with stories of people he was meeting and of conversations heard and overheard on trains, pubs, and at the studios. Meanwhile his own work schedule was becoming increasingly full. A broadcast on Joyce proved time-consuming and nerve-wracking. He complained to Evelyn about wading through dreary books for reviews and slogging away at stories that he could never seem to finish. His letters became less candid about Joan, referring to her as "the WAAF." Toward the end of April, in a letter to Evelyn, he described her as a "superb comedienne" who reminded him of Natalie. He admitted to enjoying her company but added quickly: "Lacking the only one whose company would make London drop into a background I must have women's company; somebody to link along Oxford Street on a summer evening or to look at architecture with. Otherwise I get morose and savage with loneliness." For the first time he begged her to try to come over; even his fear of air raids had begun to pale before his fear of his own dependencies.

For some reason no reviews of *Crab Apple Jelly*, published in mid-April, had yet appeared. Michael woke every day feeling that it must be an appalling book, "skinny and ragged and neurotic."[8] As usual, in situations of stress or worry, his gastritis flared up, though judging from his letters to Evelyn the primary irritant was not the book but Joan. He was by now spending every weekend with her at Hemel Hempstead. Morrow and the teacher stayed there as well, adding to the conviviality of the arrangement. Joan was stationed in London and living in quarters there; Michael kept his flat in Windsor, where he stayed during the week. On the weekends he escaped to the cottage to enjoy Joan's cooking and her company. "No frustrated female ever can cook," he wrote to Evelyn. Food and sex were, to his mind, best in the Mediterranean countries and worst in Ireland, "where sexual vitality is lowest." He should have been more careful about making such comments to Evelyn, but he could no more resist a new theory than pass by an old church.

In his letters home Michael continued to insist on the respectability of his relationship with Joan, alluding often to the "Cottage Mystery," a drama in which he was trapped as an observer and knight-errant. The plot of this mystery thickened when Joan's friend was asked to vacate the cottage by the landlady, who accused Michael of using "vile language." Since his own landlady in Windsor would not countenance cohabitation, even on weekends, Michael decided to take a flat in Thornton Heath. As always, he was candid with Evelyn about the arrangement. In June he wrote to her, ecstatic over the excellent reviews of *Crab Apple Jelly* in the *Times Literary Supplement*:

> I knew I was a great writer when I wrote that book and that was Sandymount (which you must never blaspheme at) and you and the kids; and that, Mrs. O'Donovan is how I like to live and work. I accept the present

as experience, and I am glad to have met Joan who has taught me a lot of things I didn't know, but I must get back to Sandymount.[9]

Unfortunately, by this time Evelyn had ceased to answer his letters.

About that same time, O'Connor was asked to deliver a set of lectures for the University College of Hull in July.[10] In two weeks' time he completed a draft of the lectures, but he left the manuscript on a train and had to begin again. A week later he suffered another lapse of memory and lost the black poet's hat that had been his trademark for nearly twenty years. As July approached, Michael became more and more surly, raging about the theatre, about his latest Crown Film project, and about de Valera. Though honored by the opportunity of lecturing in an academic setting, he was apprehensive about making a fool of himself. Joan did everything she could to ease his mind, from typing the manuscript to hunting down quotations; but he continued to be unpredictable: One day he would be ecstatic about what he was writing, the next day morose. Even the pleasure of their frequent walks and cycling expeditions out into the countryside began to wear thin. Preparing these lectures opened unhealed scars from the Abbey wars and kept him from his stories. Moreover, he was vexed with Evelyn; thinking she should understand, he was offended when she did not. One of his unstated assumptions was that he could sketch in other people as background to his own life, writing the scripts of their lives while playing out his own.

"The Art of the Theatre," lectures delivered nervously by Frank O'Connor to an audience of townspeople during a two-week period in July, marked the end of a twenty-year affair with the theatre.[11] He never claimed to be a dramatist himself, admitting only that some of his plays had been surprisingly effective, but by this time he had realized that writing stories and writing plays were entirely separate challenges. He held that where the storyteller holds up a mirror, the dramatist dances before it, externalizing fears as children do in play. O'Connor was convinced that the unique power of the theatre had to do with what Synge had called collaboration, or the interaction between audience, actor, and writer without which there is only boredom. His opening lecture dealt with the audience, the most unpredictable partner in theatrical collaboration. Drama, he told the small audience gathered in the Grimsby town hall, is a public art, addressed to a group rather than to an individual and dependent on the "mob" for its illusion. The audience, he asserted, "is the dramatic motor, a continuous, active throb of assent which compels the dramatist to use his invention to the utmost." Action is the basic stuff of drama, he continued, "pure activity, unhampered by circumstance . . . it is improbability, shaped to an imaginative pattern." He buttressed his elaborate argument with liberal references to Chekhov, Molière, Sheridan, Shakespeare, Ibsen, Giraudoux, and, of course, Synge and Yeats.

Turning to the writer for his second lecture, O'Connor claimed that living theatre is a writer's theatre; museum theatre belongs to actors and producers and is primarily eclectic, antiquarian, and snobbish. The best an actor can do alone is to interpret the "classics," because there is no writer around to argue about models, dirty jokes, or topical allusions. In theatre where new plays are manufactured, the stage is immediate and rough around the edges. Yeats was successful, O'Connor suggested, not because of an urgent social message or perfect craft, but simply because "he threw his theatre open to writers."

O'Connor's literary biases are obvious; he has no use for art that imposes itself upon reality, that constructs its forms *a priori*, or that assumes to enlighten "belated" races. The distinction between living and museum art appears over and over again in his critical writing. Academic or aesthetic literature, he believed, plays to pure intellect in the rarefied atmosphere of the private soul; thus he rejected any story devoid of the voice of a man speaking. Instinctive or folk literature plays to impure emotions in the clamorous, unpredictable, and ultimately ephemeral world of the communal marketplace. Ironically, at this very time O'Connor himself was moving more and more to a fiction dominated by technique, a fiction so honed and perfect that it is neither unpredictable nor instinctive.

On the last Thursday in July O'Connor concluded his lecture series by talking about actors, for whom he still held the greatest respect. His theories placed great demands on everyone, even though he spoke from a writer's point of view. Passivity on the part of an audience, abstraction or arrogance by the writer, or virtuosity among the actors, all stifle the theatre. O'Connor insisted on making the actor a creator in his own right. Acting, he suggested, is creative when it puts real people on stage; it is derivative when it imitates old gimmicks. Since the actor's currency, the spoken word, depreciates quickly with time, playing roles as they would have been played originally, whether at the Globe or at the Abbey, is like paying debts with deflated currency. To create a living role, according to O'Connor, is to pass a part through a living model. "Every artist—painter, storyteller, dramatist or actor—is bounded by his own experience, and it is out of this experience he must draw his inspiration." For him a living moment in the theatre is no more or less significant than a moment of moments in a lyric poem or an epiphany in a story; that moment is a flash point, ephemeral at best and needful of continuous renewal.

It is impossible now to tell whether or not those who attended these lectures appreciated what they had heard; his argument may have been too elaborate and his references too arcane. However, isolated in a provincial town and weary from the war, the people who came to listen found his passionate enthusiasm most refreshing. By taking his subject seriously, he had taken them seriously at a time when nothing much seemed to matter.

I I

Shortly after D day (June 6, 1944) Michael met Dona and Christopher for lunch. All over London a new feeling of optimism was gathering; people were ready to pick up the pieces and resume a life without air raids and rationing. Naturally, conversation that afternoon had to do with the future. Dona asked what each of them was afraid of. Christopher began to talk about his job but then decided what he feared most was deafness, not being able to hear music. Dona said she feared growing old and ugly. As each one spoke, Michael was unusually silent. Normally he was extremely reluctant to divulge personal feelings in conversation, but Dona's frankness forced his hand. Finally, he confided that it was his work, for he felt that with his writing he was always at the foot of an enormously high mountain that he had to get over, and his fear was that he would not.

Nothing had ever been easy for Michael. He had come from nowhere and wanted everything, more than one life could hold. He had survived a death scare, but the five years given him by Hayes had hardened him. While London hummed with visions of victory, he saw no break in the clouds blanketing his mountain. He felt trapped and unsure about his work and about his marriage. He had tried earnestly to bring Evelyn over, but the travel ban was strict owing to the concerted military efforts of that summer. His relationship with Joan had entered the cloudy area as well, past flirtation and bordering on genuine affection, no longer a diversion and not yet a commitment.

After the Grimsby lectures he found himself displaced, living between London hotels and Larry's new lodgings in Hemel Hempstead. Throughout August he cycled extensively with Joan, enduring transience for the joy of the architecture. In September Joan was transferred to Torquay and Michael's own travel pass finally came through. He accompanied her to Devon and returned to the flat he had just taken in Eton. In the emotional confusion of their parting Michael lost his sailing tickets and was forced to buy a seat on one of the early, fitful Aer Lingus flights. He arrived back in Dublin on September 28.

At first Evelyn rejoiced to have him home again, but very soon she began to ask about the Englishwoman, reminding him of his reason for marrying her—to save her from a life of promiscuity. Michael kept insisting that the relationship was innocent. His attentiveness to her and to the family must have been convincing, because the "visit" proved to be a healing time for them all. He presented Evelyn with the pounded shilling ring he'd worn ever since Gormanstown; it was the first emblem of affection he'd ever given her. He gathered the children around him and read from their favorites: *Treasure Island, The Jungle Books, Tom Sawyer*. For a short time they knew again, as Liadain would later write, "the comforting smell from his tweed jacket and his pipe, the sound of his voice, his fondness for slippers, the noise of his typewriter."[12] He even took his mother to visit Molly Alexander, whom they'd not seen in years. Unfortunately, he was due back in England by the middle of October to complete two scripts for Crown Films.

A few days after he arrived in Eton, he heard from Joan, who had been reassigned to duty in London. What first appeared great news suddenly became a nightmare when she informed him that she was pregnant. He had entered into this relationship as Sir Galahad rescuing another young lady from herself; now he felt more like Childe Roland nearing a very real dark tower. He first insisted that she have an abortion, a suggestion that she found so repulsive that she wept for days. Not even a cycling jaunt to Walton-on-Thames under sunny skies eased their panic. Michael then wrote to Evelyn explaining the situation. To justify his request that she come at once to England, he intimated that Joan was threatening suicide, a fabrication he probably believed. Somehow Evelyn secured a travel pass and sailed early in November for Wales, where she stopped to see her mother before going on to her aunt's home in Hendon. The next day she met Michael and Joan for lunch in London; it was a strained and formal occasion. Evelyn spoke in vague terms dissuading Joan from rash action, which one assumed was suicide and the other assumed was abortion. Before Evelyn left, she assured Joan that she could depend on her help. Awaiting her in Dublin was a letter from Joan thanking her for the gesture but insisting that she would manage quite well on her own. By the end of

November Michael had finished his film scripts and returned to Dublin as well.

The Christmas season at 57 Strand Road was strained. While Evelyn was in England Donny had taken the children to be baptized at Star of the Sea Chapel. Adamant that his children be anything but Roman Catholic, Michael upbraided her violently upon his return. Unable to understand the source of his animosity, the old lady refused to leave her room. Michael became sick again, and Evelyn spent more and more time at the Gate Theatre. At home she tried to maintain a good face in front of the children, who seized on the obvious discomfort of their parents to press for attention. As usual Michael showered great affection on his daughter, while ignoring his son. When Myles was accused of stealing at the Protestant school he was attending, Michael beat him unmercifully. Then one afternoon all the neighborhood children, filling their holidays with play, decided to congregate at the O'Donovan house. Myles went into the study, took all of his father's pencils, and passed them out. They were playing author. When Michael returned from town and found the pencils gone, he exploded in fury, struck Myles, and shouted at Evelyn, "Get that brat out of my sight, forever!" He stormed upstairs and slammed the door. Only the intervention of Donny, whose presence caused Michael to feel excessive guilt and shame about his liaison with Joan, restored the peace.

Evelyn maintained her composure by seeing the whole crisis in ceremonial terms, as if she were cast as one of the principals in an intense but short-run play. For the most part she played her role of courageous and forgiving wife brilliantly. She knew that Michael felt trapped by divided allegiances, and being trapped, he reacted violently. She and Michael occasionally walked in the afternoon, but she found it hard to pretend not to notice when he took a letter from his jacket pocket and slipped it into a postbox. She also found it difficult to deliver the daily letters from Joan with Michael's morning coffee. Every letter received or sent cracked the ceremonial façade a bit more, exposing painful questions about the future. Michael insisted that he would not forsake the family, but that he could not just abandon Joan and her child. Fear had paralyzed his will.

As usual, Michael coped by drawing down his veil of literature, turning to his writing to work through the turmoil within his soul. Either he sat in the front room reading a book or scribbling on a writing pad or he locked himself upstairs behind his study door. In this there was no hint of the ceremonial, nothing of the self-dramatizing gestures that often marked his public poses. For consolation he turned to his old friends Trollope and Austen, but his writing still seemed sour. He could not break the logjam of creative silence he had felt since the publication of *Crab Apple Jelly;* those stories he believed marked a change in his artistic direction, away from the emotional flavor of his earlier work to a tauter, more controlled technique.

For years O'Connor had chafed against Irish sexual attitudes. In Cork beautiful girls like Natalie Murphy and Nancy McCarthy had sent his spirits soaring while their pious chastity deflated his youthful "nature." Local gossip about bad girls of the Square and of illegitimate children outraged his sense of privacy and personal freedom. But explosive as his outrage could be, it had always been checked by a certain reticence, because Michael/Frank was anything but libertine. Riots at the Abbey Theatre over Synge's *The Playboy of the Western World* and O'Casey's *The Plough and the Stars* convinced him that the entire country was not only sexually repressed but sexually obsessed as well. The banning of his own novel *Dutch Interior* and of O'Faoláin's *Bird Alone* had infuriated him, but it was that visit of the sodality man in 1942 that had pushed him over the edge. The more trapped he felt in Ireland—by his own loyalties, divided as they were, between Joan and Evelyn; by his own scruples; and by censorship and blacklisting—the more paranoid he became about the church.[13]

The most obvious examples of this indignant voice were the stories "The Holy Door" and "News for the Church." As early as 1943 he had written a short version of "The Holy Door" from an anecdote he and O'Faoláin had heard years before in Cork, about a woman who managed to tolerate making love with her husband by imagining him as a movie star. To that tidy theme O'Connor grafted another celebrated Cork legend, about couples who went to Lourdes or to Rome hoping for some miraculous assistance in conceiving a child when actually all they needed was "carnal intercourse." The more he worked on the story, the less focused it became; the twentieth version, which was not the last, was over a hundred pages long.

Equally unmanageable was "News for the Church," a story he was busily revising under such titles as "The Sinner" and "Chorale." Though changing the treatment with each change of title, O'Connor remained steadfast to his basic story: a girl confessing a sexual encounter to a priest in a strange town. With every version the crisis tilted further from the girl and increasingly toward the priest. Just as the young woman becomes almost childlike (both in her sexual need and in her need to confess), the priest assumes the role of injured parent, punishing the "child" for being naughty. The question O'Connor seemed bent on answering was, Why, if sex was for adults, did it seem to reduce people to childish behavior?

Though O'Connor had always given his stories careful attention, it was not until this time that he began what was to become his habit of endlessly rewriting. Actually, the change had begun three or four years earlier when he concluded from the Dutch psychiatrist's interpretation of his "left-handed" dream that he must turn from emotion to technique. Once he had the story, captured in a few sentences, he devoted himself to its treatment. One of the first instances of this obsessive quest for the seamless story was "Judas," or "Night of Stars" as it was called when originally published in *The Bell* in 1942. When O'Connor wrote this story, he was still at the emotional age of eighteen in matters of sex. With each successive rewrite the focus of the story changed, shifting from a young man's sexual fantasies to the guilt he feels over betraying his mother. As the emotion edged closer to the nerve, O'Connor distilled it in ever tighter prose.

However, this habit of relentless revising was not restricted to O'Connor's stories. At the time he was also reworking his translation of *The Midnight Court* for Dublin publisher Maurice Fridberg. He knew that his translation of Brian Merriman's poem would shock Irish readers, most of whom had no idea how bawdy the original was. Polishing the final version, O'Connor savored the thought of how that sodality man would respond, almost as much as he enjoyed the artistry of his own verse translation. His refusal to soften certain sexually explicit passages had less to do with prurience than with artistic integrity. Michael was the sort of person who would react with distaste at the telling of a dirty joke. He would no more tolerate salacious remarks than he would malicious gossip. But serious as O'Connor was about things he considered absolutely important in life (and love was one of the most important), he still could not resist poking the ribs of the pious patriots whose clamor about the Irish language he believed to be as hypocritical as their moral platitudes.

Sometime before Christmas of 1944, while O'Connor was caught in the confusion of "English Miles," he received a form letter asking if he would allow inclusion of a few of his poems in a South American anthology of Irish writing that O'Faoláin was compiling. Irritated by the thought of O'Faoláin making money when he could not, he fired off a curt refusal. Seán replied that Michael was letting his bitterness at Ireland color his relationships with the people who admired him most:

> The true facts are that there is not a person of any intelligence or discrimination in Ireland or elsewhere who has come across your work who does not admire you enormously. You have established your position, your reputation, and laid the foundation of a lasting name. If you have enemies they are wholly among the undiscriminating, and since you are not of the flock you will expect that—it is part of the game; and since they are that sort you are surely indifferent to their opinions? It is the greatest tribute that I can pay you to say that even those whom you have been grossly rude to, time and again, can surmount their disgust and still admire you as a writer.[14]

O'Connor retorted savagely, in a "Dear John (May I call you John?)" letter, that the "gall and bitterness" were all Seán's. He questioned O'Faoláin's "humanitarianism," his motives, and even his honesty. "All art is single-minded, and the Bell seems to me the reflection of a mind which is swamped in a multiplicity of motives," he continued. After suggesting that O'Faoláin had cut himself off from other artists by gratifying his own creative instincts through "hacking and rewriting" the work of inferiors, O'Connor spat the final insult: "You and Dev—how you both love the second-rate!"[15] Having vented his spleen, he added that quarreling by post was silly and that instead they should meet for tea that Friday. The upshot of this latest in a series of "brotherly" quarrels was that they agreed to the publication of "The Art of the Theatre" over four issues of *The Bell,* commencing in March 1945.

Michael was short with everyone during that time, though only Evelyn really understood why. Even old friends seldom called at the house for fear of finding him in one of his black moods. One who risked it now and then was Larry Elyan, who had been instrumental in getting *The Invincibles* staged at the Gaiety, a popular Dublin theatre, in 1943, the year of O'Connor's greatest need.[16] Over a cup of tea with Evelyn one afternoon, Elyan casually mentioned reading a story by another Irish writer in a recent issue of *The New Yorker* and said that, from what he had heard, the fee was sizeable. Evelyn responded that even on a bad day Michael was twice the writer "your man" was. Elyan agreed and asked why Michael had never published in *The New Yorker.* "I don't think he has an American agent," she replied. After Elyan left, Evelyn continued to mull over what he had told her. She knew Michael would never send out the stories he was working on until he was completely satisfied. She also knew that everything had to be sent out through his agent in London. However, risking his fury, she bundled together a finished version of "News for the Church" and posted it to *The New Yorker* magazine. The story was accepted immediately and published in September. A. D. Peters was only mildly displeased at O'Connor for skirting normal channels. In August *The New Yorker* offered O'Connor a first-reading option on all of his stories.[17] A. D. Peters was more than happy to forward his willingness to accept the offer. So began O'Connor's association with *The New Yorker,* an association that would last the rest of his life.

In the next few months an astonishing chain of endings and beginnings occurred in the life of Frank O'Connor. In April Tim Buckley died at the age of eighty-three, ending something very special, Michael's own "fountain of magic." Hearing of the death of the Tailor, he wrote this tribute:

> Man is the torch that lights the tomb,
> In England now the orchards bloom.
> Where flint and rosy brick expand,
> And grey church towers on leafy heights
> These too some burning body lights
> Like Caesar's slave with burning hand.
> The torch is out that was the sun
> Which lit these lonesome hills at noon:
> And night and cold streak up the glen,
> Song, magic, bawdy, wit and truth,
> All the wild Ireland of my youth
> Is gone and all is dark again.

His old nemesis and covert supporter Bertie Smyllie published it the next day in the *Irish Times,* apparently with some assurance that just a wee poem signed by Frank O'Connor would be permissible.[18]

No sooner was the mourning over than expectation began to mount about an Allied victory, which meant the end of war, rationing, blackouts, and fear, but Mr. de Valera had already barred any celebration of the event in neutral Ireland. O'Connor wrote a poem entitled "Fiacha and the Louth Men," which told of the overthrow of a horrid tyranny. To protect himself, he described it as a translation from the original Irish. Bertie Smyllie held the poem until V-E Day (May 8, 1945), then ran it in place of the headline de Valera had banned. Beneath it were photos of the Allied leaders arranged in the shape of a V.[19] For Ireland the end of the war meant an end of isolation from the rest of Europe and from the United States. What it meant to Frank O'Connor was the possible end of his own separate war, of hostilities between himself and his homeland. The ban on his work was lifted, and since O'Connor no longer had to hide behind the mask of Ben Mayo, that covert enterprise ended as mysteriously as it had begun. In August, at Smyllie's request, he began a series for the *Irish Times,* which published, over five months, eleven articles of his on nineteenth-century novelists—Austen, Stendhal, Dickens, Flaubert, Trollope, the Russians, Hardy, and Somerville and Ross.[20]

However, the most important event of that six-month period was the birth in London during June of a child named Oliver. In Dublin Michael was anxious to the point of hysteria—mainly, it would seem, over whether or not Joan had a pram for the baby—so in August Evelyn once again travelled to London.

She found Joan, who had no money, living with her old friend the teacher (who had very little money), but cheery and resolute. Once again Evelyn offered to help, and again the young woman politely refused. She wanted Michael there with her, not his wife, whose visit to see her child had upset her deeply.

Within a week of Evelyn's return to Dublin Joan's health began to disintegrate. By September a crippling form of arthritis made it difficult for her to care for the baby, and she wrote imploring Michael to come. She had resisted the physician's advice to enter the hospital and put Oliver in a children's home—she would take care of her son in her own way and "wear her feather" with dignity. When Michael finally arrived in November he was ill at ease with his four-month-old son but more ill at ease with himself. It was clear to Joan—although he denied it—that he had either given Evelyn an understanding about her or that he himself had decided he could no longer divide himself between two women. For Joan, after all his assertions that Evelyn "understood," this was a terrible shock, and one for which he had not prepared her. He had to sleep in her bed—there was nowhere else—for three weeks; he was cold and untalkative, and did not touch her or explain why.

Also that month O'Connor was asked by Guy Schofield, editor of the *Evening News* (London) and longtime friend of Desmond MacCarthy, if he was still interested in work. Michael said he was, so on November 28 he began "The Bookman," a fortnightly review column covering everything from biography and detective fiction to poetry and children's books. O'Connor made no apologies for introducing readers to the letters of Rilke, then, two weeks later, to a set of war books. In the first few months he read and reviewed books by such personal friends as V. S. Pritchett, John Betjeman, Bill Naughton, and A. E. Coppard, and by such literary acquaintances as A. J. Cronin, Oliver St. John Gogarty, and Kate O'Brien. Though not really a labor of love—it was, in fact, labor for a price—the column proved a blessing for Michael because it diverted his energies from the tangle of his personal life while focusing his attention on what was happening in the literary world outside his own study.

Generally, O'Connor began each review with a vignette or anecdote—a conversation with a soldier on a train during the war, for instance—suggesting something vaguely relevant to the books at hand. Of course, many of these miniature conversations came directly from the very book he was having so much difficulty writing, "English Miles." Asked to review a set of books written by women, he glibly alleged: "I have always been an ardent feminist, and am never really happy unless there are women about."[21] Another review opens with this statement: "If the Lord hadn't made me what I am (whatever that may be) I think I should have chosen to be a B.B.C. war correspondent. To have been there when British and Russians met; when the survivors of the horror-camps saw their rescuers appear; when the door was opened on the Mayor's parlour in Leipzig."[22] By maintaining this personal element, he gave his literary opinions the guarantee of personal taste—at once simple and complex, provincial and sophisticated.

However, behind the civility and eccentric personal flavor moves a subtle demonstration of sensitivity to language and the art of writing. Reviewing Kipling, for example, O'Connor contended that there were only three themes in stories, and they were the same ones some natural storyteller used long ago to divert a violent bunch of cavemen: contention (what happened on the hunt), romance (how the girl was won or lost), and fear (the thing at the mouth of the cave). Natural storytellers like Kipling played on the reader's primal instincts. "The instincts are all very well in their way," O'Connor added, "but there is also judgment."[23] Oddly enough, it isn't O'Connor's judgment that blows through these reviews like salt air but his literary instincts. In his review of V. S. Pritchett's *It May Never Happen*, for instance, he expounded in great length on the differences between Irish and English fiction.[24] Perhaps nowhere else does O'Connor ever spell out quite so clearly what he and his generation of Irish writers were doing—in the absence of literary tradition, trying to describe the life around them as if writing for an "audience of educated Russians." Real-life people in Irish pubs are not only the subject to be treated but also the audience addressed, and as an audience they demand not a mirror but a distorting lens, a Hollywood romance instead of a documentary film. That as much as anything else explains the painful dilemma that, aside from his personal limitations, hindered O'Connor from realizing either great popular or critical success at home; and, too, it explains why his stories were received so readily by real-life people in England and America. O'Connor remained torn between voices outside and those within his head; dedicated to the Chekhovian reporting of mundane life, he was drawn toward a powerful inner culture full of fancy and intellectual elaboration.

Ordinarily, reviews tossed off for a few pounds would not appear crucial in a writer's life, yet Frank O'Connor's column for the *Evening News* mirrored his personal and literary uncertainty at the time. The war was over, his best stories were behind him, his family life seemed dubious. Yet 1945 was his most productive year since he had fled to Woodenbridge in 1938. While writing the Hull lectures he had begun theorizing more and more about the art of literature, challenging himself to justify his vocation. Yeats had once told him that he never considered his plays and poems his own, because what one imagines belongs to everyone and no one. What one produces from reason, Yeats believed, can be counted a possession and can be controlled, bullied, or exhibited with pride. Before the war O'Connor's critical essays were close to the nerve of his creative life, part of the imaginative flash from which he wrote his stories. After the Abbey and the tribulations of the war, he turned to criticism to prove something. At this time he thought he knew where he was as a writer; irritated by the academic mandarins, O'Connor turned to an assertive criticism, vain in its personal ownership to the point that it was very close to autobiographical declaration.

I I I

Almost as soon as Michael left for Dublin, Joan's health worsened; by Christmas she had again become bedridden. Normally a strong, self-supporting woman, it was now impossible for her to care for herself and an infant. She hesitated about spilling her woes to Michael even in her letters, recalling how unsympathetic he had been before. To him she had to remain the glib comedienne, always ready to toss off a line of poetry, a measure of song, or a tasty meal. But something must have passed between the lines of her witty letters because a few days into the New Year she received Evelyn's second invitation to come to Dublin. She capitulated, for, with Oliver, she had no other option. Within a week they were boarding a plane at Croydon.

Evelyn and Michael had prepared Donny for Joan's arrival. An old London friend of Evelyn's, they had explained, was coming to Dublin to recuperate; her husband had disappeared near the end of the war. When they arrived at Strand Road that morning, Donny came from her room to greet them. Before the awkward introduction was even begaun, she took Oliver from Evelyn's arms, exclaiming, "My, he's the living spit of Michael." From that moment on she doted on the child, allowing no one else to care for him. Evelyn's own physician saw Joan, quickly admitted her to the hospital, and supervised her medical care for three weeks. He cautioned her against returning to London until she was fully recovered. Since Oliver was apparently thriving under the lavish attention of Donny and the other children, she put aside her natural reluctance about the strange arrangement and bowed to Evelyn's insistence that she stay on with them at Strand Road.

At first the two women moved awkwardly about each other, ceremonially polite but obviously conscious of a natural enmity. While Joan acted her role as guest with cheerful deference, Evelyn played the gracious hostess with almost genuine fervor. Now and then, though, she was unable to resist the sly barb: "Oh thank you, Joan. Take the tea but come right back down"; or "Don't bother him, Joan. He's exhausted from our morning together." Joan, of course, found such comments understandable, but at the same time she felt awkward enough without being reminded of her position. By then she had come to be fairly certain that a life with Michael was out of the question. He too was nervous in the presence of the two women and spent as much time as possible in his study or in town. Gradually, however, the routines leveled out, and Michael grew somewhat smug.

Michael's mother was, as always, the ointment to heal all hurt. One day as he entered the front door he heard her gaily sing to Oliver, "Here's Daddy, so." Not believing his ears, he glanced at Evelyn, then at Joan, for confirmation. Both of them were quickly putting down teacups—not in shock but in sheer glee. The king of the castle, the smug possessor of a bevy of three fine women absolutely devoted to him, was suddenly odd man out. The worm had turned, with a vengeance; the unnatural triangle had become a box—three against one. He smiled nervously but retired quickly to his study. Later, out of earshot of his mother, he laughingly proclaimed to Evelyn that he was going to make a story of that scene. "You wouldn't," she half questioned, half commanded. "It would hurt her." "Who?" Thinking it was obvious, Evelyn didn't answer. He wrote the story anyway, titling it first "The Grandmother," then finally "Ladies of the House."

Eventually, the situation took its toll. Michael wrote with unusual frenzy, walked alone along the strand, and smoked constantly. Then one day he stopped speaking. For a week his seething silence baffled everyone. Finally, Joan broached the subject with Evelyn, who was herself just as reluctant to ask him about it. The next evening at tea he blurted something about some bastard of a writer, and both women sighed. It turned out that he had seen a new book in Eason's Bookshop, thumbed the index, found his name, turned to the passage, and found it uncomplimentary. "So that's it?" Joan asked. "What?" he queried in reply. "Why you've not been speaking all week," Evelyn answered. "Oh, go 'way," he said, laughing. That evening he read to the children for the first time in months.

Joan returned to London toward the end of February 1946, physically well but emotionally exhausted. When Evelyn began rehearsals for a new play at the Gate, Joan decided it was time for her to make her own life. She was, after all, a trained teacher, and, too, she was young and nearly healthy. Though nothing had ever been said, she knew Evelyn was pregnant, a fact that she thought indicated a decison on Michael's part to stay. But Michael was unable to make up his mind about anything—personal or professional. For two years he had vacillated not only between England and Ireland but more significantly between the work of his head—hack work and criticism—and the work of his heart—stories and translations.

Less than a month after Joan left, he went to England to meet with Schofield and to negotiate directly with Macmillan over a contract misunderstanding. (As usual, his publisher wanted a novel, not another volume of stories.) Though his letters to Evelyn never referred to Joan, she knew he had visited her. He felt a strong sense of duty about his "English family" and probably more than a slight tinge of guilt. On the other hand, Evelyn was pregnant, and his Irish family demanded his primary allegiance. He returned to Dublin a few weeks later with the assurance from Schofield that he could continue the popular "Bookman" column from there. In addition, Macmillan had agreed to publish his next book of stories, at that time tentatively titled "Holy Women," and a book about Dublin, which was eventually subsumed in *Irish Miles*.[25]

Nearly twenty years of fighting with nearly everyone about nearly everything had established O'Connor's reputation as Ireland's most abrasive voice of conscience. He believed he was standing alone, fighting a sort of guerrilla war against the forces of stupidity and vested interest. To clarify the image of Collins, to support the novels of his friends, to decry the pillorying of a public figure on the stage of the national theatre, to defend an old storyteller and his wife against hoodlum priests, were all simply moral obligations of the artist in a provincial country. This struggle against Irish provincialism became most apparent during the 1940s in his campaign to preserve the unique Irish heritage held so precariously in the monasteries, castles, big houses, and megalithic sites scattered about the country.

Irish Miles, which finally appeared in 1947, represents the culmination of that campaign. Though about his travels in Ireland, it is a travel book only as *The Big Fellow* is a biography—closer perhaps to Synge's *The Aran Islands* than to O'Faoláin's *An Irish Journey*.[26] To cycle completely around Ireland in search of ruins might have been considered a bit eccentric, but it was, nevertheless, genuine Frank O'Connor. The campaign to preserve Irish architecture obtrudes from time to time, usually as wry sarcasm directed at negligent officials; but on the whole the book sparkles with the presence of the man behind the voice. On finding another fine house gutted by "housebreakers," O'Connor, in his thinly disguised role as Alceste, quips: "Why on earth any Irish government should imagine that Ireland hadn't ruins enough and that it was their duty to fill it with more, I didn't understand, but then there is a lot about Irish governments which I don't understand." Inevitably, his love of Ireland cuts through his venomous indignation, tempering sarcasm with sympathy. About the peculiar individualism of an especially ugly church, he recalls being repelled at first and then attracted "in the way one is attracted by characters one meets in out-of-the-way places, men who superfically are all angles and oddity, but who, as you get to know them, reveal their value."

Throughout the book O'Connor manages to find the tale in the pub, to make culture a living story in which the most valuable artifacts of a people are the people themselves. Moving on ground level at cycling pace, he had nosed his way around Ireland for five years, looking at stone structures, listening to people talk, and finding bits and pieces to write about. The narrative moves at the same pace and follows this "respectable middle-aged writer with his wife and friend" from the Boyne Valley south through Leinster, west through Munster, and north through Connaught.

Through it all, the humane misanthropy of the narrator controls *Irish Miles.* Whether he is chuckling about the leverage of a literary name or complaining about another bad cup of tea, the personality, if not the character, of the author-narrator comes very much to life. For that matter, everything he experiences and everyone he makes contact with, including his cycling companions, comes to life. As always, O'Connor's ambivalent attachment to Ireland is nowhere more evident than in what he writes about Cork. Alceste explains to Célimène that "a writer who goes back to his native place is rather in the position of Heine's monkey chewing his tail. Objectively he is eating, subjectively he is being eaten."

Macmillan agreed in the spring of 1946 to publish *Irish Miles* (the title suggested by an editor to replace "No Place Like Home!") in place of the contracted novel. Though his book on architcture and cycling was finally finished, O'Connor's passion for old churches and friendly miles had not yet been satiated, nor had his ambivalent association with Ireland been resolved. The stories he was writing became more "English," as he was no longer writing with the audience of Radio Eireann in mind. Macmillan, however, had refused to consider his translation of Brian Merriman's "Cúirt an Mheadhon Oidhche" because it was too "specialized" for English readers.[27] Publishers in Ireland at the time would not touch it either because O'Connor's name was still associated with indecent and impious writing. Larry Elyan had, in the end, to approach his friend Maurice Fridberg, who agreed to take the risk, provided he could also publish a small selection of O'Connor stories. After considerable reluctance Macmillan agreed to the arrangement, and the long-awaited translation, *The Midnight Court: A Rhythmical Bacchanalia from the Irish of Bryan Merryman, with Preface,* finally appeared at the end of 1945.[28]

Apart from his stories, no other literary activity had so steadily absorbed O'Connor's interest as the translation of Irish poetry into English. That O'Connor enjoyed himself with *The Midnight Court* is obvious; working on the final draft in London, he often joked with Joan about seeing his own reflection in it. In his introduction, in fact, he called Merriman's poem a "great paean in praise of bastards," an exaggeration that struck rather close to home.[29] Yet beyond the theme of sexual freedom, a more serious idea is apparent in O'Connor's translation. Sexual impotence is part of a greater bondage, and the need for love is part of a "great hunger" for genuine freedom and natural innocence. What Merriman saw in eighteenth-century Ireland seems not too different from what O'Connor saw in the Ireland of his day.

O'Connor's exasperation with Irish civilization obtrudes more in his slightly polemical introduction to *The Midnight Court* than in the translation itself. Merriman, he explains, was born in a part of Ireland—Feakle, in County Clare—that in the eighteenth century was as barbarous as anywhere else in Europe and "isn't exactly what one would call civilized today." He died in Limerick, which O'Connor commends as "one of the pleasantest spots in Ireland," only then to condemn it for failing to mark the spot of Merriman's house out of sheer piety. He goes on to describe Merriman as a poor scholar who somehow managed in an Irish-speaking community to read the best writers of his day— Savage, Swift, Goldsmith, and Rousseau. Needless to say, O'Connor feels a kinship with this self-taught provincial whose "old utopian passion" set him apart from his time.

The story contained in the poem, at least as O'Connor summarizes it, appears innocuous enough:

> The poet falls asleep, and in a dream is summoned to the fairy court, where the unmarried women of Munster are pleading their inability to get husbands. An old man replies by telling the story of his own marriage, and of how his young wife presented him with another man's child on his wedding night. The young girl rebuts the charge and tells the story of the marriage from the wife's point of view, and then the Fairy Queen sums up and gives judgment for the women, whose first victim is the poet himself.[30]

Obviously, it was not the story that interested O'Connor so much as the attitude and atmosphere. Nor was it for the story alone that O'Connor's translation was inevitably banned, since numerous other versions escaped that indignity. It was Merriman's audacity that drew him to the poem; it was that very audacity he endeavored to capture in his translation; and it was his own audacity in rendering the poem with such uproarious exuberance that inevitably drew the ire of the Censorship Board.

O'Connor was in England when the official announcement of the banning was made, April 30, 1946.[31] To the claim that the translation was almost entirely the product of his filthy imagination, he responded in a letter to Dermot Foley that the charge was the finest compliment Ireland had ever paid him. He also wrote to Stan Stewart that day, inviting him to come cycling in England later in May. With so many Irish miles behind him, he had now turned his full attention to England. He met Stan at Euston Station, ferried him across London to Victoria Station, and caught a train to Brighton, where Bill Naughton was staying. Naughton, a young lorry driver from Lancashire who had decided to pursue his writing full-time, had been a fan of O'Connor's since hearing "Old Fellows" on the BBC three years before. He was anxious to spend time with Michael, and being athletic, he welcomed an energetic spin after a winter at the typewriter. He found plenty of talk, but not much of it took place outdoors; Stan's idea of cycling still meant moving from one comfortable public house to another with minimum haste over a minimum of miles. Exhilarated by Michael's high opinion of his work but frustrated by the ratio of railway miles to cycling miles, Naughton returned to Brighton within a week. O'Connor returned to Dublin with Stan early in June, and three weeks later, Evelyn gave birth to their third child, whom they named Owen Standish— after her father and Stan Stewart.

I V

The Emergency had been over for nearly a year, but peace did not yet prevail at 57 Strand Road. Small joy surrounded the birth of the last O'Donovan son. A new baby imposes its own order on a household and brings with it a new kind of strain, and strain was something Evelyn and Michael hardly needed any more of. The banning of *The Midnight Court,* combined with abysmal sales of the other two books he published in Dublin after the war—a thin piece of literary appreciation for a series by Metropolitan Publishers and a selection of stories for Fridberg's Hour-Glass Library Series—suggested that Frank O'Connor was slowly fading out of favor, at least in Ireland.[32] In the last half of 1945 he sold only one story, "A Thing of Nothing," to *Cornhill,* a London magazine. Then nearly everything he sent to his agent was bought. Though rejecting "Don Juan (Retired)," O'Connor's first attempt at the Irish philanderer theme, *The New Yorker* eagerly took "The Babes in the Wood," his first fictional exploration of the bastard theme. "Custom of the Country" and "The Sinner," two more stories with overt sexual subjects, were bought by *English Story* and *Argosy.* Then Reginald Moore wanted both "The Miracle" and "Friends of the Family" for his miscellany *Modern Reading.*[33]

However, "The Dead" found no takers; the story that O'Connor told A. D. Peters was the first "pure" story he had written in over a year met nothing but rejection.[34] Since only what he called his "dirty ones" seemed to interest anyone, he decided to follow his agent's advice and make a book of them. So began *The Common Chord.* Despite the deadening uncertainty of the past two years, his mind had been inordinately alive. His writing journals were full of fragments of stories overheard on his travels, sketches about England, and essays on various writers. Throughout the summer of Owen's birth the pages poured from the room behind the Author sign.

Normally O'Connor did not write much in the summertime, preferring instead to relax and "gather material." But that summer in rapid succession he finished "The Stepmother," which David Marcus used that fall in the first issue of *Irish Writing;* "Christmas Morning," a story based on an incident that had taken place one Christmas at Strand Road; and then two stories stemming from experiences in England, "Public Opinion" and "The World of Art and Reilly."[35] Nor was his interest in England confined to churches, pubs, and bedrooms, for he had been toiling almost since the day he met Joan on a book about Shakespeare, a short version of which he finished in August. His personal life may have been in a shambles during those months, but his writing seemed to have gained new direction and energy, a fact explainable only by Joan—not so much the actual person as her invisible presence. If it can be said that *Irish Miles* and *Crab Apple Jelly* were Evelyn's, then *The Road to Stratford* and *The Common Chord* were clearly Joan's books. In O'Connor's earliest work both love and literature were seen through the eyes of his frustrated romanticism as forms of escape. After the break with Nancy he wrote more and more about loss and betrayal. Now, haunted by the thought of an English "mistress" and an "illegitimate" child, O'Connor began writing about the manifold variations of the sexual life and what Yeats had called the "desolation of reality."[36]

Another reason for O'Connor's burst of literary effort that summer was the appearance in Ireland of two young scholars from Harvard University. John Kelleher, a junior fellow of the Society of Fellows, had come to spend the summer doing research and finding his ancestral home. Richard Ellmann, a young instructor recently returned to the university from the war, had come for the year to finish a book on W. B. Yeats. They were both familiar with the work of Frank O'Connor, and on the advice of friends they both called on him as soon as they got to Dublin. He was immediately enchanted by these serious and energetic young men, who seemed to know more about Irish literature than the Irish themselves. Their conversation proved to be a happy respite for him, and he spent many evenings overwhelming them with theories about his current obsession, Shakespeare. "One night he would sweep away, as interpolations, the witch scenes in *Macbeth*," Ellmann recalled, "and another he would body forth an unknown but, he assured us, perfectly conjurable collaborator of Shakespere in the problem comedies."[37] He also firmly believed that *Edward III* was written entirely by Shakespeare, an idea so eccentric at the time, so defiantly in opposition to the recognized authorities, that it left his American friends bemused. Though they were doubtful about his theories, neither was inclined to argue. Nevertheless, he captivated them and enlivened their stay in Ireland. He also encouraged their scholarly endeavors. When Ellmann's book was finished, for example, O'Connor read it, made a few suggestions, and then wrote an enthusiastic endorsement to Macmillan.

What intrigued and disturbed people like Kelleher and Ellmann about Michael/Frank was his reckless intellectual temperament, which radiated creative energy. Though skeptical about his conclusions, both men were impressed by the scope of his reading and the originality of his thinking. He was possessed of such voracious curiosity and of such prodigious assimilative capability that they could not help feeling overwhelmed in his presence. The audacious spirit so prominent in his early stories and poems now manifested itself primarily in his almost obsessive interest in literary criticism. His gigantic enthusiasm fired any subject to the melting point, eradicating all impediments and precluding all refutation. He assumed that Ellmann and Kelleher were in full agreement with whatever he was expounding at the moment, and whenever they questioned his insufficient or shady evidence, he simply resorted to the that-way-lies-madness school of confutation. It was almost as if in his relentless pursuit of the final word he were seeking some sort of absolute, some point of mental repose to offset the emotional uncertainty that dominated his personal life and emerged more and more in his fiction as a mood of desolation and loneliness.

Before Kelleher left Dublin that summer on a bicycle tour, he asked Michael if he could suggest anyone in the west who might be willing to receive his mail and hold it for him. At once the name of Stan Stewart came up. Kelleher wrote ahead asking him for this kindness. It was a very wet summer and cycling proved slow, so John took longer getting to Limerick than he had calculated. When he arrived at Stan's house, he found that the table had been set for him every day for a week; shrugging off apologies for the inconvenience, Stan took in the weary cyclist, entertained him, introduced him to his friends, and sent him on his way a week later carrying maps and introductions.

From Limerick Kelleher made his way south to the parish in West Cork where his family came from. But nobody there remembered his great-grandfather, who had stayed in Ireland and died there in 1880. After much probing, it was discovered that since the man had married outside the parish, he must have been a herdsman, and since herdsmen were so far down on the social scale, their descendants wouldn't count for much anyway. That settled that. Kelleher was graciously given some misinformation about people in the next parish who might be able to help, and was then gently dismissed. He was still sore about the entire episode when he returned to Dublin, but his account of it greatly amused Michael. One day after Kelleher had returned to the States, Michael repeated the story to a neighbor in Strand Road who had grown up in that region of West Cork. Even before he finished, she broke in: "But that man went to the wrong place. It's in Dernagree his family was. And what's more, he's got cousins in Atlantic City, whether he knows it or not." The mystery of the wild-goose chase solved, Michael wrote at once to Kelleher, who had since received the same information from a different source. Their letters crossed.

It was the beginning of a rich and rewarding correspondence between two very different men: the slow-speaking, careful scholar and the silver-tongued, audacious writer. Kelleher provided his brash Irish friend with a safety valve by giving a sympathetic ear to Michael's expression of personal discontent; his geographical detachment assured discretion. To an even greater extent, however, he provided a critical sounding board for O'Connor's literary notions. Because of his academic training Kelleher seemed freer to challenge O'Connor's untutored genius than any of his Irish friends, except perhaps O'Faoláin, and their letters were always full of literary explorations.

Shortly after Kelleher left in September, Michael went to London for a BBC broadcast, his first in nearly two years.[38] He was apprehensive abut seeing Joan for the first time in months. In response to her dilemma about what to do with Oliver while she was working, he advised that she board him out. "The kings of Ireland did," he told her. She slapped his face in pent-up rage. He returned to Dublin a fortnight later. Then, early in October, Evelyn was forced to travel to Wales because of a death in the family. While she was away Michael was walking aimlessly in O'Connell Street one afternoon when he came face to face with Dermot Foley, who introduced him to his new friend, Didicus, a remarkable Franciscan about whom he had written enthusiastically in recent letters. The three of them walked about town, Michael in between the librarian and the monk, talking about nothing in particular and everything in general. It was a sullen Dublin day in which the sky and the street seemed sewn together. After a while Michael excused himself, turned a corner, and disappeared down the quays. Dermot, who for months had talked glowingly about his friend the writer, was anxious to know what the young monk thought of him. Didicus, a sagacious and observing sort who had said nothing at all in Michael's company, replied that he thought the man was on the edge of madness. Feeling Dermot recoil, he qualified his judgment by saying he only meant that Michael seemed to be a man in great turmoil, as if he had fire in his veins that he could not put out. Knowing the present circumstances and having put up with Michael's unpredictability for years, Dermot was curious to know how Didicus could make such an appraisal so quickly. "His voice," said the Franciscan, "didn't you hear his voice?"

Frank O'Connor posed for Dermot Foley in the doorway of the Pembroke Library, Dublin, in 1930.

Frank O'Connor in the late 1930s.

Minnie O'Donovan, O'Connor's mother.

Stan Stewart took this photograph of O'Connor and Evelyn outside a hotel in Limerick during an Irish Miles tour in the 1940s. The man at center is unidentified.

TEL. 95758.

RIVERSDALE,
WILLBROOK,
RATHFARNHAM,
DUBLIN.

Thursday

Dear O Connor

I send should I asked my sister for
a proof she sent of her own accord. I have
revised one or two poems & suggested the terms,
out of one that seems to me a formula. I
think I have found some misprints in
the proof.

I suggest to your sister, my sister & print
the music for 'Repentance' as the end of
book. The broadside block fits perfectly.
she has done this with my book.

W B Yeats

I say nothing about your suggestion because
I have much to say on the subject at the
board meeting on Friday
Your book is beautiful & moving

Copy of a letter from Yeats to O'Connor written in June 1938.
The book mentioned in the last line was the Cuala Press's edition of
Lords & Commons.

*Myles and Liadain O'Donovan on Sandymount
Strand in the early '40s.*

*O'Connor with Dermot Foley and the Franciscan monk Didicus
on O'Connell Street, Dublin, 1946.*

O'Connor and John Kelleher at Duleek, County Meath, 1950.

Stan Stewart on a cycle tour in France with O'Connor, 1949.

Seán O'Faoláin in 1946, aged forty-six.

Harriet, Myles, and O'Connor at Primrose Hill, England, in December 1953, shortly after Harriet and Michael's marriage.

O'Connor with Robert Frost in Ripton, Vermont, 1952.

O'Connor in the late 1950s.

O'Connor at Cashel during filming in 1964 of Telefís Éireann series on Irish archeological and architectural monuments.

15

Prodigal Father

*All happy families resemble one another, but each unhappy
family is unhappy in its own way.*

TOLSTOY, *Anna Karenina*

SHORTLY after Christmas in 1946, Michael returned to England to script a documentary film about lifeboats, which was being shot in Hastings. Late in January he convinced Evelyn to cross with the three children and his mother. Bad
weather delayed the arrival of their train at Euston Station, where Michael and
Joan bustled everyone into a waiting taxi. After racing across London to catch a
southbound train, they found Victoria Station cordoned off by troops. Michael
indignantly asked what the matter was, and learned that the royal family would
soon board the Southampton train en route to South Africa. The children were
delighted to spend a night in a big hotel, but Evelyn only wanted to get out of
London with Michael immediately, to escape the uncomfortable triangle. Despite one of the worst snows in years, they traveled the next day by train to
Lyme Regis in Dorset, where Michael had been given the use of a cottage
owned by the wife of his boss at Crown Film, Jack Holmes.

This old coast guard cottage, situated just up the hill from the Cobb,
Lyme's justly famous breakwater, was cold and gloomy when they arrived.
Soon, however, Donny and Evelyn made things warm and hospitable. Even in
the midst of swirling snow Lyme Regis was beautiful, and Joan seemed forgotten in the newness of the place—until the first letter arrived. For a while Michael went weekly to Hastings to finish work on the film, and after that he
made fortnightly trips to London, where he was also working on a broadcast for
the BBC on Yeats. The departure of Christopher and Dona Salmon for the
United States had left him in the hands of new producers, whose criticisms he
took rather badly.[1] His stomach was uncooperative, as it always seemed to be
in February and March, and because the cottage was so much smaller than the
house in Sandymount, he snapped at the children more than usual. Because of
bad weather Liadain and Myles were constantly underfoot and irritable, and
Evelyn, accustomed to her Dublin maid, found the infant, Owen, more than an
armful to handle.

After Macmillan had flatly rejected O'Connor's Shakespeare book, he took
it back from A. D. Peters and rewrote it completely, expanding it to nearly fifty
thousand words. Early in March 1947 Methuen accepted the revised book with
an advance of sixty-seven pounds, which helped to relieve the family's financial pinch. The BBC had not used O'Connor as much as he had anticipated
when he brought his family to live in England, and his stories were not selling
well either. However, he still had the fortnightly "Bookman" column for the
Evening News, which rescued him in more than a financial way. The regular

book packets from London were something to anticipate and to talk about with Evelyn at a time when there seemed little else constructive to discuss, while reading provided him a form of legitimate escape at a time when their house seemed like a prison. Above all, writing the short reviews eased his guilt at a time when his writing seemed labored and dull. In more than one review he commented that any war marks the end of an epoch and that the fashionable writers of one moment can quickly become the old fogies of the next.

The war had obviously affected how O'Connor thought of himself as a writer, and fashion had already begun to shift; he was quite aware, for example, that the BBC had not bought a story for broadcasting in two years. His print stories were now read by more and more editors before being accepted for publication, and A. D. Peters would on occasion notify him that they were retiring a story from circulation or that they had accepted five guineas from some unlikely magazine.[2] O'Connor had never given much thought to where his stories were published, but he would no more alter his style to fit prevailing fashions than change an opinion about Killaloe or de Valera. Nor would he change his mind too easily about what he felt constituted good writing. Time and again he would warn his English readers that he was old-fashioned, that he preferred the simple to the complex, the lively narrative to the ornate symbolic form.[3]

Gradually, however, the titles of the "Bookman" reviews began to sound like the catchy leads of the Ben Mayo articles. "Writing About New Books Frank O'Connor Gets in a Rage," announces his review for April 16, which opens with a rumination about how it is that good books get reviewed at all: "Every reviewer is himself a writer or a would-be writer, and while his conscious, critical mind is wide-awake on the quest for talent, his subconscious, creative one seems to warn him off any book that might conceivably make him jealous." In May he reviews, along with a few other books, a set of broadcast stories by Eric Allen, a broadcast director at the BBC. O'Connor opens with the disclaimer that asking him to review this book is "rather like asking the vicar to review 'What the Chambermaid Saw' or Joe Stalin to write a few words on the Reminiscences of Trotsky." Allen, he goes on to explain, belongs to the "Other Side," meaning the gimmickry school of storytelling, represented by Saki and O. Henry. O'Connor, of course, puts himself squarely on the side of Chekhov and Maupassant.

Since O'Connor was working at this time on his book about cycling around England, his "Bookman" column was regularly spiced with anecdotes that appear fleshed out in the fragmented manuscript of "English Miles." Of course, the stylized characters of that unfinished book (in which Joan appears as Angélique, while Evelyn and Stan keep the familiar faces of Célimène and Géronte, which they wore in *Irish Miles*) are never mentioned, but in nearly every review the ubiquitous Irish storyteller with a ready ear for a story can be heard.

If O'Connor was relentless when on the scent of a story, he was equally restless when he was not. In Lyme Regis he felt hemmed in; the hills rising sharply above the town, and the foggy bay in front of it, gave him the unsettling illusion of living on an island, a phobia of his that seemed to grow worse every year. In April he went to Edinburgh for a broadcast, making the journey by himself because Evelyn was recuperating from a severe bout with the

mumps. Early in May she was well enough to accompany him on the first cycling tour they had made together for nearly five years. They set out with the
intention of reaching Bristol, where Evelyn could catch a train to see her family in Wales. They started on a Saturday morning, taking the Yeovil road. Near
Queen's Camel a thunderstorm hit and they took refuge and tea in the inn at
Sparkford. The next morning, Michael convinced Evelyn that instead of making for Bath, they should go out of their way to take in Devizes, if only to send a
picture postcard of the stained glass to Stan Stewart, whose passion for John
Piper windows would make him jealous enough to join them. The hills, which
kept him in a state of "dither," and Evelyn's promise of Romanesque wonders
at Lullington, lured him off the road "into delightful wooded country at the
foot of the Mendips."[4]

Diversion is the natural failing of the born storyteller, and by the third day
they had come no nearer to Bristol than when they had started. "The moment
we left Devizes we were out on the Downs, which I swear are the most magical
country in the world. . . . In the hollows black stagnant pools of elms sheltered
from the wind, and a grey churchtower peered from their depths, and when we
cycled down there was some village like Bishop's Canning with its splendid
Early English church." For a man so utterly contemptuous of formal religion,
O'Connor never seemed to tire of small churches. "At Kilpeck itself you start
mounting the circle of hills and see the church above you on your right with a
large ungainly bellcote, a finial and a cross on nave and apse—a tiny little
Celtic Church. . . . It had all the exuberance of ornamental detail you find in
Cormac's Chapel." And for a townee so suspicious of provincialism, he seemed
to gain no end of delight from the people of small towns, who he said were
"torn asunder between their natural good-nature and the respect for rules and
regulations imposed on them from birth. They will never actually break the law
for you, but if you lean hard on their good nature they can usually think up
some method of evading it." Needless to say, Michael and Evelyn reached
Bristol behind schedule.

Not long after returning from this grueling tour, Evelyn again became ill;
at the end of May she was jaundiced and extremely listless. She insisted on returning to Dublin, and Michael insisted that the children and his mother go
with her. As soon as they left, he went to London to see Joan and to put the
finishing touches on his latest book of stories, *The Common Chord*. By coincidence, galley proofs of *Irish Miles* also awaited him, marking the final curtain
to his and Evelyn's mutual obsession with cycling, old churches, and rural oddities. Almost as soon as Evelyn was settled back in Dublin, she went to see her
physician. His diagnosis was that she had a severely enlarged appendix. The
next day a specialist confirmed that opinion, and she was admitted into the
Leinster Nursing Home for an operation. A few days later she began to hemor-
rhage badly, and when she miscarried, the nurses suspected she had feigned
the appendix to hide the fact of an unwelcome pregnancy. She kept all this
from Michael until he too returned to Dublin at the end of June.

Shevawn Lynam had by that time returned to Ireland and taken a house
at the corner of Strand Road and Sidney Parade. Though she was entirely sympathetic with Evelyn about Michael's divided life, she remained close to him,
probably because she too was a writer. When he asked her to help him put together materials for his book on Ireland for the Country Book Series published

in England by Robert Hale, she jumped at the chance. Living nearby and work-ing with Michael, she began spending more time at the O'Donovan house than did most of their friends. From time to time she commented to Evelyn that Mi-chael seemed unsuited for fatherhood. For instance, one evening in her pres-ence he beat Myles unmercifully for nothing more serious than pestering Lia-dain, whom he admired and gave affectionate attention to. By the next day he had become so overcome with remorse that he took Myles instead of Liadain along on his afternoon walk and made a ceremonial stop for sweets. On an-other occasion, as he was returning up the strand from his walk, he saw Myles and his "Tram Terrace Gang" teasing an old dog.[5] Michael grabbed a stick and waded into the fray, cursing and swinging his stick at the fleeing "ruffians." He rescued the poor animal but terrorized his son and embarrassed himself in front of the neighbors by this show of uncontrollable temper. Miss Lynam found it odd that a man so adamantly opposed to violence could allow his own violent inner life to boil to the surface, striking fear in his children, who never seemed to know why he had erupted. She also found it a bit ironic that he was so bent on writing stories having to do with children and family relations.

Michael's letters to John Kelleher, his new American friend, did not say anything about his own children, but they did carry frequent allusion to the "feeling for parentage in Irish literature." It seemed especially important to him to maintain the image of himself as a good father, because, as he claimed to Kelleher, he held a Greek attitude to literature: "It's written by good guys and the better the guy the better it's likely to be for the literature." In June, responding with rage to Kelleher's admiration for Austin Clarke and James Joyce, he observed that both men approached writing from a sheerly technical angle and in so doing "destroy the moral and intellectual quality of literature; they never realize that there is such a thing as an object; a thing in itself, good or bad, and that a good thing firmly seized, with no matter what literary in-competence, is literature in a sense in which their work never is literature."[6]

O'Connor was in fact railing against what he suspected was wrong with his own stories. His writing was and always had been moral—firmly clear about right and wrong in human affairs—and his most recent obsession with children and the tortures of parentage happened to be the one moral issue clos-est to him at the time. Being a father resurrected the image of his own prodigal father and the emotional terror, the unpredictable chaos, of his own childhood. And protest as he might about the detachment of the imaginative artist from his "objective" material, O'Connor inevitably wrote out his own immediate personal agonies. But at the same time, fearful of sinking into the abyss of self-indulgence, he had become more and more obsessed with the craft of the story, often making choices in his work for technical or stylistic, rather than thematic or emotional, reasons. Almost as much as he feared the cold loneliness of being homeless, or of not having a family around him, he feared not being in control of his art.

Ever since the death of Big Mick in 1942 Michael had tried to avoid the subject of his father. Almost effortlessly that summer (1947) he wrote "The Drunkard," which was, as he told Kelleher, "about the time I came back roar-ing drunk from the funeral at the age of six." At the same time he forced him-self to finish "My Da."[7] That he had rewritten the story fifty times before sending it off reluctantly to *The New Yorker* suggests that he was strangling on his own dubious paternity. "My Da" opens with this disingenuous assertion: "It's funny the influence fathers can have on fellows—I mean without even realizing it. There was a lad called Stevie." Stevie is a "lonesome and superior" boy set apart by circumstance and character; his father had long since deserted him and his mother, and he is deadly serious about life. Then, suddenly, his "old fellow" comes back and Stevie's life is changed. His mother's weakness for drink raises old tensions between the couple, leaving the boy trapped in the middle. The eavesdropping narrator is careful to note that the old man "didn't make smithereens of the furniture or fling his wife and child out of doors in their nightclothes the way other fathers did," but, trifling as their domestic altercations were, "they left Stevie shattered." Finally, "with a fresh disillusionment to fly from," Stevie's father leaves again. "Little by little, the old air of fecklessness and neglect came back. Stevie was completely wretched— a fellow who couldn't mind a father when he got one." The dream had vanished, "robbing reality of its innocence" as it went. Stevie takes to studying in earnest, eventually becomes a priest, and goes off to America. The narrator muses at the end that he "had at last become the man his father was and left us far behind him."

By 1947 Michael had become something of a prodigal father himself. During the winter of Joan's pregnancy two years before, O'Connor had begun writing stories for an English audience (or so he claimed to Stan Stewart) about sex, sin, and illegitimate children. Until then love had emerged in his writing primarily as an adolescent illusion, a glorious haze enveloping hopelessly romantic characters. Few stories before *Crab Apple Jelly* deal openly with sex or even with the illegitimate offspring of sin. True, Mary Kate is the daughter of a prostitute and a stranger, in search of whom Mary Kate treks to Dublin (the first appearance of the theme of the bastard in quest of the prodigal father which would find so many variations in O'Connor's stories); and Eileen Madden, the most vital character in *Dutch Interior,* has what appears to be an abortion. But by and large, love in such early stories as "A Romantic," "September Dawn," and "The Procession of Life" was equated with romance. Love in the stories after Woodenbridge, stories such as "The Mad Lomasneys," "The New Teacher," and "The House That Johnny Built," was part of the social game of marrying.

One story in particular reflects O'Connor's growing uneasiness about love and marriage. Written at Woodenbridge and entitled "Mother and Son," the original version has more to do with a mother's loss than with a boy's infatuation. In subsequent versions, "The Rivals" and "Night of Stars," the story becomes more and more internalized, with love figuring as a dream world. At the time O'Connor rewrote the story as "Judas" for *The Common Chord,* all the elements had been subtly blended to show how the normal pursuit of love can be dashed, even by a saintly mother, as so much childish foolishness. That the boy, weeping in the arms of his mother for having betrayed her to selfish love, feels such guilt suggests something of the kind of conflict O'Connor himself lived with, a conflict between the demands of being a good son/husband—dutiful, punctual, thrifty—and the demands of being a good lover—dashing, sociable, expansive.

Even "Judas," however, barely approaches the gathering cynicism of the stories O'Connor had begun writing in 1945, most of which came together in

The Common Chord.[8] If there is a common chord underlying this collection, it
most surely is the need of people to offset the blight of loneliness. More than
one critic has drawn attention to the theme of human contact in O'Connor's
stories; of equal importance, however, is the amount of self-deception people
can generate in their search for love or warmth or simple communication. No
story more dramatically illustrates such self-defeating behavior than "The
Holy Door." When Eileen O'Faoláin first told Michael and Seán the story
about a Cork woman who could tolerate sexual intercourse with her husband
only by imagining him as Clark Gable, Michael felt shudders run up his spine.
His first version (1943), like O'Faoláin's story "The Woman Who Married
Clark Gable," exploited the wife's silly illusion. However, as O'Connor moved
away from Maupassant to Jane Austen in his reading, he rewrote "The Holy
Door" in twenty-seven ever-lengthening versions in order to capture both the
causes of the woman's behavior and its effects on those around her.[9] The
twenty-thousand-word version in *The Common Chord,* more nearly a novella
than anything he ever wrote, is a perfect example of the tone that had come to
dominate his writing since his affair with Joan, the same "moral hysteria" he
heard in Jane Austen.

Two women who as girls fantasized about the mysteries of marriage continue their talks after one of them has married. Polly, the one who always
avoided any mention of sex, now refuses her husband's natural advances and
wonders why they have no children. On the advice of a priest called Father
Ring she even resorts to a pilgrimage to a holy door in Rome. Her busybody
friend Nora suggests that she imagine her husband as Rudolph Valentino, but
that strikes Polly as sinful. Frustrated by her childish superstitions, her husband has an affair with the maid, who becomes pregnant and exposes the decent fellow to public shame, and the marriage comes tumbling down in a heap
of misunderstanding. The redoubtable priest intervenes again with a suggestion that he thinks will help to preserve the wronged woman's respectability. A
bolt on the door between the couple's separate bedrooms sets them apart
under the same roof until the wife's death shortly afterward. In the end Charlie
marries Nora, not the blackmailing maid. The fantasy, the confessions, and the
gossip only serve to cloud reality in a fog of self-deception, leaving people even
more isolated and unloved than they had been before.

In the small-town world of "The Holy Door" everyone knows everything
about everyone else, except the only thing worth knowing, the chord common
to them all: the need for love. Sex is "undiscussable," and Valentino is only a
word, a fanciful image interfering with rather than sustaining marital intimacy. Instead of bringing a miraculous conception, the holy door becomes a
locked door, even a tombstone. Here O'Connor again seemed to be imitating
Maupassant, who often used windows and doors as emblems of entrapment
and limitation. O'Connor linked windows and doors with the process of language, suggesting that what can bring people together most often keeps them
apart, at least in middle-class, Catholic, small-town Ireland.

Though his treatment of sex in "The Holy Door" is veiled to the point of
delicacy, O'Connor resorts to overt sexual banter in the pub talk of his "Don
Juan" stories. In "Don Juan (Retired)" two men listen jealously as a self-pro-
claimed womanizer recounts an exploit nearly twenty years past. One of the
listeners is lost in his own dreams of what-might-have-been; the other is bitter

over his wife's recent defection. When they taunt this Irish Don Juan to produce proof of his claims, he strolls off to get the girl and win the bet. But his
smug feeling of victory reveals a cynical, even jaundiced view of women;
though brutally frank about sexual conquest, the story reflects a fearful and
immature sexual mentality. "Don Juan's Temptation" is no less cynical about
the unpredictability of women. Here a group of pub friends listen to Gussie,
who they believe understands women at a level beyond them, share the secret
of his "success" with them. After bragging about his direct approach to a girl
he'd met by the canal that evening, he confesses that it wasn't always so easy
with him—as a young man he had been lonely and shy. "I sometimes think
young people are the loneliest creatures on God's earth," Gussie tells his listeners. "You wake up from a nice, well-ordered, explainable world and you find
eternity stretching all round you, and no one, priest or scientist or anyone else,
can tell you a damn thing about it. And there's this queer thing going on inside
you that gives you a longing for companionship and love, and you don't know
how to satisfy it. I used to go out at night, looking up at the stars, and thinking
if only I could meet a nice understanding sort of girl it would all explain itself
naturally." He eventually met the right girl, but she died of tuberculosis. (This
is actually the same tragic story Dermot told him in the hotel at Glendalough
where they had gone to celebrate the publication of *Guests of the Nation*.)[10]
The experience left Gussie alone but convinced that girls wanted love as badly
as he did, and in the end his opinion is vindicated when the otherwise "respectable" girl he met by the canal shows up on his doorstep.

Beneath the cynicism of both stories runs a grim faith in the ability of love
to ease the radical loneliness of men and women, to veil momentarily the terrible inevitability and cold aloneness of death. Rather than merely writing sophisticated stories to satisfy English readers, O'Connor was actually exploring
the edge of his own moral and metaphysical abyss. Larry Elyan cautioned him
that he was being called a writer of "fucking stories," and indeed most of *The
Common Chord* is a bit more shocking than the Irish common reader could tolerate at the time. But in nearly every one of these stories there is a note of
"moral hysteria" running just below the surface, indicating that the writer was
not nearly as self-satisfied or morally comfortable as the narrators in his stories
seem to be.

Michael/Frank was, in fact, still grappling with the ghosts of his past, addressing problems peculiar to people still in the shadow of the church. He had
allowed Dermot Foley's poignant story about the girl with tuberculosis to brew
all those years before telling it in "Don Juan's Temptation"; until his affair
with Joan the idea of an Irish Don Juan would not have fired his imagination in
quite that way. Had it been the only story O'Connor wrote in that vein at that
time, its personal equation would be less startling. However, "Friends of the
Family," a story about people looking for love and finding the very thing they
sought to escape—a family—also mirrors his relationship with Joan. Why, for
example, after all those years, did he return in "The Frying Pan" to Father
Traynor's confession to him—the priest had wanted to be married to the wife
of an old friend who had in turn wanted to be a priest—if not to clarify his own
nagging conviction that he was unsuitable for marriage? Apparently, O'Connor was most sensitive to those stories from the lives of his friends that mirrored the concerns of his own life, and he dredged from some source deep

within him the kinds of stories that allowed him to externalize the moral dilemmas he was having difficulty internalizing.

One reviewer remarked with a characteristic Dublin pub chuckle that there were too many bastards in *The Common Chord,* a glib observation far truer than the reviewer could even guess.[11] The theme of the illegitimate child frantically searching for a prodigal father, which was to become the one most persistent theme of O'Connor's later fiction, actually has more to do with his own quest for legitimacy than with the existence of his English son. As successful as he had become, O'Connor had still not come to terms with his past: Memories of his father's drunken rages, of himself as a boy huddling with his mother on a cold street, of an insufficient formal education, still haunted him—waking or sleeping. For years he had wondered how he could be the son of Big Mick, how he could possibly be a native-born Corkman, how he could even be Irish. The older he became, the more illegitimate and outcast he felt.

"The Babes in the Wood," a sentimental story about two illegitimate children who live in foster homes and dream of a real family, was originally titled "Outcasts." After the little boy's "aunt," who is really his mother, suddenly stops her Sunday visits, he walks in the woods with a sharp-tongued little girl, older than himself, who callously explodes his dream. She demands, from a mixture of jealousy of his aunt and compassion stemming from her own experience as an "unwanted" child, that he pledge fidelity to her. They eventually fall asleep in each other's arms, not noticing "the evening train going up the valley . . . all lit up." That image of wandering orphans, of bastards, of lost waifs of all kinds, cut off from the warmth and light of home and normal society, from security and respectability, emerges often enough in this and subsequent volumes to indicate something of deep importance to Frank O'Connor/Michael O'Donovan.[12] "A Thing of Nothing" and "The Stepmother" also suggest that where natural parents are unavailable, perfectly good substitutes seem to appear. Thus illegitimate children and unnatural parents transcend mere social pedigree by finding a truer legitimacy in the consolation of love—in fact, the same sort of consolation that their parents found in the intimacy that preceded birth.

Early in the fall of 1947 O'Connor sent to his agent for magazine publication two stories, "Don Juan's Temptation" and "Darcy in the Land of Youth," which he had decided to include in *The Common Chord,* the corrected galley proofs of which he had just returned to Macmillan. In a letter to Stan Stewart that week he hinted that he was tiring of these so-called dirty stories. Circumstances in Ireland (the banning of books and the tight publishing market) had forced him to write for an English audience, whose attitude toward sex was more cynical than attitudes in Ireland. Thus, with the submission of "The Landlady" in November, he washed his hands of stories about temporary liaisons and casual relationships and turned again to stories about children and family relations.[13] This does not mean, however, that he returned to the exuberance of his early stories. The increasing number of stories purchased by *The New Yorker* guaranteed a new market, an audience infatuated by the "experienced innocence" of stories about domestic relations and by the masterful control of his "simple" style.

It is difficult to pinpoint a more crucial time in O'Connor's artistic life than this tumultuous summer and fall of 1947. The *Times Literary Supplement*

review of *Irish Miles* (July 12, 1947) described the record of O'Connor's cycling holidays as a "picture of the aesthetic desolation of the countryside,"
meaning that "to a man of Mr. O'Connor's sensibility and patriotism the ruins
which are so characteristic of the Irish landscape are not documents for antiquarian reseach but monuments to the perennial barbarism of men who neglect their heritage." O'Connor himself is cast as the contemporary equivalent
of the eighteenth-century "man of feeling." Then, in a telling aside intended to
explain why the whimsical storyteller ("at his best when he describes these
chance conversations") turns with such savage fury on his countrymen, the
reviewer muses that maybe born artists like O'Connor sooner or later must
"leave the farm" to practice their craft and develop their genius.

Shortly after the publication of *Irish Miles* O'Connor wrote to John Kelleher about the critical reception of the book: "My self-confidence has been so
undermined that at any minute I may retire from active life altogether." Writing scripts for documentary films and turning out fortnightly reviews hardly
enhanced his artistic image either. "Of course I'd jump at a temporary job in
Harvard," he added, "being of a flighty disposition with a mass of theories inside me which I'd love to work off on someone." The lament continued: "I shall
be 44 on the 17th of September, and I feel more and more each year that I want
to make my artistic soul and that the basis of that is the advice given to a man I
knew by his old father: 'My boy, have nothing to do with nobody.' But emotionally I'm still only 24 and I face the tragedy of all provincials; that life isn't
long enough for us to grow up."[14] A month later, reviewing Mary Renault's
Return to Night, he judged the book to be at the mental age of sixteen and a
half, adding by way of comparison that Hollywood showed the mental age of
fourteen while Cork stayed at about the age of eighteen.

In the same review O'Connor confessed to having a fierce Oedipus complex: "the old lady in question is now over 82, but the complex is worse than
ever; and, what is still worse, my sons from earliest age seem obsessed with the
temptation to kill their father and marry their mother." A disingenuous notion,
to be sure, but one powerful enough that he repeated the sentence almost
word for word three months later while trying to explain his feelings about Ireland to John Kelleher. Just how powerful his attachment to his mother continued to be is illustrated by an incident that occurred on a brutally cold day in
October. Evelyn had taken the heater from Donny's room to heat the nursery.
When Michael returned from town and found his mother shivering, he exploded in savage cursing and stormed off to retrieve the heater. When he arrived at his mother's room, she was standing at the door. With her finger shaking menacingly at his chest, she chastened him with uncharacteristic fury.
Michael left the heater in the hallway, slunk to his room, and fell across the
bed sobbing. He never cursed or argued with Evelyn in his mother's presence
again.

The only person other than his mother who could make Michael think
twice about any of his actions was Stan Stewart. He often said to Dermot that
he would know when he'd gone too far when Stan disapproved. Late in August,
overcome with the feeling that Ireland was closing in on him, he went to Limerick for a week of cycling with Stan, which for Michael was the best antidote
to tarnished self-confidence or bad reviews. From Limerick he wrote a reassuring note to W. R. Rodgers who was biting his nails in Dublin for lack of a

final script for the radio version of *The Midnight Court* that he was producing
for the BBC in Belfast. Michael arrived in Dublin only a few days after the hastily scribbled script had arrived, to begin whirlwind rehearsals before setting off
to Belfast for a live transmission on September 14.[15] Michael read the part of
the Old Man with the same gusto that he'd put into the original translation,
and Bertie Rodgers was more than satisfied with the production. The *London-
derry Sentinel,* however, was distressed with the idea of allowing "this man"
on the air. "Such a country!" Michael sighed in his next letter to Stan.

His feud with Ireland continued unabated, with an outpouring of vitriolic
energy on both sides, but O'Connor could take some measure of satisfaction in
knowing that he was not alone. That fall, two young writers, Roger McHugh
and Valentin Iremonger, led a campaign against the censoring of amateur
plays in various small theatres throughout the country and even went so far as
to picket the Abbey Theatre for the heavy-handed management of Blythe and
the others. Michael gladly joined their skirmish; because he still held one hundred shares of Abbey stock, he was theoretically entitled to attend the annual
meeting. His unwelcome presence vexed the Abbey Board, but his persistent
barbs and acid questions about the McHugh controversy forced a premature
adjournment.[16]

By this time Frank O'Connor had antagonized just about everyone in Ireland, not only the pietists and the patriots but the mainsteam literati as well.
Writers like Flann O'Brien, Austin Clarke, Anthony Cronin, and John Ryan
laughed at his arrogance; anyone too aloof to frequent the pubs could hardly be
taken seriously as a writer, they mocked. That he once bodily escorted an outrageously drunk Flann O'Brien from a party at Niall Montgomery's did little for
his reputation. What few people knew was that Michael avoided the pub scene
not only in distaste for pretentious banter but also in fear of his father's ghost:
He feared loss of control, particularly the violence within that could be un-
leashed by drink. Even Patrick Kavanagh finally fell in line with the prevailing
Dublin opinion that Frank O'Connor had sold out to the English. Writing in
The Bell Kavanagh asserted that O'Connor had failed to achieve the promise
shown in his youth because he had taken the Yeatsian high road.[17] Instead of
his arrogant posing, Kavanagh argued, O'Connor should have been exploring
the ordinary life found in railway stations and smoky pubs, which is precisely
what O'Connor had done in England and precisely why he was now frowned
upon in Ireland.

Actually, Kavanagh's criticism of O'Connor is right and wrong on nearly
every count. The "actor's ability to give body and life to somebody else's ideas,"
which Kavanagh judges a weakness in the translations, is precisely what made
O'Connor a storyteller, and it does not justify condemning him as a "purveyor
of emotional entertainment." Perhaps the stories puzzled Kavanagh because
they did not seem serious enough; to his mind, O'Connor "kitchens" his material, making his comedy snide and his tragedy sentimental. The stories of *The
Common Chord* are skillful and somewhat unreal, but that did not necessarily
mean O'Connor had sold out. His satirical treatment of fraudulent piety, of
which Kavanagh was as much a victim as O'Connor, showed to Kavanagh's
mind a slightly "Calvinistic leer," but that hardly cancels out O'Connor's phil-
osophic integrity. O'Connor's moralism rests on a humanistic skepticism, as
philosophically rooted as Kavanagh's Christian cynicism. That O'Connor sel-

dom got involved with his characters is obvious in many, though certainly not all, stories. That he often surrendered tension to construction is equally true. But to infer that O'Connor's stories lack authenticity, that they are pure invention without the shock of truth, is to fall prey to their beguiling simplicity.

As devastatingly accurate as he was about what he heard in O'Connor's writing, Kavanagh seemed to ignore the reasons why he heard it. To him O'Connor was at ease neither on earth nor in the rarefied literary heavens. Kavanagh recognized that O'Connor's reputation would rest with the stories, but he wanted to dictate the script: He demanded that O'Connor get back to the vivid and the "authentic," which was what he strove for in his own writing. Kavanagh's conclusion that the result of all O'Connor's "travels in the active cultural life of this country has been futility" is so apt that one wonders why the poet of "The Great Hunger" then failed to discern that tone of desperation and moral hysteria that had begun to create in O'Connor's writing a subterranean landscape of terror and desolation. He should have heard the lonely voice because he himself was as much an outsider as was O'Connor.

On the heels of Kavanagh's article, brutal in its truthfulness but Brutus-like in its timing, came the twisting of the knife by the Irish government: On December 12 *The Common Chord* was banned. Once again O'Connor had mistaken the capacity of his audience. For years he had seen himself as an outcast in Ireland for telling the truth no one wanted to hear; unfortunately, he was unable to accept what truth Kavanagh's criticism contained. Resentful of marital antagonisms, suffering as usual from ill health, and bitter about Ireland to the point of distraction, O'Connor kept to himself most of the winter.

I I

As 1948 opened, there seemed to be very little consistency or pattern to Michael's actions or to the circumstances surrounding him. He wrote to John Kelleher that he had been ill, bored, and idle for months. Writing to Stan Stewart he blamed his dearth of writing on the deteriorating family situation, while insisting that he had to have the security of family routines in order to write. On Monday, January 12, when Evelyn brought morning coffee to the study, Michael accused her of deliberately keeping the children home from school to torment him. When she protested that the schools did not open again until Thursday, he slapped her face and caught hold of her throat. Breaking loose, she dared him to hit her again, at which point he stormed out of the room, returning in a few minutes to throw the housekeeping check on the floor. Then he yelled that she was to get out of the house before he returned; this was at ten o'clock in the morning and he was out until evening. Finding her still in the house upon his return, he simply grunted and went upstairs. Two weeks later neither he nor his mother was speaking to Evelyn. On January 27 she wrote to a friend that he was dining out that night with Shevawn Lynam—"What a man!"[18]

On February 18, 1948, de Valera's government was turned out of office by a coalition headed by John Costello. Actually, O'Connor had never paid much attention to politics, but he was glad to see de Valera gone. More than a decade of enmity had hardened him beyond reason; de Valera had become his blind spot. Dr. Collis once told Evelyn that Michael was so paranoid about de Valera that if the man was ever out of the way she should take care because Michael would have to replace the object of his fierce distrust and bitterness. For the time being, however, she had no chance to test that theory and Michael had no time to rejoice over de Valera's defeat. He left for London on the day after the national elections to begin a new BBC series, "The Critic," which called for six broadcasts in three weeks. Having promised Evelyn that he would not stay with Joan, Michael lived a nomadic life. Between broadcasts he traveled to Lancashire and Norfolk on assignment for the Central Office of Information (a new name for the wartime Ministry of Information), gathering material for another documentary film. Though admittedly a "pilgrim by nature," he found that this continual shuffling from place to place forbade any sort of serious writing.

In March he heard from Daniel Binchy, who was then at Corpus Christi College, Oxford. Binchy invited Michael to visit him and Myles Dillon, another Irish philologist, and Michael was so pleased to be given even a brief glimpse of the academic life of Oxford that he chronicled the visit in letters to most of his friends.[19] What seemed to make the biggest impression upon him was that he actually sat next to Sir Richard Livingston, the renowed Greek scholar and president of Corpus Christi College, at dinner one evening. Writing to Stan, who already knew his share of scholars, he expressed particular excitement about the fact that Binchy's rooms had once been occupied by Ruskin, a fact about which Binchy seemed nonchalant but which provoked a "scream of delight" from the wide-eyed provincial. He was also overwhelmed by the architecture of Oxford; eager to share any new discovery with an old friend, Michael invited Stan to come for a cycling holiday. Early in April the two of them joined Bill Naughton again for a week of serious cycling and drinking in the best bachelor style.

Later that month Macmillan held a special dinner in London for all of its authors. Bryan MacMahon was one of those in attendance that evening, as was Patrick Kavanagh. While chatting with Lovat Dickson, who had recently shepherded his book of stories through publication, MacMahon happened to notice the arrival of Frank O'Connor. Conversation immediately shifted. Dickson, who had also been O'Connor's editor for years, said something critical, but MacMahon would hear none of it—O'Connor had encouraged him and had even written to Macmillan on his behalf.[20] At the same time someone grabbed MacMahon's arm from behind and whispered loudly, "Do you think he'll speak to me?" It was Kavanagh, still fretting over O'Connor's reaction to his piece in *The Bell*. "He will, I'd say," MacMahon replied. "He won't," Kavanagh moaned. Unwilling to argue the point, MacMahon simply led an uncharacteristically sheepish Kavanagh toward O'Connor who gave them an uproarious welcome. Feeling rather alone and out of place, he was glad to see any Irish face, and whatever hostility he had felt over that strangely accurate article had partially dissolved over the winter. Because he was temperamentally incapable of seeking or offering forgiveness at the deepest level, Michael simply shrugged off Kavanagh's attempt to explain what he had really meant to say in *The Bell*. But he had to be gracious because he had already helped these two writers as AE had helped him, and at the time he needed no more enemies, in England or at home.

Meanwhile, Evelyn was in Wales visiting her family. The last time Evelyn's mother had been in Dublin she had found her daughter so run-down that she insisted Evelyn go home for a rest in the spring. Of course, that meant leaving the children with Donny and the maid, Ita Forde. The absence of both parents left the children with a feeling of desertion. Myles had already been disciplined twice for stealing at school. Around the neighborhood he was the infamous leader of a gang of toughs, but at home he wet the bed, except when his father was there to awaken him in the middle of the night. And Liadain, who idolized her father, developed a severe cough whenever he was away. Only Owen, who had recently recovered from a near-fatal case of pneumonia—thanks to the tireless efforts of Liadain—seemed oblivious of the domestic desolation.

Upon her return to Dublin in May, Evelyn undertook an ambitious project. Supported by money from the sale of her grandmother's house in Wales, Evelyn decided to proceed with the construction of a summer bungalow in Arklow, a small fishing village in County Wicklow about forty miles from Dublin. For nearly five months she had been corresponding with the Davidsons in Woodenbridge about such matters as blueprints and building costs. By the time Michael had returned in June, construction was well under way. He was absolutely furious with the scheme, accused Evelyn of everything from stupidity to infidelity, and sulked for nearly a week. Upon hearing her mention to Shevawn Lynam something about getting a case of beer for the workmen to celebrate capping the roof, he engineered a confrontation. "Give up the bungalow!" he demanded. "I can't," she answered. "It is the only thing between me and sanity while you are in England." "Nonsense," he sputtered. "If I said to you," she began to ask tentatively; "— if I were to say, 'you give up Joan, then I'll give up the bungalow,' what would you say?" Michael was silent for a moment and then said, "I would say that human relationships cannot be broken in that way." "But you promised me that when she was on her feet, you would not see her again," Evelyn responded. "I did, but you still can't bargain away a relationship." Nothing more was said and all decisions were deferred.

By the end of the month the bungalow was finished, and Evelyn took the children to Arklow for summer holidays. Michael returned to England to negotiate a new book of stories with Macmillan and to confer with BBC broadcast directors about a new series.[21] Joan had given up teaching in hopes of making some real money by driving a mobile canteen to the various building sites around Hemel Hempstead and by delivering fish and chips to nearby villages by night. This commercial venture struck Michael as undignified, and he chided Joan about wasting her talents. But without any word of commitment from him she had to take the future into her own hands. His irritable presence soon became vexing to Joan, who was trying to make everything comfortable enough for him to stay. "I'll be all right when I'm working," he would say with hesitant reassurance. Only his work gave him any real measure of satisfaction; only when writing did he feel any sense of ease with his existence. But these countless trips back and forth from Ireland to England disallowed settling into the sort of routine necessary to write. He may have seen himself as a born pilgrim, but in London he was actually a fish out of water. Even though he hated it, he needed the turmoil of Dublin. Dr. Collis's warning to Evelyn may have been valid, though paranoia may not have been the correct term. The fact is,

O'Connor thrived on enmity; torment and adversity often served to release his creative impulses. If idle, he would invent an adversary or magnify a trivial irritant to proportions worthy of his attention.

Ordinarily, another book on Shakespeare would have sent only minor ripples through English academic circles, to say nothing of the disinterest it would have met from the common reading public. However, the appearance in April 1948 of O'Connor's *The Road to Stratford* produced something resembling shock waves. It was not just that a mere "spinner of tales" presumed to challenge the foremost Shakespearean scholars on the authorship of *Edward III* or on various delicate textual emendations.[22] It was more that he did so with such assumptive confidence. The detachment and objective control that came to be more and more obvious in his stories disappeared almost entirely in his passionate and assertive social and literary opinions.

In his preface O'Connor proceeds at once to say that although Shakespeare's plays obviously moved his contemporaries profoundly, he himself had never been moved by them. Such disillusionment, explored first in the Hull lectures on the theatre, extended to the plays of all his "heroes"—even Chekhov, Ibsen, and Synge who were only a generation or so away—plays he loved to read but could not produce because "the collaboration between author, players, and audience that produces great theatre has ceased to exist." Thus "what we hear in a Shakespearean play today is no longer creation; it is criticism, or rather theatrical scholarship." This position is consistent with those he had taken in Cork, where he had fought O'Flynn's insipid attempt to make the bard a moral yardstick, and in Dublin, where he had upbraided Yeats for using *Coriolanus* to propagate the fascist cause. What O'Connor believed, he believed fervently and without expedient compromise. Theatre to him was a living thing, like a library: The best library was the one people used and the best theatre was the one that moved people to tears or riots. His assumption here is simply that no literary work is absolute. The medium is so imperfect, so susceptible to the passage of time, that without the lively collaboration he insisted upon, it becomes history, unintelligible to all but a few students.

Had he actually taken this idea to its limit and shown how Shakespeare could be made contemporary again, he would have anticipated the influential Jan Kott by twenty years. In fact, O'Connor only touched on the idea in his preface. His interest was to make Shakespeare intelligible by making some personal connection between him and people alive in 1948. Though he admits that there was little biographical information on the playwright, O'Connor boldly claims that "the plays themselves form a pattern of a man's existence in this world." The idea is from Yeats, who believed that the work of any writer represents "an allegory of his passage through life." O'Connor believed this to be more true of Shakespeare than of most writers, not only because Shakespeare was an "abnormally sensitive man, but also because he was, more than most writers, intuitive in his approach to literature, not governed . . . by the theoretical approach." Behind that assertion lies O'Connor's notion of the conflict between judgment and instinct, which is given literary expression in the fundamental opposition of Joyce and Yeats, Jonson and Shakespeare, Hardy and James.[23]

To attain full collaborative joy, O'Connor had to saturate himself "to the

point of identification with Shakespeare, the butcher's apprentice from Stratford who, having got into trouble with a local bigwig, made for London and became a vagabond player of ill-written plays; who learned late in life that he
could write the plays much better than anyone else, and, having acquired a little fortune, returned to his birthplace to play the gentleman amongst those
who had looked down at him." Needless to say, O'Connor identified himself
outright with Shakespeare, whose progress he calls the "story of Everyman,
written by the man of all men on whom that story seems to have made the
deepest impression"; and given that identification, his theory that what Shakespeare wrote represents an allegory of his life may be a mirror of his own life as
well.

Thus in *The Road to Stratford* O'Connor traced a pattern against which
some, though certainly not all, of the puzzling pieces of his own passage
through life can be measured, not because that pattern is necessarily true but
because O'Connor with his characteristic certainty believed it to be true. He
often called himself "only the old Cork yob!" It was somewhat narcissistic of
him, then, to view Shakespeare as a provincial outsider whose instinctive approach caused him trouble with the urbane, educated men with whom he
competed. (Another Shakespeare-obsessed Irishman, Stephen Dedalus, considered the cracked looking glass of a servant symbolic of the narcissim of all
Irish artists.) When O'Connor talks about Shakespeare's way of adopting a
manner with great facility and dropping it without fuss, he not only mirrors his
own temperament but makes a prophetic observation: "This became a real
weakness in his later years when he lightly took up subjects that he was incapable of handling, but whether as strength or weakness, it kept his work unmistakably his own and unmistakably personal in tone."

Writing about the early plays, O'Connor contends that Shakespeare
worked "piecemeal rather than wholesale" and primarily as a poet. Using line
after line from *Richard III*, which he considers the masterpiece of that stage in
Shakespeare's career, O'Connor concludes that it is "poetry that aims at a
knockout; that tries to make your hair stand on end." Later he speaks of poetry
aimed at the midriff rather than at the head. The trouble, he claims, is that it is
merely poetry, poetry as an end in itself. Every poet in the theatre, he asserts,
"has a tendency to melodrama." Then O'Connor offers a beguiling generalization: "Poetry is about oneself and other people in relation to oneself; drama is
about other people and only about oneself in relation to other people; and it is
only occasionally that the subject that makes for poetry also makes for drama."
Actually, he might have been putting forth reasons for the failure of his own
poems and plays.

From the characters in the early plays, O'Connor surmises that in life
"Shakespeare must have been an energetic, ambitious, passionate man." But
the spectacle of so many characters of that same nature "creates an extraordinarily somber effect, as though we were being smothered in an atmosphere of
subjectivity." The idea suddenly surfaces: "Drama happens only when the
poet's hard shell of subjectivity cracks, and when he is half in, half out of his
shell." O'Connor believes that during the next few years something happened
to crack Shakespeare's shell, that he reached the point of last resort where his
imagination either had to refuse to follow his characters or choose to identify
itself with them. After the shadow of the early plays emerged the excellence of

such plays as *Richard II* and, according to O'Connor, *Edward III*. By turning his back on the romantic exuberance of his early plays, Shakespeare was able finally to assert absolute control over his writing.

The secret to this spontaneous development at this point in Shakespeare's life, O'Connor contends (with the reminder that provincials develop late in life), may be found in the sonnets, which he believes tell a story of the poet's attachment to a young aristocrat and love for a "blackhaired married woman" who jilted him for the aristocrat, "leaving the poet doubly bereaved." This is admittedly guesswork, but what follows is a dazzling display of analysis. He finds the sonnets to the woman oscillating "in the most disturbing way between a sociable jocosity and a shuddering sensibility." He then disputes the standard academic disavowal of biographical connections between the poet and the voices in the sonnets. Being a storyteller, O'Connor was accustomed to invention, and being a moralist, he was prone to tamper in order to edify. The all-or-nothing tone of the sonnets suggests to him a "lacerated sensibility" in the throes of some wrenching experience that left Shakespeare disillusioned. The sonnets, "The Rape of Lucrece," and "Venus and Adonis" strike him as too "uncommonly prophetic" to be mere academic exercises presented after the fact to a possible patron.

The most important evidence for the Dark Lady theme, according to O'Connor, is *Edward III,* which he proceeds to demonstrate is entirely Shakespeare's.[24] As tenuous as his argument may seem to an orthodox Shakespearean, he presents it in the manner of a person who has seen a ghost or a UFO. For example, to prove the identity of style between *Edward III* and other Shakespearean plays of that period, O'Connor draws attention to the marked abundance in them of the reflexive rhetoric. This suggests to him nothing less than a decidedly antithetical cast of mind. "Everyone and everything contains its opposite," O'Connor asserts confidently, "by which it is saved or destroyed." Shakespeare was not just using the conventions of casuistry, he was, in O'Connor's estimation, arguing with himself, and the upheaval that prompted such doubt was not the dire social and political divisions of Elizabethan England but a personal upheaval so profound as to make Shakespeare "question all values."

O'Connor cannot, of course, put his finger on precisely what the disturbing event was, but he is certain that whatever it was it "had an immediate and pronounced effect on his work, which became more finicking, more restrained, more intellectual." The use of the reflexive conceit "seems to have satisfied some fundamental contradiction in Shakespeare's own nature." That contradiction, O'Connor believes, is between "a subjectivity so overpowering" that it regards other people (in art and in life) as extensions of itself, and an objectivity so "overweening" that it becomes all things. Torn asunder, such a personality "remains forever alone and aloof." The further O'Connor moves into this labyrinth, the surer it seems that he is recreating a crisis of his own, the "little death," or loss of innocence, that in most people happens at adolescence but occurs rarely, O'Connor confesses, "in a man of thirty."

Forcing his theory to the limit, O'Connor writes, as if in a trance, about a duality in Shakespeare that is "almost neurotic, as though he might quite easily have walked into a room and found himself sitting there."[25] As the antithesis of subject and object becomes flesh, O'Connor soliloquizes, "*I* does not cease to think and feel with the same blind human passion, but on the very summit of frenzy, *I* suddenly becomes *you* and between them a universe is born." O'Connor expounded on this idea throughout his life. It had appeared first in his aborted essay on Corkery, which he called alternately "Horses of the Sun" and "Ride to the Abyss"; and the exact phrasing actually appeared again in *The Mirror in the Roadway*, which he originally sent to his agent under the title "Ride to the Abyss."

The points of identity between the allegory of Shakespeare's passage through life and O'Connor's continue through fully two-thirds of the book. The personal note he located in the recurrent Dark Lady theme may be parallel to the illegitimate-child theme in his own work after 1945, the submerged sexuality of his domestic stories, and the lonely-voice theory in all of his critical writing. A reading of O'Connor's stories from first to last uncovers nearly the same progress that O'Connor uncovered in Shakespeare: from optimism to pessimism to resignation based on the dialectic of subjectivity and objectivity, variously expressed by Yeats (the vacillation between soul and race), by Corkery (the dichotomy between men of thought and men of action), and by O'Connor himself (the battle between the head and the heart).

Echoes of personal confession resound from piece after piece of the Shakespearean puzzle. A self-professed mimic whose speech took the sound of the people he was with, O'Connor spots the same trait in Shakespeare, whom he says "loves to break up his speeches with parody, and has a kind of chameleon quality which makes him seize on any opportunity for a change of style." Considering the impact literary heroes such as AE and Yeats had on O'Connor, it is not surprising that he notices the effect of Shakespeare on his contemporaries: "it is like the splashing of waves on the shore after the great ship of literature has sailed silently by." Whether he was discussing Collins and Parnell in the sphere of political action or Yeats and Beethoven in the arts, O'Connor could not keep his eyes and ears from genius, and perhaps the only quality he admired more than born genius was self-made genius.

O'Connor also recognizes in the history plays a "clear obsession with the idea of public order," a theme he says "haunted" Shakespeare "to the day of his death." O'Connor may not have had the same fear of mobs, but he was obsessed by a fear of violence—dating from his father's razor attacks and the brutality of the Civil War. It was a fear that "haunted" him as all of his fears and theories seemed to haunt him. Like Maupassant and so many of the writers he loved and hated, O'Connor was a driven man, possessed and obsessed. That he calls Shakespeare's fear "hysterical" echoes a persistent hysteria in his own work. About *Hamlet*, he argues that the play came at the "point in his work where Shakespeare's anxiety about the future becomes almost hysterical." Seldom does that word appear in O'Connor's work without the word *melancholy,* and in this essay he goes on to call Hamlet an "intellectual afflicted with melancholia." Refusing to speculate on the exact source of this melancholia, O'Connor instead locates echoes in the skeptical self-scrutiny of Montaigne, whose essays made such a deep impression on Shakespeare, suggesting again that Shakespeare's darkening view of existence originated in a spiritual and intellectual crisis far more profound than mere disappointment over a lady's infidelity.

In the chapters leading up to his discussion of *Hamlet*, O'Connor charts a course in Shakespeare's life, from youthful romanticism to realism, which he calls "the artistic equivalent of logical thought." In *Henry V,* for example, the poet in Shakespeare revels in war while the realist in him shrinks from its horrors. O'Connor contends that when the irrepressible Falstaff makes fun of Hotspur, Shakespeare is actually mocking himself. He begs us to remember the Falstaff in ourselves and the Falstaff in Shakespeare. Then he generalizes that wherever doubles such as Quixote and Sancho, Dedalus and Bloom, appear in literature, "they are never different characters, but different aspects of the same character, usually the author's, and usually externalizing a conflict with himself." If Shakespeare's opposite sides of the coin were Richard III and Richard II, Aaron and Shylock, then O'Connor's opposites were the bespectacled smart boy and the neighborhood gang leader, the vulnerable romantic and the tough realist. The prodigal father would become his sons by externalizing them in his stories.

Whatever O'Connor's own abyss might have been, and certainly it involved domestic tangles at the time, it is clear that he saw in Hamlet something of himself, but it is not clear what that something was. "With a purely instinctive writer like Shakespeare it is never safe to push such a question too far," O'Connor himself warns; "he exhausted a subject or method with extraordinary rapidity, and then left the premises by the window."

In the history plays O'Connor found two Englands, one romantic, the other realistic. In *Hamlet* and in the great tragedies he hears two styles, one smooth, the other harsh; he sees two faces, one the gentle face of Polonius, the other the coarse face of the grave digger. His proclamation that realism stops dead in *Hamlet* rings as something of a theatrical climax, because O'Connor believed that the play stood at a crossroads in Shakespeare's life. He quotes Sophocles—"Never to have lived were best"—to suggest that Shakespeare was struggling with the "thought of his own extinction" when he wrote *Hamlet.* No genius, O'Connor believed, ever avoided a religious crisis. Shakespeare's traditional beliefs had been shredded by Montaigne's skepticism, which O'Connor felt left him with "nothing but that sense of the utter futility of human existence by which Hamlet is haunted." Shakespeare had to ask "if reality itself be real." Thus, to O'Connor's way of thinking Hamlet's meditation on suicide was really Shakespeare arguing with himself about an idea that "was afterward never very far from Shakespeare's thought."

Nearly ten years before finishing this book, O'Connor had gone to Woodenbridge prepared to die; he had lived, but by this time had come to wonder if it was worth it or not. It is doubtful that he ever seriously contemplated suicide, but he was constantly seeking medical advice about one chronic ailment or another. The acrophobia he notices in *Hamlet* may be akin to his own recurrent falling nightmare: "it is the very dizziness of the realistic height from which Shakespeare views it which gives him the tendency toward suicide, that longing to plunge at once into the abyss."[26] O'Connor concludes that after *Hamlet* Shakespeare's attitude to death is altered perceptibly; after *The Road to Stratford* O'Connor's view of life would change radically. Contradiction would sit more comfortably, and he would find himself able to write those stories of childhood for which he would become so well known. Hamlet struggles not only with death but his own dubious lineage, wondering whether he was his father's son and whether he loved his mother and wished to kill his father. Those questions cut both ways for O'Connor, son of a prodigal father and prodigal father to four children.

After the Hamlet chapter O'Connor "left the premises by the window," and the rest of the book contains little of the writer attempting to define himself through the mirror of another man's life and work. As dazzling and arguable, as enlightening and infuriating as it is, *The Road to Stratford* remains a real mystery. The parallels between what O'Connor believed he saw in Shakespeare's life and what seems to have happened in his own life are interesting—valid to a point but not absolutely reliable. Still, the book is one of the most passionate, engaged things he ever wrote, and it is remarkably prophetic of his own pasage through life after 1948. But it is interesting to consider why, *at this time*, he felt so compelled to write *this book*. Shakespeare was not a new enthusiasm; O'Connor still owned well-marked copies of the plays and poems that went back to 1923, signed, in Irish, "M. O'Donnobhain." The ferocity of his feud with Father O'Flynn had resulted from an inclination toward Shakespeare rather than an avowed distaste. *The Road to Stratford* seems to indicate that his attachment was one of begrudging admiration, but it also represents a delayed eruption. It was not so much that O'Connor "loved" Shakespeare's works as that he felt compelled to answer for himself the overwhelming question, What makes an artist? To understand artistic genius, one must look to the highest examples of genius. *The Road to Stratford* may best be seen, then, as a personal defense of the journey of the artist, a testament of faith that O'Connor would be compelled to write again in his books on the novel, the short story, and finally the history of Irish literature.

I I I

In September 1948 the body of W. B. Yeats, O'Connor's greatest literary hero, was to be brought to Sligo from France to be buried, according to his wishes, in the Drumcliffe churchyard. Over the summer Mrs. Yeats had corresponded with Michael about making the graveside oration, but at the last minute Jack Yeats decided against speeches of any kind. When Michael arrived in Dublin from Holyhead, he found an apologetic letter from Mrs. Yeats who explained the situation and assured him that she still desired his presence on that important occasion.[27] He went to Sligo only because she had insisted he do so.

A fortnight later he was off to Belfast where he recorded broadcasts on Swift and the Ulster sagas. On the train back to Dublin he happened to find himself seated across from a drunken priest who was carrying on about the Protestants. He demanded O'Connor's opinion. O'Connor replied, "I like to live in charity with my fellowmen." "Wretched Protestant!" the priest grunted as he rose from the seat. He returned a few minutes later, acting relieved and a bit smug. He introduced himself and inquired to know whom he was talking to. Michael told him. Thoughtfully the priest reminded Mr. O'Connor that the scriptures tell us to love God and then our neighbor. "First things first," he chortled. The name Frank O'Connor, however, seemed to cause him some difficulty; in his condition all he could focus on was that he should not like the person, but he could not remember why. Then, not far from Dublin, the priest blurted: "You're not THE Frank O'Connor. The chap I mean is the Frank

O'Connor who wrote 'A Midsummer Night's Dream' and ran away with Ned Curtis' wife," thus neatly dismissing three writers with one pontifical mistake.[28] Things were not yet so bad that Michael could not enjoy the hilarious irony of it. O'Faoláin roared when he heard the story; O'Flaherty never got the chance, having cut himself off from nearly everyone. When Michael wrote to Stan with an account of the incident, he also mentioned that his marriage was near an end.

On Monday, November 15, Michael was scheduled to fly to Denmark to deliver a lecture in Copenhagen; he would return by way of Manchester to do some work on a documentary film being shot there on the cotton industry.[29] The weekend before his departure he and Evelyn had another bitter confrontation about Joan and the bungalow. By Sunday afternoon, following another incident in which Michael had become so enraged that he had struck her, Evelyn had decided that separation was the only possible recourse. She informed him that she would engage a solicitor during his absence. However, on Monday just before the plane left they "patched it up again," as she wrote in a letter to her friends the Davidsons, adding that it would be the last time.[30] He had made her, she said, an "emotional wreck."

While Michael was gone Evelyn admitted Myles to a hospital for surgery to correct the boy's bed-wetting problem. When Michael returned the first week in December and learned of the decision, he was curious about why there had been no discussion about the operation before he left. In the hospital he found Myles in great pain and wondering what he was doing there. In the boy's eyes Michael thought he saw the ghost of the boy he had seen in jail, years before, who had been beaten to a pulp. Hugging his crying son, he thought he heard his own voice screaming in hysterical desperation at a drunken father menacing a boy and his mother with a razor. There was little he could do except assure Myles that he would return the next day. He left the hospital and walked home as he had done the night his mother was injured, terror and sympathy modulating to bitter rage with every step. On the one hand, he felt the sting of guilt for always being gone when his children needed him. On the other, he blamed Evelyn for Myles's misery, but for once he bottled his fury and said very little when he arrived at Strand Road. The only thing he knew for certain was that something would have to change. The marriage was over, he felt sure of that, but he was incapable of taking any decisive action himself.

Subdued behind this cloud of uncertainty, Michael asked Evelyn to accompany him a few days later to Belfast where he was scheduled to make recordings at the BBC studios; he was to give a talk on the stories of his latest hero, A. E. Coppard, and a reading of his own story "Christmas Morning."[31] Evelyn agreed despite a neighbor's warning that Michael might try to kill her; she did promise the worried woman that she would not stand near a door on the train. Nothing calamitous happened, of course. Then, on Christmas Day, O'Connor made his first appearance on Radio Eireann in five years; he wrote to Kelleher that politics in Ireland might have been changing after all—"hurrah for liberty!"

Christmas that year was also brightened by news from A. D. Peters that an American magazine, *Holiday,* had offered $2,500 for an article on Ireland, the only catch being that the editor wanted a "good Irish-Catholic" to write it.

Michael wrote saying that he had been ceritified Irish as well as Catholic by none other than *The New Yorker*.[32] Either the editor of *Holiday* was gullible or he had not read "News for the Church," because O'Connor was given the assignment over better Catholics and more pedigreed Irishmen, and so a very bad year ended with something close to promise.

At the start of 1949 Evelyn returned to Arklow. Michael wrote sarcastically to Stan, "My wife, as usual, is in her country residence." He did not say, though, that for weeks he had barely spoken to her or that he had taken to handing the weekly household money to the maid, Ita Forde, a simple Galway girl who found it hard enough to keep accounts straight without also having to referee nasty domestic bouts. The financial pattern in the O'Donovan home was for Michael to hand Evelyn a certain sum each week—always the same—from which she would buy food. If the children needed shoes or clothes, money had to be siphoned from the household fund or disguised as five pounds of flour or some such special purchase. No extra would be forthcoming from Michael, who saw to rent and utilities himself. By giving money only to the maid, Michael pushed Evelyn into an even more humiliating position.

In mid February her mother's illness forced Evelyn to go to Wales. Before she left, she reminded Ita that the coal supply was low and told her to ask Michael for money to pay for a delivery. When Evelyn returned, she found the house cold and Donny in a flutter about "no coal for the study."[33] She learned from Ita that Michael had refused her the money and ordered her to wait until Evelyn returned. When Evelyn inquired about the coal, he exploded, claiming that such things were to be paid from the housekeeping. She reminded him of the blank checks he had always given her for that purpose, even producing a canceled check to the local coal merchant to support her claim. He replied that she was inventing all this just to sabotage his position as head of the house. She asked if he had preferred to perish from cold in order to prove his point and make her pay for a miserable load of coal. "You can find plenty of money for Arklow," he answered. Beside herself with anger, Evelyn finally said something about consulting a solicitor, at which point Michael became livid again: "You have threatened to do that before," he roared. "You will not threaten me again!"

A silly squabble over coal ignited a full-fledged domestic battle. In retaliation to threatening letters from Evelyn's solicitors Michael began withholding money and communicating only through the maid. Joan advised him to spend a few days with Stan and then to see about an English divorce. On St. Patrick's Day, exasperated to the boiling point, he left for London on the excuse of having to do a broadcast for the BBC; what he actually sought was an atmosphere conducive to writing. During Evelyn's stay in Arklow he had managed to finish one of his finest stories, "The Idealist."[34] When she had returned, he had reminded her of his warning that his writing would always come first, that he would see her in the streets before he would let her hinder his work. While she had been in Wales he had written the *Holiday* piece in less than a week. The tone of that article, vacillating between venom and veneration, signals as much about the state of his personal life as about his perennial feud with his homeland.

The editors of *Holiday* intended to use O'Connor's prose as background support for an assortment of "picturesque" photos by two of their staff photographers, but what O'Connor sent to them was hardly the usual tourist board pabulum.[35] As in his Ben Mayo articles, he is obsessed by the poverty and decay of Ireland—people in mud cabins without modern services, old churches in ruin, schools intent on cramming Irish down the throats of a generation needing modern skills, disease, and above all a feeling of despondency. In fact, reading the article one gets the feeling that instead of pulling out all the complimentary clichés about the Emerald Isle, hospitable land of saints and scholars, O'Connor has pulled out the uncomplimentary clichés about a priest-ridden, superstitious, backward land.

However, the article was written in the same spirit that motivated all of O'Connor's responses to Ireland: He loved his country too much not to hate its imperfections. Having spent twenty years saying what no one wanted to hear, he was not about to capitulate and talk about where to get a good pint or a fine wool sweater. Almost without heed of his audience (and in his journalistic writing his sense of the reader is usually impeccable), he seems to be sighing out, as if for the last time, a lament for a wasted culture whose future is slipping away. The bulk of the essay retraces *Irish Miles,* celebrating Cashel, Kilkenny, and Dublin as places emblematic of Ireland's history of foreign domination. He salutes Cormac, O'Leary, Swift, O'Connell, and Parnell as men whose genius illustrates a distinctive quality of the Irish people. About Parnell, for instance, he says nearly the same thing he wrote about Collins and Shakespeare: "a man so great that he throws a brilliant light on ordinary people and invests with all the glamour of romance old feuds and tragedies on which the eye of history would scarcely have lit."

Oddly enough, nothing in this strangely vituperative piece is quite so personal as his portrait of Swift, whose "secret terror" caused him to "fly from the spleen to the world's end." He concludes this section, headed "Swift's Progress," with the assertion that after the death of Stella, Swift "posed as The Man Who Knew Women, the celibate sour grapes with the lavatory complex." Yet he finds Swift's last pamphlets "as wonderful as the last quartets of Beethoven," which were also "filled with the utter loneliness of the deaf." The irony of Swift at the end is an "irony which no longer hopes to achieve anything; irony for its own sake; a voice muttering to itself in an empty house at night." O'Connor's heart, fed too long on enmity, had hardened, and he had come to share Swift's "secret terror" and even his misanthropy.

The remainder of the article follows the tortuous path of Irish history in the twentieth century. By the time he has reached the present, O'Connor concludes that Ireland is not a good place to live but that he would rather live there than anywhere else. He feels, first of all, that the mess could be cleared up, and that it would be "a job worth doing." But he wishes to stay primarily because of what he calls the "personal element," the close, chatty familiarity that may stifle at times but that comforts and protects as well. Having held his critical pose long enough, he relaxes into the storyteller he really is, and in a few deft sketches brightens the stage with warm, positive light. "Oh, yes, life in Ireland," he muses, "has considerable advantages! It has humanity, and poetry, and a sense of the past," and anyone lacking that sense should stay away; nobody who loves the past, "whatever our faults may be, should give us the hard word."

Now, in London and away from Evelyn, Michael threw himself into his work. Though he had sold a few stories during 1948, the few he had actually written that year had been consistently rejected by editors in England and in America.[36] Furthermore, he had produced only seven reviews for the *Evening News,* prompting his friend the editor, Guy Schofield, to ask if he seriously meant to continue the column. Stung by Schofield's reprimand, O'Connor turned out a thoughtful and focused review of books by Sylvia Townsend Warner, Mervyn Wall, and John Watney, none of whom could ever pass as a favorite of his. Reviews by Frank O'Connor appeared regularly for the next six months. In the wake of the *Holiday* article he even set himself to finish *Leinster, Munster, and Connaught,* the topographical book he had avoided for years.[37] He put aside most of Shevawn Lynam's laborious and loving research, an assignment that she later acknowledged had had as much to do with his generosity at a time when she was financially strapped as with his own inability to cope with the topic, and hastily mined *Irish Miles,* the Ben Mayo series, and other random pieces for material. In cut-and-paste fashion he constructed a lengthy, rambling, and imbalanced book on the twenty-six counties.

   Leinster, Munster, and Connaught is a massive contradiction, a testament of a love/hate relationship so intense as to defy easy solution. The book is full of sour grapes, especially the sections on the Abbey Theatre, Cork, and the Tailor. O'Connor's personal bitterness, which he seems to link with Swift's indignation when talking about Dublin, boils too close to the surface, defeating whatever validity his criticism may hold and overshadowing those moments— as when he describes a road in Kerry, a church in Tipperary, or a sunset in Clare—when his magnificent lyricism takes to the wing. His snide posturing and cute sophistication unfortunately cloud his natural ear for human stories, such as the one (also used at the end of the *Holiday* piece) about an elderly couple in a handsome Georgian manor whose lonely vigil over their Norman heritage struck him as heroic. Through the entire book runs a faint hint of regret, a veiled lament, for by now he had given up on Ireland, on marriage, and, to an extent, on himself.

   Since his return to London Michael had been moving from one friend's flat to another, from one hotel to another. Joan still shared a cottage at Picott's End with her old teaching colleague; she was finding it harder and harder to welcome him unquestioningly whenever he showed up in London, for his indecision meant continuing instability for her. She had invested her entire emotional being in him while he had kept his separate life in Ireland. The house on Strand Road was still his home, if for no other reason than his mother's presence in it. There was nothing for him to do in the end but return, solicitors or not. Evelyn and the children stayed in Arklow most of the summer, so things were quiet enough for him to finish a story and an autobiographical piece for the BBC. Alone with his mother for the first time in years, Michael used the occasion to good advantage, saturating himself in her wistful chatter about their life in Cork.

   Whenever O'Connor was in the midst of a personal crisis, his writing habits became more piecemeal, with numerous bits and pieces of ideas scribbled at random in his notebooks rather than fully formed as stories and essays. His journals for 1948–49 are full of notations about dream symbolism and sketches from his childhood. Whenever he saw Joan, he would bring up the subject of dreams. She had also begun to keep a pad of paper by her bed and to

collect books on dream interpretation.[38] Together they pondered the puzzle of
their own dreams and developed a theory of dream symbolism that relied heavily on linguistic associations (particularly puns) and numerical symbols.[39] Not
surprisingly, most of what O'Connor developed was based on family roles and
sexuality; the number one, for example, stood for father, two for mother, three
for the combination of the two in intercourse, and so on. Years before, in his
essay on Corkery, he had argued that dreams were psychological symbols, the
"private business of the author, and [had] nothing to do with criticism." But
by this time he had had come to see writing itself as a kind of dreaming, a dis-
sociated form of suggestion, and rewriting as the associating process that imposed order on what was otherwise nonsense.[40]

O'Connor left his elaborate dream theories to gestate in his notebooks,
but he transformed the sketches from his childhood into short stories. Dreams,
he believed, were part of the universal drama within each individual, which he
called "Everyman his own Family." Childhood served as the stage whereon he
could externalize the internal drama. Already in 1949 he had written two brilliant stories drawn from his experience as a boy growing up in Cork: "The Idealist" and "Man of the House," delightful accounts of a daydreaming scholar
who challenges the educational establishment, and of a helpful mother's boy
who fails in a mission of mercy because of the wiles of a pretty girl. The defiance of the one stands in contrast to the guilty tone of the other.

Both stories were extremely popular with radio audiences, but broadcast
directors at the BBC still pressed him for something autobiographical. Now,
inspired by those nostalgic conversations with his mother, he wrote a script
called "An Only Child," which begins:

> I believe that statistics have shown that genius occurs more frequently
> among younger sons of a larger family. That may well be, but I should say
> the persuasion of genius occurs almost exclusively among only children.
> I have never envied children of a large family because I feel the difficulty
> of being a genius is exaggerated in proportion to the size of the family.
>
> I have also studied only children and I am convinced we become ge-
> niuses for lack of anything better to do. Only children who aren't ge-
> niuses must find life very dull. I can't remember the time when I
> couldn't read and hadn't a private theater where I pushed about charac-
> ters.[41]

This tongue-in-cheek tone lends a detachment that allows O'Connor to look at
himself as someone else, a child long ago and far away. Beyond his fascination
with genius, this little piece carries the germ of personal history that would
later grow into his first autobiographical volume. He talks, for instance, about
reading English school stories, watching the Public Library burn during the
Black and Tan War, and liking Latin hymns at Mass. He confesses that he believed in and patterned his behavior after everything he read, and, most telling
of all, he relates the story of the magical day when a new teacher came to class
and wrote in a strange script on the blackboard. He had been hurt by Corkery
and he had struck back, but here, when honesty to oneself was the only thing
on the line, he paid tribute to his first literary father, his first conscious contact
with genius.

Evelyn returned to Dublin early in August, but only for a few days. Michael's mother must have known that something was wrong, for during that interval she suddenly decided to accept a long-standing invitation to visit her niece, May O'Donovan. When Michael returned from seeing her off at Kingsbridge Station, he found Evelyn and the children with bags packed, waiting for a taxi. She showed him return tickets for Wales. This was merely to be a holiday excursion, she pointed out, wanting him to be sure of her intention to return to *her* house with *her* children. Primarily, she didn't want him to jump to the conclusion that she was kidnaping the children, and so begin legal actions of his own. Less than a week after he saw his family board the Holyhead boat, he built a bonfire in back of the house and tried to burn his papers. But he could not bring himself to do it, because as he told Joan a few days later it would have been a kind of suicide.[42] Instead he walked the strand until midnight, then came back and hastily packed his bags. That night, leaving books, files, and a fresh case of whiskey behind, he left 57 Strand Road for good.

16

Displaced Persons

*The exile lives, mentally, at home to exactly the same extent as
the stay-at-home lives in exile.*
                                    JOHN WAIN, *Sprightly Running*

"FOR me there has always been in imagination," O'Connor wrote, "a stage beyond death—a stage where one says 'I have no home now.' " For years his
most persistent nightmare was about wandering alone cold and homeless. In
the fall of 1949 reality caught up with fantasy, and he woke to find his dreams
had come true. When he left Strand Road, even his mother had been displaced, forced to stay in Cork with relatives. For the first time in years Michael
was free from domestic cares, free to indulge in the bachelor life he had so
often wished for; but he was also without a private place to write guarded by a
dutiful wife and a sign saying AUTHOR. Over the next three years Frank
O'Connor would use twelve different addresses. It is not accidental that he had
always considered Gorky to be the prototype of the storyteller—the homeless
tramp wandering on the fringe of society telling stories to offset his loneliness.

I

For a short time Michael stayed in Guy Schofield's flat near Regent's Park and
did some more work for the BBC. He also worked out details with his publisher
for a book on France, which he jokingly called "French Lettres."[1] When Schofield returned from his holiday Michael went back to Dublin to await the decision pending in Irish courts. Action by Evelyn's solicitors aimed at uncovering
the extent of O'Connor's "fortune" stalled the proceedings, forcing him to remain in Dublin longer than he had expected. Hospitality was extended to him
by Louis Johnston, a young businessman who had met him in Belfast through
John Boyd of the BBC. Louis had some aspirations as a writer, and Michael had
given him generous encouragement and criticism. For a few days O'Connor
was so distracted that he barely spoke or ate. Marjory Johnston scolded him
gently about his miserable eating habits, but she and Louis both kept enough
distance to allow him to emerge from the depression on his own.

    The pleasant surroundings freed Michael's mind for work. Louis and
Marjory, affable and balanced northerners, reminded him of people he'd grown
up with in Cork. Their sensible approach to religion, moreover, reminded him
of a story he had tried to write years before while struggling with *Dutch Interior.* He dug back into his old notebooks and found some rough sketches about
the Cork Atheists' Club, a group of provincial intellectuals headed by a friend
of Corkery's named Dan Harrington. The only story O'Connor had extracted

from recollections of that group was "Mac's Masterpiece." Now, over ten years later, his memories were clearer and harder, and his motivation for dealing with his past was more objective. One day he joked with Louis that he was writing a story about Protestants and, true to his word, he read them the new story, "My First Protestant," a few days later.[2] They were enchanted anyway by their infamous guest, but the story seemed written for them. The narrator, Dan Hogan, is an independent-minded, self-sufficient bachelor, who fancies himself a "roaring agnostic." Dan resembles the young Michael O'Donovan only vaguely and in fact is more like the sort of fellow Michael always wished he'd been.

Unlike many of the stories O'Connor had been writing at the time, "My First Protestant" is neither satirical nor nostalgic. The narrator's tone is at once thoughtful and casual, intimate and ironic. In O'Connor's "dirty stories" the narrator is merely a convention, standing between the author and his subject and between the author and his audience; but in this story Dan Hogan is intended to reveal something about himself, not simply to pass on some cynical tale told by a character in the local pub. The gist of the narrator's story is that he had once "done a line" with a Protestant girl who threw him over for a devout Catholic. Years later, after her husband's death, he meets her coming from Mass—the Atheists' Club met on the quays each Sunday "at a time when the rest of the city was at church." Sitting over drinks in her house, he listens to her story and tries to comprehend just what had taken them in such opposite directions. "A man and a woman in search of something are always blown apart, but it's the same wind that blows them," he muses at the end. Not an earthshaking thought, perhaps, but what is important here is the cracking of the shell O'Connor spoke about in *The Road to Stratford*. Musing perhaps over his earlier loss of Nancy, who he knew would not have been right for him, he was also coming to terms with the fact that he and Evelyn had been blown apart.

Almost immediately Michael began another story about the same group of young iconoclasts. In "This Mortal Coil" a different narrator tells about the time Dan Turner, a "roaring atheist," tried to commit suicide after being jilted.[3] Though a devout rationalist, Dan Turner is, in the narrator's eyes, "as emotional as a child." Obstinacy is one thing, but suicide is quite another, the narrator argues. After failing a second time to do away with himself, this petulant genius "sees the light" and becomes such a reformed character that he avoids his old friends, as he is a "man without any proper faith." In addition to a few obvious "autobiographical" elements, the story has a startlingly personal tone. From time to time O'Connor may have contemplated suicide, particularly after the break with Nancy, but he never actually came close to taking action in that direction. In fact, the very thought of it terrified him, and had ever since he had listened to his mother's story about peering into the river Lee one night after she was once again homeless. But writing about suicide, as he said of Shakespeare in *The Road to Stratford*, seemed to externalize the whole thing for him, to put it at arm's length where he could even admit to having had the thought.

That O'Connor was in the middle of a "religious crisis" may also be seen in his final review for the *Evening News*, which amounted to a frontal assault on the claustrophobic philosophy contained in Somerset Maugham's *A*

Writer's Notebook.[4] O'Connor notices that selections from Maugham's note-books, written between age eighteen and age seventy reveal a striking simi-larity, prompting him to conclude sarcastically that Maugham's "life has ap-parently run to schedule." Maugham's dismissal of altruism, religion, and morals chills O'Connor's sensibilities. He is not bothered so much by the rela-tivism as by the attitude of "cynicism and despondency." He recalls a similar feeling when he encountered in a textbook in commercial school the sentence, "There is no such thing in business as an out-and-out free gift." Even more disturbing to him is that Maugham compromises the business of writing. To seek in one's work "nothing less than perfection" is what his mother means by living in the "presence of God" and what Carlyle meant by seeing "Eternity glaring." That sort of thing is quite the opposite of what he finds in Maugham's philosophy, which to O'Connor's mind "makes a man a creature imprisoned within his own senses, as in a cave, living only for and to himself, and throws him open to terror and the night."

Toward the end of September Hector Legge, the editor who had stuck his neck out for Michael during the war, held a small dinner party for Dermot Foley, who was in Dublin on business. The last time Michael had seen Dermot was when he had run into him walking on O'Connell Street with the Francis-can. For some reason, the idea of seeing again his old friend seemed to snap him out of his sullen mood. At the Legges' home that evening he was at his charming best, entertaining the entire company with outrageously funny stories about England. He ate and drank more than Dermot could recall his ever doing before. Then, shortly after midnight, Michael politely made prepara-tions to leave. Anxious to have a personal word or two with him, Dermot of-fered to see him out. Something about Michael's almost excessive ebullience that evening did not ring true; and Dermot was curious about Evelyn's ab-sence. When he inquired about her, Michael flippantly replied, "Oh, didn't you know, Der? That's broken up!" The news, coming so off the cuff, stunned Dermot. He continued walking up Chelmsford Road with Michael, hoping for a bit more than callous dismissal.

To break the silence, Dermot observed that they were nearing Molly Alexander's house, and began joking about the good times they had enjoyed there. Under a lamp post almost directly across from Molly's house, Michael stopped suddenly to light a cigarette, but when Dermot placed a hand on his shoulder, he broke down and began sobbing out his tale of domestic woe. He cursed Evelyn's legal maneuvering, Joan's stubbornness, and his own indeci-sion. Dermot squirmed as he heard the surprising disclosures of infidelity and revenge. Finally, unable to sympathize entirely with this barrage of self-pity, Dermot told Michael to go home and get some sleep. "Home?" Michael grunted derisively and stalked off in the direction of the Johnstons' house.

The next day Molly Alexander had an unexpected visitor. She served him tea and inquired about the family. Michael was unusually vague and left with-out ever explaining the reason for his visit. Later that afternoon he telephoned and sheepishly explained that he and Evelyn had separated. Molly didn't ask about the cause of the separation, but she wondered why he was telling her. Michael said something about having talked to Dermot the night before. Fi-nally he confessed that he was worried about his mother, with whom Molly had always been great friends, and begged her to write to Cork so the old lady would not be so lonely. Whatever else Molly might have thought about Michael's personal life, she knew that this request came from the best in him. She wrote at once.[5]

Another person on whom Michael leaned during this trying time was Shevawn Lynam. He was a daily visitor to her flat in Fitzwilliam Square. They argued about Spain—"I loathe everything about that misfortunate country," he would pontificate—and about the Arans—"God preserve me from islands!" he would moan. Actually, he had nothing against Spain except Franco and the silly dream he'd had during the war; and though he had never been on any island smaller than Ireland, he was certain that the smaller the island, the greater the constriction. Michael was astounded by Shevawn's grasp of Irish history but impatient with her detachment—about the Civil War, de Valera, compulsory Irish, and any number of topics, he could be as violent in conversation as he was harsh in print.[6] Later Miss Lynam would write that Michael, having fought for his country, reacted to talk of its problems like a "disappointed lover."

Michael introduced her to the writings of Daniel Corkery and James Joyce. While dismissing Corkery's restrictive nationalism, he commended *The Hidden Ireland,* and while dismissing Joyce as "the first of the Ph.D. novelists," he continually read passages from *Dubliners* and *Ulysses* to illustrate Joyce's stylistic brilliance. One evening he invited her to join him for dinner at the Johnstons'; his friends were entertaining guests from France. Michael admired Louis and Marjory for their cosmopolitan tastes; both spoke French and German fluently, which to Michael showed a full use of their intellectual faculties. The dinner was a smashing success, and the French guests appeared entirely at ease despite the fact that they could speak no English whatsoever. Michael was full of himself that evening and sang countless songs with Marjory and Shevawn. When one of the Frenchwomen asked about Joyce, Michael went dramatically to a bookcase, took out a copy of *Finnegans Wake,* and "started to read out loud in a broad Dublin accent; he was a superb actor." In a few minutes the entire group was caught up in laughter, and even the French guests were able to understand what they had all thought was incomprehensible.

By the first of October it was obvious that a court decision would not soon be forthcoming, so Michael returned to London. Evelyn's solicitors had filed a writ blocking publication of his newest volume of stories, arguing that "The Grandmother" libeled their client.[7] In actual fact, a story about the presence under the same roof of a wife, mother, and mistress, all conspiring against a beleaguered man, seriously upset their case against Michael as a dastardly philanderer by suggesting an element of duplicity on Evelyn's part. Time and again that fall she had threatened to drag out all the personal dirt, until in exasperation he withdrew all payments entirely, leaving Evelyn and the children hungry.

Together, Michael and Joan took a small and modestly furnished flat in Denmark Hill, a less than fashionable area of southeast London. During the week, while she worked in Sloane Square, Oliver stayed with a friend of Joan's at King's Langley. Never in his four years had the child been too long away from his mother's doting and undivided attention; he looked forward to weekends when they could be together. The sudden appearance of a vaguely familiar "daddy" upset the routine of mother and son, particularly his habit of climbing into bed with his mother on Sunday morning and playing freely about the flat. Now, it was "Shush, Daddy's working!" or "Shush, Daddy's asleep!" One morning Oliver attempted to reclaim his rightful place in his mother's bed, but his jabbering wakened Michael, who sat up roaring and struck the boy. Later in the day, feeling guilty about what he had done, Michael asked if Joan wanted him to take *her* son for a walk.

Domestic tranquility held on precariously for the rest of the month. Michael worked steadily, temporarily recharged by a change of environment. He corrected proofs of *Leinster, Munster, and Connaught* and wrote a story entitled "Masculine Principle," an almost satirical rendering of the plight of a young girl in a provincial town made pregnant by a married man. The story is told from the point of view of a cynical raconteur supposedly talking about his town and his friends but actually enjoying a good laugh at their expense. O'Connor does manage to portray the desperation of a family trying to balance scandal with respectability, and he does convey the dilemma of the young man who remains steadfast to the end and marries the girl. Even though the tone of the story is too slick, too detached, the very fact that he treated this particular subject at this particular time suggests that he was at least trying to externalize his own guilt, the burden of which was choking him.

The separation hearing was finally set for November 18, and Michael's solicitors urged him to return to Dublin to answer Evelyn's demand for seven hundred pounds a year in combined alimony and child support, a sum entirely beyond his means.* As soon as he arrived in Dublin he asked Louis Johnston to drive him down to Tipperary to visit Myles. Even before Michael had left the house at Strand Road, Evelyn had decided, on the advice of friends, to send Myles to Rockwell College, a school for boys in Tipperary run by the Holy Ghost Fathers. Michael had even taken Myles for another long walk into town to dissuade him, but the image of the place was so exciting to the ten-year-old boy that he went anyway. Once there, he was horrified: The nice lake in the brochure had been drained, so there was no boating; the discipline was brutal, and caning was not uncommon. Of greater misery to Myles was his bed-wetting problem; at Rockwell his bedclothes were never changed, and because showers were allowed only once a week, Myles could be smelt before he could be seen. Thus, when Michael went to Rockwell, he found a miserable boy. He received permission to take Myles to Stan Stewart's house in Limerick for the weekend. It took all the poise of the two Protestants, Louis and Stan, to soothe Michael's anger.

Waiting for Michael in Dublin was a note from O'Faoláin expressing "condolence" on the demise of the marriage and assuring Michael of his support.[8] Michael responded with a note explaining the "horrid mess." He bemoaned his mother's exile in Cork and Myles's incarceration, which he blamed on Evelyn's friend Charles Davidson, a very religious man who thought "it would make a good impression on the judge." The alimony and child support, combined with three pounds a week for his mother, would put a rope round his neck, he lamented. "And of course I blame myself for everything, and know that I shall tumble straight into the same sort of mess next year and I wish to Jesus I was in France, Italy or anywhere but out this kip."[9] Still, even in a per-

* Since there is no divorce in Ireland, the action was for legal separation.

sonal note the writer bobs to the surface, and he concludes with a few literary remarks: "Even de Profundis I must clamour for my Art."

The day before the hearing Michael learned from Dermot that Stan's wife, Nora, from whom he had been estranged for some time, was close to dying. Long after midnight Michael wrote to his dearest friend:

> On occasions like these we all feel guilt and remorse; we all want to turn back time; but even if we were able, things would go on in precisely the same way, because the mistakes we make are not in our judgments but in our natures. It is only when we do violence to our natures that we are justified in our regrets, and neither of us is capable of that. We are what we are and within our limitations we have made our own efforts. They may seem puny in the light of eternity but they didn't at the time, and they weren't. But I know intensely what you feel like and the way one suffers over what Emily Dickinson calls—
> > The sweeping up of the heart,
> > And putting love away
> > We shall not need to use again
> > Until eternity.
> I wish I could be with you even for a night. The case is coming off this morning and I don't know what will happen after.[10]

This expression of comfort, written in the midst of his own draining agony, not only shows Michael's capacity for genuine love but highlights his nagging awareness of "Eternity glaring."

The separation hearing did come off the next day very much as expected, though the size of the financial settlement did not quite match his fears. On Monday Michael packed his bags again, gave Louis and Marjory the one AE painting he'd salvaged from Strand Road, and boarded the mail boat for Holyhead to pick up the pieces of his private life. "When an Irish writer packs his bag," he wrote a few months later, "it is to get away from it. At home he cannot escape from reality, and reality is always five-foot-ten or thereabouts, cheerful, shop-soiled, insinuating, and insists on calling him by his Christian name."[11] The personal element had taken its toll; reality had chilled him to the bone.

Alone on the cold decks of the mail boat that bleak November night, Michael would have looked into an emptiness of his own making. He had no home. He had become what he had written about, an Irish Don Juan: "He had woken up from a nice, well-ordered, intelligible world to find eternity stretching all round him and no one, priest or scientist, who could explain it to him." Though he joked with O'Faoláin that the "demise" of his marriage was a "happy release," something within him had died. Separation had become more than a legal process, and the rope around his neck was not just financial. Not since his break with Nancy McCarthy had he felt such unvarnished dread; once again he was thrown utterly and inescapably onto himself. It was the "little death," hard enough to face for a man of thirty, like Shakespeare, but brutal for one nearing fifty; it was the shredding of a subjectivity that regarded "other people merely as extensions of itself" by the discovery that there are no such extensions, "that from the beginning to the end it remains forever alone and aloof."

In London Michael was distant and surly. He spent most of his time lying on the bed, smoking and staring vaguely at the ceiling. He began to drink heavily and would seldom even take his habitual walk. He would barely speak to Joan, let alone touch her. He cuffed Oliver without warning, then, in response to the tears of both mother and son, apologized with the explanation, "I'll be fine when I'm working." To make matters worse, British tax officials were pressing A. D. Peters about O'Connor's tax status. For years he had claimed exemption as an Irish resident, but Irish officials trying to collect his past taxes learned at the separation hearing that his legal domicile was now London. As a result, he found he owed a considerable sum to both countries, and nothing terrified Michael more than the spectre of poverty. His earnings had been modestly increasing since the war, but not enough to meet expenses; though frugal almost to a fault, he nevertheless spent a fair amount on travel and books, and his legal costs were crippling. Having no savings, he would have to write to pay tax liens from two countries; the only problem was that he could not bring himself to work.

The issue of permanent domicile may have been a legal technicality, but for one so "tenacious of roots," the domicile matter was symbolic of O'Connor's spiritual groundlessness. As a person, he was tenacious of habits and old haunts; as a writer, he was tenacious of memories. The recent emotional and legal battling only capped a tumultuous decade in which Frank O'Connor took on the entire country, and his exile in England was as much a matter of rejecting as one of being rejected, for, as Louis Johnston told him, "Michael is the architect of Frank's chaos."

I I

By mid-December things had so closed in on him that Michael was using any excuse to escape from the Denmark Hill flat. Two days before Christmas he bolted again, ending up in Avignon. Michael's flight to France may have been proof to Joan of what she called his "destructive restlessness," but it was even more a statement of his relentless need for freedom. The more isolated he felt, the less he could accept the affection he desperately craved; the more misunderstood he believed himself to be, the readier he was to leave. As a child he had escaped from the emotional chaos of his parents' life by retreating to his attic room and the variety show of his own mind, and as a man he escaped from his own domestic chaos by traveling and by burying himself in his art. Though his sense of realism enabled him to acknowledge the desolation of his existence, his even stronger romantic instincts told him he could alter circumstance. And though he had no God to turn to, what he had to offer "eternity" were his stories.

In a hotel room in Avignon O'Connor felt a burst of creative release and wrote as he had not done since Woodenbridge, when "Bridal Night" had written itself in the wake of his rage at Corkery. On Christmas Day, in the same sort of trance, he wrote "The Pretender," a variation on the illegitimate-child theme.[12] The story had come to him almost complete, and like so many of his finest stories, it was not his story at all. The woman who years before had come to Woodenbridge in desperation had eventually given her son to an old woman to be raised. The boy, then named Paddy Ritchie after the old woman, had come to the O'Donovan house for a visit and, feeling so much at home, had become like a member of the family. With the birth of Oliver, Paddy had also become a fixture in O'Connor's mind; in sculpting this poignant story of a boy's hesitant search for his "real mother," O'Connor seemed to be projecting, even justifying, the validity of his own love for his mother.

In the wake of that nearly faultless story O'Connor finished "My Oedipus Complex," which sprung from Oliver's unwillingness to share his mother.[13] Two years earlier O'Connor had jokingly admitted in a review that he had always had an Oedipus complex. In a letter to John Kelleher he confessed in a similarly disarming way to transmitting his Oedipus complex to his son Myles, "whose one ambition at the age of 8 was to kill his father and marry his mother." In "My Oedipus Complex" O'Connor resorted to a tone of humorous congeniality, an innocent, self-effacing air that disarms the reader by its wise perspective and allows the author an escape hatch.

For the past few years Michael had been exorcising the memories of his father in such humorous stories as "Old Fellows," "My Da," and "The Drunkard," transforming terror and misery into laughter. In his own sons he was now seeing a reflection of himself; in their experiences he could see his own, and thus objectified, he could write about himself without really writing about himself at all. The orphan, the bastard, and the only child were all cut from the same bolt. He had written a few childhood stories before ("First Confession"); he had already treated the subject of the outcast illegitimate child ("The Babes in the Woods"); he had even tried to capture the comedy of his own adolescence ("Judas"); but the two stories written that week in Avignon mark a turning point in O'Connor's fiction. In the "dirty stories" written after the war he had been able to edge rather close to the nerve simply by maintaining a pose of snide and satirical humor. If he had fumbled for a style in the thirties, then after the war he was fumbling for something that might be called a soul. He had worked his way back through the games of adults seeking to ease the pain of loneliness to the games of children groping for love and understanding. There he discovered the roots of which he was so tenacious, the simple values of Harrington Square which he never really abandoned.

Michael returned to England a few days after Christmas chastened and vindicated.[14] About that time reviews of *Leinster, Munster, and Connaught* began appearing, none of them very complimentary. According to the reviewer for the *Times Literary Supplement;* "This cheerful, opinionated, rambling essay on some aspects of the architecture and literary associations of some counties . . . is unfit to stand beside the *Ulster* which has already appeared."[15] He attacks O'Connor for not covering every single county and for focusing on rather eccentric features of those he does cover. Ten pages about private squabbles in the Abbey theatre strike him as "badly out of place." Instead of actually describing a manor house or ruined church, the reviewer notes, the author simply spits out a judgment: "lovely" or "shocking disappointment." Anyone who had ever cycled with Michael had heard the same things countless times; John Kelleher, for example, once recalled Michael's response to Newgrange: "pastiche!"[16] The reviewer's concluding sentence indicates exactly how alien the book was to the spirit of *Irish Miles* and *Crab Apple Jelly:* "Mr. O'Connor speaks out against the narrow puritanism of modern Ireland, but he concerns himself almost entirely with things of the intellect and has little to record of the ordinary life of the Irish." *Leinster, Munster, and Connaught* was a shabby thing, and though O'Connor knew it, he did not enjoy being reproved by a reviewer. For days afterward he sulked about the flat, not in a deep depression but in a moody restlessness.

Response to the *Holiday* article proved, however, to be even more devastating. Though it appeared only in America, copies of it deluged the desks of Irish politicians and newspaper editors, accompanied by irate letters from Irish-Americans who felt betrayed and scandalized. One editor described O'Connor's article (after quoting from it piecemeal) as a "string of falsehoods" revolting to decent Irishmen; citing Thomas Davis's "The Spirit of the Nation," he then branded O'Connor a "typical anti-Irish Irishman."[17] When Michael read these letters, his sulk turned into a wall-banging fury. The self-appointed conscience of the Irish race had blithely assumed that his unvarnished idealism would be accepted as gospel, that the people whose toes he stepped on would honor him for doing so. Although there is an admirable kind of innocence in that assumption—the innocence of the youthful provincial jousting with windmills—it also carries an element of megalomania, that inability, shared by so many gifted people, to understand that what they perceive as being ridiculously obvious is not always clear to everybody else.

Needless to say, within a month O'Connor had decided that the only place he could write, was Ireland. Joan reminded him of his success in Avignon, but he only dismissed that as a freak. He also continued to agonize over the idea of his mother being homeless at her advanced age. In February he sent the third revision of his newest book of stories, *Traveller's Samples,* to his publishers, substituting the two Atheists' Club stories for "The Grandmother" and "Ghosts," the story about John Kelleher's experiences in West Cork.[18] Originally he had intended the book to be composed largely of tales taken from his expeditions with Stan and Kelleher, but the delays caused by Evelyn's legal actions had given him time to finish stories with which he was more satisfied. Sometime in March he returned to Dublin to buy a house for his mother. Once again he stayed at the Johnstons' home and took the opportunity to visit his mother in Cork. By the end of the month he had returned to London to await his turn for a County Council house.

Almost certainly O'Connor had at the time been mining old notebooks for material, but that trip to Cork had pushed memories of his life there into the foreground of his mind. During the next few months he wrote four stories quite unlike anything he had been writing: two more or less comic treatments of rebel foolishness, "Private Property" and "The Rising"; and two rather serious stories of heroic but meaningless death, "The Baptismal" and "The Martyr."[19] Long before, Michael had eschewed the romantic violence of the Troubles; why he returned to that violence at this time of his life is almost impossible to say with any certainty. The four stories do, however, fit the picture of a man in search of himself; through them runs a thread of disaffection, of a young man's equally comic and tragic passage from romanticism to realism. Obviously O'Connor had always relied on personal experiences for his stories, but only in his two novels had he grappled steadily and profoundly with his own divided nature. When taken as part of the same "allegorical passage" as the childhood stories, these Revolution stories seem to indicate that he was now writing to survive, writing, as it were, to escape from his own abyss.

In April P. H. Newby, a program director at the BBC, rejected "My Oedipus Complex" and rather acidly asked one of his staff if there wasn't someone else besides O'Connor they could use. For years Newby had disagreed with O'Connor about what stories were suitable for broadcast.[20] He disliked O'Connor's "new vein" of childhood stories, and with O'Connor's old friends Christopher and Dona Salmon out of the picture, he had risen to a position of enough authority to cause O'Connor grief. Mercifully, John Boyd had scheduled Michael for a broadcast in Belfast; he left at once and took the opportunity to return by way of Dublin. With more impulsive enthusiasm than thoughtful caution, he signed purchase papers for an estate house still under construction on Seafield Crescent just off the Stillorgan Road in south Dublin. Thinking the house would be ready by May, he made arrangements for his mother to leave Cork at once, but because of delays in construction she was forced to stay for a few weeks with him at the Johnstons'.

During this time Michael wrote to Stan predicting that a new house would raise his mother's spirits. In that letter he also lamented the tragic situation in Belfast, adding that religious strife and bigotry had long since ceased to surprise him. He had no creed left except a belief in common, decent people. "What the hell else is there to believe in? And there aren't so many of them around." That sort of moral rumination was typical of O'Connor when he was writing to Stan Stewart. In his next letter he wrote: "You and I seem to be sharing an existence these last six months. I can't help feeling if we put them together we might get the makings of one decent existence." Only a year before he and Stan had cycled in France, and Michael was now working on a piece called "The Conversion," about that excursion.[21] The "restive and fiery" narrator and his "good-natured" companion Géronte (the same name given to Stan in *Irish Miles*) arrive in Dieppe on Holy Thursday. Cycling toward Beauvais on Good Friday, they are surprised to find all the churches locked or empty and their statues undraped. They soon learn that the area has no priest. As they cycle on they meet a young organist in the parish church and fall into conversation with him. Discovering they are from Ireland he begins to discuss James Joyce, and it is obvious to them that he is lonely for conversation; he admits that the only man he could talk to about books or music is his uncle, a severe and old-fashioned priest, who still considers Flaubert and Maupassant "immoral writers." The self-styled young atheist jokes irreverently about the vices of his uncle's parish in order to measure this odd pair. When they ask about the chances of hearing Tenebrae, he invites them to accompany him to Beauvais. The story so far is little more than casual narrative, but O'Connor never wrote without a telling occasion in mind. The odd trio enter a "great bare barrack of a church" where a young priest is conducting the Stations of the Cross in a voice at once "weak and toneless." Sitting in a pew farthest from the altar the narrator, a lapsed Catholic, finds himself "falling under a spell."

In the face of a desolate and meaningless situation, the priest improvises his own imaginary congregation.

He was not celebrating a service for three reluctant women and two small girls who had merely been dragged in to see members of their family perform in a countryside where God was dead. He was celebrating it in a crowded church in some cathedral town of the Middle Ages. The hypnotic influence he exerted came from the fact that he had hypnotized himself.

The inner power of the priest holds the service together; the only way the narrator can describe the effect is to compare it to a photograph he had been asked to take by the parents of a dead child: "the object had become the subject; the dead child had photographed the camera." It is the same "reversal of situation" one encounters in dreams.

The service over, the priest stands patiently with the cross. Only then does it dawn on the narrator that no one but himself and the organist, "an Irish agnostic and a French atheist," has any idea of what to do. Hastily he pushes himself past Géronte and down the aisle to kiss the cross. He surmises that the steps behind him are Géronte's. Instead, he turns to see the organist and muses that Maupassant's people are not so depraved after all. Outside the church after the service they find nothing remarkable about the young priest. The organist, however, is overcome with a burst of emotion and confesses that what he had thought hideous had come to be beautiful when seen through their eyes. "Perhaps that is conversion," he speculates. The narrator brusquely denies any such thing, but the young man remains steadfast. All the Irish agnostic can say, mounting his bicycle, is "I hope so."

In a story like this the personal dimension is so unforced and unaffected that it seems to reveal a side of Michael/Frank that he took great pains to mask. His cast-iron certainty and contentious arrogance melted in the face of those magical moments when ordinary people transformed life into something worthwhile, when by some creative gesture they managed, if only momentarily, to offset the loneliness of existence and nullify the terrifying silence of those infinite spaces. Walking alone to kiss the cross was his tribute to another lonely artist, the provincial priest. It was as close as O'Connor ever came to conversion.

To understand Michael at such times is to understand why Joan decided to throw up the security of her job in London and move to Dublin with him. He could be moody or even violent, but he was equally capable of being generous, charming, magnetic. The first time they walked up Baggot Street in Dublin, his hands behind his back and his head thrown back in order to amplify his great voice, there was, she felt, a certain grandeur about him. She was reluctant to be seen in public with him too much, knowing that she would probably bear the brunt of scandal; but he was all for "wearing the feather." They set up house together in June with the help of Michael's mother. Because they moved in almost before the paint was dry, they found piles of rubble about and even unfilled drainage ditches; more than one of Michael's old friends recalled seeing Joan wielding shovel or rake in the new yard. And because Michael had left everything behind when he vacated Strand Road, the house was pitifully short of furnishings. In the kitchen, for instance, was a table Michael found in town and three chairs—one each for himself, his mother, and Joan. Oliver was consigned to an orange crate. Louis Johnston came to their rescue and built some simple bookcases for his ham-fisted friend. By July the king had comfortably settled into his new castle, and by the end of the summer he had become virtually a recluse, while Joan had become virtually a slave. When a national census was taken that summer, Michael filled out the entire questionnaire in an archaic Gaelic script. When Joan asked how he explained her presence, he simply said "Housekeeper!"

John Kelleher returned to Ireland that summer along with his family. From their association four years earlier John had thought of Michael as being rather abstemious—by Irish standards—and was therefore quite surprised to find him drinking heavily now, especially whiskey. There was little drinking done by guests at Seafield Crescent, since Michael was never one to treat, except on rare occasions. But it seemed that whenever Helen Kelleher returned home from the grocer's with a bottle of fifteen-year-old Jameson's, reserved by the clerk for special customers, Michael would soon come swinging in through the gates with the unerring instinct of an army sergeant.

Twice that summer Michael and John went off cycling with Stan Stewart. One weekend they toured the Saga country of Meath. Michael was in a foul mood the entire time, finding nothing at Tara, Duleek, or Newgrange that impressed him. He kept insisting that the Irish prehistoric monuments were provincial imitations of those in England and Brittany; Newgrange he compared contemptuously with Avebury, and Tara with Maiden Castle. On another occasion, after cycling in Clare, they were drinking with some of Stan's friends in the Glentworth Hotel in Limerick. When it came John's turn to buy a round, he went to the bar, and while he was waiting there a farmer struck up a conversation by asking him the time. John pointed to the wall clock, but the man protested that he could not tell anything from electric clocks. Then he said, "You know—married sisters with children is half the history of the world." And he began a long story about his sister who had taken a house near his farm and wanted him to go partners with her husband. When John finally returned to the table, he apologized for making them wait and commenced to tell them the gist of what the farmer had been saying. Michael's response was mock outrage: "There you are," he said. "The scholar gets all the good stories and the storyteller just sits with an empty glass."

Sometime that summer Dr. Earl McCarthy, Nancy's brother, returned from Sweden after several years of study; he was to take a post at University College, Dublin. One evening he was at John's house along with O'Connor and O'Faoláin and told of trying methylated scopolamine to offset the gloom of the northern winter. "It was awful," he said. "It brought back my whole childhood, and you remember how terrible that was." Both Michael and Seán instantly said, "Get us some!" Earl sent to Sweden for the drug, and Kelleher was at Seafield when it arrived. Michael held it up triumphantly and said, "Tomorrow I'll have a whole batch of new stories!" The next day he reported with disappointment that he had not dreamt at all. Curious, Kelleher got in touch with O'Faoláin to learn what the drug had done for him. "Best damn laxative I ever had," O'Faoláin answered with a crisp laugh.

"My Oedipus Complex" and "Man of the House" were broadcast in November, despite Newby's objections, and by that time Michael had ceased, temporarily at least, to write stories about childhood. At the same time, he was becoming increasingly concerned about his children. In her father's absence Liadain had begun to cough almost constantly, and in October, when Michael visited Rockwell, Myles begged to be taken out of the school. When Michael told him that was impossible, the boy requested that at least he be able to see his grandmother at Christmas. On his return to Dublin Michael applied through his solicitor for permission to have all three children for a week after Christmas. Evelyn refused, on the advice of her solicitors, suggesting instead that he visit them at Arklow for a day. It was made clear that if he made a fuss "the moral issue" would be raised, meaning the inadvisability of her children associating with Joan and Oliver. Joan offered to go to a hotel during their visit, but Michael blanched at the thought of being alone with three children and an elderly woman for even a week. He often claimed to understand children, but he was no more comfortable with them than he was with women. He joked with Joan that children were fine before they could talk and after they had grown up, but in between they were intolerable. At Christmas he meekly took his mother to visit the children for a few hours at Strand Road under the watchful eye of Evelyn. Within a week he became seriously ill, a condition brought on by stress and exaggerated by a severe reaction to penicillin mistakenly prescribed by a physician unfamiliar with his medical history. Michael seemed to be one of those persons to whom things happen, against whom life seems in conspiracy; in fact, he preferred it that way. Time and again he forced Evelyn to take action, then retaliated with the fury of the counterpuncher, but the self-punishment such a strategy required was gradually exacting a hard toll.

I I I

The only new story O'Connor wrote that winter of 1950–51 was about young adults in Cork courting, marrying, settling into jobs. "A Romantic" is what O'Faoláin called a "Mick and I" story, which means a story about a level-headed, practical fellow and a "fiery and restive" fellow.[22] What is noteworthy in this otherwise undistinguished story is the manner in which O'Connor so neatly divides the world between realists and romantics. Mick, the realist, offers his friends stability, caution, hard work—all that O'Connor admired in Seán O'Faoláin, Sean Hendrick, Dermot Foley, and any number of male friends. Miah, the romantic with a fixation on France, offers his friends "a sense of variety and richness of life," an injection of euphoria and wonder to offset the dullness of Cork life. He drinks claret rather than stout and smokes French cigarettes. Even his marriage turns into a "romantic novel." After losing an arm—the left arm—in an accident in Glanmire Station, where he worked, Miah's personality changes; "his plunges from enthusiasm to despair" become more marked. Finally, he leaves for France but fails to get beyond England. The truth strikes his levelheaded friends back home: Miah had used France as an escape from reality all his life, and "now that it threatened to become a reality itself, he could not face it." Gradually, Miah starts to wander, "driven on by some restlessness beyond human reason." Almost in afterthought O'Connor generalizes that the tragedy of the romantic is that "reality itself becomes romance, but not until he has let it slip from his hands."

That story was written while O'Connor was estranged from his wife and children and living with a woman who had become his safety valve from the domestic and political realities surrounding him. Although not yet a tramp, he was nothing if not displaced and depressed. Throughout the winter he was so tormented by illness that he never left the house.[23] "Cluck! Cluck! No more eggs," he muttered constantly, indicating that the writing would not come. Joan's father had died the previous May, leaving her mother alone, but Michael would not allow her even to come for a visit. When Joan protested that *his* mother lived with them, he retorted: "That's different. This is her house." He went into a long discourse, angrily denouncing her mother as the source of Joan's problems. He brought up her past indiscretions and ridiculed her for not being able to make do with the five pounds he gave her for housekeeping, observing that his mother had, so she should be able to also. When Joan argued that Minnie had been able to get by because of her pension, he laughed and said, "You're mad, Joanie, stark raving mad!"

Soon this kind of emotional pressure began to affect Joan. For no apparent reason she would burst into tears and she felt totally unsure of herself. While he was sick she nursed him patiently, but as soon as he improved, she herself collapsed in exhaustion, at which point Michael insisted that she had to see a psychiatrist, the same one who had interested him in dreams. Leaving Oliver with Donny, he took her to London and arranged for her to see Philip Metman. He then quarrelled with her and left her in London without money. Eventually she borrowed her fare back to Dublin, beside herself with worry about Oliver. She had almost come to believe that he was right, that her outbursts of hysterical misery indicated schizophrenia. The psychiatrist concluded that her problems were not hers alone. To his mind Michael induced hysteria in some, though not all, people close to him. His manic-depressive behavior could bring out the worst as well as the best in Joan, in Evelyn, in his children, and even in his friends. The reason he was so quick to diagnose madness in others was that he lived constantly on the edge of it himself. He never consciously tried to cause anyone "mental anguish," he had told Nancy McCarthy years before; but somehow he always did. Perhaps he did not really give much thought to feelings because his mind was always working on a story, some new theory, or some absolute truth. When Joan returned to Dublin and reported the results of her sessions with the psychiatrists, Michael accused her of lying, then suggested a conspiracy or something more nefarious and finally went off to Limerick to visit Stan.

Traveller's Samples finally appeared in February. O'Connor had revised the volume so many times that even he hardly knew which version to expect. He had dedicated the book to John Kelleher because its original impetus had been tales gathered by the young American scholar during his travels in Cork; now none of those stories remained. O'Connor's restlessness comes out in the apparent lack of unity in *Traveller's Samples*, a collection of stories in fact resembling a commercial salesman's bag of samples. The first five, for example, are about children in the slums of a provincial Irish city. These are followed by the two Atheists' Club stories, three stories about domestic life in small towns, and four stories about the Irish in England during the war. As different as the groups are in subject matter, they are even more diverse in tone and treatment. The juvenile stories seem to fit the first-person narration quite naturally; their "confessional" tone is at once intimate and authentic, and their humor neither forced nor declamatory. In the two Atheists' Club stories the narrator compromises his reflectiveness with a slight trace of self-justification. The further O'Connor moves from the innocent "crimes" of children and the foibles of adolescents, the weaker his empathy; the closer he gets to the sins of adults, the more judgmental his tone. Third-person narration dominates the last seven stories of the volume, and the narrator's voice seems almost entirely alienated from the subject matter.

As he had done with his previous volumes, O'Connor constructed *Traveller's Samples* from recently written stories. The only exception was "First Confession," which he had written in the early thirties after hearing the tale from a girl in Belfast. On two counts it serves as an appropriate opening for the volume. In the first place, it was one of his most popular broadcast stories, having already received warm acclaim from Irish and English audiences. Many of the stories in this volume had been written originally for broadcast, deliberately forged, as O'Connor often said, with "the tone of a man's voice speaking." In the second place, "First Confession" contains a tacit recognition of guilt that seems to pervade the entire volume. O'Connor was fond of talking about the effect guilt could have on normally sane and intelligent people, how, like sickness or drink or financial pressure, it could break any man. Guilt was his own private torture, the private hell he created needlessly for himself; and his fiction would show signs of it more and more.

Michael's own greatest fear, perhaps aligned with this keen sense of guilt, was that he would let his mother down. The schoolboy in "The Idealist" eventually sees himself as a liar; the boy in "The Drunkard" gets uproariously drunk, though the guilt is thrust on the father; and the boy in "The Thief" exchanges his brother's gift for his own before his mother's tears shame him into realizing that there is no Santa Claus, only his mother trying to scrape something up from the housekeeping money. He also decides that his father is "mean and common and a drunkard," that his mother has to rely on *him* to save her from misery, and that she fears he will turn out like his father. For Michael, as for the narrator of these juvenile stories, the loss of his mother's approval would have been a death sentence.

Perhaps the juvenile stories appeal to people because in them O'Connor appears to have penetrated his own deepest emotions and because we all experience similar distress in the process of growing up. By touching chords in himself, O'Connor managed to touch chords common to all people. But when he mounted the Swiftian pulpit to "portray" people caught in one act of human weakness or another, he betrayed his natural instincts and antagonized the common Irish reader. O'Connor had in the past allowed his romanticism to run unchecked; the exaggeration that characterizes some of the early Revolution stories came to embarrass even him. What he failed to realize was that an exaggerated "realism" (the cold-storage locker of rational thought) only created another imbalance. That distinction he was so fond of carving between judgment and instinct worked best not when it created an exclusive dichotomy but when it set up dramatic tensions.

In the opening stories of *Traveller's Samples* the head and heart cooperate; in the last stories, however, the left hand does not always know what the right hand wants. "Old-Age Pensioners" and "The Sentry" are both appealing but soft stories. The loneliness of the pensioners of Caheragh is too poignant, the voice heard by the narrator too full of "self-pity like a voice from the dead. All the loneliness of the world was in it." The language of the story alone exaggerates the romanticism of pity: The effect is either "magical" or "misfortunate"; the contenders shout "derisively," yell "indignantly," pant "contemptuously," or grunt "gloomily." The priest in "The Sentry" is a living example to the formal British of the "personal element" of the Irish. O'Connor's priests all seem to represent one extreme or the other: tyrants like Father Ring (the ubiquitous priest of *Crab Apple Jelly* who appears again in "Masculine Principle") or lonely fellows like Father Michael, who lies to military officials to save a boy charged with deserting his sentry post and stealing the priest's onions. The lie, he tells a nun, was not a sin but an "act of charity." What is soft about such a story is that the characters represent principles rather than unique persons, making O'Connor's moral point of view too transparent.

On the other hand, the "dirty" stories of the volume are hardened by the facetious pose he adopts. The young Irish exiles in "Jerome" and "Darcy in the Land of Youth" blunder their "private lives" on the far side of Holyhead through a naivete so irremediable as to indicate that their mental age is frozen at eighteen. Love is represented in these stories as chivalric romance, and marriage as merely a matter of saving girls from themselves. The most alarming instance of this moral cynicism is "Masculine Principle," in which a glib narrator casually tells about a man in his town who marries a girl made pregnant by a married man, and thus wins the admiration of her father. The girl's instinctive response is to brood over her "weak character," to storm "hysterically," and finally to bolt to London in a gesture of despair. Her sisters are scandalized, her father is stupefied. The girl's old boyfriend, driven by a "sense of abstract justice," simply saves his money until he has enough for a house, then gets drunk enough to tell her that she can retrieve her "kid" from the foster home and "tell the whole bloody town to kiss [her] ass." That seems to be what O'Connor meant by "wearing your feather." The girl's father ends the story with the lament that had he exercised the same toughness thirty years before, he would be master of his house now. The narrator has so externalized the incident that it becomes cauterized into mere abstraction; what authenticity the original tale contained is lost to O'Connor's generalizing impulse.

A traveller's entertaining strangers with stories about the ridiculous antics of his friends back home is not so much confession as self-exposure. A provincial thinks everything about his home is either better than it is everywhere else, or worse. When the reviewer for the *Irish Times* suggested much the same sort of thing about the second half of *Traveller's Samples,* O'Connor was furious.[24] He sulked for days. Perhaps the reviewer, Edward Sheehy, was wrong in his belief that the failure of the adult stories stemmed from O'Connor's use of Corkery's peasant naturalism; perhaps he was wrong that O'Connor indulged mere incident and reduced his characters to puppets. However, he was right in suggesting that certain stylistic conventions, shared by other Irish writers besides O'Connor, do in fact disallow a fully human treatment of adult life. The juvenile stories contain "the ease, the naturalness, the easy intimacy of the born storyteller," Sheehy observes; but when O'Connor deals with "adult Irish life," he uses the voice of the testy, cynical storyteller so common in Irish pubs. The reviewer admits that in all of O'Connor's stories "the complexity, the unexpectedness, the variety of Irish life" is obvious, but that the *seanachie* convention obliterates any moral premise. Because the narrator seems to intend nothing more than a good laugh, Sheehy holds, there is little reason to believe that O'Connor intended anything but anecdote, "enliv-

ened with a parade of local quirks and oddities." A pub raconteur noisily holding center stage cannot be raised to the level of an "outlaw figure wandering
alone on the fringe of society." He may be lonely, but his voice is hardly a "lyric
cry in the face of destiny," the impression hardly that of one who sees "Eternity glaring."

   Since returning to Ireland, O'Connor had remained isolated from everyone. On one occasion he emerged from his self-imposed hibernation in Stillorgan and met Larry Morrow at Bewley's on Grafton Street to be interviewed for
The Bell.[25] About O'Connor's reputed distaste for public appearance, the Bellman observes that though doors are open to him in England and America, he
chooses to remain "in suburban Dublin, unclubable, almost unpubable, aloof
with the aloofness of a yogi." The two friends apparently sat down at about
"eleven o'clock on a wet Monday morning." O'Connor was pleased to receive
something other than censure; his old friend was surprised to find his subject
so agreeable. Morrow had come prepared; his tidy portrait smartly blends
background research, his own impressions, and O'Connor's lively, if only partially serious, responses to questions. A label-minded American, Morrow wrote,
might pinpoint Frank O'Connor as, variously, "The Voice, The Profile, or The
Pain." Of the three, he would have preferred to be known as the pain—"in almost anyone's neck." "Only a major prophet," the Bellman continues, "could
have achieved such reeking unpopularity in his own country. Few Irish writers
have managed to maintain at sullen heat, and for so long, such personal antipa-
thies against themselves: fewer still extracted such sweet-savoured bemuse-
ment from doing so." That summary gives a fair idea of O'Connor's reputation
in 1951.
   What O'Connor thought of himself would have been difficult to discover,
so Morrow simply checked *Who's Who* and found a defiant entry, which he described as being in the key of F-sharp major. There O'Connor ignored his detractors and listed his occupation as "Writer and journalist," adding "by profession, librarian." He made no mention of his part in the Civil War, but he
labored his reasons for resigning from the Abbey Theatre. As for his education,
O'Connor simply stated, "Christian Brothers, Cork."
   Morrow's description of Frank O'Connor in Dublin during Horse Show
week is striking. He writes that O'Connor could easily pass as "any distinguished non-Western visitor" in his customary "bawneen jacket and tussore
trousers" and blue tweed hat. His profile reminds Morrow off a "hieratic, dy-
nastic figure on an Egyptian fresco." Such an air of dignity becomes even more
pronounced on walks: "his head, flung back, fiercely-proud, flashes a startling
suggestion of the Yeats of thirty years ago—the silvered Arab steed freed from
its snaffle, sniffing the air, the lips peeled, domino-teeth in grin-grimace. And
in the darkness under the ostrich-egg brows chestnut eyes glow, burn, bra-
zier-bright."
   O'Connor carried himself majestically, but his voice was even more regal.
"To hear him appraise a Gothic arch or a tale of Turgenev's with what sounds
like 'Verray, verray lahvly!' . . . is to confuse the trilling, almost aspirated, West
Cork 'R' with the throat-clearings of the *haut monde* Parisien." V. S. Pritchett
was once asked about Frank O'Connor and replied, "Oh, yes! He's the one
with a coal-heaver's voice." Some Dublin wag reportedly described O'Connor's

voice as being "so low that barnacles cling to it *all* year round and that deep-sea divers in conversation with him have put aside their plummets and organ-tuners boomingly despaired of their diapasons."

The essence of O'Connor's discourses was often as remarkable as his voice was deep. When asked about his life, O'Connor skirted his current situation. "Pulling long and continually at his cigarette," he slowly sculpted a bit of apocryphal nonsense: "I was born reading. I don't know when I started to write, but I published—privately—a collected edition of my works at the age of twelve." Enterprising American blurb writers a few years later would swallow this personal revisionism and cast the legend in bronze. But the Bellman saw the "eyes roll and pop," the lips purse. He caught the twinkle in his friend's dark eyes and entered into O'Connor's ironic conspiracy.

When asked if he regarded himself as the *homme terrible* of Irish letters, O'Connor announced firmly: "I'm not 'terrible.' It's the Society that's 'terrible.' In a country like this, 'Pious without Enthusiasm,' like the epitaph I once came on in an English churchyard, without any standards of any sort—moral or intellectual—any normal human being appears 'terrible.' "[26] Fearing eavesdroppers, Morrow moved to politics and asked if the Irish novel might not spring from Partition or some such political issue. O'Connor grimaced, pronounced Irish politics dead, and then turned to the future of the Irish novel. He remembered that Osborn Bergin had once told him that the country had no novels in it, only some short stories. Then he said: "A great novel doesn't exist in a writer; it exists in a Society. To produce a novel you need a Society with an aristocracy—of intellect or birth."

In one broad, neatly balanced utterance O'Connor wiped out not only most of Irish fiction but most of his interviewer's line of questioning. There was nothing left but to pay the check and depart—O'Connor to contemplate how to extract fiction from his misbegotten country, and Larry Morrow to make some sense of their conversation. Both were successful. "Meet Frank O'Connor" stands out as the most reliable introduction to the writer as he was in the early 1950s. Just as some of O'Connor's own stories add a certain texture to the total picture of his life, so this eyewitness account lends a certain color. It was an authentic and unforced testimony, without American exaggeration of virtues or Irish elaboration of faults. O'Connor obviously enjoyed his moment in the spotlight, and his interviewer comes across as a living person and not a tape recorder. Not to be overlooked is the effect it had on O'Connor at the time: Appearing almost simultaneously with Edward Sheehy's ambiguous review in the *Irish Times*, Morrow's humane, light-spirited piece blew some much needed fresh and friendly air into O'Connor's claustrophobic, trouble-plagued life.

Michael returned to Stillorgan and tried to forget about those troubles. On April 20 *Traveller's Samples* was banned, but by that time O'Connor had become too calloused to care. On June 13 de Valera was returned to office, prompting Michael to joke with friends that "the old war-horse" had agreed to stand for election just to antagonize Frank O'Connor. Fortunately, his sequestered life at 86 Seafield Estate satisfied him for a time. Oliver, by then six, had taken up his father's occupation under the pseudonym Wily O'Connor; he also had his father's flair for music. Joan had induced Michael to help her with the gardening; the once bare yard now sported a few sweeps of grass, and three flower beds brightened the front of the house. Writing that summer to John and Helen Kelleher, Joan reported that at the back were "potatoes, peas, a little grass patch to sit on and one tight, bright flower bed, and my herb garden at the side, with thyme, sage, rosemary, mint, parsley, chives and horseradish, not to mention currant and gooseberry bushes, and dozens of varieties of cabbage cadged from the O'Faolain estate."[27]

Physically Michael was doing very well, having recovered from the flu and the penicillin reaction; and emotionally things between him and Joan had leveled out somewhat since her visit to the psychiatrist, though he still tried to hold a sort of Svengali sway over her. The primary bone of contention now was his feud with Evelyn. What disturbed him most was that his mother could not see her grandchildren; at eighty-six, she could not expect to live much longer, and she hated to be estranged from those she loved. He tried to vindicate himself by blaming Evelyn, but he had, after all, walked away. He had pushed Evelyn to the limit, but she had refused to break, and it was he, not she and the children, who had ended up on the streets. When he refused to pay the required child support, she retaliated by denying him access to the children. Joan argued that whatever his feelings about Evelyn were, he could not shirk his obligation to the children. "I've got to protect myself," he replied emphatically. In spite of it all, he managed to write two stories that spring, "First Love" and "The Saint."[28]

Michael and Joan ventured out for only a few social occasions that summer. At a dinner at Niall Montgomery's, where the special guest was Sidney Cox, a professor at Dartmouth College and a friend of Kelleher's, Michael talked with the man about F. Scott Fitzgerald for a time and later held forth in praise of James Stephens. Writing to Kelleher about the incident a few weeks later, Michael confessed that he had enjoyed the talk but would not have wanted to do it too often. "Dublin is simply full of the broken hearts of people who thought they were going to be allowed to talk freely of Kelleher and weren't." Michael could never hear enough good things about his friends, but even the slightest hint of criticism was too much. In that same letter he gave another account of the Dublin social circuit:

> We were dining at the French Legation the other night, and the eternal Celt turned up in the form of a pianist. There was an Italian Countess watching him with interest. He told her it was our duty to be pure. Restraining the impulse to call for her smelling salts she said with a motherly air 'Surely, Mr. T. we are put on earth to sin?' 'No,' he said indignantly, 'to follow Beauty and remain pure.' '*C'est dur*' she said with a wistful little smile at me.[29]

Nevertheless, O'Connor was busy planning two books. With Daniel Binchy, lately returned from Oxford, he was devising a memorial volume to Osborn Bergin. They reached a stumbling block when they realized that they would have to ask a number of people for essays and could not be sure what their response would be, so they contented themselves with long nights of gleeful recollections of the old philologist's eccentricities and dropped the idea of the book. Writing to Kelleher about the aborted effort, O'Connor said he was particularly fond of Binchy's description of the "Catholic ravens and wolves trying to convert the dying old man." O'Connor's second project was a book on the short story. "Provisionally," he confided to Kelleher, "I have decided that it can only be written by Russians, Americans and Irish, and that the reason is that in none of these has society set into a traditional pattern strong enough entirely to satisfy the individual." He admitted that the theory would take some working out.

He was writing to Kelleher the day after they had celebrated his mother's eighty-sixth birthday, but an even more momentous event occasioned the letter. While enjoying Donny's birthday cake, they "heard that the Abbey had been burned to the ground."[30] Michael's glee was undisguised. He and O'Faoláin inspected the site immediately and found to their disappointment "that the wretched building appeared to be intact. It was quite obvious to everybody," said O'Connor, only half facetiously, "that the burning was W. B.'s reply to the coming production of 'Player Queen' with Lennox Robinson as Septimus." The building was gutted, and Robinson's play canceled. His vendetta against the Abbey Board had gone on for so long, that this twist of circumstances must have seemed like retribution. But after seeing de Valera rise phoenixlike from the political ash heap, he could have expected the same from the Abbey.

In August Michael went to Limerick for a few days to see Stan about another excursion to France. He also visited Dermot in Ennis and went as far as Oranmore, near Galway, where Myles was spending the summer. Apparently, Charles Davidson was convinced that the boy was unruly, and suggested that Myles be sent to work somewhere. Ita, the maid at Strand Road, had always been fond of Myles, and it was she who volunteered her family's farm. With his head bent over a hoe, the lonely twelve-year-old boy did not notice his father's approach, but when the great voice burst forth in cheery salute, Myles was transformed. He buried his face in his father's tweed jacket, its tobacco smell filling his head with memories of rough affection. He was lonesome for Donny, he sobbed; he hated the thought of returning to Rockwell in the fall; he hated Arklow because of Davidson. Michael stayed with Myles only a short time— long enough to rekindle the boy's fading spirits but not so long as to antagonize Evelyn. He returned to Dublin resolved more than ever before to fight for the children in the courts, hopeless though he felt it was.

In September, while Michael was on holiday with Stan in France, Joan noticed that Donny was becoming more despondent about not seeing her grandchildren. When she found her weeping one afternoon, she decided to hire an automobile for a pleasure trip to the Wicklow hills. Driving back from town to pick up Donny and Oliver, Joan made an impromptu decision. She drove to Sandymount and, finding the children outside, convinced them, with little trouble, to come with her to see their beloved Gran. As yet they had little idea of what was happening, but when they returned from their great adventure, they were punished. Evelyn considered Joan's actions kidnaping and immediately notified her solicitors about the incident. When Michael returned and heard what had happened from Joan, he was livid.

Custody hearings began at the end of October at the Four Courts, where the children were brought in as witnesses for each session. Michael's mother learned that they were in court, and went to see the children against his wishes. She found them in the witnesses' room, but when they saw her, they moved back as if in terror. Though she begged them to acknowledge her, they did not make a move. Finally, Michael put his arm around her and took her from the room. As O'Connor recalled the incident years later, his mother stood rigid, her face suddenly ashen, and said something about turning children into devils. Michael argued that the children were only frightened of their mother, but to no avail. After Evelyn had accused them of kidnaping the children, Minnie had cut every picture of Evelyn from her photo album; after she left the courtroom, she never again spoke the names of her grandchildren, and to her son "it was clear that their photographs had been taken out of whatever album she carried in her mind."[31]

As the proceedings dragged on, the acrimony escalated. Evelyn's lawyers had gotten wind of negotiations between O'Connor and an American television producer for film rights to three of his stories, so she was asking for more alimony. Then, without warning or explanation, Evelyn backed down: She agreed to give Michael free access to the children, in effect dropping her suit. The judge advised Michael that the terms of the original separation order still prevailed, including his financial obligations.[32]

On a bleak December day Michael left the Four Courts in triumph, but he seemed neither joyful nor satisfied. He asked Joan, who had hired a car for the occasion, to take him for a drive into the country. Somewhere near Leixlip they stopped at a pub. Upon entering, Michael suddenly blurted: "That's it! We're moving." Joan argued that he had just won the right to see his children and that to leave would negate his victory, but he was adamant. He would send Donny to Cousin May for the time being and take Oliver with him to England, while Joan would stay behind for a few days to put the house up for sale, store their furniture, and sell what was left of his library. On December 10 he wrote to John Kelleher from Lyme Regis to explain the outcome of the hearings. They had been corresponding for three months about an invitation to teach the next summer at Harvard, so Kelleher was more or less familiar with the situation. Michael once again affirmed his enthusiasm about going to America; with the hearings behind him he felt he would be able to find comparative peace there. "Twice in two years I've had my home shot from under me. Ireland, the country I understand, I can't live in."

I V

While Michael was packing his bags to leave for Lyme Regis, Joan reminded him of what he had said when they left England: He could not write outside Ireland. He took the thrust, parried "What about Avignon?" and went on packing. Once he had made a decision—right or wrong—it was fixed. They both knew that bolting to England was impulsive and reckless, the result of a childish tantrum triggered by the courtroom scene between Donny and the children. The truth was that he needed someone to care for him and his mother; children were fine so long as they did not interfere with his work. He had fought for his children more out of principle than compassion; he had to prove that Evelyn was wrong in denying him access to them. Having proved his point, he fled the less heroic obligation of providing for their upkeep, even though the financial settlement was not much more than the five-pound weekly housekeeping check he had always given Evelyn. Being a long-distance

friend or part-time lover came easily to Michael; he conducted his personal relationships according to his writing schedule. It was not that he could not afford to make the support payments, but rather that he refused to be dictated to
by Evelyn about when and where he could see his children. The court order,
then, seemed like a straitjacket to him. When living in the same house with his
family, he took it for granted that he was being a good father and a good husband. He also took it for granted that such responsibilities would take little
time or energy from his writing. When Joan reminded him that he had once
said he could not work outside Ireland, she was tacitly reminding him that he
could write or not write anywhere.

Often in times of personal turmoil O'Connor turned to literary criticism,
but now he worked exclusively on stories. Since the publication of *Traveller's
Samples* he had been negotiating with Macmillan for a collected volume, tentatively titled "Stories, Old and New," which was to contain stories picked from
all of his previously published volumes.[33] For some reason, probably the relatively meagre sales of *The Common Chord* and *Traveller's Samples* in Great
Britain (the banning of those books had effectively halted sales in Ireland),
editors at Macmillan resisted the idea. O'Connor argued that Knopf had already agreed to publish such a volume, but that, unfortunately, was precisely
the problem; Macmillan had become increasingly disenchanted over the prior-
ity O'Connor had begun to give his other publishers. The incursions of Cuala,
Hale, and Fridberg, to say nothing of O'Connor's American publisher, had left
Macmillan somewhat disgruntled. With the publication of *Traveller's Samples*
his original contract with Macmillan had been fulfilled, though technically he
was to have written two more novels. Although they told A. D. Peters that
"retrospective editions" did not conform to the company's policy, it seemed
that "other considerations" were at work. When they reacted rather coldly to a
collection of juvenile stories, which was submitted in February, mere suspicions vanished; Frank O'Connor was no longer part of the Macmillan stable.[34]

At Lyme Regis he ruthlessly revised those stories about children in an
Irish slum neighborhood for a collection he called "Small Ones." They were
among the best things he had written in five or six years, and certainly among
the most popular, but what is remarkable is the extent to which he revised
them. In the past he had revised some stories between the time of initial publication and their appearance in book form. Before he ever sent a story to his
agent, he often put it through countless revisions. As an introductory note to
"Adventure" the editors of *Atlantic Monthly* quoted something O'Connor had
written to Harvey Breit of the *New York Times*:

> With me it's a difficulty of temperament. Mine is lyrical, explosive. I write
> a story with a feeling of slight regret for poor Shakespeare's lack of talent
> and wake up with a hangover that makes poteen look like cold water.
> Then having cursed life and forsworn literature, I start rewriting. If I can
> work up the Shakespearean mood often enough I may get it right in six
> revisions. If I don't I may have to rewrite it fifty times. This isn't exagger-
> ation.[35]

Indeed, it wasn't; "News for the Church," "The Holy Door," and "First Confession" all testify to his penchant for relentless revision. However, the older
he grew, the more obsessive the habit became. O'Faoláin always told him that

rewriting a story after publication was like recashing a canceled check, but the same stubborn romanticism that made him fight so viciously against injustice and stupidity in Ireland, championing one lost cause after another, also compelled him to seek the perfect story. He revised his stories for fear that he would fail as an artist, just as he lacerated himself about his explosive behavior for fear that he would fail as a human being. Yet the more he wrote, the less clearly he understood himself and others. It was as if that celebrated terror of the infinite spaces he claimed to share with Pascal was really a fear of his own imaginative silence; like two other Dublin malcontents, Swift and Beckett, O'Connor was groping for something to say in a world about which so little could be said.

Almost as if to prove his point about Avignon, Michael worked in Lyme Regis with great alacrity, revising old stories and beginning new ones. Before Christmas he finished two stories within a week, announcing after each one, "Poor Willie Shakespeare." The first of those stories, "Anchors," is a version of the Atheists' Club stories; it could have been subtitled "How Mick Dowling Lost His Faith." Actually, the story is a rather delicate handling of a father-son relationship. A young man trying to make up his mind about God expresses his doubts to his father on the way to Mass one Sunday. The wise old fellow cautions him sardonically not to confuse "anticlericalism, a view taken only by the most religious people," with atheism, a view also held by many religious people. The second story, "Adventure," is a rather unusual account of a disastrous triangle involving a young man and woman from Cork and a commercial traveler from England; the narrator is a "raw provincial boy" of twenty. A week before the young woman and the Englishman are to be married, he blows "his brains out in the hotel in Dunleary." Apparently, the Englishman's private life began at Holyhead, for he was married. His suicide has "blown to blazes" any chance the Corkman and the young woman might have had together. For the narrator, yearning for romance, it is adventure at last, though in a form he did not expect.

In January he continued in the same vein. In "A Sense of Responsibility," a mother adores one son, "a thundering blackguard," and despises the other, "a slow, quiet, conscientious chap."[36] Mick, the prodigal son, marries a "good-natured, stupid, sentimental woman" and is killed in what is said to be a "motoring accident" but is actually a suicide. (Suicide crops up quite regularly in stories written between 1950 and 1952.) The remaining son, Jack, does the respectable thing and takes care of his brother's widow; then, when his best friend takes ill and dies, he marries the girl they both had admired, though her passion and guilt never seemed to have much effect on him. When his mother has exhausted her means, he offers to take her in over the objections of his mother-in-law, "a woman of small silliness and excellent perception." (*Silly* was a term O'Connor often applied to women.) She reminds him of the responsibilities of marriage and of the need for privacy. "Marriage is a secret between two people," she tells him. "'Tis at an end when outsiders join in." (Michael had often said the same to Evelyn.) In fact, Jack's mother does nearly wreck his marriage; she knows his weaknesses in a way his wife does not. She understands, for instance, that her son has "remained temperamentally a bit of a bachelor, remote from the stresses of courtship and marriage"—"Perhaps it is only bachelors who can have a sense of responsibility." When his mother and his wife team up against him, he takes to boozing. His mother-in-law runs into trouble, and Jack once again rises to the cause and takes her in, his sense of responsiblity seemingly limitless. This time things turn out differently; his mother-in-law looks after him "as if he were a child," and sides with him in marital squabbles. When she dies, he takes complete charge of the funeral arrangements.

"A Sense of Responsibility" could have been a fine story but for the lack of an ending. Still, it crystallizes nearly every theme O'Connor had been dealing with since his affair with Joan drove the first wedge of disharmony into his marriage. As usual, he uses the primal distinction between prodigal and penitential to define character. And as in every domestic situation he had drawn since 1945, family life is seen as a place of tension, a battleground between the warring principles of male and female, judgment and instinct. What is so unusual about the story is the suggestion of a mother's divisiveness. Ever since he had been old enough to stand up to his father, Michael had given unqualified devotion to his mother; her loyalty to him had always seemed equally absolute. She had asked no questions and offered no opinions when he decided to live openly with Evelyn in Woodenbridge. After her husband died, she even found living in the same household with them agreeable, and when Michael asked the same of her with Joan, she offered no resistance.

It is possible that, despite her willingness to give him emotional support at all times, she directed tacit disapproval toward her son; it is possible that he conjectured this disapproval. Perhaps he harbored (and undoubtedly suppressed) resentment about her constant presence in his house. The pain of the disintegration of his marriage must have been aggravated by having the event occur before the very eyes of the one person in the world whose acceptance he coveted, the one person whose moral opinion he respected. Whatever moral guilt O'Connor felt about the failure of his marriage, about the misery of his children, or about the discomfort of his mother was caused by the realization that the effect of his actions did not fit his picture of himself as a decent fellow misunderstood by a terrible society and a demanding family.

The other story O'Connor wrote that January was "A Torrent Dammed," another in that line of small-town stories narrated by a faceless observer.[37] It begins with the cryptic generalization that city folks lack tenacity, from which the narrative proceeds in the manner of an example or parable. This one is about a city fellow who sets up a business in the narrator's town only to be defeated in the end by his failure to understand the "personal element" on which all small-town life rests. The main character is "not an unfeeling man"; but in the narrator's words, "like most people with an aim in life, he tended to take a subjective view of things." He sees the freak accident to the young woman he aims to marry, the daughter of the town's wealthiest citizen, as part of a cosmic conspiracy against him, so he takes up with someone else. "He was beginning to discover, as every man does sooner or later, that one woman is not enough. You need one for stability and another for sympathy." In the end he sells his business and moves to Dublin with another girl altogether. The narrator muses that apparently even two women are not enough; a third was needed for "inspiration." The rich girl recovers from the accident, which only serves to prove the narrator's original proposition: The city fellow should have stuck it out. Besides the rather obvious similarity between the ambitious pharmacist in the story and the author, a more telling theme may be found in the implication that love is a selfish contrivance and marriage a cynical arrangement of tradeoffs. Still, the narrator's facile generalizing destroys the moral clarity of "A Torrent Dammed."

The weather at Lyme Regis that winter was unusually mild. Joan and Michael took every opportunity to walk together on the Cobb or over the hill to Axminster or Collington, and in the evenings they read Jane Austen as a sort of literary pilgrimage. They faithfully recorded their dreams and discussed dream symbolism over coffee each morning. A borrowed gramophone poured out music constantly. Whenever Michael wanted to induce the proper mood for writing, he would generally put on Brahms's Barcarolle or an Irish air, such as "Slievenamon" or "Lark in the Clear Air." Joan, who had begun to write, too, preferred something like Clark's Trumpet Voluntary or Vivaldi's "The Four Seasons." When he was not trying to write, when he wished to have music for its own sake, Mozart and Beethoven dominated Michael's choice, spiced with Schubert and Hugo Wolf.

Just after Christmas Michael accepted invitations from Ellmann to teach at Northwestern during the spring and from Kelleher to teach at Harvard in the summer. On New Year's Day, 1952, he wrote to Dermot complaining that Evelyn had not allowed the children to send cards or even to accept his presents. "Apart from that I'd be aching for Dublin. Any little bit of regional passion I have is wasted on that damn place. Ba! after the next revolution."[38] As the month wore on, Michael's anticipation about the upcoming trip to the United States magnified his homesickness. The usual round of winter gastritis was complicated by internal pains, which Michael's hypochondriac mind diagnosed as cirrhosis of the liver, but Joan dismissed his fears as guilt about his heavy drinking during the custody hearings. When his mother came down with bronchitis, he decided to take her back to Cork where she could be cared for by his cousin May. Before returning to England, he stayed in Dublin for nearly a week undergoing extensive medical tests. Though nothing abnormal was found, he insisted on believing that something was seriously wrong.[39]

On this brief visit O'Connor was cornered by a reporter for the *Irish Times* in the lobby of the Shelbourne Hotel. The next day, in a story headlined "Author to Lecture at Harvard," he was quoted as confessing: "the prospect of teaching anybody anything terrifies me. I've never even been to school."[40] In response to a question about the banning of his latest book, he said that he had no intention of appealing. "This censorship is not a law," he told the reporter. "It is outlawry, and I will not be a party to the pretense that it is law." Even more remarkable than O'Connor's grumbling tone was the photo that accompanied the brief story. It shows him scowling at a newspaper, presumably frothing about the "bloody country," his face thin and blotchy, his graying hair tousled—the very portrait of a haggard, bitter man on the doorstep of exile.

Michael returned to Lyme Regis on February 11, worried about his mother, dissatisfied with the medical report, and anxious about a delayed visa. His scheduled sailing in the middle of March appeared to be in jeopardy, but every detail fell effortlessly into place. His visa was granted without question, Stan arranged for Joan, Oliver, and Michael's mother to live rent-free in a cottage on Achill Island, and all of a sudden Frank O'Connor was free to leave. On March 16, 1952, he sailed from Cobh on the S.S. *Samaria*, leaving, in Bill Naughton's words, a "great future scattered in the wake behind him."

17

The Visiting "Perfesser"

> *... his faults were too entangled in the sources of his life to be tampered with.*
>
> WALLACE STEGNER, *The Uneasy Chair*

WHATEVER destiny placed Michael O'Donovan on a ship leaving Cobh for America in March 1952 was a strange combination of circumstance and character. From the very first, Richard Ellmann and John Kelleher knew that this volcanic Irish writer was extraordinary. In 1951 Kelleher finally engineered an invitation from the Harvard University faculty for O'Connor to teach in the 1952 summer session. Ellmann then took the opportunity to have O'Connor invited to Northwestern University for the spring term. Two first-rate American scholars had respected Frank O'Connor enough to risk their personal reputations at their home institutions, but they had no way of knowing just how disjointed his knowledge was or how tangled his personal affairs had become. Michael was not so much going to the United States as he was fleeing England and Ireland. For the next two years, which would prove as disruptive as any time in his disruptive life, he was a visiting "perfesser."[1] He learned more than he taught, and he taught more than he had bargained for.

I

The extent of O'Connor's uneasiness about the prospect of teaching Irish literature to American university students was surpassed only by his sense of release from the strictures of the past. He left Ireland sick and destitute—the photograph in the *Irish Times* was the portrait of a man at the end of his rope. On board ship he did manage, however, to write a story, which was to be his last for six months. "Unapproved Route" turned out to be the most revealing story he would ever publish about his relationship with Joan.[2] O'Connor considered love a matter of wary diplomacy: "Between men and women, as between neighbouring states, there are approved roads which visitors must take. Others they take at their peril, no matter how high-minded their intentions may be." This tragedy of misalliance could have been titled "The Cottage Mystery," except that after Jim Hourigan, "a shambling, good-natured, high-spirited man, given to funny stories and inexplicable fits of morose anger," returns to Ireland, his young English lover marries someone else to escape the stigma of an illegitimate child. Hourigan is cast as a tramp who humiliates a decent girl; in a provincial English town a schoolmistress with a child and no husband would be unthinkable, but a child put away from its mother "is a question that never answers itself." The young woman, with the Shakespearean name of Rosalind, is described as a "good-looking girl with a fat and rather sullen face." She is also an excellent cook—"cooking being a form of activity associated with love-making." Her love for the Irish Don Juan is explained as "woman's vanity, the mainspring of her character." In the end she goes back again to Hourigan, and Frankie, the decent man who had rescued her, realizes "with a touch of bitterness that there are certain forms of magnanimity which are all very well between men but are misplaced in dealing with women." The story's ending is so tidy that it is as if O'Connor had written it in place of an acceptable solution to his own domestic predicament.

Frank O'Connor disembarked in New York a relatively free man. He was met by Don Congdon of the Harold Matson Agency (A. D. Peters's American representative) who had arranged for him to meet his editors at Knopf. O'Connor carried with him the typescript of the collected stories that Macmillan had rejected; he signed a contract before leaving New York for Chicago the next day. There he was met by Dick and Mary Ellmann with whom he stayed until a room became available in the Greenwood Inn close to the Northwestern campus. He was eager to begin teaching but ignorant about such details as schedules, examinations, and papers.

However, he soon found teaching two courses even more difficult than he had anticipated. A lecture was not like a twelve-hundred-word review tossed off with a flash of personal insight; ideas and facts had to fit together day in and day out; connections had to be made over and over again. He was a writer, not a scholar, and he approached literature as the product of a fraternity of writers, not as a body of theoretical knowledge. As uneven as his commentary on Irish writing seemed to students accustomed to scholarly objectivity, it came from a special vantage point. Irish literature was real to him, not something to be "examined" at a safe distance. His ideas were more personal than literary, as malicious as they were penetrating. He called O'Casey "Johnny Wet Eyes," for instance. The course, he wrote to Kelleher, was primarily Yeats; Joyce to his mind was the negation or antithesis of Yeats.[3] One young man argued continually with O'Connor, suggesting that he had not read O'Casey and was slandering Joyce. At the end of the term he discovered the heckler had failed the course. When he inquired of his assistant, he learned that this particular student made it a practice to fail any course in which he disliked the professor. O'Connor raised his mark to A—, noting that in a "pragmatic society one must be prepared to compromise."

Being Irish, O'Connor preferred to read between the lines, but Americans said what they thought, and meant what they said. Michael adjusted to this personable impersonality; his magnetism carried the day, in class and out. He found Evanston to be a large and handsome town, well-endowed with fine houses and greenery and a splendid lakefront, but he found daily walks impossible—there were no footpaths like the Marina in Cork or uninterrupted promenades by the water as he had known in Dublin. There were too many stoplights and too few "public facilities" to suit his style. But he still managed to take long Sunday-morning strolls with Fred Faverty of the English Department. He often spent evenings at the Ellmann home, where Mary went out of her way to serve his favorite dishes. He was especially taken by Dick's father, a lawyer with a wealth of stories. And from time to time he was also the guest of Walter Scott, a professor of speech, and his wife. Michael basked in the attention American universities give to visiting writers. On one occasion that spring, however, Frank O'Connor had to share the limelight. Dylan Thomas came to town for a public appearance; after the reading the Ellmanns gave a small party for him. It was a pleasant evening, not at all as sensational as some had feared or hoped. Dylan Thomas was on his best behavior, got only tolerably drunk, made no passes at any of the women present, and generally charmed everyone. O'Connor was in grand style himself. A slight competitive edge between the two eminent writers developed as they tossed quotations back and forth, Welsh versus Irish. Actually, the two hit it off quite well and kept the evening as instructive as it was sociable. Scott listened to their magnificent voices pouring forth poetry and regretted the lack of a tape recorder.

The demands of teaching once again prevented O'Connor from writing much. It was all he could do to correct proofs of the collected edition and write a brief foreword explaining his choices. There is something poignant in his admission that the chance to gather his best stories gives a writer the same glow he feels when his first good story is published. "It is something for which he has secretly always longed—the Perfect Book; the book he does not feel he really must apologize for before giving it to a friend; the book which sums up all that he has ever wished to be or do from the days when he was a penniless dreamy youngster wandering the streets of a provincial town."[4] Because he sought perfection he "included nothing from [his] first book," embarrassed perhaps by the youthful manner of those stories. For the same reason, he included five new stories and revised most of the others. Commenting about "The Luceys," a story with which he had struggled for twenty years, he admits that he is not certain that even "this tussle is our last." The words "our last" fill him with gloom. "Great cracks suddenly begin to appear across the smooth façade of my proofs . . . and my Perfect Book begins to dwindle to the proportions of Just Another Book."

As soon as the term ended, O'Connor left Evanston for Hollywood. Jerry Devine, a television producer with whom he had been negotiating for months about filming three stories, had offered to pay his expenses. Michael wrote to Kelleher that he dreaded the thought of a cross-country trek, but he wanted to see California, if only to be able to walk up to Flann O'Brien (alias Myles na gCopaleen) when he returned to Dublin and say, "You see, Myles, I KNOW America!"* To say that, he would have to visit Los Angeles. Michael was deathly afraid of flying, so he took the train. Even though railway travel was more congenial in those days, Michael suffered unmercifully. Excitement and fancy cooking had conspired to ignite his chronic dyspepsia, and the loneliness of the trip made matters worse.

He returned at last to Boston on June 16, exhausted and irritable. He soon finished "The Little Mother" and sent it off to *The New Yorker* without revision, but neither this nor the hospitality of John and Helen Kelleher could soothe him. When specialists at the Harvard Medical School found no evidence of cirrhosis or any other physical cause for his constant ill health, he raged about modern medical voodoo for a while but eventually resigned himself to

---

* One of the pseudonyms of Brian O'Nolan, longtime nemesis of O'Connor. As Myles na gCopaleen he wrote the famous "Cruiskeen Lawn" column for the *Irish Times*. As Flann O'Brien he wrote such novels as *At Swim-Two-Birds* (1939), *The Hard Life* (1961), *The Dalkey Archive* (1964), and *The Third Policeman* (1967).

uncertainty. He stayed with the Kellehers until July 1, then took a room at Lowell House in Cambridge for the remainder of the summer term.

At Harvard he taught the two courses he had done at Northwestern: Irish literature and an advanced writing seminar. The summer term was compressed, so O'Connor faced the grind of daily lectures. Once again his views on Joyce stirred some hostility.[5] In fact, after his first lecture on Joyce members of the class held a protest meeting. One night a friend of his even heard one of the campus security police groaning: "That damn fellow O'Connor is attacking Joyce. What does he know about Joyce?" A few days later he opened the door of Lamont Library, where his lectures were given, and heard a young woman passionately addressing a group of students on the steps: "I don't care what he says about Deirdre. I say she was a bitch." He said nothing at the time but did go out of his way to find out the woman's name. At a party that weekend he met her again. Though he spent most of the evening playing devil's advocate to a graduate student wrapped up in W. H. Auden, he watched her out of the corner of his eye. Not being a driver, he was at the mercy of other people to chauffeur him about, normally an irritating dependency but on this occasion a welcome opportunity. When the party began breaking up, he asked the woman for a ride and then told her to take everyone else in the car home first. He was hungry, he said, and wouldn't like to eat alone. That evening she told him that she had come to Harvard to enroll in his course after reading "The Saint" in *Mademoiselle*. Michael saw a good deal of Harriet Rich for the remainder of the summer.

O'Connor took teaching seriously. Lacking university training, he attached an eminence to it that far exceeded the reality. He approached each lecture as a night at the Abbey, a performance complete in itself. As one observer said, "He could never toss off a course of lectures in the way the professionals do." Instead he was forced to spend hours in preparation, keeping barely a jump ahead of his class. For the students this meant the transmission of fresh ideas, firsthand and alive; it meant witnessing the "effort of a man of extraordinary insight, honesty and wisdom to understand matters of passionate concern to himself." Richard Gill, a young economics instructor and junior dean, not only enrolled in the writing seminar but sat in occasionally on the lectures. He recalls: "Standing before a lecture audience with his silver-grey hair, his dark eyebrows, his eyes peering through black-rimmed glasses that always looked too small for the strong, masculine face, he was an arresting figure. When he spoke, the response was immediate, for his voice was most impressive."[6]

Much to the chagrin of some of the Harvard faculty, O'Connor became something of a hero that summer. His public lectures were packed. He was invited to speak to various Irish organizations in the Boston area; he even made a broadcast sponsored by the Jesuits. Among the students he was the subject of animated conversation; some hated him, most loved him, but few were indifferent to him. His physical appearance alone invited caricature. All summer he wore the same searsucker suit, the trousers of which hung precariously on his slim hips. In almost any cafe or bar in Cambridge that summer one could see the spectacle of a student entertaining friends with his imitation of the Irish visitor: head thrown back, rolling his *r*'s, hitching his trousers, and uttering *obiter dicta* about Joyce or Irish priests. O'Connor used two pairs of glasses, one for normal use, the other for reading. In class, students found great amusement in watching him confuse the two. Of course, as a guest in America O'Connor was also in great demand socially, and he accepted more invitations than he refused. One day he came to class hungover from a night of drinking, talking, and singing. He announced that instead of lecturing he would read poetry; in this way he transformed a potential disaster into a magical session. Such diversions, tangents, and frivolous improvisations kept his class alive to the unexpected.

If O'Connor's lectures were spellbinding, then his writing seminar was sheer torture. In the past this seminar had been conducted by Albert Guérard and Archibald MacLeish, both of whom gave students a free rein. O'Connor, on the other hand, had rather definite ideas about the short-story form. Members of the class had been selected on the basis of previous work, so he knew what their abilities were. When O'Connor required that each student submit story ideas to the class for approval before actually beginning to write, most of them recoiled in disappointment; after all, they considered themselves writers already, and this exercise seemed more appropriate for beginners. But O'Connor held his ground. They would do it his way. He hammered away at the distinction between theme and treatment. He told them that to write a story, they had to produce a theme in three or four lines. He coerced and cajoled these aspiring writers to forget fine phrases, intricate plots, symbolism; he told them to locate some incident, some moment of crisis, that changed a human being. He insisted that they eliminate all eccentricity of character, all particularity of setting. At first the resistance to his dogmatism was fierce, particularly among the older students who felt extremely vulnerable to the public scrutiny given each four-line theme. But three times a week the seminar met, and one by one students began producing ideas that took O'Connor's breath away, at which point, one student would later recall, "even the most improbable of his students would be able to see a faint line extending all the way from himself to the greatest glories of literature. What had been a private, almost despairing act became for that student at that moment an exciting reality."[7]

That student, Richard Gill, was one who produced a suitable theme almost immediately. When O'Connor pronounced it "absolutely perfect," the entire class took heart. They looked forward to the finished product. A week later he read it aloud, and as he did, O'Connor's heart began to sink. He remained silent as the class shredded the story. Gill was crushed. For O'Connor it was the signal to begin concentrating on treatment. He suggested that they get "black on white" to see what the story looked like, then back away and try it another way. He advised them to keep working at it, even if they had to listen to music to generate the right mood. Richard Gill reckoned that what O'Connor was doing was giving them "some sense of how to proceed when the impulse governing the story was not so powerful as to sweep everything before it." O'Connor's critical theories about the short story may not always have matched what he wrote himself, but his practical suggestions to his students were absolutely consistent with the way he wrote. His journals are full of four-line "themes" followed by rough sketches of one or two pages and then version after version of the same story with different characters, different narrative angles, different dialogue. The problem was that O'Connor was the sort of person who seized on some flash point instinctively; and since he was naturally more enthusiastic than disciplined, art meant a tightening of the rein, a discipline closing inward. People like Richard Gill, however, were naturally disciplined and controlled, and art for them had to be an exploding process, a freeing outward. On the next to last day of the seminar Gill returned with his story rewritten. Unlike many of the other students, who often went to coffee with O'Connor after class, Gill had had little to do with him. Still, there existed some sort of identification, most likely because of his voice, a basso profundo even deeper than O'Connor's. When Gill finished reading the story, the entire class cheered, not waiting for O'Connor, who sat spellbound. He rose dramatically, shook Gill's hand, and dismissed the class. That afternoon the two men went to coffee together.

Such obviously sincere interest in the work of his students meant that he had little time or energy left for his own. Actually, he seldom wrote much in the summer, preferring to "gather material" and relax outdoors. The sweltering heat and humidity of Boston prevented relaxation. He smoked steadily, though in concession to Harriet's concern for his health he began using Dunhill cigarette holders to cut the nicotine. On weekends she drove him to the Berkshires or the Cape beaches to escape the heat. At the end of July they went to New York for a CBS television talk on Turgenev's *Sportsman's Sketches,* which O'Connor still believed the finest book of stories ever written.

On August 18 *The Stories of Frank O'Connor* appeared. Publicity by Knopf for the new book was extensive, though not extravagant considering his already strong reputation in the United States. A handsome picture of the author standing in an idyllic wood accompanied a lead review in the *New York Times Book Review.* O'Faoláin wrote to congratulate his old friend: "By God (the other God) when I saw it I said, 'Maybe that fella is a writer after all.' "[8] He also sent regards to Stan, who had flown across for an extended holiday with Michael and John Kelleher. The trip cost Stan well over £250 at a time when his business could hardly support it. O'Faoláin had tried to dissuade him from going, but he knew that to Stan "the ideal, the HEAVENLY thing, would be to be cycling down the Rhone with you, or to be touring Ireland with John, or to be anywhere at all with both of you." Stan stayed at the home of John and Helen Kelleher, who treated him royally with sight-seeing tours of New England and special dinner parties for him and Michael. On one occasion they ventured south to Washington, D.C., Williamsburg, and the Skyline Drive in Virginia. On two weekends Harriet drove Stan and Michael to the Cape.

As fond as Michael was of Harriet, he tried to encourage something between her and Stan; he later admitted to her that he had hoped to guarantee her presence by having her marry Stan. Once again he was scripting the lives of other people to suit his own needs. Harriet, for her part, was taken with Stan, but only as one loves a jolly uncle. It was Michael she loved. Michael had been entirely open with her, never hedging on his moral obligation to Joan. He had always been fond of Joan, but it was a feeling more like sympathy than love. In addition, there was his mother, who had come to love Joan as a daughter. Of greater significance was his own sense of guilt: He had let his mother down once, he believed, by the failure of his marriage; while she lived, he could never let her down again.

As soon as classes ended at Harvard, Kelleher drove Michael and Stan up to Breadloaf for the writers' conference, where Michael was to be the guest speaker on August 23. As they were crossing Vermont, somewhere beyond White River Junction, Michael suddenly gave an imperious command: "Stop at the nearest pub." When John informed him that in rural Vermont there was no such thing, he responded with the verdict "Barbarism!" The next day John took them to Ripton, near Breadloaf, to meet Robert Frost. Richard Wilbur, the poet, was with Frost that morning and found him worried about what poem he should "say" for Mr. O'Connor. He needn't have worried. Michael, in his most Yeatsian cadence, introduced the subject: "Ah, that poem of yours, Mr. Frost, 'Stopping by Woods on a Snowy Evening.' " He began to recite it. Frost interrupted, "No, no, no! That's not how you say it!" and began his own rendition, which Michael interrupted with "No, no, Mr. Frost! You're ruining your own poem." Later, the two posed for Stan's camera.

From Breadloaf Kelleher drove Michael and Stan to New York. Michael's ship was scheduled to sail on September 4; Stan was to fly back to Ireland later. Harriet arrived in time to see Michael off. Among other people at the on-board party prior to sailing were Horace Reynolds, the critic who had given O'Connor such a splendid review that summer, Harvey Breit of the *New York Times*, Cyrilly Abels of *Mademoiselle*, Gus Lobrano from *The New Yorker*, William Cole from Knopf, and Don Congdon. O'Connor had already accepted an invitation from the English Department at Northwestern to return the following spring, and from all indications the same courtesy would be extended by Harvard as well. Harriet had already made quite clear her position regarding Stan, but the exact nature of her feelings for Michael were still ambiguous. He was returning to Joan; that much was clear. But she would see him again in a few months; that also was certain. Her personal life had been profoundly changed over the course of the summer, but she was young enough to be patient.

I I

Joan, who had been in England making arrangements for housing, hired a car in Dublin and drove south to meet the boat. Though the tone of Michael's letters had changed over the summer, she had no reason to feel anything but happy anticipation. Their reunion was uncomfortable. He gave her a necklace of pounded brass, made by a student at Northwestern with whom he had had a brief affair—one that he had candidly mentioned in letters to Joan. He had no gift for his mother, however, and Joan chided him that such thoughtlessness would hurt the old woman. Stung by guilt, he then asked for money, enough, he added, to cable the States. "Harriet?" Joan shot back. "Yes," he answered, vexed but not entirely surprised. When he returned, she asked what he had done with the thousands he had earned in America. "I left it all with Harriet," he said coldly; then, after a thinking pause, added, "to protect myself from Evelyn."

Michael's mother was overjoyed to see him, but when he handed her the bottle of Irish whiskey he had just bought for her, she was so crushed that she simply handed it back to him. Michael and Joan spent the night at the Victoria Hotel in Cork before driving on to Limerick. On the way Michael became more surly and detached as she explained about the house she had rented. He not only thought it too expensive (at eight pounds per week) but was even more disturbed that they could not have it immediately. She explained that it was the best she could do, and because he had indicated that he wanted to spend time in Ireland first, she had fixed a later date to move in. At the time they reached Stan's house, a full-blown row had already taken shape. Joan slammed the car door and went off in search of "licensed premises." Michael stormed into Stan's kitchen and sat down with the bottle of whiskey. Stan kept his composure and his sobriety; a good thing, for by the time Joan had come back, he had two very drunk people to pour into bed. The next day Michael wrote to Kelleher: "Everything is buggered up with us; all Joan's expectations of flats have collapsed and I might just as well have stayed in America until October."[9]

Three weeks later they were still feuding, but by this time they had settled in a temporary flat in Kensington, waiting for the house in Hertfordshire to become available. Michael's mother remained in Cork and Oliver in Achill. Michael was especially vexed by the delay because it kept him separated from his mother, whose health had so deteriorated over the summer that she now required constant attention. Finally, two weeks into October, they moved into High Chimneys in the hamlet of Cholesbury. He described the house in a letter to Kelleher: "two Tudor cottages knocked together, and now engaged in knocking me to pieces, with low lintels, and high chimneys as advertised, though it's only when you see what a downdraft can do that you realize they have to be high. It's better than London anyway."[10] In the same letter he confessed that he was homesick for Dublin, especially after discovering that an old friend and fellow writer, Honor Tracy, lived only a few miles away. However, the thought of Evelyn, from whom he was once again withholding maintenance payments, kept him in Cholesbury, four miles from Chesham where he walked regularly to post letters to Harriet.

Shortly after they moved into High Chimneys, Michael sent Joan to Ireland for his mother, and though he would have preferred Oliver to stay in Achill, Joan brought him back as well. By November Donny's condition had worsened; she was completely bedridden and suffering greatly. A doctor from Chesham was called in, but he offered small hope. He left morphine with Joan in case the old woman's pain became unbearable. Night after night Joan kept a fire alive in Donny's room and did what little she could to make her comfortable. In the afternoon of November 10 she asked Joan for the morphine. Before she went to sleep she whispered, "I love you." She died a few hours later in Joan's arms. Michael sat in a chair near the bed, convulsed in tears; the one anchor of his life was gone.

The next day they began the journey back to Ireland, in the manner of that taken in "The Long Road to Ummera." When they arrived at Dun Laoghaire, there was no hearse to meet them. Michael, who was already distraught, became hysterical. Joan telephoned Seán O'Faoláin, who took over the details with the efficiency of an ordnance officer, but the scene was still chaotic. Liadain had been brought by Evelyn, but memories of the courtroom incident a year before seemed to keep her from dashing to her father. She wept and crossed herself constantly; unable to bring herself to put on the coffin the violets she had been clutching all morning, she gave them to her father instead. Oliver took his cue from her and crossed himself too. Joan had all she could do in her efforts at comforting Michael. From Dun Laoghaire the body was taken to Kingsbridge Station for transportation to Cork. Myles met them at

Thurles accompanied by Stan Stewart. In Cork last-minute details for the burial were handled by Seán O'Faoláin, while arrangements for a Requiem Mass at the Dominican chapel on Sand Quay were made by the sisters of the convent school where, as an orphan girl, Mary Teresa O'Connor had once lived.

When it was all over, Michael and Joan took the train with Stan to Limerick. On the way Myles begged not to be sent back to Rockwell. Michael was too deep in his own grief to hear, but Stan and Joan noticed in the boy's voice a strange urgency. The next day, Michael talked with his son for the first time in nearly a year. The tale he heard chilled him to the bone, and Michael's moral outrage momentarily overshadowed his bereavement. He telephoned Evelyn, who agreed to let Myles return with him to England, providing he resume paying the child support. He was too upset to argue. Two days later Michael returned to England with Joan and two sons.

The morning after the return to High Chimneys he wrote to John Kelleher. "I haven't been human for a week; I don't feel it now," Michael began. He acknowledged that his mother probably could not have been "spared through the winter," but he still blamed himself for not recognizing the exact nature of her illness, for allowing her to suffer "unnecessarily," for not doing "this or that for her." Then he observes that it

> was ironic and at the same time beautiful that everything she cared most for came right at the end. She had never referred to the children after they cut her in court, but I felt that Myles at least must be at the funeral; it didn't seem fair to the child to shoulder fresh guilt on him. . . . Now Myles is sleeping in the bed in which she died, and the problems of making him happy take away some of the strain of problems that will never be solved.[11]

The simple act of writing this letter made Michael ill.

He tried to escape into his writing. He struggled to complete a script of "Masculine Principle" for the American producer who had already advanced him $1,000. He began revising stories for a second collected edition for Knopf. Every day he walked the four miles to Chesham, not only to post the mail but to get out of the house. Fortunately, his correspondence was full and lively during these few months. A. E. Coppard, whose stories Michael had so enthusiastically promoted on the BBC, wrote asking if they could meet. There were letters, too, from Joyce Cary and C. P. Snow, whose novels O'Connor had expressed substantial admiration for in his reviews for the *Evening News*. Then Val Mulkerns, a young woman whose novel *A Time Outworn* O'Connor had praised lavishly in an American fashion magazine, wrote from Ireland seeking his advice. He replied that O'Faoláin—"the one great writer you've got there"—would be of more help in matters of publishing strategy. He commended her work in *The Bell* and then cautioned her about Dublin: "It's grand if you have the hide of a rhinoceros." Then, in a fatherly manner, he reminded her that genius generally counted for less than determination when it came to writing. "Grip, as old Lady Gregory used to say, is a good dog, but Holdfast is a better."[12]

That same week he wrote a moving letter to Dermot Foley, thanking him for his help and rejecting his advice to write about something besides Ireland.

It's only in a place where one has lived for the greater part of one's life that one can have the friends who become part of one's inspiration. I don't mean who suggest subjects for stories—most of my pals don't even notice them; I mean, who are the sort of thing which is ultimately one's reason for writing stories at all. I write very little about the constricted sort of life you very properly criticize; Sean does it more than I, because Sean is that sort of objective, socially-conscious, critical writer.

At the end of the letter Michael mentioned that Joan still wished he had not sold the house in Stillorgan: "I think she pines for Dublin even more than I do."[13]

Joan, meanwhile, had taken it upon herself to teach Myles to read. The boy was not exactly illiterate, but he was decidedly behind his English class- mates. Having failed tests in the grammar school at Amersham, he had been sent to a secondary modern school (with a vocational orientation) in Chesham. Realizing that he needed no more embarrassment or pressure, Joan worked with him in a most casual way and thus turned the "tough guy" into an avid reader. For the first time, Myles was not a problem in school, perhaps because his father was genuinely attentive to him. The severity of the Rockwell trauma forced Michael for once to consider someone other than himself. Al- though his stories display an incredible sensitivity to the lives of other people, to the suffering, the desires, the emotional ambiguities of women, children, and old folks, that was his Art. And though he was certainly capable of great generosity toward such people as Patrick Kavanagh, and capable, too, of rising to the defense of the Tailor, Lennox Robinson, or the neighborhood dog sur- rounded by stick-wielding kids, that was Chivalry. However, his almost naive self-absorption often led to behavior many people regarded as selfish. For a time, though, he was undeniably unselfish toward Myles, and it probably saved his own life by keeping him from plunging into the abyss of despair.

At Christmas Evelyn made it very clear to O'Faoláin that she wanted to proceed with a formal divorce action in Britain. She refused to write to Michael except through her solicitors, so Seán had to act as a go-between. In January her solicitors filed for divorce on grounds of Michael's adultery with Joan, but owing to a confusion about his domicile, the case was temporarily withdrawn from the court lists. O'Faoláin heard by telephone from Evelyn and wrote at once to Michael: "She swears she is just as madly anxious to get the thing through as you are, and keeps on pressing her blokes for God's sake to get on with it. (Does she want to remarry?)"[14] In fact, she did.

Dermot Foley mentioned in his Christmas letter that he would be visiting London in February and wanted to see Joan and Michael. It happened that they would be in London the day he planned to arrive. Michael wrote suggest- ing they meet at Claridges and begging him to bring some Irish butter with him. Dermot was not surprised at the request for butter, but he had not known the America trip had been so fruitful as to allow Michael to stay at Claridges. Curious, he followed instructions and went directly from Euston to the plush London hotel. Joan met him in the lobby and quickly satisfied his curiosity. They were the guests of John Ford and Lord Killanin, who were interested in using "Majesty of the Law" in a film. Dermot and Joan waited in one part of the huge suite while the three men talked about the film. Dermot still had with him a hefty package of Irish butter. Ford suddenly noticed the time and beck-oned Dermot and Joan to join them. Then Lord Killanin decided that dinner for all of them could be served in the suite. Dermot squirmed nervously through-out the entire evening; he was anxious about the butter hidden beneath his chair but also curious about Michael's strange manner: He seemed somehow disoriented.

Michael was indeed adrift. His mother's death had left him without his one consistent point of reference, while Evelyn's legal maneuverings kept the wounds of his marriage open and magnified his uneasiness about marrying Joan. There was also the constant and invisible presence of Harriet; almost daily her letters came, intensifying the tension between Michael and Joan. When Michael broke his promise to her not to answer them, Joan made no ef-fort to mask her indignation. He scornfully chided her, "Be human, Joany, be human!" It was what he often would say when forcing her to swallow her pain or jealousy. Whatever it was he wanted, she did not know anymore; but it was becoming obvious that it did not involve her.

Actually, the only thing Michael wanted was freedom to write. At times when life seemed desolate, he clung to the consolation of art. Between Christmas and the middle of March O'Connor wrote two of his finest essays, both of which affirm his sense of artistic immortality. "And It's a Lonely, Per-sonal Art" defines the short story as "the lyric cry in the face of human des-tiny" and the storyteller as a tramp standing "somewhere on the outskirts of society, less interested in its famous and typical figures than in the lonely and gnarled and obscure individuals of Winesburg, Ohio, and Dublin, Ireland."[15] As always in his literary opinions, O'Connor gravitated to the personal charac-ter of the artist. The second essay, "A Lyric Voice in the Irish Theatre," also appeared on the front page of the *New York Times Book Review*.[16] Ostensibly a review of the newly published *Collected Plays*, it was essentially a tribute to W. B. Yeats, whom O'Connor called a "master of the one-act play"; that genre, he wrote, was "nearly always lyrical in inspiration; it dealt with the moment of revelation rather than with the painful evolution of character and incident." Since that definition also matches O'Connor's theory of the short story, it sig-nals a virtual identification of himself as an artist with his hero. Thus, by call-ing attention once again to the decline of the Abbey, O'Connor seems to be vindicating himself as well as Yeats:

> I mourn for that most lonely thing; and yet God's will be done:
> I knew a phoenix in my youth, so let them have their day.

O'Connor's essay is a reminder that the voice of genius is mute only when ig-nored.

In March Michael was obliged to return continually to London on legal matters. The house on Seafield Crescent had finally been sold, and his solici-tors warned him that Evelyn could lay claim to the proceeds. In order to con-ceal his assets, Michael therefore purchased a house in Joan's name. In addi-tion, he had to file various affidavits verifying domicile and financial status, as well as proof of proper schooling for Myles. At the final divorce hearing a great deal of damning testimony was given regarding the shameful life of Michael O'Donovan. Evelyn, of course, claimed absolute fidelity to her unfaithful hus-band. After the hearing Michael commented to Joan on how miserable Evelyn looked, and suggested that they take her for a drink. She balked, and once again he said, "Be human, Joany!" A decree nisi was granted on March 12, 1953. Evelyn was awarded custody of Liadain and Owen, with maintenance set at £150 per annum for each child, special provisions were granted allowing Myles to stay with his father. The decree absolute was issued on April 27.

I I I

Two days after the divorce hearing Joan hired a car and drove Michael to Southampton where he was to sail a second time for America to teach. She had wanted him to stay long enough to help with the move to Primrose Hill, the house he had purchased in Nash, near Bletchley, Buckinghamshire, but he was adamant about leaving as soon as possible. On the way to the boat he posted a quick letter to Dermot announcing that he was single again but nonetheless broke, and adding, "remember me in your prayers," a supplication Dermot thought rather out of character. This sailing marked the falling of another curtain, and Michael sighed in relief. With the death of his mother and the divorce from Evelyn, he was almost a free man, free from nine years of tension and uncertainty. Only Joan stood between him and whatever his future would be.

When he landed in New York, O'Connor was carrying a satchel full of manuscripts: four stories for Gus Lobrano at *The New Yorker,* two essays for Harvey Breit at the *New York Times,* and scripts for two television producers. After delivering his winter's work to his American agent Don Congdon, he met Harriet at the Barbizon Plaza Hotel where she was staying. They had planned to spend a day or two in New York and then drive to Boston to see the Kellehers, but something ignited a disagreement. Their shouting match ended on the sidewalk in front of the hotel with Harriet telling him in no uncertain terms that she never wanted to see him again. He went on to Chicago by train, alone. In the confusion he mislaid one of his bags, the one containing a nearly completed manuscript of his second collected edition. Fortunately, the bag turned up in Evanston a few days later and the task of revising those stories again was thus averted.

Socially, Michael was adrift in Evanston that spring because the Ellmanns were in Dublin on a fellowship for which O'Connor had written a letter of recommendation. Richard Ellmann had become, by his own admission, obsessed by Joyce. He and Kelleher and O'Connor carried on a lively dispute about Joyce through the mails, but that did little to soothe Michael in Evanston. Some friends he had made the year before were there—Fred Faverty for long walks and the bookseller Fred Roscoe with a new convertible ideal for long rides; but with the Ellmanns absent, Michael's primary haunt was the home of Walter Scott, whose wife was not only a fine cook but a singer by profession. For the most part, Michael worked hard just to keep ahead of his students, wrote very little, and drank a great deal.

O'Connor went to Boston toward the middle of June to select students for his writing seminar. Not only did he insist on doing the task himself, but he was adamant about having Richard Gill as his assistant. To the English Department's objection that Gill was an economist, O'Connor replied, "He is also a writer!" At the time O'Connor arrived, Gill had already narrowed down the applicants, among whom was a young woman named Sylvia Plath. O'Connor read her story and rejected her application at once. Gill was curious about the abrupt finality of this judgment and pressed the matter until Michael reminded him of the fellow whose madness had nearly fractured the class the year before. To his mind, Sylvia Plath's story suggested a similarly deranged mind. Later that summer his intuitions were confirmed by her breakdown, in which, ironically, he had played some part. Plath wrote to her mother that she had counted on getting into O'Connor's course.[17] His rejection had come as a brutal shock; she felt rejected as a writer. The rest is history.

Once again Michael stayed with the Kellehers until classes commenced in July. A day or two after he arrived in Boston he remarked to John that he hadn't done much preparation for the course on the modern novel and asked for suggestions. John took out a few books, among them Mario Praz's *The Romantic Agony*, which Michael read; he later announced that the book crystallized the entire course.[18] A week later they were driving out to the Kelleher house in Westwood when Michael mused aloud to John that he had at last come to realize that there was only one way to write a short story: state the theme, introduce the characters, tell the story as consecutively as possible, and reiterate the theme. John objected that his best stories—"Guests of the Nation," "Bridal Night," "In the Train," "Michael's Wife," and "Uprooted" were the few examples he mentioned—did not fit that formula at all. Michael dismissed them as immature efforts and reaffirmed the absolute finality of his theory.

Michael soon overstayed his welcome at the Kellehers. Unable to write in Evanston, he was now trying to make up for it in Boston. In his own home he insisted on quiet, but this was not his home, so the noise of the children, which Helen felt no compulsion to stifle, kept him edgy. Instead of being charming, he was morose and surly; nothing about America pleased him. He complained at length and openly about Evelyn and Joan. He still had to be driven everywhere. He had always been a finicky eater, but for some reason he was excessively demanding this summer. He ate quickly, then pushed away from the table and lit a cigarette; on more than one occasion Helen had prepared a special meal or had invited guests to meet O'Connor only to have him phone to say he wouldn't be back until late. It was this kind of behavior, based as much on Michael's lack of social grace (that innocence which many people found so appealing) as on an equally naive assumption that his talent, or genius, entitled him to special treatment, which led many people to view him as very selfish.[19]

His teaching too was generally less effective than it had been the previous year. His lectures were entertaining but eccentric and unbalanced. In the seminar he was at odds with the class from the first day because his method was bound to frustrate any budding writer. Dick Gill, knowing the emotional pressure on O'Connor, tried to act as mediator. He and his wife, Betty, saw O'Connor nearly every evening, with Michael spilling his troubles and drinking more bourbon than they thought one man could hold. Their small apartment was dominated by Betty's concert grand, and the more Michael drank, the more he wanted to sing. Whatever she played—Hugo Wolf, Hebridean songs, even Schubert—he sang, slightly off pitch but with exuberance and genuine joy. One evening Dick sang Sarastro's aria "In diesen heil'gen Hallen" from *Die Zauberflöte*. Michael went absolutely wild; he loved music, but Mozart was his greatest love.

Nearly every morning Michael came by the Gills' for breakfast, often carrying his dream notebook to regale them with his latest dream. Any letter from Joan prompted a rehashing of the saga of the "bitches" in his life. In fact, he talked so much about himself that Dick decided to find out exactly how he saw himself. He had recently come across a simple psychological test calling for a person to give three answers to the question "What are you?" According to what Dick had read, most people paused to think, but when he posed the question to Michael the answer came back at once: "I am a thick back line. I am James Joyce. I am a gnarled tree."

Toward the end of the summer Michael was talking one evening with Dick and Betty about Sylvia Plath's breakdown. Speculating that Michael might be harboring some guilt about the incident, Dick broached the subject of neurosis. Michael said that he avoided disturbed people because he could not deal with madness. Art to him was discipline, not uncontrolled emotional indulgence. When Betty commented about his own fertile dream life and uncanny intuitions, he acknowledged the thin line between sanity and neurosis. The creative person, he claimed, walks that line, balanced only by rational control. Instinct without judgment is mere subjectivity at best, insanity at worst. "And judgment without intuition?" she asked. "That, my dear," he replied, "is Auschwitz."

Michael's loneliness that summer was excessive, even for him. Harriet had elected to stay away from Cambridge because of the fight in New York, and Michael could not count on a visit from Stan either. Besides monopolizing the Gills' time, he also saw a great deal of Horace Reynolds, the critic he had met the previous summer. According to Richard Gill, Reynolds took Michael one Sunday for a stroll around Walden Pond, though Thoreau had never been one of Michael's passions. The next day Frank O'Connor stood behind the lectern, his face swollen from mosquito bites. "Nature is overestimated," he told the class before trying to talk about *Pride and Prejudice*.[20] Reynolds laughed about the incident but complained to Kelleher that once again he had had to pay for everything. "He's an interesting man and great company," Reynolds observed, "but he's a hell of a cheapskate." The next time, he was determined to wait Michael out and make *him* pick up the bill, which he succeeded in doing, but at the cost of ruining Michael's mood and the remainder of the afternoon. Actually, Michael was quite conscious of this aspect of his character—a trait resulting from the extreme poverty of his youth, as he explained it, thus absolving himself from any blame.

Early in August O'Connor got all the literary company he could have wanted when Harvard hosted a three-day conference on the novel with such writers as detective novelist Georges Simenon, Hans Holthausen, the German poet, Ralph Ellison, winner of the National Book Award for fiction in 1952, Anthony West, novelist and critic for *The New Yorker*, and such scholar-critics as Stanley Hyman, Wilbur Frohock, and Andrew Lytle. O'Connor was argumentative and petulant the entire time. Trying to define the novel struck him as a ridiculous enterprise and he said so, not mentioning, of course, that he himself had tried to define the novel countless times. He took such outrageous positions on every issue that during one panel discussion someone from the audience finally shrieked, "Will Mr. O'Connor tell us that 'Samson Agonistes' is not a poem!" O'Connor replied that he would and that it wasn't. On the second day of the conference he got on his hobbyhorse about the proliferation in the modern novel of "disassociated metaphor" *à la* Joyce. Everyone else mounted his own particular hobbyhorse about one thing or another and in the end O'Connor and Anthony West were reduced to giggling and writing notes to each other like bored schoolboys.[21] Though the formal panels were sabotaged by a general confusion of purpose, everyone seemed to enjoy the evening social gatherings. For his own part, O'Connor spent a good deal of time with Georges Simenon, one of Joan's favorite writers, and went away with a new appreciation of the famous Belgian's work.[22] Above all, he was impressed by the fact that Simenon had an American wife who sharpened his pencils for him.

True to her word, Harriet stayed away the entire summer, though apparently she had written to Michael a few times. Then unexpectedly she drove up to Cambridge from her home in Maryland during the final week of the summer session and volunteered to drive Michael to Breadloaf. That week, Michael was invited to the Kellehers' one last time. At some point in the evening Helen said to him, "I hope next time you come we'll see Joan." He laughed and said: "Ach, I don't know. I'm thinkin' now of me latther end." After a short stay in Vermont Harriet and Michael returned to New York for two days of shopping before he sailed. Unfortunately, Harriet's car was broken into and the gift Michael had purchased for Joan (a coat picked out by Harriet) was stolen. The symbolic nature of the incident made him uneasy; he told Harriet that if any student ever wrote a story with such obvious symbolism, he would reject it. Just before she said good-bye to Michael, presumably for the last time, Harriet told him to cable her when he and Joan were married—"So I can begin to forget you," she said. She also reminded him that he had to live his own life. To Harriet he was a misunderstood artist, more sinned against than sinning, taken advantage of by Evelyn and Joan, while suffering patiently through it all and trying heroically to write his stories. Her last words to him were "Think of yourself for once in your life."

IV

Joan drove to Southampton on September 8 to meet Michael, but she was far from happy and they had little to say to each other. Myles had lived with Joan and Oliver while his father was in America; now he, Oliver, and Liadain, who had stayed with Joan at Primrose Hill for part of that coronation summer, were with Evelyn.[23] Michael and Joan planned to travel to Dublin in a few days to fetch Myles and Oliver and to attend a gala celebration of Michael's fiftieth birthday organized by Dermot Foley and Mrs. Yeats. Yet another reason for going to Dublin was to attend to some legal problems concerning the birth of a son to Evelyn two days *before* the final divorce decree, apparently making the child an O'Donovan and eligible for financial support from Michael. Seán O'Faoláin, who had tried to keep him informed about the tangle of events, wrote: "In your hell there will be total peace. But you won't write a line." All

summer Michael's letters had been raging literary effusions, to which
O'Faoláin finally capitulated: "Could you exchange a bit of your lunacy for a
bit of my sanity, I'm so sick of it and it's killed my imagination?"

When they arrived in Dublin, the madness thickened. Evelyn's solicitors
besieged Michael for money; he had resumed withholding maintenance and
had failed to pay her legal costs, as required by the court. After listening to
Myles talk about his stay at Strand Road, Michael conjured a picture of deprav-
ity there and confronted Evelyn about it. She denied whatever Myles had said,
denouncing her son as a sex maniac and suggesting that the boy would probably say anything his father wanted to hear. Then she informed him of tales
Liadain had brought back from her visit to Primrose Hill, from which she could
picture an equally unfortunate situation for children. The accusations and
counteraccusations that swirled all around were so excessive and libelous that
O'Faoláin remarked to Michael that the whole thing smacked of "sodom and
begorra."

On the evening of September 17, a dinner party was held at the Wicklow
Hotel in honor of Michael on his fiftieth birthday. Guests included Seán and
Eileen O'Faoláin, Honor Tracy, Dermot Foley and his wife, Doreen, Niall
Montgomery and his wife, Hop, Denis Johnston, Stan Stewart, and Dan
Binchy. Throughout the evening Dermot noticed that something was amiss
between Michael and Joan; he abused her openly by introducing her as his
whore, then virtually ignored her while disporting himself in drunken conviviality. Dermot recalled Michael's manner a few months before in Claridges and
admired Joan's heroic composure in the face of such callous treatment. He believed that Michael had pushed Evelyn, once his devoted slave, over the edge;
now it appeared that he was pushing Joan to the limit as well.

Two days later he drove Michael and Joan to Dun Laoghaire. Myles was
returning to England with them with the consent of Evelyn, who seemed to
enjoy a tactical edge at the moment and even took Myles to the boat herself.
Before sailing, Michael became somewhat addled and kissed Joan good-bye,
then corrected himself and pecked Evelyn on the cheek. In London, Michael
instructed his solicitor to file for custody of the children before the Queen's
Proctor. For some time Evelyn had resisted his claim to legal custody of Myles.
Now his demand for custody of Liadain and Owen as well was met with even
stronger legal resistance. Evelyn had remarried, making his claim a bit weaker.
There followed a string of affidavits testifying to Evelyn's unimpeachable moral
character and blaming her financial plight on Mr. O'Donovan's refusal to abide
by the court-ordered terms of child support. Michael filed a counter suit, alleg-
ing sexual misbehavior and loss, on Evelyn's part, of all sense of responsibility
for the children. On September 30 his solicitor advised him that his custody
case would be stronger if he was to put his relationship with Joan on a "proper
legal basis." O'Faoláin said much the same thing when he advised Michael to
ignore the business of Evelyn's personal life and "stick to the cash angle"; he
begged Michael to remember that in the eyes of the court he was "no angel."[24]
This pressure to present himself to the court as a properly married man with a
stable home in which to raise his children only intensified Michael's anxieties
about Joan.

The air at Primrose Hill was poisoned by anger and suspicion. Michael refused to talk and spent hours at the pub next door.[25] When he was not drink-

ing, Michael was walking the lanes around Bletchley, chain-smoking and trying to figure out what to do. He may have felt a certain moral responsibility towards Joan—though she saw little evidence of it—but he could not continue to
live in an atmosphere of doubt and depression. By now he had convinced himself that Joan was mad, that she had no control over her actions, and that if he
married her, he would go through one ordeal after another, none of which, of
course, would have any connection with his own behavior. At the house he
needled Joan constantly about her infidelity, recoiling in anger whenever she
reminded him of his own. About Harriet he emphatically replied, "She has
nothing to do with this!" Fighting to preserve her emotional control, Joan insisted, "Harriet has everything to do with this!"

By the first week of October it had all come to an end. Joan sent Oliver to a
friend in Bristol, but stayed to clean up and make domestic arrangements for
Michael. On October 9 he wrote to Harriet telling her that at last he felt legally
and morally free to marry her; he could not promise her anything, except that
he was first of all a writer. He then walked the seven miles to Stony Stratford to
give himself time to reconsider; along the way he asked his mother in heaven
to stop him if he was wrong. He posted the letter and returned to Primrose Hill,
relieved yet fearful. The next morning, as Joan was preparing to depart, Myles
gave her his copy of *Mill on the Floss*, one of the three books he owned; he had
signed it, "To Auntie Joan." Only a day or so earlier Michael had received from
Harriet an insurance check for the coat that had been stolen from her car in
New York. Michael gave the money to Joan to set up house for herself and
Oliver. She took it but said something sarcastic about Harriet's thoughtful and
timely gift. Michael became vicious and struck her. "You're the one who is
mad," she sobbed. Myles retreated into the back bedroom where he had a sort
of seizure and began gasping for breath. As Michael was attending to the boy
Joan left the house for good. Later he took Myles for a long walk. Along the way
he talked to his son about the scene he had just witnessed and about the
meaning of all that had transpired since his return from America. Myles knew
from the tone of his father's voice that all this must be very important, but he
wanted only to rest—after two hours of walking he could no longer concentrate.

Though he felt a certain sense of relief at Joan's departure, Michael's
emotional reserves were entirely drained. For two days he paced about the
house like a caged animal, waiting to hear from Harriet. Finally a cable came
and Michael joyously placed a transatlantic call. Myles sat by quietly as his father discussed marriage plans with Harriet. Two weeks later Michael wrote to
John Kelleher about his latest turn of events in his life: "This is to anticipate
that crazy girl, Harriet, who has already shaken the fat of Stan's heart with the
news that we were hoping to get married." He then described the situation he
had come home to—one from which, "in a village of twelve houses," he could
hardly escape. He further chronicled the events in Dublin to explain that he
could not go through such ordeals again: "I know it has already done damage
to whatever little creative faculty I possess; like yourself and Stan, I have the
limitations of the normal reasonable man, but I have to put up with them and
toy with the other stuff only at my own peril." Toward Joan he felt only pity, he
claimed, adding: "it would even be a relief to feel that I was responsible, but I
can't do that either."[26] And even though he knew that marrying Harriet was

the best thing for him, he also was resolved not to abandon his children, to see his battle with Evelyn through to the end before going off to the States to "start living again."

In Bristol Joan received a formal letter from Michael's solicitors curtly requesting that she relinquish her interest in Primrose Hill, which had been purchased in her name. She answered at once that she wanted no part of the house. She also asked if Michael had yet remarried, because Harriet's mail was coming to her. Mr. Henderson responded with a warm personal letter expressing sympathy for her, disavowing any previous knowledge of Michael's plans, and suggesting his growing disenchantment with Mr. O'Donovan.

All this time Michael and Myles were together at Primrose Hill awaiting Harriet's arrival. Michael could hardly boil an egg for himself, let alone prepare a meal or wash his clothes. Fortunately, Myles proved to be eminently resourceful, and for the better part of two months he tended to the domestic details of their bachelor existence. His efforts left a great deal to be desired, as Honor Tracy discovered upon visiting them one day. After offering to prepare dinner, she found only a putrefied ham and some bread in the house. She went out and returned an hour later with groceries and fixed the two desperate O'Donovans their first decent meal in weeks. Twice in November she came to their rescue. On one of those evenings Michael became a trifle maudlin and told her that he should really have been a priest. She only laughed and replied, "You and Shelley!"

Unable to concentrate on his own writing, Michael read constantly, first the novels of Henry Green, then the autobiography of Edward Thomas (on the recommendation of Robert Frost), and finally Dickens and Trollope, again. At night he drank so heavily that Myles had to stop every evening on his way home from school to pick up a bottle of whiskey. In his confusion and loneliness Michael talked endlessly to his fourteen-year-old son, often overwhelming the boy with diatribes about old enmities or emotional evocations about events in his life which Myles was incapable of understanding. Though generally moderate in his drinking, Michael had now been on a binge for nearly a month to drown his guilt and find escape from the nagging doubts within. This usually reticent man, shy to a fault and intolerant of any hint of the salacious, held nothing back in his stupor. It was as if he were a penitent confessing for the first time in twenty years.

In one year Michael O'Donovan had been forced with wrenching clarity from the emotional stage of adolescence to the realities of middle age. In the agony of that year since his mother's death he had come to realize that he could not heal himself, that he did in fact need a woman, not just for love but for support of his creative work. The divorce, his mother's death, and the departure of Joan released him from any responsibility to the past; what he needed was not freedom from circumstances but freedom from his own character. Though Frank O'Connor saw himself as caught in the grip of overwhelming external forces, fighting against great odds and a lifetime of circumstantial insults to succeed as an artist, he had not yet resolved the destructive struggle within himself—between his head and his heart—represented always in the disassociated symbolism of his dreams as the warring principles of mother and father.

18

The American Wife

Anything that is not anonymous is all a dream.
WILLIAM MAXWELL, *The Château*

I

HARRIET RICH sailed from the United States at the end of November 1953 aboard the *Queen Elizabeth*. On Saturday, December 5, she and Michael O'Donovan were married in the Bletchley Registry Office, in a shabby but comfortable room with a coal fire in the grate and flowers on the mantelpiece. Bill and Erna Naughton were the witnesses, and Myles was the sole guest. For Michael this was one last attempt at domestic tranquility, while for Harriet it would be the first. He was an Irish writer who, at fifty years of age, stood at a crossroads, desperately trying to recover his art. She was a young American, not yet thirty, who brought with her all the poise, audacity, and innocence of the privileged. Entering the life of an older man meant unraveling scenes already acted out. For the fourteen-year-old Myles, who had fallen immediately in love with his stepmother, the marriage meant survival.

The honeymoon was brief. On Monday the new family boarded a train to London for the custody hearings. Michael told his son to tell the truth even if he thought it would hurt his father. Unfortunately, Myles was never to get the chance: The case would be decided entirely on the affidavits. Evelyn was charging Michael with desertion of the children, cruelty, and adultery. His counter suit alleged immoral conditions at 57 Strand Road, as described to him by Myles. From the outset the judge took it into his head that Myles had lied, at his father's instigation. He refused to see the boy and, upon learning that he sometimes wet the bed, ordered a psychiatric examination. The court-appointed psychiatrist came away the next day entirely convinced that Myles was telling the truth. The damage, however, had already been done. The judge discounted the psychiatrist's report, refused to cross-examine Michael, and gave custody of Liadain and Owen to Evelyn. Myles, now a ward of the court, was to remain permanently with his father, with the stipulation that he be sent to a boarding school approved by his mother, an injunction that was made over the urgent objection of the principal at Myles's school in Stony Stratford.[1]

From Michael's point of view, the outcome was a disaster. Evelyn's control over Myles's schooling made it impossible for Michael to go to America without first getting her approval. Even more painful to Michael was his failure to gain custody over Liadain and Owen. In financial terms the settlement was ambiguous: He was ordered to pay her court costs and continue child support at the previous level until a final decision was made. The judge deferred this decision until he could have a full reckoning from Michael and his new wife.

Thus Michael was left not with a clear-cut judgment, but with a continual reminder of the burden of the past.

Michael and Harriet went to London three or four times in December to consult with his agent, his solicitor, and an accountant. Harriet took advantage of these trips to buy new clothes for her two new men; she also bought draperies and linens for the house. Her enthusiasm was boundless. She was enchanted by her stepson, whom she described in her first letter home as a "lamb . . . with very pink cheeks, bright eyes, lots of curly hair and the disposition of an angel." When she mentioned the weather to any of the local residents, she was assured that it was unusually cold and damp. In credit to their veracity, it turned out to be the harshest winter in decades, with snow and temperatures below freezing for days on end.

Still, the biggest adjustment for Harriet was Michael himself. She had to adapt to his routines and meet his demands, particularly about diet (absolutely no fish, for instance). He insisted on coffee at eleven o'clock, at which time he might or might not talk. There was also his habit of walking in the afternoon: "The man is a fiend for walking," she wrote her mother, "and I'll get to be a fiend for it too or find myself discarded for sure." He rarely worked in the evening. Then he sometimes read poetry aloud to her, but never his stories, preferring to let her read those herself and comment if she wished. After Myles went to bed, they almost always listened to music, an activity he turned into a seminar. He dismissed Bach, her exclusive interest at the time, and began educating her about Mozart and Beethoven. At first she did not like, for instance, the late quartets, but as he played them over and over, insisting that she hear their sublimity, she slowly came to appreciate them. She never came to share his fondness for Hugo Wolf, however. Michael's taste was limited but direct, particularly about what he loved. In fact, he dismissed so much that Harriet soon realized she could like whatever she wished, especially Bach, so long as she gave his favorites a chance. Fortunately, she was young, impressionable, and deeply in love with him.

Stan Stewart came to spend Christmas with the O'Donovans, and Myles refused his mother's request that he join the family in Dublin for the holidays. All things considered, he and his father enjoyed their warmest Christmas together; Harriet had managed to bring some peace to their lives, and Stan's presence was icing for the cake. In January Primrose Hill received its first "official" guest: Pierre Emmanuel, with whom Michael had corresponded since their meeting at Harvard. The genteel French poet had been instantly impressed by the dynamic Irish writer whose knowledge of French literature was so rich. He and Michael sat for hours talking about Ronsard and Saint-Simon, about Joyce, and even about such obscure writers as Montherlant.

Harriet's first attempt at "literary" entertaining had been eminently successful, but soon after Emmanuel's departure her parents announced their intentions of sailing to England in March, throwing her back into a frenzy of anxiety over how they would like Michael. She should have worried more about how they would like Primrose Hill. Her mother found the damp cold insufferable, and her father kept banging his head on the low lintels; after two days they returned to London, where they entertained their daughter and new son-in-law with lavish generosity. Their reservations about Michael were partly dispelled when they met him, though they still expressed uneasiness about the age difference and wondered why Harriet and Michael could not have waited to be married the next summer in Maryland. In the end they departed with only mild assurance about the wisdom of the marriage.

Shortly after Harriet's parents had left, Michael and Harriet had their first serious disagreement. When she clamored to accept Pierre Emmanuel's invitation and go to Paris for Easter, Michael balked angrily. Her parents' visit and the nagging court action had combined to keep him from his work and upset his stomach. Not yet familiar with the signs of gastritis, Harriet thought he was angry with her. He threw out excuse after excuse, none of which diverted her. Finally, she and Myles set off without him. Harriet and Myles enjoyed themselves in Paris for nearly a week before Michael finally showed up, but when he did, they hired a car and, with Harriet driving, set out for the country. Introducing her to his "discoveries," fine old churches in out-of-the-way villages such as the Cistercian abbey in Jumièges, Michael was in his element. This was the man Harriet remembered from America, picnicking at Marblehead or driving through Vermont.

The amazing success of *Stories* had prompted Knopf to urge O'Connor to do another collection. When Harriet had first arrived in England, he had been busy revising stories for that volume. Though riding a crest of popularity in America, he was mired in dissatisfaction with his writing, and another "retrospective" collection hardly inspired his interest. He would sit for hours in front of the fire staring at his American sneakers and tinkering with his pencils and pens. Most of his earliest work displeased him, particularly the so-called lyrical stories, which he now considered too emotional. Though "Guests of the Nation," which he had revised so stringently as to make it practically a new story, was included in this new volume, the only other concession he made was the inclusion of "Orpheus and His Lute." In all, nearly half of the stories finally included in this second collection had, in fact, been written since the publication of *Stories* in 1952 (four of these had not even seen prior publication), suggesting that O'Connor believed what he had once told Kelleher: that he finally knew how to write a story. The choice of "The Mad Lomasneys" and "Judas" offered token representation of his earlier work. Actually, *More Stories* had outward order but no design, nothing of that ambiance O'Connor sought to achieve when putting together a volume of stories.[2] When he sent the final manuscript to Knopf, he was far from satisfied.

Of the new stories in this unsatisfying collection, one in particular has a special fascination. Though he used the title "The Sorcerer's Apprentice" in deference to Harriet, whose story it was, O'Connor intended it as an elaboration of the Don Juan theme that had intrigued him since the Joan years.[3] In the story, a "warm-hearted, excitable, talkative girl" with a pious streak and a penchant for gossip resists marrying the young fellow with whom she has been keeping company for five years. She runs away to Dublin where she deliberately flirts with an older man. She seduces him without very much trouble and then begins to chatter about love, at which point he chides her in an "almost clerical tone." When she returns to the home of the friend with whom she is staying, she comes to her senses:

Here she was, running away from a most desirable young man to whom she should have been married years before, and running round with a

married man who was lonely, disappointed, and poor and had to work . . .
to provide the alimony he had to pay because of a previous indiscretion.[4]

She decides to return to her orthodox young man in Cork, but as much as she
wants to reform, she falls back into the pattern of quarreling with him. She
tries to resolve their quarrel by seducing him, but he is so shocked by this that
she realizes their relationship is over, that it has changed because she has
changed. In the end she telephones the older Don Juan in Dublin; "now she
knew every man and woman is a trade in himself, and he was the only trade
she knew."

Whatever "The Sorcerer's Apprentice" may say about the dynamics of
O'Connor's relationship with Harriet—the wise old man patiently training a
flighty young wife—it reveals to an even greater extent his fundamental attitude toward women. His ideal woman had always been the mercurial, quick-
witted, impulsive girl, devoted, loyal, but greatly in need of the rational stability
of a man. On that dichotomy rests the primary tension of all his domestic fiction, between female instinct and male judgment, between Mozart's gaiety and
Beethoven's melancholy. It was that struggle between head and heart that
troubled his sleep.

The other previously unpublished works in *More Stories,* "Father and
Son" and "Lonely Rock," sprang from another deeply personal source: his
marriage to Evelyn.[5] "Lonely Rock" is the story Evelyn's solicitors had blocked
from publication in Great Britain, the story based on an incident that occurred
while Joan was living with Michael and Evelyn at Strand Road. The "unnatural triangles" that he purported to find in Joan's life in this story become delightfully funny. "Father and Son" was originally about Joan and Evelyn, but
in those lonely weeks following Joan's departure, O'Connor let the story follow
the torrential conversations with his son about the miseries of his marriage.

At the same time Myles, freed perhaps by his father's disclosures, told a
few savory tales of his own about his mother, tales designed as much to align
himself firmly on his father's side as to vent his own bitterness. One in particular struck that special chord within Frank O'Connor the writer, and after
sending off the manuscript of *More Stories,* he wrote it down in a pure, undif-
ferentiated burst of creative fury.

At Rockwell another boy from Arklow had shared his weekly parcel with
Myles, who never got one. The boy's parents took Myles back to Arklow with
them one holiday and discovered that his parents were separated and that his
mother had put him in the school as punishment. Soon after returning to
Rockwell, Myles began receiving weekly parcels too. He thought his mother
had been stung by his "hint" that other boys got parcels from home and he
didn't. In fact, it turned out that the mother of the other Arklow boy had pitied
him so much she had taken it upon herself to send him parcels of fruit, sweets,
and baked goods. When Myles discovered their origin, he angrily returned the
parcels to the boy, heroically announcing that he did not need their pity.

As so often happened, O'Connor gave the story two different titles:
"Francis" in *The New Yorker* and "Pity" two years later in *Domestic Relations.*
The story remained substantially the same, but O'Connor's emphasis
shifted—as it always seemed to when he revised a story—from the person to
the idea. In both versions the story is a small gem. In the background O'Con-

nor created a subtle disharmony through the inhumanity of the school—its crowded, filthy dormitory and sadistic prefects—and the inhumanity of the boy's family—a sister with whom he quarrels, a mother generally away from home, and a father he hardly knows. In the foreground he placed the drama of the two boys, the same two types present in so many O'Connor stories: an impulsive hooligan and a scrupulous sissy. The "crisis" of the story occurs when the wild boy discovers that the parcels are not from his mother at all. In the privacy of the lavatory he sobs to himself because he has been exposed for what he is: not tough and insubordinate, but sensitive and lonely. He could never again be friendly with Francis; "it would have been like living naked."

When hearing a story such as Myles's, O'Connor found his imagination tuned to that perfect wavelength where his concern with design blended naturally with his radical faith in human nature. At such times his art cut to the bone, the shell cracked; by listening honestly to his son he also found those interior voices of his own, and while hearing his son's agony he achieved a personal insight, a recognition of the loneliness and vulnerability they shared. For years Michael had felt much the same sort of identification with priests. Though he could never have been comfortable within ecclesiastical discipline, to say nothing of celibacy, he often said to friends that he should have joined the priesthood.[6] A month or so after finishing Myles's Rockwell story, O'Connor revived one he and Nancy McCarthy had stumbled on years before at Mount Melleray, about a monk who fled that "lonesome monastery" only to linger in the hills forlornly watching his former home until he died of hunger and exposure.

Ostensibly, "Lost Fatherlands" is one of O'Connor's many priest stories, but it is actually a variation of his Don Juan stories—without women.[7] Spike Ward, the confident ladies' man of "Don Juan (Retired)," appears here as an irascible tramp who disagrees with everyone about everything. The two other men who drive with Spike into the mountains in search of the wandering monk are also lonely souls; Linehan, the guard, and Hanagan, the Yank who owns the public house, are both isolated from the community. Though they rescue the poor fellow from the cold hills, they cannot convince him to stay on for a time to recover. Only Hanagan, who had lived for eighteen years in America thinking every day of his homeland, understands the monk's feelings.

> Spike could see that he was deeply moved, but what it was all about was beyond him. Spike had never stood on the deck of a liner and watched his fatherland drop away behind him. He didn't know the sort of hurt it can leave in a boy's mind, a hurt that doesn't heal even when you try to conjure away the pain by returning. Nor did he realize, as Hanagan did at that moment, that there are other fatherlands, whose loss can hurt even more deeply.[8]

O'Connor had by now decided that he could not earn a living in England with the constant threat of legal harassment hanging over his head. By residing in the United States he would be outside the jurisdiction of the British courts, making enforcement of any maintenance order impossible. At the custody hearing in December Myles had been made a ward of the court, though he had been allowed to live with his father. Under his ruling Michael was obligated, therefore, to obtain permission from the court before taking Myles from its jurisdiction. Since he was scheduled to teach again that summer at Harvard, O'Connor petitioned the court for permission to take Myles with him to America. Evelyn filed a counter-petition demanding that the boy spend the summer on a farm in Wales. This legal maneuver stymied Michael's departure; he was summoned to appear on June 21 for another hearing, at which he was required to present some guarantee that he would return Myles to the jurisdiction of the court. A. D. Peters himself testified on Michael's behalf, guaranteeing the return of Myles. As a result, the court allowed Myles to leave with the stipulation that Michael begin paying maintenance for Liadain and Owen.[9] On June 26 Michael, Harriet, and Myles sailed on the *New Amsterdam*. When they landed in New York, Myles went with Dick and Betty Gill to the New Jersey shore, while Michael and Harriet drove directly to Cambridge. That summer O'Connor again conducted his writing seminar and gave lectures on the novel. It was to be his last teaching stint for seven years.

O'Connor always claimed that he left teaching because he found himself more interested in his students' work than in his own, a very honest recognition of the kind of ruthlessness any artist must exercise in order to survive. But he may have had other reasons for not teaching. In the first place, he had encountered considerable friction in his relations with other faculty, some of whom were openly hostile to the arrogant, uneducated provincial. Second, his behavior on such occasions as the conference on the novel the previous summer had embarrassed even his friends. But a more crucial reason for the reversal was a simmering feud with John Kelleher.

Kelleher had begun to be disenchanted with Michael during Michael's first summer at Harvard, particularly his way of taking hospitality for granted. In addition, both John and his wife had come to admire Joan a great deal, and when Michael broke with her, they gave her their sympathy. When he received Michael's letter with its announcement of his marriage to Harriet, supported by accusations of Joan, John wrote back to Michael a violent letter of denunciation. Having heard for two summers about Michael's sufferings with Evelyn and Joan, he had been more or less prepared for the outcome, but what infuriated him was what he saw as the cold-blooded ditching of Oliver by the great exponent of the instinct and emotion of paternity. Michael had been deeply wounded by Kelleher's letter. Because he had already accused himself far worse than anybody else could accuse him, he recoiled in the face of John's presumption that he needed to be instructed in personal ethics. Just as he covered his vulnerability with a show of selfishness, his habit of self-vindication derived from a decided lack of self-assurance. Instead of answering the letter, Michael wrote to Stan condemning John's self-righteousness. Kelleher broke irretrievably with Michael and freed him from all obligations. No apologies were asked; none was given.[10]

I I

In September 1954 the O'Donovans moved to Hicks Street in Brooklyn Heights, a pleasant residential street a few blocks from the Esplanade, with old-fashioned brick and brownstone houses and apartments. Theirs was a railroad flat, one room behind the other, which they furnished in comfortable but by no means luxurious fashion. Myles attended the Brooklyn Friends School, even though his father had been ordered to return him to a boarding school in England. By ignoring the court order and by refusing to pay Evelyn's legal costs, Michael placed himself in an even more tenuous legal position. His taxes in Ireland were still delinquent and the sale of Primrose Hill was jeopardized by the lingering threat of litigation. But none of this affected him now, safely ensconced as he was in America. Contented to be in a city once again, he walked daily along the waterfront or across the Brooklyn Bridge into Manhattan. His favorite haunts were St. Paul's Chapel, the Fulton Market with its draft beer, sandwiches, and cut-rate records, and Costello's, an Irish bar then located on Third Avenue.

The quality of Michael's life and the progress of his career had always been enriched by his friends; that was true in Ireland and England, and it would remain so in America. Almost as soon as he was settled in Brooklyn Heights he heard from Carmel Snow, the editor of *Harper's Bazaar,* who in spite of his exclusive agreement with *The New Yorker,* continued to seek his work; time and again she invited Michael and Harriet to her parties, notably one that fall for the Irish celebrity Oliver St. John Gogarty. She also introduced O'Connor to Cyrilly Abels, a fiction editor at *Mademoiselle* who was instrumental in setting up Michael's first contact with Caedmon Records. The Gills had invited Michael and Harriet to Cambridge for Thanksgiving. On the way north they stopped in Connecticut where recordings of O'Connor reading "My Oedipus Complex" and "The Drunkard," were made for Caedmon. During their stay in Cambridge they and the Gills were invited to a party at Horace Reynolds's house, and among the guests that evening were the Kellehers. The tacit purpose of the occasion was to bring about a reconciliation, at the urging of Stan Stewart, between Michael and John. Unfortunately, it was sprung on Michael by surprise and the whole evening was a disaster.

Also that fall O'Connor began work on a critical study of the novel. For the most part the separate chapters of this projected book stood before him, truncated and undeveloped, in his Harvard lecture notes. What he had explored piecemeal in his lectures he now believed he could unify by his notion of the dichotomy of the head and the heart. The more he pored over his dream notebooks, the more convinced he became that in the language of dreams was a symbolic conflict between the forces of judgment and instinct, which were represented by father and mother. The more he thought about the destructive elements in his relationship with Joan, the hysteria they produced in each other, and the more he puzzled over his abiding antipathy for James Joyce, the surer he was that these problems had to be connected with some imbalance of the sort dreams were meant to signal. The idea that began to emerge, an idea he had stumbled on years before when writing about Corkery, was that when no objective standard, whether in moral or aesthetic terms, is recognized outside the individual, then the subjective imagination rides unchecked to the abyss of madness where reality is indistinguishable from fantasy.

Because his own ideas obsessed him, O'Connor assumed all writers were obsessed by one thing or another, and because he fought to control his imaginative instincts, he assumed that any writer worth his salt faced the same struggle. He approached his reading as he believed Jane Austen did: "She brooded in the way of a creative writer rather than in that of a scholar: that is, she read her own problems into the work she studied in a way that any academic critic would properly shun, but precisely because of this her criticism has to be understood if we are to understand her creative work." Frank O'Connor's agenda was not that of the scholar-critic but that of a writer; his concern was to plumb the minds of other writers, to fathom their motives and test how they solved or failed to solve the technical problems posed by the very material that obsessed them. By whichever title—"Ride to the Abyss" (O'Connor's original choice) or "The Mirror in the Roadway" (an editor's from a phrase of Stendhal's)—the book is as much autobiography as criticism.[11] For a creative writer perhaps the two are always the same.

The book begins with the admission that he grew up thinking of the nineteenth-century novel as a "contemporary art form." In the remainder of his brief introduction O'Connor attempts to define in some provisional way what the novel is and what it is not. He settles on truthfulness with regard to the material, which should be primarily domestic and civil in nature, and realism as the approach. "The novel is not only limited in material, but is also limited in outlook." He concludes his opening remarks by taking his stand: "I am afraid that the truth is that I am not only a nineteenth-century realist, but also a nineteenth-century liberal. I am not sure that either realism or liberalism is a good thing in itself, but at least I believe that they are aspects of the same attitude of mind." He then links conservatism and romanticism, symbolism and naturalism, fascism and communism, and maintains that they seem to him destructive attitudes. What O'Connor has done is to signal at once that his approach is as moral as it is literary.

About Jane Austen, to his mind the purest novelist of all time, he says: "[Her subject—] her obsession, one might say—was the imagination. . . . Truth as it is perceived by the judgment is her aim, and everything that would disturb this is eliminated." He continues: "Catherine Morland is Jane Austen, and I suspect that in real life she knew herself to be a creature of mood and fancy. For that is her one subject: the conflict between the imagination and the judgment." Commenting on the style of *Mansfield Park,* he says:

> If one glances through the pages, the rancorous, censorious tone becomes apparent in the words with which the author tries to batter our moral sense. "Disapprove," "censure," "corrupted," "evil," . . . are only a few of the words that shriek at the reader with a sort of moral hysteria that stuns and bewilders him.[12]

In the next chapter O'Connor compares Austen with Stendhal, two children of the eighteenth century who shared a sense of style and an utter integrity. "She dreaded the imagination as the source of all evil, while Stendhal remained wedded to his and, whenever he escaped for a little while from it, wondered what had gone wrong with him." This quality O'Connor attributes to Stendhal's illegitimacy, the fantasies of which are "known to every misunderstood child in the world (does this mean every child?)." Stendhal's identification with the actual model for Julien Sorel says much to O'Connor about his imagination. The character Stendhal created was a complete romantic, but *The Red and the Black* was not a romantic novel, rather "an exploration of reality by means of the romantic temperament, and it tries to explain the failure to make contact with reality. . . . Perhaps the truest thing we can say of the author is that in the conflict between instinct and judgment which he endured, his judgment constantly tended to take the form of irony."

As compelled as he is by Dickens, O'Connor brands him a charlatan for playing to the audience, thus sacrificing the sort of scrupulous fidelity practiced by Austen and Stendhal. "Victorian novels were largely bought to be read aloud, and Dickens lent himself magnificently to this." In criticizing Dickens's distortion of his character, O'Connor uses the word "impersonation." Dickens, he argues, distorts "in the manner of a character actor" who turns everything into himself. "His impersonations, like a producer's play, a conductor's symphony, most of Dylan Thomas' poetry, are composed with reference to the magnificent instrument and its resources, not to the resources of drama, music, and poetry."[13] The ease with which O'Connor draws analogies from the arts in general lends a quality of personal intimacy to his writing, a combination of sincerity and eccentricity that forces the reader to become as involved as the writer himself.

The Russians, beginning with Gogol, introduced the element of compassion into fiction, according to O'Connor. Gogol's importance was less to the development of the novel in the nineteenth century than to the rise of a distinctly Russian literature that by the end of the century would bring Osborn Bergin to claim that literature to him meant three names—all Russian. O'Connor recalls that when he heard that remark, his immediate thought was "Which three?" He calls Gogol, who started it all in *The Overcoat*, "essentially a fantasist," with an intense subjectivity. Though Gogol "gradually gained control over his own fantasy in the same way as Balzac did, it always remained there, intact and unmodified by observation and analysis. Like Goldsmith, he always writes of himself." O'Connor concludes that Gogol, pursued by guilt like Goldsmith, "was haunted by some vision of childhood and home which, in the final analysis, was a vision of his mother and an Eden to which he could never return."[14] His characters represent "life itself, his own life, above all, Russian life. For no more than Turgenev can Gogol resist identifying himself with his native land."

In Thackeray's fiction O'Connor hears "a profound, melancholy realization of historical truth, a brooding awareness of the ultimate futility of all human endeavor." *Vanity Fair* reveals to O'Connor Thackeray's ambivalence about women: "a childish strain that attracted him to women who resembled his mother, women who were soft, stupid, and indulgent. And there is no question but that the mature man in him was attracted to women of a very different type—cold, sensual, calculating women." In Thackeray the instinct seemed to O'Connor always to "represent some form of weakness, while the judgment represented selfishness." The conflict was clarified finally in *Henry Esmond*, where Thackeray was able to fuse these two elements of his personality in Beatrix and Lady Castlewood,

> so that when Esmond marries the mother he establishes a new and intimate relationship with the daughter. It is not too much to say that *Esmond* succeeds because it is the perfect solution of an Oedipal situation that underlies all Thackeray's work. That sort of situation is not at all unusual, for Stendhal analyzed it very acutely in himself, nor is it in the least abnormal; it is the way in which life resolves an inescapable conflict between a boy's love of his mother and of the woman who will be his children's mother.

O'Connor believed that in most writers "there is an adolescent element that never grows up, no matter how phenomenal their development in other directions may be."

Well over a decade before, writing about Corkery, O'Connor had talked about the embodiment of internal conflicts, the externalization of dreams. He repeats the same notion in his discussion of Turgenev and Chekhov. In a very real way he seems to externalize his own conflicting impulses. Toward the end of the book, for instance, writing about D. H. Lawrence he says: "The trouble with the oedipal relationship is that it specializes the sexual instinct. Sexual conflict is the only thing lacking between the boy and his mother, and he tends to seek this in a form where it implies nothing else, where it does not produce an actual feeling of betrayal of the mother." That O'Connor often lingered on this problem suggests some powerful, even disturbing, conflict within himself. In his chapter on Dostoevsky O'Connor's obsession with dream psychology and the peculiar energy of abnormal sexuality breaks into the open. Objects and subjects, he contends, are indistinguishable in dreams and in neurosis. The same is true of the symbolic mind apparent to him in Dostoevsky and Joyce.[15] What he had always hated so in Joyce was exactly what he feared most in himself and what he so regularly dreamed about.

The chapters on Dostoevsky, James, Hardy, and Chekhov are grouped under the heading "The Desolation of Reality." The phrase was Yeats's, but it may very well summarize O'Connor's own fundamental metaphysic. What he said about Turgenev was just as true of himself: "His theme is the mystery of human existence, of humanity faced with the spectacle of infinity. *Le silence éternel de ces espaces infinis m'effraie.*" He implies much the same about Chekhov, his other great model of the storyteller: "the last of the liberals, the last writer of fiction to attempt a synthesis of a world that is already falling into chaos about him. Such a synthesis was no longer possible to the novelist, and Chekhov perceives it only by the lightning flash of the short story, and only in solitary lives." Even before moving to the twentieth century, O'Connor has buried the novel, explained his own difficulties with the form, and justified his exclusive devotion to the art of the short story. He may have already begun to write his study of the short story, *The Lonely Voice,* based on his assertion that the "novel by its very nature presupposes a group, a social system that can absorb the lonely figure. The short story is the art form that deals with the individual when there is no longer a society to absorb him, and when he is compelled to exist, as it were, by his own inner light."

Actually, O'Connor intended to concern himself only with the novel in the nineteenth century. The few pages on the novel in the twentieth century at the end of *The Mirror in the Roadway,* therefore, amount essentially to a palinode, written to appease an editor. After Freud, O'Connor observes, novelists stepped behind the mirror, allowing subjectivity to take over. The symbolism of the subconscious supplanted fidelity to fact; "by dwelling almost exclusively on the imagination," Freudian theory "made the modern novelist doubt the existence of an objective reality behind what he writes." What he disliked about the subconscious mind was that it failed to distinguish between subject and object, the primary difficulty he had found in the "translation of dreams."

O'Connor's conclusion reveals his true colors: a moralist deeply disturbed by what he sees around him—the desolation of reality. Desperate for an answer, he recalls Christ's answer to the trick question, which of the commandments is most important?*

> For the problem that the Doctor of Laws was posing was the age-old one between subjective and objective truth, between faith and good works . . . between symbolism and naturalism, communism and fascism. . . . For Christ's reply, if I understand it, means merely that reality is inapprehensible; that if we keep our minds and hearts like clear glass, the light of God shines through us, but that we can be certain of God's presence within us only by the light it sheds on the world outside us. That, in fact, truth is subjective and objective, and that there is no truth greater than this.

Having followed O'Connor's brilliant, if frustratingly perverse, argument to such a lofty conclusion, one can only walk away feeling that the book deserves to be read again—if not for literary reasons, then surely as a portion of the allegory of one man's life.

O'Connor was amazingly productive during the winter of 1954–55. He was capitalizing on years of doing serious reading, of jotting notes in his commonplace books, of reviewing books for daily newspapers and literary monthlies, of talking about his favorite authors over the radio. In December, for example, he published his chapter on Trollope as a lead article in the *New York Times Book Review;* it was almost entirely the same as a BBC talk he had recorded before leaving England.[16] O'Connor's ideas had not changed substantially since 1945, when over five months the *Irish Times* had run eleven pieces of his on the novel, beginning with Austen and ending with Somerville and Ross. In a speech to a library group a year later, he confessed that if at age twelve he had been asked who was the greatest author, he would have said Scott, but it would have been a lie because he preferred Stevenson. At seventeen he would have answered Balzac, though he preferred Hugo; at twenty-five he turned away from Dostoevsky, whom he now thought childish, to discover Stendhal; at thirty he discovered Jane Austen; and at forty he turned at last to Trollope. But he never wavered from his belief that literature was serious business, that it bore some moral responsibility to human life.

Not only was he finally reaping the rewards of a literary life in *More Stories* and *The Mirror in the Roadway,* he was continuing to mine old journals for stories. "Lost Fatherlands" grew from a short sketch he had written in the early thirties. Shortly after moving to Brooklyn Heights, he wrote "The Teacher's Mass," based on a story Father Traynor had told him years before, and "Orphans," based on the story, heard in Lincoln during the war, about the young soldier who married his dead brother's fiancée. For years that simple story had haunted him, but he could never seem to find the right voices for it. Then a dream about an orphanage set him ablaze. He transformed the dead soldier into his mother's brother, Tim, and reversed the roles of his mother and father. The title is not accidentally the same as his mother's anonymous story in *The Bell.* Two orphaned boys had grown up so close that when the older one

---

* See Matt. 22:37–40.

dies in the war, his brother falls apart and takes to drink. Eventually he returns from a tour of duty in Egypt and asks his brother's fiancée to marry him.

The moment of crisis occurs the night before he is to leave, when she refuses to go again with him to his brother's favorite place. "We have our own lives to live," she shouts at him (the very thing Harriet had said to him at the boat). At that moment she realizes that she had already made up her mind. She knows that he loves her as "the one living link with his brother, and beyond that with a mother and home he [has] forgotten." Someday he will love her for what she is. "Like all earnest people, Hilda went through life looking for a cause, and now he was her cause, and she would serve him the best way she knew." For years O'Connor had wondered why his mother had married his father. "Orphans" suggests that the events of the past few years had caused him to ask the same question of his own marriages as well. Ten years later he wrote, "The best short stories are those one writes because one doesn't understand the incident that gave rise to them."

In the next two months O'Connor wrote two more stories about the vagaries of love and marriage. In "A Bachelor's Story" a crusty old civil servant tells his young friend Larry Delaney, now grown up and living in Dublin, a story of lost love. He had once fallen for a girl who accepted his proposal of marriage and then one from another man, fearing—because it had happened to her once before—that one or both suitors would commit suicide if she refused. When Archie drops her, his friend, Delaney, who had fallen in love with the girl's image, condemns him for his rash action. "Every nice girl behaves exactly as though she had a suicide in her past." From that moment on, Archie will have nothing to do with Delaney, severing a rewarding friendship because the man has no moral empathy. O'Connor was at his best when slicing through the layers of his own nature, and both characters are strange mixtures of Stan Stewart, Richard Hayes, and Daniel Binchy in the skins of two men very much like himself. "Fish for Friday" came from a story Dermot Foley had told him about the birth of his second child. The story is full of pub talk and nostalgia for lost youth, all of which causes the main character to forget what he has come to town for—to fetch a doctor to deliver the baby. It is a poignant story delicately balanced on the edge of humor.

O'Connor drove himself so hard that in February he collapsed. Only a week before he had written to Dermot: "I am getting old. I have heart disease."[17] He spent three weeks in bed coughing violently with bronchitis; but instead of taking care of himself or listening to Harriet, he continued to smoke. Then one evening in March he suffered a slight attack of angina; his left arm went numb and his chest felt thick and constricted. Harriet tried to frighten him into taking care of himself by insisting that he carry an identification card with him at all times so that if he dropped dead on the street, those who found him would know what to do with the body. While visiting her family estate in Annapolis at Easter, she finally got him to a doctor, who immediately prescribed medication to lower his blood pressure, and put him on a strict diet calling for low salt intake and no alcohol. When he returned to Hicks Street, he wrote "Expectation of Life," which Harriet claimed was meant to stop her nagging and worrying. The story is about a young woman with a "father fixation" who marries an older man, in spite of her friends' warning. "Women are like that," the faceless narrator wryly observes in one of those knowing generalizations O'Connor was so fond of making. Though fully expecting to be a widow soon, the young woman seems bent on keeping the old fellow alive, nagging him to give up his pipe, measuring his whiskey, and tidying up his affairs. When she herself becomes seriously ill, her elaborate scenario of life collapses. "It was the mad projectionist again, and again he seemed to have got the reels mixed up till the story became meaningless." In his obstinacy the old man outlives her after all.

Myles in the meantime had been promised a summer with Harriet's parents at Ferry Point Farm in Annapolis if his grades improved. For the last two weeks in May he spent every evening in his room studying as he had never done before, and passed every exam. In June he went to Annapolis, while his father and stepmother sailed for Ireland. Fear of a heart attack had given Michael a twinge of desire to see the old place again, to visit Cork and see old friends. He had written to Dermot that he also wanted to go up to Gougane Barra to see the grave of Tim Traynor, who had died in January.[18] But above all, he had to settle things once and for all with Evelyn, who had started fresh litigation against him for keeping Myles in America with him.[19]

As soon as they arrived in Dublin Michael and Harriet paid a visit to Evelyn in Ranelagh, where she now lived. For her own protection Evelyn had other witnesses present, which kept the conversation polite. She refused to allow him to see Liadain and Owen alone. As for the court action, she explained that it was out of her hands now; her solicitors had informed her that they would not drop the case against Michael until he paid all court costs and back maintenance, a sum of around three hundred pounds. Michael was now steaming, so Harriet tried to explain his position; but that explanation was, to Evelyn's mind, criticism of her competence as a mother. Thus insulted, she rose abruptly, terminated the conversation, and ordered them from the house. Michael stormed into the street; Harriet scurried after him petrified that his heart would explode at any moment. On July 13, 1955, in London, Judge Wallington heard Evelyn's motion that Michael O'Donovan be committed to Brixton Prison for contempt of court. The motion was granted, and a warrant for his arrest was ordered. When Joan read the announcement of the sentence in the London *Times,* she breathed a sigh of relief. Though she had not heard from him since the break, she had feared he would burst in unannounced and take Oliver. Now, facing a stiff prison term, he could not return to England at all.

III

For months now, Harriet had been begging Michael to consider a move that would bring them closer to her parents. The attack of angina in March only strengthened her argument. Upon their return from Ireland he relented, and in September they took a house in Annapolis. Myles enrolled at Annapolis High School, his fourth school in four years. Now sixteen, the boy had begun to notice girls. Walking in town one day with his first girl friend, he rounded a corner and came face to face with his father who was, as usual, wearing his tasseled Aran Island tam. Myles grimaced and at the same time the girl's face brightened. O'Connor later concluded that Myles was embarrassed that his father did not know better than to wear such a silly-looking cap, and that the girl was delighted by meeting someone who dressed as he wished. The incident induced him to write "The Duke's Children" a few months later to illustrate the idea that "falling in love always means becoming ashamed of one's own parents and admiring the parents of the boy or girl one is attracted by."[20]

Michael was irritable the entire fall. To some extent he was anxious about his "old ticker" and frustrated by his writing. But an even sharper cause for his uneasiness was a growing animosity between himself and Harriet's father. That summer Myles had innocently asked for a dollar from John Rich, who grunted in reply something about becoming "a bum like [his] father." On another occasion Michael happened to notice his father-in-law scolding one of the black maids. Because his mother had been a charwoman, Michael was keenly sensitive to the feelings of servants.[21] He assumed his patrician pose and calmly remarked that only barbarians mistreated servants, not a statement calculated to endear himself to a strong-willed man accustomed to the exercise of power. John Rich found Michael totally unlike anybody he had ever known, but he also found it difficult to accept the loss of his only daughter to a man nearly his own age. And Michael certainly was not willing to let anyone act like a father to him.

In a sense, the honeymoon was over. Early in their marriage Harriet had entreated Michael to tell her when she did something wrong. "I'm not your daddy," he replied. "I won't tell you because you should know for yourself what is right and wrong." In matters of artistic taste Michael may have been something of a mentor to her, but he refused to take responsibility for her life. "Some men do things for their wives," Harriet once told a lifelong friend, "and some men understand their wives—Michael understands me." Being married to Frank O'Connor was a taxing proposition because of the natural tension between the demands of ordinary life and the demands of creativity. "The real writer," he believed, "has to have a good streak of selfishness to get his own work done. He should throw his wife out and make his children go out and work to support themselves at a really early age."[22] After his death Harriet wrote: " [When] he was writing a story nothing else in the world mattered. He simply wasn't there."[23]

His marriage to Harriet contained an element of hero-worship, attributable more perhaps to differences in age and experience than to any dependency or passivity on her part. Her personality seemed to bring out the best rather than the worst in him. Though having few of the career aspirations of Evelyn or Joan, Harriet was considerably more assertive, perhaps even tough, in a worldly sense. She deferred to his wishes and to his writing, but she was anything but a docile woman. She took delight in listening to him talk about music or chant a new poem, but she also lectured him sternly about his health. She drove him endlessly about Ireland and France in search of monastic ruins and patiently endured his rages about the latest disaster in his native land, but she also meticulously set his affairs straight, filing his papers, handling his correspondence, and investing his money. By sheer force of will she brought peace and order to his life.

Sometime that fall, under some sort of serene inspiration, he wrote an essay for *Harper's Bazaar* in honor of Mozart's two-hundredth birthday.[24] It was a piece of sheer virtuosity, a hymn in praise of genius, far outstripping in controlled hyperbole anything O'Connor had ever written about any of his heroes. Wondering why Mozart alone defined the idea of a "unique, irreplaceable individual," he concludes that it was because of an all-encompassing way of seeing things, somewhere between tragedy and comedy. To him, Mozart represents "a human norm by which the greatest must be judged. Just as there are certain people born with perfect pitch, so there are people like Mozart born with a tuning fork in their fingers, whose business it is to render the middle C of human life."

As in nearly all of his nonfiction, O'Connor's voice is unmasked in this essay, without pose or distortion. "Let me admit that the cascade of sensuous melody in Susanna's *Deh vieni* always gives me a slight shock," he says without affectation, giving the feeling that he has a good deal of himself invested in the idea. *"The Magic Flute* is a thing apart among operas, and I am not sure that even yet I fully understand it." His theory of Mozart's artistic development is so admittedly personal that it bears at least hesitant scrutiny in light of O'Connor's own life. He compares Mozart to those natural writers "who develop rapidly and certainly, and whose first books are as excellent as their last. Maturity comes to them too soon, and they are incapable of the astonishing developments of a Shakespeare or a Yeats who change as their lives change." About the slow movement of the Violin Concerto in A-Major, written before Mozart was twenty, O'Connor wonders "where he could go from there."

That fall, O'Connor was asked by Harry Sions, senior editor of *Holiday* magazine, to write a series of pieces on the coming theatre season. He accepted, and in October he ventured to New York with Harriet to interview Arthur Miller, whose *A View from the Bridge* and *A Memory of Two Mondays* were soon to open. After customary pleasantries Miller offered O'Connor some Irish whiskey. When he raised his glass in toast, he noticed that his glass was not only a good deal smaller than Miller's but less than half as full. After that, nothing the famous American could say or write could erase O'Connor's impression of a fundamental meanness in Miller's character. The first version of the piece O'Connor submitted to *Holiday* dealt more with Giraudoux than Miller. An associate editor politely asked if he couldn't write something more personal about Miller, the sort of thing he took from the interview, which was precisely what O'Connor was trying not to say. In response, he fired off a rambling critique full of references to Hegel, Joyce, and Kafka, in which he generalized about Miller's writing from *Death of a Salesman* to *The Crucible.* In November he heard from Sions, rather than the associate editor who had been handling O'Connor's copy, clarifying exactly what he wanted: "a theater column written in a lighter—whimsical, if you will—or even a gay vein." The trouble was that O'Connor could no more be casual or whimsical about the theatre than he could about injustice. Sions advised him to pursue his remarks about *All My Sons* against the background of American life, but without the highbrow references—"we can't afford that luxury." Sions also suggested that O'Connor say something about his impressions of Miller the man. Actually, the inveterate autobiographical critic was doing everything he could to avoid the personal element.

He avoided it for the rest of the month. Finally, after returning from a trip to Massachusetts—for lectures at Amherst and Mount Holyoke, followed by another Thanksgiving with the Gills in Cambridge—O'Connor reluctantly wrote a polite article saying in effect that because a lot of people in America considered Miller a great playwright, anything he wrote deserved attention. He saw Miller as a dramatist of "American life as it is concerned with the relationship of fathers and sons," by which he meant the tension caused by the difference in moral standards from generation to generation. He assumed that it was a subject Miller "brooded upon very deeply." About Miller himself, O'Connor said only that he seemed disappointed that critics preferred *A View from the Bridge* to *A Memory of Two Mondays,* an assessment O'Connor shared. "I thought it a beautiful play," he said of the latter, adding that it seemed to him thinly disguised autobiography.[25]

Apparently this compromise met the standards of *Holiday* because his column appeared from January to May of 1956. There is little to be said on his reviews of plays by Sean O'Casey, Lillian Hellman, and Thornton Wilder, except that in each case O'Connor wrote as if in a straitjacket. Finally, he threw in the towel. He could not write to anyone else's standards, he wrote to Sions; he was a writer of feelings, not of intellect. Sions was distressed by this decision and responded with the hope that it did not mean an end to O'Connor's relationship with the magazine. O'Connor assured him that it did not and in a gesture of conciliation sent Sions a suitably whimsical piece, "In Quest of Beer," which appeared a few months later.

Two days after Christmas O'Connor delivered the finished manuscript of *The Mirror in the Roadway* to Knopf. With that project behind him, he began 1956 by writing two superb stories, and the momentum carried him through the year. "The Duke's Children" and "The Man of the World" both featured the character Larry Delaney, the narrator O'Connor had already used to great advantage in such "autobiographical" stories as "The Drunkard," "Christmas Morning," and "My Oedipus Complex." And the same young fellow, more sensitive and self-conscious than ever, appeared as the mommy's boy of "The Genius," the story O'Connor cannibalized from his autobiographical piece for the BBC entitled "An Only Child." Using the voice of Larry Delaney allowed O'Connor the freedom to appear both personally revealing and detached. In these confessional accounts of a man scrutinizing his troubled childhood in a provincial wasteland, O'Connor shifted from the moral hysteria of the Don Juan and illegitimate-child stories to something more nearly like moral confusion. Embarrassment is more pervasive than guilt. Larry Delaney continually makes a fool of himself as a boy but forgives himself with a wink as a man. About the only thing that remains morally unquestionable is the environment—the poverty of the neighborhood and the conflict between his parents.

"The Man of the World" finds Larry with an older boy spying on a married couple to learn the mystery of sex, only to feel watched himself. Words such as "ambush" and "victim" pinpoint the sense of degradation he feels, not for the couple but for himself. The reversal of observer and observed dramatizes human finitude: "always beyond the world of appearances I would see only eternity watching." The other boy, however, has not shared Larry's shattering experience, leaving the reader to wonder whether or not he will be able to tempt Larry again. As the young hero of "The Duke's Children," Larry Delaney is mortified by the commonness of his parents because he lives in a world of fantasy, induced by "interior voices" from his reading and exaggerated by an excess of adolescent nature.[26] His desperate pursuit of love—here he is reminiscent of the frantic boy in "Judas" rather than the Peeping Tom of "The Man of the World"—leaves him feeling foolish and alone. To impress his dream girl, he feigns fluency in foreign languages when all he really has are a few odd phrases, "like echoes of some dream of [his] lost fatherland." About himself O'Connor always said that he loved girls and education from afar, with the same results. Dreaming of bliss transcending the coarse humiliation of his home and job, Larry Delaney finds that his princess feels exactly the same way about her life. His fantasy is destroyed by her tears, and Delaney walks off alone down the river. It would be years, he confesses in retrospect, before he realized (and realization is the goal of every O'Connor story) that he had loved the girl because she was "one of the duke's children, one of those outcasts of a lost fatherland who go through life above and beyond themselves like some image of man's original aspiration."

For some reason O'Connor agreed to an ambitious lecture tour in February and March. Because he hated, or rather feared, flying, he and Harriet had to leave early in the month by train for California, where he spoke at Stanford University, the University of San Francisco, and the University of California at Berkeley. From the West Coast they journeyed to Michigan for more lectures, before returning to Maryland. There in March he gave a talk to a meeting of librarians in Annapolis, only to leave the next day for New York to do a television interview with Walter Kerr. In April he visited the University of Virginia under the auspices of the Peter Rushton Seminars for a series of lectures on the modern novel entitled "Ride to the Abyss." In May he met Arnold St. Suber and Richard Widmark to discuss a screenplay of one of his stories, but once again nothing came of it. All this time Harriet walked a step behind her husband, frantic about the pace he was keeping, scrutinizing his diet, and generally cautioning him about his vices—smoking and drinking. But through it all O'Connor was irrepressible; he reveled in the attention and thrived on the activity.

It is difficult to understand why O'Connor drove himself so hard, keeping more irons in the fire than one might expect of an established writer financially able for the first time in his life to do exactly as he wished—to write for himself. But O'Connor's frenetic handling of his tremendous success in America seems to indicate that he never really believed it, even when he started to receive outrageous sums from magazine editors for whimsical pieces and from university faculties for guest appearances. He could never settle comfortably into the role of "man of letters" as, for instance, his friend Seán O'Faoláin had, and being treated as a famous Irish writer did not fit his image of himself as "just the old Cork yob." He really wanted nothing more than a quiet place to write.

He once confided to O'Faoláin that he considered writing a creation of soul. "The act of imagination," he said, "is an act of self-acceptance." But that desolation of reality and the silence of infinite spaces he had come to talk about so much may have sprung more from feelings of worthlessness, magnified by his provincial, unpedigreed heritage, than from feelings of self-acceptance. His greatest fear was that of being an ex-poet. Only when he had a story banging around in the echo chamber of his mind was Frank O'Connor really alive. In company, straining to keep his public mask in position, he was out of his element but driven nevertheless by the resentment and loneliness of the outsider

to fight for center stage—only to exit with sheepish regrets for having dis-
graced himself. Even his literary criticism was a posturing attempt to prove
himself. He recoiled from the criticism of editors and even of friends, but he
returned to his study to rewrite relentlessly, obsessed by the mirage of the perfect story.

During the spring of 1956—between lectures, interviews, and random
journalistic work—O'Connor found time and inspiration to write three stories,
two of which, "The Paragon" and "The Ugly Duckling," were soundly rejected
by *The New Yorker,* with whom he still had a first-reading agreement.[27] William Maxwell confided in a note to O'Connor's agent that he seemed lately to
be more interested in didacticism than in his characters, supporting his complaint by saying, "he can set stones to talking and revealing their hearts any
time he chooses to." The one story the editors of that magazine did accept was
"The Pariah," in which O'Connor backs far enough away from his characters
to let them speak for themselves. Jack, the young narrator, is a throwback to
the Atheists' Club stories, a cynical observer trying to orchestrate his sister's
frantic love affairs. All the broken hearts and mended friendships leave the impression that in Cork love is an endless chain of unhealthy triangles, linked by
"romance and pathos." The Cork O'Connor sees from his writing desk in
America is a combination of innocence and anguish, and what was seen as didacticism by the editors of *The New Yorker* was actually a generalizing impulse
growing from nostalgia.

"The Ugly Duckling" (later published under the title "That Ryan
Woman") is another version of how Mick loses his faith, "which in Cork is
similar to a girl's loss of virtue," and loses his girl in the process.[28] Mick is
well-read, "a creature of habit who [controls] circumstances by simplifying
them down to a routine," and one who lives with associations. When his father
dies, he returns to Cork and is "suddenly plunged back into the world of his
childhood and youth, wandering like a ghost from street to street, from pub to
pub, from old friend to old friend, resurrecting other ghosts in a mood that [is]
half anguish, half delight." In his nostalgic absorption he goes to see his old
girl friend, now in a convent. Though still a die-hard agnostic, he is able to understand how she had made her own happiness: "Because of some inadequacy
in themselves—poverty or physical weakness in men, poverty or ugliness in
women—those with the gift of creation built for themselves a rich interior
world." Though susceptible in every way to the "poetry of change," Mick
leaves the lovely nun knowing that the old love affair will go on "unbroken in a
world where disgust or despair would never touch it." This last may have been
what seemed didactic to the urbane editors of *The New Yorker,* but as O'Connor wrote back sharply to them, it is a "piece of pure lyricism in which the
characters are regarded merely as voices in a bit of instrumental music." It is a
lyric story, written for his own satisfaction, "without expecting anybody in the
world to like it except [himself]."[29]

During most of the year Michael corresponded with Dermot Foley, who
was now librarian of the Cork Free Library. Though he complained at great
length about the cold shoulder he had been receiving from O'Faoláin and
about Evelyn's unreasonableness, his main topic was Ireland. He longed for
the "damp and the cold." Being an "exile from Erin" troubled him: "My work
seems to be getting more and more soft-headed; I suppose it's the price I have

to pay for 'living so far from my disgusting models' as Stendhal puts it. If I don't get home this summer I'll start becoming a second Seamus MacManus or Paddy Colum." Then suddenly he wrote in July that he would be arriving by boat in a few weeks and that he would have Oliver for a few days. He had written to Joan early in the year castigating her for keeping Oliver from him, an unreasonable accusation since she had not known his whereabouts until then. However, she agreed that if he wished to see Oliver he could do so in Dublin, but she took the precaution of going to Ireland at the same time. Because Harriet had promised her parents that she would stay in Annapolis for the summer, Michael traveled alone; actually, he wanted it that way. It had been a trying year, and he needed to escape from her watchful eye and from the fishbowl of American publicity. He once told someone that Europeans take their writers so seriously they silence them by prison or censorship, while Americans just buy them off and smother them with attention.

Dermot, always dutiful and thoughtful, made extensive plans for his old friend's visit. Since Monday, August 6, was a bank holiday, he, Sean Hendrick, and Diarmuid Hurley took Michael on a rollicking "bachelor" tour of West Cork—jugs of whiskey in Bandon, a visit to Michael Collins's house near Clonakilty, then a stop at Morris's pub in Leap and on to Bantry for a drink at Canty's. They lunched at Ballylickey, then set off for Gougane Barra, a place of many fond and frightening memories for Michael because of the Tailor. They also planned to visit the grave of Father Traynor. Dinny Cronin, the publican, told them they would still find no headstone—the bishop wouldn't allow it. When he finally realized who Michael was, he told them the enchanting story of how Traynor's friends from the area, in defiance of official policy, had buried the priest on the island at night. O'Connor left with a fine story in his pocket.

Before he left Cork the next week, Michael accidentally met Daniel Corkery on the street. "Well, if it isn't Mr. O'Connor, who only writes for American magazines now," Corkery said wryly, and kept on walking. Fearing much the same sort of condemnation in Dublin, he tried to avoid Seán O'Faoláin, but it turned out that they had both been invited to the same black-tie reception for Sean T. O'Kelly, president of Ireland. Eileen refused to speak to Michael at all, while Seán was formally polite. At some time during the evening Michael was talking to his old rebel friend Sean MacEntee, when the government minister's wife came up and took him away, making it clear, to Michael at least, that he was "undesirable." Of course, he might have been unduly sensitive to the pious whispers and callous jokes of the Dublin crowd, but years of experience had given him just cause.

After spending a few days with Oliver in Dublin, Michael went to France for a solitary excursion. In Paris he met Shevawn Lynam for a brief visit, but the sultry heat of August made him want to leave the city to the other tourists and follow sensible Parisians to the country. Frustrated by even the most banal travel details, he stormed into the Aer Lingus offices in rue de Castiglione one morning—he seemed to enter everyone's life in that way—and "flung his transport problems" on the desk of Donal Brennan, whom he soon recognized as something more than an officious public servant. An hour later the two men were lunching together on the Marché Saint-Honoré and shamelessly quoting poetry to each other. Years later Brennan still remembered that afternoon in the Belle Aurore, when O'Connor "pointed out that the French and Irish were

a match for one another in literary satire and bitterness, and he quoted Aodh-
gan O'Raithille and Leconte de Lisle with equal impressiveness."[30] People at
adjacent tables eavesdropped as he tilted back his great gray head to let the poetry tumble forth in rich, enthusiastic resonance. "There, man, there's great
stuff!" he said to his new friend upon finishing his impromptu performance.
"Sure any Irish poet might say that about Ballyex today!" O'Connor was balm
for Brennan, who felt displaced away from home, even in such a hospitable
place as Paris. The magic of shared poetry cemented a friendship that endured
until death silenced O'Connor's voice a decade later.

Even before he had left in July, Michael had decided not to return to Annapolis; the town was too provincial, too hot, and too close to Harriet's parents.
On his return from France in September 1956, they moved to New York again.
Their apartment in Columbia Heights was above the Esplanade, and from his
desk at the large front window Michael had a splendid view of Manhattan and
the Statue of Liberty. He felt comfortable in the city, not only because of the
sights, the sounds, the shops, but also because of the stimulation of the people
there. Myles meanwhile had enrolled at the McDonogh School in Baltimore,
somewhat against his father's wishes. A house without the distracting presence of a teenager, however, proved most congenial to a writer trying to produce another volume of short stories. Within a month O'Connor wrote two
more Larry Delaney stories and the volume *Domestic Relations* fell into place
almost without effort.

Though "The Study of History" and "Daydreams" feature the familiar
voice of Larry Delaney reminiscing about the foibles of his youth, they both
spring from O'Connor's obsessive quest to understand his dreams. Both stories
concern a boy who dreams of himself as someone grand only to awaken and
find his "little skin of identity" paltry and common. At the end of "The Study of
History" Delaney, having explored the fantastical notion of who he might have
been if his father had married another woman, tries to induce sleep by chant-
ing his real name and address.[31] Even that trick fails, however, for he has broken out of his established identity and somehow cannot get back into it. In his
nightmare he is lost "in empty space, divorced from mother and home and
everything permanent and familiar." Only when his mother comes to comfort
him do the terrifying spectres vanish; under her touch the terror retreats and
the "anguish of infinity" is left behind. The same disjunction of fantasy and reality occurs in "Daydreams," though in a less disquieting manner. Out of work
and short of funds, the twenty-year-old Delaney would walk the streets or read
in the library, always dreaming of women. On the occasion recreated in this
story, he stumbles into a feud between a prostitute and pimp. Like the heroes
of his reading, he rushes in to defend the lady, only to be embarrassed by his
impetuosity. Fair damsels require rescue only in books, he decides. As for the
prostitute, she has disappeared, he supposes, "to Liverpool or Glasgow or one
of the other safety-valves by which we pious folk keep ourselves safe in our own
daydreams."

Myles once told a family friend that his father was not just interested in
dreams, he was obsessed by them. This obsession rested on a nagging suspicion that the inner world represented in dreams was untrustworthy, fragile,
even dangerous. The theme of the Larry Delaney stories is a variation on the

betrayal theme of "Judas"—the fanciful innocent let down by a desolate reality or the romantic whose natural instincts betray his inflated idealism. Delaney in "The Genius" dreams of being an explorer, a writer, an opera singer, and finally a priest—all in an effort to offset the blight of his surroundings. Fantasies of love and war betray the young men of "Private Property" and "The Duke's Children," while the illusions of maturity (friendship and family) haunt the older people of "A Bachelor's Story," "The Ugly Duckling," and "Orphans."

A dreamlike sense of unreality defines the essential character of the volume of stories O'Connor finished in the first few weeks of 1957 and sent to Knopf under the title *Domestic Relations*. Though Frank O'Connor appeared, in one guise or another, in every story he wrote, the autobiographical voice presides more obviously over whole volumes than in single stories simply because the stories he chose to tell were often those of other people, refracted through his own moral lens. There is something at once highly creative and highly disturbing about the illusion of self-disclosure in *Domestic Relations*. It is almost as if the writer were trying to talk about himself without really revealing anything important about himself. The voice is sympathetic to other people and judgmental of itself—not the adult self but the self of a shadowy past; but by insisting on viewing things entirely from the outside, O'Connor has actually blurred the line between fiction and autobiography. By disassociating cause from effect, he leaves the reader wondering where the interior world of dreams ends and the desolate reality begins.

For as long as he could remember, Michael O'Donovan had been awakened by intensely vivid dreams; even the most innocent or silly dreams perplexed him. His nightmares, usually concerning some kind of domestic violence, were particularly disturbing to him. After his remarkable conversations with Dr. Metman in 1941, he faithfully kept a record of his dreams and brooded continually over them. He also read everything he could find on the subject of dreams.[32] Sometime in 1954 or 1955, while working on *The Mirror in the Roadway* and the stories for *Domestic Relations*, he also began writing his own book on dreams. The book was never finished, but enough of it survives in manuscript form and in a single article published posthumously in *Vogue* to reveal where his ideas were heading.

"I am very interested in dreams. I can sometimes even translate dreams, and one which I translated some time ago is interesting because the heroine of it is really the subject of my talk tonight." In that curious way O'Connor opened a BBC broadcast talk on the short story in October 1951.

In the dream she appears as a beautiful and intelligent girl who tells me that when Rimbaud and I were friendly we communicated by signals. It also appears that I bought her cream biscuits, which she turned into plain ones.

Now the reference to Rimbaud and to cream biscuits is interesting because it means that I began by wanting to be a poet. The cream biscuits are the poems; the plain ones are the short stories. Like the Muse herself as represented in the dream, they represent a compromise, between two sides of my nature, the poet who wants beauty out and out, and the intelligence which is liable to disintegrate any beauty it sees. The poem has to be beautiful out and out, and my intelligence is too destructive to let me get at it. The short story is a typical compromise. So you see to me it means that the story is a form of the poem, not a form of the novel. There's a very big difference represented by the approach. Poetry is a personal, lonely, anarchic art; the novel is a comprehensive social one.

Among the titles O'Connor had considered for his book on dreams were "Everyman His Own Family" and an ironically Joycean alternative, "Here Comes Everybody," both of which sprung from the assumption that in dreams one acts out a universal drama common to everyone. "I can only surmise that the individual is to an extent an integration of family influence, a fusing of the elements derived from father and mother to make a new person. Perhaps that is what the numerical symbolism means and the father's 1 and mother's 2 are combined in the symbol 3." Over the years he refined his ideas on the primal conflict represented in dreams by father and mother figures. In one of the last pieces he ever wrote—on dreams or anything else—he could thus conclude:

> The father and mother of our dreams are only occasionally the real father and mother. The dream father is a pigeonhole, a category, a principle of authority who must at the same time represent God, the government, the dreamer's human father, the dreamer as father, and the dreamer—man or woman—as conscience or judgment. He usually appears on the dreamer's right-hand side as the mother appears on the left. To put your father on the left-hand side may mean, as in one or two dreams I have read, that you are trying to use instinct as a substitute for conscience. . . . He seems to be the "public" as opposed to the "private" figure, the "front" as opposed to the "back." He is the real source and origin of life, protector of the moral law, civilization, and adaptation as opposed to the enduring, unchanging material embodied in the female principle.[33]

In 1941, the same year in which he took to recording his dreams, O'Connor had been at work on an essay on Corkery. In that essay he goes to considerable length to show that Martin Cloyne and Stevie Galvin in *The Threshold of Quiet* represent two sides of Corkery's personality, a Freudian conflict within the author given external expression. He believes that these characters were drawn from such depths of personality that the symbols chosen for externalization have all the appearance of objective reality and that it would be vain to look for subjective implications. He asserts that they are like dream symbols, "the private business of the author, and have nothing to do with criticism." Corkery, who was, of course, O'Connor's first literary father, was also, for him, the paradigm of the indulgence of the private imagination, a fatal flaw he found also in Joyce.[34]

In that Corkery essay O'Connor also recounts for the first time one of his own most haunting dreams: *I am drugged and tortured. When I wake I am tied to a post. My left arm has been stabbed in a great many places and has withered. Mussolini stands before me with a penknife in his hand. Franco is standing some distance away with his back to me. Mussolini says compassionately, 'Franco did that. These Spaniards are so cruel.'* Another version of this same dream subject came to O'Connor in a most extraordinary manner:

"as a complete short story, so vivid and exciting that I at once began to write it." Before he was done, he put it aside, seeing that it was in fact simply a version of the Jekyll and Hyde theme, demonstrating nothing more than his own "ugly character." To O'Connor the torture by Mussolini meant that he was accusing his judgment of crucifying his instincts. "So far as I understand their purpose, dreams are really a sort of built-in stabilizer that tries to reconcile the two sides of one's character, the masculine and feminine, the intellectual and intuitive."[35]

After years of dreaming, brooding, and studying, O'Connor came to believe that he understood the language of dreams, a language as capable of translation as Ancient Irish. From the dream journals of William Archer, for instance, he concluded that the man had suffered for years from some kind of gastric ailment and that he idolized his son. In Joan's dreams he found the basis for his notion of the externalized triangle of father, mother, and lover. In another place O'Connor wrote about a man who fell asleep worried about his justification for "abandoning a woman who had been unfaithful to him." His dream was this: "A man whose horse had thrown him in a race and broken its leg hadn't the heart to have it shot." Such dreams illustrated to him that the function of dreaming is to neutralize concerns that normally demand conscious attention. The distortion is less important than the verbal stream by which associations can be made to connect conscious and unconscious processes.

As certain as he was about the validity of the translation of his own dreams, O'Connor believed that without the conscious content most dreams were unintelligible. He left "snapshots" of his dream life scattered through nearly a dozen notebooks, but the details surrounding his dreams have vanished, disintegrated, as he said, "into little heaps of dust." Thus, to construct some allegory of the private life of Michael O'Donovan from those dreams would be dangerous conjecture. However, his notebooks are also full of snapshots of stories, many of which he enlarged into full-size portraits of a kind of life that does not disintegrate with time. His stories often came to him quite effortlessly, as if in a dream, whole in themselves. What the storyteller looks for, he once said, is that "lonely lyrical thing you feel at a graveside, and the first time you fall in love. It doesn't last, of course." But the stories last and from them can be discerned a great deal about the man who wrote them. "One writes in a sort of dream," O'Connor said, "and I can only hope that when I wake, I shall be satisfied with what I have dreamt."

I V

At Christmas, 1956, Michael sent a cable to Liadain and Owen in Dublin wishing them a happy holiday season. A week later, however, he received a wire from Stan informing him that the children had been alone for nearly a month and that Liadain was very ill. Assuming that Evelyn had deserted the children, he wrote to Dermot for more details. Wondering also if his daughter was reacting hysterically, he wrote to reassure her that he would be in Ireland in March as planned. However, the problem could not be solved by a simple stroke of the pen. Evelyn's husband had emigrated to Canada that fall to find work, and she had followed early in December to find a place for the family to live. Though Evelyn had left the children in the care of a neighbor, Liadain had ended up with the bulk of the responsibility for Owen and her two half-brothers. By an unfortunate set of misunderstandings Liadain was living the story "What Girls Are For" all over again. Finally, after a complex chain of negotiations involving Dermot Foley and Larry Elyan in Dublin and Michael in New York the problem was solved. Liadain, who had been in the hospital for three weeks, was released when the doctor was sure she could travel. In early February she and her three brothers left Ireland for New York. Michael and Harriet met them at Idlewild Airport and sent them to Montreal, where Evelyn was living.

In March, Liadain telephoned her father to say that there was nothing for her in Canada. Knowing that Myles was continuing his schooling, she explored with her father the idea of taking up nursing. More than anything else, she was homesick; seeing her father at the airport had erased four years of hurt and she was now reaching out for him again. Michael responded the next day by letter: He could not yet bring her to live with him. He was leaving for Europe in a few days and his flat in New York was too small for a family anyway. But he did promise that she and Owen could spend the summer with him at Ferry Point Farm in Annapolis. Until then she was to catch up on her studies at home and above all to take advantage of living in Montreal to master French. "Meanwhile, cheer up," he advised. "Everybody is as homesick as hell for the first few months in this Continent, but if you are still homesick after your first dance at the Naval Academy in Annapolis, I give you full leave to go back to Ireland and get a job as an usherette in the Metropole."[36]

Later that month, O'Connor left for Denmark, via Ireland, of course, for a writers' conference in Copenhagen. As much as he abhorred such literary gatherings, he decided to endure this one for the sake of what he jokingly called his "European reputation."[37] With his volume of stories safely in the hands of William Cole at Knopf he also couldn't resist this pilgrimage with his American wife. Dermot met their boat at Cobh and took them to the Metropole. No sooner had they sat down to a cup of tea than a call came for Mr. O'Donovan. It was Nancy McCarthy, who wanted to see Michael again and to meet his new wife. Michael was delighted by this voice from the past, but wondered how the two women would get on. He need not have worried. They met at her house outside Cork; as Michael hugged Nancy warmly the years of estrangement evaporated. Nancy and Harriet took to each other at once.

Later, Harriet asked Dermot what he meant by telling her husband on his last visit not to return to Cork. He explained, to her relief, that it had to do with the provincial atmosphere of the place; she had thought it had to do with her and the embarrassment she might cause him. They met Michael at the hotel and resumed their walking tour with Michael pointing out the Opera House, O'Faoláin's family home nearby, the locations of some of his early stories, the house in Sunday's Well where his mother had worked, and the convent where she had grown up. On the Mardyke he pointed out the seat where he had once talked to a man who was hanged a few weeks later. The rest of their stay in Cork was taken up with meeting old friends like the Hendricks and the Murphys, and a trip to Gougane Barra which, to his amusement, gave Harriet an uneasy feeling. "Too many ghosts," she pronounced. They left the next day for Limerick to spend some time with Stan before journeying on to Denmark.

Shortly after he returned to the States Michael received a desperate letter from Liadain, begging to live with him. He repeated his invitation: she and Owen could spend the summer with him, but insisted that an earlier arrival would be impossible. In a few days, he explained, he was to fly to Ireland for the world premiere of a film based in part on "Majesty of the Law."[38] Myles would be out of school at the end of the month, he told her, and she could come then. To reassure her, he promised to send the train fare the next day.

O'Connor returned from the whirlwind publicity tour at the end of May. A week later Liadain and Owen arrived from Canada. Both children were exhausted from their trip but very excited, though Liadain was quicker to hug her father than Owen, to whom Michael was a virtual stranger. The next day Harriet's father, whose relationship with Michael had warmed to respectful neutrality, drove the entire family back to Maryland. For the first time in eight years Michael was together with all three of his children. Even then his pattern of working in the morning, walking in the afternoon, and relaxing in the evening prevailed, leaving Harriet and her mother to entertain the visiting youngsters. At the end of the month Owen was treated to an American-style birthday party with cake, ice cream, soda pop, and a cowboy outfit.

Myles turned eighteen in July. That past year he had begun to take an interest in his studies. The military discipline and excellent standards of McDonogh kept his nose clean and in the books. That summer, he surprised his father by displaying a rather extensive knowledge of military history, a subject that so fascinated him that he would spend hours—like a poor boy in an attic den years before—mapping out famous battles, building model planes and ships, and reading biographies of military heroes. He pestered his father all summer for war stories and got a few hair-raising accounts of ambushes and flying-column actions during the Black and Tan War.

Oddly enough, his father was absorbed at the time in reading about the American Civil War, primarily so that he would be able to argue intelligently with John Rich, an ardent Confederate sympathizer. His birthday present that year to Myles was Bruce Catton's *A Stillness at Appomattox*. One evening on the veranda of the big house overlooking the Naval Academy, he recreated Catton's account of General Grant smoking and whittling sullenly on a piece of wood in front of his tent at Germanna Ford as he fed more troops into this crucial battle. Myles sat spellbound, listening to the voice of his father, who spoke with great animation, making the gestures of whittling, the grimaces of consternation, and then accelerated toward that moment when Grant stroked his knife faster and faster until the poor stick of wood lay in a heap of shavings at his feet. At that moment Grant knew he had won: Having made contact with Lee, he would hold on tenaciously.[39] Catton had captured the real story, Michael explained to his son, by seizing on the moment of discovery. "And that's why I wrote stories," he concluded, and there was nothing more to say. Myles somehow found time that summer to read some of those stories; he never relinquished his passion for military history, but from that moment on he also became an ardent student of the work of Frank O'Connor and two of his heroes, W. B. Yeats and Anton Chekhov.

O'Connor had already written many stories about the ways orphans, illegitimate children, and otherwise displaced children have of attaching themselves to surrogate parents while still holding some sort of instinctive bond to their biological parents. In such stories as "The Little Mother" and "The Step-mother" he had explored the other side of that mutually rewarding and wrenching relationship. That summer, he had a chance to observe at close range that very substitution process. Harriet showered Liadain with special and motherly attention, shopping with her for new clothes, introducing her to girls her own age, and taking her along to a few "ladies' gatherings." It was a new and frightening experience for Liadain, a girl whose parents' lives had kept her virtually sequestered inside the Strand Road house. Dropping out of school to work in her mother's sewing shop and tending her younger brothers hadn't made her more worldly. Evelyn had let her know that she was not to re-turn to Canada at the end of the summer with Owen. So, as warmly as she felt toward Harriet, Liadain was also torn by feelings of rejection. She had once been her daddy's darling. At Strand Road he had usually taken her for walks, rather than Myles; and when he was not writing, he had always been good for a cuddle. When he left, she had been crushed; it had not been hard for her mother to turn her against him then. Now she was being sent to live perma-nently with him, but resuming that close father-daughter relationship, as if the disruption of the past decade had not happened, proved difficult for both of them.

Michael took Liadain that summer to Cambridge to be tested by a Har-vard psychologist. Liadain recoiled when faced with the tests, her self-confi-dence so low that she feared failing something she had been carefully told had nothing to do with success or failure. She had no concept of such words as *ap-titude* or *diagnostic,* but she feared anything at all to do with school. So the man simply talked with her and found her bright but very troubled. Her experi-ences in the convent school in England suggested to him that a coeducational environment would be most advisable; he recommended two fine schools, one of which was Solebury in New Hope, Pennsylvania. "New hope!" Michael as-serted gaily. "My daughter needs new hope!"

In September 1957 *Domestic Relations* appeared, but only in America, so O'Connor was, for once, spared censure in Ireland. William Bittner, reviewing the new book in *The Nation* a few months later, remarked that in his newest work O'Connor seemed still to be Irish, "even though *The New Yorker* is get-ting into his blood."[40] In fact, of the fifteen stories in *Domestic Relations,* ten had originally appeared in that prestigious magazine. All but one of the stories ("Private Property," which appeared originally in the *Evening News* in 1950) had been written since *More Stories,* a proximity in time that also assured the volume a certain unity. All the stories in *Domestic Relations* display the seam-less craft American readers had come to expect of Frank O'Connor. The "bony structure" he often spoke about is ivory smooth. There are no rough edges, but then neither are there many shocks of immediacy, those moments of impure creative urgency that resonate from so many of his earlier stories.

By and large, reviews were laudatory. O'Connor's old friend Denis John-ston, however, writing in the *Saturday Review,* said a few things that probably could not have been said by American reviewers.[41] After acknowledging that the stories are authentic gems of craftsmanship, Johnston moves quickly to ponder the question that had baffled O'Connor's friends and admirers for years: "At what point is Frank O'Connor going to move from these artful snap-shots to the major work for which he is so eminently equipped?" Johnston is questioning not the validity of the short-story form but merely O'Connor's limited use of it. "Guests of the Nation" proved him to be a "writer of major proportions." Since then, Johnston asserts, he "might be expected to have found far more to write about during his last thirty violent years, when un-neutrally battling with the world at large, than during his first twenty-five, when he had nothing worse to bother him than the Free State Army. As yet, however, there are few clues to be found in his work to indicate that he has ever left Munster." Perhaps the reason Johnston was so baffled is that he denied what even O'Connor admitted about himself: that he was basically a provincial.

Johnston continues his critique by comparing *Domestic Relations* to Joyce's *Dubliners,* observing "the same progression from childhood—superbly etched in 'The Genius' and 'The Study of History'—to the maturity of 'Expectation of Life.' " He also finds the same autobiographical quality, though O'Connor's "observer is no single, tiresome Dedalus, but masquerades under a variety of pseudonyms." Johnston knew that one made such a comparison at the risk of losing the friendship of O'Connor, who considered Joyce "a tyrannical boss of his material," while viewing himself as an "instinctual" writer. He also knew that O'Connor, particularly when pulling the leg of a newspaper interviewer, tended to cloud the processes of his art.

> Actually, these stories confirm the view that he has a much greater sense of form and discipline than Joyce ever had. Where the magical use of language is concerned . . . there is no one to equal the old Maestro. But Joyce could never have risen to the supreme technical efficiency shown by Frank O'Connor in the construction of "Fish for Friday," every line of which is functional as regards the final effect, and which should be examined as a model by every student of the short story. If this is "instinctual," so is Euclid.

By accident or design Johnston answered the question of O'Connor's unfulfilled potential by putting his finger on the unresolved conflict in O'Connor's artistic mind—the conflict between judgment and instinct.

Almost simultaneously with the publication of *Domestic Relations* Oxford University Press came out with O'Connor's selection of Irish short stories.[42] The stories included in this anthology seem neither to prove his theories nor to be representative of much of anything, a failing attributable mainly to the way the collection was put together. It all began in April 1955 when Derek Hudson of Oxford University Press approached O'Connor about editing a book of Irish stories for the World's Classic Series. The financial prospects for such a venture were so slight, however, that O'Connor was faced with the exasperating necessity of offering nominal fees to old friends for their stories. Not many years before, he himself had quibbled with O'Faoláin about an anthology. This time O'Faoláin, not wanting to cut into his own sales, quibbled about which stories of his to reprint. As understandable as that concern was, O'Connor took it as a personal affront. Elizabeth Bowen agreed readily, but O'Casey refused altogether. Corkery would not allow use of "The Spanceled," O'Connor's favorite, but suggested "Children" instead. O'Connor countered, through Hudson, with "The Awakening." James Plunkett, who was full of admiration for O'Connor and gratitude for his help, jumped at the opportunity, but his American publisher, Devin-Adair, asked $50 for "The Trusting and the

Maimed."[43] Cape wanted 6 guineas for Joyce's "The Dead," and Longmans asked 15 guineas for the Somerville and Ross tale. Harriet insisted that he include something from *The Tailor and Ansty*. Thus, when the reviewer in the *Times Literary Supplement* suggested that the selections were questionable or unrepresentative, O'Connor could laugh without the slightest twinge of guilt or regret.

The fall of 1957 also saw the publication of Alfred Noyes's *The Accusing Ghost of Roger Casement.*[44] Casement, an Englishman who had been knighted for his humanitarian work in the Congo and the Putumayo region of Peru, had later embraced the cause of Irish freedom; because of his activities antecedent to the Easter Rising, he was hanged in 1916 for treason to the Crown. In November O'Connor wrote a lengthy piece for the *New York Times Book Review* introducing the Casement controversy to most American readers for the first time.[45] He examined at great length the probable forgery of diaries attributed to Casement, but concluded that the word haunting his mind was not so much *forgery* as *treachery*. To say that the trial of Roger Casement or the condition of Irish ecclesiastical ruins "haunted" Frank O'Connor is no overstatement. Because he believed in certain causes with such unusual ferocity, he was often laughed at by "normal" people who might have been interested in such things but not enough to allow themselves to look ridiculous. Right or wrong, dignified or silly, Frank O'Connor held his ideas with evangelistic ferocity.

The week after the Casement article appeared, Michael and Harriet boarded a train for Berkeley, California, where he was to have his "genius" tested by a team of psychologists working on the kind of intelligence peculiar to creative artists.[46] The whole thing sounded ridiculous to him, but they were willing to pay handsomely for his services. The only one of the psychologists he liked was a Jungian who simply asked him to talk about his life. At the end of their session he remarked that Michael was one of the most honest men he had ever met. Michael then asked if the man would be honest with him; he wanted to know if they had actually learned anything from their fancy tests. The Jungian admitted that a good deal of the testing, particularly by the behaviorists, was hocus-pocus, but said that they had found that the imaginative artist seems able to go further into the levels of emotional disturbance, even into psychosis, than "normal" people and still come out of it. O'Connor recalled AE's constant reference to the "dark night of the soul" and so left California reassured that he had survived his own emotional abyss.

The return to the East coast was something of an ordeal, particularly for Harriet. First of all, she was fairly certain that she was pregnant, but without medical confirmation she could not tell Michael. Second, since his remuneration came in the form of checks, they were low on cash. They had barely enough, she calculated, to make it home if they carried their own luggage, which left her in an even greater quandary because of Michael's delicate heart and her possibly pregnancy. Her loss of appetite, however, actually saved on food expenses, so they arrived in Annapolis just as the cash ran out. Her family doctor confirmed her suspicions a few days later, adding greatly to the holiday celebration at Ferry Point Farm. In a mood of anticipation, she and Michael returned to New York two days after Christmas.

19

The Storyteller's Story

Autobiography is the art of the misfit.
O'CONNOR, *Towards an Appreciation of Literature*

I

BECOMING a parent held the promise of a new beginning for Harriet but not for Michael. The prospect of becoming a father again brought mixed emotions. He was ecstatic, but he was also anxious about his ill health and advancing age. For weeks their conversation revolved mainly around the baby and its future; and the more they talked, the more worried Michael became about *his* future. At fifty-four he was at the height of his powers as a writer, but he had so much he wanted to say that he could not bring it all into proper focus. The Casement controversy, the anthology of Irish stories, and recent negotiations with Knopf for a new edition of his translations had opened a box of lifelong devotions)oo long neglected. Walking into Manhattan just before Christmas, he told Harriet he wanted to write a book about works of art that meant something to him. He began musing about chapters on Mozart and Beethoven, Degas and Rembrandt. He confessed, with a hint of worry in his voice, that he just could not seem to find a key to the puzzle; he could not see a reason why anyone would want to read about his favorite works of art. Off the top of her head Harriet said something about relating each work to some crucial moment in his life. Whatever else she said was lost to the wind, for he had already retreated into his own mind.

It was not, he told her, Mozart or Tolstoy he had to write about but himself, the one subject he had been writing around for years. The first thing he wrote was a set of vignettes about the women of his neighborhood in Cork, which he sold a few months later to *The New Yorker*, with the promise of further pieces on his childhood. But he soon put that idea aside because there were other voices in the way: voices of strangers on the Holyhead boat or the northbound train, or in the bomb shelters and pubs of wartime London; voices of friends cycling along country lanes in search of obscure ruins or sitting over tea in earnest conversation; voices of wives and lovers singing or wooing or brawling. Before returning to his childhood, he had to get the turmoil of the forties out of his system.

Ever since moving to New York, Michael had loved to watch the liners coming in; he would often muse aloud to Harriet about the people who stood on the decks of those ships, many of them immigrants. He recalled a reference in some official report to "displaced persons." The phrase intrigued him, so he made a list of his addresses from Woodenbridge to Primrose Hill. He made notes about finding his son on the farm at Oranmore and taking his mother's body back to Ireland on the mailboat. He recalled his father stumbling back onto the train, Joan standing on the docks, and his daughter arriving at the airport. His first novel in twenty years would be a working out of his life since then. "Displaced Persons" came to him as if in a dream, and he wrote it with the same inner fire that had possessed him when he wrote "In the Train," "Bridal Night," and "My Oedipus Complex." He worked steadily for about three months.[1] What he really wanted to write about was his own childhood. He joked with Harriet that her preoccupation with having a baby forced him to occupy himself with his own childhood. He took the novel as far as it led him and then, to avoid the kind of quagmire that had buried him in *Dutch Interior,* he put it aside and returned to the vignettes from his past, which eventually became the basis of his autobiography.[2]

Throughout the fall Michael had been corresponding regularly with Dermot Foley. In one letter he confessed that his present children confused him enough as it was without the addition of another, and continued:

> a poor old storyteller's head spins, and he says, taking pencil and paper: "Look, could we have a few facts!" which as EVERYBODY knows is the end of storytellers, since they are supposed to be imaginative and understand all this. Harriet—bless her—professes to understand, and starts a long, deep, dark rigmarole about the difference between men and women, which your humble servant doesn't understand since he doesn't see any serious difference between men and women, and anyhow believes that, if there is one, it's all in favour of the women.

He complains to Dermot about the exorbitant cost of the schools Myles and Liadain are attending, adding "there isn't much else to be done when kids are taken from you at the age of nine and returned at the age of sixteen or seventeen, practically illiterate." In his next letter, which amounted to a bitter harangue about Joan, Michael told this delightful story:

> Night before last the phone rings, and what I take to be my daughter's voice says "That you, father?" I say, "that's right" and it goes on "Oh, father, I have to go to a wedding tonight and I wonder if it would be all right for me to eat meat?" "My child," I reply after a pause for station identification, "You have the wrong father, but my advice would be to eat the meat first and ask permission after." Tremendous chuckles from the other end, and only the dread of getting involved with any more women makes me put down the phone.[3]

He had always believed—and nothing he had experienced could convince him otherwise—that women were the source of all joy and the source of all misery in a man's life.

Michael and Harriet stayed in New York all winter. In February they entertained C. P. Snow, the English novelist whom Michael had known for some time, and Wallace Stegner, the American novelist whom he had only just met on his trip to California.[4] He also saw a good deal of Harry Sions of *Holiday* magazine, who arranged for him to meet with Truman Capote about a film script for "Masculine Principle," and Bill Maxwell, his editor at *The New Yorker,* whom he had the privilege of introducing to Alfred Knopf. Harriet, whose pregnancy up to that point had been relatively easy, came down with the measles early in March. There was, of course, great concern that it was the kind of measles that caused birth defects, but a specialist assured them it was the harmless variety. Nevertheless, she was to remain in bed on a diet of soup. At first Michael brought the soup in bowls, then in mugs, and finally in a small vase. Harriet laughingly queried him about the last delivery. He said that everything else in the house was dirty. He had been conscientious, even solicitous, but he could not or would not wash the dishes.

Harriet's parents finally prevailed on her and Michael to come to Annapolis. They wanted her in their own house, under the care of their own doctors, close to the local hospital where John Rich was the chairman of the board of directors. Michael was not eager to be back under his father-in-law's thumb, but then neither did he want to endanger his wife and baby. On May 1 they went to stay temporarily at Ferry Point Farm, the power struggle between the expectant father and grandfather having been temporarily shelved for Harriet's sake. Her doctor was concerned because of her age and medical history.

On June 24 Harriet entered the hospital with severe labor pains. When her doctor realized he might have to perform a Caesarean section, he sought permission from her father, who gave it without consulting Michael. As it happened, the surgery was necessary, and on the next day a baby girl was born. She was named Harriet, after her mother and grandmother, both of whom were known among friends and family by the nickname Hallie. Michael, from the very first, insisted on calling his new daughter Hallie Og (*og* being Irish for "young").

When the initial rejoicing over the birth subsided and Michael learned what role his father-in-law had played, he was outraged by the indignity but held his tongue in deference to his weakened wife —for two days. Then he exploded, and the two men had it out. Myles, whose recent graduation from high school had been overshadowed by the arrival of a new sister, was trapped in the middle, an intermediary between two indignant, strong-willed men. In one of their shouting matches John Rich claimed that even Michael's son stood against him, thus distorting an innocent remark Myles had made about how much he loved the farm. Michael angrily confronted his son, saying something about "sucking up" to Uncle Jack again. Myles, who was standing at a crossroads of his own, needed the counsel and understanding of a father; instead he had to referee a bitter feud. Just after the Fourth of July he packed a bag, took a bus into Baltimore, and joined the army.

His father left town as well. He went to New York to deliver the manuscript of the first installment of his autobiography, "Child I Know You're Going to Miss Me," to Bill Maxwell and to attend the Neil McKenzie dramatization of "Guests of the Nation," which had opened on June 26 at the Theatre Marquee along with Edna St. Vincent Millay's *Aria da Capo*. The arrival of Hallie Og had forced him to miss the opening, but he wanted to see at least one performance. Three of the principal actors were Liam, Tom, and Patrick Clancy, brothers from Carrick-on-Suir who in the two years since coming to America had made a name for themselves singing Irish music. Michael was delighted with the performance and celebrated with the Clancys at the White Horse Tavern afterward. On his return to Annapolis he stayed in a hotel rather than going back to Ferry Point Farm, but as soon as Harriet felt better, they moved into town. The atmosphere inside the house on Prince George's Street was strained; the oppressive heat and humidity kept everyone on edge. Harriet's recovery from her Caesarean was slow, and even after five weeks Liadain, who needed an operation herself, was still doing the housekeeping.

As a result of his conversation with Paddy Clancy, who then headed Tradition Records, Michael was anxious to see about recordings of "In the Train" and "Guests of the Nation." Unfortunately, nothing came of the idea. Paddy turned down "In the Train" because the Radio Eireann tape was too distorted by train noises. He did want "Guests of the Nation" very much, he told O'Connor, but when he looked into rights, he learned that Neil McKenzie had somehow managed to preempt any other dramatic rendering of the story.[5] When O'Connor heard this, he confronted Don Congdon, who admitted that he had let the rights go to McKenzie. O'Connor was furious and eventually managed to sever his association with the Matson Agency. From that point on, Cyrilly Abels was his American agent.

Throughout that trying summer Michael kept in constant touch with Bill Maxwell, who was now a firm and devoted friend. Michael respected him as he had respected no other editor he had ever had, and deferred to his suggestions almost without rebuttal. Consequently, when Maxwell asked him to read the manuscript of his latest novel, Michael gladly agreed. In a sense he was returning a personal favor, since Maxwell had on his own time perused "Displaced Persons." In August Michael wrote to apologize for taking so long with the manuscript. Harriet suggested that the two of them get together when Michael went to New York at the end of the month for a television taping session. The book had Michael baffled:

> The novel you see isn't either of the novels I see: the proof of that is that the really great scenes move from one part of the state to the other—the mirror scene which first sold me on the Viennots, and the wonderful chapter when Roger pays his bill and they go off in a cloud of misunderstanding. For me, this is the high point of the book: the part where I really found myself with tears in my eyes and cursed myself for my own utter inadequacy as a writer—and yet *as a writer* I haven't the faintest idea how the effect was arrived at and I can only attribute it to those last chapters which you have written in your head and which I can't even begin to visualize.[6]

Still, he could say with certainty that it was "far ahead" of anything else by Maxwell he'd read, and left him feeling "very humble as well as very stupid."

Michael took the manuscript with him to New York, finished two days of taping, and spent some time arguing about the novel Maxwell eventually called *Château*.[7] Almost as soon as he got back to Annapolis, he developed severe head and chest pains. The doctor could not say for certain that he had suffered another attack of angina, but neither could he deny it. He advised rest, careful diet, and the elimination of smoking and drinking. For his own part, Michael concluded that the only cure was to return to Ireland. His recent letters to Dermot, who had implicitly been given the role of O'Connor's Boswell, had displayed a crankiness suitable to one playing the part of homesick exile. Absorbed in his autobiography, Michael filled his letters with memories, such as this characteristic aside: "In my youth there was a character in Cork called 'Mrs. Sorry' because of her weakness for lamenting her Machroom hoam and saying 'I'm sorry I came but ashamed to go back.' " He jokingly added: "A week or two of frosty silence had shattered the dream of my attendance at the Conference in Naples. Mention it in my biography—it was all that stood between me and a European reputation."[8]

He stayed in Annapolis for a week and then returned to New York until sailing. During that brief time Myles came back on furlough from boot camp and felt more comfortable at home than ever before. In uniform, he even felt at ease meeting prominent friends of his father. At lunch one day during this stay the guest was a well-known New York lawyer, an Irish American who had held some position in the Eisenhower administration. Myles mentioned something about being sent to Korea instead of Germany as he had requested on enlisting. The gentleman took a notepad from his vest pocket and asked for his military serial number. Apparently the man still had some influence for Myles was one of only two men pulled from an entire company being sent to Korea. A month later he was on his way to Germany.

On September 23, 1958, Michael and his two Hallies sailed for Ireland. They stayed in Cork for a few days, because Harriet wanted to see Nancy McCarthy again and Michael wanted to roam about the area where he'd grown up just to check his memories. As soon as a flat became available they went on to Dublin. Almost immediately they received welcoming visits from Bertie Rodgers, Percy Le Clerc, the only man at the Board of Works Michael had ever trusted, Niall Montgomery, and Terence deVere White of the *Irish Times*. Michael soon got in touch with Daniel Binchy and another Celtic scholar, David Greene, to discuss the new edition of his translations.

Toward the end of October Mrs. Yeats invited Michael and Harriet to lunch. She had followed his career with more than passing interest and still felt some measure of guilt about Jack Yeats's refusal to let Michael deliver the oration at Yeats's grave in Sligo. She was aware that O'Connor had been accused by some in Dublin of playing the Yeats-and-me game, but she admired his steadfast loyalty to her husband. She also knew that he had been the target of vicious personal gossip and tactfully advised him to ignore it and persist in his own work. Her confidence and counsel were precisely what he needed at the time.

In the middle of November Pierre Emmanuel was brought to Ireland by the Arts Council. Emmanuel and his wife dined with the O'Donovans while they were in Dublin, but for some reason Michael and Harriet were not invited to any of the official social gatherings honoring the visiting French poet. This apparent snub was somewhat softened when Radio Eireann sought him out for broadcast readings—in Irish as well as English. He was also asked to assist in the production of two radio dramas. It was during the first of these ambitious projects, "Country People," based on three O'Connor stories ("The Luceys," "In the Train," and "The Long Road to Ummera"), that Michael came back into association with Jim Plunkett and met for the first time Eamon Kelly, an actor who he came to believe might be good enough to rival Cyril Cusack. Years later Kelly returned the compliment he had never heard by saying that O'Connor was the most inspiring director he had ever worked with. In that interview he described how O'Connor got so wrapped up in the characters that he would interrupt and say the lines, a habit that annoyed some actors. Then he would sit with his head in his hands listening to the actors' voices, and

more often than not, Kelly recalled, the next day he would appear with revised
lines—"the man couldn't let a good thing be."[9]

O'Connor wrote steadily the entire time he was in Dublin, undistracted
by the usual public demands and public pressure. In October he began his last
story about Father Traynor. "Mass Island" tells of the nocturnal burial of an
unusual priest by his friends, a moving tribute to the moral isolation of one
man and the "submerged population" he served.[10] Unfortunately it was the
only story O'Connor published in 1959. His energies were otherwise spent on
the manuscript of *Kings, Lords, & Commons*, which he sent to Knopf just before the end of the year.

I I

Michael's health remained unstable the entire winter of 1958–59, despite Harriet's dutiful attention. He wrote to Dermot that he was feeling "low and
mean," though the stimulation of Dublin kept his mind from turning morbid.
Working with the Radio Eireann Players on a regular basis excited the active
side of him; he still loved theatre, even if he was not welcome at the Abbey. The
Casement controversy continued to engage his interest and brought him together with Roger McHugh of University College, Dublin, who shuddered at
his ferocious opinions but gave him good value in argument. In March, partly
at the instigation of McHugh, O'Connor was invited to Cork to lecture on
Casement. Years before, he had single-handedly thrust the shameful condition
of ancient ruins before the eyes of the Irish people. Now his contention that
the British government had acted with deliberate treachery toward Casement
was generating support from such reputable scholars as McHugh in Ireland,
Brian Inglis in England, and Giovanni Costigan in America.[11] O'Connor continued his earnest campaign by writing strongly worded letters to the *Irish
Times* to clear the name of this misunderstood and maligned Englishman, who
like Childers had given his life for the cause of Irish freedom, a cause that
O'Connor felt the younger generation had come to take too much for granted.

His other great passion at the time was the textual history of the *Táin*, the
ancient Irish saga concerning the exploits of Cuchulain. In this enterprise he
was fortunate to have the friendship of the foremost Celtic scholar of the time,
Dan Binchy. After Michael's death Binchy described him as a "scholar-gipsy"
whose enthusiasm about "every branch of Irish scholarship" was contagious:

> There was the fascination of watching him wrestle with a problem which
> had baffled the professionals, and after a number of wildly false starts,
> produce the right solution. "Nonsense!" he would cry out against the re-
> ceived translation. "No poet would have ever said a thing like that. It
> must be—" and he would propose something quite off the beam. "Im-
> possible, Michael, the grammar is all wrong." "Well, what about this?"
> And so on until, suddenly, the lightning struck and you said to yourself
> half-credulously, "He's done it again."[12]

Binchy, however, knew that O'Connor's work was not mere intuition; for years
Michael "worked tirelessly at Old and Middle Irish," taking valuable time from
his writing. By profession he was a writer of fiction, but the translation of Irish

verse was an equally vital ingredient in his life, an avocation he pursued in humble collaboration with acknowledged experts.

Every Sunday morning that winter and spring Binchy came to the O'Donovan home in Mespil Flats at eleven o'clock and stayed for an hour, rarely longer than two. So regular was this habit at such an irregular hour that Michael finally asked a mutual friend about it. Binchy's housekeeper, he learned, was a very pious woman, and Binchy always went out at that time so she would not know he was not at Mass. Harriet joked that it was just like an old bachelor to keep the only woman in his life off his back, but Michael rejected her cynical explanation. Years before, while visiting at Oxford, he had happened to ask Binchy why he had never married. It was nearly four in the morning at the time and the two friends were drunk and nearly talked out, but Binchy told a story that brought Michael out of his chair, a tragic story of the one love of his life. Sensing Michael's mind already at work, he then elicited a promise that O'Connor would not write the story until Binchy turned seventy. Thus Michael knew Binchy in a way no one else did, knew too that his Sunday visits were motivated by a genuine wish to avoid offending anyone.

Binchy appreciated Michael's loyalty to that pledge of years before; he appreciated the respect Michael always maintained for the way of the scholar, though he often chided him about overestimating the value of scholarship by reminding him of what Yeats had said in "The Scholars." Michael simply dismissed Yeats's distinction between learned old men and romantic young poets, believing it to be rubbish. "Your old Irish jurists," he lectured to Binchy, "were far wiser than W. B. when they numbered among the *áes dána* (artists) not merely the poet but the scholar and the craftsman, for each of them needs the same divine spark if he's to be really good at his job."[13] This unflagging sympathy for his old friend's profession encouraged Binchy to persevere in his work. Their collaboration, resumed at a time of mutual self-doubt, proved personally rewarding for each of them—and it has been said that Irish culture was immeasurably enriched by it as well.

Far beyond anything else in his life at the time, Michael's family was the source of his greatest pleasure. Christmas, 1958, was a quiet, happy affair, enhanced once again by the presence of Stan Stewart, who was almost a member of the family. Oliver's visit a week after the New Year was equally enjoyable. Harriet's genuine and ready adjustment to living in Dublin made things easier for her husband, who was free to dote on his daughter. At the least show of clear weather he pushed her pram along the Grand Canal or carried her proudly in his arms along Grafton Street, his great head cocked at a jaunty angle. When women stopped to admire the baby, they usually asked if he was the grandfather. "I am not," he replied curtly, and then, after a teasing pause, added, "I'm the father." After a glance at Harriet, now looking younger than ever, the ladies usually walked away casting dubious glances over their shoulders. Perhaps they even exchanged bemused speculation about what was becoming of the country.

Harriet's parents arrived in Ireland in April. Apparently they had developed a wary fondness for Michael since the arrival of Hallie Og, for they all survived a full tour of the West, from Cork and Kerry to Mayo and Sligo. In May Myles arrived on leave from Germany. One afternoon he got roaring drunk with Paddy Ritchie, the boy whose attachment to the O'Donovan home in Strand Road had been fictionalized by O'Connor in "The Pretender." In the course of their escapade Paddy told Myles how he had finally found his real father. He had badgered his mother until she reluctantly told him the man's name, though begging him to let the matter rest. Nevertheless, he followed the trail relentlessly, eventually locating the man in England, where he simply walked up to the door of a less than fashionable house and announced who he was.

A few days later, while walking with his own father along their old route from Sandymount through Irishtown and Ringsend to the center of the city, Myles casually asked what he tried to do in his stories. "Lay bare a person's fundamental character in one moment of crisis," his father replied. Myles looked puzzled in the face of such an abstract answer. "Let me show you what I mean," Michael said. For months Myles had been reading everything he could find about Michael Collins, an interest that amused his father. Now, instead of stopping at Eason's as usual, they continued on to the Rotunda where Michael stopped to tell the story of a British officer who had on that very spot forced a group of Irish prisoners to strip naked in full view of the nurses in the hospital. "One of the first things that Collins did when he came to power," Michael said to his son, "was to send two men to Wexford, where they shot that man down in the streets." That one act, he told Myles, said nearly everything one needed to know about Collins's ruthlessness and his sense of justice. That he wept on receiving word that his orders had been carried out, Michael added, was evidence enough of the man's monumental humanity.

On the way back toward the Grand Canal Myles asked if he could tell his father a story to see if he understood a crisis moment. When he finished telling Paddy's tale, he asked, "Well?" "Well, what?" his father answered. "Is it the kind of story you were talking about?" His father did not answer. "Well, is it?" Myles implored again. "Yes, yes," he heard his father mutter as he paced along Baggot Street faster and faster. Myles was puzzled but thought very little more about it until a year later. On the base in Germany he bought by chance a copy of *The New Yorker* and read a story entitled *"A Set of Variations on a Borrowed Theme"* by Frank O'Connor.[14] It was his father's version of the story Paddy had told him.

Early in June author's copies of *Kings, Lords & Commons* arrived from New York. For O'Connor it marked a climax of sorts, not so much a culmination of his work, though it was that, too, but a breakthrough in terms of recognition. When the book finally appeared in England, a reviewer for the *Times Literary Supplement* wrote, "O'Connor is a translator in the class of Rossetti, Pound or Waley: single-handed he has turned a literature into English."[15] The reviewer then went on to say that O'Connor had created an anthology of Irish poetry "from the bright, poignant and precise little landscapes and the religious ecstasies of the monastic poets" to "the folk poems of eighteenth-century Connaught, and Merriman's mordant and sophisticated masterpiece." What was even more remarkable to this reviewer was that O'Connor's poems were so fresh and accessible: "we cease to be conscious that it is a translation we are reading. The poems read at one and the same time like English originals but also like originals of their own time and place."

In the spring of 1959 O'Connor was approached by the BBC in Belfast to do more work for them, but since he was still liable to arrest in Great Britain, his broadcasts had to be taped in Dublin. One of these, a talk on the craft of the short story, was aired on June 24. Four days later Wallace Stegner and his wife arrived for a brief visit. O'Connor had originally given this talk at Stanford University nearly two years before, at which time Stegner had encouraged him to expand it into a book. Since then O'Connor had turned his attention to his autobiography, but he still aspired to write a book on the short story. He had also told Dermot that he wanted to make enough money to be free to write a history of Irish literature and a book on France. Finishing all that, he lamented, would require another lifetime.

On July 30 the O'Donovans flew to Paris. Michael had arranged with Joan for Oliver to be with them in France. As soon as he arrived, they hired a car and drove toward Autun where they were to meet Myles, who had secured another leave. Along the way Michael lost all their checks, discovering the error in Dijon, but everything was back to normal by the time they met Myles for a quick tour of Vézelay and Cluny. Michael was at his enchanting best, expatiating upon Romanesque architecture, telling tales of his cycling tours with Stan, and showing off his French. The night before Myles was to return to duty, they were all enjoying a leisurely meal in a restaurant at Cluny. Oliver and Harriet took Hallie Og from the table for a few minutes, and Michael turned to Myles, who had displayed some displeasure over Oliver's presence on this trip, stroked his moustache thoughtfully, and then, peering over the top of his spectacles, said in mock seriousness, "Your legitimacy was only a matter of weeks."

Oliver returned to England, while Harriet and Michael went on to Paris. Pierre Emmanuel was out of the city for the month of August, so they were able to stay in his flat. But Donal Brennan, who still managed the Aer Lingus operations in France, was there, and Michael wanted Harriet to meet the extraordinary man with whom he had spent so many memorable hours. Brennan was a great reader. He and Michael disagreed amiably about Carleton and Sartre but shared a passion for poetry in Irish. One night that August they were all together in a flat on the Île Saint-Louis when someone asked O'Connor which of his translations he considered his best. Lifting his great black eyebrows, he turned the question on Brennan, who recited some lines by Raftery in Irish and then O'Connor's translation. "Now do you hear the Connaughtman talking?" O'Connor interrupted in mock sarcasm, then continued the quotation: "the room was quiet there above the Seine as he declaimed." People always listened to O'Connor, Brennan believed, because he was "one of Nature's patricians" and because he "brought out the best in others."

Three marvelous days passed quickly in the company of Brennan and Shevawn Lynam before Michael and Harriet were forced to travel on to Le Havre for their return to the States. Early in the fall the O'Donovans returned to Brooklyn Heights, moving this time into a smaller but more luxurious apartment on Pierrepont Street with an even more spectacular view of the city than their previous place had offered. Liadain, who had graduated from Solebury in June, lived with them and worked in a Manhattan bookstore.[16] There was some talk about college, but, like her father, she mistrusted her own capabilities. What Donal Brennan observed of him—that he had an "amazing lack of self-confidence"—applied to his daughter and, in fact, to all of his children. One day, for example, Liadain bought a small painting by Augustus Peck, a simple picture of a girl in a blue coat, her eyes cast down in absorbed melancholy.

However, she was so fearful of her father's judgment, so mindful of his refined taste in art and music, that she quietly hung this prized acquisition in the room she shared with Hallie Og. When her father finally spotted the painting, he expressed such admiration for it that she let him hang it over his desk.

By November O'Connor had finished the last two installments of his autobiography. Since the inception of this project he had been a regular visitor at *The New Yorker* offices. As Maxwell recalled, they "sat at a table, with the manuscripts spread out in front of [them] or with galleys embroidered with queries from the proofreader, and talked."[17] Though his manuscripts were generally immaculate, O'Connor was not overly preoccupied with style. What concerned him was the overall design of the book and, of course, "getting the voices right." When he wandered off to recall some remark of Yeats's or to talk about the latest book he'd read, Maxwell had to bring him back to the page at hand: "Was this word right? Was that sentence what he really meant? Did he need to say that? Wasn't it implied? And weren't there too many adverbs describing how the characters said what they said?" The editor knew that left to himself O'Connor would have moved back into that echo chamber in his head rather than "laboring away at the surface of the writing." Still, he met Maxwell's perfectionism "without vanity or suspicion," accepting cuts, transpositions, and revisions so enthusiastically that Maxwell had to caution him about "unconsidered acceptance." The fact is that Michael/Frank did everything— walking, eating, reading, or writing—at the same ferocious pace, with the same expectant impatience to be finished. At the end of each session Maxwell never knew whether he would be carried off to see Michael's latest discovery—some church or gallery, for instance—taken to a nearby book or record shop, or invited to accompany him home like a small boy after school. In this spirit of collaboration O'Connor and Maxwell hammered out those portions of the autobiography serialized in *The New Yorker.*[18]

Myles came back to New York on leave for Christmas. In the course of conversation about what each of them considered home to be, the topic of Ireland and the Irish character came up. Michael told about an incident in which the son of the Irish ambassador had struck and killed a black woman with his car. Hindered by diplomatic immunity from seeing that his son was punished, the ambassador not only made a generous financial settlement but went to the funeral to extend his personal regret and to inform the congregation that he had sent his son home—small enough punishment, he admitted, but under the circumstances the best he could do. To Michael the man's gesture was born of *real* Irish character, the sort of dignity and honesty he hoped his children would exhibit wherever they lived. Home, he said, was a condition of the heart.

The next day, Michael took his uniformed son on a highly personal tour of New York, hitting his favorite shops and bars. Myles bought some detective novels at one store, prompting Michael to observe that he did not read "shockers" as much as he used to. He still admired Ngaio Marsh, Dashiell Hammett, and Georges Simenon, but he found more than enough crime in the newspapers. As they walked he told story after story of shootings and knifings to demonstrate the grisly horror of life in New York. Despite the bitter cold and the fear of being mugged, Myles enjoyed their stroll. Before catching the subway back to Brooklyn, they stopped at one of Michael's favorite bars. Upon serving them, the bartender asked, "Well, Mr. O'Connor, how does it feel to be called the greatest short story writer in the world?" To which Michael responded without hesitation, "How would it feel, Johnny, to be called the greatest bartender in the world?"

On Christmas Eve the telephone rang. Michael listened for a while as an excited young Irish voice carried on about his plans for a production of Yeats's Cuchulain plays. Finally he broke in, "Jesus Christ, boy, am I always to be afflicted by young idealists coming over from Ireland? Do you realize it's Christmas Eve night?"[19] Liam Clancy, who hadn't a clue what day it was, apologized. Then Michael chuckled and said, "Where are you?" Clancy told him. "Too far! Why don't you come here," Michael commanded. Liam was there in less than half an hour and, after a toast to the season, began talking about his plans. When the young enthusiast finished, O'Connor said "Crap!" Clancy had no way of knowing, of course, that O'Connor was given to violent language and abrasive behavior to protect himself, to keep people at arm's length. After completely devastating his guest, Michael then proceeded to talk with great alacrity about his own ideas on Yeats until four in the morning, when he agreed to work with Liam and his brothers on a production of the Cuchulain cycle. They became such friends in the coming months that Clancy years later spoke of Frank O'Connor as his "surrogate father."

On the evening of St. Patrick's Day, 1960, at the Kaufmann Concert Hall of the Young Men's Hebrew Association at Ninety-Second Street and Lexington Avenue, *Yeats and Cuchulain* came off as planned: four of Yeats's plays performed by Liam, Tom, and Patrick Clancy, Tommy Makem, Sara Farwell, and others. O'Connor vowed he would not even attend, Liam Clancy remembers, but "he was there an hour before." His introduction, delivered with all the Yeatsian sense of drama he could summon up, seemed to be an hour long to the anxious actors. Actually, here is part of what he said:

Every man's life is an allegory. God knows it, the saints live it, the poets write it. . . .

William Butler Yeats was a good son, a good husband and a good father, and that doesn't matter. What matters is that all the time he saw himself as a man who perhaps never lived, an ancient Irish hero called Cu Chulainn. . . . In the old stories it is told that Cu Chulainn killed his son. Yeats, in the first play you will hear, tells us how he too killed his son. How? Well, there are more ways than one stopping one's posterity. At the time Yeats' girl had married another man, and in the play Yeats tells us that it happened because, unlike the man his girl had married, he had listened too much to his own good sense. He says that in all of us there are two men—the clever man and the hero—and when the clever man comes on top it is just as though we had killed our children. He says even more than that. He says that each of us is both a blind man and a fool, and if the hero in us is a bit of a fool, the clever man is always blind. . . .

In the last play of all, written on his deathbed, Yeats, like Cu Chulainn, faces death alone. Everything he had loved has abandoned him. . . . But he dies not because of the one fantasy or the other but by the hand of the worldly wisdom he had all his life despised. That it is the

Blind Man who cuts his throat shows that he is still the Fool. But when the world's judgment has destroyed the Fool and the Fool still stands facing his enemy, it is the Fool and not the world's judgment that has triumphed. Yeats had proof enough of that.[20]

An aging idealist, living in exile, was speaking to strangers about the invisible presence of his surrogate father.

In addition to working with the Clancy brothers on their production of the Yeats plays, O'Connor had continued to work on his autobiography and on the story Myles had given him the year before in Dublin. Actually, "A Set of Variations on a Borrowed Theme" was the last *great* short story Frank O'Connor ever wrote.[21] It was the price he paid for living away from Ireland. He had come to believe that Joyce had put aside stories when he left Dublin; deprived of his "submerged population," his material, Joyce had turned instead to the novel to explore his own subjectivity. "This is something that is always liable to happen to the provincial storyteller when you put him into a cosmopolitan atmosphere," O'Connor stated with great authority in *The Lonely Voice,* the study of the short story that was beginning to take definite shape in his mind.

One evening at the Pierrepont Street house Michael's guest was a Jesuit. The conversation turned, as conversations with O'Connor so often did, to James Joyce. The priest began defending Joyce against Michael's harsh criticism, but as the evening matured, their positions reversed. Finally, the priest laughed and observed that whereas he'd been coming at the subject on aesthetic grounds, O'Connor's approach had been primarily moral. Quite by accident this Jesuit had put his finger on the fundamental premise of O'Connor's entire writing career, the explanation for his persistent journalistic campaigns and his passionately earnest literary criticism. He spent a life championing causes he knew to be morally right, defending the helpless, the outcasts, the easily forgotten masses, and paying tribute to those great and solitary giants of history. He steadfastly believed that good men made good literature, and everything he wrote was a statement of a faith that was entirely moral. As an epilogue to his autobiography he wrote:

> All our arguments about the immortality of the soul seem to me to be based on one vast fallacy—that it is our vanity that desires eternity. Vanity! As though any reasonable man could be vain enough to believe himself worth immortality! From the time I was a boy and could think at all, I was certain that for my own soul there was only nothingness. I knew it too well in all its commonness and weakness. I knew that there were souls that were immortal, that even God, if He wished to, could not diminish or destroy, and perhaps it was the thought of these that turned me finally from poetry to storytelling, to the celebration of those who for me represented all I should ever know of God.[22]

That attitude, however, was not achieved without some doubt. The silence of infinite spaces still terrified him. Given his penetrating honesty, he might have become an Irish Nietzsche, but his instincts tugged in the direction of Pascal. Had he been American, he might have taken the road traveled by such men as H. L. Mencken. Instead, this Irish storyteller remained torn by the wrenching conflict between head and heart; he would never achieve the sense of unity his hero W. B. Yeats seemed to have found, but he had begun to negotiate a personal truce with desolate reality, the cause of which might have been his health. Though he joked about his "old ticker" giving out, the nagging fear of heart failure was discomforting to him. His worried wife constantly begged him to be more moderate in his drinking and smoking. Though he generally smoked a pipe then, he still reached for a cigarette when he was working. He would drink with any friend who came to visit and accepted almost any invitation to appear in public. Frank O'Connor was wearing himself out in America.

I I I

In April 1960, O'Connor took the manuscript of his autobiography to Knopf. He knew it was his finest piece of sustained writing, its quality due in no small measure to the efforts of Bill Maxwell, who had edited it so carefully for serialization in *The New Yorker*. Stanley Kauffmann, assigned by Knopf to edit the book, was horrified to find that after reading the manuscript, he had nearly six pages of notes. He went to Brooklyn Heights worried about how O'Connor would react, and found eagerness rather than inflexibility. Years later, when the second volume of O'Connor's autobiography appeared, Kauffmann described the man he met on that occasion:

> A handsome, white-haired, almost rectangular head; a smile that, under his moustache, looked a little like Chaplin's; a voice that was really unfair to other men, so rich that he made others sound shrill when they piped up. An instinct for locality: he and his young wife and small child were in that apartment in the Heights, overlooking the bay, and Frank had become an enthusiast for the neighborhood; he recommended the museum down the street, and I learned subsequently that he had been in there often, boning up on Brooklyn and Long Island history. Not a big drinker, as far as I know, but a greeter of occasions with drink. The first time I walked in the door, I had a dollop of Irish whiskey inside me almost before I had finished shaking hands.[23]

One of the criticisms Kauffmann had brought with him had to do with the title of the book: No one at Knopf liked O'Connor's first title, "Invisible Presences," because it created a false impression of religious mystery; nor did they like his alternate title, "Mother's Boy." When Kauffmann explained that to Americans a mother's boy was a sissy, O'Connor replied, "That's precisely what I was." But when the editor added that *sissy* carried a hint of homosexuality, O'Connor hastily offered the title he had once used for a BBC broadcast, *An Only Child*. Kauffmann approved at once, and O'Connor moved toward the bottle for a toast. "This book has got to be a classic," he told Kauffmann as he gobbled up all six pages of suggested alterations.

Autobiography, even in the hands of the most talented and honest of writers, takes root in ambiguous soil. It can tap the deepest wells of the soul while avoiding entire strata of memories, regrets, hopes, illusions. O'Connor always said that writing was for him a creation of soul. If there is some allegory to his life buried in his stories, translations, and literary opinions, then his autobiography is the entrance to it, because everything he wrote has such a distinctive autobiographical flavor. For some writers autobiography is a creative act of self-disclosure, but for O'Connor it was an act of self-definition—the lonely artist in a desolate world improvising meaning and fighting for moral purpose. Surrounding this portrait of Frank O'Connor the artist, like a hallway of mirrors, are the various facets of the private life of Michael O'Donovan: sissy, outcast, provincial, innocent, crusader, dreamer. *An Only Child* and the posthumously published *My Father's Son* reveal not who O'Connor actually was (an impossible surmise anyway) but what he saw in the cracked looking glass.

Since O'Connor saw life through a veil of literature, what he said about autobiography gives some clue to his purpose in *An Only Child*. Shortly after the war, in the pamphlet *Towards an Appreciation of Literature,* he observed with some curiosity that the greatest books of the eighteenth century were all "autobiographies of one sort or another: Boswell's *Life,* Saint Simon's *Memoirs* and Rousseau's *Confessions.*" In each book everything is described in relation to the writer who, O'Connor surmises, is "working off some unhappiness of his own; is as it were on tiptoe, talking to us beyond his century and his circumstances as the great writers of all ages try to do."[24] O'Connor not only cracked the shell of subjectivity by taking autobiography to its limit; in the chronicle of his own life he mirrored the history of Ireland in this century—the blight of poverty and the blessing of poetry, the effects of repression and revolution, and the legacy of a divided culture.

O'Connor's life was enriched by a variety of people, in whom he eventually saw something of himself. Toward the end of *An Only Child* he tells of an old friend from Cork, a man named Breen, who believed he had been caricatured in "The Invincibles." Though the accusation disturbed O'Connor, it made him realize that "the characters in whom we think we recognize ourselves are infinitely more revealing of our real personalities than those in which someone actually attempts to portray us."[25] One has only to listen to the various voices of *An Only Child* to verify the same impulse in O'Connor. Writing about the ladies of the Square and the patriots of the prison camp, he identified himself with them, he said, because their voices were all he should ever know of God. Even more personally revealing were the portraits of his father and mother. In his eyes the father's brooding melancholy represented an unreliable masculine intellect, while the mother's stubborn gaiety and simple grace represented pure, feminine instinct. Big Mick's alcoholic violence became an emblem of a death-consciousness, while Minnie's heroic patience stood for all that is life affirming.

The issue here is not whether all he said is true or not—whether his father was really all bad, his mother all good, or even whether Cork and the church were what he said they were. The point is that the way in which O'Connor represented himself in relationship to such people as his father and his mother, his friends and his lovers, his idols and his enemies, helps us gauge something of his essential being. In one way or another every artist makes self-portraits in his work, and what is important is not what he looked like at thirty, in the case of a painter, or what he thought at forty, in the case of a writer, but how he portrayed himself. O'Connor was like an eternal child, always seeing life through the glass of a child's self-dramatization, making certain things bigger than they were and certain things smaller.

People of equal genius, talent, and dedication write differently because of the needs of the times and the leanings of their personalities. O'Connor could easily have become a first-rate playwright, given the place of theatre in Ireland, the influence of Yeats, and his own dramatic inclinations. Instead he was dominated by the lyric impulse on one hand and the narrative impulse on the other. These dual impulses came together perfectly in his short stories and translations, private and intimate forms of disclosure; they blended with somewhat less harmony in his penchant for journalism and criticism, public forms of gossip and self-dramatization. O'Connor was a born mimic who took great delight in reproducing the voices of others, an entertainer who loved the center stage, singing or reading aloud or declaiming. That's just the sort of man he was, and ultimately that's the best answer to why he wrote as he did.

As in so many of his stories, the tone of *An Only Child* is confessional yet self-vindicating, morally serious yet somehow detached from his childish weaknesses by an adult amusement. When a writer of considerable accomplishment tries to explain how he has advanced in his career over the years, to describe the passages of his life from childhood to old age, he must preserve at least the illusion of detachment and humility. There is, after all, "a sort of irresistible force behind a small spectacled boy with an aim in life."

An Only Child is a writer's life, a storyteller's story, told because the bits and fragments of the remembered life haunt him like his dreams. Words and phrases and images from a lifetime of writing still color the fabric of O'Connor's prose: hysteria, melancholy, conspiracy, genius, gloom, gaiety, loneliness, violence, hallucination, outcast, orphan, voices, Mozartean, home. It is often said that a writer has only one book, which he writes over and over again through the years, continually exploring a few basic themes. For O'Connor two fundamental ideas appear in *An Only Child* as they had in nearly everything he ever wrote: first, his perception of life as divided between two worlds, one desolate and the other elusive, and variously figured in his mind as a tension between light and dark, judgment and instinct, masculine and feminine, dreams and reality, romance and realism; and second, his certainty of the ultimate loneliness and irony of human existence, capable of being only momentarily offset by "imaginative improvisation," by which he meant some creative absorption such as music or poetry or love or even faith.

Though he had been ill most of the spring, O'Connor accepted an invitation to take part in another literary conference in Copenhagen during September. At the end of August he and Harriet sailed for France, then traveled north from there by train. In line with the aims of the conference, which was called "The Writer and The Welfare State," O'Connor had initially tried to do what serious writers do from time to time: that is, "to define what is wrong with the world." Then, realizing the futility of that endeavor, he had torn up what he had written, and then, just before sailing, he had written a speech about himself.[26]

Being a writer, he told his audience, meant that he could think only in experiences, and therefore that what he had to say about the effect of modern society on literature could best be illustrated by the particulars of his own life. He told his listeners about his orphaned mother, forced by circumstances to work as an unpaid maid, and about his "labouring father," who never earned enough to support his family, even when he was not drinking. He told about fetching medicine for his mother from the local welfare service, about having teeth extracted without an anesthetic because of the cost. He told about his schooling and how poor children were brutalized, physically and mentally. His point was not that he was poor, or that he was Irish and Catholic, though those were undeniable facts. Neither was it important that by some force of will, to say nothing of sheer ability, he had managed to escape from the gutter of poverty.

What O'Connor had ultimately to say in "The Welfare State and I" was that the whole issue struck him as unimportant. What concerned him at the time was that the sheer bulk of superstates and mass technology threatened "the most valuable thing we possess as human beings": personal freedom. Young intellectuals had no "spiritual homeland" when taste and morals degenerated to the lowest common denominator of the mass market. O'Connor concluded that the restoration of authority and quality required the restoration of the concept of God, "the concept of completeness, of the absolute opposed to the relative, of a dark sun toward which all life turns."

From Copenhagen Michael and Harriet traveled to Paris, where they spent some time with Donal Brennan before meeting Myles for another tour of the south of France. In Avignon Myles showed up for dinner in a new corduroy jacket, which he had purchased just before leaving Germany. The sleeves were a trifle too long, but he was proud of it. "Dad, how do I look?" he asked with a note of bubbly self-satisfaction. Michael looked at him and, with icy precision, said, "You look like a queer."[27] Michael knew the power of words, and in a single sentence or a mere glance he could hurt or intimidate or charm anyone he targeted. At dinner—and Michael insisted on nothing but the best food in France—he was talking about his fondness for Avignon because it was there that he had written "The Pretender" ten years before. Myles sheepishly asked why his father was in Avignon at Christmas. "You don't really want to know," Michael replied.

A week later Michael and Harriet returned to Paris to catch a flight back to New York. Michael anticipated his first transatlantic flight with horror, but because of his "old ticker" he was not permitted to drink enough to ease his fears. Donal Brennan saw them off at Le Bourget Airport, where the *commissaire de police* recognized O'Connor, addressed him as *maître*, and escorted him and Harriet through state controls. The attention pleased Michael very much and took his mind off the eight hours he would have to face in a tube high over the Atlantic. "God, Don," he joked to Brennan, "maybe the local sergeant at home will salute a poor writer one day." He laughed at the very idea. The *commissaire's* gesture of respect remained in Michael's memory and confirmed his love affair with France.

A year previously, at the instigation of Wallace Stegner, O'Connor had been invited to teach at Stanford University during the winter and spring of 1961. Though he had no great inclination to return to professoring, eight thousand dollars and five months in the sun were too much for him to refuse. That fall in New York he wrote with considerable enthusiasm and finished two stories, "The American Wife" and "Weeping Children," which would be his last for nearly three years. The proofs of *An Only Child* arrived early in December, and O'Connor corrected them with eager haste. On Christmas Day he and his two Hallies boarded a train for California. On December 30 they were greeted in Oakland by sunny skies and the smiling faces of Malcolm Cowley and Wallace Stegner, both of whom would, in the months to come, give their fellow writer unqualified support and make his stay both comfortable and rewarding.

Classes began on January 4. Four times a week O'Connor lectured to an overflow audience on the novel in the twentieth century. The lectures were so popular, Stegner would later recall, that if any students failed to show up, "their chairs were snapped up by visitors—faculty wives, random graduate students, colleagues, undergraduates from elsewhere—lurking at the doors."[28] Wallace Stegner, whose son was one of O'Connor's assistants observed that O'Connor himself was the main attraction. His magnetic enthusiasm pouring forth as he read passages from novels he had spent a lifetime reading and his dramatic interpretations of those readings stimulated as they mesmerized. Each of the forty animated lectures was a performance, part of a compelling drama of one man's way of reading. "Incurably synthetic, he leaped intuitively at truth," Stegner suggested later; "his judgments were personal, hence unhedged, hence frequently dangerous." O'Connor's abstract theories were often as outlandish as they were brilliant, but they were always uniquely his own, the product of a self-made mind and an imagination honed in a lonely writer's study. His love of books was transferred with charismatic force when he read and commented; it was then that all doubt, all rational quibbling, fled the room, and for a lyrical moment he illuminated life and literature. "No one came out of Frank O'Connor's lectures a book-scorner or a book-hater," Stegner concluded.

As at Harvard and Northwestern, O'Connor was also responsible for a writing seminar, and a far different thing it was from his lectures. He faced the two sessions each week with a feeling of dread. The students of the seminar were a select bunch of writers brought to the campus by Stegner and Cowley simply to write. Among them were Larry McMurtry, Ken Kesey, James B. Hall, Gurney Norman, Arvin Brown, Peter Beagle, and Christopher Koch, then young and promising talents who have since gone on to their own considerable artistic achievements.[29] O'Connor could no more bully them with his theories than he would have been bullied himself; he could no more make them write his way than he would write like anyone else. Many of them were as self-taught, self-possessed, and self-directed as he. They listened to their own voices, not his, which, as Stegner writes, meant "their own subject-matter, their own approaches, their own languages, and they did not seem to be impressed when he told them things that he had learned about the short story in forty years of hard application." Their casual use of obscenity disturbed him to the point that he refused to read their stories aloud in mixed company. In consequence, they read their stories themselves, as if for no other reason than to embarrass him.

One day, as recalled by Stegner in the memorial volume *Michael/Frank*, Gurney Norman put on a recording of "First Confession" before class. When O'Connor entered to the sound of his own voice, he took the joke as ridicule and was crushed. But when he returned from the spring vacation, he found them eager to resume their literary tug-of-war. They even seemed "suspiciously friendly." Norman apologized for the misunderstanding and the group followed him to the campus coffee shop to prolong the session. Stegner wryly noted that "he thought of them as a bunch of dogs pursuing a wounded fox, they thought of themselves as a bunch of puppies." He had misinterpreted their response; seeking applause, he failed to hear their muffled and begrudging respect. In the end, Stegner wrote, he might not have changed them, but he touched them somehow and "gave them an example of what humanity, cultivation, learning and sensitivity could come to in a fully matured writer, and he made them respect the combination even when they wouldn't imitate it."

By the end of the winter quarter O'Connor might well have been exhausted by lecturing and bruised by the seminar, but he now faced the ordeal of public success ushered in by the imminent publication of *An Only Child*.[30] There were almost daily telephone calls from reviewers in the East and requests from local papers and television stations for interviews. *Newsweek* sent an interviewer, and other prominent publications planned to feature another notorious Irishman in the wake of Brendan Behan's recent assault on American TV.[31] At a huge luncheon for the press sponsored by Stanford University, O'Connor beguiled his interrogators with puckish remarks on Ireland, whiskey, the modern novel, and the problems of the world in general—not in any particular order. He asserted confidently: " [Ireland] is a dying country; its literature, economy, everything. Things won't get better until England returns the north of Ireland to the Irish."[32] On the other hand, he confessed that his greatest desire was to return home and "needle the government," which he considered rather fascist. He expressed admiration of American writers, though declining to name his favorites, and envy of the climate of freedom which those writers enjoyed. At fifty-seven years of age, he felt that he was just hitting his stride as a writer. For thirty years he had goaded Ireland—it had pricked him a few times in return—and now his dream was to end his exile and resume his campaign "to save Ireland from itself."

When *An Only Child* appeared in March, O'Connor was showered with lavish praise from American reviewers. In two months over ten thousand copies of a run of fourteen thousand were gone and a second printing was anticipated. O'Connor received letters from such fellow writers as Allen Tate and Glenway Wescott. He wrote to Dermot Foley, Nancy McCarthy, and Sean Hendrick—all of whom had read the book in manuscript for errors of fact and possible libel—to share the joy of his remarkable success. Writing to Sean Hendrick, he expressed surprise about the interest shown in his portraits of people like Erskine Childers: "Wouldn't it be ironic if Childers' reputation were to be restored by yourself and myself, who went through it all in a sort of haze?"[33] About Corkery, who "got his share of the attention and praise" in the book, he only mentioned that he wished the old man were not so furious. At the end of that letter he told Hendrick of being taken by Harriet's parents to a place called The Top of the Mark—"from which one can see the whole city of San Francisco, as we used to see Cork from Dermot Nagle's house in Montenotte."

In April the spring quarter began. Even as O'Connor's writing seminar shifted to a new venue, so the subject of his lectures shifted as well—from the novel to the short story. For some time Stegner had been after him to put his ideas on the short story into book form, but not until the appearance of an anthology by Seán O'Faoláin did O'Connor actually feel compelled to do it. He even mentioned in letters to friends in Ireland how preposterous he thought O'Faoláin's book was: "I wish to God he'd get back to being Shelley, which is how I remember and like him best."[34] So, with sufficient inducement from O'Faoláin and a suitable platform provided by Stanford University, O'Connor turned his mercurial mind to a critical examination of the art of storytelling. His opinions about the theatre and the novel were those of a writer whose achievements in those forms had been only modest. No one could deny, however, that what he had to say about the short story was firmly embedded in practice and accomplishment. *The Lonely Voice,* the book that he finally made of these lectures, presents the artistic side of the storyteller's story. It was Oscar Wilde who claimed that criticism is the only civilized form of autobiography.

Actually, the book had been writing itself for nearly four decades. Over the years O'Connor's reading tastes had evolved steadily—from Corkery and Turgenev through Babel and Maupassant to A. E. Coppard and J. D. Salinger.[35] For years he had written and lectured about the world's great storytellers, spinning out theories about why the story had lost its narrative voice, about the influence upon the form of geography and social forces, about the submerged population groups of Chekhov, Maupassant, and Anderson. One of his most successful broadcast talks was "One Man's Way," an entertaining description of the "right way" to tell a story. In a magnificent review of O'Flaherty's stories O'Connor claimed with authority that a "good short story must be news." Elsewhere he wrote that it must represent a "bending of the iron bar," meaning a continuous rending of a strong emotion. In his most celebrated literary essay, "And It's a Lonely, Personal Art," O'Connor had already articulated the fundamental premise that would sound throughout *The Lonely Voice:* that by his very art the storyteller is a lonely figure, condemned to wage a losing campaign on the fringes of society and to utter his lyric cry in the face of a desolate reality.

That he took his chosen art form seriously was obvious in what he said to interviewers that spring. Loneliness, he told them, meant ruthlessness and selfishness; the real writer would revise endlessly to achieve the truest expression of his own imagination and he would let nothing come before his job, neither wife nor children nor friends. And he made it clear that his own job was producing stories, at the heart of which was the possibility of truth and freedom and integrity. The story, to Frank O'Connor and, he believed, to all the world's great storytellers, was a way of life. Time and again in the United States he had been asked why he did not write stories about America. Invariably he avoided the question by talking about his lack of knowledge, then by praising American writers, and even by launching into a discussion of why Joyce wrote only about Ireland his entire life. Finally, he concluded that what his American interviewers were asking was why he didn't write about them. His answer: "Because I can only write about ME!"[36] Thus *The Lonely Voice* amounts to nothing less than a defense of his entire life.

Admitting that he was not very good at definition ("If I were able to define a short story there would be no necessity for me to write another of the damned things," he proclaimed in his opening lecture that second semester), O'Connor insisted that he was nevertheless quite clear about what he did *not* mean by a short story. To him it was not a yarn or a squib or, as E. M. Forster put it, a piece of prose fiction of a certain length; length, in fact, had nothing to do with it. He held that though it shared with the novel a commitment to plausible reality, the short story differed from the novel in both form and attitude. Time collaborated with the novelist to establish a rhythm of continuing life, while it fought the short-story writer, who was forced to locate the "glowing center of action from which past and future must be equally visible." The crisis of a novel was the logical result of what had gone before, whereas in a short story what went before was understandable only after the crisis. The crisis *is* the story, and to that "flash point" mentality O'Connor's entire consciousness seemed to lean naturally. "The story, like the play," he said in *The Lonely Voice,* "must have the element of immediacy, the theme must plummet to the bottom of the mind."

All in all, the distinction drawn by O'Connor between the short story and the novel was not theoretical. It represented a fundamental choice in his life, the very scale of his vision. The novel, he believed, places man in society, "but the short story remains by its very nature remote from the community—romantic, individualistic, and intransigent." He saw himself as a lonely voice in a wilderness, and for this reason he saw in the story "this sense of outlawed figures wandering about the fringes of society, superimposed sometimes on symbolic figures whom they caricature and echo—Christ, Socrates, Moses." O'Connor's personal imagination sought the heroic. He wrote eloquently about the world's geniuses, but his own fiction avoided them in favor of the little people of life, the submerged population groups that obsessed all the great storytellers: "Gogol's officials, Turgenev's serfs, Maupassant's prostitutes, Chekhov's doctors and teachers, Sherwood Anderson's provincials."[37] He admitted the idea was tenuous—"It is too vast for a writer with no critical or historical training to explore by his own inner light"—but he was not exploring it, he was stating it.

Like most of his abstractions, O'Connor's theory of the short story is extremely vulnerable, but it fits his Mozartean conception of life and literature. He might have spent his life blowing things out of proportion and demanding more from life than it could possibly deliver, but when it came to short stories—reading or writing them—he was guided by a strategy of containment that insisted on narrow limits and hoped only for a momentary glimpse at truth. Above all, what he wrote in *The Lonely Voice* was as alive, as provocative, and as irritating as his lectures were that spring. Though he consistently baffled his students with generalizations, drawing smiles, frowns, and even blank stares, when he turned to read from a story, no one could miss the enchantment. The vibrant enthusiasm of his lectures emerged, too, in the individual essays of the book, where one by one he paid homage to such writers as Turgenev, Kipling, Lawrence, Babel, Hemingway. He brought Joyce to life and introduced such unknown (at least to American readers) storytellers as A. E. Coppard and Mary Lavin. By and large, his essays (like the lectures) were terse and perceptive, almost devoid of modish critical jargon and narrow academic bias. What one can hear in *The Lonely Voice* is what a crowded hall of undergraduates heard in Palo Alto in the spring of 1961: one great writer of short stories collaborating with other great writers of short stories and, in the process, defining himself.

* * *

By now nothing could assuage Michael's homesickness. Harriet loved
California and talked constantly of living there permanently. Malcolm Cowley
had arranged for them to stay in a comfortable house within walking distance
of the campus, and even Michael admitted to his Irish friends that he enjoyed
playing with his little daughter in the shade of the apricot trees behind their
attractive Japanese-style house. Still, he longed to return to Ireland, if only to
escape from the demands on his time, from his heavy teaching load, and from
the heat—he loved the sun but longed for an occasional gray respite. Under
the unusual stress of teaching and public appearances he had been suffering
constantly from gastritis. He was also smoking and drinking more and exercising less than his physician would have liked. Only in Ireland, he claimed, could
a man really enjoy a good walk. He had developed a nasty smoker's cough (he
was now up to two packs a day) and suffered from severe headaches, something entirely out of character for him.

At the end of May his stomach was in almost continual revolt, complicated
by occasional nausea and vomiting. Gas caused pressure under his diaphragm,
sending sharp pains into his left chest area, furthering his anxiety about heart
trouble. Then, on June 1, while walking to his lecture, he suddenly felt as
though the blood had been shut off from his head at the base of his neck. He
had to sit on the grass until his head stopped spinning and he could focus normally again. He was examined at home a few hours later, and though the physician found him to have abnormally high blood pressure, for which he prescribed medication, he found nothing suggestive of angina. For two days
Michael felt weak; the giddiness came and went. He told Harriet that when
everything disappeared before his eyes, he had to be still for fear that he would
disappear himself. He reported to his doctor a hammering in his chest and a
dull headache. Consultations with two other specialists led to the conclusion
that blood to a section of his brain had been cut off; he had suffered what they
termed a "cerebral incident" (he took great delight in the phrasing), which
simply meant a slight stroke.[38] He was advised to cancel all appointments and
rest for two weeks. His teaching duties were assumed by other members of the
English Department, examinations and final grading were handled by his devoted assistants, and he was free to leave.

As soon as Michael felt well enough to travel, he and Harriet boarded a
train for New York; his doctor had cautioned him not to fly and not to travel
with a child. Throughout the trip Harriet watched him anxiously, carefully
avoiding anything that would excite him. The doctor had explained that his
unusually high blood pressure had to be controlled, so she checked his pulse
and temperature regularly and administered his pills. Hallie Og, who had remained in California with friends, was flown to New York a week later. They
stayed until the end of July in the Brooklyn Heights flat, welcomed Myles home
from the army, said good-bye to the Maxwells and a few other New York
friends, and then returned to Ireland—for good.

20

Exile's Return

. . . but it is here he will return and here, no doubt, he will die.
O'CONNOR, *"The American Wife"*

I

THE O'Donovans stayed temporarily in the home of some old friends before finding a flat in an old-fashioned but conveniently situated apartment block in Wilton Place near Baggot Street Bridge. Shortly after returning to his native land, O'Connor wrote to Bill Maxwell saying, "The older I get the more I feel like a superior tramp who at one time never has with him more than he can carry." Anyone entering the flat, however, would have thought that he had more books than anyone could carry across the Grand Canal in a lifetime. And there were a lot of people who called by to welcome the stricken writer back home. Such old friends as Hector Legge and Dermot Foley saw the same restless eye and heard the storming voice but noticed that he had changed. Under the tight rein of his worried wife he was quieter, even subdued. His American exile and the fear of death had cast a more subtle light on his life, while clarifying his simple, provincial values.

The possibility that Frank O'Connor would die also sent a current of panic through many of those who had ignored him, particularly the representatives of the media, who now rushed to his door, anxious not to miss a great man. The BBC went to Cork to film a documentary on his childhood, and Radio-Telefis Eireann not only set to work on a film version of "In the Train" but also asked him to do an autobiographical piece for the inaugural week of national television service.[1] The Irish newspaper sought interviews with him, but the pieces that came out of these meetings sounded almost like post-mortems. Instead of meeting him at Bewley's, interviewers such as Frank MacManus came to his third-floor flat, overlooking the Grand Canal. Unlike O'Flaherty, who lived nearby but saw no one, O'Connor welcomed nearly everyone, but the man they met was different from the one Larry Morrow had interviewed ten years before. Instead of leaning anxiously forward in a restaurant seat, tapping his fingers nervously on the table and chain-smoking cigarettes, O'Connor now reclined in his old Morris chair and pulled thoughtfully on a handsome pipe, sending the pungent richness of Balkan Sobranie through the room. Instead of tea he now drank whiskey, whenever Harriet was not looking. Outside the flat he still wore heavy tweeds and walked at a fierce pace, but at home he relaxed in an open-necked shirt with sleeves rolled to the elbow. The only marks of his sojourn in America were an Indian string tie and sneakers. An interviewer would still observe a neatly trimmed gray moustache, great black eyebrows, and striking dark eyes. But the hair had gone white while receding toward the great dome at the back of his huge head.

Frank O'Connor in the autumn of 1961 was more secure than the desperate man interviewed by the Bellman ten years before. James Plunkett in his memoir *The Gems She Wore* observed that O'Connor "had the air of someone who had found where he belonged, not an easy thing for a writer to achieve in the Ireland of his time."[2] One sign of this security, as financial as it was emotional, was his weight, up nearly fifty pounds over those ten years. The voice had not changed, though. It still rumbled, deep and resonant, in an oracular accent marked by broad vowels and clipped or trilled consonants. Someone from Cork might have caught the vertical animation of it, but Dubliners probably heard a touch of Oxford and Yeats. (When Harriet first visited Cork, she expressed keen appreciation of the native accent she heard there. Michael seemed surprised and said, "But that's the way I speak." "Oh, come off it!" she replied in abrupt collegiate American.)

What O'Connor had to say had not changed either. Whether trying to follow his authoritative discourse while sitting in his flat, or attempting to carry on a conversation while walking at full tilt, most people were treated to a discourse on any or all of his many obsessions, which Thomas Flanagan, an American scholar and novelist who came to know him at this time, once partially catalogued:

> James Joyce, eighth-century Ireland, Chekhov, Jane Austen, pedants, the present Abbey Theatre, public figures foreign and domestic, the Church, professional patriots, the "forged" (as he believed them) Casement diaries, manuscripts and old books, eighteenth-century Ireland, the Board of Censorship, compulsory Gaelic, the ruined abbeys of Connaught and Munster, his native city of Cork, Celtophobes and Celtophiles, schools which mistreated children, the operas of Mozart.[3]

Even a partial thrashing out of these subjects was more than enough for any friend breathlessly trying to keep up the pace and far too much for any journalist trying to put together a perfunctory feature piece.

Of all these passions, the one that drew O'Connor's keenest attention upon his return to Ireland was the translation of Irish verse. Because Binchy was then teaching at Harvard, he began working with David Greene, a professor of Irish at Trinity College, on a book of texts and prose translations.[4] That O'Connor persisted in this time-consuming and demanding process of refining his old translations and creating new ones, particularly after the banning of *Kings, Lords, & Commons,* says much about his loyalty to Ireland. To him the literary heritage of Ireland represented an undaunting challenge, an ever-quickening adventure capable of holding his voracious curiosity and energy. The translation of Irish verse, then, emanated from a compulsion, no less evident in everything he wrote about Ireland, to come to terms with his home and inevitably with himself.

His imagination in boyhood had been ignited by W. Lorcan O'Bryne's *Kings and Vikings,* a copy of which he found on a back shelf of Hanna's Bookstore in Dublin a month after his return. Besides telling simple stories about the magic of ancient Ireland—Tara, Croagh Patrick, the Book of Armagh, Saint Columcille, the Battle of Clontarf, and many more—O'Byrne wove into this child's book enough translations by Kuno Meyer, Douglas Hyde, Standish O'Grady, and James Clarence Mangan to show why Ireland had always been called a land of saints and scholars, bards and poets. It was from this simple book that young Michael O'Donovan first learned about Clonmacnois, Killaloe, and Clonfert, ruins he later tried so strenuously to save. His radio play on Malachy and his collaboration with Binchy on a life of Saint Patrick probably found their impetus in O'Byrne's book as well.[5] His first encounter with Cuchulain was not in Yeats's plays but rather in O'Byrne's chapter "The Search for the Táin." And though his mother had often sung Moore's melodies to him, he first read them in O'Byrne's book. The point is that Michael/Frank might have left Cork, its provincialism and poverty, but he carried with him the passion for poetry and learning he had picked up in the little library he watched burn during the Black and Tan War.

Speaking to a meeting of Irish librarians during that first winter back in Ireland, for instance, he repeated what he had told a similar group in America: Whereas schools represent the principles of authority and professionalism, libraries and bookstores represent the principle of self-education. In America he had talked entertainingly about books and his experiences as a librarian, but now his purpose was to correct the shameful condition of books in Ireland. "Padraic Colum, the last of the great Irish writers," he told them, "recently asked angrily why in Shannon Airport he could buy a bottle of Irish whiskey but not an Irish book."[6] While it was true that many of the books O'Connor had once bought in Dublin were now out of print, it was also true that book sales were beginning to flourish in Ireland. And while it was also true that the "honor and virtue" crowd still badgered librarians and booksellers, the censorship problem in Ireland was beginning to soften. In some ways O'Connor was still jousting windmills from out of his past.

Nevertheless, to him Ireland without books was as bankrupt as Ireland without her past, her megalithic tombs and ecclesiastical monuments, her heroes and treasures. In an article for the Sunday edition of the *Independent* he proposed the establishment of a group that would "organize exhibitions and lectures, publish reading lists of Irish literature, and underwrite the republication of the hundreds of valuable Irish books that are all but forgotten."[7] This group of reasonable people might be able to influence the minister of justice and the Censorship Board to correct such inequities as the banning of *The Tailor and Ansty*—and, though he did not say as much, his own translations—and to "impress on them that every city and county library in Ireland must have every book by an Irish author . . . whether that book is banned or not." Never again should the country be faced with "the disgraceful problem of a Continental university looking for the works of Mr. O'Flaherty and discovering that in the whole of Ireland there is no such thing."

O'Connor still saw life through a veil of literature. The vast library guests found in his flat was a "Writer's Library," pruned over the years by divorce and countless moves to what he considered the indispensable: the "classics" he loved and wrote about, books of stories by rival storytellers he most admired, Shakespeare texts and a few scholarly works on Shakespeare, books on dream psychology, architecture, art, and music, books by his friends, and, of course, hundreds of books in French and Irish. Actually, cataloguing his indispensables, one wonders what he threw out or left behind, and even more, how he found time to read it all in the first place.

Though a hidebound amateur, O'Connor never ceased to amaze professional academics with his range of knowledge. Donal Brennan wrote of the time someone had compared Alain-Fournier's *Le Grand Meaulnes* to Joyce's *Stephen Hero.* O'Connor responded that such a comparison was nonsense, but went on to ask if anyone in the group had read Alain-Fournier's *Letters,* which Brennan claimed very few professional students of French literature had read.[8] Bertie Rodgers once said that walking with O'Connor was like listening to an encyclopedia; Bill Naughton called him a walking anthology. Some people have implied that O'Connor's knowledge was superficial, but in fact he was blessed not only with an insatiable curiosity but with a photographic memory. Time and again people in his presence would start to quote a poem and falter only to hear Michael finish it. Professor Philip Edwards of Trinity College, for instance, met O'Connor in College Green early in 1962. As they walked up Grafton Street Edwards mentioned something about an essay he was writing about *The Two Noble Kinsmen.* To prove a point, he groped for lines he had probably transcribed from the play that morning, but for some reason could not get them straight. "We were by the flower-seller at the corner of Duke Street," Edwards later recalled. "O'Connor stopped me and stood there and, after a moment's hesitation, declaimed the best part of the speech above the noise of the traffic."[9] Nearly anyone who ever spent more than a brief moment with him had similar experiences; many people, in speaking or writing about O'Connor, have voluntarily summoned up such incidents to illustrate his radiating charm and brilliance.

Despite his many achievements, despite all the acclaim, Frank O'Connor never received a literary prize or honor. When *Kings, Lords, & Commons* was banned, someone in Dublin said that much of it was his own invention, to which he sardonically observed that that was the finest compliment Ireland had ever paid him. Shortly after he returned to Ireland, however, the faculty of Trinity College undertook to bestow an honorary doctorate on this self-taught scholar and improvised man of letters. Thus, on July 5, 1962, dressed in formal attire and academic gown, he entered in procession with the other dignitaries. "The service," he wrote to Myles the next day, "was staggering. The hall or chapel was very cold, and I wrapped my beautiful red and blue robes round me and sat it out grimly until I had to stand up and listen to a Latin address." His old friend Honor Tracy reported: "He looked strangely unlike his bohemian self. As he went by he gave me a broad wink and a sardonic grin, which didn't fool me for a moment. This was one of the good days of his life."[10]

Before speaking at the commencement dinner, O'Connor appeared nervous and out of place. He wrote to Myles that though Harriet "drank two glasses of wine and went off the deep end," he simply "put away the brandy and made a speech about American education which produced gasps."[11] Perhaps he felt somewhat at a disadvantage, having never attended university himself, but the tone of his speech was deferential only at the beginning: "It is a great honour to be permitted to reply to the toast on behalf of the new graduates, all the more for someone like myself whose formal education ended at the age of eleven or twelve." From there O'Connor launched into stories about his experience of university life in America, all quite humorous but leading to the idea that education must be practical and personal; it must make people better human beings.[12]

Though Frank O'Connor could now append *D. Litt.* to his name, his passport still listed his occupation as "Journalist." And just as he took to translating on his final return to Ireland, so he resumed writing regularly for Irish newspapers. As a journalist, however, he was more evangelist than reporter, his concern being not to present facts but to use them to prove a point. His speeches to the librarians and the graduates illustrate this habit of using factual incidents to moralize. Though he was not a satirist, he shared Swift's moral indignation. Even in these last mellow years O'Connor possessed such an acute sense of injustice, and perhaps by then an even sharper awareness of his own ability to contribute to it, that what he wrote still burned with a focused outrage and moral assertiveness. And he worked as any journalist worth his salt must work—quickly. He told one interviewer that he usually got things done in one or two days because he wanted to keep the spirit fresh. "I have to grasp all my ideas in one big movement," he told another; "I am a violent, emotional man, and novels require meditation and a more plodding, day-to-day kind of energy." For this reason he had given up writing novels years before and had stayed with the lyric spontaneity of stories, translation, and journalism.

If his stories seemed to convey a personal sense of loneliness, then his journalistic writing invariably expressed his "old-fashioned liberalism," by which he meant a belief in the common people and a commitment to freedom, authenticity, and simplicity. His stories were generally about people trapped, frustrated, deluded, or hurting, yet finding now and then a momentary ray of insight or hope. Life to O'Connor was the amateur's game: inconsistent, diversionary, and spontaneous. He saw life through keyholes and windows, catching glimpses of the whole in the parts, and he tried to seize it as quickly as possible. He wrote as he lived, impatient for the next adventure, the next cause, impatient for the next flash of clarity, and always on the prowl for a story to light up the darkness. His notebooks and journals were not filled with notes about experiences, living or literary; rather they contained actual bits and pieces of writing and rewriting. Whether doing a short story, a review, or a feature article, he wrote on impulse; the endless revisions were themselves impulses, immediate and new, because O'Connor began everything from scratch, even the twentieth version of a story. He never invented parables to prove a point, but rather he seized on actual life to illustrate some truth about human nature in general, the Irish nature in particular. Synecdoche was a way of life for Frank O'Connor.

At a dinner party during Christmas Hector Legge asked Michael if he would do some writing for the *Sunday Independent*. O'Connor wrote now under his own name—his pen name, that is—rather than as Ben Mayo, but his voice was still assertive, angry, and sardonic. It was as if the old warrior had strapped on the armor once again to slay the old dragons of ignorance, pettiness, conventionality, and injustice. True to form, O'Connor's first four articles hammered away at the disgrace of Ireland's libraries and bookshops, the neglect of her national monuments, provincialism in art, and the mystery of the Casement diaries.[13] To readers he was dotty, just on his hobbyhorse again; while others saw in his campaigns something of a holy war.

In the spring of 1962 he wrote an extensive piece on the holy places of Ireland for *Holiday*. (It was his scathing article for this American magazine in 1949 that had been the last straw for many in Ireland.) This time, however, he said nothing of poverty, pietism, or politics; his tone seems more attentive than combative. His reason for writing about the early monastic sites of Ireland is simply that they fascinate him as nothing else in Europe. Their antiquity creates for him "an overpowering sense of mystery." Admitting that he may be adding dignity to his own enthusiasms, he persists in wondering what might happen in Ireland after his death: "Cashel excavated and restored as a world's wonder, Kildare, Clonmacnois, Clonfert and Glendalough excavated, and in the minds of young Irish men and women a new vision of the Irish past that I can only dream about."[14]

The paragraphs between are no less poignant. More than half of his attention is devoted to Clonmacnois, a place he once dismissed as rubble. And as O'Connor guides his American readers through this ancient place, one has the impression of an old man taking strangers through a ruined mansion he had lived in as a boy. Every cross, chancel arch, tower, and gravestone reminds him of a story, a name, a verse. He is free with his speculations as to why one oratory is so featureless and the next a "gem of Romanesque architecture." He draws analogies to American history, Greek mythology, and French burial customs, and before leaving Clonmacnois for Mellifont Abbey, a Cistercian monastery in County Meath, he concludes:

> Even with such little knowledge as I have to offer, it should be easy enough for you to stand here on a clear day and see not the meaningless handful of shattered ruins the casual visitor sees but a busy early-medieval town with its great cemetery; its small, beautifully decorated churches, its narrow, cobbled laneways winding between smelly rows of thatched huts and stately, carved wooden houses and a stately cross at the end of each lane. . . . And above all the library—the library that comes between me and my sleep, with the scores of books that we shall never see again and that contained the answers to all the questions about early Ireland that we shall never be able to answer in this world. Forgive me if I pause to stare in with my blind eyes.

Whatever the factual liberties or mistaken hunches, this is creative archeology, true at least to the spirit of those ancient times.

For years O'Connor had used broadcasting as a public forum, reading verse and stories, talking about writers and their work, or ruminating casually about life in general. Although his appearances on American radio and television had been largely limited to doing interview programs as a visiting celebrity, he had used his voice to great advantage on phonograph records reading from his own work and that of other Irish writers. Upon his return to Ireland after the stroke, his stock as a broadcaster soared once again. Radio Eireann asked him to repeat some of his most popular stories and his highly acclaimed talks in Irish, particularly his account of Christmas in Cork. In the fall of 1961 he made a scrapbook of reminiscences on the 1921 Civil War for BBC Northern Ireland.[15] Though the order for his arrest was still in effect in England he was allowed to travel to Belfast to make the broadcast there.

Though a Munsterman by birth and a Dubliner by conviction, O'Connor still felt a strong sense of affinity for the people of Northern Ireland. In January 1963, for example, he did a three-part series for the BBC entitled "Ulster Miles: A Journey Through the Northern Six Counties to Look at Remains of Our Historical Heritage." Besides the readings, interviews, literary portraits, and autobiographical pieces, he also gave four talks on the arts in Ulster in which he claimed that the most exciting artistic activity in Ireland was beginning to come from the North. For years O'Connor had spoken out about the tragedy of Partition, but he had come to believe that the skin-deep piety and custom-bound provincialism of the Republic was a greater obstacle to achieving a united Ireland than the parochial vehemence of Ulster Protestantism.

In the summer of 1962 O'Connor made his first television appearance in Ireland, a talk entitled "Interior Voices," under the direction of Denis Johnston's son, Michael. During rehearsals O'Connor was as jittery in the new Donnybrook studios of Radio-Telefis Eireann as he had been the night of his first broadcast. Seated behind a bare table, he looked anxiously about the room at the tangle of lights, cables, and cameras; sweating under the heat of the lights, he peered through the glare for Harriet's smiling encouragement; he ran his fingers nervously through his hair and fumbled with his well-marked script. Then, as the cameras began to roll, he focused through the lens on some imaginary listener and said with assertive familiarity, "When I was a young fellow I desperately wanted to be a writer." The face his Irish audience saw on the flickering screen was as compelling as the voice they had known for years. "Interior Voices" was O'Connor's last attempt to justify his life as a storyteller, the last verse of an autobiographical song that included *The Lonely Voice,* "And It's a Lonely, Personal Art," and "One Man's Way." He began the television talk by claiming that he became a writer by talking to himself; though his memory was still "empty of physical details," he remained "extremely tenacious of voices." After finishing *Guests of the Nation,* he said, he discovered that all he had done was to listen to the voices in his head, voices he had heard as a boy walking by the Cork Barracks, voices of fellow prisoners, voices of strangers in railway stations and friends in bars. In a few dramatic scenes he recreated a few of those voices—his grandmother's in "The Long Road to Ummera," Sean Hendrick's in "The Mad Lomasneys," his father's in "Old Fellows," and the English soldiers' in "Guests of the Nation." Then he confessed that his favorite story was "The Luceys," because for years he had struggled with it and because every time he read it "the voices in it [were] saying something new." The difficulty in writing this story, he told his Irish viewers, was that, despite the constrictions of small-town life, people in Ireland were often quite remarkable. "The difficulty in this story was to keep the issues small but the men big."

After finishing his reading of "The Luceys," the story that the actor Eammon Kelly found so moving, O'Connor concluded half boastingly that against the presences of his heroes Yeats, Synge, and Lady Gregory he had only his voices to offer. "The whole room could be full of presences," he said. "But I think I may hear a voice from the next room—one of the dead voices that I've been imitating for you—and then I know I shall get up and follow it, wherever it takes me."

O'Connor's enthusiasms were not all so positive. During 1962 he wrote four fervent newspaper articles, three of which were typically sharp and eccentric, while the fourth was unexplainably harsh and vitriolic. "Murder Unlimited" is the title of a review published in the *Irish Times* in October; its subject was Cecil Woodham-Smith's *The Great Hunger: Ireland 1845–49.* To O'Connor the Great Famine was genocide, pure and simple. He found in this book a sinister connection with the atrocities of Nazi Germany against the

Jews. Extermination, whether caused by indifference or deliberate policy, was extermination, and no amount of scholarly objectivity on the part of the book's author, a highly regarded historian, could convince him differently. Reading Woodham-Smith's quotations from high British officials rationalizing the starvation of millions of Irish men and women, O'Connor asked whether these men "were devils or merely madmen."[16]

Though acknowledging that the book was "immensely valuable," he nevertheless admitted that for Irishmen of his generation (at this time he spoke often of *his* generation) it was hard to read for personal reasons:

> I remember my grandmother's stories of what she saw round Cork Harbour when she was a girl; Petrie's description of how Ireland, the most music-loving country in Western Europe, suddenly fell silent almost overnight; and Athair Peadar's of the kindly young couple he knew, who—separated in a Macroom workhouse—heard of the death of their two children and decided to die at home themselves. He describes in a way that has haunted me since I was sixteen how the young couple—the wife dying of typhus—went to weep at the famine pit where their children had been dumped, walked the six miles back to their little cabin, and were found next day by the neighbours, the dead wife's feet inside the dead husband's shirt to warm them until the end.

O'Connor seemed bent on hearing more stories of the Famine's horrible effects, rather than a historian's balanced explanation of the forces and attitudes that caused it. Actually, he was not reviewing Miss Woodham-Smith's book so much as he was championing a book she could never have written: Asenath Nicholson's *Ireland's Welcome to the Stranger,* an eyewitness account, by a total outsider, of the Irish people "on the very eve of their own extinction." He concluded by calling for a grant from the Arts Council to republish this nineteenth century travel book.

O'Connor was haunted by the story of that dying couple and by the face of the boy beaten senseless in the Cork Gaol by his own countrymen. What horrified him about the Famine was not just the pitiful spectre of starving death, it was the thought that Ireland would forget and, forgetting, would lose something as irretrievable as the library at Clonmacnois. Like Elie Wiesel, tirelessly refusing to let the memory of the Holocaust fade from the world's consciousness, O'Connor persisted in his campaigns, often in a most tedious and antagonizing way. His idealism about the glories of the Irish past was tinged with stark terror about the future of Ireland. When he recommended a roof for Cashel, he did not have the tourist revenue in mind; he wanted to see future generations worship there if they wished, or simply go there to admire the stonework. The more the youth of Ireland knew about the past, he believed, the sooner the country would "get rid of the slave mind that expresses itself only in negation." To pretend that the Famine was a coincidence of the weather and political expediency or to ignore the contributions of Irish masons and poets was, to O'Connor, to commit cultural and spiritual suicide.

O'Connor's other blind spot was the theatre, undoubtedly for much the same reasons. In some ways he was as insecure in the theatre as he was in the university, but he believed in Yeats's dream of an Irish theatre as good as the world's best; when it failed to meet his expectations, he was not simply disappointed, he was outraged. When reviewing books, O'Connor's objective was "literary justice." Bad writing, whether from carelessness of style or misguided substance, represented to him as great an injustice to society as indifference, greed, or intolerance. Bad plays, he believed, threatened the future of the theatre by driving away young actors and young writers. Unimaginative management, restrictive censorship laws, and conventional productions all contributed to a climate of stagnant mediocrity. From his savage reviews for the *Irish Statesman* in the late twenties to his petulant letters to the editor of the *Irish Times* in the thirties, O'Connor had insisted that without new blood the Irish theatre would die. When he became a member of the Abbey Board, his primary interest was to encourage new voices. Even his theatre criticism in Britain and America eventually came back, after the fireworks, to that one simple principle: The only good theatre is living theatre, contemporaneous and regenerative.

One might, therefore, have expected him to be glowing in his praise of *Stephen D,* Hugh Leonard's dramatization of Joyce's *Portrait* and *Stephen Hero,* and the most acclaimed play at the 1962 Dublin International Theatre Festival. Instead he disagreed with everyone, saying in his review that he "thought it a poor play and an inadequate production."[17] He was most enthusiastic about Mervyn Wall's *Fursey.* Writing about the same dramatic festival a year later, O'Connor disagreed with everyone again, this time about Beckett's *Happy Days* and Hugh Leonard's *Dublin One,* a dramatizaton of six Joyce stories; and he almost single-handedly championed Conor Farrington's *The Last P.M.* at the Gate.[18] One commentator noted that this play had been "generally panned until high praise from Frank O'Connor renewed people's interest."

Buoyed by enthusiastic response to the English edition of *An Only Child,* O'Connor enjoyed Christmas in Dublin that year. In the past the holidays had always seemed to bring sickness, family strife, or some sort of uncertainty. Being an eternal child who needed to indulge emotion now and then, he usually wrote something to cheer hearts: his stirring broadcast to the English during the war, his tender Ben Mayo messages, and his poignant recollection in Irish "An Nodlaig i gCorcaigh." In 1962 his gift was a verse translation,"The Boyhood of Jesus." Just to maintain his agnostic image, however, he scribbled on the back of his Christmas card to Bill Maxwell this "Prayer for a Proper Literary Outlook":

> Lord, may all we story-spinners
> Die as we have lived like sinners
> May our wives still live in terror
> Knowing we persist in error.
> May no offer seem inviting
> To the serious forms of writing
> May we have, and air, no knowledge,
> Never get a job in college
> Never be successful when
> We write criticism—Amen!

I I

A year and a half after the stroke Michael still showed few outward signs of its effect—neither paralysis nor disability. Nevertheless, he stayed close to the flat and often napped in the late afternoon. Those friends who continued to call after the initial scare—Dermot Foley, Percy Le Clerc, Niall Montgomery, Mary Lavin, and Bill Walsh—usually arrived early in the evening. His stomach still caused him great discomfort, and his diet remained much the same as always: a light breakfast, soup or salad for lunch, and a late dinner, usually of meat and potatoes, absolutely no fish or cabbage, and few sweets, for he preferred cheese and fruit. Despite Harriet's constant attention he still smoked too much. Once, Harriet went out after dinner; when she returned, she found the bottle of wine they had opened for dinner empty and on Michael's face the look of a cat caught with the mouse.

After the publication of *An Only Child* O'Connor worked fitfully on a second autobiographical volume, finishing sketches of his library experiences in Sligo, Wicklow, and Cork. He wrote to Bill Maxwell about the book: " [It] is Hamlet's father's ghost, knocking at various points under the floor while I chase round the stage trying to pretend I perceive it quite clearly. I don't but I like to hear the knocking going on and try to encourage it."[19] He was also preparing a new collection of stories for Macmillan; his old publisher appeared to have welcomed him back into the fold. He could not seem to generate any new stories, however, and the drought obviously troubled him. In January he told Maxwell that most of his energy was being consumed by the translations he was doing with David Greene, an impractical job he felt compelled to rid himself of before he died. "Even to see the first quarter of it in proof would give me the feeling that I could mitch and write stories."

In February the first series of this "Golden Treasury of Irish Verse" began to appear in the *Independent*. Flann O'Brien, in his Myles na gCopaleen column in the *Irish Times*, poked fun at O'Connor, ridiculing the entire project. Had O'Connor intended to produce polished verse translations, O'Brien's criticisms might have been appropriate, but what he and Greene meant to do was to provide useable texts and useable translations; their purpose was more educational than artistic: a sourcebook for anyone interested in their literal translations. It is doubtful, however, considering the antipathy the two men had cultivated for years, that O'Brien would have been any less sarcastic even had he recognized the intent. One of the facts of Dublin literary life that had always saddened O'Connor, though he himself had contributed to it on occasion, particularly by his undeclared war on Joyce, was the problem that may be called the literary equivalent of Partition: the alignment into rival camps pitting the Flann O'Briens and Francis Stuarts against the Frank O'Connors and Seán O'Faoláins. In "America's Image of Ireland," which appeared a month before O'Brien's column, the prominent Irish historian Owen Dudley Edwards addressed the danger of listening only to the rejected or sensational Irish spokesmen. "It is the bitter, unfair vituperation by O'Casey rather than the reflective, dispassionate, ironic tone of O'Connor that one hears echoed."[20] Edwards suggested that in favoring O'Casey, Behan, and Joyce, Americans had chosen the worse over the better and in so doing, were apt to misunderstand or simplify such issues as censorship and the church. This was indeed wise counsel, though perhaps not entirely fair to either O'Casey or O'Connor. The British, the Americans, and even the French probably heard in O'Connor or O'Casey what they wanted to hear. The greatness of any nation's literature resides not in one writer or group of writers; the literature of Ireland is not represented by Yeats alone or Joyce alone but by them both and by all the other diverse writers, each one of them seeing Ireland in a unique way, each one of them adding to the total richness of the nation's literature.

O'Connor might not actually have read the remarks of Owen Dudley Edwards, but he had read critical attacks on O'Casey's recently published autobiography, *Under a Coloured Cap;* in May, writing for the *Independent,* he rose to the defense of the man he had once called Johnny Wet Eyes. He often told friends that most people in Ireland seemed to know better than he how to write a short story or translate a poem from the Irish, because so many had told him as much. Apparently, O'Connor writes, they had also tried to teach O'Casey how to write a play, not to mention trying to put "him right on religion, politics and sociology." He describes O'Casey as "a self-educated man," whose "weakness as an artist is his strength as a man." He admired the man for keeping his values intact: "everything with him is a cause and a crusade, and it is this integrity that has made him a sort of father figure to so many." O'Connor admonishes that it was this sort of stubborness that made O'Casey write his "great early plays, in the teeth of contempt and anger." His own anger aroused, O'Connor than declaims:

> A beaten people is a dangerous people, and after 1922 we were a badly beaten lot with all our idealism gone sour, and it was no fun to be told by an unknown Dublin slummy that all our idealism was no more than the posturing of rhetorical old cods.
>
> What we didn't know—what we couldn't know until the great autobiography appeared—was that the rhetorical old cod O'Casey had been attacking was largely himself, who had played the bagpipes and learned Irish while his heroic mother kept the little slum home together.[21]

As usual, when O'Connor is preaching at the Irish, there is a decided sense of shared guilt. He tells of having once said in the presence of Lennox Robinson that O'Casey had not written any good plays since leaving Ireland, to which Robinson had wearily replied that the only thing that mattered to him was that "Sean [was] happy at last." Recalling that reproval, O'Connor was able to view O'Casey's later works with greater empathy, particularly the moving tribute in *Under a Coloured Cap* to the son he lost to leukemia. O'Connor's admiration for what O'Casey wrote about the boy was uncompromising. It was the grief and the poetry that he heard.

At the end of the summer O'Connor traveled once again to Sligo for the Yeats International Summer School. The invitation was an honor he could not refuse. Addressing an audience of students and an eminent faculty of Yeats scholars from around the world, O'Connor was in rare form. He talked about his impressions of Yeats, what sort of man he was; he shocked some by saying that Yeats was something of a bully, then delighted them by reading from the poems in his ecclesiastic voice. He talked about Yeats's dreams for the Abbey Theatre. To some it was just another Yeats-and-me performance, but for most people in attendance it was a very moving experience.

On his return from Sligo O'Connor delivered a completed manuscript of translations to Liam Miller of the Dolmen Press. The next week, he wrote to Bill Maxwell that the book put him "straight with this distracted country." *Little Monasteries,* a thin volume of twenty dramatic lyrics from seventh-to-twelfth-century Ireland, appeared in a limited edition at the end of the year, an exquisite job of bookmaking by the publisher and by the author. Over the years O'Connor had concentrated much energy and care on his translations. Now, near the end of his life, he made one last gesture toward perfection. The descriptive impressionism of his youth found in his early translations had been gradually supplanted in revision after relentless revision by a dramatic intensity and emotional urgency.

Perhaps the sharpest example of this growth is the poem "The Nun of Beare," which when published in its earliest form in the twenties was simply an evocative lyric, a lament for the loss of youth. Nearly four decades later it had been transformed into a dramatic encounter featuring the voices of the reclusive old woman, restive about age and past love, and Saint Cummine, an adversary harrowing her patiently toward truth. The old woman, once lusty for life but now weighted by the sorrow of time, finds a moment of tragic reconciliation:

> Floodtide!
>> And the ebb with hurrying fall!
> I have seen many, ebb and flow,
>> Ay, and now I know them all.

She has reached not resignation but a kind of tragic acceptance worthy of Lear, and worthy too of the aging Irishman who translated it.

Brendan Kennelly, a young Irish poet who met O'Connor at Sligo that summer, would later muse that the real O'Connor, however, emerged in "The Ex-Poet," another poem of the lonely voice, the solitary and melancholy strain that resonates in O'Connor's finest stories. The ex-poet is "a drab spiritual pariah on the fringe of society," Kennelly observes, "moving anonymously toward a casual oblivion."[22] Indeed, reviewing the achievement of *Little Monasteries,* Kennelly argues the same point John Wain had argued a few years before when reading *Kings, Lords & Commons:* that O'Connor, in the manner of Ezra Pound, had created new poetry. The implication is that he had created something of himself as well, for it is in the lonely voice that "O'Connor's compassionate imagination is most penetrating and active, and, with terrifying bareness, he presents the fate of the lonely outcast."

A curious thing happened in Dublin that fall: Plato's *Phaedrus* was apparently banned. Peter Lennon, a writer with the *Manchester Guardian,* back home in Dublin on holiday, noticed the event and called on O'Connor, aware that of all people, he had "plenty of experience of the Irish censor."[23] In the course of the interview Harriet brought in an American magazine purchased in Limerick on their last visit with Stan Stewart, and "turned the pages to where a young woman was intent on giving some information on how to safeguard or protec- (censored). . . . She was pasted from neck to ankle with brown paper." O'Connor himself had no interest in dirty books or in the soft-core pornography of Hollywood, but he was interested in freedom and justice, without which Ireland would remain in the dark ages.

All the talk about improvement, O'Connor continued, was only wishful thinking. "It is the old Irish illusion—'hang on and things will be great in a few years.' " The death of Pope John XXIII had eliminated all hope of significant change in the Catholic Church's stand on such issues. The problem had to be tackled in education, but every attempt to bring Protestants and Catholics together, from kindergarten to university, had been stalled. "I tried to get my 5-year old child into a Catholic school but she was refused. My wife was told: 'The Archbishop wouldn't like it!' " By separating the sects, even at funerals, any exchange of views, any softening of the old enmities remained unlikely, O'Connor said, and Ireland divided remained at the mercy of the conservative establishment. Imagine "Italy without an opera house," O'Connor added, noting that practically none of the books he would be talking about in his lectures at Trinity would be available to the students. If his generation would not listen, maybe the younger generation would. For O'Connor it was the only hope.

When Philip Edwards had approached him earlier in the year about teaching at Trinity, O'Connor had been enthusiastic. He had received offers from American universities, but in view of his health he preferred to stay in Ireland. But as they talked about what O'Connor was to do, it became clear that they had very different ideas. Edwards had in mind that O'Connor would be a token writer in residence, which was precisely what O'Connor did not have in mind. They compromised eventually. In return for a weekly writing seminar, Edwards agreed "to his giving a weekly lecture on the development of Irish literature from the earliest times to the present." There was a problem about the lecturer's title, Edwards recalled, because "Irish literature" meant literature in Gaelic and "Anglo-Irish literature had limiting cultural overtones." An assistant registrar came up with a cumbersome but appropriate title; O'Connor was named Special Lecturer in the Literature of Ireland. O'Connor bought a teaching gown, which friends say he hated and treasured, and began his work in October.

Professor Edwards has described these highly popular weekly lectures thus:

My honours students, for whom they were chiefly intended, never formed more than a fraction of the big audience. The lectures were not public, and they were not advertised, but they soon began to draw in students from University College as well as interested Trinity students whose subjects were anything but literature. Visiting American academics, young writers and unclassifiable members of the public used to drop in. There had been nothing like it since the great days of Dowden's lecturers. . . .

O'Connor more or less gave up his year to the preparation of these lectures. He suffered financially and he suffered emotionally. He was always worrying about them. He was nervous before the start of every single lecture. He would come up to my room a quarter of an hour early every Tuesday, and we would talk, with much glancing at watches. Then the donning of gowns and the ritual procession to the lecture-theatre, myself as acolyte with the indispensable flask of water.

Nervous or not, he lectured magnificently. He stood at the lectern, black gown over bright blue tweed jacket, his white head thrown back, reciting in that deep voice his translation of an old Irish poem, reminiscing on something apropos which Yeats had said to him, or dogmatising on matters which made the Celtic scholars from the Institute for Advanced Studies turn and look at each other. He could never understand why at the end there were not more questions. . . .

We would go back to my room after the lecture. Tom Flanagan from Berkeley (I don't think he missed a lecture) would come with him, and there were always one or two others—Brendan Kennelly, James Carney, Mary Lavin, James Walton and others, and his wife. Relaxed *now,* he'd take charge of the talk, hearty with his admiration or contempt for whatever name came up—he enjoyed strong views. Of his anecdotes, I remember more his tone of voice than the substance: he loved mimicry, and the only thing you could have called malicious about him was his rendering of the accents of Lennox Robinson or Liam O'Flaherty.

I suspect he found his short-story class rather a bore, though he never complained. I well remember how upset he was because a rather trying American student was due to read out his story, which made a good deal of play with the main four-letter word. O'Connor was convinced that the boy was simply out to shock the respectable young Irish women of the class. He didn't want to allow the boy his triumph, and at the same time he didn't want to play the censor. It was for him entirely a question of manners and tact. How far the young ladies needed protecting, I can't say, but I was very much struck by the depth of O'Connor's concern, and I have often thought that I only really began to know him from that time.[24]

O'Connor sought the whole in the part; in this account of one small corner of his life emerge some of the primary contradictions of his entire character, those elements that were infuriating and loveable. He was arrogant and self-conscious, poised and nervous, tentative and dogmatic, friendly and spiteful. He fought against censorship and pietistic restrictions his entire life and yet held very conventional views on manners and morality. As he himself said of O'Casey, his weaknesses as a writer were his strengths as a person, and vice versa. His friend and collaborator David Greene once observed that all of O'Connor's passionate interests—politics, aesthetics, teaching, controversy—were hardly the responsibility of the creative artist, who should be tucked away somewhere writing masterpieces. However, he added, they were "part of the duty of the full man, of the zealous man, and they ate up Frank O'Connor before his time. He would not have chosen it otherwise."

As sick as Michael was himself, he nevertheless showed more concern for the well-being of his old friend Stan Stewart, now past seventy, hard-of-hearing, forgetful, and alone. A self-employed chemist all his life, Stan had little money and no pension privileges. In a letter to Myles, Michael commented that he and Harriet had brought Stan up for a visit, during which they forced him to see a doctor: "Now we are trying to get him a small flat near us in Dublin, where he will have someone to look after him. His sister has come to nurse him, but they're living over that damn shop, and so far as we can discover neither has any money, and friends and relatives have begun to desert him, 'now that he's no longer entertaining' as his brother-in-law says sarcastically." Frank O'Connor might have appeared selfish, overbearing, and aloof in public, but when it came to people like Stan, Michael O'Donovan was devoted and caring. He had spent a lifetime defending the weak and helpless, rescuing women from misfortune, and trying to save Ireland from itself; it has been said that the way in which a man prepares to die says a lot about how he has lived.

In that letter to Myles, written on Wednesday, November 27, 1963, Michael also spoke of the horrifying events of the previous week:

> With us it all began on Thursday night. We had been to dinner with some people from Cork and at 11 Hallie answered the phone and asked if I'd talk to the Irish Press. Kennedy had just given a speech in San Antonio, quoting me, and they wanted to know where the quotation was from. Naturally, I was flattered to Hell, and next day when Hallie rang her mother to congratulate her on her birthday she passed on the good news. A few hours later our neighbours rang to say that Kennedy had been killed. We both bawled. I slapped Hallie and she slapped me, and then we both realized we were behaving like Hallie Og and bawled in unison. I remained awake most of the night and next morning got off a piece about Kennedy for the Sunday paper. We drove to Killarney, where I was talking to the senior civil servants about national monuments, saw Stan for a moment and then . . . Sunday I took some of the civil servants out to Ardfert Cathedral and addressed them there in the middle of the squalor; made a further speech on Monday morning and drove back in deepening rain and gloom.

Speaking at an air force base near San Antonio, Kennedy had said, "This nation has tossed its cap over the wall of space, and we have no choice but to follow it." Proud to acknowledge his Irish ancestry, he had no fear of quoting Irish writers. In what turned out to be his last speech, Kennedy had referred to an incident in *An Only Child*. When, as young boys, Michael and his pals came to an orchard wall that seemed too high to climb, they took off their caps, tossed them over, and then had no alternative but to fetch them—and a few apples as well. Kennedy used this beguilingly simple story to illustrate the daring America would have to show in order to overcome the difficulties of space exploration, to say nothing of world peace and human rights. In his brief tribute to the American president for the *Sunday Independent,* O'Connor observed that Kennedy had been "leading the Irish in America out of the Scotch-Irish ghetto, and telling them that they were a people with a history and literature as good as the best."[25] Michael Collins, the Irish rebel leader, was gunned down in the Civil War following the realization of the Irish dream of independence. No doubt it was Collins, and perhaps Parnell or any number of other martyred Irish dreamers, about whom O'Connor was thinking when he concluded his tribute to Kennedy: "I wept as I hadn't done for years, partly for ourselves, who have lost a man who represented not only his own country but ours." To Frank O'Connor, John Kennedy was a "miracle." In December he proposed that Ireland's finest monument, Cashel, be officially designated a memorial to Kennedy, who he felt also represented the Irish character at its best.[26]

Michael's gloom persisted through the remainder of the gray, dismal winter, thickened by this latest reminder of death. At Christmas he wrote to Bill Maxwell that he was tired of students, tired of being a gowned lecturer, tired of fighting for lost causes. "For the remaining years I want to be a writer again, even a bad one. Also, I want to get to America again for a respectable holiday, and see my friends."

I I I

To dispel the gloom and escape the fierce weather, Michael, Harriet, and Hallie Og went to the south of France again early in the new year. Michael's fascination for France had in it a pilgrim impulse, an intellectual curiosity of the sort that drove Yeats to travel with Ezra Pound in search of Byzantine sites. O'Connor loved France in his later years—as he had once admired girls and education—from afar. It held the mystery of a new lover for him and, as with nearly everything else in his life, he made it grander than it actually was. On this occasion his pilgrim mentality was apparent in their choice of a hotel, the Hôtel des Anglais in Menton, where Yeats had often stayed in the last years of his life. In spite of innumerable frustrations (Hallie Og was sick most of the time and the bank in town refused to accept their Irish currency) they remained for ten days enjoying the warmth of the sun and the richness of the memories of Yeats.

On their return to Dublin they were honored by a visit from John Betjeman, a man whose poetry Michael had never ceased to admire. The next day O'Connor resumed his lectures at Trinity College. Because of the success of these lectures he began to think seriously about Thomas Flanagan's earlier suggestion that he put them together in book form. What came of it was *A Backward Look*, the history of Irish writing Yeats had told him to write thirty years before. Flanagan was a scholar keenly interested in the literature of nineteenth-century Ireland, a period O'Connor was prone to dismiss. So he conspired with Benedict Kiely, a young Irish writer much taken with the work of William Carleton, to educate "this rambling Munsterman." In the early hours of the morning Flanagan would slip scholarly notes under O'Connor's door, while Kiely would argue feverishly later in the day to assure Carleton's place in O'Connor's forthcoming book "Maria Edgeworth, poor woman," as Kiely later wrote of his and Flanagan's efforts, "they could not save—she was didactic and that was that."[27] Furthermore, O'Connor wasted little sympathy on the Gaelic poets of the nineteenth century because, in Kiely's words, "far from the little monasteries were they reared." Other friends argued for their favorites, Somerville and Ross for instance, who, judging by O'Connor's lectures, would not be given fair attention either. His views on Irish literature, whether his friends liked them or not, were his own and iron firm. The book was not meant to be the last word on the subject, just *his* last word.

As his series of lectures drew to an end O'Connor began to think about the future. He had been dissatisfied all along with the lack of connection between his subject and the rest of the curriculum, so when it became apparent that neither Edwards or Greene would be at Trinity during the academic year 1964–65, he wrote declining reappointment:

I should be glad if this appointment could be deferred to the following year, partly because I should like to have more time for my own work, but largely because my lectures would not serve the same purpose if deliv-

ered in successive years. . . . I believe the course will ultimately have to
be treated in a more ambitious manner and perhaps widened in
scope. . . . My own hope would be that the course would be widened in
scope and interest by lectures from other members of staff on such
closely allied subjects as History, Archaeology and linguistics, and would
form the nucleus of a School of Irish Studies that would give the College
an assured leadership in this field.[28]

That letter was the beginning of a new, if short-lived, cause for O'Connor. Professor Edwards supported his proposal, and a faculty committee set to work
drawing up a course of graduate and undergraduate studies "in Irish literature
(i.e., in Irish and English), the Irish language, Irish history, art, culture, and
sociology." Their pioneer scheme found great approval everywhere in Trinity,
but the Irish government failed to supply the requested funds. In his introduction to *A Backward Look* O'Connor expressed his opinion of this decision:

Ours is probably the only civilized country which has no such thing as a
chair of national literature: thousands of students pass through our universities each with less knowledge of their own culture than one would
expect to find among American students. The literature of the past is
simply ignored; the literature of our own time is either ignored or banned
by law. At the beginning of the present century the Irish theatre was
world-famous, but since effective control of it passed into the hands of
the State it is impossible to study its history in Ireland itself: the student
has better opportunities for doing so almost anywhere else.[29]

O'Connor's dream of a school of Irish studies did not vanish entirely; it is not
coincidental that within two years a very similar program was instituted at University College, Dublin.

    In the meantime O'Connor continued his crusade for the preservation of
Ireland's archeological and architectural monuments. With James Plunkett he
traveled to various sites to film a special series for Telefis Eireann. Unfortunately, these television documentaries were never finished, but O'Connor did
publish an illustrated series on Cashel, Clonmacnois, Holy Cross Abbey, and
many more, which appeared in the *Sunday Independent* in June and July.
Twenty years before, O'Connor had been a pilgrim cycling to these places; his
crusade gathered momentum in the anonymous Ben Mayo articles and hit full
stride in *Irish Miles*. Over the years he had returned time and again, not out of
a need to prove anything but out of sheer fascination for their beauty and
grace. James Plunkett called this pursuit a "search, not for a dead culture, but
a living heritage, a birthright offering personal dignity and identity, which
O'Connor found and claimed." As he guided Plunkett and the television people
on their "monastic tour," O'Connor would occasionally fulminate about the
Board of Works or the Tourist Board, whose efforts he felt had been
halfhearted at best. He seemed to take the neglect and outright mistreatment
of such places as Athassel Priory, Ardfert, and Dysert O'Dea as a sort of personal betrayal. Having spent his rage, however, he proceeded to enchant the
assembled crew with his knowledge and enthusiasm. In *The Gems She Wore,* a
book that also grew out of these filmings, Plunkett recalled that when survey-
ing the Irish countryside from the tower of Jerpoint Abbey, O'Connor had la-

mented to his young companion that it was all a lost cause. Had he lived to see such restorations as that of Holy Cross Abbey in Country Tipperary, he might have enjoyed a small measure of victory.[30]

For his part, O'Connor seemed intent on burying at least a few old enmities. Patching things up with Corkery or Hayes seemed unthinkable even now, and meeting Flann O'Brien or Ernest Blythe halfway was, of course, out of the question. His friendships with O'Faoláin and Kelleher were over, but Patrick Kavanagh, whom he occasionally noticed from his study window ambling along the banks of the Grand Canal, was still "Awkward But Alive." At the end of July he reviewed Kavanagh's newly published *Collected Poems* for the *Spectator*. Rereading the early poems, he recalled AE's judgment that they were fake. He disagreed with AE then and has remained baffled that, on the whole, "Kavanagh's poetry makes so much bigger an impact than Russell's own. They read as well as ever, and seem extraordinarily ingenious for a man who obviously had to pick up an education as best he could."[31] As so often in his critical writing, O'Connor resorts to personal anecdotes, reminiscing in this case about hearing "The Great Hunger" for the first time while walking with Kavanagh along the Liffey.

He concludes his remarks on Kavanagh by admitting that his poetry may have a touch of the charlatanism Russell found, but that "even in the heavily-laden oracular utterances . . . there are verses that echo the earlier Kavanagh who did not know the answers." He quotes from "If Ever You Go Down to Dublin Town" to prove his point. His last words on Kavanagh were: "He was. He is. He is also our greatest living poet, and I don't mean Alas!" Given a few more years, O'Connor might have ended all his wars, even the one with Joyce.

Harriet and Hallie Og had gone to America for a visit at Harriet's parents, and shortly after Harriet returned alone, Michael decided that they should take another holiday in France. They saw Donal Brennan in Paris and then toured as far as Poitiers, where they spent ten days visiting all the Romanesque churches within driving distance. Though Michael tired easily and experienced some vertigo, he was in high spirits, making it the finest trip he and Harriet had ever taken together, a distillation, as it were, of all that was good about him and about France. He returned to Dublin eager to resume writing without the distraction of teaching or broadcasting. For the first time in four years he set to work on some stories. His journals contained more four-line themes and preliminary sketches than he could have transformed into stories in two lifetimes. That fall he found an old Sligo sketch, wrote the story "A Life of Your Own," and posted it at once to *The New Yorker*. In quick succession he then brought to life the last of his Don Juan stories, "School for Wives," and a story based on the lives of an American couple which he eventually called "The Corkerys." But since neither of these two stories pleased him enough, he set them aside for revision.[32]

By the time of his stroke his writing had reached a plateau; having achieved a certain mastery of the short-story form, he faced the artistic frustration of having stories in his mind but no strength for the exhausting bursts of effort his writing demanded. Of course, he was blessed with many good friends whose company he enjoyed, but even with them conversation usually turned to one of his many enthusiasms or aversions. Thomas Flanagan and many others discovered that their role was "to offer unrelenting dissent," which meant being constantly alert and weathering "his brief, vivid rages." He also read more than ever, if that was possible, and though his response to new books was as effusive or abusive as ever, he still felt no inclination to plunder his reading for stories. The Irish newspapers more often than not only triggered his outrage because so little had really changed.

Earlier in the year while writing about Osborn Bergin for the second volume of his autobiography, O'Connor had spent considerable time talking with Dan Binchy about the great old Celtic philologists. In the course of their conversations Binchy told Michael about a colleague, an avowed agnostic his entire life, who had married a German woman. A Protestant by upbringing, she eventually converted to Catholicism to protect his reputation in town, but instead of pleasing him, it broke his heart. That fall O'Connor wrote "The Cheat," a story so different from the original that he asked Harriet not to show it to Binchy. In the past he had found that people kept a proprietary hold on their anecdotes, assuming that the reason they told O'Connor the story in the first place would be the reason he would vindicate in his version of it. Often, however, the voices he recreated were faithful to their original, but just as often what he reclaimed was a distortion of what he had been told, not less interesting or less telling but simply coherent with his own moral perspective. Binchy's sympathy had been for the wife, and he saw the husband's response as cruel and selfish. O'Connor's sympathy was for the husband, whose identity had been betrayed by his wife's conversion.

Dick Gordon, the avowed agnostic of the story, seems to be an adult version of the young heretics in the Atheists' Club stories. He is tolerant, gentle, and steadfast, but a misfit in Cork for his attitude toward religion. Moving into the crisis of the story, in which a visiting priest mentions to Dick that his Protestant wife has been taking instruction, O'Connor writes about Dick: " [He] might have a good eye for what was going on in the outside world, but he had no eye at all for what was going on in his own very house." After the priest leaves, he feels himself treacherously betrayed because a "man's loneliness is his strength and only a wife can really destroy him because only she can understand his loneliness." A few years later Dick Gordon takes ill, and fear for his soul causes a flutter of "hysteria" among his friends. A busybody priest calls by to bully him back to the faith by telling him he has only three months to live. Dick explodes in uncharacteristic fury. His wife, her patience stretched by the well-meaning hysteria surrounding them, becomes very protective of him, preferring now to let him die as he had lived.

No single O'Connor story can be seen to display a direct personal reference, but the timing of "The Cheat," to say nothing of its departure from the original incident, suggests something more than coincidence. A man like O'Connor, a professed agnostic in precarious health surrounded by people more than casually concerned with life after death, does not write a story such as this one without something in mind. A story was always a vehicle for O'Connor's restless intuitions, and this story in particular might be even more prophetic than a facetious poem he had written, called "Directions for *My* Funeral." Dick Gordon's protective wife assumes that Dick's good friend, Father Hogan, knew about the visit of the parish priest, but he explains that Dick himself had invited him over for a drink. "Am I to be held responsible for every fool and lout who happens to wear a soutane?" Hogan asks bitterly. He then reassures her that he is "not going to do anything to him—except maybe give him conditional absolution when it's all over, and that won't be on his account." He continues: "There are people in this town who'd try to refuse him Christian burial. You don't know it, but you wouldn't like it." Realizing how fragile the situation is, Hogan chooses not to disturb Dick, adding gently, "I wish I was as sure of my own salvation as I am of his." After his departure Barbara retreats into regret for her "weakness of years before." The priest, she admits, "could not afford to brood on what it all meant. He still has a duty to the living as well as to the friend who was about to die."

The prominence given to the priest in this story actually represents a more radical wrenching of Binchy's tale than the theme of marital infidelity. O'Connor had long been seen in Ireland as a notorious anticleric, yet he had always maintained very close relationships with men of the cloth. One of his newest friends, and a frequent visitor to the flat that fall, was the Reverend Maurice Sheehy, a lecturer at University College, Dublin. Because Father Sheehy's special interest was the Latin manuscripts of monastic Ireland, he and Michael had a good deal to talk about. That he was also a man of cosmopolitan refinement who had studied in Rome and Paris additionally sparked Michael's interest. Harriet, a devout and well-informed Episcopalian, enjoyed discussing intricate points of theology with Father Sheehy, an activity that amused Michael, who considered such matters irrelevant to the real business of living. Needless to say, when Father Sheehy was present, the conversation often turned to the priesthood. Michael was curious about the lives of priests, asking questions about celibacy, drink, even suicide. At the time he had been tinkering with a volume of stories provisionally titled "The Collar," to comprise mainly the relatively recent Father Traynor stories—"The Wreath," "Mass Island," "Requiem," and "The Teacher's Mass."[33] All in all, he had written nearly twenty such stories, from "Peasants," "Song Without Words," and "The Frying Pan" to "Lost Fatherlands" and "Achilles Heel," some warmly sympathetic to the humanity of individual priests and others fiercely judgmental. One day he brought from his files the story "Exile's Return" to read to Father Sheehy, laughingly referring to it as his "dipso priest" story. Sheehy's reaction prompted O'Connor to shelve the story again. He did retrieve two other priest stories from his notebooks and rewrote them during the next few months. One was a story Larry Elyan had told him, about a bishop's housekeeper, from an incident he had come across during his days as a revenue officer. O'Connor had agreed not to publish the story, "A Mother's Warning," until after Elyan had retired. The other was a tale, told to him sometime before by Daniel Binchy, about a priest who committed suicide. It was Harriet who eventually suggested an appropriate title: "An Act of Charity."[34]

The pressure of deadlines kept O'Connor busy until Christmas. Knopf wanted his second autobiographical volume and a collection of short stories for publication in 1965, the fiftieth anniversary of that publishing house. O'Connor had two possible collections in mind, "The Collar," which Knopf resisted as too narrow in scope, and "Public Relations," comprising stories written between 1957 and 1961. After his death Harriet put the two projected volumes together to form *A Set of Variations* (*Collection Three* in Britain). His autobiography, however, had no chance of going to press in 1965. As a book, it had received from him no concerted effort, though he had written occasional

pieces on Yeats, AE, and Bergin for separate publication. Primarily his time
had been spent revising *The Big Fellow* for republication by a Dublin press,
finishing another series of the "Golden Treasury" poems, which ran in the
Sunday Independent from November 1964 to January 1965, and putting his
Trinity lectures into book form.

Shortly after his in-laws had arrived for Christmas, he heard from his
agent that *The New Yorker* had rejected "The Cheat." Since "A Life of Your
Own" had been rejected a few months before, Harriet secretly telephoned Bill
Maxwell in New York to explain that these had been Michael's first stories in
some time. She felt that if the two men could only get together, Maxwell would
see what Michael was trying to do and help him bring the stories into focus.
Though Maxwell did the best he could, as an editor and as a friend, Michael
was saddened. He allowed his agents to continue placing stories he had already
written, but he never recovered enough self-confidence to begin another new
one.[35] As the winter worsened, his health and disposition declined with it. He
wrote to Myles: "My sympathy about this silly season. It makes me feel old. It
always did even when I was your age." On December 31, 1964, Daniel Corkery
died, and though Michael showed no outward signs of grief, the event affected
him deeply. Something very important had ended—for him and for Ireland.

I V

The death of a relative or close friend thrusts the reality of the end of life on a
person, with brutal and immediate clarity; behind mourning lies a hidden and
natural fear of one's own mortality, particularly for someone as subjective,
imaginative, and emotional as Michael O'Donovan. In January an old neighbor
from the Mespil Flats died, sending Michael once again into a brooding despondency. The friend was Jewish and because he detested the Irish habit of
avoiding non-Catholic funerals, Michael insisted on attending this one. Never
one to be at ease in formal situations anyway, he noticed at once that he was
the only man in the synagogue with an uncovered head. He squirmed through
the entire service, embarrassed at the thought that this innocent oversight
might be taken as irreverent disregard for the deceased and for his faith. Those
gathered only recognized in his presence something genuine and noble.

Fortunately, Michael had too much going on around him to slip into morose silence: Harriet's attentive and cheerful activity, Hallie Og's demanding
chatter, visits from loyal friends and respectful strangers, and, of course, his
work. One of his more exciting projects at the time was a BBC documentary on
Yeats being filmed during the year of the one-hundredth anniversary of his
birth. His collaborator in this project was Brendan Kennelly, the young poet
and Trinity lecturer. Kennelly was a stocky Kerryman with an exuberant
tongue and a gleeful spirit; he bounced when he walked, soared into verse
when he talked, and threw himself at ideas with the reckless abandon of a
"footballer," the word Michael used to describe him to Myles. At the time
O'Connor was also working with James Plunkett on scripts for Radio-Telefís
Eireann. Collaborating with these two very different young men kept alive
O'Connor's hope for a vigorous future, Ireland's and his own.

Early in February Michael developed severe stomach cramps, not the usual gastritis but rather a more acute pain that to his physician was an indication of a gall bladder problem. He recommended immediate surgery, but Michael was fearful that his "old ticker" would not survive the knife. Reluctantly, he finally agreed. Myles arrived from New York on February 14 and Michael checked into the Portobello Nursing Home for a routine operation to be performed the next day. Both Harriet and Myles stayed close to Michael's bed during his convalescence. Harriet, outwardly at least, spread a blanket of vibrant optimism, but Myles's demeanor showed undisguised dread. One day Michael, understanding his son's unmanageable emotions, told him to escape for a while and enjoy himself. Instead, Myles walked to their old neighborhood, retracing the walks he and his father often took along the strand. He stopped in front of 57 Strand Road but felt his body contract in anger. He went on to the Star of the Sea Church and thought of his father's old friend, Tim Traynor. When he returned to the hospital in the early evening, his father inquired about his afternoon. Myles, who found few words for anything any more, mumbled something about his journey. "That was a sad trip," Michael said, his eyes filling with the tears his son had been unable to find. He was released from the hospital on February 24; Myles returned to the States the following day.

For the better part of March Michael stayed in the flat, his recovery slowed by the same crippling pain he'd experienced before. As it turned out, the operation had not solved the problem. Throughout his recovery at home he was visited regularly by Mary Lavin, Daniel Binchy, and Dermot Foley, who was now living in Dublin. Generally, they found him cheerful enough but in constant pain and restless to get out for a walk. Every morning, shortened now by late rising, Michael tried to do some writing, tinkering with a collection of stories and polishing the later chapters of his history of Irish literature. Usually people brought or sent books to cheer him, so in the afternoon, hoping to cut into the growing pile, he read, often dozing off as daylight faded. One of the books he received was from Joan, a copy of her third novel. He read it at once and sent a note of congratulation: "You alas! Very good. Best to date. Harriet goes for Lucie but I like Len. Reminds me of someone. I wonder who." After a few general comments he concludes with a complaint: "I feel like Prometheus chained to a bog."[36]

At the end of March Michael felt strong enough for a trip to Sligo and Galway, where the Yeats documentary was being shot. Then, having failed in their efforts to induce Stan Stewart to move to Dublin, he and Harriet decided to visit him after Easter. Both men were ill throughout their reunion. A day or two after he returned home, Michael suffered a violent attack in the middle of the night. His physician came at once but was still baffled by the cause of this persistent pain. He wanted to admit Michael to the hospital immediately, but the only beds available were at the Mater Hospital in Eccles Street, and since Michael still carried a grudge from his treatment at the hands of nuns forty years ago in Cork, he chose to wait until space became available in Adelaide, a Protestant facility. Ten days later, after examination by numerous specialists, Michael was given an intravenous polygram. This attempt to diagnose the cause of his ailment produced nothing conclusive, and he was released in mid-May. He had never trusted doctors of any kind, Irish doctors especially, so their inability to come up with a definite answer frustrated him.

Of most pressing concern at the time was that he might be hindered from attending the coming services in Sligo commemorating Yeats's centenary. This time Mrs. Yeats, who was too ill to attend herself, insisted that Frank O'Connor deliver the graveside oration; he accepted the honor with some eagerness. On Saturday, June 12, he and Harriet drove to Sligo. Early Sunday morning he suffered another violent attack of nausea and colic. Harriet remonstrated, insisting that he stay in bed, perhaps the best thing she could have done, for he rose in anger, resolved to honor his hero at all costs. At the tiny church in Drumcliffe they were heralded, as were all the civil and ecclesiastic dignitaries, by a military honor guard. Ben Bulben was visible but clouded, and the crows clamored in the trees around the churchyard. When he finally entered the church, O'Connor's cold sweat had abated, but not his nervous anxiety.

The service, as in any other Church of Ireland service that Trinity Sunday, proceeded in measured and traditonal fashion: a processional hymn, the rector's announcement of the name of the person remembered on that day, lesson readings in English by T. R. Henn, director of the Yeats International Summer School, and in Irish by the headmaster of a Sligo school, hymns and prayers, and then the sermon by a longtime friend of Michael's, an authority on Swift and the bishop of Limerick, the Right Reverend R. Wyse Jackson. After recognizing Yeats's place among the immortals of English and Irish literature, his individuality, dignity, and authority, Bishop Jackson went on briefly to call attention to Yeats as a man of many aspects: the lonely man, shy and half-blind, wearing a mask of aloof reserve which few penetrated and many feared or misunderstood; Yeats the romantic, who drew inspiration from the places and the people surrounding him; Yeats the patriot, who like Swift sought integrity and hated pettiness; and Yeats the poet, who found the divine in the beautiful. After Bishop Jackson had finished speaking, the choir sang, the benediction was given, and the recessional hymn was played.

Passing from the sanctuary, the congregation assembled around the limestone tomb nearby. A laurel wreath was laid at the foot of the simple tombstone and then Frank O'Connor stepped forward. He spoke first in Irish, explaining that Yeats believed that after Greek "everything else a man needed to know could be learned from Irish." He continued in English to say a few things he thought Yeats would have wished him to say. First of all, he drew attention to the importance of Mrs. Yeats, "who made possible the enormous development of his genius from 1916 onward," and to John Butler Yeats, "because it is not every poet who has a genius for a father."[37] Next, O'Connor commemorated Yeats's "great friends and collaborators, Lady Gregory and John Synge." Only a "man with a genius for friendship" could have felt such hurt over the harm done to Synge that he withdrew from public life. Only a man with "great generosity" would have ignored the hurt and returned. "In this again, I think, we in Ireland may owe a debt to Mrs. Yeats," O'Connor added in tribute to the woman whose absence on this occasion saddened him.

O'Connor deliberately introduced the issues of love and friendship to uncover the roots of Yeats's character. The other thing to be taken into account "in the summing-up of any man's achievement," he proclaimed, was the "character of the circumstances he had to deal with." Calling attention to the very place where they were gathered—"an important Columban monastery whose history reaches back to the sixth or seventh century"—O'Connor was, according to a reporter from the *Irish Times,* getting in his usual dig at the neglect of national shrines. But to O'Connor it was a serious reminder about the sort of Ireland that Yeats had inherited, and, as he noted, "that we still inherit": "a ruined, fragmented country, divorced from its past." Cut off from "the religion of his ancestry by his father's good-natured atheism," Yeats fashioned a religion for himself; cut off from his country's heroic past by what O'Connor said was "a system of education that is still with us," he recreated in the "same patient, stubborn way" a vision of ancient Ireland by wandering around Knocknarea, Carrowmore, and Dromahair and by steeping himself in the old sagas and poems. The fragmenting, enfeebling circumstances that would have killed Joyce, had he stayed, "gave Yeats his opportunity" because he had the sort of mind "that can build happily among the ruins." He needed an eclectic mind: "strong, but full of sweetness, to build in this empty house of ours, and to see beyond the quarreling sects and factions an older Ireland where men could still afford to be brave and generous and gay."

The voice O'Connor heard did not "cast a cold eye," did not "pass by." Rather it was the voice that "chose the laughing lip," the "heart that never grew embittered." The dream he shared with Yeats was "of an Ireland where people would disagree without recrimination and excommunicaton." Turning "everything we love from our language to our religion into a test of orthodoxy" hindered the mingling of the creative forces that unify a culture. To "ensure that no young Irishman would ever again grow up so ignorant of his own past," O'Connor proposed that as a birthday present to Yeats, "his first birthday into immortality," a chair of Irish literature be established, or Sligo Abbey—"as beautiful as any Oxford college," be restored as a repository for a great collection of Yeats's relics. This was not to bury the past in a museum but to build a living monument to a living culture.

Perhaps O'Connor had fallen back on old elegiac conventions—that he may not have lived or died in vain, that we may accomplish what he only dreamed of. Perhaps he had labored a few of his own notions, even exposed a few of his own hurts. Perhaps his voice, rasping over the cacophony of the crows, sounded the wistful nostalgia of the aging, whose only remaining hope is that the dreams they fought for might in the coming days be fulfilled. And perhaps to celebrate the immortality of his hero was for O'Connor to take refuge in the only immortality he could envision, at a time when his own mortality was becoming more and more obvious to him.

For a time Michael's health improved. On June 22 he was well enough to present a staged lecture at Trinity College for the cameras filming the BBC documentary on Yeats. In the audience that afternoon were a few interested students from the summer school and many of O'Connor's friends, including Daniel Binchy, David Greene, Thomas Flanagan, and Richard Ellmann. This lecture, providing a kind of intellectual framework for the film, was spliced into footage of the Yeats country. Kennelly acted as narrator and read from appropriate Yeats poems. When finally aired in January 1966, the film bore the title, relished neither by O'Connor nor Kennelly, "Horsemen, Pass By."

Over the years O'Connor had proposed epitaphs which he thought more suitable for Yeats than the one cut in stone at Drumcliffe: these lines from "The Herne's Egg": "That I, all foliage gone/ May shoot into my joy"; and the

stanza in "The Green Helmet" about the laughing lip and the "life like a gambler's throw." Since O'Connor never really took any interest in where he
should be buried or what his epitaph should be, a poem written in 1948 when
Yeats's body was returned to Ireland for reburial takes on some degree of importance—not for what O'Connor said but how he said it. "Directions for *My*
Funeral" is a poem stipulating sarcastically what should be done if he were "to
die away from home."[38] The chief mourners would have to be Hayes and de
Valera, and for the celebrant he suggests one of the "new lay abbots, the Irish
writers," led by Patrick Kavanagh. As a much younger man O'Connor had
written an equally facetious poem called "Self-Portrait" in which he snubbed
his nose at a pious priest with a flippant, don't-give-a-damn gesture. The same
laughing defiance is heard at the end of "Directions for *My* Funeral":

> Then take me to the Ulster Border,
> And beg me a home from the Orange Order.
> A pillar of stone both tall and slender
> Frank O'Connor & "No Surrender!"

O'Connor took great delight in epitaphs found on graves in country
churchyards, and he also suggested the lines from Shakespeare that Seamus
Murphy cut in the stone over the Tailor's grave: "A star danced/And under
that was I born." Naturally, his consciousness of death had been sharpened by
his stroke, not a morbid sensitivity or brooding fear but simply an admission
that death was close enough to bear thinking about. In story after story
O'Connor wrote about realizing that "women are like that," or "war is like
that," or "small towns are like that," or "kids are like that," all of which add up
to about the same laughing, defiant, moral realism. "Life is like that," Frank
O'Connor always seemed to be saying, not as an epitaph—though it could have
served quite well—but as an affirmation of faith.

Toward the middle of July Oliver set about convincing his mother, Joan,
to go to Ireland with him. He was so insistent she could hardly refuse, though
she had writing to finish. They arrived at Rosslare and rang Harriet, who explained that Michael had had a violent attack the night before, his first in over
six weeks. She had arranged for Joan to stay in a bed-and-breakfast in Dalkey;
Oliver would stay at the flat. It turned out to be a magical holiday for them
both. Joan finished a story and even had time for a few excursions; Oliver sat
and talked with his father by the hour, mainly about his studies at Balliol. One
evening Joan came to the flat for dinner. When she arrived, Harriet took her
aside and whispered, "Flirt with him, Joan. He's feeling so sorry for himself."
Afterwards she realized that what she had been trying so hard to do in her
writing—wash away the emotional sediment of the relationship—had been futile. Through all the hurt and bitterness, O'Connor remained the one great
crystallizing presence in her life. Walking her back one evening, Michael suddenly said, "Nobody ever understood me like you." Leaving Ireland, she was
leaving something of herself behind.

Two weeks after Joan and Oliver returned to England, Michael finished
the final revisions for the new collection of stories. He had written to Bill Maxwell that he might return, manuscripts in hand, to New York in September

with Liadain, who had been staying in Dublin that summer as advisor to a group of visiting high school students. In the intervening two years Ireland had apparently become big enough for father and daughter; on several occasions that summer Michael took Liadain on long walks, often stopping at a pub to listen to her stories about chaperoning foreign students. He let her know that he was proud of the way she had weathered her storm of adolescent wildness. She returned to the States feeling reconciled at last to the one person in the world from whom she needed acceptance. In the meantime, depressed by a spate of bad weather, Michael decided to escape once again to France. He and Harriet flew to Tarbes, near the pilgrim shrine at Lourdes, which had direct Aer Lingus connections with Ireland. There they were met by Father Sheehy, who hired a car for the excursion to Moissac, Floran, and Albi. They were headed for Conques, where Michael longed to see the church of St. Foy, with its marvelous twelfth-century tympanum. Michael was in constant pain, and after an appalling attack in Albi, which frightened his companions as much as himself, they decided to return to Dublin. A week later he suffered his most severe attack yet. For the next two weeks he was in constant pain despite heavy medication. After injections of morphine he often had frightening delusions. One morning he asked Harriet if she remembered the story he tried to write earlier in the year about the priest with the D.T.'s. She said she did. Michael then commented that he now knew what the poor fellow had been through. A few days later his pain was so severe he begged for an injection of morphine. He slept for a time and then Harriet heard him talking. She went into the bedroom to see what he wanted, only to find that he was hallucinating in his sleep. "Is that the sky pilot?" he said clearly, and then quieted. She repeated what Michael had said to Father Sheehy, who was visiting at the time. "Strange," he commented, "that's an old British army saying." "Having something to do with death?" she asked hesitantly.

On September 6 Michael returned to Adelaide Hospital, where he was kept under heavy sedation and constant observation. Two weeks later an exploratory laparotomy was performed, but the cause of the pain could not be found. He remained in the hospital for another two weeks before returning to the flat. Of course, his lectures at Trinity were canceled. One of his first visitors was a man he had not seen in years, the English writer V. S. Pritchett, who was in Dublin working on a new book about Ireland. Donal Brennan, recently returned from France, called, and John Boyd, who had produced so many of O'Connor's broadcasts for the BBC, came down from Belfast. The atmosphere about the flat was as melancholy as Michael's letter to his son early in November:

Dearly Beloved Junior,
   This is my first attempt at writing anything since my discharge, and I won't guarantee that I shall finish it, but I did want to thank you for the books, which were appreciated though for most of the time I was uncertain what they were all about. Difficult to tell with four tubes sticking out of you in different parts, and what was comparative comfort for one part an outrage to the other three . . .
   I don't know what we're going to do. Though psychologically willing, I am physically incapacitated from thinking more than one week and

one mile ahead, and while I wonder whether or not I shall get round the block I find it hard to think of getting on a plane or liner to face a New York winter. When I agitate for a five mile walk the surgeon smiles pityingly. At the same time this place is dull and has got duller now that the dreams of the New Economic Miracle are fading. However the miracle seekers are still advertising unheated houses at more than American prices. . . .

Tell Cyrilly Hallie has put on a search for the M.S. of the two missing books which I sent just before going into hospital. All that is now needed is a fire in Macmillan's to cause them both to disappear from the world. Ask her if they turn up to send us a postcard.

If you come for Christmas you will be shocked to discover that our great pal is a priest who is a protege of the Archbishop's. We had gone to France on holiday with him, and he had to fire us back after a couple of days, but he saved our lives and reason. He and Hallie argue like mad dogs about religion while I look on and sigh. I have none, I'm afraid, only an intense interest in the present and a pious hope that the future may be deferred as long as possible. The faster it approaches the less attractive it seems, and I have lost the hope that the dimming of the fires would make it more a matter of indifference. Either the fires are still too strong or this is an illusion.

How I got into this melancholy vein you can guess. I feel like Emily Dickinson, too long confined to Amherst. Not comparing Amherst and this place, where flogging etc. have been fully restored to the curriculum officially. . . .

Here or there, we must meet in the next few months.

Love,
Pa[39]

O'Connor wrote many letters in his life but few quite so eloquently revealing as this one. For over half a century his life had been inextricably bound to the life of his country. As Ireland moved further toward the materialism and cynicism of the twentieth century, his dreams, the dreams of his heroes Yeats and Collins, faded. He was not really old, only sixty-two, but he felt old. Having passed from adolescence to middle age almost overnight, he had been deprived of the gradual ripening that gives men like Yeats and Picasso, Shaw and Henry Moore, the qualities of detached intensity, endurance, and resolute calm. For half a century O'Connor had carried on an affair of the heart with Ireland, both loving and hating her, sacrificing everything—his health, his family, even his art—for some unattainable abstraction of Ireland free and just and heroic. Yeats had proven that the work of an old man is simplified to the barest essentials. Unconcerned with the circumstances of past or future, the old man can isolate once and for all those few themes of his soul that have persisted in spite of all his efforts through a lifetime to ignore or fulfill them. O'Connor might have been expressing his sense of confinement and melancholy in his letter to Myles, but he had resolved to die as he had lived.[40]

Michael/Frank had struggled his entire life for freedom, but in the end Ireland had closed in on him. Even religion sat guarding the front door lest he try to escape.[41] As a boy, under the influence of his mother, he had been devout to a fault. His break with religion had been an arrogant, assertive response of the mind, an affirmation of will and self-reliance. What he rejected was not necessarily metaphysics, though he had no sympathy for any sort of supernaturalism. The mysticism of AE and Yeats, for instance, was entirely incomprehensible to him. What O'Connor rejected was the morality of the church, not the moral principles but the moral politics of constraint and negation. His faith was not in some detached deity but in the people around him who were all he could ever know of God. He was a defiant agnostic, full of doubt and dread, but also a softhearted romantic capable of crying in the face of sorrow and misery or raging in the face of injustice of indifference. He made every cause a battle between good and evil. He had no religion, but he possessed great faith, the moralist's faith, the savagely indignant faith of Swift. The good priest in "The Cheat" said that he was more sure of the salvation of the dying agnostic than he was of his own, and the wife in that story observed that if he ever relented, it would be his weakness and not him. Writing about A. E. Coppard in *The Lonely Voice*, O'Connor asserted that such pressures as poverty and guilt can push even the best of men over the edge. And in his interview for *Paris Review*, speaking about the revelation of real character, O'Connor said emphatically: "What happens if you're torturing him or he's dying of cancer is no business of mine and that is not the individual. What a man says when he's dying and in great pain is not evidence. All right, he'll be converted to anything that's handy, but the substance of the character remains with me, that's what matters, the real thing."[42]

V

The O'Donovan social calendar after the new year was crowded. On January 4 Michael felt well enough to drive to Kilkenny with his old friend Bill Walsh, whose latest project, the Kilkenny Design Center, had been loudly applauded as an example of what could be done to revive the arts in Ireland. Only his health had hindered Michael from visiting the center before. Oliver came for a few days but left a bit disappointed that his father showed no surprise at his decision to enter the Anglican ministry. To Harriet, however, he chuckled that it would have been a delightful surprise for his mother to have had an Anglican priest for a grandson. In a letter to Myles a week later Michael wrote: "I had anticipated that one, partly because the poor devil's insides had been hacked about as much as my own, and I—as I think I told you—had lost whatever little bit of religion I had left." Dick and Betty Gill, on a roundabout way to Thailand where Dick was to help set up a new university, stopped to visit Michael and Harriet. They arrived in Dublin on Sunday, January 16. On Monday evening Harriet threw a lavish party in their honor. Michael enjoyed a great night of singing and feasting, but the next day the pain he had known on and off for months became acute. He experienced dizziness, then alternating numbness and cutting pain on his entire left side. The next afternoon, on a short walk along the canal with Dick, he confessed that he feared the worst, not for himself, because he believed less in an afterlife now than he ever had, but for his wife and young daughter. Then he laughed and said he wondered what Ireland would do without his voice to prick her conscience.

O'Connor's review of another new book on Casement, appearing on the day the Gills arrived, sounded a tone of personal vindication.[43] A week later a review by Proinsias MacAonghusa of O'Connor's *The Big Fellow,* recently republished by Clonmore and Reynolds, voiced an equally strong justification of the portrait of Michael Collins he found there. Thirty years before, neither faction had liked the book, the enemies of Collins because it cast him as a tragic hero, his friends because it made him all too human. "O'Connor's Collins is no plaster saint," MacAonghusa confidently proclaimed. "The real Collins had no time for hypocritical pseudo-respectability and the pretensions of lace-curtain suburbia."[44] O'Connor had simply told the truth no one wanted to hear and if the "passing years justified Collins more and more," as MacAonghusa claimed, then time justified O'Connor's lonely stand.

On Sunday, January 23, Michael and Harriet went with Brendan Kennelly, Philip Edwards, David Greene, and a few other friends to the Donnybrook studios of Radio-Telefís Eireann to view "Horsemen, Pass By" on BBC television. In the middle of the broadcast O'Connor had a violent attack of coughing and had to leave early. The next morning his physician called by the flat and put him at once on digoxin, a medication used to strengthen the heartbeat. He also recommended that O'Connor cancel the lectures he was scheduled to give at Trinity that week. Since the operation in November had hindered him from presenting a full slate of lectures, O'Connor felt obliged to present at least these two public lectures on early Irish storytelling, and since the material was fresh, he was actually quite eager. His physician relented but warned Philip Edwards of the seriousness of O'Connor's condition. On Tuesday afternoon the lecture hall was packed. Edwards sat on the edge of his seat, ready to jump if O'Connor collapsed. Instead, Michael performed splendidly and then lectured again on Friday afternoon with inspired vigor.

On February 2 the BBC presented a dramatization of O'Connor's "Song Without Words." He wrote to Myles that Harriet would not forgive him because he had allowed it to be described as a play "by Frank O'Connor and Hugh Leonard." (Over the protests of Leonard and O'Connor, the BBC insisted on this billing in the hopes that the play would pass as other than an adaptation and win the Italia Award. It won in 1967.) "You'll be glad to know they have called it 'Silent Song' which is only because the idiots did not think of 'But Those Unheard.' " Once again there were parties and dinners for O'Connor. In fact, with every public triumph a mood of hysteria swirled around him, as if everyone were intent on not missing the last chance to honor him. The tone of his last letters to Myles and the conversation with Dick Gill indicated that he was wearily aware of this expectant mood.

Toward the end of February Michael spoke to Nancy McCarthy on the telephone. In the course of conversation she began criticizing O'Faoláin's autobiography *Vive Moi!* Michael defended the book, but she remained adamant. He thought Seán's portrait of his father was superb. "Perhaps, but he has painted a very bad picture of his mother," Nancy argued. "She was the one I knew best and I was fond of her." Not wishing to quarrel with an old friend, Michael changed the subject. "You'll never guess where I'm going tomorrow." Nancy admitted that she could not guess. "I'm off to Maynooth." "Walls of Jericho!" she screeched in delight. "You lecturing at Maynooth." To which Michael responded, "I can't blame the whoors for being ignorant if I don't go and enlighten them." The next day Frank O'Connor, accompanied by Father Sheehy, delivered his last public lecture—at Ireland's most prominent seminary, St. Patrick's College in Maynooth. February had also seen his last review, his last piece on Yeats—an elegiac essay entitled "A Gambler's Throw"—and the last installment of his autobiography, a piece on his parents entitled "My Father's Wife."[45] A few days after the Maynooth lecture he was talking to Dermot Foley, who enjoyed with him the magnificent irony of the invitation. Though their laughter was hearty, Dermot left with the sense that his old friend seemed more resigned than melancholy. In a moment of contemplative musing, for instance, O'Connor had quoted Shaw's Saint Joan: "The work is over; my voices have left me."

During the first week of March a stream of visitors called by the flat, and that Friday O'Connor went to Philip Edwards's graduate seminar to answer questions about his own work. He had never *invented* an incident, he told them. "Any scrap of conversation which came [my] way might serve as the germ of a story. . . . The core of a story must be for [me] something that had happened." He talked about his habit of endless revision. Asked about the autobiographical element in his stories, he simply repeated what he had said to so many American students: One writes what one is. "We talked a lot about the attitude of the writer to using circumstances he was involved in as a person," Edwards later recalled, "and this led to deaths and funerals: O'Connor indignantly rejected the idea proffered to him that the true writer could maintain his detachment even at his mother's funeral."[46]

On Tuesday Michael was at Trinity again to attend a lecture by Dan Binchy. By now he could hardly walk, but he felt he could not let him down. Only the week before, in the course of conversation Michael jokingly asked Binchy how old he was. All those years he had kept his promise not to write the story of Binchy's tragic love affair until Binchy was seventy, though it had haunted him as few others had ever done. Every poignant detail still resonated in O'Connor's imagination.

However, time, which had failed to diminish Binchy's story or to dampen O'Connor's passion to tell it, had finally run out. On Thursday afternoon, March 10, Michael got up from his reading, told Harriet he was not feeling very well, and went to lie down. She joined him a few minutes later. Lying with her on the bed, he put his hand over hers, and smiling he said, "I hope you don't expect me to entertain you." In the fading light he suffered a fatal heart attack.

*　*　*

At seven o'clock that evening Dermot Foley returned home from a funeral in the country. As he entered the house he heard the telephone ringing; he picked up the receiver to hear his sister say, "Michael is dead. Come to the flat at once."[47] He hadn't even taken off his coat. At the door of the flat he was met by Father Sheehy. "Would you like to see him?" Sheehy asked. "No," Dermot mumbled on his way to the kitchen, where he stood over the sink ready to vomit. Hector Legge and Brendan Kennelly propped him up. When he recovered he went to Harriet, threw his arms around her, and sobbed. Dan Binchy spoke to him a few minutes later in one corner of the living room. "Do you know what the funeral arrangements are?" Dermot asked. "Deansgrange!" came the reply. "Why not Cork, with his mother?" Dermot wanted to know. "Hallie said that Nance heard from the Cork cousins that there was no room in the grave at Caherlag." "Nonsense!" Dermot spluttered. "That's not all," Dan continued in a whisper. "Westland Row church AND Mass on Saturday."

Dermot's mind was jumping, in the face of these revelations, to O'Connor's stories, his explosive attacks on the church, his sympathy for men like the lonely priest in France. Returning to the bosom of the church would be too much out of character for Frank O'Connor, but, Dermot admitted to himself, so was dying. He asked Father Sheehy, "When did you get here?" "Within fifteen minutes," the priest replied. "She telephoned me and then the doctor." "I see," Dermot said, nodding; "then he wasn't medically dead?" "He was not, and I am perfectly satisfied with the last rites." "So there you are," Dermot wrote later in his diary, obviously not satisfied in the least.

Soon the flat was full of people, many of them strangers to Dermot. Nancy McCarthy took the first train from Cork and never left Harriet's side through the next trying days. There was a constant stream of people coming through the flat, for whom Harriet made endless cups of tea which nobody drank. Mary Lavin stayed to handle all of the domestic details. Radio Eireann broadcast a tribute by Roger McHugh and an old reading by O'Connor of "Guests of the Nation." As he listened Dermot recalled his friend's mannerisms behind the microphone, that "awful nervous tension that pervaded all his public performances." He remembered the morning the letter of acceptance had come from the *Atlantic Monthly,* and he found it difficult to believe that his exuberant friend was dead.

Yet dead he was, and what remained now for those in the flat, the widow and the friends, were the details of public remembrance. On Friday, Joan and Oliver arrived to join Cousin May and Christy O'Donovan, who had come up from Cork. As Harriet looked at the people gathered around the lunch table, she thought how Michael would smile at this oddly assorted group—Nancy, Joan, and Harriet; May, Christy, and Dermot; Dan Binchy and Father Sheehy; Brendan Kennelly and Mary Lavin—and for a moment she was glad that he had died in Ireland, where grief is naturally expressed and tears are not something to be shed in private, but openly in tribute to someone loved.

Myles arrived from New York, but Dermot hardly recognized him. The young man sat wordless in the wakeroom. Liadain would arrive from San Francisco on Saturday; Dermot met her plane and got her to the church just in time for the service. Brendan Kennelly, as good friend and representative of the young writers of Ireland, was chosen to give the graveside oration. Dermot suggested that he read from "Kilcash," and Daniel Binchy asked if he would use the lines from Yeats that Michael had quoted in Drumcliffe, the ones about the gambler's throw. Finally, Dermot and Father Sheehy hastily arranged to have a death mask done—in the dim light of the mortuary after the service Friday night—by a local sculptor named Broe.

Father Sheehy had arranged for the coffin to be met at the Westland Row church by the parish priest and an old friend of his, the Reverend John McCarthy. The hearse arrived early and another priest approached to inquire by what authority they were bringing the body into the church. At that moment Father McCarthy appeared, saluted Father Sheehy, and the coffin was taken in. Less than an hour later a small crowd poured into the little mortuary and stood around the walls. Harriet sat in a front seat, flanked by Myles and Oliver. Dermot stood with Seán O'Faoláin and James Dillon. David Greene and Proinsias MacAonghusa were there and, of all people, Ernest Blythe.

The requiem Mass on Saturday morning, March 12, was celebrated in stately fashion by Father Sheehy. Michael's friends, old and new, were all there. A few dignitaries were present as well, including Michael Yeats and Sean MacEntee, but no other government officials. De Valera's representative conveyed formal condolences and apologized for the president's regrettable absence. They were burying a man who had done more than almost anyone else to preserve, reveal, and nurture the glories of Ireland, and the nation's president was opening an extension of Colaiste Mhuire in Parnell Square. Outside the church television cameras tried to capture the arrival of any notable. And afterwards there were those who went home to gossip about how many women were there to mourn him. Patrick Kavanagh, with tears for a lost friend and indignation for the mood of vapid condescension, turned to Sean White and whispered these lines from Yeats:

> I mourn for that most lonely thing; and yet God's will be done:
> I knew a phoenix in my youth, so let them have their day.

The funeral procession wound south along Merrion Road to Blackrock to Dean's Grange Road. At the cemetery a small group of friends gathered. "A lovely morning of sun and cold wind for a cold job," Dermot scribbled later. First there were prayers by Father Sheehy, and then Brendan Kennelly's voice rose over the wind.

> What shall we do for timber?
>   The last of the woods is down.
> Kilcash and the house of its glory
>   And the bell of the house are gone,
> The spot where the lady waited
>   Who shamed all women for grace
> When earls came sailing to greet her
>   And Mass was said in the place.

The young Irish poet paid stirring tribute to the master, to his dreams and his battles, and then offered as an epitaph the lines O'Connor chose for Yeats:

> And I choose the laughing lip
> That shall not turn from laughing whatever rise or fall;
> The heart that grows no bitterer although betrayed by all;
> The hand that loves to scatter;
> The life like a gambler's throw.

Dermot stole a glance at Seán O'Faoláin, buried in a wool scarf, and knew that "with the corpse went a piece of Seán into the grave." He noticed Liadain weeping openly, Myles rigid and stony-faced, Oliver attentive to the microphone he was holding to record Kennelly's oration. Nancy stood close to Harriet and gave silent support. Joan stood somewhere in the background. After all the words had been said, Harriet put a bouquet of flowers into the open grave and withdrew in tears. Suddenly it was all over.

Montaigne, in his essay "On Not Judging Men Until After Their Death," mused about the fortune that lies in wait to surprise us in our final hour, to nullify or vindicate what was years in the making. Fortune commented with sardonic irony when within a few months of O'Connor's death the Abbey Theatre opened its new and impressive building. Within a few weeks of his death an old enemy, Flann O'Brien, died, and a year later Patrick Kavanagh; then, in quick succession, Paul Vincent Carroll and Bertie Rodgers. When Austin Clarke died in 1974, the generation of the "strayed revellers" of the Irish Literary Renaissance had all but ended. Irish writing is flourishing today, however, and for that O'Connor would rejoice. Compulsory Irish vanished a few years ago, and its demise brought a renewed interest in things Gaelic. Irish music is enjoyed for its own sake, and the native arts are now even popular. The national monuments not only are protected by law but are undergoing extensive restoration. And programs of Irish studies, structured along lines once proposed by O'Connor, now exist in each of the national universities.

Frank O'Connor never cared much about reputation; but writing in 1960 on the centennial of Chekhov's birth, he looked with more than passing concern at the fact that the reputations of most writers pass under a cloud after they have died. "The cloud is finally scattered only by the patient work of critics and scholars, but even then, the figure that reappears is never that which his contemporaries saw."[48] The reason, he surmised, was not simply literary fashion. "Most great writers have a streak of the charlatan in them," by which he meant the posing and self-advertising that fade at death. "Tolstoy sold himself to his generation as a latter-day saint, Dostoevsky as a mystic, Kipling as the bearer of the white man's burden and Yeats as the vague creature who saw darling little leprechauns in every corner." Chekhov was the only writer, O'Connor believed, who did not pose or pretend, and because of that his reputation did not suffer at all. Chekhov regarded himself "as a minor writer and never attempted to emulate his famous contemporaries in the writing of long novels," but O'Connor went on, his stories have been placed "among the major achievements of Russian literature." Obviously, O'Connor identified himself with Chekhov and refused to bend to pressure for the big work, continuing stubbornly to practice his lonely art in shorter forms. Michael O'Donovan strove to be a good man; indeed he had to see himself and present himself as a good man. Frank O'Connor strove to be an artist, and in his art there is little posing.

"Nothing outlives the man that wrote it," he once wrote. However, that which he produced at his best seems very much alive and capable of sustaining his memory, with or without the critics and scholars. The years immediately following his death saw a vigorous campaign of posthumous publication. David Greene carried out the completion of A Golden Treasury of Irish Poetry, and O'Connor's agents sold nearly all of the articles and stories sent them by his widow, who eventually began putting together his letters and unpublished manuscripts. Macmillan and Knopf brought out the collection of stories he was working on after his return to Dublin. Father Sheehy shepherded two of O'Connor's books through publication: the history of Irish literature, A Backward Look, and the second volume of the autobiography, My Father's Son. He also edited a memorial volume of essays by O'Connor's friends, the title of which came from Mrs. Yeats's affectionate nickname for him: Michael/Frank. That book would prove to be a fitting and worthy tribute to the man and to the writer.

In the years since his death, Frank O'Connor's reputation has shifted with the uncertainty of an Irish summer sky. His stories, as one might expect, have held their appeal and find their way regularly into new collections, anthologies, and even stage and television adaptations. The novels came back into print in Ireland for a time and then disappeared. His translations, though out of print in full volume, appear in numerous anthologies but survive mainly by continual imitation and criticism. That some among the present generation of poets and translators feel compelled to ridicule O'Connor's translations says something about the staying power of his work. That others rush to brand his writing "soft" and "stage-Irish" while cheering the demise of the "myths of O'Connor and O'Faolain" gives some indication about the strength of his memory. Two of O'Connor's plays have seen revivals on the stage of the Abbey Theatre, proving perhaps that even a thorn in the flesh can be admired—once it's out. Whether or not the clouds darting over his reputation will scatter, only time will tell.

Michael O'Donovan is dead, his voice stilled forever, but the voices of Frank O'Connor endure. In London during the war he came across a story that haunted him for years after. It was told to him by his old friend Cyril Cusack. Toward the end of his life, in the television broadcast "Interior Voices," he recalled the story, laying a heavy curse on anyone who would lift it from him:

> My friend, who is a famous actor—probably the greatest of Irish actors—was in a publichouse one night when a young Commando trooper approached him, and said "I know you're a famous actor, and I just wondered how you act a part. Do you meet somebody casually in a pub, just as you're meeting me, and then play the part as you think he'd have played it?" "I suppose that roughly that's exactly what I do," said my friend. "You think you could play me, for instance?" "I think so," said the actor, and I know he wasn't boasting. Sometimes in a few minutes one gets an overwhelming impression of a personality as I got from the voice of the young man I thought of when I was writing "The Luceys." "Would you play me?" asked the soldier. "Why?" asked the actor. "Tomorrow," said the soldier, "I'm going off on a job, and I don't think I'm going to come back. You know the way you get these hunches. I'd just like to feel that when I'm gone, I could come back again, even for a while, and people would see that I was still real, as I am now. Would you do it?"
>
> Many of these voices I've talked to you about, like that of the young soldier are gone forever, but for me they are still alive in the pages of my books, and sometimes as now when I've been looking back on these stories, I find myself saying over Thomas Moore's loveliest lines—
>
> And as Echo far off through the vale my sad orison rolls,
> I think, O my love, 'tis thy voice from the kingdom of souls,
>   Faintly answering still the notes that once were so dear.

Acknowledgments

EXPRESSING one's gratitude adequately can be nearly impossible. A few published words to a group of people are poor substitutes for a personal gesture — a handshake perhaps, a hug or a drink together, a hearty salute. Nevertheless, I should like to thank some of the people who have helped in the making of this book and to apologize for its weaknesses, which are mine alone.

My gratitude first, of course, to the members of Michael O'Donovan's family on both sides of the Atlantic for their support, cooperation, and forbearance in an enterprise that must have seemed both interminable and impertinent to them: to his widow, Mrs. Harriet Sheehy, who, although she gave me access to the private papers and manuscripts and was generally helpful, does not agree with a number of the conclusions I have drawn; to the two other important women in his life, Evelyn and Joan, whose present surnames must remain private; and to his two eldest children, Myles O'Donovan and Liadain O'Donovan Cook.

My thanks also to those who gave with such trusting generosity their memories of Frank O'Connor—and information and advice—to a bumbling stranger who had only more questions to offer in return for their candid conversation, thoughtful letters, and helpful documents: Mrs. Molly Alexander, Mrs. Berry Allitt (Nancy McCarthy), General Tom Barry, Sir John Betjeman, Professor Daniel Binchy, Mr. John Boyd, the Clancy Brothers (Liam, Bobby, and Paddy), Mr. Lovat Dickson, Professor and Mrs. Richard Ellmann, Mr. Larry Elyan, Mr. Gabriel Fallon, Professor Thomas Flanagan, Mr. Dermot Foley, Mr. John Garvin, Mr. and Mrs. Richard Gill, Professor David Greene, Mr. and Mrs. Sean Hendrick, Mrs. Mary Manning Howe, Mr. Hugh Hunt, Denis Johnston, Mr. Louis Johnston, Professor and Mrs. John Kelleher, Eamon Kelly, "Quidnunc" Kelly, Brendan Kennelly, Mary Lavin, Mr. Hector Legge, Shevawn Lynam, Norah McGuinness, Professor Roger McHugh, Mícheál MacLiammóir, Bryan MacMahon, William Maxwell, Val Mulkerns, Mr. and Mrs. Seamus Murphy, Bill Naughton, Mrs. Geraldine Neeson, Seán and Eileen O'Faoláin, Mrs. Aurelia Plath, James Plunkett, Professor Walter Scott, Sir Charles Percy Snow, Mr. Mervyn Wall, and Mr. Sean White. (Some among this number are now deceased; to them my regret that this book took so long.)

To those whose personal support is beyond measure: Jim Crane, Del and

Tru Williams, Peter Sexton, Saul Field, and Jean Townsend; to Jean Schultz for typing this thing in too many drafts, and to those friends and editors who read a few of those drafts to weed out errors, my firm assurance that I am to blame for whatever errors remain; to my former colleagues who wondered why and my former students who often proved that good students make good teachers; to my family for always being there, and to my wife, Holly, for always believing. If I have failed to mention anyone for whatever forgotten gift, it is only because I owe so much to so many.

For courtesy extended and competent assistance rendered my gratitude to the staffs of the following libraries and archives: The Mugar Memorial Library, Boston University; The Bancroft Library, University of California, Berkeley; The Humanities Research Center, University of Texas at Austin; The Suzzalo Library, University of Washington; The Eckerd College Library, St. Petersburg, Florida; The National Library of Ireland, Dublin; The Library of University College, Cork; The Library of Trinity College, Dublin; The Chancellery, Archbishop's House, Dublin; The Cork Museum; The Cork Archives Council; The Crawford Gallery, Cork; The British Library, London; The Written Archives of the British Broadcasting Corporation, Reading.

For financial assistance I wish to thank The National Endowment for the Humanities, The American Philosophical Society, and the Faculty Development Fund of Eckerd College.

Finally, for permission to quote, my gratitude to the following: Mrs. Harriet Sheehy, for the unpublished and published writings of Frank O'Connor, and to his publishers, Knopf and Macmillan London, Ltd.; Mr. Michael Yeats and Miss Anne Yeats for poems and plays by W. B. Yeats, and to his publishers, Macmillan and Macmillan London Ltd.; Mr. Seán O'Faoláin for unpublished letters and for the published writing for which he holds copyright, and to his publishers, Little, Brown & Co., and Longmans Green and Rupert Hart-Davis; to the Executors of the James Joyce Estate and to his publishers, Viking Penguin Inc. and Jonathan Cape.

Notes

THESE NOTES are meant to provide the scrupulous reader with information supplemental to the text as well as basic documentation of sources. The notes also must serve as a limited bibliography, since it would be presumptuous to duplicate the generally adequate listing of material in the memorial volume *Michael/Frank* (New York: Knopf, 1969; Dublin: Gill and Macmillan, 1969) or to anticipate the extensive and "official" bibliography now in preparation by Professor Sherry. In the interest of space, citation of quotations from the published writings of Frank O'Connor has been kept to a minimum; citation of unpublished material has been done primarily to state location. The job of editing the O'Connor letters and, I presume, the unpublished papers, as well, is presently in the hands of his widow, Mrs. Harriet Sheehy. Obviously, a good deal of the information used in the making of this book has come from conversation and correspondence with people who knew O'Connor, though only a small portion of it has been actually noted here. A complete listing of the people to whom I am indebted for information may be found in the Acknowledgments.

The main locations of unpublished material pertaining to Frank O'Connor (with abbreviations to be used in the notes) are:

Frank O'Connor Collection, Mugar Memorial Library, Boston University: MMB

Seán O'Faoláin Papers, Bancroft Library, University of California, Berkeley: UCB

A. D. Peters Papers, Humanities Research Center, University of Texas, Austin: UTA

National Library of Ireland, Dublin: NLI

Library of University College, Cork: UCC

Library of Trinity College, Dublin: TCD

Written Archives of the British Broadcasting Corporation, Caversham: BBC

Cork Archives Council: CAC

Cork Museum: CM

In the private possession of Mrs. Harriet Sheehy: HS

Unless otherwise stated, all letters from O'Connor remain in the private possession of the addressee: PP

Special abbreviations used here include:

Frank O'Connor (when identifying authorship of letters). FOC

An Only Child. New York: Knopf, 1961; London: Macmillan, 1962. *AOC*

My Father's Son. New York: Knopf, 1969; Dublin: Gill and Macmillan, 1968. *MFS*

Michael/Frank: Studies on Frank O'Connor. Edited by Maurice Sheehy. New York: Knopf, 1969; Dublin: Gill and Macmillan, 1969. *M/F*

"A Frank O'Connor Miscellany." *Journal of Irish Literature,* January 1975.
JIL
The Cornet Player Who Betrayed Ireland. Dublin: Poolbeg, 1981. *CP*

CHAPTER ONE

1. Daniel Corkery, *The Threshold of Quiet* (Dublin: Talbot Press, 1946), p. 3.
2. Seán O'Faoláin, *An Irish Journey* (London: Longmans and Green, 1940), p. 90.
3. Frank O'Connor, "In Quest of Dead O'Donovans," *Three Old Brothers* (London: Nelson, 1936), p. 26.
4. Benedict Kiely, *Modern Irish Fiction* (Dublin: Golden Eagle Books, 1950), p. 52.
5. O'Faoláin, *An Irish Journey,* p. 85.
6. Frank O'Connor, *Leinster, Munster, and Connaught* (London: Hale, 1950), p. 175.
7. O'Faoláin, *An Irish Journey,* p. 78.
8. Frank O'Connor, *An Only Child* (London: Macmillan, 1961), p. 49 (herefter cited as *AOC*).
9. *AOC,* p. 77.
10. Ibid., p. 78.
11. The official birth certificate provided by the Southern Health Board, Cork, gives the name Michael John Donovan, whereas the baptismal record in the family possession reads Michael Francis Xavier O'Donovan. See ibid., p. 8. Michael and John were the names of the two grandfathers. At this time, the names "O'Donovan" and "Donovan" were, as O'Connor notes, "almost interchangeable. English officials insisted on the latter form, and it was always used familiarly." Ibid., p. 13.

CHAPTER TWO

1. That description closely resembles the titular heroes of such early stories as "Lofty," "Alec," and "The Late Henry Conran," all of which appeared in *Guests of the Nation* (London: Macmillan, 1931).
2. O'Connor's account in *AOC,* pp. 34–35, only dramatized an event that took place on many occasions.
3. Ibid., p. 36. His mother's earnings were about two shillings per week; his father's fitful earnings as a navvy averaged about five to seven shillings per month. With the monthly pension of one guinea, that meant the family income was about thirty-six shillings per month. By comparison, rent was four shillings and six pence per month.
4. James Larkin, who founded the Irish Transport and General Workers' Union, championed the cause of unskilled workers in Ireland. His general strike in Dublin in 1913 was as crucial in liberating Ireland as was the Easter Rising of 1916, though the eventual rebellion was dominated more by nationalistic fervor than labor sentiment.
5. Frank O'Connor (hereafter cited as FOC to indicate authorship of letters)

to William Maxwell, editor at *The New Yorker,* ca. December 1956, from 60 Cornhill, Annapolis, Md., PP.

6. "The Genius," originally titled "The Sissy," was eventually published in *Domestic Relations* (New York: Knopf, 1957).

7. AOC, p. 120. In his adult life Michael was haunted by dreams of falling from great heights and by a very keen sense of claustrophobia. He disliked air travel, tall buildings, elevators, and, most of all, islands.

8. From an interview with Seán and Eileen O'Faoláin, September 1976.

9. "My father and both my uncles had been in the British Army, and, though I differed from them and from most of the children round me in that I was fond of reading, the papers and books I read were English public-school stories. I do not decry these stories, nor am I worried as much as Mr. Orwell seemed to be about whatever bad principles they may have been supposed to inculcate. . . ." O'Connor, *Leinster, Munster, and Connaught,* p. 171. He is referring here to Orwell's essay "Boys' Weeklies," published in *Horizon,* March 1940.

10. O'Connor's account of Christmas in Cork first appeared in *The New Yorker,* December 19, 1959, before taking final form in AOC, pp. 129–37. It also appeared in Irish: "An Nodlaigh i gCorcaigh," *Comhar,* February 1960.

11. AOC, pp. 141–42. See also his interview with Harvey Breit in the *New York Times Book Review,* June 24, 1951.

12. Sean Beecher gives this description of the school: "The Order of the Christian Brothers was founded in 1811 in Waterford by Edmund Ignatius Rice to provide education for the poor. . . . It was, and indeed still is a truism to say that the civil service is run by Corkmen and many of these civil servants are products of the schools of the Christian Brothers and in particular the 'North Mon'." *The Story of Cork* (Cork: Mercier, 1971) pp. 30–31.

13. About the mind and mood of Irish schoolboys at the time, Ernie O'Malley had this to say: "We told our school chums stories of Fionn and Cuchulain, but they laughed at us. They had read the latest Buffalo Bill, could talk of the red varmints of Indians, Colt's-emptying frontier fighters, of split-up-the-back Eton suits and the rags of that other public school life of the Magnet and Gem. Only to ourselves now did we talk about the older stories." *On Another Man's Wound* (London: Rich & Cowan, 1936), p. 16. Young Michael O'Donovan's nascent awareness of the Irish past was, therefore, not uncharacteristic of the children of the time.

14. The influence on O'Connor's stories, particularly those about Irish priests, of the fiction of Canon Sheehan should not be overlooked. Among the novels that young Michael no doubt read were *My First Curate* (London: Longmans, 1899) and *Glenanaar* (London: Longmans, 1905), both of which are about priests in peasant villages. Sheehan was also a fervent patriot, best illustrated in two other novels that Michael O'Donovan read: *Lisheen* (London: Longmans, 1907) and *Graves of Kilmorna* (London: Longmans, 1915).

CHAPTER THREE

1. The Easter Rising has attracted the attention of the best writers and historians of Ireland in this century because it was the culmination of the entire history of the Irish. The most indelible eyewitness account was James Stephens's *The Insurrection in Dublin* (Dublin: Maunsel, 1916). A number of books were written by actual participants in the fighting—Liam Deasy, Frank Gallagher, Tom Barry, Charles Dalton, Darrel Figgis—but the one that stands out as the most impressive literary effort, and the one that O'Connor considered the best book to come out of the Troubles, was Ernie O'Malley's *On Another Man's Wound.* Also see Desmond Ryan's *The Rising* (Dublin: Golden Eagle Books, 1949), and *1916: The Easter Rising,* edited by Owen Dudley Edwards and Fergus Pyle (London: MacGibbon & Kee, 1968).

2. O'Connor referred to the Troubles as a "crisis of the imagination." See *AOC,* p. 155. One account of the imaginative dimension of the Easter Rising is William I. Thompson's *The Imagination of an Insurrection* (New York: Oxford University Press, 1967).

3. In O'Connor's phrasing, the "whole country was on the edge of a volcano." "The Patriarch," in *Guests of the Nation.*

4. *AOC,* pp. 160–161. *A Munster Twilight* (Dublin: Talbot Press, 1916) contains twelve compact, almost mystical tales including: "The Spanceled," "Solace," "The Cry," "The Return," and "The Ploughing of Leaca-na-Naomh," as well as a sequence of loosely connected vignettes entitled "The Cobbler's Den." It was Corkery's first published work.

5. *AOC,* p. 195. References to music pepper *AOC* as they do nearly everything O'Connor ever wrote about himself. Corkery also tried to introduce him to art; he got Michael into the Crawford School of Art where the boy copied casts, drew from live models, and argued with his teachers about perspective and chiaroscuro and other subtleties of painting. Probably Michael's poor eyesight and impatience had something to do with his brief career as a painter, though he dabbled with sketches most of his life.

6. *AOC,* p. 163.

7. Seán O'Faoláin, "A World of Fitzies," *Times Literary Supplement,* April 20, 1977, p. 502. O'Faoláin says much the same thing in his autobiography, *Vive Moi!,* (Boston: Little, Brown, 1963), p. 169.

8. In that same interview (October 1976), Mrs. Neeson said affectionately about Michael O'Donovan: "We called him MickMehawl then."

9. *AOC,* pp. 197–98. Corkery at the time was an assistant in the Office of Irish Instruction.

10. Sean Hendrick, "Michael O'Donovan's Wild Son," in *Michael/Frank: Studies on Frank O'Connor,* ed. Maurice Sheehy (New York: Knopf, 1969; Dublin: Gill and Macmillan, 1969), pp. 5–15 (hereafter cited as *M/F*). Hendrick made this particular statement in a speech delivered on December 29, 1966, at the presentation of an O'Connor memorial to the city of Cork.

11. *Vive Moi!,* p. 175. As O'Connor wrote in "The Patriarch," they were all "glad to have been young in such a time."

12. The best account of the Treaty negotiations is still that of Frank Pakenham

(Lord Longford), *Peace by Ordeal* (London: Cape, 1935). Another important source is Frank Gallagher, *The Anglo-Irish Treaty* (London: Hutchinson, 1965).

13. Corkery's contribution to the first number (May 6, 1922) was a polemical essay "Larkin or Ford?" Seán O'Faoláin reviewed a production of Lennox Robinson's *The Round Table* at the Abbey Theatre, Dublin, and a new novel in Irish. Sean Hendrick's poem "To Walt Whitman" appeared in the third issue of *An Lóng* (July 15, 1922) along with "Un Peu de Musique" and an essay in Irish, "Solus," by Michael O'Donovan. In UCC. An account of the Twenty Club and its other publication *An Lá* ("the day") appears in *Vive Moi!*, pp. 170–71.

14. *An Poblacht* was a national publication; what Childers supervised was the "Southern Edition." O'Connor passes over his first few months with the Republican forces in *AOC*, but Sean Hendrick in his essay in *M/F* has most thoughtfully filled in the details. Two other eyewitness accounts are Eoin Neeson's *The Civil War in Ireland, 1922–1923* (Cork: Mercier, 1967) and Ernie O'Malley's *The Singing Flame* (Dublin: Anvil, 1978). A useful historical study is Carlton Younger's *Ireland's Civil War* (London: Muller, 1968).

15. *AOC*, p. 215. Also see the last two chapters of Andrew Boyle's biography, *The Riddle of Erskine Childers* (London: Hutchinson, 1977).

16. *AOC*, pp. 217–24. The incident became one of O'Connor's first stories, "War," published in the *Irish Statesman*, August 7, 1926.

17. Years later O'Connor wrote the story "Baptismal," which appeared in *American Mercury*, March 1951. Carlton Younger repeats the episode in *Ireland's Civil War*, p. 393.

18. *AOC*, p. 227. See Younger, *Ireland's Civil War*, p. 412.

19. Younger, *Ireland's Civil War*, p. 431. On August 9 Collins began an inspection tour of the West but returned when Arthur Griffith, prime minister of the Free State government, died on August 12. After the funeral Collins resumed his tour; on the Macroom-Bandon road, not far from his home, Collins was killed.

20. For a fuller account of this amazing episode than space permits here, see Boyle, *The Riddle of Erskine Childers*, and O'Malley, *The Singing Flame*.

21. *AOC*, p. 237. Daniel Corkery (using the pseudonym Reithín Siúbhalach) dedicated his *Rebel Songs* (Cork: Lee Press, 1922) to Erskine Childers.

CHAPTER FOUR

1. Frank O'Connor, "A Boy in Prison," *Life and Letters*, August 1934, p. 525.

2. Ibid., pp. 526–27. "Nightpiece with Figures" appeared in *Guests of the Nation*.

3. *AOC*, p. 244. Corkery even signed a copy of Heine with the name Martin Cloyne.

4. O'Connor, "Boy in Prison," p. 529.

5. The following letter (TS, Corkery Papers, UCC) from Corkery to a friend in Dublin corroborates O'Connor's memory:

1 Auburn Villas
Ashburton, Cork
2–11–23

A Chara

I forwarded your letter to Jim Bierne & knew that he received it—I
hope he has written to you. When last heard of he was still hunger striking—but later news from the camp seems to show that some there have
gone off the strike. I do not know whether friend Jim is among them.

M. O'Donovan has not been on hunger strike: he was in hospital
with bronchitis when the strike began, and is now as far as I know, attending on the others. He was never robust. He is in confinement for
nine months. His address is   Michael O'Donovan
1121
Hut B
Gormanstown Internment
Camp

I buried my poor mother a fortnight ago. She was 80 years of age but
never felt more than 40. R.I.P.

If ever I go to Dublin I hope to call on you—I trust you and your
people are well and happy.

Le meas mor'
D. Ua Corcra

6. *AOC*, p. 248. Ernie O'Malley, who was interned at Mountjoy Prison in
   Dublin, also got a good education while serving time in a Free State
   prison. See O'Malley's *The Singing Flame*, p. 232.
7. While working together in Dublin, Gallagher and Childers were arrested
   by British authorities in 1921. In Wellington Barracks Gallagher went on a
   hunger strike, after the example set by Terence MacSwiney. Later, Gallagher became editor of *The Irish Press* and wrote an account of the Troubles, *The Four Glorious Years* (1953) and a study of Partition, *The Indivis-
   ible Island* (1957).
8. O'Malley wrote: "We had been refused the Sacraments whilst on hunger-
   strike. Church and State were united in breaking us. Then suddenly the
   priests decided to administer them, and some of us were able to receive
   Holy Communion every morning. . . . Their demeanour had changed.
   They had come to visit us with adamantine minds; were we not criminals,
   looters and robbers?" *The Singing Flame*, pp. 255–56.
9. Frank Gallagher, one of the strongest advocates of the hunger strike as a
   political weapon, later wrote a journal of his hunger strike: *Days of Fear*
   (London: John Murray, 1928). A detailed account of the November hunger strike can be found in O'Malley's *The Singing Flame*.
10. AE's editorial in the *Irish Statesman* of November 10, 1923, not only
    questioned the thinking behind the hunger strike but also the thinking of
    those who allowed it to continue; to AE, stupidity seemed to be rampant on
    both sides. On December 1, 1923, AE announced joy at the end of the hun-
    ger strike, adding, "We hope that this political weapon will now be dis-
    carded for ever in Ireland."
11. Published in a special O'Connor miscellany in the *Journal of Irish Litera-*

ture, January 1975, p. 21 (hereafter cited as *JIL*). A typescript of the poem and a number of other documents (poems, letters, manuscripts) were donated to the Cork Museum by Sean Hendrick in 1969.

12. MS, CM.

13. MSS, CM.

14. *JIL,* p. 24.

15. In *Irish Statesman,* March 14, 1925.

16. In *Irish Statesman,* January 14, 1928.

17. Recently, in the O'Faoláin papers (UCB) the typescript of a poem titled "Cork" turned up. It was probably written by Frank O'Connor between 1924 and 1927, according to O'Faoláin.

CHAPTER FIVE

1. Frank O'Connor, *My Father's Son* (New York: Knopf, 1969; Dublin: Gill and Macmillan, 1968), p. 13. Hereafter cited as *MFS.*

2. FOC to Sean Hendrick, ca. 1924, from County Book Repository, Sligo, CM Published in *JIL,* pp. 44–46.

3. *MFS,* pp. 34–35. Robinson's story was "The Madonna of Slieve Dun," which appeared in the first number of *To-Morrow,* in August 1924. The storm over Robinson's story might have been minor had not Yeats given the editors his poem "Leda and the Leda," a version of the same heresy. Yeats also wrote a scathing editorial, under a pseudonym, deploring the cultural standards in Ireland and the narrow vision of the clergy, who had only to look to Rome in order to see the marriage of art and religion. See Francis Stuart in *The Yeats We Knew,* ed. Francis MacManus (Cork: Mercier, 1965).

4. *MFS,* p. 13. The incident was corroborated by the late Seamus Murphy, the stone carver, in an interview in Cork, in August 1970.

5. For another version of the meeting, see Henry Summerfield's biography of AE, *That Myriad-Minded Man* (Totowa, N.J.: Rowman and Littlefield, 1975), p. 234.

6. In *Irish Statesman,* March 14, 1925.

7. O'Connor's letter of protest was signed "Micheal O Donnabhain." *Irish Statesman,* June 13, 1925, p. 427–28.

8. *MFS,* p. 50. Because the second volume of O'Connor's biography was "put together" after his death by Maurice Sheehy, it bears the stamp of the editor's hand. For the rest of this delightful story, see the original piece, "Bring in the Whiskey Now Mary," *The New Yorker,* August 12, 1967.

9. The *Irish Tribune,* a weekly published in Cork from March to December 1926, briefly provided Corkery and his circle a local platform for their endless debate on "The National Tradition." In that short-lived paper also appeared the first stories by O'Faoláin ("Calf Love" on May 14) and O'Connor ("Sion" on August 6 and "The Peddler" on November 26). In UCC.

10. O'Connor's first contribution was a review of O'Faoláin's thesis study (for the Celtic Faculty of University College, Cork) on David Bruadair: "The Poet as Professional," *Irish Statesman* October 2, 1925.

11. "An Irish Anthology," *Irish Statesman,* June 12, 1926, suggests that he had made translations of "The Old Woman of Beare," the pantheistic nature poems "Winter" and "Spring," Saint Columcille's lament, and the Suibhne Geilt series. If Phibbs's letters to O'Connor are reliable, then O'Connor had already begun to translate the poets treated by Corkery in *The Hidden Ireland* (Dublin: Gill, 1925).

12. O'Faoláin writes in his autobiography, that at this time O'Connor was already "writing exellent poetry" under his pen name. Michael had urged him to send something to AE, which he did; and it was his short story called "Lilliput," which AE published in the *Irish Statesman* of February 6, 1926, "beside a translation of a Gaelic poem by O'Connor." See O'Faoláin's *Vive Moi!,* p. 240. O'Connor's poem, "Celibacy," was a song by the priest Geoffrey Keating, which O'Connor sent to Hendrick with the note, "It may amuse you." See *JIL,* p. 48.

13. Both poems are highly dramatic. Another example of O'Connor's penchant for the dramatic is "At the Wakehouse," in *Theatre Arts Monthly* of June 1926. He was probably prompted to send this dramatic vignette, of barely one hundred lines, to the American publication because of the appearance of Corkery's play *Resurrection* there in April 1924.

14. In 1927 O'Connor wrote a lengthy essay entitled "Sinn Fein and the Irish Cultural Revival" for *Vox Studentium,* a student publication at University College, Cork. The essay is noteworthy primarily as O'Connor's first substantial statement on the debilitating relationship between nationalism and provincialism. UCC

15. The records of the Cork County Library Committee (including minutes, abstracts of accounts, contracts, and letters) are held by the Cork Archives Council, the Courthouse, Cork. The archivist and secretary, Ms. Ann Barry, kindly supplied copies of this material, which is extensive. On November 26, 1977, she wrote: "Cork Co. Library adopted the Library Acts on Nov. 5th 1925. Michael O'Donovan was appointed 1st County Librarian on Dec. 19th 1925. His salary was £20. 16s. 8d. per month. . . . The Library premises were at 25, Patrick St., Cork. Initially the scheme was funded by the Carnegie Trust, and then taken on by the Cork County Council at the rate of 1/3 penny in the pound. M. O'Donovan resigned as from Dec. 28th 1928."

16. *MFS,* pp. 53–54. According to the minutes, this comedy of errors took place on March 13, 1926. In CAC.

17. A photograph of the new library van appeared in the *Cork Examiner* on September 11, 1928.

18. FOC to Geoffrey Phibbs, n.d., on letterhead of Leabharlann Charnegie Chomhairle Chonntae Chorcaighe, PP. The letters of O'Connor to Phibbs were in the possession of the late Norah McGuinness, who sent copies to me in March 1977. Letters from Phibbs to O'Connor in MMB.

19. *Evening Press,* July 23, 1962, p. 10. AE mentions Michael's hospitalization in 1926 in a letter to Seán O'Faoláin. See *Letters from A.E.,* ed. Alan Denson (London: Abelard-Schuman, 1961), p. 172. On August 19 O'Connor wrote to Phibbs outlining his trip with O'Faoláin. He also sent a copy of the *Irish Tribune* with his story "Sion," mentioned AE's kindness during his hospital stay, and spoke somewhat disparagingly of Liam O'Flaherty, with whom O'Faoláin had recently become acquainted.

20. O'Faoláin, *Vive Moi!*, pp. 264–65. O'Connor's idea for a black hat may have come from a piece by H. L. "Larry" Morrow, which was printed next to O'Connor's essay on O'Bruadair in the *Irish Statesman,* October 2, 1925.
21. Michael Farrell, "Drama in Cork City," *The Bell,* December 1941, p. 215.
22. MacLiammóir's version of this first meeting appears in *All For Hecuba* (London: Methuen, 1946), p. 42. In O'Connor's journal is this entry, dated August 15: "Wilmore (MacLiammor)—fuzzy hair which he is obviously proud of but doesn't wash often enough; brown about the eyes—an actor's face—actor's complexion, that is to say complexion wiped off. Insincere as hell. Talented. Went to the stage at the age of ten with an English company. Speaks of his training as a complete wiping out of personality, the imposition of another personality and so on. In his own character there are a half dozen personalities." Journal 1, HS.
23. "Wild Boy," in *M/F*, p. 14.
24. Ibid.
25. *MFS,* pp. 58–59. Corroborated in interviews with Mrs. Barry Allitt (née Nancy McCarthy), Mrs. Neeson, and Mr. Sean Hendrick.
26. Material pertaining to the Cork Drama League taken from a scrapbook compiled by Mrs. Allitt.
27. TS in possession of Mrs. Allitt.
28. That summer O'Connor wrote two poems to Nancy McCarthy. One entitled "Sonnet" speaks about how in only five months "one woman" has changed his life. TS, CM. The other poem, "The Hawk," was published in the *Irish Statesman* on August 18, 1928.
29. From there O'Connor wrote to Eileen O'Faoláin about the possibility of his leaving Cork because of the claustrophobic effect it was beginning to have on him. FOC to Eileen O'Faoláin, n.d., ca. September, 1928; Flying Horse Hotel, Nottingham. UCB.
30. Father O'Flynn struck first on December 21, 1927. Micheal O'Donnabhain rose to Lennox Robinson's defense on December 24 and also to the defense of fellow Corkmen Corkery and T. C. Murray. On December 28 the theatrical priest leveled his sights on Mr. O'Donovan and his reputation for associating with the "Dublin muses." His refusal to give the name of his adversary in Irish was that it is probably assumed but obviously insincere. In his reply on December 31 Michael deigned only to correct the misguided priest's Irish, leaving it to Sean Hendrick, disguised as "The Spectator," to attack from the flank.
31. *Moke* is slang for "ass." See Shakespeare's use in reference to Bottom the Weaver in "A Midsummer-Night's Dream." The irony is that O'Connor had been reading Shakespeare avidly for nearly ten years. In the possession of O'Connor's daughter, Liadain, are Chiswick pocket editions of *Troilus and Cressida* and *Poems,* both well marked and signed "M. O'Donnabhain 22.5.20."
32. *Cork Examiner,* November 28, 1928.

CHAPTER SIX

1. Dermot Foley wrote of his years with O'Connor in the Pembroke Library in "The Young Librarian," *M/F*, pp. 50–63.

2. *MFS*, p. 66. Foley's version of the meeting may be found in "A Minstrel Boy with a Satchel of Books," *Irish University Review*, Autumn, 1974, p. 205.

3. *M/F*, p. 50.

4. O'Connor's letters to Nancy McCarthy, numbering over a hundred, are currently in the hands of his widow, Mrs. Harriet Sheehy, who has undertaken editing the letters.

5. From O'Connor's *The Saint and Mary Kate* (London: Macmillan, 1932), p. 152.

6. FOC to Nancy McCarthy, p.m., September 14, 1930, HS.

7. The administration which formed the Free State government from September 19, 1923 until 1932 was led by W. T. Cosgrave, President of the Executive Council, or the prime minister. The title now used in Ireland for head of government is *An Taoiseach* but it was not used until the adoption of the new Constitution in 1937.

8. See John Ryan, *Remembering How We Stood* (New York: Taplinger, 1975; Dublin: Gill and Macmillan, 1975), p. 17.

9. In 1928 Sean O'Casey's *The Silver Tassie* was rejected by Yeats and the Abbey Theatre. The matter received a good deal of publicity in the Dublin press before O'Casey finally left for London. Writing to Gabriel Fallon on November 7, 1928, O'Casey took a blast at Higgins, Gogarty, Clarke, O'Connor, Phibbs, and AE in a bit of doggerel verse about the old age of the Abbey. *The Letters of Sean O'Casey,* vol. 1, ed. David Krause (New York: Macmillan, 1975), p. 320.

10. For a full account of the issue of censorship, see Michael Adams, *Censorship: The Irish Experience* (University, Ala: University of Alabama Press, 1968).

11. A detailed history of the *Irish Statesman,* including complete chapters on the censorship issue and the libel action which led to the demise of the publication, may be found in Edward D. Smith, "Survey and Index of the Irish Statesman (1923–1930)" (Ph.D. diss., University of Washington, 1966). Particularly helpful is a complete checklist of all writers who published in the *Irish Statesman* and the index of titles, subjects, and authors.

12. Speech delivered to the Library Association, Dublin, 1962. See *JIL,* p. 162.

13. O'Connor's account in *MFS,* pp. 74–77, is supported by T. S. Matthews in *Jacks or Better* (New York: Harper & Row, 1977), pp. 119–24. Laura Riding pilloried the lot of them in her book *14A,* which Norah McGuinness blocked at publication.

14. O'Connor recounted this incident a number of times. Once in a broadcast talk on Joyce he told the story and W. R. Rodgers included it in his *Irish Literary Portraits* (London: British Broadcasting Corporation, 1972). On a postcard to Nancy McCarthy, postmarked "Paris 1.4.29," he wrote: "Today we go to Beauvais. Jonty remains to see Rose Marie and the Follies Bergers. I wrote this sipping St. Raphael citron in the street outside the station. Oh, Life! as Joyce says. He has asked me to come to see him." Jonty was his nickname for Daniel Cronin, assistant in the Cork Library. Joseph Holloway, the ubiquitous Dublin diarist, wrote in his diary on Tuesday, April 9, that Kenneth Reddin had just returned from Paris where he saw Joyce and "also saw the person who writes verse under the name of

Frank O'Connor in *The Irish Statesman*. Joyce is friendly with him for literary purposes, but the other doesn't see it and is flattered by Joyce's attention." In *Joseph Holloway's Irish Theatre*, vol. 1, 1926–1931, ed. Robert Hogan and Michael O'Neill (Dixon, Calif.: Proscenium Press, 1968), p. 47.

15. *M/F*, p. 51.
16. Ibid., 52.
17. The *South Dublin Chronicle* for the years 1929 to 1931 carried frequent announcements of events in the Pembroke District Library. NLI.
18. Because he could not read staff notation O'Connor used the tonic sol-fa method of transcribing music, which meant capturing the sounds of the scale in do-re-mi fashion. Thus his journals are full of otherwise strange markings, such as "d-t-t-d-r-etc.," often taking up full pages. HS.
19. *M/F*, p. 57. O'Connor's interest in music was boundless. In August 1929 he went to Salzburg on holiday, primarily to take in a Mozart festival.
20. O'Connor scribbled ideas for stories in bound journals, available in most bookstores in Ireland. His stories began as short sketches, which he then expanded in ever-lengthening drafts at the typewriter. Most of these journals are in the possession of his widow, Mrs. Harriet Sheehy, though a few are found in the material sold to Boston University by O'Connor's first wife.
21. In *Irish Statesman*, August 7, 1926. The story remained buried until O'Connor's widow included it in *The Cornet Player Who Betrayed Ireland* (Dublin: Poolbeg Press, 1981), a collection of hitherto uncollected and previously unpublished stories (hereinafter cited as *CP*).
22. FOC to Nancy McCarthy, p.m., April 3, 1930, from 34 Chelmsford Road, Ranelagh, HS.
23. O'Connor could joke about Garnett's rejection; but in a letter to O'Faoláin congratulating him for *Midsummer Night Madness*, for which Garnett wrote a glowing introduction, O'Connor ended with this postscript: "Garnett is a fool. AE joins me in this." UCB.
24. AE to Macmillan and Company, Ltd., July 30, 1930, from 17 Rathgar Avenue, in *Letters from A.E.*, p. 180.
25 FOC to Nancy McCarthy, p.m., September 18, 1930, HS.

CHAPTER SEVEN

1. O'Connor later wrote: "Moore was the only Irish writer of his time who was in touch with continental fiction. He was the first writer in these kingdoms who realized what it was all about and introduced to English fiction the principle of French naturalism. There is no doubt at all in my mind that Joyce was deeply influenced by him." *A Short History of Irish Literature: A Backward Look* (New York: Capricorn, 1968), p. 196. (Hereafter cited as *Backward Look*.)
2. Though O'Connor had tried to learn Russian, most of his reading was done in translation, including the Constance Garnett translations of Chekhov and Turgenev, and the Nadia Helstein translation of Babel's *Red Cavalry* (1929).

3. O'Connor's first critical work was on Turgenev; written in Irish, it won a prize from the Gaelic League, but unfortunately it has been lost.

4. Kiely, *Modern Irish Fiction,* p. 14.

5. TS, CM, published in *JIL,* p. 19.

6. "September Dawn" is the centerpiece of *Guests of the Nation* in the same way that "Fugue" is the centerpiece of O'Faoláin's volume *Midsummer Night Madness* (London: Jonathan Cape, 1932): not the finest story in either case, but the emotional core of the volumes. Michael's letters to Nancy at the time indicate that he and O'Faoláin were still close and still very competitive. O'Faoláin wrote a wildly enthusiastic letter commending the beauty of "Nightpiece" and "September Dawn," the two most lyrical stories in the book, MMB. Michael, in turn, defended Seán's volume of stories to Nancy, particularly "The Small Lady" and "Fugue," both of which combine adolescent vigor with melancholy rumination. FOC to Nancy McCarthy, February 26, 1932, from Trenton, HS.

7. Kiely compared this story to Sartre's story "The Wall," observing that the difference between them "is not in the distance between Spain or Paris and these two islands, but in the distance between the mind of the man who wrote *The Saint and Mary Kate* and the mind of a man moving in a world peopled solely by perverts, and producing a novel like *L'Age de Raison." Modern Irish Fiction,* p. 11.

8. O'Connor developed his ideas about the art of the short story in *The Lonely Voice* (Cleveland: World Publishing, 1962). But this one sentence in "Guests of the Nation" represents nearly everything that needs to be said about his theory of the "crisis" of a story, the moment of realization that radically alters a person's perception of the world or of himself.

9. In a television talk entitled "Interior Voices" O'Connor claimed that the voices of the two English soldiers in "Guests of the Nation" were based on what he had heard as a boy playing about the Cork barracks. As for the actual source of the story, he said: "One day as I was sitting on my bed in the camp preparing my lessons for the next day, I overheard a group of country boys talking about two English soldiers who had been held as hostages and who soon got to know the countryside better than their guards."

10. In Gormanstown O'Connor had read the prison journals of John Mitchel and Michael Davitt. It is probably not coincidental that the dogmatic rebel commander, Jeremiah Donovan, resembles that Fenian hero, Jeremiah O'Donovan Rossa, friend of Mitchel and Davitt.

11. In a letter dated January 30, 1930, Michael wrote to Nancy McCarthy: "Life is very queer. It consists in having dreams, in falling in love with a woman when you are 18 and meeting her at 26 and finding her just as beautiful as ever, in creating spiritual homelands, in visiting them, in leaving them again and getting back to the world which for want of a better word we call real." HS.

12. *M/F,* p. 53.

13. In *Letters from A.E.,* p. 238n. Joseph O'Neill (1878–1952) was a Celtic scholar and friend of Osborn Bergin, AE, and Yeats. He was also a novelist whose *Wind from the North* (1934) won the Harmsworth Award of the Irish Academy of Letters. O'Connor wrote a glowing review of the novel for the April–June 1935 issue of the *Dublin Magazine.*

14. FOC to Nancy McCarthy, ca. December 1930, from 123 Anglesea Road, HS.
15. Mary Manning was publicity manager at the Gate Theatre as well as a writer of plays and novels. Anne Crowley was a teacher in Bantry and a highly skilled musician. Irene Haugh, like the other two women about three years younger than Michael, was a poet and journalist; she served as AE's assistant at the *Irish Statesman.*
16. *M/F,* p. 54.
17. From an interview with Mrs. Alexander in November 1972. She has since died and all papers in her possession relating to O'Connor (letters, photographs) were sold to the Boston University Library.
18. FOC to Nancy McCarthy, ca. January 1929, HS.
19. FOC to Nancy McCarthy, p.m., January 20, 1930, from 34 Chelmsford Road, HS.
20. FOC to Nancy McCarthy, p.m., July 5, 1929, HS.
21. FOC to Nancy McCarthy, January 1, 1931, HS.
22. Olga Knipper was the young actress with whom Chekhov corresponded for some time before marrying near the end of his life. Michael saw great similarities between the relationship of Chekhov and Olga Knipper and his relationship with Nancy. He instructed Nancy to read the Garnett translation of Chekhov's letters (Chatto & Windus, 1926) which he thought laid bare the artist's soul.
23. FOC to Nancy McCarthy, ca. June 1931, HS.
24. FOC to Nancy McCarthy, ca. June 1931, HS.
25. A reviewer in the *Observer* of September 13, 1931, wrote: "Mr. O'Connor's themes are grim and unrelenting. His medium is iron—the iron that has bitten into the soul—and he beats out of it a few bright and tragic sparks." Reviews in the *Daily Express* of August 26, 1931, and the *New Statesman & Nation* of October 17, 1931, were moderately commendatory. The *Irish Press* of September 25, 1931, called it a powerful book, then spent most of the review talking about the literature of the war and comparing O'Connor to the Russians. "What wonder if Russian writers and this Irish writer depict a sort of dislocation of the soul?"
26. FOC to Nancy McCarthy, ca. September 1931, HS.
27. FOC to Nancy McCarthy, p.m., February 1, 1932, from Trenton, HS.
28. The essay on Corkery, entitled "Ride to the Abyss" in various versions, holograph and typescript, remains unpublished and in the possession of Mrs. Sheehy.
29. A two-story tenement occupied by six to eight families, the Dolls' House was located just off the North Mall near St. Vincent's by the quays.
30. *MFS,* pp. 67–69.
31. Realizing with AE's help that his theme was still the crisis of growing up in Cork, O'Connor published two stories just before beginning his novel. "The Ring," published in the *Irish Statesman* on July 28, 1928, was a Chekhovian account of a tale told by a woman—orphaned as a girl and resembling Michael's mother—about settling for the first man who asked to marry her. In "The Awakening," which appeared in the *Dublin Magazine* of July 1928, another young woman—equally daring, gay, and carefree—

comes to life and leaves her empty home and saintly boyfriend. The title
was borrowed from Corkery.

32. O'Connor, *Saint and Mary Kate,* p. 194.
33. FOC to Nancy McCarthy, p.m., May 1, 1932, HS. In that same letter
O'Connor mentions a book in his head about Irish literature, but then
rages about the banning of O'Faoláin's book. "But Oh for Turgenev!
Oh for Chekhov!" he laments, adding that he is reading *War and Peace*
again.
34. O'Connor included a vignette of Minnie Connolly, along with two other
women of Harrington Square, in "I Know Where I'm Going," a section of
AOC first published in the *New Yorker,* February 14, 1959.
35. In April he wrote to Nancy that he had found in Chekhov's letters that
Ivanov was Chekhov's "Saint," meaning it was the work he suffered agonies over because no one understood it. The character Ivanov in the play
by that name falls in love with Sasha, but in spite of his good intentions he
brings pain to those around him and in the end commits suicide. See
Chekhov's letter to Alexei Suvorin, dated December 30, 1888, in *Letters of
Anton Chekhov to His Family and Friends,* trans. Constance Garnett
(New York: Macmillan, 1920), pp. 111–19.

CHAPTER EIGHT

1. *MFS,* p. 89.
2. Ibid., p. 29.
3. John Eglinton, *A Memoir of AE* (London: Macmillan, 1937), p. 105.
4. *M/F,* p. 53.
5. A recent biographer of AE observes that this "mutual attachment" between AE and O'Connor developed "despite a clash of personality." See
Summerfield, *That Myriad-Minded Man,* p. 234. Alan Denson in his edition of AE's letters is somewhat fairer. For instance, he quotes Joseph
O'Neill's contention that even when he disagreed with O'Connor ("as I
most definitely do in his theory that AE was schizophrenic"), he found
him "full of illumination." "Frank may have penetrated more deeply into
AE's mind than the rest of us." *Letters from A.E.,* p. 238.
6. Frank O'Connor, "Two Friends—Yeats and AE," *Yale Review,* September
1939, p. 64.
7. From an early draft of the *Yale Review* article, entitled "Two Poets." TS,
HS.
8. *MFS,* p. 91.
9. Quoted by O'Connor in "Two Poets," p. 10.
10. *MFS,* pp. 88–89.
11. A slightly different wording of this conversation appears ibid., p. 87.
12. FOC to AE, January 1, 1931, from 123 Anglesea Road, TS 3859, TCD. According to Denson, AE was in the United States from October, 1930 to
April 1931 on a lecture tour. *Letters from A.E.,* pp. 190ff.
13. Joseph Holloway in his diaries comments time and again about O'Connor's negative reviews. On Wednesday, February 5, 1930, Holloway notes
that O'Connor prefers plays by Ibsen and Chekhov to Shakespeare and
seems to think Cork people act better than the Abbey players. See *Joseph*

Holloway's Irish Theatre, p. 58. Holloway also mentions seeing Ruth Draper, a Gaiety actress, with O'Connor.

14. FOC to Sean Hendrick, n.d., CM; published *JIL,* pp. 49–52. This is a pastiche of Emily Dickinson's poem number 1755, published in 1896. In a letter to O'Faoláin following the publication of *Midsummer Night Madness,* AE expressed the hope that O'Connor and O'Faoláin would do for their generation what Yeats and others did for his own. UCB.

15. *MFS,* p. 107.

16. From an interview with Professor Binchy in September 1976. Additional memories may be found in his essay "The Scholar-Gipsy," in *M/F.*

17. Frank O'Connor, "Adventures in Translation," *Listener,* January 25, 1962, p. 175. Originally broadcast for the BBC on January 17, 1962.

18. According to Liam Miller in *The Dun Emer Press, Later the Cuala Press* (Dublin: Dolmen 1973), *The Wild Bird's Nest* was no. 48 in the Cuala series; 250 copies were printed and the book appeared on July 12, 1932, at ten shillings and six pence. The volume contained one of O'Connor's poems, "The Lament for Art O'Leary," which was issued by Cuala in a separate volume with drawings by Jack Yeats in May 1940 (no. 64 in Cuala series).

19. Douglas Sealy, writing about O'Connor's verse translations, argued that it is "when the poetry turns into drama, that O'Connor is at his best. His personality has something of the ranting, roistering blade about it; he likes to hold the centre of the stage and declaim." "The Translations of Frank O'Connor," *Dubliner,* Summer, 1963, p. 80.

20. According to the information supplied by the Archbishop of Dublin, Timothy Joseph Traynor was born May 1, 1899, in Mitchelstown, County Cork. He entered Holy Cross College, Clonliffe, in 1917 and was ordained at the Pro-Cathedral on June 6, 1925, by the Most Reverend Dr. Byrne. After holding various positions in Dublin, he was appointed curate of Star of the Sea Church in Sandymount on September 26, 1935.

21. *MFS,* p. 147.

22. Ibid., p. 154.

23. According to *The Dictionary of Irish History,* ed. D. J. Hickey and J. E. Doherty (Dublin: Gill, 1980), Richard Hayes was born in Bruree, County Limerick, in 1878 where he was a boyhood friend of Eamon de Valera. He fought with the Irish Volunteers at Ashbourne and was sentenced to twenty years' imprisonment. As a member of the first Dáil Éireann representing East Limerick, Hayes supported the Treaty but did not sever friendships with anti-Treaty supporters. He qualified for medicine in 1906, held a number of public appointments, including the Donnybrook No. 2 Dispensary post, but was essentially retired after 1930 to pursue his scholarship on France and Ireland. In 1951 he was awarded the Cross of the French Legion of Honor. He also received an honorary doctorate (D.Litt.) from the National University of Ireland. He was a member of the Irish Academy of Letters and the Royal Academy of Surgeons. He served as a director of the Abbey Theatre from 1934 and as film censor from 1940. Richard Hayes died on June 16, 1958.

24. Seán O'Faoláin, "Falling Rocks, Narrowing Road, Cul-de-sac, Stop," *Foreign Affairs and Other Stories* (Boston: Little, Brown, 1975), pp. 156–57.

25. *MFS,* pp. 139–40.

26. Hayes's first work was *Ireland and Irishmen in the French Revolution* (Dublin: Gill, 1932). Then in fairly quick succession he published *Irish Swordsmen of France* (Dublin: Gill, 1934); *The Last Invasion of Ireland* (Dublin: Gill, 1937); and *Old Irish Links with France* (Dublin: Gill, 1940).

27. *MFS,* p. 136.

28. In O'Connor, "Two Friends," p. 72. The Yeats portion of the essay appears in E. H. Mikhail, ed. *W. B. Yeats: Interviews and Recollections,* vol. 2, (London: Macmillan, 1977), pp. 260–69.

29. Frank O'Connor, "What Made Yeats a Great Poet," *Listener,* May 15, 1947; originally broadcast for the BBC May 4, 1947.

30. From a BBC broadcast cited in Rodgers, *Irish Literary Portraits,* p. 19.

31. O'Connor claimed that the "phantasmagoria" of Yeats was inspiration, but "there was too little daylight in AE to nourish poetry." *MFS,* p. 51.

32. O'Connor, "Two Friends," p. 76.

33. O'Connor's account in *MFS,* pp. 116–17, gives some indication of his own role in this fiasco. See also Adams, *Censorship,* pp. 47–50; and Mikhail, *Interviews and Recollections,* p. 270n.

34. MFS, p. 111.

35. For complete information about the formation and organization of the Irish Academy of Letters, see *The Yeats Centenary Papers,* ed. Liam Miller (Dublin: Dolmen Press, 1965), Appendices A, B, and C.

36. FOC to Nancy McCarthy, p.m., March 27, 1934, PP. O'Faoláin's account of the dreadful evening is in *Vive Moi!,* p. 353.

37. Mikhail, *Interviews and Recollections,* p. 270n. O'Connor's account of the confrontation over O'Malley appears in *MFS,* p. 120.

38. *MFS,* p. 122.

39. O'Connor, "Two Friends," p. 84. He repeats the anecdote in *Backward Look,* p. 164.

40. MFS, p. 212. References to O'Connor in Yeats's letters to his friends suggest a definite familiarity. AE's letters to Yeats mention O'Connor regularly, particularly his feeling for Gaelic culture and his ear for literary gossip. Both AE and Yeats were concerned about O'Connor's ill-health. Yeats even convinced him to read Shelley's theories on vegetarianism. O'Connor reported that he didn't understand the philosophy but he would try the diet; by this time he was desperate for anything to soothe his stomach. Yeats reported to Edith Shackleton Heald (August 10, 1937) that O'Connor had been on the diet for nearly a year. See *Letters of W. B. Yeats,* ed. Allan Wade (London: Macmillan, 1955) and *Letters to W. B. Yeats,* Vol. 2, ed. Richard Finneran et al. (New York: Columbia University Press, 1977).

41. Richard Ellmann, *The Identity of Yeats* (New York: Oxford University Press, 1962), p. 280.

42. See Norman Jeffares, *Commentary on the Collected Poems of W. B. Yeats* (Palo Alto: Stanford University Press, 1968), p. 464. He notes Yeats's debt in the third line ("The lovers and the dancers are beaten into the clay") to O'Connor's "Kilcash" ("The earls, the lady and the people beaten into the clay.") Nearly identical phrasing occurs in Yeats's "Under Ben Bulben." Jeffares also refers with some skepticism to O'Connor's role in the genesis of "Lapis Lazuli," the story of which O'Connor told in various places, including *Backward Look,* p. 174.

43. Ellmann has carefully listed the imprint of Yeats's hand on O'Connor's translations. *Identity of Yeats,* pp. 195–200.
44. *MFS,* p. 11. The story is repeated in *Backward Look.*
45. Jeffares, *Commentary,* p. 366.
46. Ellmann, in *M/F,* p. 26.
47. Frank O'Connor, "W. B. Yeats," *Critic,* December 1966, p. 50.
48. Ellmann, *Identity of Yeats,* p. 201.

CHAPTER NINE

1. The *Irish Press,* for example, ran a frontal attack on the book; the reviewer was a Jesuit. L. A. G. Strong, writing for the *Spectator,* was mildly enthusiastic; and Ralph Strauss wrote in the London *Sunday Times* of April 24, 1932, that though O'Connor calls himself a realist, "he is more than a bit of a poet, and a rich beauty is to be found in his work even at its   most drab and sinister moments." However, the best review of the novel came from a fellow Corkman, P. S. O'Hegarty; writing for the *Dublin Magazine* of October–December 1932, he called it a masterpiece of imaginative realism.
2. W. B. Yeats to Olivia Shakespear, July 8, 1932; in *Letters of W. B. Yeats,* 799–800. From Rathfarnham at the end of the month he wrote to Miss Shakespear again, with even stronger praise of O'Connor's novel.
3. After reading the book O'Connor wrote to O'Faoláin, then teaching in Middlesex, praising the book and explaining a few of the criticisms he made in a review in the *Dublin Magazine* (April–June, 1932). O'Faoláin was not to be placated and about the ensuing row Michael wrote to Nancy: "I am appalled by the thought that I possibly cause all my friends as much mental anguish as I seem to cause him." HS.
4. *MFS,* p. 127. Michael wrote a letter to Norah McGuinness from Glengarriff full of sketches and stories about two artists who taunted AE. FOC to McGuinness, ca. August 10, 1932, from Stella Maris, Glengarriff, PP
5. On August 10, for example, he wrote to Nancy that he had been with Anne to Dunboy; in the letter is a sketch of a man kissing a woman while writing behind her back. On July 23 he had written about Anne and her contralto voice, remarking, "How inconstant I am!" HS. According to Norah McGuinness in an interview (January 1978) O'Connor's image of himself as a sexual innocent is not accurate.
6. FOC to Nancy McCarthy, ca. September 27, 1932, from Trenton, HS.
7. FOC to Nancy McCarthy, p.m., October 24, 1932, HS. O'Faoláin he considered "superficial—in the best sense of the word," while about Dermot he wrote: "I am always attracted by those quick joyous minds who see almost everything significant even if they lack profundity—my own particular weakness."
8. FOC to Nancy McCarthy, ca. December 30, 1932, from Trenton, HS.
9. Reprinted in CP. In March 1933 another unusual story, "Seagulls," appeared in the *Quarryman,* a student literary magazine put out in Cork. Perhaps the most nearly Chekhovian story O'Connor ever wrote, "Seagulls" is simply a young man's account of his conversation with an old man in St. Stephen's Green.

10. From an interview with Denis Johnston and Mrs. Mary Manning Howe in September, 1976.

11. This letter, addressed "Sweetheart" and written when he felt very much in love—"at the hour of 10:10 pm 12.6.33"—was by Nancy's own reckoning the only real love letter Michael ever sent to her.

12. Though Michael's letters to Anne Crowley (nearly forty in all, written between 1930 and 1939) are full of his usual complaints about women and the "queer business of life," they read more like a running commentary on his love of music, a passion he had in common with Miss Crowley. PP.

13. Cumann na nGaedheal, the pro-Treaty party ousted from power in 1932, merged its identity with O'Duffy's military organization to mobilize Catholic opposition to a feared Protestant uprising. Internal dissension brought an end to this alliance in 1934, and by the next year Cosgrave had organized the party that is now called Fine Gael. Yeats flirted with O'Duffy's fascist movement for a while, even to the point of writing marching songs and appearing publicly in a blue shirt. O'Connor's hatred of the Blue Shirts was unmuted, particularly in his letters to Nancy McCarthy. His account of Yeats's involvement with the Blue Shirts appears in MFS, pp. 124–25.

14. Ibid., p. 131.

15. AE to Osborn Bergin, August 2, 1933, from London, in *Letters from A.E.,* p. 206.

16. FOC to Nancy McCarthy, August 5, 1933, HS. Externalizing oneself was a flaw O'Connor criticized in Corkery after their break, while nourishing one's interior life was the trait he most admired in his newest literary fathers, AE and Yeats.

17. FOC to Nancy McCarthy, p.m., October 22, 1933, from 43 Raglan Road, HS.

18. Early in 1934 one of his letters contains some crude verse about hunchback men, "crippled with fantasies," masturbating away their souls. A few weeks later (p.m., February 14, 1934) he laments, "Sometimes I think women don't know what love means."

19. FOC to Nancy McCarthy, p.m., April 19, 1934, HS.

20. Frank O'Connor, "The Man Who Stopped," *Bookman,* August 1934. That entire issue of the *Bookman* was given over to Irish writing, with essays by O'Faoláin, Lennox Robinson, Stephen Gwynn, and Samuel Beckett (under the pseudonym Andrew Belis). Also in that issue was the essay "Two Languages," under the name of Michael O'Donovan.

21. Frank O'Connor, "A Boy in Prison," *Life and Letters,* August 1934. Desmond MacCarthy, editor of *Life and Letters,* was impressed enough to ask for more writing from O'Connor and to introduce his name to Lovat Dickson, editor of *Fortnightly Review,* who immediately requested a story from O'Connor for his publication *Lovat Dickson's Magazine.* For an account of London literary magazines in the 1930s, see Lovat Dickson's *The House of Words* (New York: Atheneum, 1963).

22. FOC to Dermot Foley, n.d., no. 9 in series of letters, PP. These letters, numbering over 130 and dating from 1931 to 1961, form a solid bridge across O'Connor's career. Another man with whom O'Connor corresponded regularly in the 1930s was Arnold Marsh, headmaster of the

Newtown School in Waterford. Judging from O'Connor's letters, Mr. Marsh was a great source of stories. TSS and MSS, TCD.

23. According to the files of O'Connor's agent A. D. Peters, the story was written on October 6, 1934, and remained unsold. It was published only in *Bones of Contention* (London: Macmillan, 1936). At about this time O'Faoláin was at work on a biography of Daniel O'Connell and often sought O'Connor's opinions about the great patriot and orator. See *Vive Moi!*, p. 369. O'Faoláin eventually dedicated that book, called *King of the Beggars,* to Frank O'Connor.

24. In O'Faoláin's story "How to Write a Short Story" in *Foreign Affairs,* a young writer and county librarian named Morgan Myles decides to "out-Maupassant Maupassant." O'Faoláin's famous description of the real-life Michael/Frank is to be found at the end of *Vive Moi!*, pp. 368–70.

25. "Repentance" appeared in *Lovat Dickson's Magazine* in January 1935; "Michael's Wife" in February. "The English Soldier" was published in the *Yale Review* of December 1934 and "May Night" in *Life and Letters* of April, 1935. The latter story was recently republished in *Cornet Player;* a reviewer commented that it seemed to foretell Beckett's *Waiting for Godot.* According to Deirdre Bair, Beckett had met Desmond MacCarthy, original editor of *Life and Letters* and then advisory editor, in 1934. See *Samuel Beckett* (New York: Harcourt, Brace, Jovanovich, 1978), p. 181. Whether or not he actually read the O'Connor story is difficult to say.

26. Frank O'Connor, "In the Train," *Lovat Dickson's Magazine,* June 1935. In "Interior Voices," O'Connor embellished the genesis of the story but gave essentially the same details as Foley, adding that he rewrote it even as it was going to press at Macmillan to allow for the entry of another "voice," the drunk.

27. "Peasants" had been published in *Lovat Dickson's Magazine* in October 1934, while the other so-called *seanachie* story, "Majesty of the Law," appeared first in the *Fortnightly Review* of August 1935. O'Connor's sudden use of the techniques of the native Irish storytellers has been admirably examined by Daniel J. Casey in "The *Seanachie*'s Voice in Three Stories by Frank O'Connor," *Anglo-Irish Studies* 3 (1977); 96–107. Whatever his reasons and whatever his influences (Casey suggests Corkery and Tim Buckley), O'Connor had obviously found a voice that fit his theme of justice in rural Ireland. On March 3, 1934, before the Irish Academy of Letters, meeting in the Abbey Theatre, O'Connor delivered the lecture "Irish Democracy and the Gaelic Tradition," in which he argued that the ancient bards had adopted the fatal policy of live and let live, making the Irish system of law a "vast piece of self-deception." O'Connor saw the Blue Shirts movement and the increasing strength of the Censorship Board as new threats to justice and democracy in Ireland, and in the months following he took every possible opportunity to decry the situation.

28. In 1936 O'Connor made his first radio broadcast, a review of books for Radio Eireann; for the rest of his life he talked to eager audiences in Ireland and Great Britain. Reading his own stories over the wireless convinced him that the written word had robbed the short story of its narrative voice, and he began concentrating on putting that voice back into his stories.

29. *MFS*, p. 47.

30. The words *hysteria* and *melancholy* continued to appear frequently in O'Connor's writing, suggesting something like schizophrenia, a term O'Connor himself used in reference to Corkery and AE. For an anthropological and psychological investigation of the unusually high incidence of schizophrenia in Ireland, see Nancy Scheper-Hughes, *Saints, Scholars, and Schizophrenics: Mental Illness in Rural Ireland* (Berkeley: University of California Press, 1979).

31. In his review of *Three Old Brothers* F. R. Higgins anticipates the general disregard of O'Connor's so-called original poetry by suggesting that the book would hardly enhance O'Connor's reputation. "Let us hope," Higgins concludes with mild sarcasm, "he has published these poems as an act of affection towards early work—the affection of a father, even for his illegitimates." In *Dublin Magazine,* September 1936, pp. 69–70.

32. FOC to Nancy McCarthy, March 12, 1932, from Trenton, HS.

33. In his acknowledgments Hayes wrote: "And I am under no small debt to Frank O'Connor who, in the midst of his busy literary work, was kind enough to read the proofs and made many valuable suggestions." Hayes's book about the role of the French in the famous 1798 Rebellion anticipated the best-selling novel *The Year of the French* (New York: Holt, Rinehart and Winston, 1979) by Thomas Flanagan, a friend of O'Connor toward the end of his life.

34. Piaras Beaslai, *Michael Collins and the Making of a New Ireland,* 2 vols. (London: G. Harrap, 1926). Even Beaslai, who had edited *An t'Oglach,* had been unable to gain the cooperation of some Hayes convinced to see O'Connor. Beaslai's monumental study, O'Connor admitted, should be read as a corrective to his own.

35. Unlike O'Connor's writing journals, which were suited for table writing, these notebooks were the vest-pocket variety. Consequently, they are very difficult to read because of the usual untidy scrawl and the cramped space and pencil smudging. HS.

36. In his foreword O'Connor wrote that Pakenham's book was one that he had "shamelessly pillaged." He also acknowledged debt to Dorothy Macardle for lending him proofs of her book *The Irish Republic*; to Batt O'Connor's autobiography *With Michael Collins* (London: Peter Davies, 1929); and to Hayden Talbot's *Michael Collins' Own Story* (London: Hutchinson, 1923).

37. Ernest Blythe was an early Sinn Fein organizer who later served the Free State government in the Ministry of Finance; he was also on the Boundary Commission with Kevin O'Higgins and has quoted O'Higgins as saying: "That crooked Spanish bastard will get the better of that pasty-faced blasphemous fucker from Cork." Edward Broy, who had worked for Collins as a double agent inside Dublin Castle, quoted Collins as telling him: "One side of your brain shouldn't know what your left is doing."

38. *MFS*, p. 140. In the foreword to his biography of Collins O'Connor mentioned not this incident involving O'Reilly but a similar one involving Tom Gay. *The Big Fellow* (London: Nelson, 1937). Hypnosis was one of the subjects Traynor had gotten O'Connor interested in, particularly the phenomenon of self-hypnosis.

39. Mr. Dermot Foley showed me Traynor's own copy of *The Big Fellow,* signed by Frank O'Connor: "For Father Tim, who is partly responsible." Traynor's copious marginal notes are surprisingly critical of O'Connor's treatment of Collins and his use of the sources.

40. FOC to Dermot Foley, n.d., from 84 Northumberland Road, PP. O'Connor moved to the flat on Northumberland Road shortly after his return from a holiday trip to Italy. (A letter to the *Irish Times* protesting the banning of O'Faoláin's *Bird Alone* was dated September 19, 1936, with the Trenton address.) Apparently, Mrs. O'Grady, his landlady at Trenton, had sold the house in June, but O'Connor had resisted all attempts to get him to vacate, claiming that he could not be disturbed from his book.

41. O'Connor believed that Anglo-Irish literature, beginning with Swift, was "linked with the immediate reality of politics." See *Backward Look,* p. 121. Unfortunately, the best book on the subject—Malcolm Brown's *The Politics of Irish Literature* (London: Allen & Unwin, 1972)—stops with Yeats and Joyce, saying only that literary Parnellism is a dominating theme of the work of O'Connor and O'Faoláin.

CHAPTER TEN

1. *Irish Times,* July 22, 1935.

2. Peter Kavanagh, *The Story of the Abbey Theatre* (New York: Devin-Adair, 1950), p. 171.

3. Kavanagh's position is largely supported by the recent "official" history of the Abbey: Hugh Hunt's *The Abbey: Ireland's National Theatre, 1904–1979* (New York: Columbia University Press, 1979; Dublin: Gill and Macmillan, 1978).

4. *MFS,* pp. 177ff. For the most part O'Connor's account of his years at the Abbey agrees with Kavanagh and Hunt. For additional information on the characters in this real-life drama, see Mikhail, *Interviews and Recollections,* p. 394, and *Letters of Sean O'Casey,* p. 348. Professor William Magennis was not only in the department of metaphysics at University College, Dublin, but on the Irish Censorship Board, as well.

5. *Irish Times,* February 26, 1935. The letter was signed by O'Connor and O'Faoláin, and Joseph Holloway, the Dublin diarist who seemed to record everything pertaining to the theatre, mentions it. See *Joseph Holloway's Irish Theatre,* vol. 2, *1932–1937,* ed. Hogan and O'Neill (Dixon, Calif.: Proscenium Press, 1968). Volume 1 of this helpful edition of Holloway's copious diaries covers the years 1926 to 1931; volume 3, the years 1938 to 1944 (hereafter cited as *Holloway* 1, 2, or 3).

6. According to Hugh Hunt, his contract commenced on August 19, 1935. *The Abbey,* p. 152.

7. *Holloway* 2, p. 46. However, the best account of this affair is found in *Letters of Sean O'Casey,* pp. 576–80.

8. Peter Kavanagh, *Story of the Abbey,* pp. 169–71, and Hunt, *The Abbey,* pp. 151–52, both agree substantially with O'Connor's account in *MFS,* pp. 179–80. See also *Holloway* 2:46–47, and *Letters of Sean O'Casey,* pp. 582–89.

9. *MFS,* p. 182. In 1935 Frederick R. Higgins (1896–1941) was co-editor

with Yeats of a monthly series for Cuala called *A Broadside* and that year
published with Yeats a collection of songs called *Broadsides*. He had already published volumes of poetry and a play for the Abbey; he was Yeats's
closest friend and obvious protégé.

10. *MFS*, p. 184.
11. O'Connor is depicted as an arrogant bully who hated actors and knew
    nothing about writing plays in *Holloway* 2:56f.
12. *MFS*, p. 186.
13. Hunt, *The Abbey*, p. 152.
14. Hunt observes that the Abbey could not be rescued by challenging the se-
    lection of plays performed at the Gate. His production of André Obey's
    Noah (November 11, 1935) was successful, but his *Coriolanus* (January
    13, 1936) pleased no one. Yeats wanted the play to be performed in col-
    ored shirts as he had seen it done in Paris, but O'Connor and Hunt ob-
    jected that another riot would not save the Abbey either. See Hunt, *The
    Abbey*, p. 153, and *MFS*, pp. 187–89.
15. *MFS*, p. 185. Hunt was made manager and not managing director.
16. According to Hunt, "The School of Acting was reorganised under Ria
    Mooney's direction, and from its pupils past and present arose a lively Ex-
    perimental Theatre in the Peacock in which new plays were tried out."
    The Abbey, p. 154.
17. O'Connor's shares were dated June 11, 1936; they are now in the hands of
    his daughter, Liadain. An extensive file of Abbey material (including min-
    utes of Board meetings, financial accounts, contracts, corrected play
    scripts, and correspondence) is to be found in MMB.
18. Hunt, *The Abbey*, pp. 154–55. Also *MFS*, p. 215.
19. *MFS*, p. 201. Hugh Hunt wrote to me in November 1978 to explain that
    O'Connor had exaggerated to some extent; Hunt did not take Mac-
    Liammóir's part, though the idea was suggested.
20. *MFS*, p. 215.
21. Ibid., p. 189–90. *In the Train* has been published in a Samuel French edi-
    tion (New York: 1960) as a "drama in one act" by Hugh Hunt, "adapted
    from the short story" by Frank O'Connor.
22. From an interview with Mr. Hunt on July 12, 1976.
23. *Holloway* 2:70.
24. *MFS*, p. 190.
25. The departure of Higgins with the First Company gave Yeats the opportu-
    nity to make O'Connor the managing director. Peter Kavanagh, *Story of
    the Abbey*, p. 171.
26. *MFS*, pp. 161–63.
27. Peter Kavanagh, *Story of the Abbey*, pp. 172–73. The Abbey repertory in
    New York (October 2 to December 18, 1937) included O'Connor's *In the
    Train*, O'Casey's *Juno and the Paycock* and *The Plough and the Stars*,
    Lennox Robinson's *Drama at Inish* and *The Far-Off Hills*, Teresa Deevy's
    Katie Roche, George Shiels's *The New Gossoon*, and Synge's *The Playboy
    of the Western World*.
28. Holloway was highly critical of the plays produced at the Abbey in the ab-
    sence of the First Company. See, *Holloway* 2:72–74.
29. From an interview with Mr. Gabriel Fallon in October 1972. Mr. Fallon

was for years an Abbey actor and a friend of Sean O'Casey's. He later became a well-known Dublin theatre critic for the *Catholic Standard.* For a full account of these lesser-known Abbey playwrights, see Robert Hogan, *After the Irish Renaissance* (Minneapolis: University of Minnesota Press, 1967), pp. 21–63.

30. On May 6, 1882, Lord Frederick Cavendish, newly appointed Chief Secretary for Ireland, and his under secretary, an Irish Catholic named Thomas Burke, were attacked by a group of men wielding long knives outside the viceregal lodge in Phoenix Park. A splinter group calling themselves the Invincibles claimed responsibility for the assassination.

31. *MFS,* pp. 203–206.

32. Hugh Hunt, *Irish Independent,* September 3, 1967.

33. *Holloway* 2:75.

34. *MFS,* p. 205.

35. Roger McHugh, "Frank O'Connor and the Irish Theatre," in *M/F,* p. 67.

36. *Holloway* 2:75.

37. From TS, HS. A text of *The Invincibles,* edited by Professor Ruth Sherry, appears in the New Abbey Theatre Series published by Proscenium Press (1980).

38. *Holloway* 2:76.

39. *MFS,* p. 205. The debate, called by the Actor's Guild, was about the danger posed to the safety of everyone in the theatre by the threatened demonstrations.

40. Ibid., p. 207. "Lennix" was Yeats's way of saying Robinson's first name.

41. Hunt, *The Abbey,* p. 159.

42. Among the protesting players: Ria Mooney, Shelah Richards, Ann Clery, Cyril Cusack, Fred Johnson, W. O'Gorman, and Eric Gorman. See ibid., p. 160.

43. *Holloway* 2:77. For the other side of the story, see also O'Faoláin's preface to the published version of *She Had to Do Something* (London: Jonathan Cape, 1938), pp. 7–24. David Sears, in the *Irish Press,* called the play a "sneer at Irish life," and Andrew Malone, in the *Irish Times,* complained about the plot, development, and theme, which to O'Connor and O'Faoláin were the "bamboozling abstractions of theatre."

44. From an interview with Evelyn in August, 1977. Conversation about marriage and Speaight telegram quoted verbatim from letter from her dated April 21, 1979. *Murder in the Cathedral* opened at the Mercury Theatre in London on November 1, 1935, following its premiere at Canterbury. Speaight then brought the play to the Gate in May 1936. See *Holloway* 2:54. At a party held for the cast, O'Connor first met Evelyn Bowen. Letters from FOC to Evelyn Bowen in 1937 reveal a developing intimacy, while letters from Robert Speaight to his wife suggest that he was not only aware of the situation but indifferent to it. MMB.

45. Annulment proceedings are confidential, so the exact grounds on which Speaight was basing his claim remain unclear. Furthermore, the issue is so complex as to defy analysis, and any conjecture would only cause hurt to the people concerned.

46. This preface is found in one of O'Connor's writing journals. HS. A partial text of *Moses' Rock* in typescript is also in the hands of Mrs. Sheehy. In

that preface O'Connor stated that the play, which he called a fantasy, came to him while writing the biography of Collins and listening to the men who had fought with Collins.

47. Entry dated March 1, 1938, *Holloway* 3:7. Holloway actually found O'Connor's play interesting—"good entertainment and amusing lines." The incident with Murray is contained in an entry dated Sunday, March 6.

48. Though Holloway puts O'Connor's resignation from the library at March 1, 1938, the fact is that O'Connor went on a leave of absence on that date. The formal date of retirement was actually April 1, 1938. At the time his salary was £383 6s. 8d. and, according to his income-tax statement for April 1937 to April 1938, his literary earnings were £126 5s. 9d. The pension is verified in every income-tax statement filed by Michael O'Donovan between 1939 and 1949. MMB.

49. Lennox Robinson, ed., *The Irish Theatre* (London: Macmillan, 1939), p. vii. This book includes texts of all the lectures given from August 8 to August 20.

50. *MFS*, p. 165.

51. Ibid., p. 220. The unpublished letter from Yeats is in MMB. The book to which Yeats referred, *Lords and Commons* (no. 60 in the Cuala series), was finished the last week of August; 250 copies, priced at 10s. 6d., were published on October 25, 1938. See Miller, *Dun Emer Press*, p. 115.

52. For an account of the intrigues surrounding the first Abbey Festival, see Peter Kavanagh, *Story of the Abbey*, pp. 174–76. On May 26, 1938, Eric Gorman wrote to O'Connor an official letter on Abbey letterhead stating that *Thomas Muskerry, The Player Queen*, and *In the Train* were all being dropped from the Festival program. MMB.

53. Hunt, *The Abbey*, p. 162–3.

54. *MFS*, p. 225.

55. Corkery's study of Synge was the basis for the M.A. he received in 1929 from the National University of Ireland; in 1931 he was named Professor of English at University College, Cork. Corkery's now famous statement about finding the true national mind of Ireland at a hurling match at Thurles was made in *Synge and Anglo-Irish Literature* (Cork: Cork University Press, 1931), p. 12. In *The Irish Renaissance* (Syracuse: Syracuse University Press, 1977), Richard Fallis further explores the distinction made by O'Connor and missed entirely by Corkery: that Irish literature could be national without being nationalistic. He also raises the most conspicuous contradiction in Corkery's nationalism: namely, that though he insisted that only those writing in Gaelic could be considered legitimate Irish writers, he had to do so in English, the primary language of intellectual exchange in Ireland.

56. The O'Connor lecture, like the other lectures delivered during the Festival, was published in Robinson, *The Irish Theatre*, pp. 31–52. Joseph Holloway attended all of the lectures as well as the plays. On Thursday, August 18, he wrote commending Walter Starkie and Denis Johnston for answering questions so courteously, "not like F. R. Higgins and Frank O'Connor earlier in the week. They just simply insulted the questioner to show off!" *Holloway* 3:12.

57. Hunt, *The Abbey*, p. 163. About *Purgatory*, Holloway lamented that Yeats

had fallen in step with modern attachment to the sordid. "Now the old poet's thoughts are turned to war and desolation and the ugliness of life." *Holloway* 3:12.

58. After Higgins's lecture on Thursday, August 11, Terence Connolly, the drama critic for an American Jesuit magazine who had in 1935 led the fight in Boston to ban O'Casey's play *Within the Gates,* asked what *Purgatory* was supposed to mean. Father Connolly admitted that he had read the play and attended the performance but still had no idea what it symbolized. Considerable heat but very little light was produced in the ensuing debate. Yeats responded succinctly in the *Irish Independent* of August 13, 1938, denying any allegorical intent. O'Connor then wrote a slashing letter published in the *Irish Times* of August 16, 1938, defending Yeats's play and Higgins's lecture against Father Connolly's sarcastic and hostile manner. He particularly objected to the subterfuge by which an outsider had been given a text of the play. Maurice Leahy defended his friend Father Connolly by attacking O'Casey during Walter Starkie's lecture that afternoon; his objections to the anti-Catholic sentiments of Yeats and O'Casey appeared in the *Irish Times* the next day, August 17, 1938, which brought a rebuttal from O'Casey—who was still living in England—which appeared in the *Irish Times* of August 19, 1938.

59. In September O'Faoláin published two articles in the *Irish Times* on the policy of the Abbey and on the conflict between the artist and the mob. O'Connor responded on October 3 with a letter to the editor about the idea of a national theatre, prompting O'Faoláin to write a letter, challenging O'Connor while at the same time commending his work in the Abbey. The barrage continued between the two until Flann O'Brien entered the battle on October 25 and November 8, condemning both of them. The letters ceased until the production on December 26 of O'Connor's play *Time's Pocket,* which was slated so badly that O'Connor and O'Faoláin both wrote letters defending it. On January 14, 1939, Lily Yeats wrote to her brother, W. B., who was in France: "[O'Connor and O'Faoláin] are still writing letters to each other and have got to the stage where they say 'Go home and wash your face' to each other so I think they ought to stop—also they are much too long-winded for letters in a paper." *Letters to W. B. Yeats,* 2:606.

60. For further consideration of the departure of theatre people from Ireland after the death of Yeats, see Cyril Cusack's essay "Every Week a Different School" in *Flight from the Celtic Twilight,* ed. Des Hickey and Gus Smith (Indianapolis: Bobbs-Merrill, 1973), pp. 23–35.

61. MFS, p. 183. Hunt's version is neutral (*The Abbey,* pp. 160–61), but everyone else blamed O'Connor for Carroll's departure. Herbert Kenny in *Literary Dublin* (Dublin: Gill, 1974), pp. 280–81, quotes Carroll's letter to the *Irish Times* defending himself by attacking O'Connor, the only one who had taken the trouble to write him personally. That letter shows precisely how Carroll misrepresented O'Connor's intentions by suggesting that O'Connor asked him to suppress the play for the sake of his reputation, when actually he suggested making a few changes. MMB.

62. O'Faoláin's letters in MMB. O'Connor's letters in UCB.

63. Yeats had edited five issues of the *Arrow* between 1906 and 1909. The

issue planned for Christmas, 1938, was to have been a special commemo-
rative issue to Yeats, who had himself asked O'Connor to be the editor.
As it happened, Lennox Robinson edited the sixth and last issue of the
Arrow (Summer, 1939), a "W. B. Yeats Commemoration Number." See
O'Casey's letter to Gabriel Fallon of May 8, 1939, disavowing any intention
of entering into O'Connor's controversy over the editorship of the *Arrow*
but affirming that the whole thing had been Yeats's idea. *Letters of Sean
O'Casey*, p. 796.

64. *MFS*, p. 231. Hunt mildly challenges O'Connor's notion that the medioc-
rity of the theatre could be attributed to the Board by suggesting that the
war was an insurmountable burden to creative activity in Ireland. See
Hunt, pp. 164–65. Peter Kavanah's version of the controversy agrees with
O'Connor's; in fact, his chapter on the intrigues following the death of
Yeats (pp. 179–84) is entitled "Betrayal."

65. O'Connor was attacked mercilessly by the critics, partly because of his ostentatious display of letters that fall. He was accused of knowing nothing
about the theatre and of being an "egotistical nobody." On January 6,
1939, he responded in kind with another letter to the *Irish Times* stating,
among other things: "Literary movements begin in a conspiracy between
an author and a small section of his audience. The critics have no part in
the conspiracy; they think only of 'construction' and 'action' and 'development' and 'psychology'—all of which have about as much to do with the
theatre as the man in the moon."

66. When Speaight's annulment request was denied, he sued Evelyn for divorce on the grounds of adultery, claiming Michael O'Donovan co-respon-
dent. Full documentation of this action is in MMB.

67. FOC to W. B. Yeats, n.d., letterhead Westminster Hotel, Chester, MMB.
Yeats died in Cap Martin, near Menton in the south of France, on Saturday, January 28, 1939. He was buried in Roquebrune, and not until after
the war was his body returned to Ireland.

68. All the letters between O'Connor and Eric Gorman, corresponding secretary of the Abbey, may be found in MMB. According to Peter Kavanagh,
the Articles of Association were altered on August 18, 1939, to empower
the members of the board to dismiss a director. When O'Connor refused to
relinquish his shares in the theatre, the Articles of Association were
changed again, on January 25, 1940, to deny any shareholder access to
books or documents of the company. See Kavanagh's *Story of the Abbey*,
p. 180.

69. O'Connor, "Two Friends," p. 88.

CHAPTER ELEVEN

1. *MFS*, p. 219.
2. Frank O'Connor, "Mac's Masterpiece," *London Mercury*, May 1938. The
story sold for fifteen pounds; at the same time O'Connor's agent returned
"The Miser," a story rejected by fourteen magazines. "Mac's Masterpiece" has been republished in *CP*.
3. From his essay on Corkery, "Horses of the Sun," first written in 1938. See
Journal 3, HS. A later version was titled "Ride to the Abyss." TS, HS.

4. "That the Provincial Writer Should Stay at Home," BBC broadcast discussion with L. A. G. Strong on March 10, 1938. BBC.
5. FOC to Evelyn Bowen, ca. September 15, 1938, from Thackeray Hotel, MMB.
6. Dermot Foley, in *M/F*, p. 62.
7. In 1939 Easter fell on April 9; the competitions lasted the week.
8. FOC to Evelyn O'Donovan, ca. April 12, 1939, from Grand Hotel, Sligo, MMB.
9. O'Connor gives a slightly sarcastic and perhaps condescending account of the Sligo festival in *Leinster, Munster, and Connaught* (London: Hale, 1950), pp. 255–56.
10. Among the many literary visitors to Woodenbridge was Elizabeth Bowen, the novelist, who wrote glowingly of O'Connor to her friend William Plomer. See Victoria Glendinning's *Elizabeth Bowen: Portrait of a Writer* (London: Weidenfeld and Nicolson, 1977), p. 119.
11. Review of *The Fountain of Magic*, by Frank O'Connor, *Times Literary Supplement*, March 18, 1939. O'Connor wrote a heated letter accusing the reviewer of a "literary vendetta" and received a polite letter denying the charge. MMB.
12. FOC to Seán O'Faoláin, ca. May 1939, from Lynduff, UCB.
13. Carmel Snow, the Irish-born editor of *Harper's Bazaar* from 1932, bought her first O'Connor story, "The Storyteller," in 1937. In 1938 she bought "Flowering Trees," and in 1939 "Bridal Night," which she also commissioned Norah McGuinness to illustrate. Mrs. Snow's letters to O'Connor in MMB.
14. *MFS*, pp. 166–67.
15. Macmillan published *Dutch Interior* in London in 1940; and later that year Knopf published it in the United States. The Harold Matson Agency, the New York affiliate of A. D. Peters, was then handling O'Connor's writing in America. However, both Matson and A. D. Peters were struggling to place his stories.
16. FOC to Seán O'Faoláin, ca. Summer, 1939, from Lynduff, UCB.
17. FOC to Dermot Foley, no. 43 in series, n.d., from Lynduff, PP,
18. A reviewer for the *Irish Times* of June 29, 1940, wrote that the descriptions are French and the tone is Irish, but that the unity of the novel is Cork itself. A reviewer for the *Times Literary Supplement* of June 1, 1940, suggested that "the pattern of life in the poor quarter of a southern Irish city is drawn together quietly and closely," but it is a world to which none of the characters seem to belong.
19. Years later in an interview for *Paris Review* O'Connor explained that to him "a novel is something that's built around the character of time, the nature of time, and the effects that time has on events and characters." In *Writers at Work*, ed. Malcolm Cowley (New York: Viking, 1959), p. 165.
20. From *The Mayor of Casterbridge*, by Thomas Hardy, quoted in *The Mirror in the Roadway* (New York: Knopf, 1956), p. 246.
21. William Tomory argues that the grotesques and silhouettes of *Dutch Interior* and the episodic form indicate the influence of Sherwood Anderson's *Winesburg, Ohio*. See Tomory's *Frank O'Connor* (Boston: Twayne, 1980). The idea is beguiling, but O'Connor made no reference to Anderson in anything public or private that he wrote before 1952 (when he went to the

United States). He did write in a draft of the Corkery essay that *The Threshold of Quiet,* a novel it is certain he was trying to write out of his system, resembled Alain-Fournier's *Le Grand Meaulnes* and dealt with "another form of suffering: the resignation and loneliness of the provincial intellectual."

22. The title, however, which baffled every reviewer of the novel, remains baffling, and one wishes O'Connor had been a bit more firm with his editors and kept his original title, "The Provincials."

23. Horace Reynolds, in the *New York Times Book Review* of November 17, 1940, saw in the episodic structure of the novel, which he termed "a series of loosely related sketches," the influence of James Joyce.

24. O'Connor, *Backward Look,* p. 229. Professor Scheper-Hughes, for example, considers schizophrenia in Ireland to be largely a cultural phenomenon, caused by the peculiar "double-bind" facing so many people there— that paralyzing ambivalence between conflicting allegiances (between the Irish language and the English language, or between Anglo and Celt values) or the fatal choices offered between equally disagreeable alternatives (between sin and celibacy, between farming or civil service). *Saints, Scholars, and Schizophrenics,* pp. 164–66. See also Michael Sheehy's chapter "The Irish Dualism," in *Is Ireland Dying?* (New York: Taplinger, 1968).

CHAPTER TWELVE

1. Yeats and Lennox Robinson formed the original Dublin Drama League in 1918 with the aim of producing a wider range of plays than the typically Irish repertoire offered by the Abbey. It ceased to exist in 1929 when the Gate Theatre opened with the same policy. See Hogan, *After the Irish Renaissance,* p. 112.

2. Frank O'Connor, *Irish Miles* (London: Macmillan, 1947), p. 72.

3. Letters to Dermot Foley show that O'Connor went over Foley's stories meticulously and got O'Faoláin to publish one of them, "The Verger," in *The Bell.* In 1940 Joseph O'Neill, the philologist, educator, and novelist, wrote to O'Connor commending his "generous sympathy" for the work of other people. MMB.

4. Patrick Kavanagh, *The Green Fool* (London: Michael Joseph, 1938), p. 241. Kavanagh's letters to O'Connor in MMB.

5. O'Connor, *Irish Miles,* p. 46.

6. Ibid., p. 177. On May 22, 1940, gardaí raided the home of Stephen Carroll Held, an Irish businessman of German parentage, and found traces of a parachutist, a wireless transmitter/receiver, code books, and maps. It was assumed that Germany would use Ireland as a base for an assault. Churchill believed this firmly and took every opportunity to decry the irresponsibility of Irish neutrality. See Joseph Carroll, *Ireland in the War Years* (New York: Crane and Russak, 1975), and *Ireland in the War Years and After: 1939–51,* ed. Kevin B. Nowland and T. Desmond Williams (Dublin: Gill and Macmillan, 1969). For a sense of what it was like to live in Ireland at this time, see James Plunkett's novel *Farewell Companions* (London: Hutchinson, 1977).

7. O'Connor's original title for these humorous chats was "Tales of the Pub." Material pertaining to O'Connor's work for Radio Eireann (contracts, receipts, letters, and scripts, including a complete typescript of "Malachy") may be found in MMB.

8. Frank O'Connor, "At the Microphone," *The Bell,* March 1942, p. 415.

9. Christopher Salmon, a talks officer at the BBC, began his association with Frank O'Connor in 1938 with the broadcasting of "The Climber" (March) and "Orpheus and His Lute" (April); the latter story was scripted for broadcast by Denis Johnston. O'Connor's letters to Salmon and his wife, Dona, also a broadcast director, are in the Talks File of the O'Connor papers in BBC. Salmon's letters to O'Connor in MMB.

10. FOC to Dermot Foley, no. 58 in series, ca. July 1940, from Lynduff, PP.

11. For further details on the genesis of the Mount Melleray story, see *Leinster, Munster, and Connaught,* p. 165.

12 O'Connor, *Irish Miles,* p. 108. The cycling adventures in the book, it must be remembered, are a composite of many excursions.

13. Ibid., p. 112. In the poem "Demon and Beast," in *Michael Robartes and the Dancer* (1921), Yeats uses "barren Thebaid" to describe the harsh nature of early Christian monastic sites in Egypt. See Jeffares, *Commentary,* p. 237.

14. O'Connor, *Irish Miles,* p. 114.

15. O'Faoláin wrote with great affection about Dan Flavin in *An Irish Journey,* p. 148.

16. From an interview with Mr. MacMahon in September 1976 in Listowel.

17. Other characters in *Irish Miles* include Angélique from *The Hypochondriac* (referring to a woman from Cork, probably Nancy) and Orgon from *Tartuffe* (probably Dermot Foley). See O'Connor, *Irish Miles,* p. 32.

18. Reviews of *Dutch Interior* began appearing in June in England and Ireland but not until November in the United States.

19. *Dutch Interior* was banned by the Irish Censorship Board and placed on the *Register of Prohibited Publications* on July 12, 1940.

20. See letters between O'Connor and Salmon for October 1940 in BBC and MMB.

21. Lennox Robinson's modernization of Maupassant's "Boule de Suif," which he called *Roly Poly,* was staged at the Gate on November 20, 1940. Maupassant's hatred of the Prussians was well-known, but that story was particularly uncomplimentary of the German soldier.

22. Micheál MacLiammóir to Frank O'Connor, November 21, 1940, on Gate letterhead, MMB.

23. James Plunkett in *Farewell Companions* notes that young intellectuals at the time would have been reading "cross channel magazines." By 1940 *Ireland-Today,* the magazine edited by Edward Sheehy, had gone out of business, leaving only Seamus O'Sullivan's *Dublin Magazine* as an outlet for young Irish writers and readers.

24. The opening editorial is obviously O'Faoláin's, though the tone is similar to that of the abortive *Irish Tribune* of the 1920s. "This is Your Magazine," *The Bell,* October 1940. As with everything O'Connor and O'Faoláin stood for, *The Bell* was to be national but not nationalistic, catholic but not exclusively Catholic.

25. O'Connor, *Irish Miles,* p. 129.

26. According to Joseph Carroll, in *Ireland in the War Years* (p. 34), Mr. Frank Aiken, minister for co-ordination of defensive measures, was so extreme in his censorship of the press during the war that it became a great joke in Dublin. People like R. M. "Bertie" Smyllie, editor of the *Irish Times*, felt the censorship most keenly; his paper was still considered the arm of the old, Anglo-Irish ruling class. Radio Eireann was a government-controlled station, directly under the jurisdiction of the minister of posts and telegraphs.

27. Published in *JIL*, pp. 146–51.

28. The "Curtain Up!" discussion series ran from January 17, 1941, to February 21, 1941, with an additional discussion (April 18) with Val Gielgud on radio drama. According to a copy of a letter from Salmon to O'Connor (January 1, 1940), O'Connor received 150 pounds for the series, plus expenses and a room in Cotswold House, Chipping Campden, Gloucester. BBC.

29. O'Connor was also the guest of L. A. G. Strong, the novelist and literary editor, and of Desmond MacCarthy, another editor who had been supportive of O'Connor during the 1930s.

30. Apparently the psychiatrist was Philip Metman who had written a book on psychology and the Greek myths: *Mythos and Schicksal* (Leipzig: Bibliographisches Institut Ag, 1936); in England during the 1940s and 1950s he wrote a number of pamphlets on psychology for the Guild of Pastoral Psychology.

31. Verified by O'Faoláin in an interview in January 1974.

32. Phibbs's letters in MMB. O'Connor's letters to Phibbs after 1929, if they exist, remain in the private possession of his family.

33. Phibbs to FOC, December 2, 1940, from Airton House, Tallaght, MMB. About his friend's sloppy spelling, O'Connor wrote: "sometimes I thought he misspelled deliberately to keep me occupied. 'You will die of sintactical exactniss of the mind,' he once wrote to me. 'I believe it is a very slow and paneful death.' " *MFS*, p. 22.

34. Cuala Press correspondence in MMB.

35. Carbon of FOC to R. M. Smyllie, April 24, 1941, from Lynduff, MMB.

36. Seán O'Faoláin to FOC, ca. early May 1941, MMB.

37. Frank O'Connor, "Stone Dolls," *The Bell*, June 1941, pp. 61–67.

38. Denis Johnston's offending remarks had been made in his theatre column. See *The Bell*, April 1941, p. 91.

39. Louis D'Alton's reply appeared in the Public Opinion section of the July issue.

40. In fact, O'Dea had gone out of his way to ask Johnston, well-known as a lawyer, if he thought the role slanderous; unfortunately, Johnston was never called to testify in behalf of the defendants at the libel trial. From an interview with Johnston in August 1976.

41. "Standards and Taste," *The Bell*, June 1941.

42. Hayes to O'Connor, May 3, 1941, from 26 Herbert Park, Ballsbridge, MMB. Hayes did not deny that he voted to change the Abbey Articles of Association nor that he was the one who in August 1939 had put forward the motion to dismiss O'Connor. O'Connor's letter to Hayes did not survive. There may have been a subtle reference to Hayes in the "Stone

Dolls" article, specifically the phrase "some Censor of the soul." In 1940 Hayes became film censor. See "Meet Dr. Hayes: or the Genial Censor," by The Bellman (Larry Morrow), *The Bell*, November 1941, pp. 106–14. For a different portrait of Richard Hayes see O'Connor's story "Hughie" published only a month before in the October 1941 issue of *The Bell*.

CHAPTER THIRTEEN

1. In an undated letter to a neighborhood association that was resisting the Dublin Corporation's plan to build a park along the strand, O'Connor wrote: "In an essay I wrote on Ireland many years ago I explained that the two things the strand represented to me were its association with the medieval Irish saga *Togail Bruiden da Derga* and 'Ulysses'." MMB.
2. See Carroll, *Ireland in the War Years*, for an explanation of the causes and effects of rationing in Ireland. For a contemporary picture, see Alex Comfort, "Letter from Ireland," *Horizon*, April 1943, pp. 265–70.
3. Soon even cigarettes were not available in Ireland, forcing O'Connor to carry large quantities back from England.
4. *MFS*, p. 167.
5. Ibid. According to the death certificate, Michael O'Donovan was seventy-three years old when he died. Official cause of death was given as pneumonia. Whether or not Big Mick died face down in a gutter is unclear (the stain in the chest suggests so).
6. FOC to Dermot Foley, no. 93 in series, ca. April 1942, PP.
7. *MFS*, p. 168. During the D'Alton furor, O'Connor received a letter from Irene Haugh, AE's assistant at the *Irish Statesman*. After stating her fundamental disagreement with Michael about the D'Alton matter, Miss Haugh went on to talk about AE, how he might have had a wider audience in Ireland had he been Catholic. Then she recounted AE's resistance to the bothersome priests who had circled about him like vultures as he neared death. He had once told her that pain might bring a man to do anything, even to fall in line with the church. AE's courage and spiritual integrity at the end was, in her words, "his death bed non-conversion." MMB.
8. Of the 90 percent extraction loaf that passed as bread, James Plunkett in *Farewell Companions* observed that it tasted like sponge and sawdust. Plunkett's novel and Brian Moore's *The Emperor of Ice Cream* (New York: Viking, 1965) present vivid pictures of Ireland (both Eire and Ulster) during the war years, especially what people actually did on a day-to-day basis.
9. On February 5, 1941, O'Connor wrote to Mrs. Yeats from London. The same day he wrote to Evelyn: "She asks me to come in as joint-editor of Cuala and I shall, just to keep up my association with the institution." MMB. The Cuala Press file in MMB contains material from 1939 to 1948, including letters from Mrs. Yeats, Jack Yeats, and John Piper; financial statements; cost estimates, royalty statements; Betty Rivers's illustrations for *A Picture Book;* and page proofs for *Irish Miles,* corrected in O'Con-

nor's hand. On O'Connor's brief role on the advisory board of Cuala Press, see Miller, *Dun Emer Press,* pp. 97–98.

10. From 1936 to 1938 Denis Johnston was a scriptwriter for the BBC in Belfast, returning at the beginning of the war to work in Dublin. Though a lawyer by training, Johnston was a man of the theatre by heart, a writer by profession. He was a prime mover in the revival of the DDL, and with his departure in 1942 to serve as a war correspondent for the BBC, the organization began to crumble.

11. The letter from Mrs. Yeats was signed "Love, George"; n.d., from 46 Palmerston Road, MMB. Carbons of affectionate yet businesslike letters from Michael to Mrs. Yeats are also in MMB.

12. In 1940 O'Connor had submitted the play to the Abbey only to have it returned with a few comments by Roibéard O'Farachái n, newly appointed director, to the effect that it would offend the MacSwiney family. O'Connor replied that he refused to rewrite the play according to a scenario laid down by "Hayes and Co.," who by the same principle would demand that Synge's *Playboy* be rewritten so that the boy would *really* kill his father. FOC to O'Farachái n, n.d. 57 Strand Road, MMB.

13. *The Statue's Daughter,* subtitled *A Fantasy in a Prologue and Three Acts,* was produced by the DDL at the Gate Theatre, December 8–13, 1941. However, the text published in *JIL* was probably the one used for a production at the Gaiety staged by Larry Elyan in 1943; it had four acts. TS, HS.

14. According to one reviewer, the play "hardly fills the bill for the opening night of a revival movement in the Irish Theatre." *Irish Independent,* December 9, 1941.

15. According to a letter from Evelyn to Dermot Foley, dated November 10, 1941, both Connolly and Stephen Spender, the poet, visited 57 Strand Road. O'Connor knew both men from recent assignments in London for the BBC. Connolly and Spender had together launched *Horizon* in January 1940.

16. Peter Kavanagh speaks of the incident with mixed pain and amusement in his autobiography *Beyond Affection* (New York: Peter Kavanagh Hand Press, 1977), pp. 56–57.

17. Frank O'Connor, "The Future of Irish Literature," *Horizon,* January 1942, p. 55.

18. The Censorship Act provided for the prohibition of not only published material but films as well. In an interview published in *The Bell* in November 1941, Richard Hayes stated that he censored all films for propaganda, though he believed most American films were vulgar anyway. He feared an Americanization of Irish standards; his opinion that divorce, abortion, birth control, and illegitimacy were "definitely banned subjects" was not shared by his former friend Frank O'Connor.

19. O'Connor, "Future of Irish Literature," p. 62.

20. Among the letters was a postcard from the Reverend R. Wyse Jackson of the Church of Ireland in Limerick congratulating O'Connor on his "masterpiece of Oomeragh." In his review of O'Connor's *Collected Stories* (New York: Knopf, 1981), Denis Donoghue recalls how as a boy in Ulster forty years earlier he had listened eagerly to the wireless. "News of the war was not so memorable . . . as "The Long Road to Ummera," a dramatized

version of O'Connor's story, which I heard on Radio Eireann." *New York Times Book Review,* September 20, 1981. Unfortunately, O'Connor's popularity was not matched by his financial reward; he received a scant one pound for each of the three January broadcasts, according to accounts records in MMB.

21. Set of letters, no. 28 in Talks File la, 1936–42, BBC. O'Connor and Denis Johnston were not the only Irish writers working for the BBC. Louis Mac-Neice, a poet from the north of Ireland, went to work for the BBC in 1941. A superb picture of broadcasting during the 1940s may be found in Barbara Coulton's *Louis MacNeice in the B.B.C.* (London: Faber and Faber, 1980).

22. The official silence seems permanent. The Radio Eireann archives contain next to nothing. And in his *Forty Years of Irish Broadcasting* (Dublin: Talbot, 1967), Maurice Gorham mentions Frank O'Connor only once and then simply to note that Cyril Cusack took the lead in a production of *The Invincibles* in 1951. According to the title page, Gorham's book was published for Radio-Telefis Eireann. All documentation of O'Connor's association with Radio Eireann, therefore, derives from MMB, and some material in BBC. Additional verification from interviews with Mr. Gabriel Fallon, Mr. Hugh Hunt, Mr. Denis Johnston, and Mr. Eamon Kelly. See also O'Connor letters to O'Faoláin, UCB.

23. John Betjeman went to Dublin in 1941 as press attaché. According to Carroll, in *Ireland in the War Years* (p. 112); his duties were to persuade the Irish that Germany was anti-Catholic. O'Connor's telegram to Christopher Salmon dated July 3, 1942, BBC.

24. According to material in MMB, Evelyn had steady work from September to December 1942.

25. In his review of O'Brien's book O'Faoláin presented his own list of censored writers which amounted to every writer of consequence in Ireland. *The Bell,* August 1941. He followed that piece with articles by himself and others on the subject of censorship: "Sex, Censorship and the Church" (September 1941); "Censorship: Principle and Practice" (January 1942); and "Censorship, Law and Conscience" (July 1942). He kept *The Bell* clanging.

26. Ryan, *Remembering How We Stood,* p. 17. In his chapter on Irish censorship, "Behind the Emerald Curtain," Ryan not only listed a few of the banned books, he mentioned the closing of art galleries and the ban on jazz music. Herbert Kenny wrote that the censorship of the early 1940s was an example of "Catholicism grown implicitly heretical." See Kenny, *Literary Dublin,* p. 271.

27. Eric Cross, *The Tailor and Ansty* (London: Chapman & Hall, 1942), was placed on the *Register of Prohibited Publications* officially on October 2, 1942, though the Board's decision was made on September 28. O'Connor's letter was dated October 8, 1942, and published in the *Irish Times* on October 9, 1942.

28. See letters from Cross to O'Connor in MMB.

29. For a summary of the entire proceedings, see Adams, *Censorship,* pp. 84–95.

30. Ibid., p. 89.

31. FOC to Sean Hendrick, ca. January 1943, from 57 Strand Road, CM. Published in *JIL.*
32. FOC to Stan Stewart, July 1943, from 57 Strand Road, HS.
33. According to Joseph Carroll, de Valera's government, by the same score, could not let it be known that British espionage and recruiting agents were operating in Dublin—with his blessing! *Ireland in the War Years,* p. 113.
34. *A Picture Book* by Frank O'Connor, with fifteen illustrations by Elizabeth, was published in September 1943; the 450 copies of this edition were priced at £1 1s. Miller, *Dun Emer Press,* p. 118. O'Connor's brief text (less than 80 pages) was a version on the book on cycling and architecture, which eventually became *Irish Miles.*
35. See FOC to Stan Stewart, December 16, 1942, HS. Here O'Connor wrote, "I sint in me ould book and dedicated it to you; please note that anyone I ever dedicated a book to fought with me."
36. Frank O'Connor, "James Joyce: A Post-Mortem," *The Bell,* February, 1943, p. 370.
37. Set of letters in January 1943 about a broadcast from Wales, "What is a Welshman," with V. S. Pritchett and others for the "Living Opinion" series. BBC.
38. O'Connor describes the incident in a letter to Stan Stewart. FOC to Stewart, no. 20 in series, January 30, 1943, HS. "The Sentry" eventually appeared in *Harper's Bazaar* in January 1950.
39. Hector Legge to Frank O'Connor, March 9, 1943, letterhead of *Sunday Independent,* MMB. See also "When Frank O'Connor was Treated Like an Outcast," by Hector Legge, *Sunday Independent,* April 13, 1969. O'Connor received two guineas for each article at first; his pay was raised to three guineas later.
40. A few of these Ben Mayo articles have been republished in *JIL.*
41. Ben Mayo, "Our Irish Towns Have Their Attractions," *Sunday Independent,* July 18, 1943.
42. Ben Mayo, "A Book Industry That is Greatly Neglected," *Sunday Independent,* August 22, 1943.
43. In February Louis D'Alton produced *The Invincibles* at the Gaiety, before taking the play on tour in Ireland. A letter from D'Alton on February 27, 1943, shows gate receipts of £557 for the week just ended. MMB.
44. *Leinster, Munster, and Connaught,* p. 179.
45. *Irish Miles,* p. 103.
46. Ibid., p. 106.
47. Peter Kavanagh, *Beyond Affection,* p. 49.
48. FOC to Stan Stewart, ca. July 1941, from Lynduff, HS.
49. "Flowering Trees" and "Grandeur" had both appeared originally in *Ireland-Today,* and "The Climber" and "The Storyteller" were both published by *Harper's Bazaar.* (Of those four stories, only "Grandeur" was not included in *CP.*) When a volume of stories failed to materialize, all the stories went back into his creative bin for rewriting (often under different titles), meaning that O'Connor may have actually written twice as many stories as those actually published.
50. In a letter to Christopher Salmon he answered a query about his favorite books: Chekhov's *Duel,* "his only novel, in which he thrashes out magnifi-

cently the whole battle between instinct and reason"; Saint Simon's *Memoirs*, "the most astonishingly complete picture of the world there is." FOC to Salmon, n.d., received BBC March 31, 1944, BBC.

51. Journal 6, HS.

52. Kiely, *Modern Irish Fiction*, p. 144. Actually, it is the split-mindedness of O'Connor's treatment of priests that is so remarkable; he considered the priest a surrogate artist and felt empathy as well as hatred for the clergy. His use of priests is the subject of the chapter "Island of Saints" in Maurice Wohlgelernter's *Frank O'Connor: An Introduction* (New York: Columbia University Press, 1977), pp. 41–63. Much has been written on the stifling effect of Catholicism on Irish life, including Paul Blanchard's *The Irish and Catholic Power* (Boston: Beacon, 1953) and Michael Sheehy's *Is Ireland Dying?* A fairly moderate view may be found in Scheper-Hughes's *Saints, Scholars, and Schizophrenics* (pp. 119–21).

53. In Robert Schumann's *Dichterliebe* opus 48 there is a song ("Ein Jüngling liebt ein Mädchen," no. 11) about a lad who loves a girl who loves another lad who loves another still; so in angry rebound she weds the first man who crosses her path.

54. When O'Connor sent the first batch of stories for *Crab Apple Jelly* to his agent in July 1943, he stated that he considered "The Mad Lomasneys" the best of the lot. UTA. "The House That Johnny Built" was the Castleblayney story mentioned frequently in letters to O'Faoláin; it was Nancy's story about answering an advertisement for a job in a chemist's shop in Castleblayney.

55. "Interior Voices," Telefis Eireann, June 13, 1962. HS.

56. Ibid. "Interior Voices" was first given at the Library of Congress on November 21, 1960. See *Library of Congress Information Bulletin*, November 7, 1960.

CHAPTER 14

1. Salmon wrote to Jack Beddington at the Ministry of Information on January 20, 1944, suggesting that they employ O'Connor as a scriptwriter. Recommendations also came from Desmond MacCarthy, John Betjeman, and Nicolas Mansergh, BBC.

2. FOC to Evelyn O'Donovan, February 14, 1944, from Norwich. MMB.

3. TS, HS. The same incident is told in the story "Orphans" (not the anonymous story in *The Bell*), published in *Mademoiselle* of July 1956.

4. The lines quoted by O'Connor were from the poem "Ireland with Emily," published in *New Bats and Old Belfries* (London: Murray, 1946). O'Connor and Betjeman shared a lifelong passion for ruined churches. FOC to Evelyn O'Donovan, p.m., March 6, 1944, from Rothesay Lodge, Windsor, MMB.

5. On three occasions A. D. Peters had to write to British revenue officials explaining that O'Connor was a citizen of the Republic of Ireland. Full transcripts of the legal decisions on the tax matter may be found in UTA. The correspondence with Mrs. Yeats may be found in the Cuala Press file in MMB. In April 1944 Cuala published *Dafydd Ap Gwylym*,

Collected *Poems,* translated by Nigel Heseltine, with a preface by Frank O'Connor. See Miller, *Dun Emer Press,* p. 118. O'Connor's correspondence with Mr. Heseltine is also in MMB.

6. FOC to Evelyn O'Donovan, p.m., March 8, 1944, from Rothesay Lodge, Windsor, MMB. In that letter O'Connor expressed pride that L. A. G. Strong had dedicated his novel *The Director* (published by Methuen) to him.

7. Both Dona and Christopher Salmon worked with the Talks Department of the BBC's Home Service. "As I tell Dona, half of me is Dona Salmon and the other half is Christopher Salmon and they've always got to box it out." FOC to Christopher Salmon, n.d., received BBC March 31, 1944, BBC. See also carbon copy of Dona Salmon to O'Connor, April 18, 1944, BBC.

8. *Crab Apple Jelly* was featured as the first choice of recommended reading in the *Times Literary Supplement* of May 6, 1944. The reviewer observed that O'Connor's stories bring "into view a way of peasant or small-town life rooted in seclusion, poverty, religion, drink, a sense of Irish locality," and that because his characters are born-story-tellers they "do the imaginative work for him." Less expansive but equally positive was Kate O'Brien's review in the *Spectator* of May 26, 1944.

9. FOC to Evelyn O'Donovan, p.m., June 19, 1944, from Picotts End, Hemel Hempstead, MMB.

10. The Registrar of the University of Hull (known in 1944 as the University College of Hull) informed me in 1978 that records of those years had been destroyed, but that the lectures were probably part of a series sponsored by the university for local residents during the war. The invitation was probably engineered by Desmond MacCarthy.

11. Between 1941 and 1944 O'Connor wrote an essay, probably meant for broadcast, entitled "A Storyteller Writes a Play." Journal 6, HS. "The Art of the Theatre" was published first in *The Bell* as a four-part piece appearing between March and June 1945 and then in pamphlet form by Fridberg (1947).

12. Liadian O'Donovan Cook, "Michael O'Donovan, Frank O'Connor & Me," *Frisco,* December 1981, p. 31.

13. The explosion of stories about priests in 1943 and 1944 finds parallel in O'Connor's bitterness toward priests evident in letters to Dermot Foley and Stan Stewart following his father's death, the visit of the Legion of Mary man, and the treatment of Tim Buckley by priests after the banning of *The Tailor and Ansty.*

14. Seán O'Faoláin to O'Connor, January 30, 1945, from Killiney, MMB.

15. FOC to Seán O'Faoláin, January 31, 1945, from 57 Strand Road, UCB.

16. Lawrence Elyan, a tax official for the Irish government, had known Michael in Cork. Being Jewish, he became acquainted with Maurice Fridberg at the synagogue in Dublin.

17. Verified in A. D. Peters file in MMB and UTA.

18. "In Memory of Timothy Buckley, The Tailor," *Irish Times,* April 25, 1945. Seamus Murphy, the stone-carver from Cork, asked O'Connor for an epitaph for the Tailor, and O'Connor immediately answered, "Benedict's lines from *Much Ado About Nothing:* 'A star danced/ And under that was I born.' " Those words, a slight misquotation from Shakespeare, are on the stone over the Tailor's grave in the cemetery in Gougane Barra.

19. Peter Kavanagh explains how the censor was fooled on V-E Day by this lay-out of pictures. Apparently few understood O'Connor's poem. *Beyond Affection,* p. 74.
20. "Shakespeare of the Drawing Room," an essay on Jane Austen, appeared on August 11, 1945. The last in the series for the *Irish Times* was "Somerville and Ross," published on December 15, 1945. Most of this material also appeared in the pamphlet *Towards an Appreciation of Literature* published by the Metropolitan Publishing Company of Dublin in 1945.
21. "She left a fortune at 69," *Evening News,* May 28, 1947.
22. "The Dark Lady (and the dark horse)," *Evening News,* June 5, 1946.
23. "There are only three stories," *Evening News,* March 13, 1946.
24. "Paper Puppets," *Evening News,* January 2, 1946. O'Connor and Pritchett had spent a good deal of time together in broadcasting particularly in Wales "The Clerk's Tale" sounds very much like one of O'Connor's own anecdotes in "English Miles," while "The Voice" could have been Pritchett's own peculiar rendering of O'Connor's impressive voice. However, the one story in *It May Never Happen* that raises the eyebrows of any reader even vaguely familiar with the stories of Frank O'Connor is "The Oedipus Complex."
25. A. D. Peters file in MMB and UTA.
26. Asenath Nicolson's account of her travels in Ireland in 1844 and 1845 to study the plight of the poor was originally titled *Ireland's Welcome to the Stranger.* It was republished in 1927 as *The Bible in Ireland.* Evelyn wrote two broadcast scripts about this remarkable book in 1941 but they were rejected by O'Faracháin at Radio Eireann. *Irish Miles* shares with that book a sense of a traveling campaigner, though his interests were matters aesthetic and cultural rather than those hygienic, nutritional, or theological; his campaign was not against poverty or for the Bible but against indifference and for the National Monuments.
27. According to A. D. Peters, Lovat Dickson at Macmillan rejected *The Midnight Court* as unsuitable for English readers. MMB. O'Connor had already published portions of the poem in *The Bell.*
28. O'Connor sold *The Midnight Court* to Maurice Fridberg for twenty-five pounds, which A. D. Peters considered tantamount to an out-and-out free gift. Fridberg published the poem in a slim volume for his Hour-Glass Library Series. The name of the author, it must be remembered, is spelled variously as Merriman and Merryman.
29. Henry Reed, reviewing *The Midnight Court* for the *New Statesman and Nation* of April 13, 1946, praises the poem and O'Connor's "lively and malicious preface." The reviewer quotes O'Connor himself as saying the poem was "a great paean in praise of bastards," because in the poem "the bastard is used as a symbol of natural innocence." Scheper-Hughes uses O'Connor's translation of *The Midnight Court* to illustrate the fear of intimacy and the "low-energy sexual system of the rural Irish." *Saints, Scholars, and Schizophrenics,* p. 116. She fails, however, to note such stories as "Bridal Night," "The House That Johnny Built," or "A Life of One's Own."
30. Preface to *The Midnight Court* (Dublin: Fridberg, 1946), pp. 6–7. O'Connor was also unrelenting in his attack on Corkery's *The Hidden Ireland,* a

study of Gaelic Munster in the eighteenth century, which all but overlooked Merriman.

31. According to Adams, the banning of this translation represented "the only
banning to date of a book published in Ireland." *Censorship,* p. 249. Arland Ussher's translation appeared in 1926 (with an introduction by
Yeats) and was not banned; nor was David Marcus's translation in 1953.
O'Connor's translation received scathing treatment at the hands of Austin
Clarke. O'Connor, Clarke wrote, "uses Merriman as a stick to beat the en-
emies of common sense. . . . It must be admitted, however, that Mr.
O'Connor's variations are as witty at times as they are clandestine." In the
end Clarke judged the translation of Arland Ussher not only superior to
O'Connor's but "the finest translation from the Irish of our time." *Dublin
Magazine,* January–March 1946, pp. 53–56.

32. O'Connor received almost no royalties on *The Midnight Court* and *Towards an Appreciation of Literature.* Fridberg's Hour-Glass Library publication of *Selected Stories* made no money either.

33. A. D. Peters sold six stories in 1946, including "Lady of the Sagas," which
the American magazine *Today's Woman* bought for $750, a great deal of
money considering that Reginald Moore paid 10 guineas for "Friends of
the Family." UTA.

34. O'Connor wrote to A. D. Peters about the story in December 1945. In Jan-
uary it was rejected by William Maxwell of *The New Yorker,* with whom
O'Connor had just signed another lucrative first-reading agreement. Max-
well told Matson, the American agent, that it was "just not a good story."
The story has disappeared or else was rewritten under a different title.
UTA.

35. A. D. Peters received "Public Opinion" and "The World of Art and Reilly"
in October 1946. In August O'Connor had submitted a 25,000-word version of the Shakespeare book. UTA.

36. *Towards an Appreciation of Literature* contains in nascent form nearly all
the major critical and philosophical ideas that dominated O'Connor's
thinking for the rest of his life, particularly loneliness and dreams. There,
for instance, he quotes the lines from Yeats's "Supernatural Songs" that
summarize his own view of things:

> Man's life is thought,
> And he, despite his terror, cannot cease,
> Ravening through century after century.
> Ravening, raging and uprooting that he may come
> Into the desolation of reality.

In the very next sentence he talks of dreams and the conception of existence, which "some censor of the soul" endeavors to hide from us. See
Roger Chatalic, "Frank O'Connor and the Desolation of Reality," in *The
Irish Short Story,* ed. Patrick Rafroidi and Terence Brown (Atlantic High-
lands, N.J.: Humanities Press, 1979), pp. 189–204. The phrase "desolation of reality" appears in "Don Juan's Temptation," a story written that
same year.

37. Richard Ellmann, "Michael-Frank," in *M/F,* p. 24.

38. "Human Nature," a Third Programme broadcast on November 1, 1946.
BBC.

CHAPTER FIFTEEN

1. In August Salmon wrote to O'Connor that he and Dona were taking positions at Trinity College in Hartford, Connecticut. BBC.

2. Reginald Moore edited the *Modern Reading* series for Big Ben Books, which were cheap (nine pence) paper editions of stories, poems, and essays sold at newsstands. Moore published "The Sinner" in 1945 and "Friends of the Family" in 1946. Another paperback series that bought O'Connor stories was *Penguin New Writing,* which published "A Story by Maupassant" in no. 24 (1945) and "The Landlady" in no. 37 (1949).

3. *The New Yorker* rejected seven stories between the end of the war and the beginning of 1947. Concerning *Irish Miles,* a Knopf editor wrote: "It is strictly limited in interest, and would surely bore anyone not intimately familiar with Ireland's churches as much as it bores me. O'Connor's fine writing does not redeem it." Matson also notified A. D. Peters that he could not interest an American publisher in the Shakespeare book either. UTA.

4. MS, HS. The only thing that came of this fragment was a Home Service broadcast "John Bull and his own Island," April 25, 1948, BBC.

5. Just as O'Connor had gone to Lyme Regis because of its literary association (Jane Austen), so he returned to Sandymount, where Yeats had grown up. The Tram Terrace Gang is mentioned in O'Connor's story "What Girls Are For," probably the most telling story he ever wrote about life at 57 Strand Road. It has been republished in *C.P.*

6. FOC to John Kelleher, ca. Summer, 1947, from 57 Strand Road, PP.

7. According to the A. D. Peters file in MMR, "My Da" and "The Cornet Player Who Betrayed Ireland" were received in March 1947. Why O'Connor suddenly started to write about his father is unclear, but he once said that Shaw avoided any attempt to understand his father, a drunkard, because the memories were strangling him. "When he begins writing about his father, he writes about him from a funny point of view, but each reference to his father, as he goes on in life, becomes more mature in its realisation of what was really happening." Quoted in Rodgers, *Irish Literary Portraits,* p. 120.

8. Sin is the subject of both "News for the Church" (originally titled "The Sinner") and "Custom of the Country" (originally titled "Adam and Eve"). Yet sexual morality in both stories is less a matter of principle than a matter of social respectability, the crux of which is the ever-present eye of the church. Respectability is also the theme of "Public Opinion," written in October 1946. UTA. *The Common Chord* (London: Macmillan, 1947) bore no dedication.

9. It is not coincidental that O'Connor at this time was deeply buried in the nineteenth-century novel, which abounds in female heroes and their sins. O'Connor's criticism of the novels of Flaubert, Austen, Thackeray, Trollope, and Hardy is entirely moral. His stories, too, at this time carry the same moral edge. "The Holy Door," for example, is the closest O'Connor ever came to Jane Austen, a novelist he believed exhibited "moral hysteria."

10. In *The Common Chord* (New York: Knopf, 1948), pp. 276–277. In a letter

to Nancy McCarthy, O'Connor once described Dermot's story as "one of the most tragic things I have heard outside literature." See FOC to Nancy McCarthy, p.m. July 5, 1929, HS.

11. Kiely, *Modern Irish Fiction,* p. 143. English reviewers were cautious. The reviewer in the *Times Literary Supplement* of November 15, 1947, said *Common Chord* was pursuing the point of Irish puritanism with such tenacity that the stories became unreal. James Stern in the *New York Times Book Review* of February 15, 1948), describes O'Connor launching "his wild, irreverent attacks on Puritanism with a shillelagh in one hand, a glass of porter in the other, and his eyes alight with a compassionate smile."

12. A few years later, in *The Lonely Voice,* O'Connor wrote that Maupassant's subject, his obsession, was a submerged population of the nineteenth century: prostitutes and girls with illegitimate children. "His life itself may be considered an allegory, for scarcely had he attained fame than he was destroyed by the disease that ravaged the whole submerged population he wrote about."

13. On November 22, 1947 A. D. Peters received "Mildred and Min," a story that had grown out of the strange triangle between Joan, Evelyn, and himself. UTA. He later told his son, Myles, that it had Shelleyan overtones. O'Connor's own absorption in dream theory and his gnawing guilt about his father and his illegitimate son bear a curious resemblance to Shelley's romantic agonies, his burden of guilt and his obsession with the idea of the antithetical self, the ghostly doppelgänger haunting his dreams. See, for example, Richard Holmes, *Shelley: The Pursuit* (New York: Dutton, 1975), specifically chapter ten, "Three for the Road: Europe 1814," about the triangle of Shelley, Mary Godwin, and Jane Clairmont. "Mildred and Min" did not sell, but O'Connor published it in a new version, "Father and Son," in *More Stories* (1954).

14. FOC to John Kelleher, p.m., July 29, 1947, and review in *Evening News,* August 20, 1947.

15. FOC to Bertie Rodgers, ca. September 1, 1947. UTA.

16. In November 1947, during a performance of O'Casey's *The Plough and the Stars,* Roger McHugh, a professor at University College, Dublin, and Valentin Iremonger, a young poet who had won the AE Memorial Prize in 1945, protested that the policy of the Abbey Board was debasing the original ideal of the theatre.

17. Patrick Kavanagh, "Coloured Balloons—A Study of Frank O'Connor," *The Bell,* December 1947.

18. Evelyn O'Donovan to Charles and Kathleen Davidson, January 27, 1948, from 57 Strand Road, PP. In a letter card to Evelyn from London (p.m., March 3, 1948) O'Connor said he would be seeing Elizabeth Bowen the next day, MMB.

19. See FOC to Stan Stewart, March 9, 1948, HS. Daniel Binchy was a Senior Research Fellow at Corpus Christi College, Oxford from 1945 to 1950.

20. Lovat Dickson, who had published so many O'Connor stories in the mid-1930s, had joined Macmillan in 1938 as assistant editor of general books.

21. A. D. Peters notified O'Connor in November 1948 that they were having trouble placing his stories, especially in England. *The New Yorker* turned

down every story he wrote in 1948, after having paid $625 for "The Drunkard" in February. UTA.

22. O'Connor bibliographic note acknowledged his debt to Sir Edmund Chambers, Professor J. D. Wilson, and to Dr. G. B. Harrison. *The Road to Stratford* (London: Methuen, 1948) was dedicated to his son, Oliver. In a letter to Christopher Salmon he wrote, "What I've tried to do, eschewing imaginary biography, is to describe the curve of the man's mind." FOC to Salmon, ca. August 1946, BBC.

23. In an earlier piece he spoke of the four fatal archbishops of literature, four writers to be afraid of: Jonson, Flaubert, Henry James, and Joyce, whom he called "writers in spite of themselves," writers of the head and not the heart. "Pleasure from Pain," *Evening News*, September 3, 1947.

24. Professor Wohlgelernter effectively explodes O'Connor's pose of certitude by observing, "had O'Connor merely consulted the small, but very solid volume on Shakespeare by Marc Parrott, published some thirteen years before *The Road to Stratford*, he would have read" a cautious explanation for the appearance of lines from the sonnets in *Edward III. Frank O'Connor: An Introduction*, pp. 141–42.

25. In *Is Ireland Dying?* (p. 118), Sheehy finds this dualism (between puritanism and humanism, mind and matter) in such writers as Swift, Berkeley, Joyce, Synge, Yeats, and AE. See Scheper-Hughes, *Saint, Scholars, and Schizophrenics*, pp. 133, 193.

26. O'Connor was also quick to diagnose the mental conditions of real people: AE he thought schizophrenic, Joan he pronounced mad, Richard Hayes he branded a latent homosexual. His diagnosis of Hamlet's acrophobia is curiously similar to his own fear of heights, his persistent falling nightmare, and his own claustrophobia and fear of islands.

27. Mrs. George Yeats to FOC, August 21, 1948, from 46 Palmerston Road, Dublin, MMB. The body of Yeats was disinterred from the cemetery in Roquebrune and brought by a ship to Ireland. The ceremonies were held at the Drumcliffe churchyard on September 17, 1948. The Irish government intended to send Minister of External Affairs, Sean McBride (son of Maud Gonne McBride) but stipulated that Frank O'Connor not be the one to give the oration. Jack Yeats, therefore, decided that no speeches of any kind would be allowed. See the Cuala file in MMB for the letters of Jack Yeats to O'Connor.

28. FOC to John Kelleher, p.m., November 26, 1948, PP.

29. Francis Hackett and his Danish wife, Signe Toksvig, left Ireland when his novel *The Green Lion* and her novel *Eve's Doctor* were banned. They settled in Denmark. O'Connor had protested the banning of Hackett's novel in a fierce letter to the *Irish Times*—the book had as its hero the bastard child of a mountain girl. Hackett in turn kept in touch with O'Connor over the years. It is likely that Hackett was behind this invitation to Copenhagen.

30. Evelyn O'Donovan to the Davidsons, November 11, 1948, PP.

31. BBC Third Programme broadcast on the stories of A. E. Coppard, November 27, 1948 BBC.

32. On December 27, 1948, the editor of *Holiday* wrote to A. D. Peters: "We

would prefer to have a writer who is Catholic and whose relations with the church have not been strained." MMB.

33. Evelyn O'Donovan to the Davidsons, February 28, 1949, PP. A canceled check in the amount of £8 17s. to Dohertys Ltd. (Coal Merchants), dated December 2, 1947, suggests that Michael did, in fact, take care of the coal payments.

34. FOC to A. D. Peters, p.m., February 19, 1949, UTA.

35. Frank O'Connor, "Ireland," *Holiday,* December 1949.

36. As a diversion from his writing, O'Connor appeared regularly on the popular BBC Third Programme series "Brains Trust." BBC.

37. According to the A. D. Peters file, O'Connor had been contracted since 1945 to do this book. UTA.

38. Many of O'Connor's dream journals for the years 1948 to 1953 contain Joan's handwriting. HS.

39. In *Towards an Appreciation of Literature* O'Connor had already concluded that the abnormalities of Joyce's style were caused by the sort of disassociation evident in dreams: "almost every word and sentence is distorted as it is in dreams in which we can dream the word 'umbrella' and know perfectly well that it really means 'whiskey', some censor of the soul having endeavored to conceal from us the fact that we like whiskey" (p. 55).

40. In *The Road to Stratford* O'Connor wrote: "It is possible that all literature is in origin sub-conscious and based upon fantasies of dreams with which the conscious, intellectual mind wrestles until it has given them 'a local habitation and a name'; but certainly with poets and instinctive writers, like Shakespeare, Dickens and Ibsen, any decline in creative power at once causes the shadows of the fantasia to take over control and reduce the writer almost to a state of somnambulism" (p. 137).

41. Journal 9 (with "Annals" written on cover and over twenty pages of material on the annals for John Kelleher) contains a fragment of "An Only Child," which was intended for broadcast on the BBC Scottish network (October 11, 1950). HS.

42. On August 11, 1949, O'Connor wrote to Stan Stewart about his thoughts of fleeing to the United States or England. He also mentioned that his mother had recently remarked that she wished he was with Stan, adding "Little she knows!"

CHAPTER SIXTEEN

1. See FOC to Stan Stewart, p.m., August 26, 1948, HS. In January, 1952 Macmillan wrote to A. D. Peters asking about O'Connor's book on France, with a reminder that he had signed the agreement in September 1949, UTA.

2. Published only in *Traveller's Samples* (New York: Knopf, 1951). Sketches of Dan Harrington, Denis Breen, and other members of Corkery's circle are found in Journal 1 (dating from 1927), HS. See also AOC, pp. 191–95.

3. "This Mortal Coil," *New American Mercury,* December 1950. The title had been used previously by Julian Maclaren-Ross, whose *Memoirs of the For-*

ties (London: Alan Ross, 1965) gives a spicy picture of the London publishing scene at that time.

4. "Nothing for Nothing," *Evening News,* October 6, 1949.

5. Among the material supplied by Molly Alexander to MMB are two letters from Minnie O'Donovan, dated November 9, 1949 (from 7 Hill View, Cork), and September 20, 1950 (from Seafield Crescent, Dublin).

6. At the time O'Connor had little good to say about women writers. "No woman can write, except perhaps about love. It's about the only thing they know anything about." Years later, after he had championed the work of Val Mulkerns and Mary Lavin, he looked aghast when Miss Lynam reminded him of his misogyny, and disclaimed the remark. See "A Sparring Partner," *M/F,* pp. 89–90.

7. See letter from A. D. Peters to O'Connor (March 20, 1950) advising them of the libel action, in UTA.

8. Seán O'Faoláin to O'Connor, ca. November 1949, MMB.

9. FOC to Seán O'Faoláin, ca. November 1949, from 11 Palmerston Road, UCB.

10. FOC to Stan Stewart, November 18, 1949, from 11 Palmerston Road, HS.

11. Frank O'Connor, "What the Neighbours Think," *Spectator,* November 24, 1950, p. 564.

12. In the introduction to his first collected edition O'Connor said of the "The Pretender," " [It seems] as good as it seemed when I wrote it down in a hotel room in Avignon on Christmas Day." *Stories* (New York: Knopf, 1952), p. vi.

13. In 1952 at Northwestern University O'Connor met a graduate student named Daniel Weiss who eventually wrote an essay on the Freudian implications of some of O'Connor's stories. "Freudian Criticism: Frank O'Connor as Paradigm," *Northwest Review* (Spring 1959). According to Weiss O'Connor wrote to him denying that he was aware when he wrote "Judas" that it "dealt with an Oedipal situation" and that he had even read Freud at that time. He did, however, admit to knowing Freud quite well when he wrote "My Oedipus Complex." David Marcus, literary editor for the *Irish Press,* originally published "The Cornet Player Who Betrayed Ireland" in his magazine *Irish Writing* (April 1948); he also published "My Oedipus Complex" in *Irish Writing* (November 1952).

14. In the afterglow of Avignon, O'Connor wrote a story about Liadain's motherly attention to her sick little brother, Owen. Called "What Girls Are For," it was published in the March 17, 1951 issue of *Collier's.* It remained uncollected until *CP.* In April he learned that though it had been rejected by *The New Yorker* (which bought "The Pretender") "My Oedipus Complex" had sold for $850 to *Today's Woman.*

15. *Times Literary Supplement,* January 12, 1951, p. 23.

16. It was O'Connor who interested John Kelleher, a scholar, in pre-Viking Ireland (the period A.D. 432–825). O'Connor had the *Annals of Ulster* and the *Annals of Loch Ce* and was full of theories about the effects of the Viking raids on ninth-century Ireland.

17. "The Poison Pen," *Irish Press,* December 15, 1949.

18. See UTA. "Ghosts" was eventually published in *CP;* and "The Grandmother" appeared under a new title, "Ladies of the House," in *Harper's*

(October 1954) and under yet another title, "The Lonely Rock," in *More Stories by Frank O'Connor* (New York: Knopf, 1954).

19. "Private Property" appeared in the *Evening News* (June 1950); "The Rising (later titled "Eternal Triangle" and "The Tram") in *Cornhill* (Autumn, 1951); "The Baptismal" in *American Mercury* (March 1951) and, under the title "A Spring Day," in Reginald Moore's *Modern Reading* (February 1952); and "The Martyr" in *John Bull* (December 15, 1951) and in *Harper's* (February 1953).

20. In March O'Connor heard from his old friend at the BBC in Belfast, John Boyd, who was trying to arrange a broadcast in April. BBC. O'Connor wrote to his agent on March 9, 1950, requesting that a copy of "My Oedipus Complex" be sent to Boyd. UTA. In the meantime Boyd sent a copy of "Old Age Pensioners" to London and received this reply from P. H. Newby the new talks director: "Is there anyone except O'Connor we could find a place for in Third?" On April 12, 1950, Newby turned down "My Oedipus Complex" for broadcast. BBC.

21. "The Conversion," *Harper's Bazaar,* March 1951.

22. "A Romantic," *Evening News,* September 4, 1951. When O'Connor sent the story to A. D. Peters, it was entitled "Frenchy" (the name given to Miah Reidy by his friends). On December 21, 1951, O'Connor told his agent, "I'm going to do that book on France if it takes me ten years." UTA. A different story with the same title appeared in *Bones of Contention.* Two other stories were, in O'Faoláin's view, "Mick and I" stories: "First Love," written in the summer of 1951 and published in *The New Yorker* (February 23, 1952), and "Anchors," written that fall and published in *Harper's Bazaar* (October, 1952).

23. O'Connor did write two long letters to Peter Kavanagh on the publication of his book on the Abbey. On January 31, 1951, he wrote to thank Kavanagh for his references to him in the book and on February 17, 1951, he responded to a letter from Kavanagh answering a list of questions. See Peter Kavanagh, *Beyond Affection,* pp. 123–30.

24. Edward Sheehy, "In the Arena," *Irish Times,* March 20, 1951. In many ways his review was closer to the truth than the cautiously polite review in the *Times Literary Supplement* of February 23, 1951, and the reviews in the United States.

25. The Bellman, "Meet Frank O'Connor," *The Bell,* March 1951, pp. 41–46.

26. Ibid., p. 45.

27. Joan to the Kellehers, July 22, 1951, PP.

28. "The Saint" was bought by *Mademoiselle* magazine for $300.

29. FOC to John Kelleher, ca. July 19, 1951, from 86 Seafield Estate, PP.

30. The Abbey Theatre building burned on July 18, 1951, destroying the stage and the greenroom; the exterior shell was left standing.

31. *AOC,* pp. 84–85.

32. The actual amount of child support O'Connor was obliged to pay varies from document to document, depending on the tax. In 1949 he was required to pay £18 4s. per month for each child, or £416 per annum total (less tax). HS.

33. On September 24, 1952, Lovat Dickson at Macmillan wrote to A. D. Peters stating quite firmly, "We will not publish *Stories Old and New,* because of the Knopf contract." UTA.

34. *The Stories of Frank O'Connor* was published in England in 1953 by Hamish Hamilton. The dedication read: "To the Memory of Mary O'Donovan (1865–1952)."
35. Frank O'Connor, introduction to his story "Adventure," *Atlantic Monthly,* January 1953, p. 47.
36. "A Sense of Responsibility," *The New Yorker,* August 2, 1952.
37. "A Torrent Dammed," *The New Yorker,* September 3, 1952.
38. FOC to Dermot Foley, ca. January, 1952, from 7 Cobb Terrace, Lyme Regis, PP.
39. The examining physician was Dr. Earl McCarthy.
40. *Irish Times,* February 4, 1952.

CHAPTER SEVENTEEN

1. O'Connor used the term *perfesser* in a letter to Dermot Foley, ca. April 10, 1952, from Department of English, Northwestern University, PP.
2. "Unapproved Route," *The New Yorker,* September 27, 1952.
3. See FOC to John Kelleher, p.m., April 25, 1952 from Evanston, PP.
4. "Author! Author!," *The Stories of Frank O'Connor* (New York: Knopf, 1952). At the end of that introduction O'Connor quotes (slightly misquotes actually) from Shelley's "Hymn to Pan."
5. Though O'Connor had expressed firm opinions about Joyce before, it was not until 1952 that his attitude became noticeably hostile. According to Kelleher—in interview and letter—O'Connor's fear of Joyce's symbolism and subjectivity had become almost pathological. A particularly ugly portrayal of O'Connor at Harvard may be found in a story by M. M. Liberman, "O'Malley," in *Four Quarters,* Autumn, 1972, pp. 3–8.
6. Richard Gill, "Frank O'Connor in Harvard," *M/F,* p. 40.
7. Ibid., p. 46.
8. Seán O'Faoláin to O'Connor, August 30, 1952, HS. The review was by Horace Reynolds, "Told Out of a Love for Irish Life," on the front page of the *New York Times Book Review* of August 17, 1952. Horace Reynolds had reviewed *Dutch Interior* in 1940; it was Reynolds who had brought O'Casey to Harvard in 1934. O'Casey had written to Reynolds (March 31, 1940) recommending that he read Seán O'Faoláin and Frank O'Connor. See *Letters of Sean O'Casey,* p. 856.
9. FOC to John Kelleher, ca. September 10, 1952, from Moyvane, Limerick, PP.
10. FOC to John Kelleher, ca. October 1952, from High Chimneys, Cholesbury, PP.
11. FOC to John Kelleher, p.m., November 22, 1952, PP.
12. FOC to Val Mulkerns, ca. December 1952, from High Chimneys, PP. O'Connor's praise of Miss Mulkerns's novel *A Time Outworn* appeared as a prologue to an excerpt from that novel published by *Harper's Bazaar* in August 1952.
13. FOC to Dermot Foley, p.m. December 11, 1952 from High Chimneys, PP.
14. Seán O'Faoláin to O'Connor, ca. January 1953, HS.
15. "And It's a Lonely, Personal Art," *New York Times Book Review,* April 12,

1953. It is here that O'Connor mentions Sherwood Anderson for the first time.

16. "A Lyric Voice in the Irish Theatre," *New York Times Book Review,* May 31, 1953.

17. See Sylvia Plath, *Letters Home,* ed. Aurelia S. Plath (New York: Harper & Row, 1975). On June 8, 1953, Sylvia Plath wrote to her mother, "Have a horrible feeling I probably won't get into O'Connor's course" (p. 116). In her commentary Mrs. Plath writes that she dreaded telling Sylvia "that she had not been accepted as a student in Frank O'Connor's short-story writing class" (p. 123). On May 6, 1981, Mrs. Plath wrote to me to explain that the story her daughter had submitted to O'Connor was "Sunday at the Mintons," published in *Mademoiselle* in August 1952, adding that Sylvia "never learned *why* the story was turned down." The story is included in *Johnny Panic and the Bible of Dreams* (New York: Harper & Row, 1978), and in his introduction Ted Hughes quotes Sylvia Plath as saying of O'Connor's stories, "I will imitate until I can feel I'm using what he can teach."

18. Mario Praz in *The Romantic Agony* (London: Oxford University Press, 1933) had explored, among other ideas, the conflict of realism and romanticism in the nineteenth century. O'Connor sent the Italian scholar a copy of *Mirror;* from Rome on October 27, 1957 Praz wrote to O'Connor expressing admiration for the book, particularly "the connecting of genre painting with the novel." Praz's own book on the novel, *The Hero in Eclipse in Victorian Fiction,* trans. Angus Davidson (London: Oxford University Press, 1956) contained an introductory chapter entitled "Genre Painting and the Novel."

19. On one occasion Michael was the guest of Jack Sweeney, curator of the poetry room at Lamont Library, and his wife, Máire, the daughter of the famous Celtic scholar and revolutionary, Eoin MacNeill. It being Friday, fish was served, but Michael protested that he never ate fish, causing his hostess further offense by pouting when she refused to serve him meat. Máire MacNeill later published a classic study of Irish folklore—*The Festival of Lughnasa* (London: Oxford University Press, 1962)—which O'Connor reviewed glowingly in the *Irish Times* of September 12, 1962.

20. In *M/F,* p. 39.

21. See "The Novel Approach," *New York Times Book Review,* August 23, 1953. Another version of his "giggling" may be found in *Writers at Work,* p. 172.

22. O'Connor had already spent some time that summer with Pierre Emmanuel, who introduced him to Marcel Aymé's *Le confort intellectuel,* which O'Connor read and spent the winter writing about in letters to Seán O'Faoláin: "a wrong-headed book which has had an enormous influence." Among other things, he was fascinated with Aymé's notion that Baudelaire "began the rot of the modern novel." UCB.

23. Elizabeth II succeeded her father, George VI, on February 6, 1952; she was crowned on June 2, 1953. Coronation festivities were spread through the summer as the new queen traveled in England to accept the good wishes of her subjects.

24. Seán O'Faoláin to O'Connor, ca. September 1953, HS.

25. "When an Irishman goes to a pub it is usually to get away from women," O'Connor later wrote. "Drink is his escape from the emotional problems which . . . he now evades more successfully than any male in Europe. He wants nothing suggestive of love, family and home." See "In Quest of Beer," *Holiday,* January 1957, p. 72.

26. FOC to John Kelleher, ca. October 1953, PP. In that letter O'Connor claimed that the money he had made the previous year in America, close to $10,000, had gone into Primrose Hill. A letter to Joan on June 19, 1953, verifies that figure for earnings, but letters from his solicitors about the eventual sale of the house suggest that a good deal less than that went into the purchase of Primrose Hill, HS. Furthermore, his letters to Dermot Foley, from whom he had been forced to borrow money for his mother's funeral, also attest to Michael's refusal to convert his dollar holdings to sterling. "I have dollars, dollars everywhere, and not a quid to spend," he wrote in February 1953.

CHAPTER EIGHTEEN

1. Mr. J. Read of St. Giles' school in Stony Stratford, Buckinghamshire, opposed taking Myles out of school because of his progress and "manifest happiness." Other court documents in this case reveal that on November 21, 1953, O'Connor's gross American earnings were $14,447, or £5,170, with British earnings of £139 plus the £76 from the library pension. Furthermore, O'Connor had a U.K. tax lien of £994. HS.

2. *More Stories* did not appear in England. C. P. Snow has argued that the 1860s were Trollope's "decade of maximum fortune." In *Trollope: His Life and Art* (New York: Scribner's, 1975), p. 117. In many ways the 1950s were O'Connor's decade of maximum fortune; it was during the ten years following his marriage to Harriet that he was the best property for publishers and had his greatest popularity.

3. A notebook dated 1952 to 1954 lists a string of Don Juan stories long enough to comprise a full volume, including "Don Juan Married," "Don Juan in Fetters," "Don Juan to the Rescue," "Don Juan in Trouble," and "Don Juan in Hell." HS. A possible literary influence on this rash of Don Juan stories was the publication in an English version of Chekhov's play *Don Juan in the Russian Manner,* translated by Basil Ashmore, with a preface by Sir Desmond MacCarthy written just before his death (London: P. Nevil, 1952).

4. "The Sorcerer's Apprentice," published in *Harper's Bazaar* of August 1954, was originally entitled "Don Juan's Apprentice." The quotation used here is from the version in *More Stories,* p. 104.

5. The other previously unpublished story in *More Stories* was "Unapproved Route."

6. In 1815 at Bishopsgate Shelley said much the same thing to Thomas Love Peacock. According to Holmes, "Peacock answered in his usual mode of gentle irony that he thought Shelley would find 'more restraint in the office than would suit his aspirations.' " In *Shelley: The Pursuit,* p. 288. When O'Connor felt pushed to the wall by women, he imagined a safe re-

treat in celibacy, but friends like Honor Tracy and Bill Naughton played the part of Peacock.

7. The story, simply labeled "Melleray," is no. 13 in a notebook (dated 1953–57) full of four-line themes which formed the basis for most of the stories O'Connor wrote during the next ten years. In another journal the story in a longer draft is titled "The Returned Yank." HS.

8. "Lost Fatherlands," *The New Yorker,* May 8, 1954. The quotation here is from the version in *A Set of Variations* (New York: Knopf, 1969), p. 271.

9. O'Connor had consistently resisted the original maintenance settlement, insisting that his American earnings were irregular. In spite of earnings in 1953 in excess of £5,300 he was still holding out for £150 per annum per child. Thus, this latest incident convinced him that Evelyn was only using Myles as a wedge to force him to pay the required sum. When her solicitors began hounding A. D. Peters for money, O'Connor simply notified his agent to send all funds to Stan Stewart.

10. When Stan heard of the break with Kelleher he wrote to John (but not to Michael) begging *him* to patch up the feud; reluctantly Kelleher wrote a note apologizing for the tone but not the content of his previous letter. He received a nose-bloodying reply, which pre-empted any future reconciliation.

11. Frank O'Connor, *The Mirror in the Roadway* (New York: Knopf, 1956). It was published the following spring by Hamish Hamilton in London. On September 22, 1956, O'Connor was the featured "Author of the Week" in *Saturday Review,* which published a brief sketch of his life and career by Thomas Cooney and a review of *Mirror* by Howard Mumford Jones. Jones apparently had difficulty with the distinction between judgment and instinct, which he took to be a problem of philosophy, and the metaphor of mother and father in dreams, which he saw as "a Freudian excursus into biography."

12. The Knopf editor assigned to the book (probably Herbert Weinstock) pointed out a contradiction that bothered him throughout the book: "In general, judgment and sensibility, realism and romanticism, liberalism and conservatism, the male principle and the female principle (derived from the Oedipus situation) are used as related pairs of opposites, with God on the side of the first of each. But here, as one example of the way the system breaks down, Jane Austen fails in *Mansfield Park* because she leans on judgment to the detriment of imagination and the emotions, on the male side of her nature at the expense of the female." HS.

13. It was this facile weaving together of literature and the other arts that appealed to Mario Praz when he read *The Mirror in the Roadway.* See Praz to O'Connor, October 27, 1957, HS. Lord David Cecil wrote to O'Connor on November 26, 1956, praising O'Connor's view of Trollope but questioning his ideas on Jane Austen, HS. Cecil was the one critic of the nineteenth-century novel O'Connor admired.

14. Years later O'Connor wrote about Gogol again, saying that the man was more interesting than his stories: "Here he is again, a murky, sinister psychopath, with his sickly childhood, his religiosity, his self-abuse, his theft and flight abroad. . . . Perhaps you may then feel inspired to write the true biography of Gogol as I suspect it may have been, and describe how a des-

perately sick man, with a sickly childhood, an Oedipus complex, a castration complex, an onanistic complex *and* a religious mania, laughed himself and a sickly society into health." *New York Times Book Review,* September 6, 1964.

15. Though O'Connor announces himself the enemy of all direct moralizing in fiction, he is quick to judge the failure of Gide, Woolf, Joyce, and Proust as one stemming from sexual abnormality. For example, he agrees with Gide's admiration of Dostoevsky's *The Eternal Husband,* though to his mind it is the first example of the "eternal triangle of husband, wife, and lover, or husband, wife, and mistress, as it presents itself to the mind of the adolescent and neurotic."

16. "A Matter-of-Fact Problem in the Writing of a Novel," *New York Times Book Review,* December 12, 1954. "Architect of His Own Reputation," BBC, July 24, 1954, BBC.

17. FOC to Dermot Foley, ca. end of January 1955 from 136 Hicks Street, PP. On January 26 he wrote to Liadain at Our Lady's Convent, Foxbush, Hildenborough, Kent. Besides telling her about Christmas he complained of a poor production of his story "The Martyr" on television. One of the actors who particularly vexed him was Ronald Reagan.

18. FOC to Dermot Foley, ca. March 1955 from 136 Hicks Street, PP. Father Traynor died on January 5, 1955. Michael said in his letter to Dermot: "I didn't even know he was ill, much less dead until I got your letter, and it's ironic for the Atlantic has published this month or should be publishing his story about the priest's death that I've tried for years to write and which even now keeps on coming a cropper on me, and the N.Y. is doing a story about him, of which you know the subject, though it wasn't connected with him. No doubt all the American Catholic associations will rise in their wrath and say these things never happened among the Irish priesthood." "The Wreath" appeared in the *Atlantic Monthly* in November 1955; "The Teacher's Mass" was published by *The New Yorker* on April 30, 1955.

19. Because Myles was still a ward of the court, Michael's refusal to return him to England constituted grounds for contempt charges. In January Evelyn, desperate to get some money from Michael, who still refused to pay anything until a permanent settlement had been reached, had her solicitors file a write of attachment against his royalties and the sale of Primrose Hill (completed in September for £2,650).

20. O'Connor told of the Annapolis incident in "One Man's Way," a broadcast for the BBC (made in Belfast) on June 24, 1959. See *JIL,* p. 152.

21. Commenting on the element of compassion in Russian literature, O'Connor has even paid tribute to these servants by recalling their names. In *Mirror in the Roadway,* p. 98.

22. In *Newsweek,* March 13, 1961.

23. Harriet O'Connor, "Listening to Frank O'Connor," *Nation,* August 28, 1967.

24. "For a Two-Hundredth Birthday," *Harper's Bazaar,* January 1956. Carmel Snow asked him to do the article.

25. "The Most American Playwright," *Holiday,* February 1956.

26. The title "The Duke's Children" came from Trollope's novel of the same

name. A similar story is one he heard from Hector Legge during the war, which he eventually wrote as "An Out-and-Out Free Gift."

27. According to the files of A. D. Peters (and the affiliate office in New York, Harold Matson) O'Connor signed a first-reading-option agreement with *The New Yorker* on June 23, 1952, for $100, then on December 10, 1953, for $550, and on December 13, 1956, for $1,200. Three years later the sum increased to $2,500.

28. Frank O'Connor, "That Ryan Woman," *Saturday Evening Post,* January 19, 1957.

29. FOC to William Maxwell, p.m., September 9, 1957, from 160 Columbia Heights, PP. An even more didactic story is "The Paragon," published in *Esquire* of October 1957, about one of his sons, a "tall, gangling, good-looking boy," with a fine tenor voice and the highest marks in Ireland.

30. Donal Brennan, "Reminiscences from France," in *M/F,* p. 115.

31. In Journal No. 8 the story is given two titles: "The Realist" and "The Meditation of Buddha." HS. Like most of the stories he was writing about children, "The Study of History" was another version of the conflict between what one inherits from his father and what from his mother. The Irish proverb *Is treis dutcas na oileamaint* means that what a child inherits is stronger than how it is raised. Professor Scheper-Hughes explores this conflict in terms of the distinction in the Irish language between *dutcas* (nature or breeding), which is associated with the father, and *naduir* (upbringing), which is associated with mother's milk and all the nurturing qualities of mother. See *Saints, Scholars, and Schizophrenics,* pp. 168–69.

32. References in O'Connor's dream journals and drafts of essays for his book on dreams indicate extensive research. Though Father Traynor had tried to interest him in Freud, O'Connor had avoided the so-called father of psychoanalysis until after his meeting with Philip Metman. By the mid-fifties he had read Rene Allendy, *Rêves expliqués* (Paris: Gallimard, 1938); Emil Gutheil, *The Language of the Dream* (New York: Macmillan, 1939); and Wilhelm Stekel, *Sex and Dreams: The Language of Dreams,* trans. James S. Van Teslaar (Boston: Badger, 1922). *Die Sprache des Traumes* is the original title. Other than his own dreams and Joan's, O'Connor relied on the dreams recorded over a ten-year period by the famous drama critic and translator of Ibsen, William Archer in his book *On Dreams,* ed. Theodore Besterman, with preface by Gilbert Murray (London: Methuen, 1935). Freud's *Interpretation of Dreams* in the translation by A. A. Brill had been available since its publication in 1913 by Allen & Unwin.

33. "In Dreams: Does Seven Mean Conception?," *Vogue,* November 1, 1967, p.165.

34. See O'Connor, *Towards an Appreciation of Literature,* p. 55. His abnormal sensitivity to "abnormal" conditions in other people indicates that he was at least fearful of falling into the same traps himself.

35. *Vogue,* November 1, 1967, p. 236. In his autobiography O'Connor contrasted the gaiety of his mother and the melancholy of his father as "the two powers that were struggling for the possession of my soul." *AOC,* p. 20.

36. FOC to Liadain O'Donovan, ca. early March 1957, from Ferry Point Farm, PP.

37. In 1957 Elisabeth Schnack published *Er hat die Hosen an* (Munich: Nymphenburger Verlagshandlung). Two years previously she had included O'Connor stories in her general anthology of Irish short stories: *Irishe Meister der Erzählung* (Bremen-Horn: Walter Dorn Verlag, 1955). In 1949 Mrs. Schnack had written to O'Connor requesting exclusive translating rights; they were granted and her efforts have given him a large German audience. In addition, O'Connor was translated into Danish by Harold Engberg, *Den hellige Dør* (Copenhagen: Gyldendal, 1954). His reputation in other European languages is still nascent.

38. *The Rising of the Moon* was a production of Four Provinces Films under the direction of John Ford and backed by Brian Hurst, Lord Killanin, Tyrone Power, and Michael Scott. The section "Majesty of the Law" (for which O'Connor received £500) was played by Noel Purcell and Cyril Cusack. The film was not censored, though a number of groups protested its showing. However, while O'Connor was in Dublin censorship did raise its ugly head. On May 23 an English director, Alan Simpson, was arrested for producing Tennessee Williams's *The Rose Tattoo* at the Pike Theatre. O'Connor and Brendan Behan took part in a demonstration protesting the arrest of the cast the next day. See Simpson, "The Rose Tattoo: Arrest and Trial," in *Flight from the Celtic Twilight,* pp. 128–33. Years later O'Connor repeated the incident in an admiring portrait of Behan– –O'Connor, "He Was So Much Bigger Than Life," *Irish Independent,* March 22, 1964.

39. See Bruce Catton, *A Stillness at Appomattox* (Garden City, N.Y.: Doubleday, 1953), p. 64.

40. William Bittner, review of *Domestic Relations,* by Frank O'Connor, *Nation,* January 11, 1958.

41. Denis Johnston, "If You Like Them Short," *Saturday Review,* September 21, 1957.

42. *Modern Irish Short Stories,* selected and with an introduction by Frank O'Connor (London: Oxford University Press, 1957). It was as much O'Connor's introduction as the stories in the volume that prompted the unusually long review "Thereby Hangs a Tale" in the *Times Literary Supplement* of December 20, 1957.

43. It was O'Connor who had given this American edition wings by recommending to an American editor that he give it a review. For some time O'Connor had pushed Plunkett's writing, even recommending him to his own agent, A. D. Peters.

44. Noyes was the man Yeats had implored years before to uncover the truth about Casement. Only a year before this book was published a conflicting account appeared: Rene MacColl, *Roger Casement: A New Judgment* (New York: Norton, 1956). The book by Noyes was largely a defense of Casement, while MacColl accepted Casement's guilt. The crux of this complex argument was the infamous "Black Diaries," which many believed had been forged by British authorities to discredit Casement as a shameless pervert.

45. Frank O'Connor, "At the Heart of the Martyr's Myth, a Haunting Mystery," *New York Times Book Review,* November 17, 1957. Just before this review appeared, O'Connor heard from Roger McHugh, with whom he had corresponded about the Casement business; McHugh apprised him of the excellent work of Professor Giovanni Costigan of the University of

Washington. On December 19, 1957, Costigan wrote to O'Connor commending his review and inviting him to hear a paper he would be giving on the subject in San Francisco at Christmas. On January 2, 1958, he wrote again, expressing regret that O'Connor was unable to make it: "The thesis I present in my paper was that the 'Black Diaries' are genuine diaries of Casement's, into which the authorities interpolated indecent passages, perhaps from the criminal record of some now nameless pervert, which was lying in the files of Scotland Yard for use at just such a moment." The correspondence continued for some time. HS. Costigan, a historian with very impressive achievements in a number of fields, including a book on Freud, has since written *A History of Modern Ireland* (New York: Pegasus, 1969).

46. Apparently, this reseach was being done in conjunction with the famous Stanford studies by Lewis Madison Terman (who died in 1956, but whose work had been carried on by M. H. Oden at Stanford), a leader in the study of the gifted. See Lewis Madison Terman and M. H. Oden, "The Gifted Group at Mid-Life," *Genetic Studies of Genius,* vol. 5 (Palo Alto, Calif.: Stanford University Press, 1959).

CHAPTER NINETEEN

1. From the edited copy of the manuscript I saw, "Displaced Persons" is a novelistic version of the battle between subjectivity and objectivity carried on in literary terms in *The Mirror in the Roadway* and *The Road to Stratford,* and in psychoanalytic terms in the dream writings. In the novel a painter from Cork named Denis goes to England where he meets a writer (resembling O'Connor's Don Juan character) and has an affair with a young Englishwoman, which eventually falls apart because of *her* sexual infidelity. MS, HS.

2. *The New Yorker* had bought "I Know Where I'm Going" in May 1958, according to correspondence with Maxwell. PP.

3. FOC to Dermot Foley (January 12, 1958). PP. O'Connor claimed to object to women writers in general. In "It's All in the Telling," published in the *New York Times Book Review* of April 12, 1959, reviewing a book by Ralph Cusack, O'Connor distinguishes between writers who stick to the point and writers who don't: "Mr. Cusack belongs to the latter group, in the distinguished company of Joyce, Faulkner, Samuel Beckett, and *all* women, and his book bears a distinct resemblance to a woman's idea of a good yarn." This from a man who considered *Emma* the perfect novel. See *M/F*, pp. 89–90.

4. In February O'Connor managed another attack on Joyce, this in a review of Stanislaus Joyce's book *My Brother's Keeper;* see the *Nation,* February 1, 1958.

5. According to FOC to Evelyn, ca. August 1958, MMB, "In the Train," a script of which he had requested from Evelyn, had been turned down.

6. FOC to William Maxwell, ca. August 1958, PP.

7. William Maxwell, *The Château* (New York: Knopf, 1961).

8. FOC to Dermot Foley, September 2, 1958, PP. In that same letter he praised Brendan Behan's *Borstal Boy*.
9. From an interview with Mr. Kelly in July 1976.
10. O'Connor's journals indicate that he was tinkering at the time on a volume of stories about priests, the bulk of which were Father Fogarty stories (from Tim Traynor). HS. The volume itself, which was to be called "The Collar," never materialized, but most of the stories appeared in *A Set of Variations*, a posthumous volume of stories put together by Harriet (New York: Knopf, 1969).
11. Giovanni Costigan's review of the Grove Press edition of Casement's *Black Diaries* appeared in the *Herald Tribune Book Review* of April 26, 1959; also an extensive essay was published in the *Irish Press* of September 6, 1959. The publication of the diaries cemented O'Connor's belief that they had been tampered with by British authorities. This position was seriously questioned by Brian Inglis in "Saintly Sinner" (*Spectator*, March 6, 1959), to which O'Connor responded with a letter setting forth proof that the ambiguous passages had to be interpolations by someone other than Casement (*Spectator*, August 28, 1959). Inglis has since written an extensive biography, *Roger Casement* (London: Hodder and Stoughton, 1973), the final section of which is entitled "The Ghost of Roger Casement."
12. *M/F*, pp. 18–19.
13. Ibid., p. 22.
14. "A Set of Variations on a Borrowed Theme," *The New Yorker*, April 30, 1960. The story was titled "Variations on a Theme" when published in *Winter's Tales*, II (1965). Other titles were "The Hireling," and "Variations on a Theme by William Maxwell." MSS, HS. O'Connor has written that he first became aware of the plight of illegitimate children while living in Wicklow; later in Dublin he saw dozens of girls appear in the "Green Street court-house to be indicted and sentenced to death for the murder of their babies." He goes on to say, "Out of that experience I must have written a dozen stories." In *Backward Look*, p. 227.
15. Actually, *Kings, Lords, & Commons* did not appear in England until 1961. It was reviewed along with *AOC* in the *Times Literary Supplement* of June 30, 1961, perhaps by John Wain. The reviewer observed that *AOC*, though perhaps not a profoundly revealing self portrait, was a highly skillful one.
16. On February 20, 1959, O'Connor wrote to Liadain at Solebury: "No, I won't be in the U.S. for commencement; we plan to get back in September if we CAN get back, which is another matter. We were both delighted with your reports, which are excellent. And I feel very proud of having spotted your capacity before anyone else did." His refusal to make it to her graduation hurt Liadain greatly.
17. William Maxwell, "Frank O'Connor and the *New Yorker*," in *M/F*, p. 142.
18. James Atlas tells a similar story about Maxwell's efforts, particularly in salvaging "The Track Meet," a story that Atlas argues "remains a tribute not only to Delmore's persistence in the face of madness and disintegration but also the editorial talents of William Maxwell." See his *Delmore Schwartz: The Life of an American Poet* (New York: Farrar, Straus & Giroux, 1977), p. 328.

19. See Rosemarie Doyle's interview with Liam Clancy in the *Irish Times* of May 17, 1980.
20. From the printed program. HS.
21. Eight stories were published after "Set of Variations," which came out in April 1960; four of those stories had appeared in journals in one form or another before 1960. HS. Four of the eight stories were published posthumously by O'Connor's widow. Four more stories appeared in the 1970s—see *CP*—but all seem to have been written, at least for the first time, before 1960.
22. *AOC*, p. 276.
23. Stanley Kauffmann, "O'Connor Seen by Himself and Others," *New Republic,* November 29, 1969.
24. *Towards an Appreciation of Literature,* p. 44.
25. *AOC*, p. 193. During the final editing process in 1960 O'Connor even sent a copy of the book of Sean Hendrick who, along with Seamus and Mairgread Murphy, went over the book scrupulously; one change of fact they made was in the scene with Breen and Corkery.
26. "The Welfare State and I," paper delivered at "The Writer and the Welfare State," a conference held in Copenhagen, Denmark, September 8–14, 1960. MS, HS. Iris Murdoch and Kingsley Amis were among those attending the conference.
27. O'Connor's abnormal sensitivity to sexual abnormality suggests a certain insecurity; he was heterosexual to be sure, but perhaps he avoided any recognition of the masculine and feminine sides of his personality. In a story written after 1961, "The Corkerys," O'Connor described a character as being "the very type of the homosexual—the latent homosexual." It was also obvious to him that Roger Casement was a latent rather than a practicing homosexual. Writing about Casement he defined the difference: "In the practicing homosexual, sex is diverted; in the latent homosexual, emotion is diverted." He then asserted that some of the finest people he had known "could be described as latent homosexuals; people who have diverted sexual emotions into religion, teaching, or art." *Irish Times,* June 6, 1964.
28. Wallace Stegner, "Professor O'Connor at Stanford," in *M/F,* p. 95. Actually, as O'Connor wrote to Sean Hendrick, he hated "professoring," adding that O'Faoláin seems to have "taken to it in wonderful style." FOC to Sean Hendrick, ca. March 1961, CM. Though no dramatic break occurred between O'Connor and O'Faoláin, it was obvious that after 1954 (the marriage to Harriet and the break with Kelleher) they saw each other infrequently.
29. *M/F,* pp. 98–99.
30. *AOC* was probably O'Connor's most widely reviewed book—in England and the United States, of course, because he had insisted that no copies be sent to newspapers in Ireland. Granville Hicks reviewed the book in *Saturday Review* (March 11, 1961); Valentin Iremonger, the Irish poet and diplomat, wrote about it for the *Guardian* (June 23, 1961); V. S. Pritchett, a friend and fellow writer, reviewed it in the *New Statesman* (June 30, 1961). Other important reviews appeared in *Time,* the *Times Literary Supplement,* the *New Republic,* and the *Nation,* but perhaps the most

penetrating, thorough, as well as laudatory review was that by Vivian Mercier, "The O'Connors of Cork," in the *New York Times Book Review* (March 12, 1961).

31. "Artist as Boy," *Newsweek,* March 13, 1961.

32. These glib statements, appearing in San Francisco area papers, were typical of O'Connor's way with American journalists. For instance, a reporter for the *Washington Post* interviewed him after his performance of "Interior Voices" at the Library of Congress on November 21, 1960. The next day, under a picture of O'Connor and Harriet was the headline "Irish Author Bemoans Popularity of Scotch," and true to form, the brief article focused on O'Connor's appeal to President-elect Kennedy to start drinking Irish whiskey in the White House because it would set an example for other Irish Americans.

33. FOC to Sean Hendrick, ca. March 1961, from Palo Alto, Calif., CM.

34. O'Faoláin's book, *Short Stories: A Study in Pleasure,* was published also in 1961 by Little, Brown. In that letter to Hendrick in March, O'Connor not only derided O'Faoláin's academic posing— denying, of course, that he was being malicious—but also told of protesting the latest incarnation of the Stage Irishman in Brendan Behan. In *Towards an Appreciation of Literature* (p. 16) O'Connor had written: "Swift, Wilde, Yeats, and Joyce have certain characteristics like insolence, introspection, and a tendency to wear a mask which are not uncommon among writers brought up in Ireland." Not only could O'Connor diagnose mental disorder with relative ease, but he was also quick to spot phoniness—in other people.

35 In 1956 O'Connor wrote an essay, originally entitled "The American Story," which appeared in the *Nation* of November 10, 1956, as "Prospectus for an Anthology." In it he argued that storytelling had always seemed to him *the* most characteristic American art form.

36. Frank O'Connor, "Why Don't You Write About America," *Mademoiselle,* April 1967.

37. O'Connor's theory of submerged population groups seems similar to what Professor Scheper-Hughes calls "a residual population," a category of marginal people "left behind after generations of sifting away through marriage-out, internal migrations, and emigration abroad." In *Saints, Scholars, and Schizophrenics,* pp. 70–71. Throughout her book Professor Scheper-Hughes refers to the "lonely resolution" of such people, their escape into dreams, alcoholism, masturbation, and even suicide.

38. The brief report filed by these specialists represents one of the few medical clues to the puzzle of O'Connor's lifetime of ill health. Few physiological abnormalities were found, nothing suggestive of angina or any other chronic disorder. The stroke was described as an "episode of vascular insufficiency or slight hypertensive encephalopathy," with the hypertension listed as "essential" (blood-pressure reading: 180/120). Note was made of his "smoking more and drinking more wine, exercising less." His gastritis was mentioned as associated with heavy drinking, smoking, and "nervous strain and tension." Nothing congenital was suggested.

CHAPTER TWENTY

1. A filmed interview on the program "Monitor" was broadcast on BBC television on November 19, 1961. "Self-Portrait" was aired in the very first week of broadcasting by Telefís Eireann in January 1962.
2. James Plunkett, *The Gems She Wore* (London: Hutchinson, Arrow, 1978), p. 41.
3. Thomas Flanagan, "The Irish Writer," *M/F*, p. 148.
4. Eventually published posthumously as *A Golden Treasury of Irish Poetry, A.D. 600 to 1200* (London: Macmillan, 1967).
5. "Malachy," an unpublished radio script, MMB.
6. Speech delivered at the Library Association dinner, Dublin, June 1963, TS, HS. See *JIL*, pp. 168–71.
7. "What Shall We Do Without Books?," *Sunday Independent*, March 25, 1962.
8. *M/F*, p. 117.
9. Philip Edwards, "Frank O'Connor at Trinity," *M/F*, p. 131.
10. Honor Tracy, "King of the Castle," *M/F*, p. 4.
11. FOC to Myles O'Donovan, ca. July 1962, from 34 Court Flats, Wilton Place, PP.
12. Speech delivered at commencement dinner, Trinity College, Dublin, July 5, 1962, TS, HS.
13. Articles published in the *Sunday Independent* between March 25 and September 9, 1962. See *M/F*, pp. 184–85.
14. Frank O'Connor, "The Holy Places of Ireland," *Holiday*, April 1963.
15. "Scrapbook for 1921—Irish Civil War," BBC, October 2, 1961. Between October 1961 and his death almost five years later, O'Connor made over twenty broadcasts for the BBC in Northern Ireland, mainly through the efforts of John Boyd. BBC.
16. Frank O'Connor, "Murder Unlimited," *Irish Times*, October 10, 1962. According to Shevawn Lynam, Miss Woodham-Smith was astonished by O'Connor's review and asked her to arrange a meeting with him; O'Connor had years earlier expressed to Miss Lynam his desire to meet Miss Woodham-Smith. The meeting apparently took place in Dublin sometime after his strident review, but it "solved nothing." See Lynam, "A Sparring Partner," *M/F*, pp. 92–93.
17. Frank O'Connor, "Plays: The International Theatre Festival, Dublin," *Sunday Independent*, September 30, 1962. The festival had evolved from An Tóstal but not without great difficulty. In 1958 Archbishop McQuaid disapproved of plans to stage a premiere of O'Casey's *Drums for Father Ned* and Alan McClelland's dramatization of Joyce's *Ulysses*, called *Bloomsday*, and he refused to give the votive Mass to open the larger celebration, An Tóstal. In protest Beckett withdrew permission to stage his mimes, which collapsed the entire festival. It was revived later by Lord Killanin and Brendan Smith. For fuller details on this whole unfortunate business, see *Flight from the Celtic Twilight*, pp. 134–51, and Hogan, *After the Irish Renaissance*, pp. 186–87.
18. Frank O'Connor, "Plays: The International Theatre Festival, Dublin," *Sunday Independent*, October 7, 1963.

19. FOC to William Maxwell, ca. November 1962, from 22 Court Flats, PP.
20. Owen Dudley Edwards, "America's Image of Ireland," *Irish Times,* January 11, 1963.
21. Frank O'Connor, "Are We Being Fair to Sean O'Casey," *Sunday Independent,* May 12, 1963. O'Casey responded a few weeks later with a letter to the editor: O'Connor, he wrote, was kind to say a word or two for him, "and brave, too, for it is never easy for one to take the part of one who is out of favour."
22. Brendan Kennelly, "Little Monasteries," *M/F,* p. 107.
23. Peter Lennon, "For Decency's Sake," *Manchester Guardian,* October 9, 1963. According to Michael Adams, Lennon wrote four more articles in January 1964; Adams suggests that Lennon was often "mistaken in his facts and tendentious in his judgments." In *Censorship: The Irish Experience,* p. 253.
24. *M/F,* pp. 132–33.
25. Frank O'Connor, "A Tribute to John F. Kennedy," *Sunday Independent,* November 24, 1963.
26. Interview in *Irish Times,* December 11, 1963.
27. Benedict Kiely, "Men Who Wrote Like Angels," *New York Times Book Review,* June 25, 1967.
28. Edwards, *M/F,* p. 133.
29. *A Backward Look,* p. 1.
30. See Plunkett, *The Gems She Wore,* p. 86. The Irish sculptor John Creagh has observed that O'Connor had been the one voice over the past twenty years crying out to preserve the national monuments of Ireland. He included in his plea to continue a preservation effort a picture of O'Connor at Athassel Abbey, a particularly ruined gem of ecclesiastical architecture. In "Save Our Heritage from Neglect," *Sunday Independent,* November 26, 1967.
31. "Awkward But Alive," *Spectator,* July 31, 1964.
32. "A Life of Your Own," was rejected by *The New Yorker;* it was published in the *Saturday Evening Post* on February 13, 1965. Both "School for Wives" and "The Corkerys" were published posthumously in *The New Yorker.*
33. The one priest story he might have been working on at this time was "The Call," published eventually in the *Irish Press* of August 21, 1971, and included in *CP.*
34. "A Mother's Warning" was rejected by *The New Yorker* and published in the *Saturday Evening Post* of October 7, 1967. "An Act of Charity" was published posthumously in *The New Yorker.*
35. O'Connor's widow, Harriet Sheehy, claims that the story he was "working on" at the time of his death was "The Grip of the Geraghtys," a story that probably dates back to 1948 along with the story "Ghosts" (originally entitled "Distinguished Visitors"). See the A. D. Peters files, UTA. The two are together at the end of *CP* and form an admirable conclusion to the book, for in his final days O'Connor was indeed still chasing ghosts, the ghosts of Cork particularly. In "The Grip of the Geraghtys" a good deal is made of epitaphs and romantic solutions, like suicide, for the interminable blight of Cork. If indeed it was the last thing O'Connor wrote, then its closing lines are a hell of a way to end: " 'Women and ghosts!' he said

mournfully over his lonely drink in the pub. 'Isn't that a man's life for you?' "

36. Richard Ellmann has since referred to Frank O'Connor as the "Flaubert of the bogs." See "O'Connor's Crab-Apple Jelly," *New York Review of Books*, October 8, 1981.

37. Michael Foy, "Graveside Tribute to W. B. Yeats," *Irish Times*, June 14, 1965. O'Connor's address is reprinted in *JIL*, pp. 173–78. One of the last things O'Connor wrote on Yeats was published under the simple title "W. B. Yeats" in the *Critic* of December 1966–January 1967. Only a few days before his tribute to Yeats at Drumcliffe, his final word on Cork appeared; it was called "A Place in the Mind: Regency Cork," which shows that in many ways O'Connor never escaped from his hometown at all. In *Spectator*, June 11, 1965.

38. "Directions for *My* Funeral," *Atlantic*, February 1969, p. 120.

39. FOC to Myles O'Donovan, ca. November 1965, PP. The manuscripts referred to in the letter were *A Backward Look* and *A Golden Treasury of Irish Poetry*.

40. According to international data (1960) cited by Professor Scheper-Hughes, Ireland ranked high in coronary heart disease, hypertension deaths, and gastric and duodenal ulcer deaths, all of which suggests that O'Connor's self-destructive habits (Ireland also ranked high in cigarette consumption and daily caloric intake) almost make a composite picture of Irish deaths in general. See *Saints, Scholars, and Schizophrenics*, p. 57.

41. Years before, during *The Tailor and Ansty* furor (recently recalled to O'Connor, for in 1964 he wrote an introduction for a republication of the book), O'Connor had received a letter from Irene Haugh describing AE's "death-bed non-conversion." Now the wolves of religion, as she called them, circled O'Connor too.

42. In *Writers at Work*, p. 177.

43. Frank O'Connor, "The Case for Roger Casement," *Sunday Independent*, January 16, 1966.

44. Proinsias MacAonghusa, "O'Connor's Collins Is No Plaster Saint," *Sunday Independent*, January 23, 1966.

45. Frank O'Connor, "My Father's Wife," *Saturday Evening Post*, February 26, 1966.

46. *M/F*, p. 135.

47. From the personal diary of Dermot Foley, March 10, 1966 through March 12, 1966, comprising twenty-three handwritten pages.

48. "A Writer Who Refused to Pretend," *New York Times Book Review*, January 17, 1960.

Index

James Matthews was born and raised near Seattle, Washington, graduated from Seattle Pacific College in 1964, and received a Ph.D. from Vanderbilt University in 1968. He taught for two years at the University of Tulsa, where his interest in Irish literature began, and then for eleven years at Eckerd College in St. Petersburg, Florida. Now a lapsed academic, he has returned to the Pacific Northwest, and lives on a farm outside Stanwood, Washington, with his wife and three children.